W9-BRF-270

The Supreme Court

The Supreme Court

An Essential History

Peter Charles Hoffer
Williamjames Hull Hoffer
N.E.H. Hull

University Press of Kansas

© 2007 by the University Press of Kansas

All rights reserved Published by the University Press of Kansas (Lawrence, Kansas 66045), which was organized by the Kansas Board of Regents and is operated and funded by Emporia State University, Fort Hays State University, Kansas State University, Pittsburg State University, the University of Kansas, and Wichita State University

Library of Congress Cataloging-in-Publication Data

Hoffer, Peter Charles, 1944–
    The Supreme Court : an essential history / Peter Charles Hoffer, Williamjames Hull Hoffer, N.E.H. Hull.
    p.   cm.
    Includes bibliographical references and index.
    ISBN 978-0-7006-1538-4 (cloth : alk. paper)
    1. United States. Supreme Court—History. I. Hoffer, Williamjames. II. Hull, N. E. H., 1949– III. Title.
    KF8742.Z9H64 2007
    347.73'26—dc22
                                        2007016900

British Library Cataloguing-in-Publication Data is available.

Printed in the United States of America

10 9 8 7 6 5 4 3 2 1

The paper used in this publication is recycled and contains 50 percent postconsumer waste. It is acid free and meets the minimum requirements of the American National Standard for Permanence of Paper for Printed Library Materials Z39.48-1992.

Contents

A photograph section appears following page 238.

Preface

Early in the preparation of this book, a caustic reader asked why another book on the Supreme Court was necessary. Weren't there enough already? Wasn't it self-indulgent to write another? As the number of volumes on the Court in the bibliographic essay at the end of this book testifies, that comment needed a response. Here it is—a question answered with questions. When is enough examination of our democratic institutions enough? When should we become content with the stories told of our past? When do we no longer need any more histories? When does rethinking history become, in the words of a president of the United States, the evil of "revisionism"? The answer is: Never!

There is a second question, a more important and more relevant question, that our skeptical reader did not ask. Why should a reader choose this book over all the others in the pack? As we go to press, we are more up-to-date than other books, but soon enough other scholars will present new interpretations or carry the story further than we have here. As we suggested a moment ago, as long as we have memory and the will to inquire, new histories will appear and demand our scrutiny.

But we hope that we have achieved something useful in the pages that follow—a concise and readable account, an account that is clear but does not oversimplify, an account that is fair and neither overly critical nor overtly celebratory. For in the story of the United States Supreme Court there is much to admire, and just as much to draw back from in dismay. Its opinions are sometimes Olympian and sometimes pedestrian. Some of the justices stand among the most admired figures in our history. Others were ambitious, prejudiced, and lazy; overstayed their usefulness on the Court; treated their colleagues with disdain or worse; or regarded the public interest as something to be pillaged by members of their own circle, class, party, and state.

Our view of the Court and its legacy grows out of our experience editing the Landmark Law Cases and American Society series of our publisher, the University Press of Kansas. In those books and in this one, legal history lies at the intersection of intellectual, social, cultural, economic, and political events. The books in the series focus on a single case or a group of closely related cases. Although the time span and cast of characters in *The Supreme Court: An Essential History* is far broader than any single book in the series, like the authors of the books in the series, we view the Court in the context of time, place, and personality. A study of the justices' views opens a portal between their world and ours. We have also followed the format of the series, forgoing the formal apparatus of citations (endnotes) in favor of a detailed bibliographic essay. The sources of quotations in the book from the cases appear in the text.

Although every history must root its narrative in a past time and place, we confess to some degree of "presentism" in our selection of cases and quotations from the justices' opinions. Historians are wary of presentism, decried by David Hackett Fischer in his *Historians' Fallacies* (1970) as "the mistaken idea that the proper way to do history is to prune away the dead branches of the past, and to preserve the green buds and twigs which have grown into the . . . forest of our contemporary world." Actually, pruning away old growth to allow new shoots to bloom is good horticulture and can be good history. An account of the Court that dwells overly on issues and ideas that are no longer relevant to our world would be antiquarianism, not history. We value history precisely because it speaks to our concerns, and that voice makes history a living mentor. Thus we have spent more time with those cases and quarrels that today's reader will understand and, even more important, will see as still relevant. The same way that light bends in a prism, our account is angled to reveal how the story of the Supreme Court is essential to us.

We have tried to let the justices speak for themselves, preferring their explanations for their opinions to ours. Nevertheless, it was impossible to provide more than a small portion of their writing in any one case, for obvious reasons of space. To the best of our ability we drew from the entire opinion its core thinking. Some of the justices' views may surprise or jar modern readers, but bear in mind that they lived in very different times from ours. We indicate at the end of the book where the full texts of Supreme Court opinions can be found.

One more apology of sorts: every major case in this book could be a book in itself. Many in fact have generated book-length treatments. Thus our pages, or in some cases single paragraphs, can never really do justice to all the nuances of a case's history. But by epitomizing, summarizing, commenting, and contextualizing, we have tried to fit these cases into the longer history of the High Court. The bibliographic essay at the end of the book suggests where to look to find more detailed accounts of individual cases and justices' lives.

Although we have fully collaborated on this book, reading one another's chapters from the first outline to the final draft, Peter Charles Hoffer was the primary draftsman for the first part, N. E. H. Hull was the primary draftsman for the second part, and Williamjames Hoffer was the primary draftsman for the third part. Collaboration is often difficult, but the members of our family of scholar-teachers have been collaborating on books, editorial projects, teaching materials, and educational planning for many years, and we found working together on this book especially enjoyable. For a slightly different reason, a few very short excerpts from the authors' other published forays into the Court's life appear in the following pages. Every scholarly enterprise stands on the shoulders of its predecessors, and *The Supreme Court: An Essential History* is no different.

We want to thank the many readers who have helped us with this volume. Richard Bernstein, Daniel Hulsebosch, William Nelson, and the members of the New York University School of Law legal history seminar in 2005–2006 commented on the introduction and chapters 3 through 5. They helped focus our account. Lawrence Friedman, David O'Brien, and Melvin Urofsky read a working draft of the entire book. Their insights were invariably helpful. We acknowledge also the research assistance provided N. E. H. Hull by Dr. George Yacoubian and the contributions of Professor Hull's legal history seminar students in the fall semesters of 2005 and 2006. If there are still errors of interpretation or exposition, they are ours alone.

Fred Woodward, the director of the University Press of Kansas, supported the project throughout. Michael Briggs, the editor in chief, worked with the authors as manuscript became printed page. His abundance of patience and insight improved the book in untold ways. Our thanks go to both of them, to production editor Larisa Martin and copy editor Dorothea Anderson, and to all the good folks at the University Press of Kansas.

The Supreme Court

Introduction

In these years of hotly contested Supreme Court nominations, marches and demonstrations on the Supreme Court building's steps, and controversial High Court rulings, can there be any doubt that the U.S. Supreme Court's decisions affect the lives of ordinary Americans? Or that the Court has become an incredibly powerful part of our system of self-government? But why does the Court have the final word on the meaning of the United States Constitution, and why can it nullify federal and state legislation and overturn federal and state court decisions?

The answers to these questions lie in the history of the High Court. History is an essential place to look for answers for three reasons. First, the justices of the Supreme Court themselves are continually looking to history to help them decide cases. They examine "precedents," earlier decisions of the Court on past cases similar to the one they must decide at the moment. They also survey the events leading up to the case, in effect the case's own little history. If the case in front of them raises constitutional questions, they ask an additional set of historical questions: What did the framers of the Constitution and its amendments mean to say when they wrote those words? What did the words mean to people who lived then? Have those meanings changed over time? If the parties in the case are disputing the application of an act of Congress or a state legislature, the justices pose a similar set of historical questions about that piece of legislation.

The second reason that a history of the Court is an essential aid in understanding its function in our political system and the meaning of its decisions is that the Court is itself a historical actor. Sometimes what it does and says is even more important than what Congress or the president does or says. When a bitterly divided Court opined, in 1857, that Congress could not prevent a slave owner from taking his or her property into the western territories, its decision brought the Civil War closer. The Court's refusal to allow New York to regulate its bakers' hours, in 1905, spurred reformers to find other ways to safeguard workers. When a unanimous Court announced, in 1954, that segregation in public schools was illegal, it opened a new chapter in the civil rights saga. By deciding that a woman had a right to determine whether to end a pregnancy, in 1973, the Court created a political furor that has continued to this day.

Third, and not least, a history of the Court is essential because its operation, so vital to our system of checks and balances, is often obscure. The complexity of the cases the Court chooses to hear and decide cannot be easily explained to laypeople. The deliberations of the Court are kept secret, which veils its operation and thinking from our inspection. The arcane language of the law in its opinions adds another layer of incomprehensibility to the Court's operation, leaving most Americans bewildered about the Court. The result may be incomprehension and anger—as when House majority leader Tom DeLay, infuriated by a High Court action he did not understand, called a press conference to denounce the High Court as "an arrogant, out of control, unaccountable judiciary" and warn that "the time will come for the men responsible for this to answer for their behavior."

A history of the Court can lift the veil on that obscurity. By placing the justices' words in their historical context, going back to the time and occasion of their writing, one can gain a better and clearer perspective on the Court's labors. In effect, one can see behind the words to the ideas and intentions of the justices themselves.

But a historical inquiry into the Court poses two difficult questions. The first is whether the Court is just another political institution swayed by the partisanship of the justices and the political currents of the day. The second question is whether, as time has passed, the justices have changed the meaning of our fundamental laws—in effect, remade the Constitution. These two questions are the themes that frame the rest of this book, but they require some explanation here.

THE HIGH COURT AND POLITICS

Long ago, an aristocratic French visitor to our shores, Alexis de Tocqueville, wrote: "There is hardly a political question in the United States which does not sooner or later become a judicial one." From the controversies over taxation and slavery in the founding era to the most recent disputes over the detention of suspected terrorists in offshore compounds and the definition of prenatal life, the rulings of the High Court touch sensitive political areas. Does that mean that the justices are politicians and their decisions are politically determined?

Shortly before he died in 1954, Justice Robert H. Jackson wrote that "the constitutional convention [of 1787] deliberately withheld from the Supreme Court power that was political in nature." In his first year on the High Court, longtime political activist and law teacher Felix Frankfurter did an about-face and insisted that "no duty of judges is more important nor more difficult to discharge than that of guarding against reading their personal and debatable opinions into the case." The two justices denied that the Court was a political institution, that its members were chosen for political reasons, and that its decisions were framed according to the justices' political preferences. If, as many at the time complained, both Jackson and Frankfurter were highly influential political advisors to the president who nominated them, their views about politics and the Court demonstrate their aspirations to a nonpartisan stance.

Guarding the justices from the influence of political fads and fears was an announced design by the framers of the Constitution. The Court was supposed to be, in the words of founding father Alexander Hamilton, the "weakest branch" of the new government precisely because it had no political base. Its members were chosen by the president and confirmed by the Senate rather than directly elected by the people, steps intended to insulate the Court from political currents. The justices had no role in selecting lower federal court judges or any other federal official. To further immunize the justices from the demands of impatient majorities and outside interests, tenure on the Court was for life, with removal only for official misconduct after impeachment in the House of Representatives and conviction in the Senate. After all, one of the Court's major purposes, again according to Hamilton, was to restrain the popularly elected branches of government from overstepping their powers and violating the Constitution.

At times, the Court has gone to great pains to avoid making political decisions. In 1849, the Court adopted a self-denying "prudential" (judge-made) rule that it would avoid hearing cases that the legislative branch, or the people, could decide for themselves. Such "political questions," according to Justice Levi Woodbury in *Luther v. Borden* (1849), "depending often . . . on policy, inclination, popular resolves, and popular will, and arising not in respect to private rights . . . but in relation to politics . . . belong to politics, and they are settled by political tribunals." Giving to the justices, or the justices taking for themselves, the authority to decide political questions would create "a new sovereign power in the republic, in most respects irresponsible and unchangeable for life, and one more dangerous, in theory at least, than the worst elective oligarchy in the worst of times." In 1946, Frankfurter reiterated this principle in *Colegrove v. Green.* The apportionment of state legislative districts "is one of those demands on judicial power [in] which . . . this Court, from time to time, has refused to intervene. . . . It has refused to do so because due regard for the effective working of our Government revealed this issue to be of a peculiarly political nature and therefore not meet for judicial determination."

As with all rules the Court imposes on itself, however, the aversion to "political questions" was subject to later revision. In a famous footnote to *Carolene Products* (1938), Justice Harlan Fiske Stone promised that the Court would pay particularly close attention to state actions that discriminated against "discrete and insular minorities," precisely because they were not protected by democratic "political processes." In the 1940s, the Court struck down state laws denying persons of color the right to vote in election primaries, distinguishing primary voting from other kinds of political questions. Later decisions barred states from drawing legislative districts intended to dilute the votes of minority citizens. By the 1960s, the Court's abstinence in political questions had worn thin. In a series of *Reapportionment Cases*, the Court determined that states could not frame state or congressional electoral districts unfairly. Sometimes called the "one man, one vote" doctrine, the High Court's rulings remade state and federal electoral politics.

What is more, from 1789 to the present, the president and the Senate have imposed their politics on the composition of the Court. The very first members of the Court that President George Washington named had had political careers before they took their place on the federal bench. They were major figures in the American Revolution and served in elective office in their states or in the Continental Congress. What was more, they were all "federalists"—supporting the new federal Constitution when it came to the states for ratification.

Subsequently, presidents who nominated justices to the bench and members of the Senate who consented to the nomination well knew the political preferences of the nominee as well as his or her personal history. Henry Abraham's definitive study of the appointments process reports that well over 85 percent of the nominations presidents have sent to the Senate have come from the president's own political party. Federalist John Adams picked John Marshall as chief justice in 1801 because the president was confident that the nominee's political views matched Adams's own. Democrat Andrew Jackson chose Roger Brooke Taney as Marshall's successor because Taney was Jackson's loyal supporter. Republican Abraham Lincoln's choice of Democrat Stephen Field for the High Court was the first time that a president selected a justice from a different political party, but Field was a fierce unionist and hated the confederacy. Before President Franklin Delano Roosevelt named Frankfurter to the Court, he had been a strong supporter of the New Deal and a frequent guest of the president. Frankfurter remained loyal to the president's wishes. Justice Abe Fortas was President Lyndon Johnson's longtime legal advisor, a relationship that continued after Fortas became a justice and ultimately caused both men grief.

Members of the Court sometimes flaunted their own political ambitions. While on the Court, Chief Justice Salmon Chase and associate justices Stephen J. Field and William O. Douglas explored their chances for the presidency. Chief Justice William Howard Taft had served one term as president of the United States before he joined the High Court, and his successor as chief justice, Charles Evans Hughes, had earlier quit the Court to run for the presidency.

Nor can one ignore the political inclinations of the individual justices in explaining how they made law. It is important to remember that "the Court" is really nine people and not to confuse the shorthand reference to "the Court" with some sort of uniform, single-minded, entity. For example, *Bush v. Gore* (2000), growing out of contested ballots in the presidential election of that year, divided the members of the Court along partisan lines. There was plenty of precedent for that schism. As far back as 1803, Chief Justice Marshall was accused of reading his Federalist Party principles into his decisions. His successor, Roger Brooke Taney, was similarly attacked for interpreting the Constitution to favor the Democratic slaveholding South. Chief Justice William Howard Taft was accused of being a partisan for big business, and Chief Justice William Rehnquist faced criticism for his support of Republican presidential initiatives and his opposition to Democratic presidential policies.

In addition to personal loyalties and ideologies, major political events—galvanizing moments in public life—have influenced members of the Court. Congress's inability to settle the issue of slavery in "Bleeding Kansas" contributed directly to Chief Justice Roger Taney's over-the-top opinion in *Dred Scott v. Sandford* (1857). So, too, Franklin D. Roosevelt's landslide victory in the 1936 presidential race, coupled with crippling sit-down strikes at automobile manufacturing plants, followed by FDR's plan to "pack" the High Court influenced at least one member of the Supreme Court to change his views on the constitutionality of New Deal legislation.

Even Justice Jackson conceded that when politically charged cases came to the Court its authority to interpret the meaning of statutes put the Court squarely into the political arena. And at the very time he wrote his memo about impartial judging, Frankfurter was in the middle of a highly political case involving a religious group's refusal to salute the American flag in schools. The Court has sometimes issued broad decisions of political moment precisely because its members thought that the legislative and executive branches had stalled or were incapable of resolving national crises. *Dred Scott v. Sandford* and *Brown v. Board of Education* are arguably the most historically significant events in the Court's long history precisely because of the political stakes in both.

Some observers of the Court, including members of Congress and political scientists, have accordingly concluded that the High Court should be regarded as a political institution little different from Congress and the presidency. U.S. senator Charles Grassley (R-Iowa) candidly commented, on the occasion of the nomination of Samuel Alito Jr. to the High Court: "Now we have four liberals, four conservatives, and a moderate," as though the Court was simply a political body whose membership was to be apportioned according to the division of political views in the country as a whole.

Senator Grassley's comment demonstrates that the politics of the Senate spill over onto the Court. Senate confirmation hearings are sometimes political free-for-alls. The Senate confirmation hearings on Louis Brandeis, in 1916, were especially nasty because Brandeis's politics seemed so left wing at the time (he supported the rights of labor unions to organize and strike, for example), but Brandeis was confirmed in a narrow and partisan vote. He went on to become a much-respected jurist. Some presidents had poor luck with their nominees in the Senate—for example, Richard M. Nixon's first two choices to replace Abe Fortas, Clement Haynsworth Jr. and G. Harrold Carswell, were turned down. It appeared to many in the Senate that both of these southern judges had poor records on civil rights and were little more than a payback to that section of the country for Nixon's successful "southern electoral strategy" of 1968. His third selection, Harry Blackmun of Minnesota, became one of the most beloved members of the Court. So, too, Ronald Reagan's first choice to replace Justice Lewis Powell, Robert M. Bork, was turned down by a 58-to-42 vote after a bitterly divisive set of hearings, because Bork's views on civil rights seemed at odds with mainstream ideas. President George H. W. Bush's selection of Clarence Thomas ran into trouble when his alleged sexual harassment of an employee became part of the hearings record. The confirmation hearings of Samuel Alito were frankly and bitterly partisan, with both sides conceding that he was well qualified as a judge but disputing his anticipated views on key political issues. Although some observers lament the apparent rise in partisanship in recent confirmation proceedings, history shows that partisanship—and rejection by the Senate—is nothing new.

At the same time, it will not do to reduce the explanation of the Court's interpretation of the law to simple partisan politics—whether the politics of the justices or the politics of the country. Even if justices sometimes behave like political animals, their legal education, law practice, and fidelity to legal principles are never far away. What is more, were we to see politics everywhere in the history of the Court, we must discount what the justices themselves said. Most of the time most of the justices regard themselves as legal craftspeople making good law. This was particularly true in hard cases, cases whose mixture of fact and law was novel. As Laura Kalman has written in a wise and informed essay:

We should speak in terms of law and politics. We should remember that the Court can be at once a legal and a political institution. We should stop arguing about which account is correct and see how both together are. Our accounts are not mutually exclusive. Just as some speak of life in terms of body and soul, so law and politics create the life of the Court. Like objectivity and subjectivity, form and substance, public and private, law and politics are interdependent.

What is more, the members of the Court, whatever their political allegiances, are almost always zealous defenders of the Court's final authority to interpret the Constitution. When the governor of Arkansas openly defied the Court's order to desegregate a city school system, in effect interposing himself and the state government between the High Court and the citizens of the United States (those who happened to reside in Little Rock), the Court spoke with one voice. It did not matter that Justice William O. Douglas and William Brennan were Democrats or that John Marshall Harlan and Charles E. Whittaker were Republicans. In a unanimous opinion, *Cooper v. Aaron* (1958), the Court proclaimed that it was "supreme in the exposition of the law of the Constitution," and no state or federal official, elected or otherwise, could refuse to obey its command.

THE COURT AND THE CONSTITUTION OVER TIME

The second question that occurs in a historical study of the Court is whether the justices have changed their interpretation of the provisions of the Constitution. Dissenting in *Home Building Association v. Blaisdell* (1934), Justice George Sutherland wrote that "the whole aim of construction [of the meaning of the Constitution] . . . is to discover . . . the intent of the framers." If this cannot be done with any precision, it is nevertheless a historical task. When attempted, however, does it prove that the justices' view of particular constitutional clauses have changed as the times changed? Can one determine the meaning of the words of the Constitution to those who wrote them? This historical task was assigned the justices by Justice Antonin Scalia, dissenting in *Roper v. Simmons* (2005). "What a mockery" the Court makes of the founders' Constitution, he warned, when it supplants the "original meaning" of the document with its own preference for "evolving standards." In a 2006 address to the Federalist Society, he insisted that the only way to read the Constitution was "as it was originally written and intended." Those who could not see this simple and necessary truth, including members of the High Court, were "idiots."

Justice Sutherland was as appalled at this prospect as Justice Scalia. In 1936, Sutherland wrote for the majority of the Court in *Carter v. Carter Coal*:

It is urged that the question involved [that is, government-imposed minimum wage laws] should now receive fresh consideration, among other reasons, because of 'the economic conditions which have supervened'; but the meaning of the Constitution does not change with the ebb and flow of economic events. We frequently are told in more general words that the Constitution must be construed in the light of the present. If by that it is meant that the Constitution is made up of living words that apply to every new condition which they include, the statement is quite true. But to say, if that be intended, that the words of the Constitution mean today what they did not mean when written—that is, that they do not apply to a situation now to which they would have applied then—is to rob that instrument of the essential element which continues it in force as the people have made it until they, and not their official agents, have made it otherwise.

Not all of the justices subscribe to Sutherland's view of constitutional interpretation. Some adopted a more fluid style of interpretation of our fundamental law. In a much-cited 1985 address, Justice William Brennan said that Americans have a "living Constitution," changing to fit their needs and reflect their values. In *Roper*, Justice John Paul Stevens wrote that "the evolving standards of decency that have driven our construction of . . . the Bill of Rights foreclose any such frozen . . . reading. That our understanding of the Constitution does change from time to time has been settled since John Marshall breathed life into the text." As President Franklin D. Roosevelt told the nation in his fourth inaugural address, on January 20, 1945, "Our Constitution of 1787 was not a perfect instrument; it is not perfect yet, but it provided a firm base upon which all manner of men, of all races, and colors, and creeds, could build our solid structure of democracy."

Students of the Court have given names to Justice Sutherland's and Justice Brennan's philosophies of judging. The former is called "judicial restraint" and the latter "judicial activism." In fact, only a few of the justices have consistently hewed to one or the other of these styles of judging. Sutherland, like Oliver Wendell Holmes Jr. before him and Felix Frankfurter after him, was consistent in his belief that courts should not try to go beyond the case before them or intrude on the functions of the other branches. This partitioning of the function of courts and the elective branches is called deference. A few justices have been openly activist, Chief Justice Roger Taney for one, and Justices Frank Murphy and Arthur Goldberg as well. For them, results were more important than doctrinal consistency.

A history of the Court also provides an answer to the question of whether the justices, over time, have in fact changed their view of the Constitution. History cannot prove that the Constitution is a living document that changes its meaning, but the historian of the Court can say that the Court is a living institution whose members have changed their view of the Constitution. As Justice Stephen Breyer has wisely written, "The fact that members of historically different Supreme Courts have emphasized different constitutional themes, objectives, or approaches over time allows us to characterize a Court during a period of its history and to speak meaningfully about changes in the Court's judicial 'philosophy' over time."

Indeed, when one looks closely, one can see strong ties between the shifting constitutional readings of the justices and larger changes in American life and thought. Historical actors themselves, the justices do not stand outside of time. Instead, as Benjamin Cardozo revealed to a Yale University audience in 1921, eleven years before he was elevated to the Court, judges reach into their own values and experience to decide how to apply precepts and precedent to the cases coming to the Court:

There is in each of us a stream of tendency, whether you choose to call it philosophy or not, which gives coherence and direction to thought and action. Judges cannot escape that current any more than other mortals. All their lives, forces which they do not recognize and cannot name, have been tugging at them—inherited instincts, traditional beliefs, acquired convictions; and the resultant is an outlook on life, a conception of social needs.

These forces find their way into every justice's opinions, and in turn become part of the political, intellectual, and cultural history of our land.

The justices are not always entirely candid about admitting the essential role of their own history in their view of the law, however. Chief Justice John Marshall, one of the most creative of our lawgivers, consistently denied that he was doing anything other than pronouncing what the law was. Jurist and later judge Jerome P. Frank wrote in *Law and the Modern Mind* (1930) that most judges are in thrall to the "self-deception" that they could not make law and that judicial lawmaking was "improper." The result was a series of "circumlocutions" and confusions. Some modern critics of the Court have accused the justices of "hiding the ball" in their decisions, concealing their true motives and desires.

THE STORY OF THE COURT IN FIFTEEN CHAPTERS AND THREE PARTS

To demonstrate the historical relationship between the Court and politics and to track how the justices' ideas of the Constitution have changed over time, *The Supreme Court: An Essential History* adopts a narrative approach. In other words, we tell a series of stories. These tales are dramatic in themselves, tracing the Court's beginnings, with six men living in a clapboard boardinghouse, meeting in a series of drafty mildewed anterooms, and riding thousand-mile circuits in rickety coaches, to what has become the most closely watched and admired tribunal in the world, with its own "marble palace" and thousands of lawyers, law professors, journalists, and historians hanging on its every word.

We tell of the law the justices made, with its evolving conceptions of human rights and human dignity, its shifting readings of the role of business and commerce in our law, and its often contentious relations among the various branches of government and among the various levels of government. We have included discussions of the "doctrines" or ideas of law that the justices enunciated and surveyed contemporary commentary on the merits of the Court's work.

We follow how the High Court's decisions weave into the larger history of our nation. In times of war, class strife, and moral revolution, the Court sometimes spoke the conscience of the nation and sometimes seemed to lose its moral compass, sometimes ahead of popular opinion, seeing the future, and sometimes lagging seriously behind changing mores and attitudes.

To organize this narrative, we have adopted a "chief justice synthesis," a way of breaking up the story similar to the conventional "presidential synthesis" found in American history textbooks. Each chief justice's tenure occupies its own chapter. Such a scheme has the virtue of simplicity and definitude, though we know that not every chief justice was a John Marshall or an Earl Warren, and all chief justiceships did not last the same number of years. Thus our chapters vary in length.

We provide thumbnail sketches of every associate justice appointed to the Court and longer biographies of the more important members and those members who sat in more recent years. Although some justices contributed relatively little to the Court's work and even less to the law, they all belong here, for they all served. To be complete, a history of the Court cannot omit any of them. For the same reason, we relate something about the everyday life of the Court and its members—where the Court met, how the justices worked with one another, and how they balanced family and occupation.

We analyze the Court's handling of cases, but we do not discuss every case the Court heard and determined. That would have been impossible. Even the pre–Civil War Courts averaged over 50 cases per term (the time the Court sits each year). By the end of the nineteenth century, the docket had grown to 250 cases a year. After Congress decided, in 1891, to let the High Court limit some of its caseload and then, in 1925, to allow the Court to select its docket, the caseload evened out at about 200 to 210 cases per year. In recent years, that docket has come down to 80 or so cases a year, but the number of majority opinions, concurring opinions (agreeing with the decision of the Court but adding or subtracting something from the majority opinion), and dissents has grown immensely. In fact, during the Warren Court years, there were more concurring and dissenting opinions than majority opinions. That pattern persists.

We selected those cases that were most reflective of the way the Court saw the law and those cases that had the most impact on the everyday lives of ordinary Americans. This rule of selection seemed best to fit our idea of an essential history of the Court for today's citizen.

We have added a larger framing device to the fifteen chapters by dividing the work into three parts. This division is not entirely arbitrary, nor merely a housekeeping device. The three parts correspond to three deep sea changes in ordinary Americans' relationship to their government (and vice versa).

In the first section, we cover the Court from its inception into Reconstruction, in 1873. From the founding of our nation through the Civil War, our system of democratic republicanism remained a great experiment. Undertakings of state and federal government might lead to a more secure America, or to division, controversy, and ultimate dissolution. No one could be sure which road we were traveling. The key legal mechanism holding the nation together was itself a novel innovation of the Constitution—federalism. Federalism is the concept that both the national and the state governments were sovereign. A brilliant experiment offering something to both nationalists and localists, federalism nevertheless posed difficult legal questions about state laws and court rulings that conflicted with federal law, and about states having different laws from one another. The Constitution did not resolve these questions, other than to allot certain powers exclusively to the federal government and to make the Constitution the supreme law of the land. To the Court fell the job of defining and defending the boundaries of federalism.

In the second section, we trace the Court's thinking from the Gilded Age through the end of the New Deal. Union victory in the Civil War seemed to answer the most vexing puzzles of federalism. The nation was one and would survive. Amendments to the Constitution ended slavery and defined federal citizenship. Under this new Constitution, the nation would prosper. These were the days of increasing concentration of wealth in corporations and giant financial and industrial institutions; the appearance of sprawling cities, filled with millions of immigrants; and the country's rise to international power. These changes heightened the struggle between labor and capital and between old ideas of competition and new forms of economic combination. All sides turned to the Court, and its attempts to resolve these immensely contested issues would shape politics for the next sixty years.

In the final section, we cover the history of the Court from World War II to 2006. A third great shift in American government in the 1930s posed new challenges for the justices. The nation adopted liberal reforms and governmental welfare policies—a "safety net" for workers, the elderly, the infirm, children, and the poor. All of these government initiatives were challenged in court. Under pressure from reformers inside and outside the other branches of government, the Court had to rethink its earlier posture on private rights and public policy. At the same time as the Court was deferring to legislative reform initiative, it confronted questions of the rights of racial and other minorities. The Court also heard cases concerning First Amendment freedoms of worship and speech. It began to view gender as a legal category and considered whether privacy was a constitutional right.

Surely no story is more essential for Americans to know or for historians to retell.

Part One

The Heroic Courts

Politics and constitutional law came together from the first sitting of the first U.S. Supreme Court and continued to infuse one another through the last sessions of the Civil War–era Courts, in 1873. Chief Justices John Jay, Oliver Ellsworth, and John Marshall grew to political maturity in a time when the word "party" was synonymous with conspiracy and faction; yet each man was a committed federalist and approved of the new national government. Each contributed on the Court to making that nation stronger. All saw the Court as a crucial agency in that process, changing the Constitution from the shell holding together a federation of states into the core document of a central government. In short, they changed the role of the Court and the meaning of the Constitution.

Chief Justice Roger Taney and Chief Justice Salmon P. Chase came from parties undreamed of at the time of the ratification of the Constitution, but both men served at the highest levels of those parties before taking the center seat at the High Court. The Jacksonian Democrats and the Lincoln Republicans shared a robust concept of democratic republican politics that none of the founding fathers would have recognized—or approved of. Taney's version of states' rights, however, had its origin in the Jeffersonian protests against an overweening Federalist Congress, and Chase's version of civil rights had its origin in the enactments of the Civil War Congress. Political change and legal change thus fed the ideology of the High Court well into its fourth and fifth generations.

The so-called Reconstruction amendments—the Thirteenth, Fourteenth, and Fifteenth—have been rightly called a new Constitution, but that text, like the prewar document, had to be interpreted. It was a heroic effort in an age of larger-than-life jurists and politics. For the Court not only helped found the nation—it helped save the nation from itself.

CHAPTER 1

The Origins of the U.S. Supreme Court

From the very first moment that the American colonists established judicial tribunals to hear and determine cases, the connection between politics and the courts was clear and important. In the revolutionary crisis that ended the colonial era and in the rise of new state governments that followed independence, the courts were as much political actors and as influenced by political currents as any of the other branches of government. In other words, the struggle for power and the operation of courts continually overlapped. This contest shaped the framing of Article III of the federal Constitution, the article creating the Supreme Court of the United States.

At the same time, the judges who sat on the bench and the lawyers who brought cases to court believed that the rule of law—neutral, fair, and well-understood principles applied evenhandedly to those who stood before the court—should govern the operation of the courts. Rule of law confuted the appetite for power, saved courts from factions and parties, and elevated judging above favoritism and corruption. This ideal of impartial justice, with safeguards against the politicization of the law and the courts, also found its way into Article III.

COLONIAL AND REVOLUTIONARY PRECEDENTS

Although colonial law and colonial law courts were based on English models and in the main relied on the outward forms of English law and courts, from their inception they differed from their English counterparts, and that difference resulted from practical politics. There were many law courts in England at the beginning of the seventeenth century. The law was written in a combination of English, Latin, old French, and jargon. In America, by contrast, there were only a few kinds of courts and they were conducted in everyday speech.

The down-to-earth quality of American courts reflected the fact that the colonial court was an extension of the power relationships in the colony itself. Royal charters giving the colonists the privilege to make and enforce laws were contracts that the crown's lawyers drafted, but the colonists viewed them as constitutions of self-government. Grants to the colonists to hold courts became occasions for locally important men to sit as judges concerning their fellow colonists. This they could do because the colonists, in general, willingly accepted the judgments of the colonial upper classes. In turn, the judges, drawn from the landed and mercantile elite, did not flaunt their power. Colonial courts relied on the politics of deference and reciprocity.

The colonial court from the beginning was political, sensitive to local opinion, and open to the people. When courts met, the parties to civil suits and the judges all knew one another, and the social and economic distance between the highest and the lowest in society (except for the slaves) was not nearly as great as in England. True, in theory, the ultimate authority for all law and judging still lay across the Atlantic. But the crossing was long and difficult, and for most purposes authority lay on this side of the ocean.

The shape of the colonial courts system, like its function, mirrored local political arrangements. Unlike the English array of a great many very narrow and specialized tribunals, almost all of the colonies developed a very simple overlapping hierarchy of courts. Petty sessions held by the justices of the peace were the lowest level of official tribunal. Above them sat county courts. Supreme or superior courts were the highest courts in the colony. Often the same men sat as justices in local courts and judges on the high courts. There was no bar to multiple office holding in the colonies. In some of the colonies, notably Connecticut, the legislatures performed the role of high courts. Individuals could petition the assembly for redress, and the assembly would pass a "private bill" that took the place of a court hearing and decision. Legislatures also passed "bills of attainder" that named a person as a criminal and convicted him of the offense without any trial. Finally, some legislatures sat as collective tribunals to hear cases that touched on public order or the political process. All of this brought politics into court and the courts into politics.

The colonial high court judges were laymen, men of affairs and authority in their communities who were acquainted with law but rarely trained in it. Moreover, they were never full-time jurists. After three-quarters of a century of operation, the highest courts of Massachusetts and Virginia rarely included more than one well-educated lawyer. The legal skills of the judges in Pennsylvania were no higher. Only New York had a legally literate bench. This pattern continued well into the eighteenth century in most of the colonies.

Because the judges did not possess their own store of legal expertise, they were prone to being influenced by the lawyers who practiced before them, on the one hand, and by blatantly political considerations, on the other. Lawyers like William Smith of New York, George Wythe of Virginia, and Oxenbridge Thatcher of Massachusetts gained great authority as teachers of law as well as its practitioners because they knew how to navigate the shoals of political bias in the courts and because they were living repositories of their colonies' case law.

Some judges were openly partisan. When James DeLancey, chief justice of the New York Supreme Court in 1735, presided over the trial of John Peter Zenger (accused of libeling governor William Cosby), DeLancey made no pretense of objectivity. Appointed by Cosby, he was Cosby's man, and he even refused to let Zenger's New York lawyers argue the case for him, disbarring them when they complained of Cosby's high-handedness. Colonial high court judges had to sit with juries, unlike the English high courts. American juries could and did ignore the law ("jury nullification"), and even when they bowed to the judges' instructions, they were not as tame as juries today. DeLancey told the jury to convict Zenger, but he got off because his new lawyer (Philadelphia's Andrew Hamilton) convinced the jury that telling the truth was a defense against the charge of libel, and the jury did not care much for Cosby.

By the early 1770s, American lawyers and jurors had worked out in their own minds what their rights and privileges were in the grand scheme of the empire, creating a kind of American constitutionalism within the framework of empire. In this, they blended and transformed English and earlier colonial legal ideas, philosophical conceptions of governmental rights and duties, and religious notions of the good state. This native constitutionalism did not appear in the opinions of colonial supreme court justices, most of whom were appointed by the crown and some of whom remained loyal to it when the revolutionaries declared independence from the British Empire. Instead, American constitutional notions surfaced in lawyers' briefs, revolutionary pamphlets, and newspaper articles.

Many of the best and brightest of the revolutionaries were lawyers, and they took part not only in the legal defense of revolutionary activity but also in the framing of the new states' governments. It was a lawyer, Thomas Jefferson, who wrote the Declaration of Independence that the delegates to the Continental Congress signed. It was another lawyer, John Dickinson, who drafted the Articles of Confederation to bind the thirteen new states of the United States together. In those states, no sooner were the shackles of the British thrown off than revolutionary leaders drafted constitutions and asked the voters to ratify the new documents and then reopened the courts as republican institutions.

Then, irony of ironies, the revolutionary lawgivers decided that their new courts must be safe from politics. In fact, one of the most important parts of their new system of republican legalism was a concept of separation of the judicial branch from the legislative and executive branches, monitored and maintained by checks and balances.

The notion of separation was first discussed by John Adams in his *Thoughts on Government* (1776), written to influence the shape of a new constitution for Massachusetts. He hated multiple office holding and advised that no official should be allowed to hold more than one. According to Adams, separation of powers would safeguard the republic from corruption—by reserving the making of the laws to the legislature, the execution of the laws to the executive, and the adjudication of disputes to the courts. The legislature was no longer to act as a court nor was the governor to sit as a judge.

Adams insisted that the independence of the judiciary in the state was essential to prevent its capture by the legislature or its domination by the executive: "The dignity and stability of government in all its branches, the morals of the people, and every blessing of society depend so much upon an upright and skillful administration of justice that the judicial power ought to be distinct from both the legislative and executive, and independent upon both, that so it may be a check upon both, as both should be checks upon that." One can see in Adams's explanation of separation of powers the origins of the concept of checks and balances, not only as a foundation of later American constitutional thought but also as a protection of the courts from the other, more political, branches.

The idea of separation of powers caught on in a big way. After the federal Constitution was drafted, three of its proponents, Alexander Hamilton and John Jay of New York and James Madison of Virginia, set about to defend it in a series of newspaper articles. Later named the Federalist Papers, these serialized essays explained the need for checks and balances in language that would become a part of American political heritage.

The Federalist Papers regarded the separation of the judiciary from the other branches as a vital safeguard in republican governance. As Madison wrote in Federalist Number 47, "The accumulation of all powers legislative, executive, and judiciary in the same hands, whether of one, a few, or many, and whether hereditary, self appointed, or elective, may justly be pronounced the very definition of tyranny." How to avoid it? Madison returned to the topic in his Number 51: This could be done "by so contriving the interior structure of the government, as that its several constituent parts may, by their mutual relations, be the means of keeping each other in their proper places."

Adams had already concluded that courts must be a source of moral authority. Although he knew that the laws did not embody moral precept (that was left to churches, families, and other institutions), he insisted that judges, particularly high court judges, not only spoke the law; they must be seen as the embodiment of the authority of the law: "The judges, therefore, should be always men of learning and experience in the laws, of exemplary morals, great patience, calmness, coolness, and attention. Their minds should not be distracted with jarring interests; they should not be dependent upon any man, or body of men." In short, they should have a judicial temperament. Hamilton, like Adams, a lawyer, made the same point in his Federalist Number 78: "The benefits of the integrity and moderation of the judiciary have already been felt in more states than one. . . . Considerate men of every description ought to prize whatever will tend to beget or fortify that temper in the courts; as no man can be sure that he may not be to-morrow the victim of a spirit of injustice, by which he may be a gainer to-day."

Adams's call for judicial tenure during good behavior (as opposed to the English system of tenure during the pleasure of the crown) would become the rule for federal judges and was true of the first state court judges as well. Massachusetts's new constitution expressly stated that "it is essential to the preservation of the rights of every individual, his life, liberty, property, and character, that there be an impartial interpretation of the laws, and administration of justice. . . . the judges of the supreme court should hold their offices as long as they behave themselves well." Pennsylvania's Supreme Court judges were barred by its constitution from "holding any other office, civil or military, not to take or receive fees or perquisites of any kind" but on good behavior could be reappointed to office every seven years and were to have a fixed salary.

Both the Massachusetts and the Pennsylvania state constitutions featured a bill of rights. All the new state constitutions (with the exception of those of South Carolina and Georgia) included one form or another of bills of rights guaranteeing freedom of speech and assembly, jury trial, the presence of counsel at trial, prohibitions on illegal searches and seizures, and the right to own and bear arms. The protection of those rights fell to the state's highest courts. These bills of rights did not appear in the federal Constitution the delegates drafted in Philadelphia, but they did figure in the ratification debates. In fact, the Federalists (the pro-Constitution party) explicitly had to promise to propose amendments to the Constitution comprising a bill of rights when the first Congress met.

THE SUPREME COURT BECOMES PART OF THE FEDERAL CONSTITUTION

There was no supreme court in the confederation the states framed during the Revolutionary War. The reason was political. The new states did not want their own courts overshadowed by a central or national court. In fact, the Articles of Confederation, first drafted in 1776 and finally ratified by all the states in 1781, did not mention any courts. Disputes among parties within the states would be handled by the appropriate state court, and those who fled from the judgments of those courts were to be delivered back to the state from which they fled. Boundaries or other disputes between states would be heard by the confederation congress, when and only when one or more of the states petitioned the congress to hold a hearing. Commissioners agreed to by the states or appointed by the congress, with the states having the power to strike from the list objectionable names, would decide the issue. The same procedure would be used when disputed land claims by citizens of different states came to the congress. In effect, these were arbitration boards, not true courts, and certainly not national supreme courts. Unlike regular courts, they did not sit at regular terms, nor have a fixed, salaried membership, nor have their own docket (list of cases to be heard).

Although a confederation supreme court could not have gained the approval of the states at this time, the absence of a national court was keenly felt by lawyers and litigants. As Hamilton wrote at the beginning of Federalist Number 78, "In unfolding the defects of the existing confederation, the utility and necessity of a federal judicature have been clearly pointed out." There was no court to handle disputes arising on the high seas (vitally important for a nation dependent on its overseas trade), disputes over the finances of the confederation (in particular, the laxness of some states in providing their share of funding for the confederation), or disputes in which foreigners sued American citizens (in particular English merchants owed money by Americans).

But the same states whose representatives to congress rejected the idea of a national supreme court provided the model for it. Although the new state constitutions varied a good deal, they all had some form of supreme court. Historians have not given enough credit to the state constitutions' influence on the federal Constitution. Much that would appear in the document the framers drafted that spring and summer of 1787 in Philadelphia came directly from the state constitutions. As Madison would write in Federalist Number 39, the guide the delegates used for the new federal Constitution was the states' constitutional provisions. For example, "the tenure of the ministerial offices [in the federal government] will be a subject of legal regulation, conformably to the reason of the case, and the example of the State Constitutions."

When the delegates to the Constitutional Convention met, the Virginia delegation proposed a plan to create a national government. Although the confederation congress had called the convention to prepare amendments to the

Articles of Confederation, all the delegates knew they would be going beyond these instructions to formulate an entirely new government. The so-called Virginia Plan included a national judiciary. Its judges would serve during good behavior for a fixed salary so that the new high court would be independent of the other branches. Its jurisdiction would include those cases that only a national judiciary could hear and that had especially vexed the old confederation—piracy and other crimes on the seas, disputes over ships captured from the enemy, cases in which foreigners were suing Americans or citizens of one state were suing citizens of another, cases involving the national revenue (the same sort of cases that the kings' high courts heard), and cases of impeachment of federal officers.

The impeachment provision offers a clue to where the Virginians' idea for a national supreme court originated. It came from the Virginia Constitution of 1776. Under it, any officeholder could be impeached upon the vote of the legislature that the official had violated his public trust or committed a crime in office. The penalty for impeachment was removal from office and disqualification from holding office again. So, too, the provisions for a national supreme court were modeled on the state's constitution. Thus a combination of necessity arising from the absence of a judicial arm of the confederation and familiarity with the provisions of its state constitution shaped the Virginia delegation's vision of a national judiciary.

Delegates from New Jersey were not happy with the Virginia Plan. They did not care for the idea that both branches of the national legislature would be based on the "free population" of each state. Slavery was legal in New Jersey, and its delegates did not oppose the Virginia Plan because of opposition to slavery but because Virginia, a larger state with a larger population than New Jersey, would automatically have more weight in the proposed national legislature.

But the so-called New Jersey Plan that its delegates offered also included a national judiciary, and it was very similar to Virginia's. The New Jersey delegation framed its plan in response to the same dismay over the weakness of the confederation and relied upon the same kind of corresponding or analogous borrowing from state law as did the Virginians. New Jersey's Constitution created a supreme court whose members were named by the legislature and commissioned by the governor for renewable seven-year terms. The justices could hold no other office and might be removed by impeachment. According to the New Jersey Plan, the federal judiciary was to be appointed by the executive and to hold office during good behavior at a fixed salary and was to hear and determine all cases of impeachment, disputes over ambassadors, cases of captures of enemy shipping, cases in which foreigners were parties, and cases involving federal laws on revenue or trade.

Later in the debates, Hamilton offered his own plan. His views were in most ways unacceptable to the body (he wanted a lifetime president, for example), but in his proposal for a national judiciary, he clove close to his colleagues. Its twelve judges were to handle impeachment cases and cases involving the capture of vessels at sea and to hear appeals from the state courts' rulings on federal revenue cases and cases involving foreigners. The judges were to hold office during good behavior and to have fixed salaries.

In the ensuing debate over various plans for the federal government, comparatively little was said about the courts. A general agreement on the need for a national court rested upon recognition that state courts should not be deciding admiralty (piracy, capture, and salvage) and diplomatic cases, cases with foreign parties, and cases involving the federal revenue. What was more, when citizens of two different states or the states themselves sued one another, there had to be an impartial tribunal to decide the matter. The confederation's version of arbitration was workable but unwieldy.

The most contentious issue was how to select the members of the high court. James Wilson of Pennsylvania, who would serve on the first Supreme Court, begged that the legislature not name the judges. It would lead to "partiality and intrigue," he feared. Anyone familiar with the highly partisan politics of Pennsylvania's legislature would naturally worry about giving the national legislature sole control of the nominating and confirming of federal justices. John Rutledge of South Carolina disagreed. He represented the "lowland" elite of the state, which controlled its legislature, and he had no reason to object to legislative control of the judiciary. Rutledge's fellow South Carolinian Charles Pinckney supported Rutledge's position.

James Madison of Virginia, one of the authors of the Virginia Plan and a frequent contributor to the debates (some have called him the father of the Constitution), worried that the Rutledge plan gave the legislature too much of the judicial power. Madison was a fan of checks and balances. At the very least, he wanted the Senate to have the power to appoint rather than the lower house. A month passed, and Madison came up with another idea. On July 18, he proposed that the executive should nominate and the Senate should confirm the justices, but he could not persuade his comrades, and the issue was again set aside.

Madison was a canny operator at the convention. He had served in the confederation congress, and he knew how hard it was to get the states to give up any of their prerogatives. He was also a strong believer in national power and the need for an independent national judiciary. So he bided his time until

September 12, in the meantime working with the Committee of Detail to get his proposal for the appointment of justices into their report. He succeeded. By the time the delegates got finished with it, that report looked exactly like Article III in the final version of the Constitution. Indeed, because the new court was to have jurisdiction over controversies between states, between a state and a citizen of a different state, and between citizens of different states, the other members of the Committee of Detail were even more determined to place a check on the appointment power in the Senate. That house (under the Great Compromise struck earlier in the convention) would represent all states equally, and each state legislature would select its two U.S. senators.

In the proposed Article III, the entire judicial function of the new federal government was vested in the Supreme Court and in inferior courts to be created by acts of Congress. This gave to the U.S. Congress some check upon the judiciary. Although tenure of federal judges, including the justices of the Supreme Court, was during good behavior (and not at the pleasure or whim of the president or the Congress), justices could be removed by impeachment in the House of Representatives and conviction in the Senate. This did not mean that the justices had to stay in office their entire lives, and in the early years of the Court, many nominees either refused to accept appointment to the court or resigned after a short period of service.

JUDICIAL REVIEW

There was another wrinkle in the fabric of the proposed new Supreme Court, a kind of jurisdiction not mentioned in Article III. The objects of the new court's purview were clear—but was the Court to have sole or even primary authority to rule on the meaning of the new Constitution's provisions? William Samuel Johnson of Connecticut, a lawyer with a huge practice (he was the number-one debt collector in his state) and some credentials as a scholar (he would take part in the codification of his state's laws), offered an amendment to the Committee of Detail report adding "all cases arising under this Constitution" to the jurisdiction of the new court. Madison worried aloud that this might give the high court the power to issue advisory opinions, that is, to interpret the Constitution when it did not have a case or controversy before it. Such a provision in Article III might encourage the justices to meddle in the operations of the other branches.

Elbridge Gerry, a Massachusetts delegate and as close to a democrat as anyone at the convention, argued that the judiciary should only rule on the constitutionality of laws pertaining to judicial matters—whatever they might be (he did not say). The problem, unexamined in the brief debates on the new court, was that any matter might be deemed "judicial" by the court once it sat, even purely political issues that were best left to the elected branches. Ironically, fourteen years later, Madison would find himself in the middle of a sensational case in which the High Court appeared to meddle in politics, a case that would once and for all establish the power of the Court to say what the Constitution meant.

The authority to lay any federal or state legislative enactment, as well as any decision by a lower federal or state court, against the text of the Constitution and decide whether the act or the lower court ruling was constitutional is now called "judicial review." It is the single most controversial power that the High Court exercises. There could be little objection to the proposed federal Supreme Court deciding that a *lower court* had read the Constitution wrong— that ability was explicit in the Constitution and implicit in the very concept of a supreme court. The highest English courts exercised it over inferior courts in the realm, and England's judicial officers exercised it over colonial legislative enactments and colonial supreme court decisions. The real question in the new nation was whether judicial review of *legislative enactments* violated the idea of separation of powers, elevated the unelected justices of the Court above the elected representatives of the people, and placed courts above legislatures.

The new states' high courts had exercised a form of judicial review over their state's legislative acts in a handful of cases between 1776 and 1787. Almost all involved denying loyalists or suspected loyalists the right to a jury trial as guaranteed in the new state constitution. Most recently, Daniel Hulsebosch's research has found such cases in Virginia, New Jersey, North Carolina, New York, Connecticut, New Hampshire, and Rhode Island. Rather than striking down the offending legislation as unconstitutional and therefore null and void from the moment of its passage—and initiating a constitutional crisis in the process—the state high courts overturned the rulings that lower courts had made, based on some fault in the statute. Although in almost all of the cases the assembly bridled at the courts' rebuke, the supreme courts insisted, at least by implication, that they were the final judges of the constitutionality of legislation. Thus the precedent of state courts' judicial review could be read in two opposing ways—either to support the necessity of judicial review or to warn against it as improvident.

Hamilton tackled the issue of judicial review in Numbers 78 and 81 of his Federalist Papers essays. He came up with two ingenious but mutually exclusive defenses of judicial review. First, he cast the high court as the virtual representatives of all the people. Virtual representation was an English idea, that members of Parliament did not speak only for their constituents but for all the people. The revolutionaries rejected the concept. Hamilton, a great lover of English conservative political ideas, brought it back to life: "No legislative act therefore contrary to the Constitution can be valid. To deny this would be to affirm that the deputy is greater than his principle . . . that the representatives of the people are superior to the people themselves," that is, that the legislature at any given sitting could overrule what the people wanted in their constitution. In America, "it is far more rational to suppose that the courts were designed to be an intermediate body between the people and the legislature, in order . . . to keep the latter within the limits assigned to their authority." Hamilton assumed (or at least he argued) that such a high court would never be activist, creating law or turning its ideas of good political policy into law. Instead, it would be a "bulwark of a limited constitution against legislative encroachments."

Hamilton's second argument ran at right angles to his first. In Federalist Number 81, he insisted that "there is not a syllable in the plan under consideration which *directly* [italics in original] empowers the national courts to construe the laws according to the spirit of the Constitution." In other words, if the authority was not spelled out in the Constitution, it could not be exerted. How odd that only a few years later Secretary of the Treasury Hamilton would assay a "loose construction" of the Constitution's language in order to support his plans for a national bank. As he wrote in 1791, "If, then, a power . . . in any case be deducible, by fair inference, from the whole or any part of the numerous provisions of the Constitution of the United States," its constitutionality could be established.

In arguing "in the alternative," that is, putting forward two views that were themselves not consonant, Hamilton was acting the role of lawyer, his client being none other than the Constitution itself. For he, and also those who opposed the Constitution, knew that the Committee of Detail's report gave to the new high court the power to reverse state court decisions (under the Supremacy Clause of Article IV): "This Constitution and the laws of the United States which shall be made in pursuance thereof, and all treaties . . . shall be the supreme law of the land, and the judges in every state shall be bound thereby." The practical application of this injunction, coupled with the language that emerged in Article III defining the appellate (appeals) jurisdiction of the Supreme Court as extending "to all cases . . . arising under this constitution, the laws of the United States, and treaties . . . both as to law and fact," was a plain acknowledgment of the power of judicial review.

At the end of consideration of the Committee of Detail's report, William Samuel Johnson added to Article III's grant of jurisdiction the phrase "in law and equity." Although Johnson was probably thinking about his own experience in Connecticut, the two words "in equity" would prove to be a remarkable piece of farsightedness. Many states had separate courts of law and equity. In them, equity did not equate to abstract fairness. It meant that the court could provide certain types of relief or remedies not available in law courts. Equity of this sort originated in the medieval English court of chancery when a party claimed that he or she needed the help of the chancellor to gain justice. The chancellor used his power as the king's secretary to compel the other party to the case to do or not do something—for example, to produce documents or to answer questions. The most potent of these remedies was the injunction. Johnson's few words would, in time, come to be tremendously important to the Supreme Court and the nation. For example, enforcement of Supreme Court civil rights decisions almost always involves injunctions.

The delegates voted to accept the recommendations of the Committee of Detail on September 12, then left for home, except for a handful of delegates, led by Gouverneur Morris of New York. These men formed the Committee of Style, and it was this committee that added the Preamble to the document. Thus the notion of a perfect union, in effect a perpetual union, did not arise from the debates in the convention. Nor had the majority of the delegates agreed to the language that "we the people" had spoken. The rest of the hortatory language of the Preamble, its commitment to domestic tranquility, justice, the common defense, and the general welfare, and above all the blessings of liberty, were the handiwork of the Committee of Style, not the convention.

Preambles to legislative acts are not generally taken to be part of the enactment, but this Preamble would play an increasingly large role in the history of the Constitution, for it was the only statement in the Constitution of the purposes for forming the federal government and, beyond that, of the aspirations of a new and untried kind of nation. At the end of the twentieth century, some scholars would argue that the Preamble prefigured a government far more concerned for the rights and dignity of its citizens than existed anywhere else in 1787 and that the High Court was responsible for interpreting this language.

THE SUPREME COURT IN THE RATIFICATION DEBATES

Like the state constitutions, the federal Constitution would not be the fundamental law of the land until it was ratified. The document provided that the new government would begin operation when two-thirds of the states agreed to the Constitution. All but one of the states held elections to ratification conventions (South Carolina's legislature gave itself the power to sit as a ratifying convention).

Article III of the draft constitution was not a major topic at the ratification conventions in the states. From this relative silence, one should not conclude that the framers' generation of political leaders trusted courts or that the arrangements in Article III satisfied everyone. At the same time, the ratifiers knew that the Supreme Court would have an important say in the future of the country.

For example, the Constitution made several concessions to states that had slaves, including guarantees that fugitive slaves would be returned, that three-fifths the number of slaves in a state would be counted in determining that state's representation in the House of Representatives, and that Congress would impose no bar on the importation of slaves from abroad until 1808. But other states had already ended slavery, and it was prohibited in the newly organized Northwest Territory. These matters would surely come before the High Court at some time. The language of Article VI, making the Constitution and the laws of Congress supreme in the land, did arouse suspicion among those who favored states' rights, and certainly the Supreme Court would have to handle cases arising from that grant of authority.

Long ago, legal historian Julius Goebel suggested that the reason why the judicial portions of the draft Constitution escaped relatively unscathed from the ratification controversy was their vagueness. Of course, it is also possible that there were more discussions and more objections than have survived in the records of the debates and the pamphlets and newspaper articles on ratification.

It might be added, as Hamilton hinted when he called the federal courts "the weakest branch," that the High Court was to have no say in the choice of any officials, including its own membership. Unlike the legislative branches, it had no way to censure or exclude any of its members. Members of the High Court had no formal say in the selection of lower federal court judges, should Congress create such courts. When Congress did create inferior federal district and circuit courts, in 1789, the president nominated and the Senate confirmed or refused to confirm federal judges. Nor did the U.S. Supreme Court ever have a formal role in selecting, disciplining, or removing any other member of the federal government, for the powers of impeachment and trial resided with Congress. The single exception was that the chief justice was to preside over Senate impeachment trials of presidents.

Lawyers played a major role in the debate over ratification of the Constitution. Some were frankly worried about a Supreme Court that could overturn state court decisions. George Mason, a Virginia lawyer who had written his state's constitution, wrote to George Washington on October 7, 1787: "The Judiciary of the United States is so constructed and extended, as to absorb and destroy the judiciarys of the several states; thereby rendering law as tedious intricate and expensive, and justice as unattainable, for a great part of the community, as in England." Mason, like Luther Martin of Maryland, another leading lawyer, would have preferred to limit the U.S. Supreme Court's jurisdiction to national matters only, but they could not object to its existence. In reply, federalist lawyers like Hamilton and Connecticut's Oliver Ellsworth denied that the federal courts would interfere in purely state matters, a denial that was not entirely forthright.

Although all the men who would become members of the new Court in 1789, and many who would serve before the decade was over, sat in their respective states' ratification conventions, only a few of them spoke about the provisions for the Supreme Court. James Wilson of Pennsylvania argued that the new High Court must have the power to restrain the federal legislative branch, even to void acts of Congress, but he stopped short of saying that the Court could restrain state legislatures, although Pennsylvania anti-federalists raised this specter. John Jay of New York would write a handful of the Federalist Papers essays and was Hamilton's able partner in gaining New York ratification, but his contributions to that project did not require defense of Article III. Sitting as an associate justice on the Supreme Court in 1795, John Blair of Virginia would support judicial review of legislation. Seven years before, at the Virginia ratification convention, he supported the new Constitution, but on neither occasion did he offer elaboration of his views. William Cushing of Massachusetts favored ratification at his state convention, but he did not address the objections that anti-federalists raised to the supposed "tyranny" of federal courts. In Connecticut, Ellsworth lauded the idea of a union. He did not discourse on the merits of the new judiciary, though he would play a major role in framing that judiciary when Congress met. The silence of the future justices made sense—why rise to defend what was not attacked? Save for the near-universal demand that jury trial be guaranteed somewhere in the Constitution, the federal courts at first flew under the anti-federalists' radar.

The achievement of the framers, pulling together the experience of colonies and new states and creating a national court, yet leaving to Congress the creation of inferior federal courts and the fine tuning of the High Court's procedure and appellate jurisdiction, was the work of true statesmanship. Politics played a part, but so did the genuine desire of lawyers for a fair and final national tribunal. How would their plan function?

CHAPTER 2

The Jay and Ellsworth Courts, 1789–1801

The Constitution may have created the Supreme Court, but congressional acts defined and empowered it and the president named its inaugural members. From the first, thus, the new Court was not really independent of the other branches. Within the first long decade of its existence, experience would prove that the line between the legal and the political was almost invisible to the eye and easily crossed.

At the same time, the justices made every effort to locate their opinions on high ground, placing legal precedent above the waves of partisanship that rocked the new nation. Though all of the justices were federalists and supporters of the Constitution, they eschewed obvious connections with the emerging two party system. They thus established another kind of precedent that had nothing to do with law—the ideal of a court above parties.

CONGRESS FRAMES THE OPERATIONS OF THE FIRST SUPREME COURT

In March 1789, Thomas Jefferson pleaded with his younger friend and trusted political ally, James Madison, to draft amendments to the federal Constitution and submit them to the first session of Congress. Both men knew the dangers of legislative tyranny, and both believed that even limited government needed to be curbed. Both knew the nation had been greatly divided during the ratification debates and understood that one of the points of contention was the absence of a bill of rights in the Constitution. Madison had already, grudgingly, conceded as much to the voters who elected him to the first Congress. Precisely when he became a convert, to use Julius Goebel's term, is unclear, but over the course of the fall and winter, he culled a list of prospective amendments from the suggestions various states had made. When the first Congress met, he promised to introduce a list, and on June 8, 1789, three months after Jefferson pressed him, Madison submitted them to Congress.

Madison proposed nine changes, only five of which had to do with personal liberty and civil rights (the other four would have altered the Preamble), and he wished to include them in the body of the Constitution. Debate over these in Congress swelled their number to seventeen, and twelve were passed and sent to the states to be added to the end of the document. The first of them began "Congress shall make no law" establishing a religion or preventing the free exercise of religious worship, nor was it to abridge freedom of the press, speech, assembly, or petition. Additional amendments included the right to own and bear arms, not to be forced to house soldiers, and to be protected against illegal searches and seizures (probable cause was required, and the search warrant had to be specific).

The other nine amendments ratified by a sufficient number of states to go into effect in 1791 included trial by jury, grand jury indictment, right to counsel, public and speedy trial, no double jeopardy, no self-incrimination, right to confront witnesses and to compel the production of evidence, and no excessive bail or cruel and unusual punishment. The Ninth Amendment was a catchall, specifying that the enumeration of rights in the first eight amendments did not exhaust the rights retained by the people. This amendment would find new life in modern concepts like the right to privacy.

Finally, a tenth amendment reserved to the states and the people those "powers" not "delegated" to the federal government. The last amendment opened the door to what would later be called "states' rights" and was clearly a sop to the anti-federalists. The federal government could not function if the anti-federalists of 1787 refused to acknowledge the new nation's authority. One must bear in mind that in 1789, Rhode Island and North Carolina still had not ratified the Constitution. In point of fact, there was no organized resistance to the federal government by the anti-federalists. A number of them secured election to the Congress. They would become a "loyal opposition" within the government, demanding literal and strict adherence to the limitations on Congress and the presidency written into the Constitution.

Only the First Amendment explicitly addressed Congress. It is not clear if Madison or other members of Congress voting for the amendments intended them to apply to the states as well. In 1819, the Supreme Court decided that the Bill of Rights did not apply to the states, but after the Civil War—when the Fourteenth Amendment explicitly required states to ensure due process, equal protection of the law, and privileges and immunities of U.S. citizens residing in the state—justices, lawyers, and legal scholars began to discuss the "incorporation" of the Bill of Rights into the Fourteenth Amendment.

Although they were not explicitly directed to the High Court, the Bill of Rights would find in it its ultimate definer and defender. But not at first. Indeed, the High Court operated for two years before the Bill of Rights was ratified. One of the basic guarantees of liberty Jefferson extolled was the judicial check upon the other branches, but the Court was not, at first, eager to undertake this role. Indeed, within the next decade, just such a challenge to freedom of speech and freedom of the press would arise from acts of a partisan majority in Congress (the Alien and Sedition Acts of 1798, discussed below), and the Court never ruled on it.

Some commentators on constitutional history have argued that the Bill of Rights amounted to a new constitution, based on rights rather than government power, but there is little evidence for this in the historical record. Instead, they were the extension of guarantees in the state constitutions that predated the federal Constitution, another example of the influence of state constitutions on the federal Constitution. Although they would, in later years, become the basis for a defense of personal dignity, at the time they were directed to the protection of personal property.

The second contribution the Congress made to the functioning of the Supreme Court was the Judiciary Act of 1789 and the Process Act of 1789. It can even be said that the judiciary acts completed the work of Article III. Together they fulfilled the promise of Article III to establish a system of federal trial courts ("such inferior Courts as the Congress may from time to time ordain and establish"), define their jurisdiction ("with such exceptions, and under such regulations as the Congress shall make"), and then lay down rules for bringing suits (called "civil procedure"). The acts provided the means by which suits in lower federal courts could be appealed to the High Court. In many of these, the High Court had no choice but to hear the appeal. Thus much of the business of the first Court involved private actions rather than matters of real public importance or the interpretation of the Constitution.

The Judiciary and Process Acts concerned both procedure—how to bring a suit and which courts heard which kinds of suits (jurisdiction), in short, the forms of the law—and content. Teachers of law make the distinction between procedure and content in law a major one. In fact, the line between the two is often blurry. It certainly was in the two acts.

The new High Court was to have six members. They were each to join with newly appointed federal district court judges to hold the "circuit courts." (The district court was held by the district judges sitting alone.) The circuit courts were to hear cases of crimes under federal law (a subject of controversy about which we will hear more shortly), suits brought by citizens of one state against citizens of another (so-called diversity suits), suits brought by a citizen of one state against another state (even more controversial—it would lead to the Eleventh Amendment), and suits brought by foreigners against U.S. citizens or states (the most controversial of all, because it concerned suits by British creditors to recover prewar debts from Americans). The Court was not to weigh factual assertions but only to interpret law. In short, it was to be a true appeals court.

The committee that wrote the Judiciary Act was led by Oliver Ellsworth of Connecticut and William Paterson of New Jersey, but on it sat two of the most vociferous of the anti-federalists, Virginia's Richard Henry Lee and William Maclay of Pennsylvania. Both had campaigned against the Constitution but now served in the new Congress. They would ensure that the new federal courts did not take a big bite out of the business of the state courts.

As a result, the two pieces of legislation were a patchwork of compromises. They gave to the federal courts those powers that the confederation experience dictated national courts must have, but they limited federal courts to a small portion of the jurisdiction they might have claimed under the Constitution. For example, although the federal courts gained diversity jurisdiction, and these cases might end up on the Supreme Court docket, section 25 of the Judiciary Act stated that the law of the state in which the federal court sat was to determine the outcome of diversity suits. This was a major concession to those in Congress who feared that federal courts operating under purely federal law would undermine state sovereignty.

District courts were to hear admiralty cases (for example, disputes over salvage and confiscation on the high seas, navigable rivers, and the coast), the collection of the federal revenue, and "prize cases" (cases of ships taken during war, brought into U.S. ports, and claimed as prizes by their captors). But neither the district court nor the circuit courts had broad jurisdiction over suits arising under federal law because the Judiciary Act did not confer this jurisdiction. This was another major concession to the localist forces in the Congress.

The debate in Congress over the Judiciary Act galvanized the legal community. Anti-federalist lawyers maintained a steady correspondence with their allies in Congress on the subject of how the new courts would operate. Although many of the letters worried about the imposition of federal court tyranny, underneath one can read the lawyers' genuine concern about how the new courts would affect legal practice in the states. James Sullivan of Massachusetts wanted to know whose laws would govern disputes in the new courts. Edward Shippen of Pennsylvania worried that the proposed circuit courts would be "inconvenient" for him and his clients. Samuel Chase of Maryland voiced objections to using "chancery" procedures in federal court (particularly, taking depositions instead of hearing witness testimony in open court).

These kinds of practical concerns anti-federalist lawyers shared with federalist lawyers. Although the federalists supported the creation of inferior federal courts, they were also uncertain how the new courts would operate. Fisher Ames of Massachusetts knew that "the lawyers" were going to dispute every point, and John Jay of New York urged the circulation of "useful hints" among lawyers to allay their concerns. This kind of very practical back-and-forth demonstrates that the lawyers, most of whom would have to practice before the new courts, had a set of priorities apart from political ideology and party identification.

There is some evidence that supporters of the two acts were not so interested in the supposed impartiality of federal courts (for example, protecting out-of-state parties in suits against the partisanship of state courts' judges or juries) so much as in using the federal courts to collect revenues and punish those who committed federal crimes. Although these functions were both vital if the new federal government was to prosper, at the time there was no federal law of crimes and no federal revenue to collect. Nevertheless, listening to Ellsworth and Paterson talk about the need for strong federal courts could not have been comforting to defenders of local courts.

The Judiciary Act once again soothed local fears. The act placed a monetary threshold on federal jurisdiction—in civil cases $2,000 and in admiralty cases $300. In fact, monetary provisions in the new legislation truly constrained the new federal courts. The federal government was already in debt, and in any case the congressmen believed that expensive government, government that had lots of offices with high salaries, was an open door to corruption. The funds allotted to the new High Court under the Compensation Act of 1789 were but $21,500, all for salaries. No fees. No expenses. This parsimony continued until 1819, when total compensation package for all the justices was raised to $33,000. The salaries grew bit by bit over the next century. Still, many nominees to the Court refused to serve because they could not support their families on the salaries the government offered.

This same penny-pinching attitude influenced Congress to refuse to create a separate body of judges to ride circuit—laying instead this duty on the shoulders of the justices of the Supreme Court. The justices hated circuit riding. One wrote to his brother that he felt like a "Post boy," and another's wife complained that it turned him into a "traveling machine." In 1793, some of this burden was eased—only one Supreme Court justice had to attend the circuit court sessions instead of two.

An entirely rational, indeed already overdue, reform was passed by Congress in 1801 that created an intermediate layer of federal appeals courts staffed solely by circuit court judges. It would have ended the burden of riding circuit and clarified the duties of the Supreme Court. But the Judiciary Act of 1801 was so tainted by politics—all the new circuit court judges were from one party—that the very next Congress, now with a majority from the opposing party, voided the act. Supreme Court justices had to ride circuit until 1891.

THE FIRST SUPREME COURT MEMBERS

In addition to setting the number of the justices and creating the inferior federal courts, Congress had a direct role in the appointment of the justices. The Senate had to confirm all nominations. Lawyers who intended to practice before the Court wanted justices who were educated, competent, and trustworthy. The party in power in the presidency wanted justices sympathetic to its aims and goals. In 1986, Justice William Rehnquist argued that there was nothing wrong with the president trying to "pack" the High Court with justices friendly to presidential aims.

The majority party in the Senate likewise was looking at nominees' political affiliations. The vast majority of Senate votes on Supreme Court candidates have followed party lines. The senators' preferences might clash with the president's. This happened as early as 1795, when the Senate rejected President George Washington's nomination of John Rutledge as chief justice. In fact, over the course of our history, the Senate has often challenged and occasionally rejected a nominee, though sometimes the process is far more openly partisan than at other times. Of the 157 nominations to the U.S. Supreme Court between 1789 and 2006, 35 were not at first confirmed by the Senate. Of these, 5 were eventually confirmed.

There were no well-organized, sharply divided national parties in 1789, when Washington submitted the first roster of nominees to the Senate. The federalists and the anti-federalists both sought seats in the new government and pledged themselves to make it work. But all of the nominees for the first Court as well as their successors in the 1790s were federalists. They lobbied for ratification of the Constitution. All of the nominees were also well-known lawyers. Almost all of them had had some hand in drafting the Constitution and the Judiciary Act. Some had experience as state court judges, but others, like James Wilson and John Jay, had very little experience on the bench. Still, as South Carolina federalist Ralph Izard wrote when he learned that his friend John Rutledge had been chosen, "The judges of both the Supreme Court and the district courts are chosen from among the most eminent and distinguished characters in America, and I do not believe that any Judiciary in the world is better filled."

Washington sought the advice of people he trusted in making the appointments, but likely candidates were not shy about petitioning him for his support. James Wilson, who would be appointed, wrote to the new chief executive: "But how shall I now precede? Shall I enumerate reasons in justification of my high pretensions . . . and inform you that my aim rises to the important office of chief justice?" Wilson stopped there, knowing that the Pennsylvania delegation in Congress would sing his praises.

Pennsylvania lawyer and judge Edward Shippen had to promote himself, and he was not shy about it: "I promise you to execute the Trust with assiduity and fidelity and according to the best of my abilities," he told Washington. The salary would also help him support his eight children. Washington did not choose him. Virginia lawyer Arthur Lee also offered his services—as one Virginia gentleman to another: "It is not without great apprehension of presuming too much on the favor you have always shown me, that I offer you my services, as a judge of the Supreme Court." Washington agonized over this offer, but in the end declined it because Lee was an anti-federalist and known to be testy.

The process of solicitation and choice of the first justices set a number of lasting precedents. Because the Senate had to confirm the nomination, many of those who expected to serve asked their state's U.S. senators to put in a good word with Washington or with John Adams, the new vice president and presiding officer of the Senate. To this day, the senators from the potential appointee's state are consulted about the appointment, a "senatorial courtesy."

The barrage of letters and personal pleas also set a precedent—the first six weeks of every president's term are still spent trying to fill posts. Before the Civil Service Act, just about every federal office was a patronage post and up to the president to fill. Washington selected those men whose views were substantially in accord with his own. He did not appoint men known for contentiousness, assuming that the federal judges should have a judicial temperament. In a pattern of choice that set a precedent lasting to this day, President Washington also based his nominations on geographical considerations. New England, the Middle Atlantic, and the southern states were all represented. When a justice from one of these regions left the Court, Washington and his successors in the presidency tended to nominate a successor from the same region. The reason behind this was the circuit-riding requirement.

The average age of the first Court's members was a little over fifty. At a time when the average life expectancy was under forty, the Court's members were exceptional for their longevity. As if in proof, shortly after their nominations, two of the six became too sick to serve. As rule, justices from the Tidewater lasted a shorter time than those from New England—the brackish marshland of the Chesapeake was home to malaria and typhoid. There were even outbreaks of yellow fever as far north as Philadelphia.

Still, Washington's preference for the more mature jurist set a precedent. The average age of the Court's members throughout the nineteenth century never dipped below fifty years and often was over sixty. The result was that much of the time a slot or two were unfilled, some members were too sick to attend sessions, or justices were infirm while they sat. Some were nearly blind; others almost deaf; and some thought more about their own mortality than the cases before them. Looking to fill seats on the Court, President William Howard Taft remarked that one of the incumbents was deaf, another blind, and a third slept through the oral arguments.

The last precedent that Washington set in the appointments process was not properly within the job description of the justices, but then much that shaped the country's first federal government was extralegal. He had picked men he thought he could trust on a wide variety of matters, and he did not hesitate to ask members of the Court for advice on matters touching on diplomacy and policy as well as on law. They supplied him with information and guidance. This close personal tie between individual justices and presidents continued well into the twentieth century. In 1793, the Court refused to issue formal advisory responses to the president's queries, a refusal that has endured to this day, but the back door to the president's office was always open to his friends on the Court.

Just as George Washington was chosen president in part for his accomplishments and in part for his demeanor—truly being as well as acting the part of father of his country—the first chief justice set the tone for the office by his background and his manner. John Jay came from one of New York's most wealthy families and had a significant law practice all during his adulthood. He was a revolutionary, but a moderate, wise, and prudent one, much respected among the new state's members of the bar. His caution and wide experience of law made him a natural diplomat, and the mission to Spain during the war was, if not entirely successful, proof that he could perform his job in the most trying of circumstances. He would repeat the performance as head of the U.S. delegation to Britain, in 1795, to negotiate a treaty between the two countries.

During the confederation period, Jay had served as secretary for foreign affairs (precursor to the office of secretary of state in the federal government), and this experience confirmed what his trials overseas had taught—the necessity of a strong national government if the revolutionary experiment in republican self-government was to succeed. He joined with Hamilton and Madison to write the Federalist Papers and urged the New York convention to ratify the Constitution. His was the first name submitted by Washington to Congress, and two days later, on September 26, 1789, Jay was confirmed by the Senate.

Jay would serve until 1795, when he resigned to become governor of New York. He stepped down from that post in 1801 after two terms (following the precedent for executives set by President George Washington) and lived twenty-eight more years in retirement on his Hudson River estate. Calling him a conservative is easy in one sense—in his views of social and political events he was hardly a democrat. But he was not conservative in his role as chief justice, expanding the purview of the Court and the power of the federal government. And in some areas of law, for example, criminal punishment, he was a reformer. He also urged the abolition of slavery.

Washington's second appointment to the High Court was an embarrassment to him and to the reputation of the Court. John Rutledge of South Carolina had a distinguished career as a South Carolina judge and revolutionary governor. What was more, he had strongly supported the Constitution. But there was a mercurial streak in him, perhaps because his father had died when he was young and then a succession of uncles and teachers died suddenly. In any case, he resigned his post on the High Court without ever having sat on it.

In 1795, Washington appointed Rutledge to replace Jay as chief justice, but Rutledge violently denounced the pro-English policy of Washington's administration. He was reported to have said that he preferred going to war with England once again rather than bow to its demands. The Senate, a majority of whose members strongly supported the administration's foreign policy, refused to confirm the appointment. Even his friend Ralph Izard commented that the death of Rutledge's wife had left his "mind so much deranged, as to be in a great measure deprived of his senses." Libeled by other federalists as a "Jacobin" (a supporter of revolutionary French radicalism), Rutledge was actually an aristocrat who had little liking for democracy. He simply liked the English, against whom he had fought in the Revolutionary War, less. He died in his beloved city of Charleston, in 1800.

William Cushing's nomination was even more troubled than Rutledge's, but not because of Cushing's temperament. Instead, he had a rival from Massachusetts who, in effect, ran against him for the post. John Adams favored John Lowell, with whom he had close ties, but Cushing won out. He was hardly the aristocrat that Jay and Rutledge were, instead coming from an upwardly mobile middle-class family. He was, typical of some Americans of that day, a man "on the make"—ambitious and eager for personal and financial advancement. His talents and opportunism took him from rural Massachusetts to rural Maine (then a province of Massachusetts) and back, and finally to a place on the colonial supreme court (while not abandoning his private practice of law). He served the crown, then the new state, with equal avidity. In financial and legal matters he was a conservative, with no affection for the farmers of his birth region. Once confirmed to the High Court, he served on it until his death in 1810.

The tenure of Robert Harrison of Maryland on the Court was as short as Cushing's was extended. At first he did not accept the post, even after the Senate had confirmed him. Reconsidering, he agreed to serve but never reached the first meeting of the Court. Ill health, the ostensible reason for his initial decision, overcame him, and he died three months after he returned home. His career was similarly obscure though admirable. Rising from the local gentry, through law practice in Virginia, and distinguished service in the Continental Army, he became Washington's military aide in 1775 and remained at Washington's side through all the hardships of the war. He returned to Maryland after the war, choosing a quiet life as chief judge of the state supreme court. Washington trusted him and told him so, but his health, so carefully guarded in the postwar era, gave out before he could serve his chief once again.

James Wilson was in many ways Harrison's opposite—outspoken, fulsome, and egocentric. He was born in Scotland and educated for the ministry. He came to Pennsylvania to make his fortune, read law in John Dickinson's law office, and practiced law on the colonial frontier. There he became an avid revolutionary politician and propagandist. He could be a long-winded speaker, but what he said was often brilliant. He made major contributions to the debates at the Constitutional Convention and shepherded the Constitution through the Pennsylvania ratification convention. At the same time as his political career flourished, his law practice grew. Unfortunately, he engaged in a number of highly speculative land deals and was deeply in debt by 1789, when his appointment to the Court was confirmed. He was hounded on circuit by lawyers representing his creditors, sometimes missed sessions to rush back to Philadelphia to refinance his debts, and in 1797 was briefly jailed for nonpayment of nearly $200,000. In broken health and poverty, he died in 1798.

John Blair Jr., of Virginia, unlike Wilson, came from one of the most prominent families in the state and was a wealthy man when he was tapped for the Court. Long favored by the royal government, he was a reluctant and conservative revolutionary, but his high status and ability gained him high office in the judiciary of the new state. At the Constitutional Convention he sided with the federalists, again with no great enthusiasm. He served on the High Court until 1795 and died in 1800.

Harrison's place on the Court was taken by James Iredell of North Carolina. Iredell had come from Bristol, England, in 1768 to serve as a customs collector in North Carolina. His brother was a minister in the Church of England, and his family was well-off but not gentry. He read for the bar in North Carolina and began practicing law there in 1773. By the next year he was writing antiparliamentary pamphlets, but he was not in favor of independence (like many of the Carolina professional and merchant class) until it was declared. He served his new state's government as attorney general and judge and continued his private practice. He strongly supported the right to private property against almost all comers, and he saw the new Constitution as a bulwark of that right. A strong and outspoken federalist, he was a natural replacement for Harrison and sat on the Court until his death in 1799, at the age of forty-seven.

In 1791, Washington tabbed Thomas Johnson of Maryland to replace Rutledge. Almost sixty at the time, from one of the best and oldest families in the state, Johnson was a land speculator, lawyer, politician, and early opponent of royal taxes. He represented Maryland in the Continental Congress and was an avid supporter of independence. He became governor in 1777. His private interests and his seven children drew him away from public service for much of the 1780s, but he did support the Constitution, and he returned to public life as a justice on the state supreme court in 1788. He was hesitant about accepting the invitation to serve on the U.S. Supreme Court, however, and after two circuits and one session of the High Court, he resigned in 1793. Healthier in retirement than he had ever been in office, he lived in comfort on the estate of one of his granddaughters and died in 1819.

The next replacement was William Paterson of New Jersey. Paterson was born in Ireland but came to Delaware at age two. His family was not well-to-do, and he had to work his way through the College of New Jersey. No friend to the royal government, he was an early and consistent advocate of independence. As attorney general of New Jersey, he vigorously hounded the loyalists while carrying on a private law practice. His role in the Constitutional Convention led to the Great Compromise (the bicameral legislature with equal representation for every state in the Senate), and he pushed for ratification in New Jersey. Its legislature named him a U.S. senator, and he was the first from that house to serve on the High Court, from 1793 until his death in 1806. He was also the first of the justices to leave a distinct mark on the jurisprudence of the Court.

Samuel Chase was another of the first justices whose views of the law were soon widely known. Like Paterson, many of whose views he shared, Chase came from relative obscurity to high office. And as in Paterson's case, the catapult was the American Revolution. Chase's father was a clergyman, and the family always had trouble making ends meet (even when Chase's law practice was going well). He did not marry into wealth and never felt comfortable around the rich. He did find friends in the revolutionary crowd however, and he was as close to a rabble-rouser as anyone who held office under Washington. He was most at home in the legislature of his own Maryland, and he was the only anti-federalist that Washington appointed. But by 1788 he had changed course: he gained office on the bench and became a staunch federalist. His support for Jay's treaty brought him to Washington's attention, and Chase, one step ahead of bankruptcy, was happy for the salaried position. He served from 1796 to 1811 and was involved in many of the most politically divisive cases coming to the Court.

The last of Washington's appointments was Oliver Ellsworth. When the Senate rejected John Rutledge as chief justice and Cushing turned down an offer of the post, Washington turned to the Connecticut lawyer and legislator. Ellsworth had attended Yale and Princeton and, unlike Chase, married well (the daughter of a former governor). He preferred farming and legal practice to hobnobbing with the rich, however, and walked to the nearby county court rather than ride a horse or drive a chaise. He was adept at committee work in the Continental Congress and duplicated the feat at the Constitutional Convention in Philadelphia. He mastered detail, learned how to work well with others, and gained the respect of people of all parties. He was a federalist during the ratification debates and was selected for the U.S. Senate in 1789. There he drafted the Judiciary Act of 1789. During his service as chief justice, from 1796 to 1799, he worked for unity on the Court. Journeying to France in 1799, he helped heal the rupture of relations with the former ally of the United States and prevented war, an accomplishment for which pro-English politicians like Alexander Hamilton never forgave him. Citing ill health, Ellsworth retired in 1800. He died at home in 1807.

The last of the appointments in the 1790s was Bushrod Washington, John Adams's choice in 1799. Washington was the late president's nephew and lasted the longest of any of the first nominees, until 1829. He studied law at William and Mary, served as a private in a cavalry unit during the last days of the Revolutionary War, practiced law in Richmond, Virginia, and supported the Constitution in the Virginia ratification convention. Like his good friend and fellow lawyer, John Marshall, Washington was also a student of the law, publishing reports of cases and delving into the principles behind the precedents. He thus became a well-respected law teacher—Henry Clay was his student. Washington was less an original thinker on the Court than a meticulous and reliable one. He died in 1829, on circuit.

The second of Adams's appointments to the High Court was Alfred Moore of North Carolina. Moore came from great wealth, and he was early and consistently a federalist. He was also a power in North Carolina politics and an ardent nationalist, even though that state did not enter the Union until after the first Congress had met. He replaced Iredell in 1800 and served until 1804. He did not make a major contribution to federal case law, authoring only one opinion during his tenure. He did have the dubious distinction of being the least physically imposing of all the justices, standing no more than four and one-half feet tall and weighing in at less than one hundred pounds.

The appointments process—the who and how behind the staffing of the High Court—demonstrates that the founders of our constitutional regime did not see the Court as part of a democratic system. The nominees for the Court were drawn from the elite ranks of the legal profession (though not necessarily from the wealthiest families in the country). They did not equate the doctrine of "sovereignty of the people" on which the republic was theoretically based with ordinary people running the government. For them, the Constitution was not an act of popular will except in a general sense. Instead, the High Court was the epitome of a trusteeship in which "the people" were supposed to defer to their betters.

PARTY FORMATION, POLITICAL FACTIONALISM, AND THE SUPREME COURT

Two distinct types of political controversies influenced the Supreme Court's docket and output in the 1790s. The first was the struggle between localism and nationalism. Despite the creation of a national government, the American people's sense of nationhood in 1789 was weak. Over 90 percent of the population of four million lived in rural areas. Roads connected only a small portion of these localities, and travel along rivers, the major highways in the country, was dangerous in spring and impossible in winter. Most Americans thought of themselves as members of their villages, towns, parishes, churches, and states before they thought of themselves as citizens of the United States. Indeed, the new Constitution did not even define national citizenship.

Although most of the nation had united behind the new Constitution and would send representatives to Congress in the temporary capital of New York City, the political unity of the country was a fragile one. Creditors and debtors were vying for control of state governments, eastern bankers and western farmers had different political agendas, and, most troublesome, it appeared that there were "sectional" (large-scale regional) differences between the North and the South over slavery and expansion of the nation to the west. But the most telling of these controversies in the early days of the Court was the tussle over jurisdiction between federal and state courts, and the focus of the struggle was suits by citizens of one state against the government of another. Such suits put the sovereignty of the states at risk—the very peril that the opponents of the Constitution and the Judiciary Act had warned about.

Eight of these cases came to the Court between 1791 and 1798. Most of them arose because of a simple unpaid debt or a very convoluted dispute over land titles. The debt or transfer of title might have predated independence or arisen because a state had not paid for something it had purchased from an out-of-state vendor or because the state now owned the property that the out-of-state plaintiff claimed.

In the first of the cases, Maryland and New York agreed to be parties. In all but one of the remainder, governors and state attorneys general refused to participate, despite subpoenas from the High Court. They were backed by their state legislatures, who saw the suits as a violation of state sovereignty. In a number of the cases, the states told the plaintiff that he would gain justice if he applied to the state courts or to the state legislature instead of the federal courts.

The lead case in the widespread resistance to this branch of federal jurisprudence was *Chisholm v. Georgia* (1793). In *Chisholm*, the Court heard a suit by a South Carolina citizen seeking to collect a debt from the state of Georgia. Alexander Chisholm could have gone into the Georgia courts to seek payment, but he brought the suit in federal circuit court instead (assuming that the state court would rule in favor of the state). This fear was one of the reasons why the Judiciary Act had given diversity jurisdiction to the federal courts. But at the circuit session, Justice Iredell ruled that his court had no jurisdiction in the case and dismissed it. Chisholm then filed the suit in the Supreme Court, not on appeal, but under the Court's original jurisdiction in cases "in which a state shall be a party."

In effect, he was asking the High Court to act as a trial court to hear his case. The suit directly pitted the High Court against the sovereign state of Georgia, and it refused to participate in trial. On the jurisdictional issue, Chief Justice Jay reasoned that if one state could sue another in the Supreme Court, then a citizen of one state could sue another state. Georgia's sovereignty, which the Constitution guaranteed and Jay conceded, did not protect it from a lawsuit. He went on to suggest that the purpose of the federal court system was to protect litigants from the "errors" of state courts, a strong version of the federalist position. Justice Wilson agreed.

Justices Cushing and Blair did not press as hard for total supremacy of the "national courts" over state courts (this would have crushed the sovereignty of the state) but found grounds for jurisdiction in the plain language of Article III. If the Supreme Court had original jurisdiction in suits to which a state was a party, and Chisholm was suing the state of Georgia, then the High Court had to hear the case. Iredell dissented. The Judiciary Act did not spell out jurisdiction when a private citizen sued a state, and, since the act came after the drafting of the Constitution, it should control or provide the meaning of the grant of original jurisdiction in Article III.

Moreover, if the Supreme Court opened this door, then it would have many cases of this type coming directly to it, and its docket would overflow with trivial matters. What is more, because all of these cases were not coming on appeal, the High Court would be acting as a trial court, with a jury to determine matters of fact, more often than it would sit as the highest appeals court in the land. Perhaps the paucity of cases on the docket at that moment misled the majority; a more prudent stance would have renounced or qualified their jurisdiction in such cases.

Congress almost immediately stepped in to change the Court's jurisdiction. It could have responded by statute, but, instead, members of Congress from Massachusetts and Georgia, acting at the behest of their state governments, proposed an amendment to the Constitution that the judicial power of the federal courts not "be construed to" extend to suits against a state by citizens of another state or foreign nationals. Both houses of Congress passed the proposed amendment in 1794. By 1795, enough of the states had ratified to satisfy the three-quarters requirement, but the Eleventh Amendment did not go into effect until 1798, simply because states did not notify president John Adams.

In later years, the Court itself expanded the bar on suits versus states to include suits by a citizen against his own state and suits by states versus states when the state was acting for one of its citizens. In turn, plaintiffs seeking aid in federal courts got around the Eleventh Amendment by suing state officials by name rather than suing the state. In 1908 (*Ex parte Young*), the Supreme Court gave this exception its seal of approval. Then the Rehnquist Court narrowed the opening for such suits in *Seminole Tribe of Florida v. Florida* (1996).

Chisholm was also the first of a number of important cases overruled by constitutional amendments. Many of the Court's rulings upholding slavery and the forced return of fugitive slaves were overturned by the Thirteenth Amendment, which made slavery unconstitutional. The High Court's income taxation opinions were revised by the Sixteenth Amendment, which permitted an income tax not based on apportionment. The Court's deference to state laws barring women from voting were reversed by the Nineteenth Amendment, which gave women the constitutional right to vote; and the Twenty-fourth Amendment, barring poll taxes, overturned earlier Supreme Court decisions allowing poll taxes that effectually prevented blacks from voting.

A second type of local-versus-national politics erupted with a conflict over federal revenue acts. Most of the money to run the new government came from customs duties, but these did not begin to pay off the Revolutionary War debt. In 1791, Secretary of the Treasury Alexander Hamilton proposed a series of excise taxes, principally on distilled grains, that would close the shortfall. These fell disproportionately on western farmers, who could not get all of their crops to market and therefore distilled grains for home use and local sale.

In 1793, a group of disgruntled western Pennsylvania farmers refused to pay the excise taxes and attacked the collectors. In attacking federal officials, the so-called Whiskey Rebels were committing a federal crime. President Washington led a force of over ten thousand men over the mountains to quell the rebellion, and its leaders surrendered. Nine of them were held for trial in circuit courts in April 1795, but only seven were tried and only one was convicted. Washington pardoned him. *U.S. v. Hamilton* (1795), the only High Court case to come out of the affair, simply ruled that one of the rebels could not have a special court to hear his case. No one raised the Second Amendment (the right to own and bear arms) as a defense of the conduct of the rebels.

Political party factionalism was far more virulent than the local-national contest, but, unlike the latter, the High Court took no part in it. Political parties tried to silence one another by passing laws denying their opponents' free speech and freedom of the press, but leaders of the two parties did not bring to the Court cases testing the constitutionality of these statutes. It was the dog that did not bark in the night.

In the political ideology that the founders inherited from Britain, political parties were never acceptable. At best, they were seen as self-interested cliques; at worst they might be cabals or conspiracies to pull down the government. Organized opposition to government, even a "loyal opposition," was proscribed by law. When the opposition published its criticisms of the ruling party, the rulers prosecuted the dissenters for seditious libel.

The national party system that emerged here in the 1790s violated all of these precepts. The government party, the Federalists, dominated the executive and legislative branches, but the opposing Republican Party was also inside the government. The two parties thus contested the making and execution of policy at every turn. Out of this two-party contest, rather than out of the formal language of the Constitution, would come the basics of democratic politics—rotation in office, the right to criticize those in power, and the right to organize opposition at the polls.

The origins of the parties lay in part in Secretary of the Treasury Hamilton's program to place the nation on a sound financial footing. Reading the Constitution loosely ("loose construction") to allow Congress to create a national bank, provide bounties for home industries, and pass excise taxes, Hamilton hoped to jump-start the national economy, pay off the national debt, and reward the confidence of creditors. Taken together, his proposals also favored the wealthy citizens of the Northeast over the farmers of the West and the South. Representatives of debtors objected that Hamilton's ideas would favor a few over the many, in particular the "money power" over the poor farmer. Madison was among these opponents. So was Secretary of State Jefferson. The battle in Congress spilled out into the electoral districts, as Hamiltonian Federalists and Jeffersonian Republicans vied for votes.

Foreign policy issues made the party divisions even sharper. The center of the controversy was the United States' position on the wars that raged between England and France in the 1790s growing out of the French Revolution of 1789. The Hamiltonian Federalists supported England; the Republicans supported France.

When England and France went to war, Washington asked Chief Justice Jay to lead a delegation to Britain to resolve disputes over the neutral rights of the United States. The resulting treaty so displeased Washington that he concealed its terms for some months. When revealed, they infuriated the Republicans. The Federalists had a majority in the Senate and consented to the treaty in 1795. In the House, the Republicans threatened to hold up the appropriation necessary for the treaty but finally acquiesced. In the streets, however, Republicans paraded effigies of "that damn'ed arch-traitor, Jay."

Both sides started newspapers to gain voter allegiance and plead their causes. In 1797, after they retained control of both houses of Congress and elected John Adams president, the Federalists turned to law to suppress Republican dissent. Pointing to the growing nastiness of Republican newspaper attacks on Adams and other Federalist leaders, Federalist majorities in Congress passed a series of Alien and Sedition Acts in 1798. The Enemy Aliens Act allowed the president in time of war to deport or jail noncitizens deemed spies or saboteurs. The Enemy Friends Act gave him the same powers in time of peace. The Republicans saw both acts as aimed at the Irish and French immigrant supporters of their party. The Naturalization Act extended the period of residence required for citizenship (and the right to vote) from five to fourteen years, another step in preventing pro-Republican immigrants from participating in politics.

The Seditious Libel Act made statements and publications that opposed "any measure or measures of the United States" liable to criminal prosecution, with a maximum of a $5,000 fine and five years in prison. Truth was a defense, and there was no prior censorship of these statements, aspects of the law that, the Federalists alleged, allowed it to pass muster under the First Amendment. Ten of the seventeen Republican editors tried under the law were convicted. Some were imprisoned.

It was a legal crisis of unprecedented proportions and threatened to throw the new nation into civil war. Madison and Jefferson formalized their objections to the Alien and Sedition Acts in the "Virginia" and "Kentucky Resolves," respectively. The first, introduced by Madison in the Virginia House of Assembly in 1798, followed a statewide protest movement. Madison argued that the Federalists had illegitimately imported the English law of seditious libel into the federal Constitution. Jefferson, writing the Kentucky Resolves anonymously, went even further, to say that the states had the right to "interpose" themselves between the federal government and the citizens of the states when Congress violated the Constitution. The language of the resolves would be retrofitted to suit secessionists in later years, though neither man continued to hold these views after 1801 and Madison condemned extreme states' rights positions during the Nullification Crisis of 1828–1833.

Behind the two men's thinking was the concept that the federal Constitution must be interpreted "strictly" to confine the powers of the federal government to the letter of the document. They rejected the notion that the Constitution could be read "loosely" to expand the powers of the federal government.

All of this might have come to the High Court, either through a challenge to the Jay Treaty or through appeals of the convictions under the Seditious Libel Act. More than one member of the Court had prepared opinions on these issues in the event they arose. Both Paterson and Chase had ready drafts of opinions that would have upheld the Federalist legislative program—a foretaste of the Court's rulings on freedom of speech and press in the World War I era.

Still, if the Court upheld the Seditious Libel Act as constitutional, it would place itself in the center of the political maelstrom. If it struck down the law, it would isolate itself from the Federalists in Congress. Either ruling posed the threat of a self-inflicted wound from which the young Court, with little saved-up credibility (after *Chisholm*), might never have recovered. The Court could also have refused to hear the cases, claiming that they did not raise legal issues that the Court was competent to decide, or that it did not have jurisdiction in the cases, or that it was deferring to the elected branches of government. In later years, the Court would offer similar prudential (judge-made) excuses for not taking particular cases. Here, however, these claims would have rung false.

One may hypothesize, however, about arguments on both sides, had the issue come to the Court. Had the Court agreed to hear these cases, defenders of the Seditious Libel Act might have argued in court, as they did on the floor of Congress, that the law did not impose prior censorship on anyone, and thus did not prevent anyone from exercising freedom of speech or press. The First Amendment, if one accepts this argument, simply prevented Congress from operating a censorship bureau. Opponents would reply that the threat of prosecution for uttering political opinions would (and did) have a chilling effect on freedom of speech. No one at the time believed that freedom of speech was absolute, but the law penalized all criticism of the government that could not be proven, not just vile and unfounded lies (or, to borrow the language of *Sullivan v. New York Times* [1966], statements in reckless disregard of the truth).

A second issue would have arisen: whether Congress could import (or "receive") the English law of seditious libel, or any other of the English criminal laws. On the one hand, the Seditious Libel Act was not the first time that Congress had passed law based on English precedent. What was more, in a few cases that federal circuit courts heard involving crimes by diplomats, the courts had ruled that they also had such authority. The Judiciary Act of 1789 said nothing about this, but judges always try to expand their jurisdiction. Ellsworth in particular thought that the federal courts could impose common law penalties without congressional acts. Presiding over one circuit court session, he told the jury that there were "frequent references, in the Constitution, to the common law as a living code . . . brought from the country of our ancestors." Neither statement was exactly true. The Constitution did not mention the common law, and England was not the country of origin of two of his colleagues on the Court—Paterson was Irish and Wilson was a Scot.

On the other hand, Madison had told the Virginia assembly that such laws were bloody and barbarous and had constituted one reason why the colonies had rebelled. That was why he, Jefferson, and other leading Virginia lawyers had led a movement to create and codify new laws in Virginia. Federalists could reply that everyone assumed that the federal government had as much right to receive the common law as the states (many of which did receive the common law). In the alternative, they could argue that the same loose construction of the Constitution that permitted Hamilton's financial program to pass muster would permit Congress to enact the English common law of crime. The Supreme Court finally put the matter to rest in 1812, when it ruled that there was no federal common law of crime. Nothing prevented Congress from copying

English criminal laws, however, so long as the American version did not violate the Constitution.

Members of the Supreme Court heard Seditious Libel Act prosecutions on circuit. It is clear from their rulings in these cases and their summation of the law to the juries how they would have decided an appeal to the High Court. When one defendant argued (as permitted by the statute) that his criticism of the government was true, Justice Chase told the jury that the defendant "showed that he intended to dare and defy the government, and to provoke them," and that was enough to warrant his fines, jail time, and muzzling.

But neither Jay Treaty cases nor seditious libel cases came to the High Court, and Adams's own sense of right and wrong intervened to prevent disunion. He had no love of Hamilton, whom he saw as ambitious and unprincipled, and did not want a large standing army. In 1799, over the other Federalists' objections, he sent a second mission to France, led by John Marshall. The new mission settled most outstanding disputes. Adams would later reward Marshall by naming him secretary of state and, still later, chief justice of the U.S. Supreme Court. In the latter office, Marshall would serve with distinction until 1835, asserting the power of the High Court to review the constitutionality of state and federal legislation and establishing the supremacy of federal law.

But the furor over the Seditious Libel Act led to a split in the Federalist Party. Hamilton and his followers bolted and ran a candidate against John Adams. The same furor enabled Jefferson and his party to gain much popular support. With his victory in the 1800 presidential race, the idea that a free press could be silenced by law with the complicity of the federal courts was dealt a severe blow. In times of war and public fright, however, many Americans and not a few judges have proved more than willing to silence opinions they found unpalatable.

THE PRECEDENTS OF THE JAY-ELLSWORTH YEARS

The first sessions of the High Court had little business. Indeed, until 1791, no cases came to the Court under its original jurisdiction or its appellate jurisdiction. Over the course of the decade, from 1790 to 1801, only eighty-six cases appear on the High Court's docket. Half of these cases were actually "reported" in the first volumes of Supreme Court reports, edited by Philadelphia lawyer Alexander James Dallas. The largest number were admiralty cases, fitting the notion that the most pressing need for federal courts lay in the areas of piracy, privateers, and prize or capture cases. The justices were far busier riding circuit than sitting in New York, later Philadelphia (when the capital was moved there), and finally Washington, D.C., to hear cases. In fact, the Court had no permanent home in these years, holding sessions for a time in the city hall of Philadelphia.

But the cases that the Court heard, and those they refused to hear, were of great significance. They established precedent on the jurisdiction of the Court, the relation between the states and the federal government, and the powers of Congress and the presidency. In all of them, the Court's decision tended in the same direction: supporting the supremacy of federal law and federal courts over corresponding state law and courts.

In the first of these, *Hayburn's Case* (1792), the Court refused to sit as a pension board to hear petitions of Revolutionary War veterans. The justices believed that this onerous delegation of authority was not judicial, nor, according to the statute, would their determinations be final. The justices' decision came in the form of individual letters to President Washington rather than opinions from the bench. In *Glass v. Sloop Betsy* (1794), the justices agreed that all federal courts had admiralty jurisdiction and that jurisdiction could not be weakened by intervention of state courts or the courts of foreign countries. In *Ware v. Hylton* (1796), the Court ruled that treaties were not to be flouted by state laws. In *Hylton v. U.S.* (1796), the Court determined that a tax on carriages was not a direct tax (which under the Constitution had to be proportional to population) and was therefore constitutional. The decision protected the various federal excise laws. It also hinted that the Supreme Court had the right and duty to determine the constitutionality of federal legislation. In *Calder v. Bull* (1798), the Court read the constitutional ban on ex post facto laws narrowly (the ban only applied in criminal matters) and found a Connecticut law about wills unexceptionable; but Justice Chase hinted that state acts might be found unconstitutional if they violated a broader and more shadowy collection of basic republican principles. Taken together with the Ninth Amendment, Chase's opinion could become the basis of privacy rights.

There was one opinion that Justice Wilson and circuit judge Richard Peters delivered in 1793 that should have become a signal precedent in the years to come, but did not. In *Elkay v. Ives and Moss*, a free black father in Massachusetts sued two Connecticut slave traders for carrying off his daughters and selling them. The circuit court took the case under its diversity jurisdiction, and a jury awarded Elkay damages for the false imprisonment of his daughters, found to be free. They were returned to his custody. The precedent was clear: a black man could be a citizen of Massachusetts for the purposes of federal diversity jurisdiction, and he could bring a suit against white men who violated his family's rights. The case was widely reported in newspapers at the time, and no one suggested that the circuit court had gotten it wrong. In 1857, Chief Justice Roger Taney, writing in *Dred Scott v. Sandford*, said that a person of African ancestry living in America could never be a citizen of a state (hence could never invoke federal diversity jurisdiction) because the framers of the Constitution would never have allowed it. Wilson was an important framer of the Constitution. Taney's history was wrong.

There was one body of law that did not come to the Court whose absence is worth noting. The Court heard no cases involving religion. This was noteworthy for two reasons. First, the nation was very religious—all of the justices belonged to churches and the sessions of the Court began with "God save this honorable court" and a religious invocation—but the First Amendment barred Congress from establishing a religion or preventing the free exercise of religion. Did this apply to the states as well? Could Congress support religion in a neutral way (for example, arranging for parcels of land in the national domain to be set aside for churches) without violating the amendment? The Northwest Ordinance did just that.

Second, there was a very controversial movement under way to disestablish religion in the states. Led by Jefferson and Madison in Virginia, it had resulted in a state law ending the official position of the Protestant Episcopal Church. Could the ministers or the vestries of that church bring suit in federal court on First Amendment free exercise grounds? Could they litigate ownership of church property under the amendment? But no case came to the Court.

The colonial courts were riven with intense partisanships, but the High Court, with little precedent to guide it, ably handled national security cases and supported the other branches of the federal government. The Court tried to avoid controversy but could not always do so, and it may be that the Court's reputation and authority were protected by what did not come before its bench. Nevertheless, within two years, newly named Chief Justice Marshall would lead the Court into one of its most active and controversial periods.

CHAPTER 3

The Marshall Court, 1801–1835

David Hume, perhaps the greatest philosopher and one of the finest historians of the second half of the eighteenth century, wrote that republics are distinguished from other forms of rule by one fact: they are governments of laws, not of men. Hume's writings on politics were required reading for the framers of the Constitution, and their work was in a way a tribute to his insight. Our nation was founded on the rule of law. But it was the task of men to interpret that law, and John Marshall and his Court, a second generation of framers, would inherit the task of defining the meaning of the federal Constitution and the role of the High Court in our republican system. In the process, they introduced powerful and lasting readings of the supremacy of the federal government over the states and the Court over the other branches of the federal government.

JOHN MARSHALL'S COURT

Marshall was a remarkable combination of doting husband, frontier jokester, gentleman, folksy town lawyer, entrepreneur and speculator (he had a huge law practice and invested in land schemes), deep thinker, principled believer in the prospects of the new nation, and political opportunist. In short, he embodied many of the contradictions and ironies of early national America.

Marshall was born to the gentry in western Virginia and inherited a plantation—but preferred to live and work in Richmond. He saw combat as a young officer in the Revolution and served as a diplomat and later as secretary of state (1800–1801). He never sought high elective office. Simple in dress, manner, and tastes, he rarely stood on ceremony and had little attachment to the aristocratic pretensions of the great Virginia Tidewater aristocracy.

He was never a great fan of slavery, though he owned a few and did not free them at his death. He supported the American Colonization Society plan, whereby slaves would be purchased from their owners, freed, and returned to Africa—a prospect that pleased few masters and even fewer slaves. He wrote in *The Antelope* case (1825) that slavery violated natural law and that the slave trade offended "the feelings of justice and humanity," for "every man has a natural right to the fruits of his own labor . . . and no other person can . . . appropriate them against his will." Then he proceeded to rule against freedom in a variety of cases.

Though an indifferent speaker and, in person, lacking the intellectual flair of others of his generation, notably his great rival Jefferson, he had great honesty and personal courage, along with the ability to see to the core of others' arguments. Though a Federalist and nationalist, he was also a student of older republican ideals of disinterested public virtue. His family life was warm, and he was devoted to his often-ill wife, Polly, and his many children, four of whom died young.

Marshall gave no clue to his personal views when he wrote opinions. He wrote as though the law dictated the course of his pen, worked hard for consensus on the Court, based his decisions on the broadest possible grounds, and pioneered in switching the Court from "seriatim" opinions, in which every justice read his own, to "opinions for the Court," in which justices "signed on" to one another's opinions. Opinions were published as written rather than read aloud. In no decision was this method of proceeding more important than in the first major ruling Marshall rendered for the Court—*Marbury v. Madison* (1803).

MARBURY V. MADISON *AND JUDICIAL REVIEW*

Marbury came to the Court in the middle of its first great crisis. When they came to power, the Jeffersonians not only repealed the Federalists' Judiciary Act of 1801, but the new Republican majority in the Congress passed another Judiciary Act, in June 1802, postponing the next session of the Supreme Court until February 1803. Thus, while the Republicans debated among themselves how to counter Federalist influence on the High Court, the case that was to establish the Court's preeminence in the review of the Constitution hung fire. It was not decided until nearly two years after it was filed. By that time, party passions had cooled somewhat, and Marshall had time to think of a way to defend the role of the Court while still protecting it from a congressional backlash. As legal scholar William Nelson has written of the case, Marshall would use it to take the Court "out of politics."

The facts of the case are relatively simple: William Marbury, an Annapolis financier, Federalist supporter, and tax collector for the state of Maryland, was supposed to receive a commission as a justice of the peace for the District of Columbia. It was another of the Federalists' "midnight" moves to fill the judicial offices with Federalists. Marshall, outgoing secretary of state, failed to send it on, and the incoming secretary of state, Madison, with the assent of President Jefferson, did not remedy Marshall's oversight. When he did not get the commission, Marbury filed suit with the clerk of the Supreme Court under the provisions of the Judiciary Act of 1789. Section 13 of the act gave to the Supreme Court the power to issue a writ (a judicial command) "of mandamus, in cases warranted by the principle and usages of law, to any courts appointed, or persons holding office under the authority of the United States," to perform some act, in this case requiring the secretary of state to send the commission to Marbury.

Thus the case went directly to the Court. Over the long course of the Marshall Court, less than 1 percent of its cases were based on original jurisdiction. The vast majority of cases came through other channels—writs of error from federal courts or state courts (when the dispute involved interpretation of the Constitution, a treaty, or federal law), certification of division (when the district court judge and the Supreme Court justice sitting in the circuit court disagreed, often a contrivance), appeal from a lower court, and other writs (including habeas corpus in criminal cases).

Charles Lee argued Marbury's cause. He had served as attorney general under Adams and thought the issue was clear: the secretary of state had the duty to deliver the commissions. Lee's arguments were presented orally. Until 1833, counsel for parties did not have to submit written briefs prior to their appearance before the Court. Thus great orators like Daniel Webster and Henry Clay could take many hours to present their client's case. (The Court limited these oral arguments to two hours per side in 1848, and then to one-half hour, in the twentieth century.) The justices, including Marshall, took notes during oral argument, and the points counsel made and authorities they cited found their way into the justices' opinions. From 1849 on, briefs were to be printed and distributed to the parties as well as submitted to the Court.

The justices had their own law libraries. Marshall, on whom legal pedantry made little mark, routinely consulted English reference works like William Blackstone's *Commentaries* and Matthew Bacon's *Abridgment* of the laws of England, Virginia's statute books, and Daniel Call's, St. George Tucker's, and Bushrod Washington's reports of Virginia cases (including those argued by Marshall). For a time, Marshall kept his own reports of cases, jotting down the arguments of counsel and the rulings of the state's court of appeals. These focused on practical matters, however, more than being displays of arcane learning.

At the start of the nineteenth century, opinions—including Marshall's—rarely included references to earlier cases other than those directly on point.

Early federal law was heard as much as written, and the opinions of the first justices reflected the relatively greater importance of legal rhetoric over legal scholarship.

The issue before the Court, as Marshall framed it, was whether the Court had jurisdiction over the case. He intentionally ignored the political context of the suit. Nothing better demonstrated Marshall's command of his Court and his ability to rise above party than this deliberate shift from the political to the constitutional, though everyone knew that the issue was political. The Judiciary Act of 1801 provided jobs for forty-two Federalists, an example of political patronage that Jefferson and Madison decried as corruption. Jefferson's Congress had removed all of the newly appointed judges and magistrates at one stroke in repealing the Judiciary Act of 1801. (A companion High Court decision in *Stuart v. Laird* found that the Judiciary Act of 1802 was constitutional and, in effect, that newly appointed judges did not have a constitutionally protected property right to their offices.)

It would take considerable prudence as well as intellectual ability to navigate these political shoals, but Marshall was up to it. In a very long opinion for that day (twenty-six pages), Marshall wrote for a unanimous Court. He ruled that the justices could not issue the writ because it was not one of the kinds of original jurisdiction given the Court in Article III of the Constitution. The Constitution controlled or limited what Congress could do, and in particular prohibited the Congress from expanding the original jurisdiction of the Court. Congress had violated the Constitution by giving this authority to the Court. In short, he struck down that part of the Judiciary Act of 1789 as unconstitutional.

The power that Marshall assumed resided in the Court to find acts of Congress unconstitutional, and thus null and void, was immensely important. First, it protected the independence of the Court from Congress. Jay's Court had done this when Congress and President Washington wanted the Court to act like an administrative agency in the matter of pensions. Marshall made this a foundation of the Court's place in the constitutional scheme.

Second, Marshall implied that the Court was the final arbiter of the meaning of the Constitution. This vital pronouncement of "judicial supremacy" would be elaborated and extended in the coming years to include state legislation and state court judgments. The other branches of the federal government might engage in some sort of constitutional self-scrutiny when they acted, asking themselves if they had exceeded their power, but the final voice in contested cases must be the High Court's. Here it applied rather narrowly to a matter of the Court's own powers. That is, in the particular case, Marshall was simply saying that the Court had the final say on its own jurisdiction.

Finally, Marshall reminded everyone that the Constitution was the supreme law, and that every act of Congress had to be measured against it. To be sure, the Court had no intention of involving itself in the everyday details of the other branches' operations, for example, how the secretary of state ran his office, and giving the High Court the power to do this through writs of mandamus would violate basic tenets of separation of powers.

It was an awesome power that Marshall arrogated to his court, and one the early Court used very sparingly. Indeed, although from 1791 to 2000 the Court overturned 156 acts or parts of acts of Congress, it found only one—section 13 of the Judiciary Act of 1789—unconstitutional before 1866. (*Dred Scott* did not fit this description because Taney's comment that the Missouri Compromise was unconstitutional was dicta, not part of the opinion of the Court, and the Kansas-Nebraska Act had already superseded the Missouri Compromise acts.)

The opinion could have gone the other way. Marshall could have stretched the definition of "public ministers" in the Court's original jurisdiction to apply to Secretary of State Madison; or Marshall could have rejected Marbury's claim without explicitly overruling section 13. Some scholars have suggested that Marshall was looking for a way to assert the Court's primacy as interpreter of the Constitution and cynically twisted the law to attain that result. But he did not need to manipulate the law to get to judicial review. It was plain, as he wrote, that "the province and duty of the judicial department is to say what the law is." And if the Constitution was the higher law, then a statute in conflict with the Constitution must fall.

Although Marshall would have been the first to deny it, he had substantially enlarged the jurisdiction of his Court and thereby changed the meaning of Article III of the Constitution. Its framers had not given to the High Court the authority to strike down acts of Congress. The framers did make the Constitution the supreme law of the land and allowed for High Court review of state court opinions. They could have given the Court the authority to review federal law, but did not. *Marbury* did.

The problem that contemporary critics of the decision, including Madison and Jefferson, had was finding a forum in which to challenge Marshall's opinion. One answer lay in the political approach to law that Marshall tried so hard to avoid. Anticipating the wave of democratic reforms of the 1820s and 1830s (as well as twenty-first-century scholarship about popular constitutionalism), some of the first commentators on *Marbury* decried judicial tyranny and others complained that the opinion was colored by Marshall's party affiliation.

Other critics denounced the very principle of judicial review, preferring the revolutionary era orthodoxy of legislative supremacy in all things. This notion too has a long history, becoming, in the twentieth century, the "countermajoritarian dilemma." How in a democracy can the final word on the Constitution rest with a body that is not popularly elected? Some presidents have numbered among the opponents of judicial review, openly attacking the Court, attempting to "pack" it with justices more amenable to the party line, or undermining its judgments by refusing to enforce them.

Marshall was aware that *Marbury* opened wider his conflict with Jefferson, and he protected the opinion in two ways. First, he wrote as if everyone knew the truth of his logic. This defused any claim that he was abusing his discretion or that (to borrow modern terminology) he was an "activist" judge, inventing law. Like all judges in his age, he did not believe that judges should make law. Instead, they "found" it. The Mosaic tone of the opinion would add to its oracular status over the years. Second, he made the ruling self-executing. That is, because the Court refused to help Marbury, its ruling did not require Madison or Jefferson to do anything. They might thus reject Marshall's arguments but they could not directly countermand them by refusing to obey a Court order.

JEFFERSON AND MARSHALL

The Jeffersonians had other means to oppose Marshall and his Court beyond repeal of the Judiciary Act of 1801. The Republicans did not build a courthouse for the justices—perhaps an oversight or a deliberate slight. State supreme courts had their own facilities, but the justices of the nation's highest tribunal ended up in a drafty, mildewed, damp antechamber in the basement of the new capitol building.

And in a series of impeachments and trials, the Jeffersonian majority in the two houses aimed to remove Federalists from judicial office or at least to curb their partisanship on circuit. None of the Jeffersonians had forgotten how Paterson, Chase, and their brethren handled the seditious libel cases on circuit. The impeachment campaign only netted the addled and inebriated Timothy Pickering, a district court judge. Justice Chase avoided conviction in the Senate by a mere handful of votes. In 1821, Jefferson was still fuming: "The germ of dissolution of our federal government is in the constitution of the federal Judiciary . . . working like gravity by night and by day, gaining a little today and a little tomorrow, and advancing its noiseless step like a thief, over the field of jurisdiction, until all shall be usurped."

Many scholars believe that the impeachment campaign itself, though it fell short of removing the obnoxious and opinionated Chase, still frightened Marshall and the other justices enough to curb their view of their own powers. That view is not born out by the first rounds of the Marshall Court's decisions. From 1803 until well into the 1820s, the Supreme Court consistently defended its own jurisdiction, its primacy as interpreter of the Constitution, and the subordination of the state courts and legislatures to the U.S. Supreme Court's reading of the Constitution. But the Jeffersonian direct attack on the justices did persuade them to curb their tongues when it came to politics. It would take the onset of the Civil War for a chief justice to use his office to berate an incumbent president.

Marshall found a way to pay Jefferson back in kind. Jefferson hated ex–vice president Aaron Burr, the New York politician whose past history included the attempt to sneak away with the presidency in 1801, when he got as many electoral votes as Jefferson. In 1804, Burr had escaped punishment for killing Hamilton in a duel by fleeing from prosecution. No longer vice president, Burr's next scheme was an expedition attacking Spanish possessions in the Southwest, which may or may not have had the goal of making Burr a little despot over federal territory. When his coconspirators turned him in, Burr faced trial for treason in federal circuit court.

Jefferson licked his lips at the prospect of ridding American politics of Burr, but Marshall's rulings on the case at trial at the Richmond session of the circuit court on August 31, 1807, saved Burr. After disposing of the commentaries of judges and other authorities on treason and a review of prior cases, Marshall discoursed on the "plain meaning of the Constitution" once again, "trusting to the dictates of reason." The prosecution could prove that Burr may have had a "treasonable design," but the evidence against Burr consisted of letters, meetings, and promises for a still-vague armed expedition.

Jefferson took the evidence as true, as it may have been, but for Marshall proof of treason under the Constitution—"levying war" against the country or giving "aid and comfort to its enemies"—should be strictly construed. A plan or a plot to raise rebellion was not treason. Even gathering supplies and hiring men, without an overt act of "the application of force or violence," fell short of the constitutional requirement. Burr was not present when any overt act occurred.

What was more, reversing the Federalists' position on common law crimes (remember the Seditious Libel Act), Marshall rejected the English idea of a "constructive treason" that included conspiracy within the definition of the offense. He denied that any federal court had placed such a construction on the Constitution. (In fact, earlier circuit courts in the Whiskey Rebellion, Fries Rebellion, and other mob violence cases had found grounds for treason charges against conspirators.) In any event, the bottom line was that Burr had to have been there, with the armed body, when it acted, or the case must fail. So instructed by Marshall, the jury found Burr innocent of the charges.

Marshall won the battle with Jefferson this time, but Jefferson orchestrated a newspaper campaign against Marshall, and the two great Virginians never forgave one another. Marshall's skirmishing with Jefferson continued to the end of Jefferson's second term as president. Court historian Herbert Johnson believes that Jefferson's assaults on Marshall and his Federalist allies on the Court created greater harmony within it and gave to Marshall more authority than he might have had otherwise.

JOINING MARSHALL'S COURT

After 1801, every member added to the Marshall Court was a Republican. By 1819, only two of the seven members of the Court were openly Federalists (Marshall and Washington). Still, many of the new members had Federalist backgrounds or affiliations. These included Henry Brockholst Livingston (appointed 1806), scion of one of the most politically astute families in New York. He had served in the Continental Army, with John Jay in Spain, and in the New York assembly. He dabbled in banking and land speculation but made his living in the law. When he condemned the Jay Treaty he had no place to go but the Republican Party, though its democratic tendencies did not appeal to him. Elegant in manners (though he reputedly had a wicked temper and fought a number of duels), married three times and divorced twice, he valued collegiality on the Court above all. He died in 1823, in almost all ways Marshall's trusted ally.

So too was Thomas Todd (appointed 1807), a Virginia-born lawyer and judge who emigrated to Kentucky and there established a reputation as an intelligent and able jurist. Quiet and often ailing, he missed many sessions of the Court and dissented only once before his death in 1826. Gabriel Duvall of Maryland (appointed 1811), like Livingston, served in the Continental Army and then chose a legal career and ended up in the Republican Party during the tumultuous 1790s. He sat briefly in Congress before returning to Annapolis to finish his career as a much-respected state judge. Or would have, but Madison needed to fill two High Court seats in 1810 and 1811 and chose Duvall for one. He would sit on the Court from the age of sixty until his retirement in 1835, deaf during the latter portion of those years, the author of only fifteen opinions, and loyal supporter of Marshall throughout his tenure, except on one notable occasion. When Marshall refused to allow hearsay testimony (word of mouth about what witnesses had heard) in the case of a slave claiming her freedom, Duvall dissented. "People of color," he wrote in *Mima Queen v. Hepburn* (1813), "from their helpless condition, under the uncontrolled authority of a master, are entitled to all reasonable protection" against fraudulent enslavement. He died in 1844.

Madison's second appointment, in 1811, Joseph Story of Massachusetts, provided Marshall with more than a loyal subordinate. Story was in every way Marshall's intellectual equal and with him provided a one-two punch unmatched until the Oliver Wendell Holmes Jr.–Louis Brandeis alliance in the twentieth century. Story's support of Marshall's nationalist program showed how time had changed the political map.

Story came from a large family and found his way to Harvard and the law through diligent study. Indeed, he had a scholarly bent that he carried through his entire career. His frequent illnesses and the tragic deaths of his father and his wife drove him further into his books and his law practice. His second marriage was a happy one, although only two of his seven children survived to adulthood. A man of great personal honesty and conscience, he was an independent-minded Republican in state politics, and his brief term in Congress saw him oppose Jefferson's foreign policy, an opposition that many New Englanders shared.

Story's first contact with the High Court came when he successfully represented Fletcher against Peck, discussed below. President Madison was not planning to name him to the Court, but his first three choices declined. Marshall came to respect greatly Story's learning, and Story came to greatly admire the chief justice. Though they sometimes disagreed in the details (for example, Story favored stern government measures against the British during the War of 1812 and Marshall wanted to protect the American property of British nationals during the conflict), they shared a vision of a great nation bounded by law. There were other differences of policy. For example, Story more strongly opposed slavery than did Marshall and found ways to free slaves when he could, a course that Marshall did not adopt.

A born teacher, Story was named to a chair in law at the newly established Harvard Law School in 1829. His lectures became famous, and he turned them into much-quoted commentaries on the law. These publications include treatises on equity and conflict of laws, two subjects that connected private transactions to public law. He brought the same didactic style to the conferences of the Court, sometimes monopolizing the conversation. After Marshall died and the Court was dominated by Andrew Jackson's Democratic appointees,

Story would carry the spirit of the Marshall Court into the new era. He died in 1845.

The only Jefferson appointee without some Federalist connection was South Carolina's William Johnson, whom Jefferson appointed in 1804, at the height of party disputes about the Louisiana Purchase and foreign policy in the Napoleonic Wars. Johnson's youth (he was thirty-two, the same age as Story was upon appointment), his eccentricity and contrariness, and his early advocacy of states' rights should have made him the odd man out on the Marshall Court. But party affiliation no longer mattered as much as it had in 1801. Story's views seemed to draw Johnson's fire more readily than Marshall's. After all, Marshall was a fellow southerner and a man of such geniality and amity that it would have been hard for even so temperamental, stubborn, and impatient a man as Johnson to stay mad at Marshall.

In many cases involving interstate commerce, contracts, and other matters, Johnson went along with the majority. He was miffed and angered by his state's dismissal of his views in the Denmark Vesey conspiracy case (he thought the free black lay preacher and his friends had gotten a raw deal) and by South Carolina's decision to nullify the Tariff Act of 1828. He died a sad and lonely man in 1834, estranged from the Court and from his home state's proslavery policies.

THE CONTRACTS CLAUSE CASES

From a distance of two hundred years, it seems as though the jurisprudence of the Marshall Court covered every major legal topic in profusion—a flood of great cases, profound lawmaking, and audacious vision. In fact, the key cases totaled no more than a dozen, spread over the thirty-four years of Marshall's chief justiceship. Various historians have divided these cases by topic, by period, and by legal doctrine or philosophy. They defy easy categorization but are held together by Marshall's vision of the Court's role, the relationship between the federal government and the states, and by a focus on the rights and privileges of private persons balanced against the public good.

Fletcher v. Peck tested all of Marshall's skills. In 1789, a corrupt Georgia state legislature passed an act allowing four land companies to purchase almost the whole of the Yazoo territory of the state (thirty-five million acres, now the states of Alabama and Mississippi) for a penny-and-a-half an acre. Profiteers included three governors, a multitude of judges, and other notables (including Justice James Wilson). The original purchasers almost immediately resold their grants to other speculators, rightly anticipating that the entire fraud would be revealed and the land grant act repealed, as came to pass in the 1796 Rescinding Act. The federal government had an interest as well—the lands were occupied by Indians who had no say in any of these deals. Congress and Georgia worked out an arrangement—the land was made part of the national domain for a one-time payment of over a million dollars to Georgia. A federal commission settled the outstanding disputes among private claimants in 1814.

But speculators could not know that they would fare well under this evolving administrative solution to the problem. Over their heads in debt already, they wanted the windfall that would come with title and subdivision of the land into parcels for sale. They turned to the federal courts, asking that the Georgia act rescinding the grants be declared null and void and their own purchases of the disputed land from the original companies upheld. The secondhand purchasers of the Yazoo lands followed the precedent of the original purchasers—not only did they buy up land, they bought political allies. But what were the rights of the people who purchased the land from those illegally granted it? Aside from the political questions—corruption, fraud, and self-dealing—was there a legal question on which the High Court could base its decision?

Alexander Hamilton, recently retired as secretary of the treasury, represented a group of these buyers, and he argued that the Georgia statute of 1796 was a violation of the Contracts Clause of the Constitution. (Article I, section 10, clause 1, reads: "No state shall . . . pass any . . . law . . . impairing the obligation of contracts.") Georgia might reply that the plain meaning of the language was that the state could not step into a private agreement and undo it; but state courts did that all the time when contracts were based on duress, misrepresentation, and other forms of misconduct by one of the parties.

In any case, the Eleventh Amendment prevented anyone from suing Georgia without its consent, so the various speculators executed an end run around the amendment. Robert Fletcher of New Hampshire had bought a parcel of the land from John Peck of Massachusetts, whose company had bought it from the original purchasers. Fletcher alleged that Peck did not have title to the land because of the Georgia Rescinding Act. The money that supposedly changed hands was just enough to qualify for federal jurisdiction, and the two parties met the diversity requirement as well. Both wanted the federal courts to set aside the Georgia Rescinding Act, a decision that would have validated both Fletcher's and Peck's titles.

The case, filed in 1803, was decided in 1810. Marshall was not interested in the states' rights case or the arguments about immoral legislators and under-the-table deals. The letter of the Constitution was clear. According to the oral argument of counsel, Fletcher was a good faith buyer—as Peck was before him, without notice of the fraud—and had paid good money. As neither side raised the issue of corruption in the Georgia assembly, Marshall blithely noted that it had not been raised by the parties and so was not before the Court: "It would be indecent in the extreme" for the Court on its own "to enter into an inquiry respecting the corruption of the sovereign power of a state." He also winked at the collusion among the parties—in the seven years between 1803 and 1810, Marshall must have heard rumors about Fletcher's and Peck's games. (Justice William Johnson, newly appointed to the Court, referred to the collusion in his concurring opinion.)

But purely as a legal question, Marshall decreed that Georgia's granting of land was a contract; and as such it came under the purview of the Court. By rescinding that contract in 1796, the state was taking away private property. State governments were not powers answerable only to themselves: "Georgia cannot be viewed as a single, unconnected, sovereign power, on whose legislature no other restrictions are imposed than may be found in its own constitution. She is part of a large empire; she is a member of the American Union." The federal Constitution limited the powers of the state legislators, particularly that power to "take" from citizens of the United States what the Constitution had guaranteed to them. A unanimous Court found for Fletcher, and all but one of the justices signed on to Marshall's opinion that made land grants into vested property rights.

Georgia may have winced at language somewhat reminiscent of the crown's objections to colonial legislative claims; and in the Civil War years, Marshall's reasoning would echo in Abraham Lincoln's views of secession. Justice Johnson refused to found his concurrence upon such nationalistic and unionist grounds. Instead, he argued that the right to personal property was imbedded in nature. Johnson, from a state with more slaves than free persons, may have had another form of personal property in mind when he inveighed against a state taking away what a man owned. He added that he thought Marshall's reading of the Contracts Clause was overbroad, for states were all the time regulating contracts to protect public safety (another important point for a man from a state with a black majority).

Like *Marbury*, *Fletcher* did not require the Court to open itself to disobedience issues. Georgia had already ceded its claims (thankfully, from the Court's point of view—the last time that the Court had told Georgia to obey had resulted in the amendment of the Constitution). Peck was happy that Fletcher won, for in effect the ruling protected both of them. In fact, they, like all the land speculators involved in the deal, were now able to make their case before the U.S. commissioners.

The Court's opinion in *Fletcher* had an immediate and lasting extralegal dimension. Well into the nineteenth century, land and land speculation con stituted the number-one economic enterprise in the country. With the danger removed of state intervention in land grants, sales, resales, and other public and private transactions involving the national domain—the vast expanse of lands in the West—lands could be surveyed, sold, recorded, and developed more swiftly and with less controversy. Marshall, a trained surveyor and a land speculator in Virginia, probably anticipated these results from his decision in *Fletcher*, and his views in later land law cases support this supposition.

Next in this "line" of cases on the Contracts Clause (bearing in mind that such lines are actually templates that later students of the Court lay over a much messier mix of cases) was a suit by the trustees of Dartmouth College against the state of New Hampshire. *Dartmouth College v. Woodward* (1819) touched on another area of American business life—the corporation. Under older English and colonial rules, private corporations resulted from legislative charters. They created a quasi-monopoly in some area of economic activity because the corporation served a public interest. There were few corporations. Most enterprises were partnerships or sole proprietorships at that time. The old college was based on a charter of incorporation from the crown that forever vested control of the college in a board of trustees that chose its own replacements.   ·

In 1816, the state legislature rescinded the charter and proposed to change Dartmouth College into Dartmouth University. State politics were again involved, just as in Georgia's land grant policies. The college had a Federalist board of trustees, and the legislature was solidly Jeffersonian Republican. The law would have enlarged the number of trustees, allowing for a Republican majority. The old trustees hired Daniel Webster to argue their case. He lost before the state supreme court, which unanimously ruled that the Contracts Clause did apply to corporations, but only those whose purposes were private. Public service corporations, like Dartmouth, could be regulated by the state.

In *Fletcher*, the Marshall Court had blurred that distinction between public and private purposes of contracts, and Webster took the case to the Supreme Court in the hope it would extend its *Fletcher* reasoning from land companies to corporations. The Court obliged. The charter was a contract under the Contracts Clause that bound the state and protected the trustees of the private college. They and the donors who supported the college were not an agency of the state but a private body whose purpose was a public and charitable one, to be sure, but was never meant to be changed as radically as the 1816 state law intended.

Marshall was no more pro-commerce, pro-business, or pro-capitalism than others with his background in Virginia politics. He certainly was no visionary who sought to establish a laissez-faire (free market) regime in the new nation.

That the framers of the Constitution did not intend to retrain the States in the regulation of their civil institutions, adopted for internal government, and that the instrument they have given us, is not to be so construed, may be admitted. . . . But if this be a private eleemosynary institution, endowed with a capacity to take property for objects unconnected with government, whose funds are bestowed by individuals on the faith of the charter; if the donors have stipulated for the future disposition and management of those funds in the manner prescribed by themselves; there may be more difficulty in the case.

And there was. For the College was private, its funds were private donations, and "this charter was accepted, and the property both real and personal, which had been contributed for the benefit of the college, was conveyed to, and vested in, the corporate body."

One of the great intellectual achievements of the founding fathers was drawing a sharp line between public and private, between privileges subject to public rescission and private rights. No private right was more sacrosanct to these framers than private property. That is one reason why men so committed to notions of liberty and freedom from British tyranny were able to accommodate chattel slavery. Slaves were private property. Involuntary manumission of slaves would be taking private property, thus violating the rights of the owners.

The Constitution protected contracts from the exactions of state governments precisely because contracts conferred private property rights. Corporations were simply collections of individuals, and charters for them were simply contracts. As Story added, in his concurrence, "It will hardly be contended, that even in respect to such corporations, the legislative power is so transcendant [*sic*], that it may at its will take away the private property of the corporation, or change the uses of its private funds acquired under the public faith."

There was a virtual explosion in volume of business and the capital invested in business in the twenty years after *Dartmouth College* was handed down. The notion of contract itself altered from one of fair exchange of goods, services, or monies, to a simple bargained-for exchange, a meeting of minds that courts would enforce. The Court's protection of corporate charters from state regulation did not lead to a flood of corporate activity—the partnership remained the standard form of doing big business well into the 1850s—but banks, insurance companies, and transportation firms did turn to corporate forms of doing business, knowing that the Court would protect their interests.

THE COURT AND THE STATES

Behind the Court's limitations on what states could do in matters of contract and incorporation was a far-broader vision of the relationship between the federal government and its courts, on the one hand, and the states on the other. Part of this vision grew out of the position of the High Court in the federal system. It was the advocate of the federal Constitution. Had Marshall sat on the Virginia Supreme Court, like the great Virginia states' rights judge Spencer Roane, one wonders where his loyalties might have lain. But he did not, and in a series of cases he upheld the preeminence of Congress and the primacy of national law.

Some of these cases came in the form of appeal from state supreme court rulings. If federalism had created two sovereignties—the states retaining theirs alongside the new federal government—could a state high court reverse or refuse to give effect to a U.S. Supreme Court order? That is what lay at the heart of *Martin v. Hunter's Lessee* (1816).

The case involved the largest land dispute of the colonial period, the so-called Fairfax grant in the Northern Neck of Virginia. The simple holding of the High Court, in Justice Joseph Story's opinion, was that "the appellate power of the United States [courts] does extend to cases pending in the state courts. . . . we find no clause in [the Constitution] that limits this power." To provide for uniformity of decisions, to protect foreign plaintiffs against untoward prejudice in state courts, and to give effect to the Supremacy Clause, the High Court had to have final say in state cases. This did not prevent states from hearing suits by foreigners against the state's citizens or giving judgments based on federal law or the Constitution, it just left the final decision to the High Court if the High Court took the case.

Story's rationale looked simple—indeed it so resembled the kind of clean and authoritative logic Marshall used that some scholars have argued that Marshall wrote or at least heavily edited the opinion. For Marshall had a personal interest in the Fairfax lands and had recused (removed) himself from the case because of the conflict of interest. This history was long and convoluted. Virginia had taken the lands during the Revolution because the Fairfax claimant was a loyalist. Marshall, counsel for the Fairfax interest, had argued in the Virginia courts that the Treaty of Peace of 1783 prohibited such seizures. Story's opinion agreed with Marshall's side of the case but based it on the Jay Treaty. Either way, the individuals who gained the land from the state of Virginia (the state supported its war effort in part by selling confiscated loyalist and British property) would be out of luck.

In 1813, the Supreme Court ordered Virginia to return title to the original holders. The Virginia Court of Appeals, in an opinion that Spencer Roane authored, refused to comply. Roane, long Marshall's rival (Roane would have been Jefferson's choice for chief justice of the High Court), argued that the High Court was simply a department of the federal government, not superior in any way to the Virginia high court. Story (with Marshall's eager support) retorted that the Constitution, not the federal government, created the High Court and gave it supervisory jurisdiction.

A parallel case arose when state courts denied that criminal prosecutions were subject to federal review. In *Cohens v. Virginia* (1821), Marshall had another chance to explain what federalism meant. The brothers Cohen were selling D.C. lottery tickets in Virginia. Congress had authorized the lottery for the District, but Virginia forbade such lotteries. They were indicted, tried, and convicted in a Virginia court of law and appealed their conviction to the Supreme Court. Marshall had no quarrel with the Virginia law and dismissed the Cohens' appeal against it. Virginia could criminalize conduct that was legal elsewhere if it chose.

But Marshall did not stop there. Counsel for the state had argued that the High Court did not have jurisdiction over the appeal. Marshall disagreed. The High Court had jurisdiction in "all cases in law and equity arising under . . . the laws of the United States." It was entirely proper that the Cohens appeal to the High Court, even if they lost on the merits. The nation and the Constitution would be rendered powerless, the law uncertain, and citizens of the United States subject to the varying whims of state governments if appeal to the High Court was blocked. "The general government, though limited as to its objects, is supreme with respect to those objects," another example of the Constitution's imposition of "many express and important limitations on the sovereignty of the states."

Marshall knew that he and the Court were rapidly spending the political capital invested in the Court at its creation. Devices like self-executing decisions, as in *Marbury* and *Cohens,* saved the Court the potential embarrassment of having a party refuse to obey. Winking at collusive cases like *Fletcher* or piggybacking jurisdictional rulings on cases that turned on technical points averted some criticism. In fact, long before Felix Frankfurter and Louis Brandeis developed formal "prudential" ways of avoiding deciding a case on constitutional grounds (for example, the plaintiff lacked standing to bring the suit, the suit was already moot or not yet ripe, the Court preferred statutory interpretation to constitutional interpretation), Marshall had pioneered methods of averting conflict. But if Marshall was adept at avoiding head-on collisions, he also believed, as he wrote in *Cohens*, that "the judiciary cannot, as the legislature may, avoid a measure because it approaches the confines of the Constitution." *McCulloch v. Maryland* (1819) was such a case.

The case had none of the rich narrative history of *Martin's Lessee* or the bare-knuckle political confrontation of *Marbury*, but at stake in *McCulloch* was the very essence of the federal republic. In 1819, that republic was mired in one of the worst economic panics it had ever experienced. Land speculation had led to overheating of the economy, and banks all over were going belly-up. The Second Bank of the United States, chartered in 1816 after the federal government's financial troubles during the War of 1812, was supposed to prevent such collapses before they occurred, but the overseers of the bank were themselves speculators, and many of the bank's practices were inefficient and corrupt. A number of states, including Maryland, passed laws regulating the Bank of the United States branches in the state. James McCulloch was the cashier of the Maryland branch of the Bank of the United States, and he was fined for trying to do its business without paying the licensing fee of $15,000 to the state. When his conviction was upheld by the state supreme court, he appealed to the U.S. Supreme Court.

The Bank of the United States was something of a misnomer from its inception. A project of ambitious financiers like Robert Morris and fierce nationalists like Hamilton, it had a private board of directors (unlike the Federal Reserve Bank today), and it could sponsor private projects on its own initiative. Nothing in the Constitution specifically allowed Congress to charter the bank; and the debate over the charter of the first bank, in 1791, followed the contours of the party wars. Hamilton insisted that governments must read their powers broadly in order to perform their duties. The discretion Congress exercised in creating the bank could be found, by implication, in Article I, section 8, clause 1, "to lay and collect taxes," in clause 3, "to regulate commerce," and in clause 18, "to make all laws which shall be necessary and proper for carrying into execution the foregoing powers." Without such a bank, Hamilton argued, the huge national debt could not be managed and the credit of the new nation would lie at the mercy of the states (the same problem that had doomed the Confederation). This was a "loose construction" of the Constitution, but it won the day in Congress and convinced President Washington, at first hesitant to sign the act, to set aside his reservations.

Madison and Jefferson opposed it, claiming that the framers of the Constitution had considered and rejected authorizing Congress to create such a bank. Scholar Daniel Farber has called this argument the first example of "originalist" constitutional theory, in which the purposes and intentions of the framers would govern assessments of any act's constitutionality. They also argued for the strict construction of the Constitution, limiting the power of the federal government to those objects named and those functions specifically delegated in the Constitution.

At oral argument, originalism reappeared. Representing the state of Maryland in *McCulloch*, Luther Martin (who had taken part in the Constitutional Convention) reminded the Court that he had been a framer, and he knew for a fact that the framers understood that the power of the state to tax was "absolutely unlimited." Counsel for the bank, including Daniel Webster, retorted that the Constitution was created to restrain the very kinds of activity Maryland attempted.

The debates of 1787 were not the only source of originalist authority. At oral argument, Maryland's counsel, Joseph Hopkinson, returned to the arguments of the Virginia and Kentucky Resolves of 1798: "Can it be contended, that the State rights of territory and taxation are to yield for the gains of a money-trading corporation; to be prostrated at the will of a set of men who have no concern, and no duty, but to increase their profits? Is this the necessity required by the Constitution for the creation of undefined powers?" Walter Jones, also appearing for the state, made the argument sharper still: The Constitution was "a compact between the States, and all the powers which are not expressly relinquished by it, are reserved to the States." Hopkinson and Jones introduced what would become the anthem of proslavery constitutional thinkers: "the compact" theory of the Constitution. Though most often associated with John C. Calhoun's argument for states' rights in the 1830s, the compact theory arrived, fully developed, in *McCulloch*.

In *McCulloch*, the decision of the Court was unanimous, and Marshall wrote a magnificent summary of all his earlier admonitions that "it is a Constitution we are expounding." Marshall rejected the compact theory of the Constitution, writing that, instead, it reflected the will of an entire people. It followed that the federal government spoke for that people, not for the concurrent will of the independent states. He then recalled and recast Hamilton's arguments for the bank. The federal government could not be bound by the narrowest confines of strict construction because it could not respond to exigency nor take advantage of opportunity. The Bank of the United States was constitutional; it enabled the federal government to tax, to borrow, and to carry out other economic policies; it fit the very definition of "necessary and proper."

Marshall could have avoided the storm of protest against the decision by using the case to reiterate his view of the national union and then allowing Maryland some wiggle room. But insofar as "the power to tax is the power to destroy" and the state licensing fee would "annihilate" the bank, Marshall had no choice but to strike down the Maryland law. Not to do so would be to subject the whole of the Constitution to the whims of state legislatures.

Marshall's opinion was almost Olympian in its tone—principled, authoritative, brooking little dissent. He never once hinted that a great national crisis over another subject entirely was looming in the capitol chambers above the basement room where the Court met, and that its decision directly affected that crisis:

The subject is the execution of those great powers on which the welfare of a nation essentially depends. It must have been the intention of those who gave these powers, to insure, as far as human prudence could insure, their beneficial execution. This could not be done by confiding the choice of means to such narrow limits as not to leave it in the power of Congress to adopt any which might be appropriate, and which were conducive to the end. . . . Let the end be legitimate, let it be within the scope of the constitution, and all means which are appropriate, which are plainly adapted to that end, which are not prohibited, but consist with the letter and spirit of the constitution, are constitutional.

No one in oral argument over the Maryland bank law mentioned slavery, but everyone knew that Congress was coming to an impasse over the admission of Missouri as a slave state. On February 13, 1819, during a House debate over the motion to admit the Missouri territory to the Union as a state, James Tallmadge of New York proposed that no slaves might be permanently brought into Missouri after its admission and that all slaves in the state be freed at their twenty-fifth birthday. The advocates of slavery rose in united fury. Such an act of Congress would take from the slaveholder his property without compensation; it would violate the will of the people (Missouri voters had prepared a constitution legalizing slavery); it would give the free states a majority in the Senate; and it would become the opening wedge of an attack on slavery in all the southern states. Southerners muttered the words "civil war" and "disunion." A compromise was reached in 1820, followed by another the next year. Missouri entered as a slave state; Maine entered as a free state.

The *McCulloch* decision was met with fury in many parts of the South, including in Marshall's own Virginia, because of the Missouri crisis. The notion that the High Court could strike down state law violating federal law was denounced in newspapers and in state legislative halls throughout the South. Spencer Roane, writing as "Hampden" (a figure from the English civil wars of the seventeenth century), called up all the anti-federalist rhetoric against a tyrannous court. Marshall penned a defense of the decision and had it published, anonymously.

For if Marshall's view of the Constitution and the powers of Congress was right, then Congress could exclude slavery from the territories and perhaps even end it where it existed. White southern politicians would not swallow this, but when the debate over Missouri went their way, they could push the unpalatable meal of federal supremacy to one side. It remained on the table, however, and would until the ratification of the Fourteenth Amendment in 1868.

THE COURT AND INTERSTATE COMMERCE

In the 1820s, the Marshall Court found itself facing a new set of difficult cases. These revolved around state regulation of commerce and transportation. In *Gibbons v. Ogden* (1824), the issue was not a state directly confuting a federal law, but a state intruding into an area of activity that the Constitution seemed to assign to Congress. The Commerce Clause (Article I, section 8, clause 3, of the Constitution) gave Congress the authority to "regulate commerce . . . among the several states." In fact, the problem of mediating states' disputes over riverine traffic was the occasion Madison and Hamilton used to bring together delegates from various states interested in a federal union in 1785. That conference led the next year to another, at Annapolis, and then to the Constitutional Convention of 1787. But was the grant of authority over interstate commerce to Congress "exclusive"? Could the states not share in it (the same issue as in *Martin's Lessee*)?

The particulars of the case remind us of the importance of technological as well as entrepreneurial innovations in the early nineteenth century. New York sought to tap the agricultural riches of its upstate region and the newly opened Northwest Territory. That required cheap, safe, and speedy navigation of the Hudson River. Inventor and entrepreneur Robert Fulton and his steamboat won the state's competition for that navigation, and New York rewarded him with the monopoly. He allowed licensees like Aaron Ogden to run a line, but the monopoly was challenged by Thomas Gibbons and others, who were already operating steamboats along the coast under a federal license.

The litigation began in the New York courts, in 1812, where Fulton's monopoly won. Gibbons was told to not run his boats up or down the river. The result was that New York and its neighbors (Connecticut and New Jersey, where steamboat operators connected with New York) were soon embroiled in their own litigation. The tiff recalled the colonial land wars that New York waged against Connecticut and New Jersey farmers over who held title to which parcels of land on the borders of the colonies. Gibbons turned to the Supreme Court.

In fact, states already regulated many items of commerce that crossed state borders and supervised multistate enterprises. As Thomas Oakley, counsel for the state of New York, insisted, the very essence of sovereignty was command of the waterways, and the Hudson was entirely within the borders of New York. The argument may or may not have rested upon a compact theory of the Constitution, but it certainly ran against earlier holdings of the High Court in *Martin's Lessee* and *McCulloch*.

Daniel Webster was counsel for Gibbons, and his formulation of the issues—and options—was brilliant. He proffered four lines of analysis, all leading to victory for his client: exclusive federal jurisdiction, whether or not Congress acted; jurisdiction when Congress acted (trumping any existing state laws); concurrent jurisdiction in all matters; and partial state jurisdiction in relatively minor matters.

Marshall saw *Gibbons* as another occasion in which national authority and the need for uniform standards outweighed state interests. For a unanimous Court, he wrote that the ratification of the Constitution began a new era of federalism, and the states must bow to the dictates of the document they had ratified. He did not conclude that interstate commerce was Congress's exclusive domain, however. Some reasonable state regulations were acceptable, but in this case Congress had preempted those regulations by passing the act that licensed Gibbons. When Congress passed a law regarding commerce, it barred the states from acting on the same subject.

Marshall did not discourse upon the state's inherent power to restrict commerce in order to protect the health and welfare of the state's citizens, but by stopping short of the extreme position in Webster's first option, Marshall and the Court left the door open for states to act when Congress had not and for the Court to uphold the "police power" of the states in later cases. Thus, while a state could not cloak its imposition of tariffs on imported goods by appearing to regulate commerce (*Brown v. Maryland*, 1827), a state could charter a dam on a creek when Congress had not legislated on the issue (*Wilson v. Black Bird Creek Marsh Company*, 1829).

THE SECOND MARSHALL COURT

Although it is a fact that many of the most significant decisions of this remarkable thirty-four-year run of cases bear Marshall's signature style, even more remarkable is the relative unanimity of the Court in these cases. Of course, Marshall did not do it all alone, and even more striking is the fact that, by 1821, the Court had changed its personnel almost entirely. Gone were Federalist stalwarts like Paterson and Chase. On board were the appointments of Jefferson, Madison, and Monroe, all Virginia Republicans. Indeed, by the end of Marshall's tenure, he was the only Federalist on the Court.

Newcomers after 1821 included Smith Thompson of New York (appointed in 1823), a former student of the great New York jurist James Kent. Thompson became a leading Jeffersonian Republican in the state and served on its supreme court. Although the rest of his political career was spent on the bench, he remained an active participant in national politics. While on the Court, he ran, unsuccessfully, for governor of New York.

John Quincy Adams, president from 1824 to 1828, nominated only one justice, Robert Trimble of Kentucky, in 1826. Trimble was the first genuine frontier-bred justice. Educated at Transylvania College, in Lexington, he practiced in a small town, married, had ten children, followed the course of many successful small town lawyers and entered politics, but then chose not to stand for the U.S. Senate (the legislature would have named him) and accepted a seat on the state supreme court instead.

In many ways he was as typical of the contradictions of the 1820s and 1830s as Marshall had been of an earlier generation of lawyers: he was a promoter of education and libraries and a slaveholder. Named to high office repeatedly, he repeatedly declined; his large family dictated that he could not abandon his lucrative law practice for long. As a federal district court judge, his nationalism rankled his Kentucky neighbors. He refused to allow his court to be hamstrung by Kentucky debt relief laws, though he believed that the state could pass bankruptcy laws and would say so in *Ogden v. Saunders* (1827). When Justice Todd died, John Quincy Adams named Trimble. He served only two years before dying, in 1828. In most matters, he agreed with Marshall, with the exception, notably, of *Ogden.*

The new president, Andrew Jackson, nominated three justices during Marshall's tenure, John McLean (in 1829), Henry Baldwin (in 1830), and James M. Wayne (in 1835). McLean served until 1861, Baldwin until 1844, and Wayne until 1867. McLean was something of a throwback to men with backgrounds like

Chase and Paterson. He came from the "middling" classes, farmers who moved to Ohio seeking to better themselves. McLean clerked with a practicing local lawyer, entered politics at the bottom rung of the ladder, and found inspiration and strength in evangelical Methodism. Much of his view of the world came from the egalitarian strains in Methodism, reinforcing his own salt-of-the-earth background. He opposed slavery and favored democratic reform in his terms in Congress and on the Ohio court. He would run for the presidency as, first, a Free-Soil Democrat (Free-Soilers opposed the expansion of slavery into the western territories) and later under the new Republican Party banner (the new Republicans formed in 1854 to oppose the spread of slavery). He left relatively little impact on the law, however, though he wrote 247 opinions for the Court and died while serving, in 1861.

Connecticut's Henry Baldwin, like John McLean, came from a hardworking but hardly well-off family (his father was a blacksmith). But unlike McLean, Baldwin's modest family beginnings did not lead him to egalitarian views. After Yale and reading the law he moved to Pittsburgh and a successful law practice. He represented the growing manufacturing interest in the city, and when he was elected to Congress, in 1816, he supported a protective tariff. He defended Andrew Jackson against factually correct accusations that Jackson abused his authority in chasing Indians into British Florida, where Jackson hanged two British subjects for aiding the Indians. Baldwin stumped for Jackson's presidential campaigns, and Jackson named him to the Court. There he was as irascible as Johnson and far less predictable in his views. He supported the slave interest, denied Indian claims, insisted that the Court not make law in the Marshall manner, and disagreed with just about everyone on the bench. He died in 1844.

James M. Wayne of Georgia grew up on his father's rice plantation. These were among the most successful large-scale agrobusinesses in the early republic. But he was sent north for his education, to Princeton, and then returned to read law in Savannah, near the family home. He served with a volunteer company in the War of 1812. He gained a seat in the Georgia legislature campaigning for states' rights and carried these views onto the Georgia bench and to Congress in 1828. He supported Jackson's (and Georgia's) efforts to displace the Indians. He did not agree with South Carolina's attempt to nullify the Tariff of 1828, and once on the Court, he changed his view of the federal union. In a series of opinions, he supported economic nationalism and the power of Congress to regulate interstate commerce, and, finally, when the Civil War erupted, he was a unionist stalwart. He died in 1867, aged seventy-seven, while at work.

SLAVERY AND THE COURT

The Court that met after the Missouri Compromise could see clouds on the horizon of domestic tranquility and the Union, clouds "no bigger than a man's hand," as Jefferson once called them. They would test the Court in Marshall's final years and throughout the tenure of his successor, Roger Taney. These cases revolved about a new concept, indeed a concept without a name then. Today we would call them civil rights cases, for they involved isolated and powerless minorities who sought the aid of the Court to protect their rights or gain equal treatment.

Slavery was an old institution when the American colonies were founded, but nothing in the common law encouraged or implied the legality of "chattel slavery," bondage in which the slave was merely property and had no personality in the law and whose offspring were automatically slaves. Indeed, in *Somerset's Case* (1772), Lord Mansfield, chief justice of England, opined that there was no place for chattel slavery in the common law. Instead, the colonists adopted modified versions of other European nations' slave codes. Although all northern states either ended slavery or provided by law for its gradual disappearance by the early nineteenth century and the Confederation had barred slavery from the Northwest Territory in 1787, southern states did not end slavery. Some made manumission (the owner freeing the slave) easier, and some southern revolutionary leaders either freed their slaves or expected slavery to die out.

The Constitution compromised on the issue of slavery. Though some would call it a pact with death and scholars today debate whether it was a proslavery document, in fact it accepted slavery rather than promoting it. The Constitution did not use the word slave or refer directly to slavery, but in three places it did acknowledge slavery's impact on the country. First, in the "three-fifths compromise," it permitted states to include three-fifths of the total of "other persons" in its population counts for apportionment purposes. Second, Congress could make no law ending the international slave trade until 1808. Finally, under the Rendition Clause of Article IV ("no person held to service or labor in one state, under the laws thereof, escaping into another, shall, in consequence of any law or regulation therein, be discharged from such service or labor, but shall be delivered up upon claim of the party to whom such service or labor may be due"), runaway slaves could be recaptured in free states and returned to their masters. The Rendition Clause would spawn the most controversial federal laws of the pre–Civil War era—the Fugitive Slave Laws of 1793 and 1850. These effectively denied to persons of color the legal and procedural rights of whites, making dark skin presumptive evidence of slave status.

The framers may have hoped that slavery would die out of its own accord. In fact, the very reverse occurred. When South Carolina senator Henry Hammond boasted in 1858 that "cotton is king," he was not far from the truth. The spread of cotton cultivation and its growing importance in the national economy was little short of astounding. From 7 percent of the value of the nation's exports in 1800, it had become nearly 60 percent of the value of all exports by 1860. In 1790, only 4,000 bales were produced. By 1860, over 3.8 million bales were picked, packed, and shipped. Slaves were not necessary to the planting or harvesting of cotton. In fact, nearly 50 percent of cotton farmers had no slaves. But slavery and cotton did go together because profits depended upon the amount of cotton grown, and slave labor could increase the yield in direct proportion to the number of slaves employed. Slaves in the South thus multiplied from a little under 700,000 men and women in 1790 to nearly four million by 1860. High cotton prices convinced the children of the older inhabitants of the South to relocate west. The internal immigration also spurred the domestic slave market, making it profitable for planters in Virginia and South Carolina to sell slaves they did not need "down the river." In the period up to 1850, Mississippi (1817), Alabama (1819), Missouri (1820), Arkansas (1836), Florida (1845), and Texas (1845) joined the Union as slave states.

As slavery spread throughout the South, an era of intense moral self-examination was sweeping the North. A "ferment" of reformism changed the way Americans thought about themselves, and communal experiences as widely divergent as revival meetings and labor union meetings shared the notion that the human spirit could be perfected and society as a whole could be improved. Over time, the reform ideal moved from persuading the individual to repent, to fostering reform associations and utopian religious sanctuaries, to seeking the aid of governments in imposing reform measures. The impetus to reform covered all manner of subjects, from education of the very young to improvement of insane asylums, the demand for women's rights, and the temperance movement against alcohol abuse—to the most imposing and divisive of all the reforms, the abolition of slavery.

Opponents of slavery had founded the American Colonization Society in 1817 to remove emancipated slaves and free blacks from the country by sending them to the colony of Liberia that the society had purchased in West Africa. Few slaves sought this option, preferring to remain with family and friends in America. In 1821, a new stage in the antislavery movement began when Baltimore Quaker Benjamin Lundy began publishing the *Genius of Universal Emancipation*, a model special-interest newspaper featuring stories of slave atrocities and calls for political action. In 1828, he was joined by a young Bostonian,

William Lloyd Garrison. In 1831, Garrison published the first issue of *The Liberator* in Boston, promising, "I will not retreat a single inch—and I will be heard." Lundy had pressed for gradual emancipation. Garrison demanded immediate emancipation. Moreover, he welcomed women and blacks to join him in the New England Anti-Slavery Society and with them founded the American Anti-Slavery Society in 1833. Such radical attacks on widely held racialist views raised the wrath of northern conservatives. In 1835 Garrison himself was chased and nearly lynched by an antiabolitionist mob in Boston.

The rise of immediate abolitionism led to growing southern intransigence on the issue. Southerners announced that only white solidarity could prevent slave uprisings. Planters like Thomas R. Dew of Virginia argued that slavery was a positive good for the whites and the blacks, and found justification for it in the Bible, science, and the laws of society. Indeed, he and those who came after him believed that slavery alone enabled a society to rise to the heights of nobility and achievement. As Dew wrote in 1832, "It is, in truth, the slave labor in Virginia which gives value to her soil and her habitations; take ways this, and you pull down the Atlas that upholds the whole system."

Recognizing that slavery was a legal minefield, the High Court's slavery jurisprudence avoided the kind of sweeping language that it favored in other cases involving private property. The personal aversion or at least unease with slavery that many of the justices shared may have dictated this course of action. As Marshall said over and again, "However the personal feelings of the individual [justice] may be interested on the part of a person claiming freedom," the issues had to be viewed purely in a legal light. If the domestic law of the state in which the case arose treated slaves as property, then the Supreme Court had to follow suit; if international law gave possession of slaves to foreign claimants, the Court could not deny those claimants their rights.

THE COURT AND THE NATIVE AMERICAN "PROBLEM"

In the closing years of Marshall's tenure, a second group of potentially divisive cases arrived at the Court. These concerned the baffling problem of Indian rights. The United States claimed absolute legal title to Indian lands under a number of legal doctrines, including conquest by war and cession by treaty, as well as by private purchase. All of these involved some degree of coercion, misrepresentation, or fraud. Indian customs included forms of communal land use, common hunting and gathering rights, and means of punishing crime that were distinct from Anglo-American common and statute law, but state and federal legal authorities imposed American law on the natives wherever and whenever they could.

Representatives of the federal and state governments also employed questionable methods of gaining Indian assent to treaties, many of them originating in British colonial policy toward the Indians. First, the American negotiators designated large areas of Indian settlement as "tribes," an arbitrary and misleading category. The actual units of Indian life were villages and clans. Next, the federal spokesmen found and suborned the cooperation of a handful of "chiefs," even though in Indian culture chiefs could not speak for or command Indian peoples. The negotiators then convinced these chiefs, sometimes by bribery or misrepresentation, to sell or cede ancient Indian lands to the United States. Early national leaders defended these methods as a form of "benevolent paternalism" meant to "civilize" the savage native. Sometimes the justification was simply the absolute sovereignty of the national government, as in legislation like the Indian Removal Act of 1830.

Two considerations governed these treaties. Neither of them treated the Indians as true sovereigns over their own lands but instead as tenants at the pleasure of the United States. The first was a desire for security from Indian attack. This dictated fixed boundary lines between Indian lands and federal or state territory and characterized the treaties made before 1815. The catch-22 was spelled out in the Treaty of Greenville, in 1795: "The Indians, who have a right to those lands, are quietly to enjoy them [that is, without outside interference] . . . but when those tribes, or any of them, shall be disposed to sell their lands, they are to be sold only to the United States," with U.S. courts deciding whether the sale was legal. In *Johnson v. McIntosh* (1823), Marshall wrote for the Court that Indians might be sole possessors of the land, but for purposes of sale, they did not hold absolute title. He later added, in *Worcester v. Georgia* (1830), that concessions to Indian occupiers were based on a sense of natural justice and a conciliatory attitude rather than on the Indians' legal rights.

The second consideration was the Americans' unquenchable need to acquire more land for farming, mining, and other domestic purposes. This required the removal of the Indians or the constriction of Indian territory and dominated Indian policy for much of the rest of the nineteenth century. For some western political leaders, the treaty-based removal of Indian tribes was too slow and unpredictable a way to occupy Indian lands. Andrew Jackson, of Tennessee, a lawyer, politician, planter, and chief justice of the state's supreme court, had fought in Indian wars, and even when these died down, he continued his war on the Indians by other means. As president of the United States, he was an avid supporter of the Indian Removal Act, claiming that it would protect the Indians from the animosity of the Georgia and Alabama state governments, though these were the governments violating the treaties. He offered the assistance of federal forces to states that wanted the Indians "removed" west, "beyond the Mississippi."

There were over 125,000 Indians living east of the Mississippi when Jackson took office, most of them in the South. The Cherokees were the most "civilized" (that is, least traditional) of all these peoples. Sequoyah had fashioned an alphabet of the Cherokee language, an Iroquoian dialect, and Elias Boudinot, another Cherokee, published a Cherokee language newspaper. In 1827, the Cherokees adopted their own constitution, including an assembly to make laws for the entire people. The Cherokees assumed that, as provided in treaties with the U.S. government, they were not subject to the laws of Georgia, where most Cherokees lived. Georgia state authorities disagreed, and in 1828 passed laws subjecting all the Indians to state regulation and declaring that no Cherokee could own land. All of them were tenants and could be dispossessed at the will of the state. When gold was discovered on Cherokee lands later in the 1830s, the state allowed miners to drive the Indians from their homes.

Marshall's Court had consistently found that Indians occupied rather than owned the land on which their villages and fields stood. No tribe had the kind of title that any white person could gain through purchase, deed, and the recording of the deed in a local court. Indians' occupancy was a kind of privilege granted by Congress and confirmed by treaty, ironically much like the privilege under which the colonists had held title (subject to revocation by the crown).

Who then could speak for the Indians? For example, who among them could sell or surrender their lands? And who could obtain title to the lands? These were questions without easy answers. The High Court insisted throughout the 1820s that the Indians could not be removed except by their own will, but left the back door open to removal by act of Congress. And the southeastern tribes occupied so much land that speculators wanted and that settlers squatted on that the pressure to remove the Indians was almost irresistible.

A states' rights' argument, on the other hand, gave the Georgia courts, legislature, and governor the power to remove the Indians whenever the state wished. Georgia refused to take part in Supreme Court cases challenging this right (shades of *Chisholm*). The High Court could not compel or punish the state, a harbinger of more serious constitutional crises to come. Indians could bring suits to the Supreme Court and even vindicate their rights against the state, but without the intervention of President Jackson the Court was powerless to enforce judgments against the state.

In *Cherokee Nation v. Georgia* (1830), Marshall, writing for a divided Court, refused to enjoin Georgia from enforcing its laws on lands guaranteed the Cherokee under the treaties of Holston and Hopewell. The Cherokee were not a sovereign nation but a "domestic dependent nation" and so could not claim that their treaty rights were violated. It was a unique relationship, like "a ward to his guardian." Marshall's claim had some basis in historical fact—the colonial governments and the American treaty negotiators often spoke as if Indians were children—but according to common law, guardians protected the property rights of wards. This the Court refused to do. The High Court did not have jurisdiction in the case, he concluded, a view somewhat at odds with his Court's long course of aggressively claiming jurisdiction in matters touching on the supremacy of the federal government.

Marshall knew that Congress had spoken in the Indian Removal Act, that Jackson's opinions were not easily changed, and that Georgia would not have obeyed an injunction. The Court had to protect its small and precious store of political capital. And no judge is eager to issue an order that cannot be enforced. "If it be true that wrongs have been inflicted, and that still greater are to be apprehended, this is not the tribunal which can redress the past or prevent the future."

Marshall's views were not entirely antagonistic to justice for the Indians, and he was not ready to deny the Cherokee all remedies. Story lobbied for the Indians on the Court and dissented strongly in the case. Thompson wrote for the two of them. Back in Georgia, the Cherokee continued to look to the federal courts for aid when Georgia arrested two missionaries on Cherokee land. In violating Georgia law, Samuel A. Worcester was practicing the same kind of civil disobedience that Concord, Massachusetts, writer Henry David Thoreau would make famous fifteen years later in opposition to the Mexican War. Again Georgia refused to appear before the Court when it heard the appeal from the state court prosecution.

No matter. In *Worcester v. Georgia* (1832), Marshall, joined by Story, Thompson, and Duvall, found that the Georgia law was unconstitutional—the state could not pass laws regulating what happened on lands reserved to the Indians by federal treaty. Georgia responded in a fashion whose echoes would be heard from the Nullification Crisis of 1828–1833 to the civil rights era. It refused to obey. Governor Wilson Lumpkin, a lawyer, was heard to say he would rather hang the missionaries than free them, a somewhat more extreme position than Governor Herman Talmadge's resistance to school desegregation in the 1950s but uttered in the same spirit of lawlessness. When the missionaries petitioned the governor for a pardon, implicitly endorsing his states' rights position and the power of the state to legislate for the Indian lands, Lumpkin gloated and then allowed them to go free.

Lumpkin had an ally in a high place. Jackson, his hands full fighting off South Carolina nullification, expressed his support for the relocation of the Indians. He never said, "John Marshall has made his decision, now let him enforce it," but he was worried that a confrontation with Georgia over the Cherokee might throw that state into the arms of its neighboring South Carolina in opposition to the federal government. What was more, he had little sympathy for the Indians, having gained a reputation as a ferocious Indian fighter during the Creek Wars of nearly twenty years earlier. The practical result of Georgia's intransigence was that the Cherokee would be "removed" from Georgia in the winter of 1838. Along the Trail of Tears to the Indian Territory, in present-day Oklahoma, thousands perished.

If they had felt that the Court had erred in its view of the Constitution, did President Jackson or Governor Lumpkin have a duty to resist it? Or at least did they have legal grounds to refuse to enforce it? Jackson said that "the decision of the Supreme Court has fell stillborn, and they find that it cannot coerce Georgia to yield to its mandate." It is true that the Court was the weakest of the three branches of the federal government, but at the time none of those branches could force a state to obey the federal courts. Would Georgia have yielded to the decision if Jackson had called upon it to obey the Constitution? Georgia had refused to enforce the Supreme Court's rulings before, for example in *Chisholm*, and had not suffered for its assertion of state sovereignty. To its credit, Maryland had acquiesced in *McCulloch*.

On what legal grounds might the president or the governor base their refusal to obey the Court? Simple refusal did not appeal to Jackson or Lumpkin. Both were lawyers and former judges; both believed in the rule of law. They hinted that they were merely democratically elected magistrates in a democratic system and that their decision was an exercise of democratic governance. The word "democracy" does not appear in the Constitution—nor would one have expected it to be there, given that most of the framers were afraid of a truly democratic government. But times had changed. Jackson and Lumpkin were both extremely popular politicians, elected by large majorities. Had a referendum on the removal of the Indians been taken in the United States at the time, Georgia's position would surely have won by a large majority. In a democratic system, should not the will of the majority trump the view of a majority of the Court, none of whose members were elected or faced reelection? Played out in this way, as an example of the countermajoritarian dilemma, perhaps a democratic system should not vest final say on the law in the hands of justices appointed for life.

Jackson could also have argued that the justices' view of the Constitution was not the final word. He was entitled to have his say. What Marshall had pronounced in *Marbury* about the Court being the final arbiter of the Constitution could not be found in the plain text of the document. If the Court asserted its role as interpreter of the Constitution, might not Congress and the executive also have had the duty to construct the meaning of the Constitution? This authority was nowhere denied them in the Constitution. This is just what Abraham Lincoln said in 1858, when he objected to the Supreme Court's decision in *Dred Scott*, and what he repeated when he was inaugurated as president in 1861.

Marshall had, by force of personality, a reputation and political skill unmatched on the Court until William Brennan arrived in 1956, and his ability to make friends persuaded the justices to seek consensus. Many scholars regard him as the greatest of the chief justices. According to Herbert Johnson's count, of the 1,426 opinions delivered over the period, Marshall wrote 632. Only Story, Marshall's right-hand man, came close, with 302. What had perhaps been simply Federalist views in 1801 became, by 1835, a judicial orthodoxy. Indeed, as the fortunes of the Federalist Party declined, so the concept of judicial review that Marshall championed became less divisive. Federalism without Federalists flourished on the Court.

Many of the newer appointments of the 1810s and early 1820s were Republicans of convenience, having switched their nominal allegiance during the 1800s. In the era of one-party rule sometimes called the Era of Good Feelings, many conservative legal thinkers—like John Quincy Adams, the former president's son, Daniel Webster, the New Hampshire and Massachusetts politician and lawyer, and Henry Clay, of Virginia and Kentucky, another leading politician and attorney—became National Republicans.

Another phenomenon may help explain why the Republicans' first choices for the Court went along with much that Marshall decreed. The vast majority of the Court's cases involved real estate, commercial law (including contracts), and court jurisdiction. On the former subjects, moderate Federalist notions of private property jibed with those of moderate Republicans. On the subject of jurisdiction and the authority of federal courts, justices of the Supreme Court, like all other judges, were naturally protective of their authority and mindful that they were the supervisors of the entire federal court system.

But the justices coming to the Court in the late 1820s and 1830s differed from Marshall and his first colleagues in an important way—they had not known the travails of the Revolution, nor served in the Continental armies, nor watched, firsthand, as the great experiment in federal government launched itself. They took the republic for granted, regarded popular politics as normal rather than a dangerous novelty, and assumed that parties would always divide the nation. They were a new generation schooled in capitalism, free markets, and competitive enterprise. Above all, they recognized that slavery was not going to simply vanish. Whether for good or evil, it seemed part of American law.

And with Marshall's passing, the Court was theirs.

CHAPTER 4

The Taney Court, 1836–1864

In a famous essay on the causes of the Civil War, historian Roy Nichols blamed the excesses of democracy for accelerating the movement toward disunion. Too many elections, too much stump speaking by politicians eager to court the popular will, and too few real statesmen doomed the young republic to the agony of disunion and the horror of four years of devastating conflict. Although it may be unfair to the politicians, including those who served on the High Court in these years, to accuse them of bringing on a catastrophe they could not have foreseen, Nichols's argument could have been applied to the High Court as well as to the elected branches.

Indeed, some of Marshall's successors on the High Court had no such fear of a catastrophe. Buoyed by a confidence in democratic republicanism that no man of the revolutionary generation would have indulged and motivated by political aims that went far beyond the passions of the 1790s and 1800s, the justices of the Supreme Court in the era of Roger Brooke Taney did not see disaster looming before them. Some of the blame for this tragedy of errors belongs to Marshall's successor as chief justice, but, in all fairness, it may have been impossible for the Court to avert such an "irrepressible conflict" as the Civil War.

ROGER BROOKE TANEY AND HIS COLLEAGUES

Jackson selected Taney of Maryland to replace Marshall for the same reason that John Adams had named Marshall. Both presidents wanted men who had served them well, who could be trusted to protect the presidents' policies, and who shared the presidents' view of the world. Taney did all of these.

Like Marshall, Taney was a man of many faces. Taney came from the planter elite. Like the leaders of that class in Maryland, Taney was a Roman Catholic in a nation that barely tolerated Catholicism. Despite the discrimination against Catholics in America, however, Taney was never a great fan of the underdog. He freed his own slaves but would become a defender of slavery. His career in public office included important posts in the federal government, but he balanced states' rights constitutionalism with nationalism. And then, when the South seceded, Taney chose the Union.

A man who owed his high office to politics, Taney had a gift for misreading political currents. As attorney general of the United States (1831–1833) and secretary of the treasury (1833), he so infuriated members of the Senate that they refused to confirm his permanent appointment to the treasury and denied him a post on the High Court the first time Jackson submitted his name. In 1836, the Senate finally confirmed him as chief justice, in which post he served until his death, in 1864.

During Taney's term of office, the High Court became even more political than it had been in the early years of Marshall's tenure. The Judiciary Act of 1837, increasing the size of the Court to nine justices, permitted Jackson and his handpicked successor in the presidency, New York's Martin Van Buren, to make the Court even more a Democratic creature. To join Taney and Virginian Philip Barbour, also appointed in 1836, Jackson was able to get Tennessee's John Catron through the lame-duck Congress. Like Barbour, who defended Jackson and upheld a stronger version of states' rights than either Jackson or Taney (Barbour believed that states could carry on their own foreign relations and that a state's police powers within the state are "not surrendered or restrained by the Constitution of the United States"), Catron was Jackson's personal friend and political ally in the state and, later, against the Second Bank of the United States.

Barbour died in 1841, having left little mark on the law. Catron was longer lived. Like Jackson, Catron came from hardscrabble beginnings and rose in the Tennessee bar and politics through his mastery of real estate law, his shrewd choice of allies in state politics, and his steadfast attachment to the Jacksonian party. Though he believed in states' rights and supported slavery, Catron was a unionist and had to flee from Confederate Nashville in a swift carriage ride ahead of a mob. Perhaps this experience made him a staunch supporter of the war effort in the North. He died in May 1865.

It was inevitable that the Democratic justices would be so staunch in their political allegiances, for in the antebellum years politics was king. In fact, the newly organized Whig Party lambasted Jackson as "King Andrew." But the political process in the Jacksonian era was entirely different from that of the first party period, when the leaders of the parties were intellectuals and much of their disagreement was ideological. In the 1830s and after, the contest for office was just that—a contest for the spoils of victory. Politics welcomed the backroom party managers, the candidates who could appeal to everyone, and the vacuous symbolism of log cabins, dark horses, and military honors. One often could not tell the Jacksonians from their Whig opponents, so much did the parties pander to popular demands. There were differences in the platforms, to be sure—the Democrats stood for less state intervention and the Whigs for state-sponsored reforms—but there were conservatives on both sides and liberals on both sides.

These included the justices added to the Court during the remainder of Taney's tenure. Van Buren's appointment of James McKinley of Alabama was pure politics. When McKinley's support for Henry Clay brought McKinley no joy, he became a Jacksonian and delivered the state's electoral votes to Van Buren in 1836. His reward was a seat on the High Court. His strongest attachments were to the southwestern farmers (he favored federal land grants to squatters), and his opinions generally favored states' rights over federal courts and absolute state sovereignty over banks (notably that Alabama could bar the operation of out-of-state banks). As his service continued, however, following the lead of Taney, he was willing to compromise and joined the majority in allowing federal regulation of interstate trade. He died in 1852, worn out from riding circuit throughout the West. In his fifteen years on the Court, he authored only twenty opinions for it.

As had Jackson with Catron, Van Buren was able to add one more justice to the Court in the waning days of his presidency. Peter V. Daniel would serve until 1859, dying a year later. In his jurisprudence, he was a far more consistent and vocal defender of states' rights, the legality of slavery, and the limitations of federal jurisdiction than anyone else during Taney's tenure.

Daniel regarded himself as the epitome of slaveholding aristocracy, although he was not a planter. That aristocracy was conservative in social ways but not necessarily so in politics. Although he was not able to win highest elective office (he contented himself with the lieutenant governorship of Virginia for seventeen years), he was a loyal supporter of Jackson and Van Buren and was rewarded with the High Court seat.

History might have regarded Daniel as a great dissenter. He led the Court in dissents and wrote in dissent about as many times as he wrote for the majority of his brethren. This role on the Court is an honorable one, filled by such luminaries as John Marshall Harlan, Oliver Wendell Holmes Jr., and William Rehnquist. But Daniel's quarrels with the Court's majority had an antique and brittle quality, and scholars have not given him high marks for the opinions he wrote. The last agrarian, he never accepted the emergence of a commercial, corporate economy, internal improvements (particularly government assistance to transportation), or the expansion of federal power. He preferred to think of "this confederacy" of states rather than the nation. Unlike many of his predecessors, he did not silently bow to the majority or withhold a dissent in the interests of unanimity. In his personal correspondence and frequent anonymous contributions to the political pamphlet wars, he could be corrosively insulting, and on more than one occasion, he was challenged to a duel over what he wrote or said.

President John Tyler had immense trouble getting his nominees through the Senate. The reason lay in an excess of partisanship on both sides. Tyler was elected as vice president on the Whig ticket with William Henry Harrison. Harrison died shortly after his inauguration, in February 1841, and Tyler succeeded to the office but not in it. Not actually a Whig—but instead a conservative Virginia politician whose views of states' rights and expansion to the west were much closer to the Democratic Party—he dumped all of the Whigs in the new cabinet, with the exception of Daniel Webster (who stayed on to negotiate a treaty with Great Britain establishing the U.S. border with Canada), and set about creating his own party. Nothing of this endeared him to the Whigs in the Senate. Consequently, the vacancies on the High Court went unfilled until Tyler got New York's Samuel Nelson, his fourth nominee, through the Senate in February 1845, another lame-duck session appointment.

Nelson was a veteran jurist, having served for over two decades on the New York bench. He was chief judge of the state's supreme court when Tyler tapped him. He was courteous, learned, and moderate in his opinions and his lifestyle, favoring a middle-of-the-road version of the Democratic states' rights position. His opinions departed from the majority of his colleagues' in only one way—he cited authorities (including treatises) in notes, a style that would become fashionable in later years and is standard now. He sat until 1872 and died a year later.

In 1844, both Tyler and the Whig candidate, Henry Clay, were beaten by an obscure Democratic senator from Tennessee, James K. Polk. He was sometimes dismissed as Little Hickory because of his close ties to his mentor, Andrew Jackson. Polk was a man of little humor and workaholic habits. He literally worked himself to death in office, dying a short time after stepping down in 1848. He too had trouble getting his nominees for the High Court through the Senate. Two made it. Levi Woodbury, of New Hampshire, served from 1846 to 1851, and Robert C. Grier, from Pennsylvania, served from 1846 to 1870.

Woodbury was a disciplinarian, demanding as much of himself as of others. He kept lists of his own faults. Riding the rising tide of Democratic Party popularity in the state, Woodbury held just about every kind of high office in his native New Hampshire, from state assemblyman to supreme court judge to governor. He was a U.S. senator, a secretary of the navy, and a secretary of the treasury (replacing Taney) as well. As a Democrat, he supported the annexation of Texas in 1845 and the war with Mexico thereafter. Some scholars speculate that had he not died in 1851, he, rather than his Democratic colleague from New Hampshire, Franklin Pierce, would have been the party candidate for president in 1852.

But Woodbury could not fill the shoes of Joseph Story, whose seat he took on the High Court. His rigid adherence to the Democratic orthodoxy of states' rights led him to opine that the Court could not review a state law unless it explicitly annulled a law of Congress, a stance at variance with the Court's precedents and the views of his fellow justices, including Taney. The only time he voted to expand federal jurisdiction over the states came in slavery cases, when northern state governments tried to undermine federal fugitive slave laws.

By contrast, Grier was a moderate in matters of federal-state relations. Easygoing and able, his credentials as a Democrat were impeccable, and his desire for higher office did not match Woodbury's. He spent much of his career in the courts of his native Pennsylvania and was a craftsman on the Court rather than a partisan. His thoughtful views on matters as intricate as state police powers, bankruptcy law, and slavery gained him the respect of his fellow justices. He tried to follow the Court's old precedent of avoiding sweeping decisions on slavery and in the leading case of *Dred Scott v. Sandford* urged the Court to write a narrow and technical opinion—in effect calling for judicial restraint—advice that other members of the Court did not take. When the war came, he was a strong unionist, supported President Lincoln's powers in wartime, and denied that states could "leave" the Union. He died in 1870, a few months after retiring.

Benjamin R. Curtis, the next justice to join the Court, arrived in 1851, the choice of President Millard Fillmore. Fillmore's presidency was another accident, like Tyler's. Louisiana planter and military hero Zachary Taylor had been the Whig victor in 1848, but he died in 1850. Fillmore, a New Yorker with southern-leaning interests, was able to fill Woodbury's slot with Curtis. Curtis was a highly respected Whig lawyer and politician in Massachusetts. In fact, his intellectual appetite and his learning should have made him the successor to Story's "professor" seat on the Court, just as he replaced Story on the Board of Overseers of Harvard. His opinion in *Cooley v. Board of Wardens* (1852), a Pennsylvania case in which the Court permitted the state to police its own harbors, was not only a model of learning but also a proof that a balance could be struck between federal and state regulatory powers.

At the same time, Curtis won Court approval for extending federal admiralty jurisdiction to inland waterways, in *Steamboat New World v. King* (1854).

Although he had defended the federal government's right to pass fugitive slave laws, he was no friend to slavery, and he would write in strong dissent in *Dred Scott*. Shortly thereafter, he resigned his seat and went back to his substantial law practice, probably for financial reasons. In private life, he was a doting father and loving husband, though his first two wives died before him. He had twelve children by his three wives. He argued over sixty cases before the High Court. He died in 1874.

COMMERCE AND THE TANEY COURT

Although the Democrats and the Whigs had opposing opinions on the role of government in the economy, the Taney Court's handling of commerce and contract cases did not reflect political alignments so much as the explosion of enterprise and the problem of state regulation, on the one hand, and private property interests, on the other. The first of these cases came hard upon Taney's taking up the reins.

In *Charles River Bridge Company v. Warren Bridge Company* (1837), the Court had to decide if a state's incorporation of a company was a grant of a monopoly or merely gave a boost to a particular enterprise. In 1785, the Massachusetts state legislature passed an act granting the Charles River Bridge Company the opportunity to span the Charles River. The charter gave them the right to charge tolls for forty years. The project benefited both the company and commerce as communities on both sides of the river grew in population and wealth. In 1828, the state arranged for the Warren Bridge, a span close to the Charles River Bridge. The Warren Bridge would also charge a toll, but after six years the bridge became state property and toll collection would cease. The old bridge company's directors brought suit in the state to stop construction of the rival span and failed. They then appealed to the U.S. Supreme Court, on the grounds that the state was violating the Contracts Clause of the U.S. Constitution.

Oral argument took place in 1831 and then again in 1837. By the latter year, the new bridge had become vital to the economy of the region. But it cut into the profitability of the old bridge and the Charles River Bridge Company had suffered financial losses because of it. Hence its lawyers shifted their request for relief from an injunction barring construction to a suit for damages. Daniel Webster argued for the old bridge, as he had for Dartmouth College, that the charter was a contract. The state had destroyed the value of the contract by underwriting the building of the new bridge.

Simon Greenleaf, representing the new bridge, denied that the charter said anything about giving the old company exclusive rights or a monopoly. What was more,

Every act of a public functionary is merely an exercise of delegated power, entrusted to him by the people, for a specific purpose. The limits of the power delegated to the legislature, are to be sought, not only in the constitution, but in the nature and ends of the power itself, and in the objects of government and civil society . . . providing safe and convenient ways for the public necessity and convenience . . . without which no community can well exist.

In short, the legislature, representing the will and the interests of the people, had simply acted to comply with public needs.

The Court split sharply over the case, Taney and three other justices finding for the new bridge and Justice Story, with two colleagues, writing in dissent for the old company. Taney's opinion was his first important foray into constitutional law from the bench. He held that legislative grants must be read strictly, and the one at issue did not include a noncompetition provision. More important, legislatures represented the will of the people (the bedrock of Jacksonian ideology)—the initial grant was not exclusive, indeed, it could not be without unduly limiting the sovereignty of the people expressed in the acts of their legislature. Finally, he reckoned that economic progress must be a consideration: "The millions of property which have been invested in rail roads and canals, upon lines of travel which had been before occupied by turnpike corporations, will be put in jeopardy. We shall be thrown back to the improvements of the last century, and obliged to stand still." The prosperity and happiness of the community trumped any narrow reading of the rights of private property, at least private property created by public acts. It was a view that paralleled the course of southern legislatures on slavery—for they had limited the right of slaveholders to free their slaves (a right grounded in property law) in the name of public order.

Story disagreed. Following the Marshall line of cases on the Contracts Clause, he insisted that the legislature could not take away what it had given, or no one's property would be secure. "There must be some pledge that property will be safe." Story's view harkened back to a time when all incorporation was limited and charters (or "vested" rights) were protected from competition. But this was a new age of enterprise and technological advances, and Story's reasoning, while based on sound precedent, had an old-fashioned quality.

Story's voice was more clearly in tune with a changing America in *Swift v. Tyson* (1842). At the time, the case was not controversial or even much noticed, although it involved issues crucial to the conduct of commerce in the nation. One of the most important sectors of that commerce was the sale and development of land. Land speculation had been the number-one business in America since its founding. Maine timber and farmland was about the only untapped agricultural resource in the Northeast by the 1830s, and unscrupulous speculators in Maine, along with conspirators in commercial centers like New York City and Boston, engaged in fast-and-loose deals with titles, financing, and, when all else failed, litigation.

In earlier years, Maine land shenanigans had led to gunplay, but by the 1830s, the crooks had become more sophisticated. To kite their speculation they used commercial paper (in this case "bills of exchange") that were endorsed (a promise to pay, like endorsing a bank check) and circulated far beyond the circle of original entrepreneurs. The problem came when a creditor received an endorsed bill of exchange, without notice of the underlying fraud, and tried to pass it on for payment. If the new recipient "dishonored" it, refusing to accept it, the entire chain of transactions could come under the scrutiny of the courts. That is what happened with increasing frequency after the Panic of 1837 brought banks crashing down and spurred creditors to demand payment on notes.

Swift was a bank cashier who presented to Tyson a bill of exchange growing out of one of these illicit Maine land schemes, and Tyson refused to honor it. Swift probably knew (by other means) and Tyson had already discovered that the underlying debt was based on a fraud, and in New York's federal district court, Tyson presented evidence of the fraud. Under New York law, such a defense was permissible, and the federal court was bound by Article 34 of the Judiciary Act of 1834 to use the law of the state in which it sat.

Case closed—or not, when Swift's counsel appealed to the U.S. Supreme Court. Justice Story, writing for a unanimous court, knew all about these frauds from his travels on the New England circuit. He also knew that the negotiability (legal circulation) of commercial paper was vital for business dealings. Constitutional scholar Melvin Urofsky has called Story's opinion in favor of Swift "a triumph" for judicial nationalism, for Story found a way to get around the New York law, and with it, the confusion that various state laws imposed on interstate commerce. He argued that there was a general law of commercial dealings that the High Court could prefer to New York's. To arrive at this result, he distinguished state supreme court decisions from state statutes—implying that only the latter were "law" as defined in Article 34.

Story's decision was seen at the time as limited to commercial law. Certainly states' rights advocates on the Court like Taney and Daniel would not have signed on if they thought that the state courts' decisions would not bind federal courts in other matters. But the case was soon cited as precedent in the much wider area, and the much more contentious area, of substantive law, including contracts, labor law, and even the sale of slaves. The notion that there was a federal common law extended even further in the post–Civil War period to tort liability for railroads and other industries. The precedent of *Swift* was not overruled until 1938, in *Erie Railroad v. Tompkins*. But even that unanimous decision permitted some exceptions.

New York v. Miln (1837), the so-called *License Cases* of 1847, and the so-called *Passenger Cases*, decided in 1849, demonstrated how easily the slave question could infect Contract and Commerce Clause cases. In *Miln*, state law required shipmasters to post bond for immigrants. The Court allowed the New York law to stand as a police measure, though in effect it regulated interstate commerce. Reading the latter term narrowly, the 6-to-1 majority decided that people were not objects of commerce. Hidden behind the facts in the case was the southern states' (particularly South Carolina's) desire to prevent free persons of color from working ships in their harbors or entering their states as passengers.

In the *License Cases*, the Court examined a Massachusetts law requiring a license for the sale of small quantities of alcohol. The license was not on the tavern (an old colonial practice) but on the object sold. The case dragged on until 1847, when a majority accepted the state's argument that it was using its police powers in the public interest. In the *Passenger Cases*, however, New York and Massachusetts taxes on incoming passengers to pay for hospitals were invalidated. If states could impose taxes like this, could they not also effectively bar the entry of slaves, even those coming into the states with their southern masters? Plainly, the justices were looking ahead to harder cases.

THE COURT AND SLAVERY, ONCE AGAIN

The real division in the country was one that the two-party system was designed to hide rather than exploit. That was the division over the expansion of slavery. The Jacksonian Democrats desired expansion into the West. Their opponents, the Whigs, wanted to limit expansion. The independent Republic of Texas's request to become part of the United States tied the expansion of the country to the issue of slavery. American immigrants to the Mexican state of Texas had raised a rebellion and won their independence in 1836. One of their grievances with their Mexican governors had been that Mexico did not permit slavery. The leaders of the new Republic of Texas expected to be incorporated into the United States. President Martin Van Buren, fearing that the admission of slaveholding Texas would throw the nation into turmoil, resisted. When Tyler became president, he vowed to annex Texas. Congress went along with him at the very end of his term.

Polk promised to further expand the Union to include the Oregon territory (shared with Great Britain), California (a part of Mexico), and much of the Southwest. He kept his word. The British agreed to a treaty dividing Oregon along the forty-ninth parallel. Polk sent a covert force that successfully incited rebellion in California. But no easy solution to the Texas-Mexico border region presented itself. There, Texans with strong memories of Mexican war crimes and Mexicans who resented American arrogance, slavery, and anti-Catholic prejudice were spoiling for a fight. War began in 1846, lasted two years, and ended with the Mexicans ceding California, New Mexico, Arizona, Colorado, and Nevada to the United States and accepting the Rio Grande boundary of Texas in return for a monetary payment.

With the annexation of Texas and the war with Mexico, antislavery opinion in Congress saw a plot to expand "the empire of slavery." In August 1846, during a debate over the funding of the war, David Wilmot, a Pennsylvania Free-Soiler, proposed a "proviso" to the bill that no land taken in the war be open to slavery. Wilmot's amendment twice passed the House in highly charged sectional voting and was twice defeated in the Senate, which again voted not by party but by section. All but one northern state legislature passed resolutions supporting it, fearing that territory taken from Mexico and given to slavery would be "poisoned."

It was in this vitriolic climate of opinion that the Taney Court heard a series of slave cases, *U.S. v. Claimants of the Schooner Amistad* (1841), *Prigg v. Pennsylvania* (1842), *Jones v. Van Zandt* (1847), and *Strader v. Graham* (1851). In June 1839, a Cuban schooner carrying forty-nine slaves sailed from Havana to another port on the island. Along the way, the slaves rose up, killed the captain and all but two of the crew, and ordered the two to sail for Africa. Instead, the surviving crew members managed to bring the ship into U.S. territorial waters, where it was boarded by American sailors and berthed in Providence, Rhode Island. A sensation in the newspapers, the case was eagerly watched by abolitionists in the North and slaveholders in the South.

The *Amistad* presented familiar issues both of salvage (that is, who could legally benefit from the saved ship and cargo) and the legality of the slave trade in American waters. As a salvage case, the question was whether the cargo of the ship—the Africans—belonged to the men who came aboard (two naval officers) and brought the ship into the American port, the Spanish owners, or the two Spanish men who in fact had purchased the bulk of the slaves and who were to have sailed the ship to Africa under the orders of the slaves. The queen of Spain petitioned the federal court in support of the Cuban owners, who were Spanish subjects, resting the case upon a maritime treaty between Spain and the United States ratified in 1821. Under it, the ship belonged to the Spanish citizens who owned it. As a question of salvage, the case was of little importance and would have ended in the lower court with a decree that the ship be returned to its Cuban owners.

But the alleged slaves also petitioned for their freedom, arguing that they were free when the ship crew kidnapped them and carried them from their homeland to Cuba. Helped by abolitionists and ultimately represented by John Quincy Adams (who had written the treaty with Spain in 1819), they raised vital questions about the slave trade's legality, the morality of bondage, and the right to rebel. The case was politically explosive, for Van Buren's secretary of state, John Forsyth, was a virulent Georgia slaveholder and tried every trick to return the slaves to their owners by executive decree. Adams, by contrast, was waging what seemed to be a one-man war in the House of Representatives to lift the "gag order" that the Congress had placed on antislavery petitions. (Congress, led by John C. Calhoun and other defenders of slavery, saw the petitions as insulting and denied that Congress had any power to legislate on slavery. Adams claimed that the gag rule violated the petitioners' First Amendment rights.)

The Marshall Court had already determined that slavery only existed where domestic law permitted it, Justice Story had written powerfully on the immorality of slavery in earlier cases, and the lower federal court judge hearing the case noted that Spain had outlawed the slave trade in 1817. He decreed that the forty-nine alleged slaves were in fact free and should be given to the president of the United States to be returned to their homes in Africa. The circuit court concurred. But the owners wanted the slaves, and again with the support of the queen, appealed to the Supreme Court.

The High Court had before it evidence that the human cargo were not Cuban slaves by birth (and thus slaves under Cuban law), and simply en route from one Cuban port to another, but were newly taken from Africa. What was more, the documents that the ship's master carried were a fraud to get around Spain's agreement with Great Britain not to trade in African slaves. But Story's nationalism and his fear that the debate over slavery could destroy the Union (a fear that had become far greater in 1841 than it had been in the early 1820s) cautioned him against any eloquent denunciation of slavery. Indeed, he did not even cite or repeat his earlier condemnation of it.

Instead, he wrote a technically clear but limited opinion based on his wide-ranging knowledge of conflict of laws. When one jurisdiction (the United States) was bound to render judgment under the laws of another jurisdiction (Spain), the Spanish law should govern. Story read Spanish law and the Treaty of 1819 as barring transatlantic trading in slaves. He agreed with counsel for the Africans that the evidence proved they had been taken in Africa. He affirmed the lower court ruling except for one item: the Africans were not to be delivered to President Van Buren (and thus to the mercy of the Spanish) but were free to go immediately.

Prigg v. Pennsylvania presented a far-more-vexing political question to the Court. In 1826, Pennsylvania had passed a law requiring that anyone seeking to recapture a runaway slave must get a certificate from the state that the person sought was in fact a runaway slave. Margaret Morgan and her children were either runaway slaves or free persons of color (the census listed her as free) from Maryland living in Pennsylvania. Professional slave catcher Edward Prigg found her, her husband, Jerry (a free black), and her children and returned them to Maryland, but he did not get a certificate from Pennsylvania. For violating its laws, he was indicted, and Pennsylvania sought his extradition from Maryland to stand trial. The two states agreed that he would be tried, and his conviction was appealed to the Pennsylvania Supreme Court, which upheld the lower court trial verdict. The two states now directly appealed to the Supreme Court.

Article IV, section 2, of the Constitution mandated free states' rendition of fugitive bondsmen and women to their owners, and the federal Fugitive Slave Act of 1793 based on this clause permitted slave catchers to bring alleged runaway slaves before any state magistrate prior to taking them from the state. In theory, the Pennsylvania anti-kidnapping law did not apply to such fugitives. It merely protected free persons of color from being carried off illegally.

Story wrote for a very divided Court. He knew that the Rendition Clause was of utmost importance to South Carolina and Georgia in the drafting and ratification of the federal Constitution, and that the slave South regarded the return of its wayward property as essential to its welfare and wealth. At the same time, *Prigg* was an agonizing case for Story. As "a judge from the constitution" he wrote to a friend a year later, he could not have written otherwise. The law could not be sidestepped. In his opinion, the duty to return runaways was absolute and the rights of southern property holders must be secure. Applying this to the Pennsylvania law, he found it in violation of the federal Constitution. Prigg's conviction was reversed and the law voided.

Story inserted two additional arguments in his opinion that were unnecessary for the judgment on the merits. The first was that the power to compel rendition was exclusively federal. States could not add to it; neither were they required to assist in it. Abolitionists who excoriated the opinion would nevertheless later claim that *Prigg* barred states from giving the slave catcher any aid, including allowing him to come into state court seeking redress against people who helped a fugitive escape. Second, Story opined that states could not interfere to protect persons of color resident in their boundaries, except when the slave catcher breached the peace or used illegal means. This was a concession of sorts to southern concerns.

There was no shortage of interpretations of the latter two points. Other members of the Court, notably Taney and Peter Daniel, signed on to Story's view of the Rendition Clause but resisted his view of exclusivity of remedy. They wrote that every state had the duty to assist slave catchers. Justice McLean dissented, agreeing with abolitionists that Pennsylvania law did not apply to slaves, only to free persons illegally treated as slaves. The purpose of the law was to ensure that the slave catcher had evidence. One of Morgan's children had been born in Pennsylvania, making that child free by the state law. Maryland law, under principles of comity, should have regarded that child as free, but she was enslaved along with her mother and siblings. Using *Prigg* as its authority, antislavery majorities in northern state legislatures barred state magistrates from assisting in the recapture of alleged runaways. Even Story's son, William Wetmore Story, tried to spin the decision as a "charter for freedom" allowing the free states to escape the burden of enforcing a policy that was abhorrent.

Prigg made clear that the Court was no friend to the runaway slave or her abettors. In *Jones v. Van Zandt* (1847), the Court ruled that an Ohio man aiding and abetting the escape of runaway slaves had violated the provisions of the Fugitive Slave Act of 1793. He had to pay a fine. Writing for the Court, Levi Woodbury did not find the case novel or especially difficult to decide. It was simply a matter of protecting the right of private property. Indeed, the case was made a cause célèbre not by its facts or law but because counsel for Van Zandt, including Ohio's Salmon P. Chase and New York's William Henry Seward, both Whigs with higher political ambitions and superb legal skills, had argued that Congress lacked the power to enact the Fugitive Slave Act. Both were U.S. senators, and in less than a decade they would help found the Republican Party. In 1864, Chase would become chief justice of the High Court.

A unanimous Court in *Strader v. Graham* ruled that the abolitionists who helped a group of slave musicians to run away from their Kentucky owner were liable for damages under Kentucky law. The defendants' counsel argued that the men were not slaves at all, because they had been taken to perform in Ohio and the Northwest Ordinance of 1787 banned slavery there. The Supreme Court decided that it had no jurisdiction in the case (and thus could not hear the appeal).

Taney stopped short of saying that the Northwest Ordinance's provisions against slavery were unconstitutional. Still, the growing expansiveness of the Taney Court's slave decisions, a departure from Marshall's largely successful effort to decide slavery cases on the narrowest and least political incendiary grounds, made many of the justices uncomfortable. Justice Catron, for example, saw in Taney's opinions an incipient antinational thread, and it worried him. McLean's aversion to slavery led him to dissent in *Prigg*, but his belief in the rule of law and his commitment to national unity caused him to apply *Prigg* in cases of slave runaways he heard on his circuit riding. Still, he agonized over the gulf between higher morality and settled law. Curtis quietly seethed at Taney's bullying tactics in the slave cases and would ultimately resign rather than continue to sit with Taney.

As potentially disruptive as these decisions already were for a nation divided over slavery, the Court was stumbling toward an even-more-critical dilemma. Could Congress bar slavery from any territory? Could any state strip slaveholders of their human chattel? When the gains of the Mexican War, including California's admission as a state and the settlement of the interior plains (Kansas and Nebraska), became political issues in the 1850s, democracy could not contain sectional discord. Some historians agree with William Seward, the Republican senator from New York, who in 1858 called the conflict between slavery and freedom "irrepressible," and Abraham Lincoln of Illinois, who warned in the same year that "a house divided against itself cannot stand."

Successive concussions in Congress over the admission of California as a free state, the passage of a strong federal fugitive slave law, the eruption of antislavery-versus-proslavery violence in the Kansas Territory, and an abortive movement in the South to secede in 1850 proved that traditional party politics and congressional compromise could not contain the slavery controversy. A new party, the Republican Party, appeared on the scene and opened its arms to those who opposed expansion of slavery. By the late 1850s, the Republican platform's centerpiece was free soil. The Republicans would also build state party machines so strong that all presidents from 1860 to 1880 were members.

Against this background of intensifying partisanship and sectional passion, the Supreme Court might elect to follow its 1849 rule against deciding political questions or it might take the lead in finding legal solutions to intractable political problems. In 1856, newly elected Democratic president James Buchanan asked the Court to find a comprehensive solution to the controversy.

There were three sources of law the Court might cite to accommodate Buchanan. The first was the Comity Clause of the Constitution. If northern states could be made to give "full faith and credit" to the "public acts, records, and judicial proceedings" of southern courts, as specified in Article IV, section 1, of the federal Constitution, and to follow the provisions of section 2 of that article, requiring the return of persons "held to service or labor" in southern states, perhaps the South would be satisfied. If, in turn, the southern states (as they had before the 1850s) allowed slaves freed in the North to return to the South as free persons, the dispute might be mitigated. The Comity Clause did not look like a promising place to find a solution, however, for northern states were busy passing personal freedom laws to undermine the Fugitive Slave Act of 1850, while "fire-eaters" in the South were opening mail from the North to be certain that it did not contain abolitionist literature.

The next source of law was congressional legislation. Congress had long prescribed the conditions under which territories might become states. Under section 3 of Article IV, Congress had "the power to dispose of and make all needful rules and regulations respecting the territory or other property belonging to the United States." This power was expressed in the Missouri Compromise in 1820 and the Kansas-Nebraska Act of 1854. The former barred slavery in lands acquired in the Louisiana Purchase north of 36 degrees 30 minutes north latitude. This would have included Kansas. The Kansas-Nebraska Act in effect repealed the Missouri Compromise and gave to the settlers of the territory the privilege of deciding whether it would join the Union as a free or slave state. The Court could simply have deferred to Congress, but by 1857, it had become clear that Congress could not control the passions that slavery and antislavery engendered.

Finally, the Court might have found legal grounds to settle the slavery controversy in its own precedents. But in the past the Court had prudently steered away from the sort of sweeping ruling that Buchanan wanted. Basing expectation solely upon these precedents, one might have expected the Court to move very cautiously. But when the Court answered Buchanan's request in *Dred Scott v. Sandford* (1857), it gave Buchanan far more than he bargained for.

THE "SELF-INFLICTED WOUND"

Dred Scott was the slave of U.S. Army doctor John Emerson and was taken with him from Louisiana to posts in free states and free territories. There Scott married a slave named Harriett and had children. In 1843, Emerson returned to a family home in Missouri, a slave state, and Scott went with him. In 1846, for himself and his family, Scott sued for freedom. Two trials and four years passed, and a Missouri trial court ruled in his favor. The Missouri Supreme Court reversed that decision in 1852. In the midst of the crisis over slavery in the territories, a majority of that court abandoned its own precedents that if a slave was freed in the North, the individual's return to Missouri did not re-impose bondage. Northern personal liberty laws, the response to the Fugitive Slave Act of 1850, angered Missouri slaveholding interests, and the new policy the state's supreme court adopted in *Scott* reflected that anger.

But Scott's cause had also gained new friends, free-soil and abolitionist interests that saw his case as raising crucial issues. Because Dr. Emerson's estate had a New York executor, John Sanford (the name is misspelled in the official report of the case), Scott could bring his suit for freedom in federal court under the diversity clause of the Judiciary Act of 1789. Of course, this litigation could only go forward if Scott were a citizen, but the federal circuit court sitting in St. Louis heard the suit. In 1854, however, the federal court agreed with the Missouri Supreme Court and ruled that under Missouri law Scott was still a slave.

The U.S. Supreme Court agreed to a full dress hearing of Scott's appeal in 1856. Why it did this remains a mystery. It could have refused to hear the appeal, leaving the lower federal court's holding in place. Perhaps the case had now become so widely discussed and so important to the debate over slavery in both the North and the South that the High Court had to take it on. But this explanation is not entirely credible. No case forces itself upon the Court. In fact, a number of the justices wanted to hear argument on the issues. Oral argument took four days, and the Court's final ruling was delayed another year, until after the presidential election of 1856.

The historian is obligated to give the members of the Taney Court a fair shake, to weigh their words in light of the time and place in which they were uttered, but, as Justice Charles Evans Hughes later wrote, the Court's opinions in the case were a "self-inflicted wound." Chief Justice Taney elected to cast the Marshall Court's and his own Court's prior slavery jurisprudence aside, replacing judicial restraint with judicial activism. By not deferring to the elective branches and in seeking to settle the slavery issue once and for all, he put the Court into the center of the most divisive issue ever in U.S. national politics.

Joined by six of the other justices, Taney ruled that the lower federal court was correct—under Missouri law Scott had no case. The case should not have come to the federal courts, for Scott was not a citizen. The law behind this decision was clear, and it was enough to resolve the case. But Taney was not done. He added two dicta, readings of history and law that were not necessary to resolve the case but would, if followed, have settled the political questions of black citizenship and free soil.

Taney wrote that no person of African descent brought to America to labor could ever be a citizen of the United States. Such people might be citizens of particular states, but this did not confer national citizenship on them, for "they were not intended to be included, under the word 'citizens' in the Constitution, and can therefore claim none of the rights and privileges which that instrument provides for and secures to citizens of the United States." Adding gratuitous insult to injury, Taney continued: "[Blacks] had for more than a century before [the drafting of the federal Constitution] been regarded as beings of an inferior order, and altogether unfit to associate with the white race, either in social or political relations; and so far inferior that they had no rights which the white man was bound to respect."

Taney's dictum about citizenship and race was another instance of originalism, the attempt to determine the meaning of the Constitution by reference to the thinking of the framers. Whether he meant it to reflect (as many of his fellow white Americans believed it did) historical fact or whether he selectively mined the writings of the framers in search of views supporting his own, his opinion appeared to give the stamp of the High Court's approval to an uncompromisingly racialist reading of American constitutionalism.

Taney did not regard himself as a judicial activist, as making new law. Instead, he wrote as if he could divine exactly what the framers had in mind. But as with much originalism, whether of the illiberal or liberal kind, his history was overgeneralized. The men who wrote and ratified the Constitution also wrote and agreed to the Northwest Ordinance's bar on slavery, including in it the possibility that African Americans could be citizens of the states fashioned from that territory. Free blacks could not vote in much of the North, but then neither could women—and they were citizens. In *Elkay* (1793), a federal circuit court had determined that a free black could be a citizen of a state.

Still, Taney's judicial activism had changed the meaning of the Constitution. Nowhere in it was national citizenship defined. Taney now had defined citizenship in racial terms. Whites could be citizens. Blacks could not. Only one other member of the Court, Peter Daniel, subscribed to Taney's opinion on this point. Thus it was not a ruling "of the Court" (that would have required a majority to agree to this part of his decision) and had no weight as precedent.

Even if Taney's dictum on race and citizenship did not become constitutional law, it so offended the usually cautious and polite Curtis that he wrote, in dissent: "When a strict interpretation of the Constitution, according to the fixed rules which govern the interpretation of laws, is abandoned, and the theoretical opinions of individuals are allowed to control its meaning, we have no longer a constitution; we are under the government of individual men." In effect, this was also a debate over an activist style of judging (Taney's) and judicial restraint (Curtis's).

But Taney had not finished. In a second dictum, he opined that the Fifth Amendment to the Constitution, guaranteeing that no man's property might be taken without due process of law, barred Congress from denying the expansion of slavery into the territories. Although Article IV, section 3, of the Constitution had explicitly given to Congress full and untrammeled authority to set laws and regulations for the territories, it could not rule out slavery because the Fifth Amendment was added to the Constitution after ratification, and it must be read to modify Congress's powers over the territories. In effect, Taney retroactively declared the Missouri Compromise of 1820, barring slavery in territories north of 36 degrees 30 minutes north latitude, unconstitutional.

Taney's interpretation of the Constitution was certainly arguable. The entire document made concessions to slavery. Why would the Fifth Amendment not constrain Article IV, section 3? But the implications of this line of argument were troubling to many in the North. Did it mean that states could not bar slavery within their own borders? The Supremacy Clause of the Constitution might be read to impose the Fifth Amendment on state governments. The Rendition Clause of Article IV had already occasioned federal government intrusion into states under the Fugitive Slave Act of 1850. As McLean put it, in dissent, "I must be permitted to say that it seems to me the principle laid down will enable the people of a slave state to introduce slavery into a free state."

The opinion was celebrated in the South and excoriated in the North. Northern public opinion, never friendly to abolitionism, now found the possibility of slavery moving north frightening. As one angry editorial in the *New York Times* railed, "Slavery is not longer local; it is national . . . and when the time for the next step comes, we shall have it in the logical sequence, that no state government has a right" to bar slavery. Lincoln used it to undermine his rival for the Illinois Senate seat, Stephen Douglas. Lincoln, no mean lawyer and debater, asked Douglas whether he accepted the *Dred Scott* decision. If he did, how could he hold to the notion of popular sovereignty—for under *Dred Scott* voters in a territory could never bar slavery. Lincoln lost the race (Douglas and the Democrats controlled the legislature), but he won the debates and found an issue on which to campaign for higher office.

LINCOLN'S COURT

It is an old adage that in war the laws are silent. This was not true of the American Civil War. Its roots lay in illegal acts punished by law, and its inception was an attempt to create a legal alternative to the federal Constitution. Upon learning that the "apelike" Lincoln, as he was caricatured in the South's newspapers, had won the presidency, the South Carolina legislature ordered an election for a convention to discuss secession from the Union. It met on December 20, 1860, and was unanimous in its support for secession. The state relied on the compact theory of the federal Union first hinted at by Jefferson in the Kentucky Resolves, explored by counsel for Maryland in *McCulloch*, and later fully developed by John C. Calhoun in the Nullification Controversy of 1828–1832. The Constitution was supposedly a "contract of alliance" among the various states, in effect a treaty. The North, led by the Republicans, had violated the terms of the contract, leaving South Carolina, and any other state that so wished, free to leave the Union.

By February 1, 1861, Alabama, Florida, Georgia, Louisiana, Mississippi, and Texas (the states whose delegates had walked out of the Democratic convention in April 1860 when northern Democrats clung to popular sovereignty) had seceded. With South Carolina, they announced that they had formed a new country, the Confederate States of America. A constitution was prepared that resembled the federal Constitution but guaranteed states' rights and slavery. The strongest support for secession had come from the counties with the largest concentration of great plantations and slaves.

On February 18, 1861, Jefferson Davis of Mississippi, a former U.S. senator and a hero of the Mexican War, was named president of the Confederacy. Davis, no lawyer, borrowed the compact theory of the Constitution in his farewell address to the U.S. Senate. After the Civil War, Davis's vice president, Alexander H. Stephens of Georgia, a lawyer, explained why he felt he too could take part in the Confederate government. He opined that the bedrock of the Constitution and American constitutional thinking was the "absolute right of local self government, or state sovereignty."

Neither Davis's nor Stephens's interpretation was historically or textually sound. The Constitution does not look like a treaty, and in it the enumerated and explicit powers of the federal government (including the power to defend itself against internal insurrection) were plain as day and not constrained by state sovereignty. In the Virginia and Kentucky Resolves of 1798 and during the Nullification Controversy, versions of the compact theory were proposed, but they never gained great adherence and were not law.

Lincoln kept silent during secession, and when he finally spoke in public at his March 4, 1861, inauguration, he called secession illegal. He would always regard it as a federal crime and never recognized the Confederacy as a separate nation. But he offered the hand of friendship to those who had seceded: "The mystic chords of memory, stretching from every battlefield and patriot grave, to every living heart and hearthstone, all over this broad land, will yet swell the chorus of the Union, when again touched, as surely they will be, by the better angels of our nature." He pledged, as he had in the Lincoln-Douglas debates, not to touch slavery where it already existed, but he would not budge on the issue of free soil.

Lincoln had hoped that cooler heads would prevail and that secession would fail of itself, but as president he had to act immediately if he was to fulfill his oath of office to preserve and defend the Constitution. One of the first acts of the Confederates was to occupy federal forts and seize the weapons and ammunition in federal arsenals in the South. In one sense, southerners had reenacted John Brown's raid on the Harper's Ferry arsenal, only this time they justified the action as legitimate because all men had the right to rebel against a tyrannous ruler. (Slaves, not in a "state of society," did not have this right.) Of the posts that the South wished to seize, the most important was Fort Sumter, which was under construction in Charleston harbor. Its garrison, under Major Robert Anderson, would run out of food in a matter of weeks, and it was ringed by Confederate batteries and impossible to defend if attacked. It surrendered on April 13, 1861, after one day of bombardment.

War had come. Lincoln, having maneuvered Confederate president Jefferson Davis into firing the first shot, called for seventy-five thousand militia men to put down the rebellion. Virginia, North Carolina, Tennessee, and Arkansas seceded, and the Confederate capital was moved from Montgomery, Alabama, to Richmond, a partial payment for the Virginians' change of heart that was to prove a mixed blessing for the people of the state. Virginia would become, as its unionists had warned, the cockpit of battle for the next four years.

Lincoln moved swiftly against supporters of secession in areas under federal control. On April 27, 1861, he gave to military officers the authority to arrest individuals supporting secession by word or deed, in effect suspending the right of habeas corpus. In Maryland, pro-Confederate mobs had rioted and pro-South political leaders were drilling antigovernment militias. One ringleader was Maryland assemblyman John Merryman, a terrorist who had helped destroy bridges to prevent the movement of federal troops south. He was arrested by military order and held without bail for a military tribunal. Merryman had important friends, however, including Chief Justice Taney, who rushed to Baltimore to order Merryman released on a writ of habeas corpus. But Lincoln had suspended the operation of the writ in Maryland. This set the stage for the first of a series of confrontations between the old Democratic members of the Court and the new Republican president and congressional majority.

The role of the Supreme Court in the Civil War was not minor, but neither was it as important as it had been when it rendered judgment in *Dred Scott.* Lincoln's first inaugural address not so subtly warned the old Democrats on the bench that "if the policy of the government upon vital questions affecting the whole people is to be irrevocably fixed by the decisions of the Supreme Court, the instant they are made in ordinary litigation . . . the people will have ceased to be their own rulers." He, and the incoming Republican majority in Congress (as southern Democrats resigned their seats and returned to serve the new Confederate states), would not tolerate another *Dred Scott* decision.

In the meantime, Taney was livid when the military refused to honor the writ in Merryman's case. On the spot he declared that the president had no power to suspend the writ; the military had no authority to supplant the normal course of justice or to disobey the courts in an area not in active rebellion; and Union officers could not arrest anyone except army personnel. The Constitution provided that the writ might be suspended in time of "rebellion or invasion" or when "the public safety might require it," but this provision was included in Article I, under the powers of Congress.

Although the question of who could suspend the writ was a genuine constitutional issue, the rest of Taney's views, if allowed to stand, would have fatally crippled the federal government's efforts to quell the revolt and restore the Union. Some antiwar Democrats in the North hailed his opinion, and prophetically so, for their support of the rights of the Confederacy would soon bring their own arrests and they would end up before the High Court. Republicans reviled the opinion, calling it *Dred Scott* revisited. In any case, Merryman had committed criminal acts under civil law and was delivered to a criminal court but not prosecuted. Similar controversies over military detainment of civilians occurred in all the border states still part of the Union, for in these slave states there was much prosouthern sentiment.

The Court, Merryman notwithstanding, did not challenge Lincoln's conduct of the war. The war occasioned cases of first instance—novelties like what to do with Confederate raiders and how to read Congress's confiscation laws. These cases began to arrive after Lincoln had had the chance to add Republicans to the bench and after the Court supported the administration's policies. Ohio's Noah Swayne was the first of the Republican justices, arriving on the

Court at the beginning of 1862, shortly followed by Samuel F. Miller, an Iowan, in July of that year, and then David Davis of Illinois, in October. Stephen Field, a strongly unionist Democrat from California, was the last addition to the Taney Court, coming in March 1863. These were relatively young men, free of the taint of proslavery and secession.

Swayne, originally a Quaker from Pennsylvania, came by his dislike for slavery naturally. His parents were antislavery activists. After reading law, Swayne started his practice in central Ohio and won a seat in the statehouse as a Jacksonian Democrat. When Swayne married a Virginian, he and his wife agreed to free her slaves. Long service as the U.S. attorney for the federal district court sitting in Ohio followed, but Swayne broke with the Northern Democratic Party over its willingness to let slavery into the territories. By 1856, Swayne was a Republican stalwart, and in 1860, he backed Lincoln. At fifty-eight, he was considerably younger than his fellow justices, and he steadfastly supported the emergency war powers that Lincoln exercised. A robust figure of a man, he would also support a robust version of freed slaves' civil rights and liberties after the Civil War. Swayne served until 1881 and died in 1884.

Lincoln's second appointment to the Court did not see eye-to-eye with Swayne on some matters. Swayne favored business interests, but Samuel Miller was the advocate of farmers. He was not the nationalist that Swayne was, nor the advocate of federal power. Born in Kentucky to a farm family that had come from North Carolina, Miller trained as a doctor and practiced in a small town. This reinforced his native sense of equality. He read law on his own and joined the Kentucky bar in 1847, at the age of thirty-one. He opposed slavery, but Kentucky did not, and he moved his practice to Iowa, where he freed his slaves. An impressive figure in the courtroom (he was the size of a football lineman), a wonderful storyteller, and with a very sharp intellect, Miller became a leader in the antislavery movement and joined the Republican Party at its inception, in 1854. He did not have the credentials as a judge, political figure, or legal scholar that many other appointees sported, but he delivered the state to the Republicans and was confirmed by the Senate in record time (under an hour). He sat on the Court until he died in 1890. From almost the first time he sat, he was a firm friend to the older members, a mentor to those named to the Court after him, and the author of many opinions.

David Davis was even larger in life than Samuel Miller and Noah Swayne, a veritable giant at nearly three hundred pounds. Born and reared in Maryland, his family had slaves and property, but he paid his own way through college and the first year of law school. He went west to find his fortune, and though he never became a rich man, he did establish a solid law practice in Bloomington,

Illinois, followed by a judgeship. On circuit, he became close friends with Lincoln. Both men were Whigs, and they became Republicans at the same time. Davis was Lincoln's campaign manager in 1860 and close advisor during his presidency. He remained a politico on the Court, thought about running for president himself, and resigned in 1877 to become a senator from Illinois. He died in 1886, of complications from diabetes.

Given the imposing physical size of the new appointees, it was a good thing that the Court was able to move out of the basement of the Senate into the old Senate chamber. A major ten-year rebuilding project had added wings to the Capitol for the two houses of Congress, and the old chamber was now available. It offered a robing room and a reception area, as well as a much larger space for the counsel and for observers to watch oral argument. The judges sat behind a raised bench facing a semicircular space. The chamber itself was larger and more elegant, and its acoustics were a great improvement over the basement hall. No longer did the justices suffer from the drafts, dampness, and mildew of the basement.

As nimble and slight as Miller and Davis were solid, Stephen J. Field of California more than matched the behemoths in judicial stature. Field came from a remarkable Connecticut family. His parents were from old Puritan stock. His father was a minister and missionary, and one brother, David Dudley Field Jr., became a leader of the New York City bar and one of the most prosperous lawyers in the nation. Another brother, Cyrus Field, became one of the most successful merchants in the country and supervised the laying of the first transatlantic telegraph cable.

Like Miller, Field went west, all the way to California during the Gold Rush of 1849. He soon had a prosperous law practice and served as a judge on the new state's supreme court. He was the primary author of the state's legal code (an achievement his brother had pioneered in New York), and at forty-six, in 1863, he became the last of Lincoln's additions to the Court. It took an act of Congress enlarging the number of justices to ten (and giving Lincoln the chance to ensure an antislavery majority) to open the way for Field. The new justice was supposed to handle a new circuit composed of California and Oregon—perfect for Field. He would sit until 1897, returning to his Democratic instincts (opposing government regulation of the economy and a strong national government) once the crisis of the Union was over. He died in 1899.

Although the Court had a reliable prowar majority, in 1863 the outcome of the crisis was far from determined. Lincoln had imposed a blockade on southern ports, preventing Confederate vessels from leaving and other nations' ships from entering. Blockade was governed by international laws of war, and legal disputes about southern blockade-runners, raiders, and European nations' aid to the Confederacy required sharp legal thinking. Were the Confederate ships at sea pirates or the vessels of a sovereign power? Could European goods intended for southern ports and carried on southern vessels be confiscated as contraband? In both of these matters, federal courts reversed the United States' long defense of neutrals' rights on the high seas and adopted once-despised British notions of blockade going back to the Napoleonic wars.

The crew of the Confederate ship *Savannah*, which was captured on the high seas as opposed to U.S. territorial waters, were tried as pirates, implying that they were still citizens of the United States violating its laws. Trial resulted in a hung jury—not a bad thing, for it forestalled retaliation by the Confederate government against federal prisoners of war. In these cases, however, as well as in the cases of "prizes" (Confederate ships captured at sea), the High Court ruled that Lincoln's imposition of the blockade was legal, even without an act of Congress or a declaration of war, and that confiscation of southern property was justified by the Constitution and the international laws of war. Grier wrote for the majority that Lincoln was bound by his oath and the Constitution to respond to the insurrection. Taney, Nelson, and Catron dissented, with Nelson continuing to use language redolent of states' rights.

The reconstituted Court also permitted a temporary curtailment of certain individuals' civil rights in the North. Congress did not ratify Lincoln's suspension of the writ of habeas corpus until 1863, but, earlier, Lincoln used military courts to stifle and muzzle opposition to the war all over the North. In infamous military trials of prosouthern politicians Clement Vallandingham and Lambdin P. Milligan, in Cincinnati and Indianapolis, respectively, military courts clearly usurped the role of civil courts when the latter were in full and safe operation. Only after the war was over did the High Court, in *Ex parte Milligan* (1866), declare that such violations of the Constitution were intolerable when the civil courts were open (incidentally freeing Milligan). Thus Mark Neely Jr. has found that the decision was "irrelevant," but in context, as Harold Hyman notes, the case was a "blow" to Republican plans for reconstruction of the South.

In 1864, Taney was eighty-eight years old, had long been in ill health, and had regular premonitions of his death. Indeed, he had far outlived his contemporaries and his times. Feeble, in constant pain, and unable to digest his meals, he died quietly, without official ceremonies, though his body was "attended" by Lincoln, Seward, and other high federal officials as it was transported from the capital to his Maryland home. Massachusetts Republican senator Charles

Sumner, who had crossed swords often with the chief justice over slavery, remarked that the latter's "name is to be hooted down the page of history. . . . an emancipated country will fasten upon him the stigma which he deserves." Justice Miller, though no friend to Tancy's proslavery views, thought him a man whose conscience and principles activated his actions and whose sense of duty, rather than his personal interest, motivated his thinking.

When all was said and done, Taney had left a deep impress on federal law. He was a nationalist in many ways, and progressive at times, but as Sumner's bitter comments suggest, a single case had come to stand for Taney's entire long tenure. Had the slavery issue not so dominated national politics and public opinion during that tenure, leading to a civil war, Tancy's reputation at his death, and today, would undoubtedly have been more positive. But history's verdict cannot be changed, even by the most pliant of historians.

CHAPTER 5

The Chase Court, 1864–1873

The Supreme Court in the last years of the Civil War and during most of the Reconstruction period—under Chief Justice Salmon P. Chase—faced momentous and complex challenges. Just as secession had raised profound legal issues at the outset of hostilities, so the end of the war and the protection of the rights and freedom of the former slaves required legal creativity of the highest order. And what was to be done with the former Confederate states? With those individuals who had aided and abetted the insurrection? How were the freedmen and freedwomen to be introduced to the privileges and duties of citizenship?

All of these constitutional issues were fraught with political consequences, for they had arisen from highly partisan circumstances. The Civil War was both a political and a legal (or illegal, depending on where one stood with respect to the Mason-Dixon Line) crisis. From the inception of presidential and congressional plans to end the war and restore the Union in 1864, the guarantee of genuine and permanent reform lay in a new regime of constitutionalism, but the political will and skill to make this happen—to push legislation through Congress, to get the president to enforce that legislation, and to convince the Court to support the new regime of law—had a chancy prospect.

The Court that reassembled under the leadership of its new chief, Salmon P. Chase, was the most political of all the Courts. In part, this could not be helped—for hanging over all appointments to the Court as a brooding omnipresence was the partisanship of the war years and its immediate aftermath. In part, the political shadow over the Court was cast by its leading members—Chase wanted to be president and so did Field. Both men wrote opinions, from opposite sides on many issues, with one eye on the law and one eye on the electorate.

PROSPECTS AND PROBLEMS

Three great amendments to the Constitution, the Thirteenth, Fourteenth, and Fifteenth, accompanying a fleet of civil rights and enforcement acts, had the potential to shift the relationship between the states and the federal government, expand the area of civil rights and liberties, and redefine the very nature of citizenship. The Thirteenth Amendment (1865) ended slavery, a massive transfer of wealth from haves—slaveholders—to have-nots, the slaves themselves. There was no precedent and no parallel for such a vast shift in private property or the right to it before the amendment, though Lincoln had confiscated slaves from rebels early in the war, and in the Emancipation Proclamation he freed slaves in rebellion as of January 1, 1863.

The Fourteenth Amendment (1868) guaranteed state citizenship to all citizens of the United States and prohibited states from denying to their citizens equal protection of the law, due process of law, and all the privileges and immunities of citizens of the United States. Through gradual and selective "incorporation," the Court, through the Fourteenth Amendment, has imposed the Bill of Rights on the states. Federal courts were at first hesitant to extend the Fourteenth Amendment to cover the full range of public institutions and institutions that served the general public (for example, amusement parks, banks, hotels, and restaurants), as these did not result from "state action," but over time that hesitancy has eroded.

The Fifteenth Amendment (1870) barred states from denying the right to vote based on "race, color, or previous condition of servitude" but did not guarantee anyone the right to vote. The Republicans in Congress assumed that access to the political process would be the ultimate guarantee of full equality and civil rights for blacks. But the reformers underestimated the ingenuity and determination of southern lawmakers and lawbreakers to deny to freedmen the vote. With poll taxes, unfairly imposed literacy tests, and simple violence, white southerners kept their black neighbors from registering or casting their votes. Like the Thirteenth and Fourteenth Amendments, the Fifteenth included the invitation for congressional action. Voting rights acts in the latter half of the twentieth century, aided by a massive federal voter registration drive, has enabled blacks to go to the polls in safety.

These amendments were also political devices, the work of one of the two great political parties—the Republicans—to ensure Republican dominance in the South. They were imposed over the objections of almost all of the Democrats. Thus the Court, when it had to weigh the meaning of this vast addition to federal law, was also weighing in on a political contest. Because the Republicans were not, at first, a majority on the Chase Court, and because the cases almost always pitted the Republican justices against the Democratic justices, the interweaving of politics and law became almost impossible to untangle. The history of the Chase Court raises, in its starkest form, the question of whether the justices' readings of law were dictated by their political affiliations.

The challenges that the end of slavery and Reconstruction posed to the Court's prudence and creativity were not the only ones the Court encountered. In the course of the fighting, certain prewar commercial and industrial trends were accelerated. These involved the deployment of a wide variety of financial schemes to support the war effort. Public and private bond issues and the introduction of a federal paper currency ("greenbacks") as legal tender changed the way the nation paid for its business and labor. Added to these, former Confederates' fiscal dealings had to be confronted. Were the public bond and currency issues of the Confederacy and its member states to be honored? What about their courts' decisions in private matters?

On top of everything else, the caseload for the justices, added to the circuit court riding now that the nation stretched from ocean to ocean, was almost too much to bear. The Court in those days did not have the luxury today's Court has of picking and choosing its cases. Any state dispute in which a federal claim was made and denied, and any lower federal court case from which a party appealed, came to the High Court. From an average of around 50 to 60 cases per year before the war, the High Court decided 169 in the 1869 term, 193 in the 1873 term, and 248 in the 1877 term. Many of these concerned private matters rather than major constitutional issues.

The Court, with carry-over members from the antebellum period, was not prepared to face the novelty of these questions or the backbreaking travail of their jobs. They complained of being slaves to their work. Circuit travel by train was an improvement over carriages on dirt roads, but the journey was nevertheless exhausting. Back in Washington, the justices had no clerks to help them research and write opinions. The old Senate chamber where they robed and sat was far more comfortable than the drafty basement room their predecessors had occupied, but it had no library and no offices. The reporting system of cases still depended upon private contractors, and there was no systematic reporting of lower federal court cases or easy access to state appellate court reports. (The West Publishing Company began to introduce its "National Reporting System"—in reality a collection of regional federal district and circuit court opinions and state high court opinions—in 1876.)

POLITICS AND POLITICIANS ON THE COURT

The Republican majority in Congress and President Lincoln recognized the obstacles that the sitting Democratic members of the Taney Court posed to full prosecution of the war. A redrafting of the judicial circuits and the addition of a tenth justice, along with the appointment of justices whose support for the war could be trusted, ensured that the Court would back Lincoln's war aims. In the process, the High Tribunal's divisions became openly political.

The prime example of the shifting politics of the Court was Lincoln's appointment of Salmon P. Chase of Ohio to replace Chief Justice Taney. Chase was an obvious choice for political reasons only. He certainly was not a legal scholar or an accomplished litigator, though he was well known for his anti-slavery activities in court. His legal education rested on reading law rather than formal study, and his practice was largely confined to the cause of the slaves.

But he had won high office in Ohio as both governor and U.S. senator. He opposed Lincoln's nomination for the presidency but then agreed to serve as secretary of the treasury. Though he had put aside his own presidential ambitions to support Lincoln, Chase always hankered for higher office. This self-importance immediately revealed itself on the Court. He never did become its real leader and only grudgingly acceded to the limitations of his new office.

Chase was not a particularly elegant or learned thinker. His passionate antislavery beliefs did not include the idea of social or economic equality. He did believe in legal equality for the freedman, however, including the notion that the freedmen should have the right to participate in politics and civil life. He supported giving the freedmen the vote and ensuring their right to sue and be sued, to serve on juries and in political office, and to enter the professions.

Beyond that, Chase saw little role for government in social or economic life. He was a nationalist rather than a states' rights advocate and voted with the Court to ratify Lincoln's wartime exercises of power but opposed any long-term government involvement in the economy. He was a laissez-faire theorist, believing in the immutability of the unwritten laws of the marketplace (even though such "laws" might in fact be based on court decisions and legislative enactments).

During Chase's term as chief justice, intellectual leadership on the Court came from Stephen J. Field, Samuel Miller, and Joseph Bradley. Field was as political as Chase and campaigned for the Democratic presidential nomination in 1884 and 1888. A brilliant small man with a large ego (he posed for portraits with his hand inside his vest like Napoleon Bonaparte) and strongly fixed notions of liberty and freedom, he made the High Court a platform for his politics.

Field derived his notions of law from prewar ideologies of free labor and Jacksonian democracy. These did not lead him to question whether concentrations of wealth in the hands of a few, or corporate monopolies in the marketplace, could be as oppressive as any government. Whenever he wrote opinions, concurrences, or even dissents, he favored large business interests and railroads over smaller businesses, labor, and farmers. When the Fourteenth Amendment was ratified, Field found in its Due Process Clause a hook on which to hang his economic ideas. He developed the idea of "substantive due process" (though the term itself did not gain currency until the 1940s), a test the High Court could impose on all state regulation of resource use, market conduct, pricing, labor relations, and just about everything else. For him, most of the state regulations would fail that test.

Field was opposed to slavery but no friend to people of color, including Indians, African Americans, and Hispanics. Miller, a man of more settled habits and conservative personal conduct, was no more solicitous of the rights of the new freedmen and freedwomen. And in his own fashion, he was just as political in his view of the world as Chase and Field. But unlike these two men, Miller truly believed in the importance of collegiality on the Court, and he often hid his strong opinions when he feared they might lead to acrimony. In return, he was highly regarded by his brethren and assigned to write the bulk of the Court's constitutional decisions when he was in the majority. Like Field, he had no hesitation about deciding cases on moral grounds rather than on some strict or technical letter of the law. But, unlike Field, Miller adhered to the plebeian strain in Jacksonianism, speaking for the common man.

Other new justices were not quite so overtly political in their approach to judicial matters. Joseph Bradley of New Jersey was self-taught and spent his career as a counsel for railroads and other business clients in Newark. A conservative Republican, he was not an abolitionist, had no judicial or significant legislative experience, and was not new president Ulysses S. Grant's first choice upon his first chance to appoint in 1869. Former secretary of war Edwin Stanton got sick before the Senate could confirm him. Attorney General E. Rockwood Hoar could not get the necessary votes. And thus Bradley was nominated and confirmed in 1870. He would serve for twenty-two years, dying while still on the Court.

Bradley's legal views were based not on exceptional learning or quickness of wit but on an unshakable belief that old ways were best. He was the truly old-fashioned conservative voice on the Court, as opposed to what may be called Field's neoconservatism. Bradley thought that the line between public and private concerns was uncrossable. Government could not dictate what people did with their private lives, businesses, or beliefs. Women belonged in their traditional roles, as did racial minorities. Nature, not law, governed the relationships of the races and the sexes, and nature had determined a rank ordering that manmade law could not and should not try to alter.

When a business or a private group attempted to affect the public interest, however, the state or the federal government might legitimately intervene to protect the people. This was not a Jacksonian view—even though some scholars suggest that Bradley would have been more at home in the Democratic Party than in the Republican—so much as a throwback to the era of the founding fathers. Serious in person, with wide-ranging (if somewhat eccentric) intellectual interests, Bradley was not a particularly easygoing sort. The only time he ran for national office he was soundly defeated.

The next to the last of the Chase Court additions was Connecticut's William Strong. Not himself a lawyer, Grant depended upon others in his administration to select nominees, much as another war hero, President Dwight David Eisenhower, would. In general, Eisenhower's appointments were splendid. Grant's were less successful. If Bradley was a throwback to the era of the founders, Strong was a remnant of an even-earlier Puritan age of New England. Strong, like Bradley, had Democratic affinities. Indeed, Strong had represented a Pennsylvania congressional district on the Democratic side of the aisle. But he was opposed to slavery and switched to the Republican Party at the outset of the Civil War. He was never in tune with the Radical Republican ideas of Reconstruction and narrowly construed the civil rights acts. He did not believe, for example, that the fact of persistent exclusion of blacks from civil rights in the South indicated illegal discrimination. A Presbyterian evangelical, his chief contribution to constitutional thought occurred before he was named to the Court. He proposed to amend the Constitution to proclaim "the Lord Jesus Christ the ruler of all nations, and his revealed will as the supreme law of the land." During his tenure on the court, from 1870 to 1880, he made no effort to include that language in his opinions. He devoted his retirement to Christian causes. He died in 1895, his reputation as an able but unimaginative jurist intact.

When Justice Nelson stepped down, Grant had no trouble getting the Senate to go along with his choice for Nelson's replacement, Ward Hunt, a successful New York State lawyer and judge. Hunt was one of the pillars of the Republican Party in the years before the war, and on the Court he would support the moderate Republican Reconstruction program. Hunt had moved with the flow of public opinion in upstate New York from Democrat to Free-Soiler to Republican. He played no role in the Chase Court and a stroke in 1879 cut short his participation on the bench. Though partially paralyzed, he did not resign until he was provided with a pension, in 1882. He died four years later.

UNFINISHED BUSINESS FROM THE CIVIL WAR

Even with the desperate times of the fighting now behind the country, the Court still had to deal with a series of issues growing out of the conflict. First among these were the various tests of loyalty to the Union that the wartime Congress and the various state legislatures had placed on citizens. Some of these were fashioned during the war. Others came with Republican victories in 1865 and 1866. The former were wartime measures to ensure public safety; the latter were political measures to ensure the continued dominance of the Republican Party.

In *Cummings v. Missouri* (1867), a bare majority of the Court, including all of its Democrats and none of its Republicans, struck down a Missouri law prescribing a "test oath" for lawyers, local officials, clergymen, teachers, and other professionals. No one who had helped the southern cause or fled from another northern state to avoid the draft or even expressed "disaffection" with the Union in the past could take the oath. Without the oath, an individual could not practice his profession. There was a fine of $500, as well as jail time, for falsely taking the oath.

Father John Cummings, a Roman Catholic priest, was sentenced to pay a fine because he performed his religious duties without taking the oath. His counsel, Democratic Senator Reverdy Johnson of Maryland, had served as U.S. attorney general and had successfully argued *Dred Scott.* He was an opponent of secession but did not support the end of slavery. He made a strong case that the law violated constitutional bans on both ex post facto laws and bills of attainder. An ex post facto law punished a person for doing what had not, before the law, been criminal, and the bill of attainder was a legislative criminal proceeding without any of the trappings of a trial at law (including the presence of the accused). A similar Missouri law would have made sense in the terrible times of guerrilla warfare in that state from 1861 to 1865, but the statute in question was passed in 1865, when the war was over. It could only be read as a naked attempt by the Republicans to punish Democratic southern sympathizers once the war was won.

Oddly, had the case come to the High Court after the ratification of the Fourteenth Amendment, Johnson might have argued that Missouri had violated Cummings's right to practice his religion, as protected by the First Amendment. The First Amendment only applied to Congress and the federal government until the Fourteenth Amendment barred states from denying to citizens of the United States due process of law. But the "incorporation" of the

Bill of Rights, in other words, the application of the Bill of Rights to the states via the Fourteenth Amendment, lay in the future.

Field's opinion for the majority hinted that the law could have been invalidated for being overly broad and vague. After all, the oath included the individual's sworn statement "that I have always been truly and loyally on the side of the United States against all enemies." Might it not be applied to someone who opposed a foreign war? Or supported Indian rights? Or sided with the runaway slaves? Instead, he parroted Johnson's brief. Chase disagreed, along with the other Republicans on the Court. The powers of the federal government and its courts had profoundly changed—not only during the war but as a result of the war. Insofar as congressional supervision of Reconstruction was part of this new mandate, test oaths were a regrettable necessity. Allowing the prewar southern elite to return to power would surely doom the congressional program.

The same lineup of justices heard and decided *Ex parte Garland* (1867). In *Garland*, the majority overturned a federal law requiring lawyers who practiced in federal courts to swear that they had not supported the Confederacy. Upheld, it would have effectually disbarred much of the South's legal community. Plainly, it was a Republican attempt to punish economically those whom criminal penalties could not reach.

Augustus H. Garland was a practicing lawyer in Arkansas before the war, and though he had supported the Confederacy (he served in the Confederate Senate), President Johnson pardoned him in 1865. The new law barred him from practicing in the federal courts. Reverdy Johnson again argued for the appellant: "Authorities show that the people intended to, and in fact did, clothe the President with the power to pardon all offences, and thereby to wash away the legal stain and extinguish all the legal consequences of treason—all penalties, all punishments, and everything in the nature of punishment."

Field wrote for the majority—again all the Democrats on the Court once more bought into Johnson's view of the matter. Miller wrote in dissent for the four Republicans that the test oath was a necessary expedient in turbulent times. The right to practice law in federal courts was "a privilege" not a right, and all that the law did was prescribe the conditions of this privilege. Surely they might exclude those who had engaged in treason against the federal government. Miller's dissent applied to *Cummings* as well as *Garland*, denying that the laws in both cases were ex post facto or bills of attainder but instead were merely ways of ensuring that the moral qualities of certain professionals measure up to the mark that the legislature prescribed. The presidential pardon might relieve Garland from any of the penalties in the federal law but it did not allow him to enjoy the privilege of practicing in its courts.

One can begin to see from Field's opinions his later absolute defense of private property, because engaging in a profession was a kind of property. Miller was not opposed to this kind of reasoning, nor was Chase. Chase voted with the dissenters because he saw the local political impact of the oaths. They would give to the forces of reform a tool to use in the local law courts against entrenched interests. Although the Court divided along partisan lines, the precedent of these *Test Oath Cases* stands—individuals who have repudiated membership or participation in outlawed groups cannot later be prohibited from working or holding office by ex post facto laws.

In *Cummings* and *Garland*, Miller stated that his views grew out of the late, desperate struggle the Union had waged for its survival. In the course of this struggle, civil rights of whites were second to military necessity, and that necessity the military itself determined. In a second series of martial law cases, the Court unanimously ruled that when the civil courts are in operation, military tribunals were not to arrest or try civilians. The best-known of these cases was *Ex parte Milligan* (1866).

Lambdin Milligan was a lawyer and Democratic politician who was more than sympathetic to the southern cause. Like Merryman before him, Milligan actively sought to raise rebellion within a Union state. Unlike Clement Vallandingham, Milligan's support for the Confederacy did not consist only of words. He was alleged to be part of a conspiracy to free Confederate prisoners of war, purchase arms, and take over the Democratic presidential convention of 1864. Although nothing came of the plot, there were acts that furthered it, largely the work of Confederate agents. Milligan, along with others, was arrested and tried in a court-martial in Indianapolis and condemned to death.

Lincoln was not eager to sign the death warrants, and, after the assassination, Johnson first commuted the sentences to life at hard labor and then ordered the release of the men. In the meantime, the condemned (three others in addition to Milligan) sought to move their cases to the civil courts under a writ of habeas corpus. The Constitution incorporated this old English privilege. Anyone detained by government authority might bring a writ of habeas corpus to the courts requiring the arresting officer to show cause for the arrest. Here, Milligan was arguing that the military tribunal had no jurisdiction to hold, try, convict, or sentence him.

In 1866, the Court unanimously favored the "return" of the writ, in effect saying that the Constitution barred the military trial of the conspirators. The war was over, and not only was there some desire for an end to the harsh military regime throughout the country but also the Court now had the luxury of reasserting its preeminence over that of Congress and the president in the realm of criminal law. In addition, the array of talent representing Milligan and his codefendants was impressive, including Justice Field's brother, David Dudley Field. By contrast, the government's case was not impressive, for the passions and the fears of the war years had become muted. Davis wrote for the majority that the federal government could not ignore the plain language of the Constitution, save in the most dire event. There was no danger of rebellion in Indiana in 1864, and the suspected conspirators should have been turned over to the civil courts for trial if the government wished to prosecute.

Chase wrote an opinion for the four Republicans concurring in the ruling but basing it on statutory rather than constitutional grounds. The military tribunal had not complied with the provisions of the Habeas Corpus Act of 1863, which gave the president the right to suspend habeas corpus during wartime but allowed federal judges to issue it when a federal grand jury was sitting. In effect, it was what the lawyers call "a nice point," a technical out for the Republicans to hold for Milligan and still not condemn the wartime martial rule or the current Reconstruction program. The latter issue was paramount, for as the Court was hearing Milligan, Congress was preparing to reoccupy the South with troops and give to the occupying army the power to enforce congressional statutes.

In all of these holdover wartime cases, it would seem that party politics determined how individual justices regarded cases. Surely the brooding omnipresence of the late war influenced the Court, and its members were voting their old party allegiances. But merely looking at the vote conceals the agonizing crosscurrents of opinion in the minds of some of the justices. In particular, both Chase and Miller did vote out of their loyalty to the Republican Party, but the two men were sympathetic to many of the federalism and property rights arguments that petitioners' counsels made and Field repeated in his opinions.

The Court faced a different but equally divisive series of questions arising from the issuance of greenbacks during the war. In these *Legal Tender Cases*, Chase broke from his Republican brethren and, even more remarkably, from his wartime views as secretary of the treasury. Then, he had supported the issuance of the paper money under an 1862 act of Congress. Fifteen state supreme courts had heard suits on the greenbacks, and all had decided they were legal tender for all debts. But all of the state judges deeming the law constitutional, as it happened, were Republicans. Those who dissented were Democrats. State courts had always possessed the power to decide questions arising under the federal Constitution. When creditors lost these cases in the states, they had grounds to come to the Supreme Court. The first case, *Griswold v. Hepburn*, came to the Court in 1868.

There were two issues the Court faced, the constitutional and the practical. The former returned to the question of loose and strict construction. Did Congress have the authority to issue paper money? It had the sole authority to coin money. It could borrow. Its bank could issue currency when it had a national bank. But nothing in the Constitution specifically mentioned the issuance of paper money. The second issue was practical. What would happen to the economy (not to mention the dockets of courts) if every debt called in and paid in wartime paper were deemed unpaid? There were about 450 million notes circulating. Were they to be made worthless at a stroke?

Then again, there had always been a strong voice against paper money in America, raised by those who did not want debts owed them paid in depreciated paper. This was a sound money party, and Chase belonged to it before he was presented with the terrible necessity of funding a war effort. That required money for the troops, their ordnance, and their food and clothing, and money to pay the expanding federal bureaucracy. Wars always cost more than any profit they caused. He had acquiesced then but later regretted it.

Only eight justices heard the case. Grier retired before it was decided. And though Strong and Bradley had just been confirmed, Chase did not schedule it for rehearing with them on the bench. According to the story, one of the reasons Grant chose them was that they would uphold the legal tender acts, and Chase knew it. He hurried to dispose of the case before they arrived and wrote for a bare majority of four. He argued that it would be a violation of the Due Process Clause of the Fifth Amendment to make the greenbacks legal tender for debts contracted before the act was passed. That left the matter of post facto debts up in the air. But not for long.

The very next year, with Strong and Bradley sitting, the Court heard two more *Legal Tender Cases*, *Knox v. Lee* and *Parker v. Davis* (1871), and in a 5-to-4 vote, reversed itself. Or rather, the majority in *Hepburn* became the minority in the next cases, as Strong wrote for Bradley and for the three dissenters in *Hepburn*. Strong's argument was simple: the government had to have the contingency powers in wartime that in fact it exercised; the issuance of a paper currency was implied in Article I; and terrible dislocation of the national economy would occur if the greenbacks were not legal tender. Strong's loose construction–implied powers–elastic clause deference to the legislative branch has a distinctively Hamiltonian sound, though in the post–Civil War atmosphere, Strong's defense of the implied powers was as much a restatement of nationalist principles as of any constitutional doctrine.

As expected, Chase dissented but covered no new ground. It was Field's dissent that rang loudest, for he claimed that the already-depreciated greenbacks would surely harm the creditor class. "A large part of the property of every commercial people exists in . . . private debts. . . . and the principle which excludes a stranger from meddling with another's property which is visible and tangible, equally excludes him from meddling with it when existing in the form of contracts."

It was the old Democratic platform of sound money, to which Chase adhered, retrofitted to the postwar era. "No one, indeed, is found bold enough to contend that if A. has a contract for one hundred acres of land, or one hundred pounds of fruit, or one hundred yards of cloth, Congress can pass a law compelling him to accept one-half of the quantity in satisfaction of the contract."

Finally, the Court had to decide what to do with the Confederate currency and other financial obligations that individuals in the Confederate states had incurred during the war. Chase disposed of both issues in *Texas v. White* (1868). It seems at first a simple case—can a state sue its bondholders? In this case, the bonds were drawn on the federal government as part of the settlement of the Mexican War. To be negotiable, the bonds had to be endorsed in Austin, Texas. At the outset of the war, nearly 800 of the 5,000 bonds, each in the sum of $1,000, sat in the Texas treasury. Near the end of the war, to help finance Texas's part in it, 135 of the bonds were sold to George W. White and another investor. The U.S. treasury thus had the distinction of financing the rebellion.

White never delivered the goods he promised, the bonds were "dishonored" when they were presented for payment after the war, and Texas, reconstructed, wanted them back. White had cozied up to President Johnson in an effort to dispose of his bonds. In the meantime, a complex game of find-the-bonds began, intertwined with Reconstruction politics and the buying and sale of politicians as well as commercial paper. The whole mess landed in the lap of the Court under its original jurisdiction, for Texas was suing the bondholders, citizens of others states, for return of the bonds.

Lawyers for the bondholders argued that Texas had a right to revolt based on the Declaration of Independence, among other sources, and that the Confederate state government could dispose of bonds in its possession as it wished. They also argued that since Texas was not a state when the Constitution was written, the High Court could not have original jurisdiction in the case. These were hardly persuasive arguments, and the Court gave them little credence.

Chase used the case to explain the nature of the Union. It was "an indestructible union composed of indestructible states." Texas and the other states in the

Confederacy had not ceased to exist, but they had strayed. The Reconstruction acts restored them to full membership in the Union, and the Reconstruction acts were legal under the Guarantee Clause of the Constitution, ensuring to every state a Republican form of government.

Grier, Swayne, and Miller dissented. They termed Chase's account fiction, not fact. They objected to the assertion that the Court did not have original jurisdiction because Texas was not a state and therefore could not bring a suit against the bondholders in the High Court. If this were true, then Texas had ceased to exist for the five years of the conflict and the ensuing period of Reconstruction. And if Texas did not exist, then neither did the other ten states in the Confederacy. Were they then a foreign country, as they claimed?

Grier did not speculate. Legal fictions were long a part of legal reasoning, precisely for the purpose to which Chase had put his. When law did not change as fast as facts, sometimes a little invention was necessary. The Constitution did not contain a right of secession. Secession had failed. The legal fiction that Chase wove allowed the Court to honor the normal operations of the Confederate state courts (for example, in cases of probate, contract, debt, criminal prosecutions, and the like), while annulling all the public acts of the same state governments during the war. Not a bad compromise.

On the merits of Texas's suit, as opposed to the jurisdictional question of Texas's right to bring the suit under the original jurisdiction of the Court, Chase may have made an error. He ruled for Texas on the grounds that the purchasers of the bonds should have informed themselves that they needed to get them countersigned. Ordinarily, if one pays good money for a legal thing, without notice that the title to the thing is in some way impaired, the purchase will stand. (Receiving stolen goods is an exception.) Actually, White and his fellow purchasers knew that their title to the bonds was faulty, but that did not stop them. In any case, within a decade, Chase's novel theory of negotiable instruments was reversed by the Court. But not until successive holders (the original payees had sold the bonds to others) started suing one another, with Texas hot on all their trails.

Chase's willingness to promote a speedier end to the uncertain state of the Confederate states, so long as the larger purposes of Reconstruction were not obstructed by the former Confederate states, was pragmatic. Some commentators have suggested that his stance reflected a return to his pre-1850s Democratic leanings, and others have carped that he was trying to curry favor in the South for a presidential bid. In any case, judicial statesmanship is always a plus. One need only remember how far Taney's lack of statesmanship in his *Dred Scott* dicta had sunk the Court to appreciate the value of Chase's words.

RECONSTRUCTION

As Chase stated for the majority in *Texas v. White*, as far as the Court was concerned, the Union had never been dissolved; it was indestructible. But the reconstruction of the Union, or as Chase preferred to call it, its reorganization, faced formidable obstacles. The issue was not just the Confederate war debt, but the rights and privileges of the freedmen and freedwomen. Lincoln and the majority of the Republican Party were not abolitionists. They were Free-Soilers opposed to the expansion of slavery into the territories. Lincoln called for volunteers after the surrender of Fort Sumter not to free the slaves but to restore the Union. In the course of the war, it became evident that black troops might well tip the balance in the Union's favor, and Lincoln began to consider freeing all slaves in territories in rebellion. This is what the Emancipation Proclamation did, under Lincoln's war powers. He confiscated the slaves—chattel—from their owners in territory still in rebellion.

But the war galvanized abolitionist opinion in the North among the Republicans and within the Union armies. The end of slavery became a northern war aim. Thus moderate and even conservative Republicans joined in Congress to support the Thirteenth Amendment. Had a Gallup Poll been taken in the North, the vast majority of men and women would have been in favor of ending slavery. Most white southerners would have objected, but all black southerners, even those who remained loyal to their masters during the war, would have applauded the end of human bondage. Indeed, the United States, pledged to liberty and justice, was one of the last of the civilized nations of the world to give up slavery.

Going beyond simply freeing the slaves was both the key obstacle and the opportunity in Reconstruction. The "first Reconstruction" of the former Confederate states began with President Lincoln's and President Andrew Johnson's resolve to restore the Union as expeditiously and seamlessly as possible. Lincoln had no desire to punish individual white southerners for secession. He did not want a long and bloody guerrilla war to follow the formal surrender of the South. Thus, in his second inaugural address, he promised a swift and merciful restoration of the Union, "with malice toward none and charity for all." He promised also a general amnesty for all but the leaders of the Confederacy. His one condition was that white southerners accept the end of slavery, and this meant that the newest citizens, freedmen and freedwomen, would have to fend for themselves without any protection from the federal government.

The Thirteenth Amendment stated that Congress would have the power to enforce the end of slavery by legislative means. We will never know how

Lincoln and his Congress would together have crafted Reconstruction. On April 14, less than a week after Lee surrendered the Army of Northern Virginia to Grant, Lincoln was assassinated by a bitter southern sympathizer.

Vice President Andrew Johnson from Tennessee, chosen in 1864 to balance the ticket, was left in charge of "presidential reconstruction." Although he grew up poor and had no love of the planter aristocracy, he had equal contempt for people of color. He absolutely opposed giving black people the vote, believing them only one step removed from "barbarism." In politics he had been a unionist Democrat, and he preferred limited government to the vast expansion of federal power that the war brought. With Congress in recess, there was no one to slow his pace as he took the lead in bringing the confederate states back into the Union as swiftly as possible.

Johnson named provisional governors for the former Confederate states, and they called constitutional conventions. The new states had to ratify the Thirteenth Amendment. Former slaves could not vote in these elections, and the old southern elite returned to power in their states and in Congress. At home, they immediately passed a series of "black codes" that imposed virtual slavery on the newly freed men and women, denying them basic rights that whites possessed. White vigilante groups burned the homes of blacks who sought full equality and killed those who did not learn their lesson.

Learning of violence against the freedmen and seeing the sacrifices of the war to free the slaves going for naught, the Republicans in Congress embarked upon a Reconstruction program of their own. They passed the Civil Rights Act of 1866, which protected the legal rights of all citizens and permitted the "removal" of certain kinds of legal actions from state to federal court. This would become the basis of much later civil rights litigation, and the remedies of the acts are still on the books. Next came congressional passage of the Fourteenth Amendment to the Constitution. The Fourteenth Amendment revolutionized federal-state relations, but it was not clear whether it was limited to state actions against freedmen (like the black codes) or if it was meant to apply to individuals who acted with the covert consent of former Confederate state leaders as well as to the states themselves. To protect the freedmen from both overt and covert dangers, Congress added to the amendment the provision that Confederate leaders could not hold federal or state office until two-thirds of Congress approved—a club held over the heads of the ruling class in the South.

Public opinion in the North, influenced by Republican newspaper accounts and eyewitness reports of the continuing mistreatment of former slaves, demanded further action from Congress. The first Reconstruction Act in 1867 carved the former Confederacy into five military districts, each containing one, two, or three states, with Union generals and federal garrisons supervising elections and keeping order. Freedmen could vote and hold office. Each state was required to write a new constitution, which Congress had to approve, and to ratify the Fourteenth Amendment. More enforcement acts followed, providing for protection of freedmen at the polls.

On their face, the acts were simply guarantees that the democratic process in the South would not be derailed by violence. The acts asserted Congress's primacy in the Reconstruction process and repudiated Johnson's methods. At the same time, in a more partisan sense, the acts ensured that the Republican Party's own interest in southern government would be promoted. Still, the acts committed the federal government to the ideal of justice for all.

The High Court was well aware that many white southerners did not regard the freedmen and freedwomen as having any legal rights worth maintaining, much less protecting in state law courts. The full measure of violence that hooded criminals exacted against the former slaves was never brought to light, but even when local law officers brought prosecutions for assault, battery, manslaughter, and murder against whites whose victims were blacks, local juries refused to convict. The civil rights, Reconstruction, and enforcement acts that the Republican majority in Congress passed provided federal legal remedies for such injustices, but the High Court could hardly indulge in the fantasy that the white South would accept the civil rights, much less the economic and social equality and the political role, of the freedmen.

As political as the Court's members were, one would expect the Republicans on the Court to adopt an "activist" role in promoting congressional Reconstruction. Instead, the Court proved to be the institution least inclined to radical reform. Its members, including Chase, found narrow technical means to decide, or avoid deciding, controversial cases. *Ex parte Yerger* (1869) was typical of these. A white Mississippi planter with a violent temper and a long habit of getting his own way murdered a Union Army officer in the occupying forces. His family hired counsel to urge that his case be heard by a civil jury rather than a military tribunal as provided by the Reconstruction Act of 1867. In the nearly monthlong hearing, his insanity was well proven and the fact that he had committed the crime was established without doubt. (In fact, it was the testimony of a former slave that best proved his violent temper.) His counsel argued that this anger management problem was a form of insanity.

The constitutional issue that brought the case to the High Court was whether, as in the case of Milligan, Yerger was entitled to be tried in a state civil court. Chase and the other justices tried to dodge the issue—they did not want the confrontation with Congress. Still, Chase wrote for the Court that it, not Congress, had the final say on the constitutionality of all the provisions of the Reconstruction Acts, including habeas corpus relief from military trials. As a matter of fact, Mississippi was readmitted to the Union in 1870, and the provisions of the much-controverted Reconstruction Act no longer applied to it. Thus the military proceeding ended with a whimper. Yerger was never tried in a civil court. He left Mississippi and took his act to Baltimore, where he started a newspaper. He got away with murder in the figurative and literal senses of the term. In that, his case was little different from those of thousands of violent men who could not be brought to justice in Reconstruction days. Attorney General Ebenezer Hoar was right when he argued for the prosecution in *Yerger* that the war had never ended.

The Chase Court had not lost interest in the project of Reconstruction, but the majority was not willing to follow the implications or the inclinations of the Radical Republicans in Congress. Law could be used to protect the gains of freedom but not expand its boundaries. Had Chase so desired, the nine years of Chase's superintendency of the High Court might have witnessed the beginning of a true revolution in federal-state relations and through the latter the institution of a constitutional regime of civil and human rights for the oppressed. It would have been, as Lincoln had told the nation during the war, "a new birth of liberty." Instead, the Court inched its way uncertainly, patching older ideas together into narrowly conceived and often contrived rationales to avoid innovation. Chief Justice Rehnquist wrote that the High Court has no "generalized mandate" to do justice, and the Chase Court certainly did not seek such a mandate.

SUBSTANTIVE DUE PROCESS AND THE ECONOMY

The majority of the Court was as unwilling to expand the law in the commercial arena as it was in civil rights, though a coalition of new and old conservatives was forming around a project to protect certain kinds of economic activity against state regulation. It was still in a nascent state in the Chase Court, but the outlines of the alliance and its aims could be seen in the debates and outcome of the *Slaughterhouse Cases*.

The *Slaughterhouse Cases* (1873) came to the Court on appeal from the federal circuit court in Louisiana and to the latter from the state's supreme court. The issue, like so many the Court faced in this decade, was transformed by Reconstruction and the Fourteenth Amendment. The state had incorporated a livestock butchery as part of an effort to clean up the industry. Abattoirs polluted the waters in New Orleans, posing a major health risk. But the legislature was playing favorites in its regulation efforts, assigning the profits of the entire business to one company in which a number of politicians had a personal interest. Butchers left out of the deal joined forces to seek injunctions in local courts against what in effect was a monopoly. Citing the impairment of their own property and professional enterprise (in effect, the same argument successful in the *Test Oath Cases*), the butchers sued and lost. State courts upheld the legislation as a legitimate exercise of the state's police powers.

With new legal counsel in the form of former Supreme Court justice John Campbell, the butchers turned to the federal courts, alleging that the state law violated their federal constitutional rights under the Fourteenth Amendment, in particular their "privileges and immunities" as citizens of the United States. Campbell argued that the right to labor freely was one of these national privileges. He continued that the statute had reduced the excluded butchers to a state of involuntary servitude in violation of the Thirteenth Amendment. In effect, he equated race with class, turning amendments meant to uplift an oppressed racial minority into protectors of the rights of oppressed economic groups. (Not that he was defending the poor worker—the butchers owned the slaughterhouses.)

Campbell might also have argued that the law violated the equal protection and due process provisions of the new amendment, but he had said enough to move the case into federal court. Justice Bradley, riding circuit, agreed—the state had violated the Fourteenth Amendment. Although the state had immunity from suit under the Eleventh Amendment, the butchers could shut down the Crescent City slaughterhouse the state law created, achieving the same goal.

When the case arrived at the High Court in 1873, Bradley's circuit court opinion raised a host of difficult problems. Not surprisingly, the Court divided on the case and the issues. For the majority, Miller wrote that the statute as a matter of fact did not deny to butchers their trade; instead it stated that "the butcher . . . is still permitted to slaughter, to prepare, and to sell his own meats; but he is required to slaughter at a specified place and to pay a reasonable compensation for the use of the accommodations furnished him at that place." Such state regulation of health and welfare was not only common but well established in law: "This power is, and must be from its very nature, incapable of any very exact definition or limitation. Upon it depends the security of social order, the life and health of the citizen, the comfort of an existence in a thickly populated community, the enjoyment of private and social life, and the beneficial use of property."

That might have settled the issue, but Miller wanted to deal with the novel Thirteenth and Fourteenth Amendment claims. He summoned Clio to his aid and offered a gloss on what Congress wanted:

In the light of this recapitulation of events, almost too recent to be called history, but which are familiar to us all; and on the most casual examination of the language of these amendments, no one can fail to be impressed with the one pervading purpose found in them all . . . we mean the freedom of the slave race, the security and firm establishment of that freedom, and the protection of the newly-made freeman and citizen from the oppressions of those who had formerly exercised unlimited dominion over him.

Field wrote for the dissenters. He insisted that the state could have stopped with the regulation of butchering and accomplished its purposes legitimately. The creation of the monopoly was not necessary, a mere "pretense" for corruption. The sweeping phrases of the two amendments that Miller read in context of the war, Field looked upon instead as an invitation to laissez-faire economics:

It is evident that the language of the amendment is not used in a restrictive sense. It is not confined to African slavery alone. It is general and universal in its application. Slavery of white men as well as of black men is prohibited, and not merely slavery in the strict sense of the term, but involuntary servitude in every form. . . . the compulsion which would force him to labor even for his own benefit only in one direction, or in one place, would be almost as oppressive and nearly as great an invasion of his liberty as the compulsion which would force him to labor for the benefit or pleasure of another, and would equally constitute an element of servitude.

Whatever one may think of Field's analogy between chattel slavery before the war and the butchers' servitude, he had taken a great stride toward what would, in later years, be called "strict scrutiny" of state laws. Field and his allies lost the battle, but in the Gilded Age his view of the amendment would become orthodoxy on the Court. It would adopt his prudential (that is, judge-made) notion that the amendment required the Court to engage in substantive due process analysis. In this, the Court entered the very arena that Miller tried to avoid, setting itself up as final arbiter of all state economic and police regulations.

One of these regulations that did pass muster on the High Court was Illinois's ban on women at the bar. Leading feminists had lobbied hard for women to be included in the Reconstruction Amendments' guarantees of rights and privileges, particularly the Fifteenth Amendment's right to vote. They had failed. Women were still second-class citizens—afforded some rights but not others. The common-law restrictions on women remained in place in some states, including bars to their practice of the professions, entry to schools, and ability to hold office, serve on juries, and control their own property. For feminists, *Bradwell v. the State* (1873) was a landmark case.

Myra Bradwell had a law degree, but the Illinois state bar association denied her the right to practice law. Otherwise qualified by education and moral character, only her subordinate status as wife and woman denied her the privilege of earning a living. The Illinois court ruled that "God designed the sexes to occupy different spheres of action, and that it belonged to men to make, apply, and execute the laws." Behind the invocation of the divine may have been more mundane reasons to bar women. They represented competition, and members of the bar were jealous of their profits. It was assumed as well that they would be directed by their husbands or distracted by their children, to the detriment of their clients, though no one offered proof of those assumptions.

Bradwell appealed to the Supreme Court under Fourteenth Amendment arguments that the butchers in the *Slaughterhouse Cases* had pioneered; in fact, the two cases were decided together. Justice Miller's refusal to read the amendment broadly doomed Bradwell along with the butchers, and he made the same point in his opinion in *Bradwell v. State* as he had in the *Slaughterhouse Cases*. The power to license belonged to the state, and the licensing of women as attorneys was no different from the licensing of slaughterhouses.

But the Court was not finished with the issue. Justice Bradley wrote a concurrence in which Field and Swayne joined. "Nature itself," Bradley wrote, "has always recognized a wide difference in the respective spheres and destinies of man and woman. Man is, or should be, woman's protector and defender. The natural and proper timidity and delicacy which belongs to the female sex evidently unfits it for many of the occupations of civil life."

Chase dissented from the judgment of the Court and from all the opinions, but he did not say why. He had been partially disabled by a stroke in 1870 and was growing feebler with each day. Harold Hyman attributes Chase's later thinking to a desire to "privatize" Reconstruction—an odd way for Chase to read what was from the first a public program, imposed from above. Chase died on May 7, 1873, after a second stroke.

The Chase Court stood astride the transformation of American government. Small, inexpensive, limited government was changing over to more expensive, administratively adept, larger government. The time when most legal subjects were matters of private law was changing to a time when public policy and law intruded into the most intimate and hitherto-untouchable regions of ordinary life. The end of slavery and its consequences both symbolized those shifts and forced the Court to assess how far those shifts would go. Riven with political partisanship and often poorly led, the Court gave no answers to the questions of Reconstruction.

But, by 1873, the High Court was no longer an immature and untried institution. It had developed its own conventions and fully asserted its place in the federal system. Although *Dred Scott* and the *Legal Tender Cases* had impaired the reputation of the Court in certain quarters, neither these cases nor other unpopular decisions took from the Court what its first eighty-four years of operation had established—an estimable role as a full partner in federal government and a praiseworthy record in constitutional adjudication.

Part Two

The Classical Courts

The Waite, Fuller, White, Taft, and Hughes Courts shared a vision of a powerful Court fully in tune with the increased authority and reach of the federal government after the Civil War. It could and did strike down acts of Congress and state legislation that violated prudential—judge-made—doctrines. Although these Courts claimed to discover doctrines like substantive due process and liberty of contract in the Fourteenth Amendment, in fact the justices invented these concepts. With the assurance and elegance of classical philosophers, the majority of justices on these Courts then wove arguments to protect capital and commerce from organized labor and government regulations.

In the process, the Court was able to reverse the pre–Civil War Courts on a key point. Marshall and his Court declared that the Bill of Rights did not apply to the states. Bit by bit, the classic courts incorporated the Bill of Rights into the Fourteenth Amendment, and in so doing imposed the Bill of Rights on the states. At the same time, the Court majorities steadfastly refused to read the Reconstruction amendments broadly, leaving disfavored African Americans to the not-so-tender mercies of racist local courts and state legislatures.

Surely politics played a part in these decisions, but the patterns of alliance and dissent were not entirely dictated by party. Conservative Republican jurists found common cause with conservative Democratic justices in pro-business, antigovernment stances. Liberal Democrats like Louis Brandeis and John Clarke and liberal Republicans like John Marshall Harlan, Charles Evans Hughes, and Harlan Fiske Stone joined to inch the Court toward greater deference to legislatures and reform. In the struggle between these two viewpoints, the outlines of a new kind of jurisprudence, and a new role for the Court, began to emerge.

CHAPTER 6

The Waite Court, 1874–1888

The role of the chief justice does not allow him to dictate the course of his Court. Chase's tenure in that role proved as much. But a chief justice with vision and character can do much to make the Court a more coherent and respected political and intellectual institution, as Marshall demonstrated. Morrison R. Waite certainly had the attributes of character—modesty, loyalty, a willingness to work hard, and a fidelity to the rule of law—that might in other times have ranked him among the finest of American jurists. But new legal problems and dramatic shifts in climate of opinion called for a bolder thinker to lead the Court than Waite.

The post–Civil War era was a period of dramatic change. In the wake of the carnage, a national legal regime emerged, founded on the Reconstruction amendments and the civil rights acts. But the promised shift in federalism and the regime of racial justice did not develop as its advocates anticipated or intended. Instead, the amendments and enactments that were meant to ensure the full panoply of legal rights for the freedmen and freedwomen became the basis for a different legal revolution—the rise of big business and the protection of new kinds of private property. In biological "niche theory," new species evolve because there is a space in nature for them. In the years of the Waite Court, the evolving economy created a niche that new legal conceptions of corporations, trusts, and commerce filled.

CHANGING TIMES

The rise of big business, the display of opulence, and the power grab of the very rich in these years gave the epoch a nickname—the Gilded Age. Mark Twain coined the term to describe a time when the appearance of wealth was all and the display of wealth could cover the most scandalous corruption. There was no shortage of the latter—from Grant's closest advisors down to federal Indian agents, railroad stock salesmen, and the lowliest office seeker. But ostentatious flaunting of wealth contrasted sharply with the spread of abject poverty. In the cities, the moguls' lavish palaces of marble and fine imported wood stood but an avenue away from the squalid tenements of the "ragged newsboy, the rag-pickers, the street vermin . . . a battle field . . . amid which men moved, sooty, grimy, sullen, and sickly," as described in novelist Frank Norris's *The Pit.*

In such an age, the passion of prewar reform, the sharp divisions of the war itself, and the remnants of reform energy that went into Reconstruction were soon bankrupted. Whether this shift in focus was destined to occur or not, the classic period Supreme Courts, from the Gilded Age to the New Deal era, shared the view that the law and the courts' highest purpose was to protect private property against the excesses of legislative intervention, workers' agitation, and public regulation. The Court did not insist on the maintenance of the status quo—quite the contrary. It allowed many innovations in finance, corporate organization, and industrial activity to go forward unhindered. But all of these were private initiatives rather than public programs.

Nor can one say that the Court was simply conservative, although its views of race, class, and gender were certainly not liberal. Instead, in these days, the Court clearly reflected a new kind of politics, the politics of economic laissez-faire. There were laws of capital and labor, price and consumption, and supply and demand; and government intrusion into the economic arena, imposing collective policies on individual choice, would invariably cost more than it gained. The marketplace would regulate itself.

A nationwide religious revival played in complex fashion into this view of private initiative and government regulation. The Gilded Age was, despite its veneer of indifference to morality, a time of religious renewal. Evangelists like Dwight L. Moody in Chicago built up huge followings. On a single day in 1893, observers counted over one hundred thousand worshipers at one of his revival meetings. His was a reassuring reading of the Gospels, focusing on the healing power of the Holy Spirit, recognizing sin but offering salvation to those who sought it. Liberal theologians launched the "social gospel" movement, calling for religion to assist the weak and the poor. Ministers like Solomon Gladden asked their parishioners to volunteer to be reformers, curing the sins of society.

Many of the justices were deeply religious. But that religion did not turn them into social reformers in robes. Instead, it reminded them that salvation lay in individual choices and individual responsibility. The law must free men and women to make such choices but could not save them from their own sin. Thus even the staunchest advocates of laissez-faire in the marketplace believed that government could and should regulate morals and punish sin.

WAITE'S COURTS

The Waite Court has been called a "transitional court," but this term might be applied to any chief justice's tenure. More accurate would be the "postwar court," for even more than Chase's Court, Waite and his brethren inherited the problems and opportunities that congressional acts posed.

Waite, an Ohio lawyer when Grant picked him to replace Chase, was a transplanted New Englander and not prominent in law or politics. Though well known and respected in his state, he had failed in his efforts at elective office and fell back on an appointment to the state supreme court. He was opposed to slavery but not particularly friendly to the rights of the freedmen and freedwomen. He was not a particular friend of Grant either, though the two men apparently respected one another. His relative lack of intellectual talents fit him perfectly for a Court dominated by Field, Miller, and Bradley. He rarely dissented and only slightly more often wrote for the Court himself.

Unfortunately for him and the Court, his nomination to succeed Chase came at the end of a season of embarrassing misfires in appointments. When Chase died, Grant struggled to find a willing (and acceptable) chief justice. He asked Ward Hunt's New York friend, the master of political patronage in the Republican Party, Roscoe Conkling, to accept the chief justiceship. Conkling declined, and Grant also floundered with his next picks. Those Grant approached were likely to fail at confirmation or they turned him down. In the meantime, Bradley, Miller, Swayne, and Field all lobbied for the center seat.

Finally, eight months after the chief justice's seat had been vacated, Waite was named and confirmed. He gave up a far more lucrative practice in Toledo (estimated at $25,000 a year) to move to Washington and accept the newly raised salary of $10,000 authorized for him by Congress. He still had to borrow to make ends meet. He thought of himself as a steady, no-nonsense manager of his more opinionated and volatile brethren and set them an example with his diligence, modesty, and even temper.

But Waite's work habits were sorely tested as the Court's caseload jumped from about 600 a year in 1874 to over 1,200 by 1880. The number of cases awaiting decision rose proportionally—by the end of his term it stood at 1,500. The Court was churning out many hundreds of opinions a year, up from the double digits of the prewar period, but still losing ground. The backlog in the federal courts increased 89 percent, from 29,000 to 54,000 cases. The reason for the rise in caseload was an act of Congress in 1875 giving the federal courts "federal question" jurisdiction. That meant, in addition to admiralty, piracy, federal crimes, and diversity suits, litigants could bring to federal courts any dispute arising from or raising a question under the laws of Congress. In addition, the rule for removal of a suit from state court to federal court originating in the Civil Rights Act of 1866 was liberalized.

At the same time, the workforce available to hear the cases declined. Justice Clifford, a Democratic holdover from the prewar court, refused to resign until a Democrat was elected president, but he was infirm through most of the 1880s and did not do his share of the work. Hunt's stroke in 1879 prevented him from carrying his load. Some of the justices, notably Clifford and John Marshall Harlan, insisted on writing long opinions, which delayed their arrival and added to the burden on the other justices. On top of this, until 1891, the justices still rode circuit. Waite tried to shoulder more than his share of the opinions, and in March 1888 he collapsed in Court and died a few days later.

The first addition to the Waite Court, John Marshall Harlan, was in many ways like his namesake—confident of his powers of reasoning, perfectly willing to substitute real world facts for legal fictions and doctrine, and deeply committed to both the Constitution and his moral beliefs. He had been born into a well-to-do Kentucky family, was the owner of slaves, and for a time was a vocal member of the nativist Know-Nothing Party. There was little in his early career to distinguish him from others in the border state elite.

During the war, however, Harlan switched to the Republican Party, accepted a commission in the Union Army, and raised troops to fight the Confederacy. In 1863, he reentered private life to take on his late father's legal business. Later, he ran, unsuccessfully, for state office. In 1876, he represented the state at the Republican presidential convention and carried his delegation for the eventual victor, Rutherford B. Hayes. Hayes never forgot a friend, and when Justice Davis's seat fell vacant, Hayes put up Harlan for it. Although some Republicans suspected Harlan's late conversion to the cause (he had opposed the Thirteenth Amendment for a time), the nomination sailed through the Senate on a voice vote in early 1877.

Unlike the justices of the prewar Court, who lived quietly and inexpensively, Harlan occupied a mansion that covered nearly a block in an elegant section of the District of Columbia. He had servants, brought out his daughters as debutantes, and sent his sons to Princeton. He saw public service as a private obligation, and often his decisions were hailed for their sympathy to ordinary people. But like many addicted to "conspicuous consumption" and "pecuniary emulation"—terms the sociologist Thorstein Veblen coined to describe the Gilded Age's vices—Harlan could not deny himself grand displays of social prominence.

Harlan was a maverick on the Court, so often and so powerfully dissenting that others claimed he had "dissent-ery." His dissents in the *Civil Rights Cases* and later in *Plessy v. Ferguson*, his defense of Congress's imposition of an income tax and passing of antitrust laws, and his belief that the Fourteenth Amendment incorporated the Bill of Rights endeared him to later generations, even as these positions put him at odds with his brethren. But he did not mind, more than once shouting down, shaking a fist at, or pointing a finger at a colleague. He died in 1911, in office, having served three chief justices and the nation with honor.

Justice Strong's replacement was William B. Woods, an Ohio-born Democrat who switched to the Republican Party, fought on the Union side, and joined the "carpetbaggers," Union men who moved south after the war and gained high office. Woods relocated to Alabama, where he became a planter and lawyer, and Grant named him to a federal judgeship in 1876. In 1877, he moved once again, this time to Atlanta to serve on the fifth circuit court. Hayes, in 1880, nominated him for the High Court. Though he had fought with Sherman's command in the South, Woods was acceptable to the southern Democrats in the Senate, and his nomination went through smoothly in 1881. On the Court, he joined the majority in all of its major decisions, showing as much ability to blend in on the bench as he had in his prior political career. He worked hard, writing nearly one hundred decisions in his tenure and almost never dissenting, but he left little impress on the law. He died in 1887.

Stanley Matthews's nomination was tainted by partisanship and patronage. Matthews's politics mirrored much of the Republican Party's history. Though born in Kentucky, Matthews became an abolitionist when he moved to Ohio, changed from a Democrat to a Republican on the eve of the war, and served in the Union Army with his college friend, Hayes. A deeply religious man, Matthews led the Presbyterian Church to officially condemn slavery. Above all, he was Hayes's staunch ally, and this fact, rather than his stature as a lawyer or judge, led Hayes to look to Matthews when Swayne retired, in 1880.

Appointment to federal offices and the distribution of patronage was still in the hands of the president, and to the victor went the spoils. This system consumed much of the president's time, however, and each appointment had the potential to be divisive. Because he was not a party regular, Matthews's candidacy was rebuffed by the Republicans in the Senate when the nomination was made in January 1881. Some of the animus against Matthews was personal; but another source was his unabashed representation of the railroads at a time when revelations of railroad misconduct (gouging, price-fixing, and the paying off of politicians) was a major political issue.

Matthews's candidacy seemed dead. But, quite unexpectedly, Hayes's successor in the White House, Republican James A. Garfield of Ohio, renominated Matthews in March 1881. Matthews had paved the way for this turn of events—contributing money and influence to Garfield's presidential run. The Senate voted 24 to 23 to confirm, with only nine Republicans in the yes column. Matthews, like Woods, did not serve long, but he was a force until his death in 1889. He wrote over two hundred opinions and rarely dissented, and, as his long career representing the railroads would lead one to predict, he believed that government-imposed railroad regulations slowed economic progress.

Horace Gray was the second of the professorial justices. Like his predecessor in that role, Joseph Story, Gray was from Massachusetts. A little heavy-handed and pedantic and given to opinions based on great learning and overflowing with citations, Gray produced miniature treatises from the bench. Gray came to the Court from the chief justiceship of the Massachusetts Supreme Judicial Court, in 1882. He was originally the choice of Garfield; and when Garfield died from an assassin's bullet, President Chester A. Arthur honored this wish. Massachusetts senator George F. Hoar ran interference for Gray—they were Harvard College roommates—and Gray joined the Court with little fuss. Because of his attention to detail, Gray's opinions did not come quickly, and as his health declined, he became even more dilatory. To assist in his research, he hired young Harvard Law School graduates as clerks, sent to him by his half brother, John Chipman Gray. Among these men were Louis D. Brandeis, a future justice.

Gray was a strong believer in the authority of the state to regulate its economy and protect the health and welfare of its people. He dissented when the Court used the Fourteenth Amendment Due Process Clause to strike down state health and welfare regulations. To his great credit, he was the author of the doctrine that every child born on American soil, of whatever provenance or ancestry, was a full citizen of the United States (*U.S. v. Wong Kim Ark* [1898]). Gray died in 1902, while still a member of the Court.

Gray was widely read in many subjects. Samuel Blatchford, his colleague on the bench from 1882 to 1893, was an expert in only a few—but in those few, including admiralty, he was without parallel. A craftsman and lawyer's lawyer, he had been a child prodigy (graduating from Columbia College at age thirteen) and a staunch Whig, later becoming a Republican. His patron was Senator William H. Seward, a Radical Republican, but Blatchford preferred the quiet and certainty of the judiciary to the rough-and-tumble of electoral politics. His New York City law practice rivaled that of his great Democratic contemporary, David Dudley Field. He would make signal contributions to constitutional law in his opinions for the Court on the application of state law to regulation of business enterprises, anticipating later ideas of the limits of delegation of authority to independent commissions. He died in 1893, during his service on the Court.

L. Q. C. Lamar was the last of the Waite Court appointees. Unlike his predecessors, he was a Democrat, the pick of Democrat Grover Cleveland in 1887. A much-traveled lawyer and politician from Mississippi, he had served the federal government as a senator and diplomat, the Confederacy (after having drafted the Mississippi Ordinance of Secession) in the Army of Northern Virginia, and again the federal government as a congressman and Cleveland's secretary of the interior, gaining the nickname "the great pacifier" for his call for the end of sectional animosity. For that very reason, his nomination symbolized the road to reconciliation. He was an able lawyer, having taught law at the University of Mississippi, but not a brilliant or even a persuasive lawgiver. Like Gray and Harlan, he disliked judicial activism, preferring to defer to popularly elected legislatures. He died in 1893.

As these appointments to the Court demonstrated, party affiliation and personal loyalty were still the most important considerations of presidents and senators when selecting justices. Like their prewar predecessors, almost all of the members added after 1865 had political experience. The justices were fully aware of the partisan nature of the appointment process, as they demonstrated during the tumultuous election of 1876. In the presidential election that year, Democrat Samuel J. Tilden led Republican Rutherford B. Hayes in popular votes and, 184 to 165, in the electoral college, but disputed electoral votes in a number of states left twenty electoral votes in doubt. Congress created a fifteen-member electoral commission of ten congressmen and five Supreme Court justices, divided by party, and the commission gave Hayes all twenty votes. The three Republican justices who served voted for every Hayes elector. The two Democratic justices voted for every Tilden elector. Both sides complained about the partisanship of the other.

UNCIVIL RITES

The Waite Court faced the task of determining the constitutionality of the civil rights acts and the meaning of the Reconstruction amendments. Under the enforcement acts, which the Republican majority in Congress passed, federal prosecutors protected black voters in the South, contributing in part to the landslide reelection of Grant in 1872. The Democrats regarded the enforcement process as purely partisan, a way of ensuring Republican victory at the polls in contested southern elections. Counsel for the defendants in these prosecutions, themselves Democratic politicians, appealed the convictions, hopeful that the High Court would narrow the scope and operation of federal law enforcement in the former slaveholding states.

Outside of the courts, "Redeemers" implemented the "Mississippi Plan," designed to regain control of the South from the Republicans and their African American allies. The plan was simple—frighten or assassinate the black voters; persuade white Republicans to switch allegiance; regain control of the southern state governments; and bluff the Republican administration in Washington out of military or legal responses. White "gun clubs" and "bulldozers" kept blacks from the polls. The plan worked in part because the North was tired of fighting for black rights, because the Depression of 1873 had undermined the Republican Party in the South, and because the federal courts all the way up to the High Court were unwilling to enforce the law.

In the hotly contested presidential election of 1876, the Republicans traded a promise to end military occupation of the South for House Democrats' agreement not to force the election into the lower house. The Court played its part in the retreat in the cases of *U.S. v. Hiram Reese* and *U.S. v. William Cruikshank et al.*, decided in 1875 and 1876. In the former, a Kentucky state voter registrar refused to allow blacks to register without paying a poll tax. In fact, in the particular case, one Garner, an African American, did offer to pay, but the registrar refused to accept the money because the man was black. The motive was as much political as racial because the state was Democratic and the party leaders assumed that every black voter was a Republican. A circuit court had dismissed the indictments. The High Court affirmed the lower court. In the latter case, a mob of whites attacked blacks guarding a courthouse in New Orleans. Again, the federal circuit court had found the indictments wanting. The High Court agreed. The chief justice wrote for the Court in *Reese*:

The Fifteenth Amendment does not confer the right of suffrage upon any one. It prevents the States, or the United States, however, from giving preference, in this particular, to one citizen of the United States over another on account of race, color, or previous condition of servitude. Before its adoption, this could be done. It was as much within the power of a State to exclude citizens of the United States from voting on account of race, &c., as it was on account of age, property, or education. Now it is not.

The Kentucky law did not on its face deny to black people the right to vote. Everyone had to pay the same poll tax. In effect, however, it disenfranchised more blacks than whites, because the newly freed slaves did not have the cash to pay.

Every justice understood this—the impact and the purpose of the law was to disenfranchise black voters. Such disparate impact of a state law might be obvious, a matter of simple statistics or of anecdotal evidence, but the High Court did not weigh impact. Similarly, an inquiry into the purposes of the legislators might have revealed their intent to deprive black voters of their rights, but the Court has never agreed that legislative intent must be included in analysis of a law's constitutionality. Some justices, notably Hunt in *Reese*, did look at legislative intent, but others refused to engage in such inquiry.

Was the Court concerned about the political implications of the two cases? They were heard in 1875, but the decisions were not announced until the next year. Justice Clifford wrote the first drafts of the opinions, basing his decision on the poor drafting of the indictments. Waite and the other members of the majority thought that the constitutional question should be addressed, and he stepped in to write for the Court. His opinion straddled the issue—the enforcement acts were legitimate exercises of legislative authority but must be construed narrowly, particularly because they represented a "radical" departure from prewar federal criminal jurisdiction.

Clifford dissented, offering as his dissent the draft he had proposed originally: the indictments were poorly written, and therefore there was no need to get to the constitutional issue. In this, he was anticipating a doctrine that later justices, particularly Felix Frankfurter, would raise to the level of rule: dispose of cases on statutory interpretation rather than constitutional grounds whenever possible.

Hunt also dissented, but on far different grounds. He looked behind the face of the law to see what had actually happened—a conspiracy to deny to the freedmen the right to vote. The poll tax was the excuse only, a filter put in place so that the registrars could determine the color of the potential voter before registering him. What is more, he also looked to the purpose of the enforcement act to determine how to read it:

The intention of Congress on this subject is too plain to be discussed. The Fifteenth Amendment had just been adopted, the object of which was to secure to a lately enslaved population protection against violations of their right to vote on account of their color or previous condition. . . . Congress determined to meet the emergency by creating a political equality, by conferring upon the freedmen all the political rights possessed by the white inhabitants of the State. It was believed that the newly enfranchised people could be most effectually secured in the protection of their rights of life, liberty, and the pursuit of happiness, by giving to them that greatest of rights among freemen,—the ballot.

In his opinion for the Court in *Cruikshank,* Waite introduced the concept of "state action," a limitation on the reach of the Fourteenth Amendment's Due Process and Equal Protection Clauses. The New Orleans mob was not an agent of the state. So the Fourteenth Amendment did not apply: "The Fourteenth Amendment prohibits a State from depriving any person of life, liberty, or property, without due process of law; but this adds nothing to the rights of one citizen as against another." Then the logic of *Reese* took hold. The federal prosecution of the mob for conspiracy to deny the right to vote to the black victims must fall. In any case, here was a sop to Clifford: the indictments for conspiracy were defective, for "it is nowhere alleged in these counts that the wrong contemplated against the rights of these citizens was on account of their race or color." But Clifford, still upset that his opinion was not the one that his fellows adopted, once more dissented on the grounds that the defective indictments were sufficient to sustain the lower court ruling.

The application of the state action doctrine in *Reese* and *Cruikshank* was relentless. In *U.S. v. Harris* (1883), the Court disposed of a prosecution under the KKK Act of 1871, using the logic of the *Voting Rights Cases.* The statute had criminalized violent Klan activity. Twenty white Tennesseans belonging to the Klan attacked blacks in the custody of a sheriff, beating one of the prisoners to death. When the Klan members were indicted by a federal grand jury, their counsel argued that the statute overextended the power granted to Congress by the Fourteenth Amendment. The federal circuit court members agreed to disagree, passing the case on to the Supreme Court. The Court then struck down the portions of the act involved, because the Klan violence was private, not state-sponsored.

Relying on *Reese* and *Cruikshank,* Justice Woods found the case an easy one to decide. Despite the U.S. solicitor general's argument that the Equal Protection Clause of the Fourteenth Amendment permitted the federal government to prosecute the murderers, Woods concluded that "the section of the law under consideration is directed exclusively against the action of private persons, without reference to the laws of the State or their administration by her officers[;] we are clear in the opinion that it is not warranted by any clause in the Fourteenth Amendment to the Constitution." The Thirteenth Amendment did not apply, because beating a man to death was not the same as enslaving him.

But there was a long line of purely federal criminal laws, beginning with the statutes on piracy in the 1790s, that justified certain kinds of civil rights prosecutions. In *Ex parte Yarbrough* (1884), Justice Miller wrote for the Court that it did not ordinarily review the criminal cases of the lower federal courts, but when imprisonment was unconstitutional, it would intervene:

Stripped of its technical verbiage, the offence charged in this indictment is that the defendants conspired to intimidate Berry Saunders, a citizen of African descent, in the exercise of his right to vote for a member of the Congress of the United States, and in the execution of that conspiracy they beat, bruised, wounded and otherwise maltreated him; and in the second count that they did this on account of his race, color, and previous condition of servitude, by going in disguise and assaulting him on the public highway and on his own premises.

Although the violence was perpetrated by private individuals, and therefore its prosecution in a federal court under federal law might be overturned under *Cruikshank*, Miller took a different line: "That a government whose essential character is republican, whose executive head and legislative body are both elective, whose most numerous and powerful branch of the legislature is elected by the people directly, has no power by appropriate laws to secure this election from the influence of violence, of corruption, and of fraud, is a proposition so startling as to arrest attention and demand the gravest consideration." There was no need for a discussion of the Fourteenth Amendment, and in fact that amendment was nowhere mentioned in Miller's opinion, for the case could be brought and the statute upheld on far more traditional grounds—the right of all governments to preserve themselves: "It is as essential to the successful working of this government that the great organisms of its executive and legislative branches should be the free choice of the people as that the original form of it should be so." A more cynical observer might note that the difference between *Yarbrough* and the *Voting Rights Cases* was that the former could be decided without explicit reference to race.

The near unanimity of the court in these decisions bears comment. Why did the Republicans who signed on to Miller's majority opinion in the *Slaughterhouse Cases* no longer see the Fourteenth Amendment in explicitly racial terms? The answer to this puzzle lay in politics. Hayes had made it plain that he would accede to the end of Reconstruction. In turn, the South would accept Hayes's election. Hayes kept his end of the bargain, removing federal troops from the South. The last Republican Reconstruction governments in the South collapsed, and the Redeemers, determined to make southern politics lily-white once again, had their way. In practical terms, there was no way that the Court could impose the Reconstruction legislation on the South.

But even that dire conclusion did not explain the majority opinion in *Hall v. DeCuir* (1877). The reconstructed state of Louisiana had passed a statute barring racial segregation on its common carriers—rails, carriages, and passenger boats. The owner of a Mississippi steamboat refused to accommodate a black woman in a cabin reserved for whites. The Supreme Court, with Waite writing for the majority, found that the state could not regulate its waterways—that was left to Congress, for steamboat travel was interstate commerce, and only Congress could regulate it. More precisely, the state's law impressed a "direct burden" on interstate commerce. Yet the Louisiana law simply followed the language of the federal Civil Rights Act of 1875, barring discrimination in public accommodations. Waite wrote: "Commerce cannot flourish in the midst of such embarrassments" as the Louisiana law. Had Congress made such a law, its provisions would have been "uniform," Waite opined, simply ignoring the congressional Civil Rights Act of 1875, which did have uniform provisions. Instead, he noted wrongly that Congress had "refrained" from such legislation.

Justice Clifford went further, recognizing the obstacle that the federal enactment posed to Waite's somewhat lax reading of the law: "Vague reference is made to the Civil Rights Act [by the state's counsel]. . . . but it is clear that . . . it was not intended to accomplish any such purpose." In fact, it was. Although the Civil Rights Act of 1875 rested not on the Interstate Commerce Clause but on the Fourteenth Amendment, its manifest purpose was to bar racial discrimination by a private individual operating a public conveyance.

Hall was the first prong of a very elegant tool to undo civil rights enforcement, the first in a series of what may be termed "catch-22" readings of federalism. The state could not guarantee the rights of its minorities when those rights touched on interstate commerce. All matters relating to interstate commerce were exclusive to Congress. In its *Civil Rights Cases* (1883) opinion, the Court would reveal the other prong—Congress could not act unless the offender was the state itself or its agents. Thus private discrimination of all kinds must be left to the state to remedy. But the state could not legislate against those forms of discrimination touching interstate commerce because Congress had exclusive jurisdiction.

All of which makes the occasions when the Court did protect minority civil rights the more perplexing. Over the dissent of Field and Clifford, the Court held unconstitutional a state law limiting jury duty to whites (*Strauder v. West Virginia*, in 1880), and, again over Field's dissent, the Court found that the federal government could prosecute a state judge for excluding blacks from juries on his own authority (*Ex parte Virginia*, also in 1880).

But the Court refused to assume that such a state policy existed simply because no blacks appeared in the jury pools (*Virginia v. Rives*, again in 1880). As Field explained the entire matter, dissenting in *Ex parte Virginia*,

The law, in thus providing for the preparation of the list of persons from whom the jurors are to be taken, makes no discrimination against persons of the colored race. The judge of the county or corporation court is restricted in his action only by the condition that the persons selected shall, in his opinion, be 'well qualified to serve as jurors,' be 'of sound judgment,' and 'free from legal exception.' Whether they possess these qualifications is left to his determination; and, as I shall attempt hereafter to show, for the manner in which he discharges this duty he is responsible only to the State whose officer he is and whose law he is bound to enforce.

Never shy about ignoring law that constrained his views, Field returned for authority to the Constitution as it stood before the Reconstruction amendments: "The government created by the Constitution was not designed for the regulation of matters of purely local concern. The States required no aid from any external authority to manage their domestic affairs. They were fully competent to provide for the due administration of justice between their own citizens in their own courts." He conceded that the Reconstruction amendments had ended slavery and given rights of citizenship to the freedmen, but went on to argue: "Nor should it be forgotten that they [the Reconstruction amendments] are additions to the previous amendments, and are to be construed in connection with them and the original Constitution as one instrument. They do not, in terms, contravene or repeal any thing which previously existed in the Constitution and those amendments." Field thus reversed the rule that later laws supersede earlier ones, and, at a stroke, he nullified the three amendments as they applied to race.

Field's old Democratic states' rights sympathies were here in evidence, but hidden not very far behind them was another extralegal kind of reasoning. The federal indictment in *Ex parte Virginia* had presumed "that [the local judge's] failure to [include blacks on the jury lists] was because of their race, color, or previous condition of servitude. ... In the face of this ruling no defense could be made by the accused, although he may have exercised at all times his best judgment in the selection of qualified persons." Field hinted that the county judge had good reason to think that blacks were not as suitable as whites for jury duty. They were not fit—not as individuals and not as a group. To underline the freedmen's collective incapacity, Field linked the logic of denying to freedmen full participation in civic life to the Court's denial of the same rights to women: "But the privilege or the duty, whichever it may be called, of acting as a juror in the courts of the country, is not an incident of citizenship. Women are citizens ... yet they are not allowed in Virginia to act as jurors." Two wrongs, apparently, made a right, or rather, denied one.

Field's dissents in the first two cases are an important indicator of where the Court was going, and it arrived there in the *Civil Rights Cases* (1883)—a collection of five cases, arising in Kansas, California, Missouri, New York, and Tennessee, four of which involved federal prosecution of individuals operating public commercial enterprises who refused admission or service to people of color in violation of the Civil Rights Act of 1875. With only Harlan dissenting, the High Court found that the Civil Rights Act of 1875's public accommodations provisions exceeded the power given to Congress under the Thirteenth and Fourteenth Amendments.

Bradley wrote for the majority that public conveyances, inns, parks, and other facilities run by private individuals could not be brought under the umbrella of federal law. The Thirteenth Amendment did not extend to gaining service at an inn or amusement park, and the Fourteenth Amendment only applied to state actions and actors: "It is State action of a particular character that is prohibited. Individual invasion of individual rights is not the subject-matter of the amendment." Bradley's sharp distinction between public and private had a distinguished pedigree, going back to the American revolutionaries' resistance to parliamentary acts. But there were exceptions, for example, licensing laws, Sunday closing laws, and public health inspection laws. The amusements, inns, and conveyances were open to the general public (except the minorities), licensed and taxed by the states, and subject to the state's police and regulatory activity. Still, Bradley found both absurd and alarming the prospect that "Congress [might] proceed at once to prescribe due process of law for the protection of every one of these fundamental rights, in every possible case, as well as to prescribe equal privileges in inns, public conveyances, and theatres."

Bradley insisted that the separation between public and private could not be crossed by federal civil rights acts of any kind, for "in this connection it is proper to state that civil rights, such as are guaranteed by the Constitution against State aggression, cannot be impaired by the wrongful acts of individuals, unsupported by State authority in the shape of laws, customs, or judicial or executive proceedings. The wrongful act of an individual, unsupported by any such authority, is simply a private wrong, or a crime of that individual." In short, *Reese*. The Civil Rights Act of 1866 had made the violation of a person's civil rights into a federal offense, but Bradley stopped short of striking down those enactments, because they did not rest on the Fourteenth Amendment—they preceded it.

Bradley conceded that pre–Civil War laws on slavery did not observe this public-private boundary. But "when a man has emerged from slavery, and by the aid of beneficent legislation has shaken off the inseparable concomitants of that state, there must be some stage in the progress of his elevation when he takes the rank of a mere citizen, and ceases to be the special favorite of the laws, and when his rights as a citizen, or a man, are to be protected in the ordinary modes by which other men's rights are protected." This was the language of free men, free soil, free labor, in which men made their way forward through their own merits, gained and used their property in the way they pleased, and need not open their businesses to everyone. Bradley offered that those disfavored by discrimination must seek redress in the state legislatures.

Harlan's dissent borrowed from the same store of ideology, but came to a different conclusion:

The opinion in these cases proceeds, it seems to me, upon grounds entirely too narrow and artificial. I cannot resist the conclusion that the substance and spirit of the recent amendments of the Constitution have been sacrificed by a subtle and ingenious verbal criticism. . . . Constitutional provisions, adopted in the interest of liberty, and for the purpose of securing, through national legislation, if need be, rights inhering in a state of freedom, and belonging to American citizenship, have been so construed as to defeat the ends the people desired to accomplish . . . in their fundamental law.

Harlan, like Hunt in *Reese*, looked for legislative intent. In the years before the Civil War, the federal government had acted directly and forcefully to protect the master's property in his slave. The fugitive slave laws trumped all state legislation: "With all respect for the opinion of others, I insist that the national legislature may, without transcending the limits of the Constitution, do for human liberty and the fundamental rights of American citizenship, what it did, with the sanction of this court, for the protection of slavery and the rights of the masters of fugitive slaves."

Had the Thirteenth Amendment "involve[d] nothing more than exemption from actual slavery? Was nothing more intended than to forbid one man from owning another as property? Was it the purpose of the nation simply to destroy the institution, and then remit the race, theretofore held in bondage, to the several States for such protection . . . as those States, in their discretion, might choose to provide?" Harlan knew firsthand that southern Democratic leaders never intended to treat the freedmen as full citizens, much less equals. Discrimination based on color violated the spirit of the Thirteenth Amendment by reinstituting "burdens and disabilities which constitute badges of slavery and servitude," against which Congress could legislate.

Did denial of public entertainments and forms of transportation to blacks fall under this rubric? Could federal law force owners and operators of such amusements and facilities to serve everyone?

Such being the relations these corporations hold to the public, it would seem that the right of a colored person to use an improved public highway, upon the terms accorded to freemen of other races, is as fundamental, in the state of freedom established in this country, as are any of the rights which my brethren concede to be so far fundamental as to be deemed the essence of civil freedom. . . . In every material sense applicable to the practical enforcement of the Fourteenth Amendment, railroad corporations, keepers of inns, and managers of places of public amusement are agents or instrumentalities of the State, because they are charged with duties to the public, and are amenable, in respect of their duties and functions, to governmental regulation.

Harlan had one more string to his bow. He objected to the majority reasoning because it usurped the role of the legislature. He believed in deference to the elected bodies:

But it is for Congress, not the judiciary, to say that legislation is appropriate—that is—best adapted to the end to be attained. The judiciary may not, with safety to our institutions, enter the domain of legislative discretion, and dictate the means which Congress shall employ in the exercise of its granted powers. That would be sheer usurpation of the functions of a co-ordinate department, which, if often repeated, and permanently acquiesced in, would work a radical change in our system of government.

Harlan was making the case for judicial restraint on separation of powers grounds. One could trace this argument all the way back to the earlier Supreme Court's refusal to act in an executive capacity—and it would reach all the way to the present.

Although Bradley did not say as much, it may be that the Court was not entirely pleased with the growth of the federal government that the Civil War had required and the Reconstruction had entailed. The justices had entered government service when governments were smaller, cheaper, and more limited in their operation. In the *Trademark Cases* (1879), Miller, for the Court, held that the federal government could not criminalize the forgery of trademarks, unless such a power could be found in the Constitution:

As the property in trade-marks and the right to their exclusive use rest on the laws of the States, and, like the great body of the rights of person and of property, depend on them for security and protection, the power of Congress to legislate on the subject, to establish the conditions on which these rights shall be enjoyed and exercised, the period of their duration, and the legal remedies for their enforcement, if such power exist at all, must be found in the Constitution of the United States, which is the source of all the powers that Congress can lawfully exercise.

But that power was not implied in the patenting and copyright authority, for nothing in a trademark was creative, inventive, or a discovery. The other putative source, the Interstate Commerce Clause, did not apply either to trademarks for products that were not in the stream of commerce. Plainly, trademark and other matters of intrastate commerce must be left to the states. Miller even used *Reese* as precedent on the limits of congressional criminal jurisdiction. Such an absolutist view of the boundaries of federalism harkened back to the prewar jurisprudence of Taney's Court and looked forward to important limitations on congressional action on business monopolies and income taxes.

THE COURT AND THE ECONOMY

Despite the serious depression in 1873, the American economy was rushing forward like a runaway locomotive, with the railroad industry in the lead. Between 1865 and 1900, thirty-five thousand miles of rail track had grown to two hundred thousand, and the lines employed over a million people servicing the nearly two million freight and passenger cars and locomotives that linked the nation together. The rails brought western timber and mine resources east and enabled midwestern industries to flourish.

A transportation system that was chaotic and sometimes deadly (company bankruptcy was common, train car couplings did not work, brakes were inadequate, signals were haphazard, bridges were not properly constructed, and horrific accidents were almost everyday occurrences) became regular and reasonably safe. Westinghouse air brakes and Janney automatic couplers saved thousands of rail worker and passenger lives. New techniques of management and professional accounting helped railroads make fortunes for their owners, reduced freight costs for shippers and consumers, and pumped capital into the economy.

The rail boom spurred and in turn was supported by the growing size and complexity of the coal and steel industries. Inventions like the Bessemer converter had made Andrew Carnegie's steelworks more profitable and shifted control of production from master "puddlers" on the plant floor to money managers in corporate offices. Other innovations, for example, the introduction of electricity, telephones, and other communications and power systems, gave to industrial leaders mastery of information—allowing them to control sales and production. Industrial productivity for the first time exceeded agricultural productivity.

To complete their mastery of production, distribution, and sales, the great enterprises needed the aid of government and of lawyers. Railroads in particular could not have assumed their ascendancy in the national economy without the aid of government. State and local government promoted rail depots and lines by issuing bonds and underwriting stocks and granting right-of-way lands. The federal government dipped into the national domain and gave to rail companies nearly two hundred million acres as right-of-way. In turn, the rail companies spread their largesse over Congress, leading to some of the most notorious of all the Grant-era corruption trials and giving the epoch the name "the big barbeque."

Lawyers played their role in the industrial boom and its government subsidy program. They helped create new forms of financing and control for the industrialists. The large corporation called "big business" was a legal creation, a person under the Fourteenth Amendment, and thus protected from state actions denying it equal protection and due process of the laws. Equally important was the role that lawyers played as counsel for their big business clients. Increasingly, the corporation lawyers were no longer politicians. Instead, they were full-time attorneys, partners in major firms.

Led by the example of men like David Dudley Field, the Gilded Age lawyers were far more technically polished than their pre–Civil War counterparts. They mastered the arts of removal of suits from state to federal courts and stalling tactics, favoring their corporate clients over poorer suitors. Paid by the hour instead of according to a fee schedule, educated at major law schools like Harvard, Yale, Columbia, and Penn, they brought a sophistication and learning to the Supreme Court bar. They also earned more in retainers and hourly billing than did their predecessors, joining with the upper-level management of the corporations they served in a new professional elite. The founding of the American Bar Association by Simeon Baldwin in 1878, bringing together "the best men of the bar" from all over the country, signaled the arrival of this elite bar. Not surprisingly, these elite lawyers had major railroads as their clients—neatly tying together the circle of rails, law, and the federal courts. Railroad lawyers, like Stanley Matthews, became Supreme Court justices.

Some state legislatures assayed checks upon the financial dealings and competitive tactics of the largest businesses. State-mandated or controlled prices and rates was not an innovation. Colonial governments had set wages and prices as well as rates. But the Fifth Amendment to the federal Constitution found that any taking must be for public use and that it must be compensated by fair market return. Did the Fourteenth Amendment imposition of due process on the states impose the Fifth Amendment on them? And did rate setting fall under that imposition?

The case that showed how far the High Court was willing to let states go in regulating business was *Munn v. Illinois* (1877), the first of the *Granger Cases*. The most common occupation on the plains was wheat farming. Employing machinery like the McCormick reaper allowed midwestern farmers to increase their productivity, and the extension of the rails out of the metropolis of Chicago made it the center of wheat warehousing. But the grain storage operators, in concert with the railroads, sometimes tried to gouge the farmers. This, added to the declining prices for food grains (because of increased supply), led farmers to resent the elevator operators as middlemen who made exorbitant profits.

The farmers formed associations called Granges to protect themselves against the railroads and the grain elevator (a storage facility) operators. The Granges helped elect friendly state legislators. The Granger movement would, in short order, merge into a larger political crusade called Populism, an alliance of northern and southern farmers demanding reforms in politics and a curb on the power of railroad and other "combinations." The Illinois act regulating the grain elevators was one of the Granger laws.

Ira Munn and George Scott were members of the Chicago Board of Trade, from its inception in the 1850s a promoter of price-fixing, gouging of suppliers and consumers, and monopoly. They ran a grain elevator business in Chicago, storing and reselling one third of all the grain that came into the city from the surrounding farms, but they did not have a license from the state, as required by law, nor did they comply with the statutory controls on prices. Ironically, by the time they found themselves in court, their business had gone bankrupt.

But Munn and Scott appealed their $100 fine levied under the state law to the federal courts, using the argument that the law violated their Fourteenth Amendment due process rights. Justice Field's minority opinion in the *Slaughterhouse Cases* had laid the ground for this appeal: The Fourteenth Amendment had created a kind of substantive due process right, quite different from simple fair procedural practices envisioned in the older idea of due process. The High Court should be willing to lay state legislation alongside this substantive due process template to see if the state violated the Fourteenth Amendment.

The argument did not win in 1873, and it did not win in 1877. In fact, so long as Waite was chief justice, the argument never won. Instead, Waite wrote for a majority of the Court that the state's police powers were integral parts of government, inherent in the very idea of self-government and necessary for government to be effective. It was consistent with the Court's opinion about elections in *Ex parte Yarbrough*, and in some sense, it anticipated the *Civil Rights Cases* and could be extended to certain kinds of economic regulations:

Under these powers the government regulates the conduct of its citizens one towards another, and the manner in which each shall use his own property, when such regulation becomes necessary for the public good. . . . To this day, statutes are to be found in many of the States upon some or all these subjects; and we think it has never yet been successfully contended that such legislation came within any of the constitutional prohibitions against interference with private property.

How then were the acceptable actions of states regarding private property to be determined? Was there a formula? For Waite, yes: "Property does become clothed with a public interest when used in a manner to make it of public consequence, and affect the community at large. When, therefore, one devotes his property to a use in which the public has an interest, he, in effect, grants to the public an interest in that use, and must submit to be controlled by the public for the common good, to the extent of the interest he has thus created." Waite did not, indeed could not, define when a private act would become "clothed" with public interest. That was for the Court to decide, case by case.

Waite offered some clues to his thinking, however. The grain elevators in Chicago were huge. They serviced a vast area and a vital industry. They held enough wheat to feed Europe, and they were part of a transportation system that spanned two continents. In short, Waite was not just looking at the law, he was looking at the global economy. In that economy, American farmers had always taken a part, but their return was controlled by others—middlemen, freight haulers, bankers, and distant markets. He knew that the largest elevators were owned by a handful of men like Munn and Scott, and their power constituted a "virtual monopoly" of the storage trade. Waite knew all about farmers and their travails, having lived in a rural part of New York State in his youth. He also knew that they had political clout when they chose to use it and that "this indicates very clearly that during the twenty years in which this peculiar business had been assuming its present 'immense proportions,' something had occurred which led the whole body of the people to suppose that remedies such as are usually employed to prevent abuses by virtual monopolies might not be inappropriate here."

Field dissented: "The principle upon which the opinion of the majority proceeds is, in my judgment, subversive of the rights of private property, heretofore believed to be protected by constitutional guaranties against legislative interference." He drew the line between public and private sharply, just as he would in the *Civil Rights Cases* and in a different place from Waite: "The defendants were no more public warehousemen, as justly observed by counsel, than the merchant who sells his merchandise to the public is a public merchant, or the blacksmith who shoes horses for the public is a public blacksmith; and it was a strange notion that by calling them so they would be brought under legislative control." Field's objections sounded like the older prewar Courts' battle with legislatures: "If this be sound law, if there be no protection, either in the principles upon which our republican government is founded, or in the prohibitions of the Constitution against such invasion of private rights, all property and all business in the State are held at the mercy of a majority of its legislature."

The opposite danger, that the Court might set itself up as a super legislature to judge every state regulation that a defendant argued had taken property without due process, did not worry Field. The reason was that he thought the line very clear between health and safety, on the one hand, and confiscation, on the other. Health and safety was no more than that—regulation of inherently dangerous activities. Confiscation was a form of redistribution of wealth, taking from the deserving enterpriser and giving to the undeserving. Let the market decide how wealth was to be distributed. Field could summon to his side both moral and economic arguments behind laissez-faire for staying the hand of the state—so long as that hand hindered the growth of enterprise.

Miller had joined with the chief justice in protecting the states' regulation and the next year made his position even clearer. In *Davidson v. New Orleans* (1878), Miller complained about the spate of cases like *Munn* that challenged entirely reasonable state regulations. But he did leave the door ajar for such challenges when a state acted arbitrarily or unreasonably. The notion of reasonableness had no textual basis in the Constitution, but as part of the balancing test that Waite assayed in *Munn,* reasonableness could find a place in Fourteenth Amendment challenges. Again the question was, who would decide what was an unreasonable exercise of the powers of the state? State legislatures presumably did not act unreasonably, and Miller was willing to defer to them, but if the Court assigned to itself the authority to decide what was reasonable, it would be flooded with even more cases. And it was—over seven hundred between 1878 and 1918 that tested state regulations.

For a time, Waite managed to hold the line, and *Munn* seemed likely to become the first major "balancing test" case of its day. That is, the Court would balance the private property claim against the state's assertion of police powers, the fulcrum being the "clothed with a public interest" test. Such balancing tests were very common in nuisance suits, where the court attempted to balance the rights of plaintiff and defendant, rather than seeing right on only one side. But as Waite repeated in *Stone v. Farmer's Loan Company* (1886), "If there is a reasonable doubt, it must be resolved in favor of the existence" of the power to regulate. "The power is granted to fix reasonable charges, but what shall be deemed reasonable in law is nowhere indicated."

Some states delegated the power to regulate rates, and in effect prices, to special commissions. Congress did this when it established the Interstate Commerce Commission in 1887. Although these could (and often were) "co-opted" by the very enterprises they were supposed to regulate, their discretion was no more safe from Court scrutiny than legislative rate setting. Even when the Waite Court allowed such delegation by the legislature to an administrative body, as it did in *Stone*, the acquiescence included the warning that the power to regulate was not the power to destroy or confiscate. In other words, private property was still safe and profits were private property. Lest anyone assume that private property could only be protected by individuals, the Court, in what amounted to an aside, in *Santa Clara County v. Southern Pacific Railroad Company* (1886), announced that "the court does not wish to hear argument on the question whether the provision in the Fourteenth Amendment to the Constitution, which forbids a State to deny to any person within its jurisdiction the equal protection of the laws, applies to these corporations. We are all of opinion that it does."

Although the Waite Court would continue to balance the ledger in favor of state regulation, powerful business interests had already registered their concerns. They lobbied hard in Congress and in the Republican Party for a shift in the Court's views, particularly on state and federal regulation of the rails. Especially infuriating to the railroad owners was the Court's insistence, in the *Sinking Fund Cases* of 1879, that the rail men pay what they owed their bondholders, including the federal government. President Garfield, sensible of the gifts the rail men gave to his campaign and eager to please so generous an interest group, made sure that the next vacancy on the Court in 1880 went to a railroad lawyer—Stanley Matthews. But Chester A. Arthur's picks, Blatchford and Gray, were no more beholden to the railroads than Arthur himself, and they sided with Waite on federal regulation of rail rates.

PERSONAL RIGHTS AND WRONGS

With the passage of the Reconstruction amendments, individuals sought federal court aid when states denied personal rights. Surely civil privileges that states conferred, like the right to vote, were now federal civil rights? At the Seneca Woman's Rights Convention, in 1848, Elizabeth Cady Stanton and Susan

B. Anthony added a provision to the Declaration of Rights calling for woman suffrage. Women agitating for the right to vote were outraged when the Fifteenth Amendment was limited to men of color. They felt betrayed by their former allies in the abolition movement. In 1872, Virginia Minor, a leader in the woman suffrage movement, tried to register to vote in Missouri. The state registrar, one Reese Happersett, refused to list her name. Her husband, Francis Minor (a leader himself in the woman suffrage movement), sought damages from Happersett based on the Citizenship Clause and the Privileges and Immunities Clause of the Fourteenth Amendment.

The former, Waite held in *Minor v. Happersett*, did not confer specific rights, only the general membership in the community. Specific rights, like the right to vote, must be conferred by the states. The Constitution had left to the states the authority to determine such matters before the Reconstruction amendments. The Privileges and Immunities Clause had been gutted by the *Slaughterhouse Cases* decision. Above all, Waite was unwilling to do by judicial fiat what states and Congress had refused to do by legislative enactment. He deferred to the elected bodies, as he had in *Munn*. The concept of citizenship continues to vex the High Court today. For example, does it include the right to an education? Yes. A quality education? No.

Absent from the brief of counsel was the Equal Protection Clause, which today would be the obvious choice for a suit against sexual discrimination. Though the case resembled *Bradwell* in outcome, Waite's opinion had none of the Victorian condescension of the justices in *Bradwell*. Nevertheless, the presumption of the Court was that the most basic of all political rights, at least according to Congress when it debated and passed the Fifteenth Amendment, was not part of citizenship. In fact, Congress had explicitly omitted sex from the Fifteenth Amendment despite a proposal from the floor to do so. Perhaps the men on the Court agreed that women did not have the independence of judgment to cast ballots—hinted when Waite went out of his way to write that "no argument as to woman's *need* of suffrage can be considered [italics added]."

Minor was explicitly overturned by the ratification of the Nineteenth Amendment, in 1920, based on language that Susan B. Anthony had supplied in 1878. The amendment was introduced in every session of Congress until 1919, when it passed by two-thirds in both houses. By this time, Wyoming, Utah, Colorado, and Idaho had granted women the franchise. As ratified, the amendment read: "The right of citizens of the United States to vote shall not be denied or abridged by the United States or by any State on account of sex."

The same unwillingness today to extend the protections of the Fourteenth Amendment to domestic relationships marked the Court's handling of race issues. After the Redeemers had regained control of Alabama, its legislature imposed far-stiffer criminal penalties for a mixed race couple than for a man or a woman cohabiting with a person of the same race. The same law made any intermarriage a crime. Two white people or two black people living together without benefit of clergy had to pay a fine of $100. A white person marrying a black person or living with a black person subjected both to a jail term of two to seven years at hard labor.

In 1881, Tony Pace, a black man, and Mary Cox, a white woman, were convicted under the Alabama law and appealed their case all the way up to the High Court, arguing that the Alabama law used race in a discriminatory fashion, violating the Equal Protection Clause of the Fourteenth Amendment. Justice Field, writing for the Court, denied their petition. The law did not discriminate on the basis of race, he concluded. It simply distinguished between miscegenation and intermarriage, on the one hand, and adultery, on the other. "Whatever discrimination is made in the punishment prescribed in the two sections is directed against the offense designated and not against the person of any particular color or race. The punishment of each offending person, whether white or black, is the same." What seemed, on its face, a straightforward reading of statutory law, was actually the first of many decisions in which the Court upheld Jim Crow—a system of laws and ordinances designed to keep the races separate. Field personally favored this American version of apartheid: For him, it was morally better for both races that they be separated.

The same deeply held moral views were applied to religious sects the members of the Court found obnoxious—specifically, Utah Mormons and their practice of polygamy. George Reynolds was facing a bigamy conviction in the territory of Utah in 1870, and he claimed, in his defense, a religious obligation to marry more than one woman. The Church of Christ of the Latter Day Saints in the territory encouraged this conduct, which the High Court dismissed with scorn.

Waite wrote for the unanimous Court: "Congress cannot pass a law for the government of the territories which shall prohibit the free exercise of religions. The first amendment to the Constitution expressly forbid such legislation." But before Reynolds or any other Mormon could conclude that religiously inspired polygamy might be exempt from bigamy laws, Waite continued: "The word 'religion' is not defined in the Constitution. We must go . . . to the history of the times in the midst of which the provision was adopted." In 1791, when the amendment was ratified, there was no Church of Christ of the Latter Day Saints. Indeed, in those days, religious toleration was a new and largely untried notion. Waite's return to times of bigotry for precedent was another adventure in "originalism." In trying to determine what Jefferson, Madison, and other defenders of freedom of religion had in their minds when they crafted the Virginia Act of Toleration and supported the First Amendment, Waite turned to the very common-law sources that Jefferson and Madison had denounced in 1798 as "that bloody code."

The First Amendment says that "Congress shall make no law . . . prohibiting the free exercise" of religion. Short of announcing that the Church of Latter Day Saints was not a religion (and in effect violating the Establishment Clause of the First Amendment by deciding what was and what was not religion), Waite simply argued that Congress could not proscribe belief, which was "mere opinion." It could, however, make criminal "actions which were in violation of social duties or subversive of good order." In short, religious thought was safe from government prosecution, but religious practices were not.

Polygamy was such a practice, according to Waite. Ignoring polygamy among the biblical Jews, Waite stated that it "has always been odious among the Northern and western nations of Europe." It was "almost exclusively a feature of the life of Asiatic and African people." A well-tuned ear will catch here echoes of the contemporary philosophy that race or "blood" distinguished the superior or "ruling races" from the inferior races. Polygamy was not only morally reprehensible; it was scientifically dangerous.

Waite's final argument was that marriage was not a religious union but instead a civil contract, and that all civil proceedings could be regulated by law. He went on to suggest that, as a civil institution, monogamy led to democracy, while polygamy "leads to the patriarchal principle, and . . . fetters the people in stationary despotism." If presented as historical truth, this argument fails. The very same English common-law sources that Waite had cited to denounce polygamy had protected patriarchal domestic relations in England. Monogamy in England went hand in hand with "coverture," in which married women had no separate identity from their husbands, fathers had complete control over their daughters, and even widows and spinsters had little in the way of legal rights. In the United States, a democratic regime founded upon monogamy, according to Waite, women could not claim the right to practice a profession, vote, hold office, or, in most states, act without the consent of their husbands. If Waite was trying to protect the "weaker sex" against victimization, a Victorian duty, he did not say so in the opinion. A year later, in *Minor,* Waite would prove that he had no interest in trying to protect women's rights.

In fact, it was the sexual immorality of Mormon men that aroused Waite's ire. The last analogy that he offered in his opinion revealed its motive force: "Suppose one believed that human sacrifices were a necessary part of religious worship, would it be seriously contended that the civil government . . . could not interfere to prevent a sacrifice?" It was a powerful analogy revealing Waite's own horror at polygamy. But he could have far more modestly upheld the prosecution by simply deferring to the act of Congress which criminalized the practice of polygamy. Such a rationale would have been fully in keeping with his Court's precedents.

Waite had nothing against the Mormons' "beehive" of economic activities, however. Freedom to pursue an occupation, gain a legal living, start or operate a business, or make a profit, so long as the activity did not endanger public health or welfare, was protected by the Constitution. The city of San Francisco, California, in 1880, passed an ordinance requiring all commercial enterprises in the city to be licensed and then used the law to shut down all Chinese laundries. Yick Wo and Wo Lee found counsel to take their complaint to the High Court. The facts were plain: under the ordinance, over eighty non-Chinese laundries were licensed, while two hundred Chinese laundries were not, and their owners were fined when they remained in operation. Running a laundry was one of the few business enterprises that the Chinese had enough capital to operate, and the purpose of the statute was to drive the Chinese from the country. The California Supreme Court found the ordinance, and the fines under it, unexceptional.

The High Court disagreed. Justice Matthews, in *Yick Wo v. Hopkins* (1886), explained: "In the present case we are not obligated to reason from the probable to the actual, and pass upon the validity of the ordinances complained of, as tried merely by the opportunities which their terms afford, of unequal and unjust discrimination in their administration." The Court, in other words, did not look behind the neutral language of the law to find the malign intent. Doing this would have opened a Pandora's box of Jim Crow laws. Instead, "the cases present the ordinance in actual operation, and the facts shown establish an administration directed so exclusively against a particular class of persons as to warrant and require the conclusion that, whatever may have been the intent of the ordinances as adopted, they are applied . . . with a mind so unequal and oppressive as to amount to a practical denial by the state of that equal protection of the laws." Racism was not unconstitutional. Denial of equal economic opportunity was.

Private property's sanctity was again the Court's lodestar in a search and seizure case that laid the groundwork for the "exclusionary rule." The rule states that evidence obtained in an unconstitutional manner may not be admitted at trial. It is not only the foundation of Fourth and Fifth Amendment jurisprudence, but it also tutors the police forces in their constitutional duties.

In *Boyd v. U.S.* (1887), importer E. A. Boyd sued the Customs Office for uncon-stitutionally entering and searching his warehouse. In shades of the 1761 *Writs of Assistance Cases*, in which James Otis Jr., among others, argued that a man's house was his castle and thus safe from illegal searches and seizure, counsel for Boyd argued that the customs officers did not have the proper warrants to invade his client's place of business.

The Court agreed. Bradley, writing one of his last opinions, found that the use at trial of the papers taken from Boyd's establishment violated not only the Fourth Amendment protection against warrantless search but also the Fifth Amendment rule against self-incrimination. These were "the very essence of constitutional liberty and security," for in their breach, "private property" could never be safe from government. The opinion echoed the sentiments of the founding fathers as they inveighed against royal customs officials in the revolutionary crisis. Evidence produced at trial gained through illicit means must be excluded—it was poisoned by the manner in which it was obtained.

In the course of his opinion, Bradley inveighed against such invasions of "the privacy of life." It was a "sacred right," but a right nowhere mentioned by name in the Constitution. In effect, Bradley constructed the right to privacy in the overlap of the Fourth and Fifth Amendments. The right was not absolute but certainly applied to unreasonable acts of government agents. Privacy was a concept of personal liberty that would in time flower into a much more robust notion. Nearly a hundred years later, it would be the basis for a right to practice birth control in *Griswold v. Connecticut* (1965), the right to end a pregnancy in *Roe v. Wade* (1973), and the right of adults to engage in consensual sexual activ-ity in *Lawrence v. Texas* (2003).

Shortly after Waite died, the *Magazine of American History* ran a story on his home life in the District of Columbia. The author's assessment of the chief justice was more a eulogy than a dispassionate account, but in a few sentences the piece captured what Waite had tried to do: "Few of us appreciate as it de-serves the enduring work the Supreme Court performed in the reconstruction period. It aimed to eliminate old issues by settling them. It was the court that saved the country." The Court had not saved the Union, but its refusal to finish the business of racial justice preserved unity among whites in both sections. It preserved what scholars have called the *Herrenvolk* nation—the nation of the ruling race.

At the same time, the Waite Court had quietly introduced key and novel concepts to the reading of the Constitution, balancing rights to liberty with needed government regulations. Waite recognized that the elected branches of government must be allowed to govern. This deference to Congress and to state governments ran like a red thread throughout his leadership of the Court.

But neither balancing nor deference to the popularly elected branches turned aside the tide of violence roaring across the land. As workers organized into larger and larger unions and the unions took on the great railroads and manufacturing companies, confrontation hardened into homicide. At the end of the McCormick reaper strike in April 1886 in Chicago, after police and Pinkertons forces had fired into the strikers and killed five, union leaders and anarchists called a protest meeting. A rainy day did not deter thousands from converging on Haymarket Square to hear speakers, but as the event wound down and people were turning for home, a squadron of police arrived and someone threw a "homemade bomb" into the ranks of the police. The bomb killed one, injured dozens, and led to a wild melee—with people shooting, running, and fighting.

There was an outcry from the major newspapers—foreign agitators had invaded America's shores intending to destroy the very fabric of capitalism. Seven of the anarchists were indicted and condemned to death by a jury and judge (an eighth was sentenced to fifteen years at hard labor). Even Clarence Darrow, the great attorney for the unions, and Jane Addams, the urban reformer who had founded the Hull House settlement, were convinced of the anarchists' guilt. Four were hanged, but Illinois governor John Peter Altgeld pardoned three.

Could the High Court, the symbol as well as the source of law and order in the nation, find safe ground in the raging storm? Could it mediate between labor and capital? Could it end racial discrimination? Could it define the constitutional boundaries of government involvement in the economy? Waite's successor would face those tasks.

CHAPTER 7

The Fuller Court, 1888–1910

No U.S. Supreme Court in our history, including the Marshall and the Warren Courts, made a greater impress on the politics, the commerce, and the law in its day than Melville W. Fuller's Court. No Court, including the often-disparaged Taney Court, had more of its key decisions overturned or narrowed to the point of invisibility by amendments to the Constitution, later High Court decisions, or legislative action than the Fuller Court.

Though in the main the Fuller Court's justices were suspicious of government involvement in the economy, feared radical ideologies, and distrusted organized labor, most also resented the power that the super rich flaunted and opposed monopolistic schemes. In all of these attitudes, they differed little from the educated elite of their time. The legacy of the Court lies not in its jurisprudence, thus, but in its view of the power of the judicial branch. Under Fuller, the Court made itself into a super legislature, taking up a highly activist role. What was more, certain justices cloaked their activism in highly technical and neutral-sounding language, what historians have called "legal formalism," as if an objective, neutral law dictated their decisions.

BIGGER IS BETTER

In 1831, the famous German poet Johannes Wolfgang von Goethe wrote, "America, you have it better." Had he looked again in 1900, he would have written, "America, you have it bigger." Everything had become outsized. Immigration from Europe had reached flood tide. The cities had grown in number and size. Manufacturing had passed from craft and shop to factory lines in cavernous plants. The rich had gotten considerably richer, and the poor—far more numerous than ever before—were even poorer by comparison.

In the 1890s and early 1900s, immigration averaged over five hundred thousand newcomers a year, totaling more than twenty million in the forty-year period from 1880 to 1920. Stepping off the rudely appointed ships, these newcomers seemed the embodiment of Emma Lazarus's "huddled masses, yearning to breathe free." Most immigrants came to the cities. By 1900, four-fifths of

Chicago residents were foreign-born. African Americans had moved in large numbers from the rural South to New York City and Chicago, as well as into former border state cities like Cincinnati, St. Louis, and Baltimore. From 1860 to 1900, the rural population had doubled; but the population of the cities had increased sevenfold. By 1900, one-third of Americans lived in the cities.

Cities were more than just densely packed warehouses of people. They flaunted their size vertically and horizontally. Innovations in construction, like the all-steel frame and the electric elevator, enabled builders to invent the skyscraper, "a soaring thing, rising in sheer exultation," according to one turn-of-the-century architect. From the top floor of these twenty-plus-story towers one could see how the cities' "suburbs" sprawled into the countryside.

The city and its suburbs boasted huge manufacturing plants as well. Nothing so embodied the material ambition of the nation as its factories. Carnegie's Homestead Steel Works on the outskirts of Pittsburgh employed over seven thousand workers in mills and furnace works. The new wealth from manufacturing spawned a new class of super rich—the number of millionaires grew to four thousand from perhaps three hundred over the years from 1860 to the 1890s. Some fortunes made in speculation were lost in the collapse of 1893, but men like John D. Rockefeller of the Standard Oil Company and Andrew Carnegie, whose holdings became U.S. Steel, did not fear recession. Their companies were like octopuses, controlling every step of the manufacturing and distribution process. With the aid of bankers like J. P. Morgan, the industrial giants built financial empires large enough to match their industrial capacities.

The corporation had become the preferred legal shield for giant business ventures. And they too grew larger. Between 1897 and 1904, 4,227 firms merged to form 257 corporations. By 1904, 318 companies controlled about 40 percent of the nation's manufacturing output. A single firm produced over half the output in 78 industries. At the top of these pyramids of industry was the trust, holding companies that enabled the tobacco, sugar, oil, steel, and other industries to reduce competition and control the labor market. Against such "combinations" that restrained free trade Congress passed the Sherman Antitrust Act of 1890, but the law had to be tested in court.

The other side of the story of bigness was labor unrest and poverty on a hitherto-unimagined scale. Economic progress rested upon cheap labor. To increase workplace safety and gain higher wages and shorter hours, workers organized, but the companies had enough clout with local and state government, and enough wealth, to beat down the unions. The Homestead Strike of 1892 and the Pullman Strike of 1894 were proof that the state had to intervene as broker or conciliator if labor and capital were to avoid all-out war.

In this maelstrom, the High Court could have acted as a coolant. It could have carried on the balancing tests that the Waite Court had introduced, political in the best sense of the word, reflecting democratically diverse interests in a win-win solution. As constitutional commentator Jeffrey Rosen has written about later Courts, the justices could have "encouraged bilateral dialogue and cooperation" among various contending parties. Instead, the Court took one side and claimed that its choice was dictated by the law, when in fact it was not applying established law but making it.

FULLER'S COURT

Although friendly and easygoing, Fuller was neither an intellectual leader nor a workhorse. He was, in fact, a purely partisan choice, like Waite, of little political distinction. He was selected for the chief justiceship by Democratic president Grover Cleveland in the hope of gaining Illinois support for his reelection in 1888. Fuller had gone west to seek his fortune when prospects in native Maine paled. During the Civil War, he had flirted with Illinois Copperhead Democrats, and with the war's end, he built a very lucrative legal practice representing business interests in Chicago.

Fuller combined prewar states' rights philosophy with an even stronger pro–private property stance reminiscent of certain Jacksonians. Unlike the Jacksonians, however, Fuller had no love for democratic majoritarianism. He did not defer to elected bodies. He had none of Waite's hesitation about substituting the will of the majority of the Court for the will of the majority of the people. Some scholars see Fuller's motivation as a faith in economic individualism and the sanctity of private contract, but Fuller's fierce antagonism to unions, perhaps a result of his corporate law practice in Chicago during the Haymarket riots, demonstrated that his laissez-faire views were limited to entrepreneurs' activities and did not extend to the actions of working men. Mergers of giant firms were permissible. Leagues of laborers were illegal. And Fuller was almost immediately surrounded by like-minded allies on the Court.

Republican Benjamin Harrison, elected president in 1888, named four men to the bench whose views of property rights differed only marginally from the Democrats who had dissented in *Munn*. David J. Brewer was the first of these, named to the Court in 1889. In academic and legal attainments, he was clearly superior to the Democratic justices. A Yale grad, he had studied at Albany Law School and then apprenticed in his uncle David Dudley Field's office. There he learned firsthand how the greatest of all the corporate lawyers of his time plied his trade.

Like many of the Civil War Court's justices, Brewer went west to make his fortune, settling in Leavenworth, Kansas, and representing the railroads. A strong unionist and antislavery Republican, he had little use for "the paternal theory of government" and opposed government regulation of rates, prices, and anything that took from business its profits. He believed as well in "freedom of contract," allowing workers to agree not to form unions, to work longer hours, and to accept dangerous working conditions. He opposed statutory hours and wages legislation. But he was not opposed to all government intervention—he believed that the courts should and could intervene to protect private property. For example, he strongly supported the "labor injunction" by which courts could, at their discretion, enjoin workers from striking and criminally punish any worker who violated the injunction.

A deeply religious man raised by missionaries, he opined that the United States was "a Christian nation." He found state laws banning lotteries, prostitution, polygamy, and Sunday "blue laws" (closing businesses on Sunday) legitimate exercises of state police powers. But his version of Christian morality did not include even a paternal interest in black civil rights. As a judge in Kansas, he had ruled in favor of the Kansas system of segregation in the schools—a direct forerunner of *Brown v. Board of Education of Topeka, Kansas* (1954). He cited the overriding importance of local control of the schools, which in fact amounted to white control of blacks' rights. He would get the chance to vindicate his views in *Richmond County, Georgia, v. Cumming*, in 1899.

Like his uncle, Stephen Field, Brewer had no hesitation in viewing the Constitution and the role of the Court through his own lenses, but, unlike Field, Brewer hid his personal predilections behind formal doctrine and technical jargon. Brewer was an ideologue, but he was not doctrinaire. He made exceptions and distinguished cases when he found good reason. For example, even though he resisted most regulation—state and federal—of the railroads, he voted to uphold an Illinois statute requiring trains to slow as they passed through cities. Though he might have invalidated the act because the trains were part of interstate commerce (and hence the state must bow to the Commerce Clause), he found that, until Congress spoke to the contrary, the state's intervention was a reasonable exercise of its police powers. He served on the High Court from 1890 until his death in 1910.

In 1890, Henry Billings Brown replaced Samuel Miller, the last of the Civil War Republicans. Miller had been an intellectual giant with vision. Brown was a man much liked on the court but without much of a philosophy of his own, except for his dislike of the moneyed classes and monopolies, his belief that social mores and values could not be changed by court decisions or acts of Congress, and an aversion to any government burdens on commerce. Brown's friendship with Brewer (they both went to Yale and then west) influenced much of Brown's judicial writing on the Court. He was as much opposed to federal intervention in civil rights as Brewer, and only once, in the *Income Tax Cases*, did he break ranks with the conservative majority. He resigned in 1906, leaving as quietly as he had arrived—and with as little impact.

The old order changed once more in 1892. Joseph P. Bradley died, and President Harrison named George Shiras Jr. to the seat. Shiras, a Pennsylvania Republican, appreciated the value of railroads and big business. Like Brown, Shiras found the dormant Commerce Clause (a Court-invented doctrine in which state actions affecting interstate commerce are suspect even if Congress has not legislated on the matter) to be a convenient doctrine to strike down state regulations. He joined as well in the liberty of contract ideology. Like Brown, whose opinion established the "separate but equal" doctrine underlying legal segregation in the states, Shiras believed that there was no constitutional bar to literacy tests for voting, even when they were patently misused to deny blacks the chance to vote. He resigned from the Court in 1903.

Howell E. Jackson was Harrison's fourth appointment, and, like Brown and Shiras, he added little to the luster of the Court. But Jackson had an excuse. In ill health when named in 1893, he stayed at his Nashville, Tennessee, home during much of his short tenure and died in 1895 from tuberculosis. He had opposed secession but served in the Tennessee government when the state was part of the Confederacy. Though he was nominally a Democrat, and as such went to the U.S. Senate, he was more suited to the judicial branch. His long service as counsel to railroads and his personal friendship with both Cleveland and Harrison gained him a place on the federal bench and then appointment to the High Court. His conservative views found favor with both men and made him a logical successor to Samuel Blatchford.

When Grover Cleveland was reelected, in 1892, he resumed packing the Court with like-minded Democrats. Edward D. White, named in 1894, had served in the Confederate army and had entered Louisiana politics as a "Redeemer" when the state returned to its prewar lily-white politics. He was a tool of the sugar trust, a lawyer who had served his wealthy clients with fierce loyalty as a senator from Louisiana for three terms. He joined the Court in 1894 and in 1910 was elevated to chief justice, the first internal appointment for that post.

Though not as well known or as closely associated with a style of judging or a judicial philosophy as some of his contemporaries, White left his impress upon federal law and constitutional adjudication. In simplest terms, he believed that the Court was the defender of the Constitution against those who would use it for private or self-interested ends. Though today we regard government as the protector of the individual against corporate interests, in White's day the enemy of limited government was the legislature.

White was a believer in consistency and rules. He was an opponent of expanded national power when it took power from the states, a throwback to the states' rights ideology of his beloved Confederacy. He believed in the extension of national power over foreign enemies and to make distant conquests. He believed in reason when it curbed regulation, but only because the "rule of reason" gave to the courts the final determination of the reach of legislative enactments. He opposed government intervention in the economy on the side of labor and joined the opinion striking down the federal ban on child labor. Consistent in his support for racial segregation, he opposed civil rights and equal protection for blacks, Asian Americans, and Indians. He wrote the first of the opinions holding that U.S. acquisitions abroad were not entitled to any of the protections of the U.S. Constitution but could be governed by martial law.

Rufus W. Peckham, nominated and confirmed in 1894, was a New Yorker from a family of lawyers and a personal friend of Cleveland. On the state court, he had consistently opposed regulatory legislation and the protection of laborers. He was stridently antiunion and pro-business. For him, private property was "sacred," and to aid the poor was an invitation to class warfare rather than a way to avert class struggle. Reform would "array class against class," a prospect that chilled Peckham.

Peckham sided with the majority when it denied civil rights to minorities. His writing in civil rights cases showed a certain almost-studied indifference to the way in which law operated on those who did not share his notion of "privilege." As he wrote in one civil rights case, "There can be no just fear that the liberties of the citizen will not be carefully protected by the states respectively," referring to southern states' laws that imposed a type of bound labor on black people. Peckham died in 1909.

To what may be called the second Fuller Court, Presidents McKinley and Roosevelt named four justices. The first, confirmed in 1898, was Joseph McKenna. A California Republican, he had little formal legal schooling, but he was a quick study as a district attorney, a beneficiary of the powerful railroad interest in California, a fierce partisan in the party wars, an opponent of Asian immigration, and an indefatigable advocate for patronage for his congressional district. He surmounted anti-Catholic agitation to become a power in state politics. Appointed to the Ninth Circuit Court of Appeals soon after the new appellate circuits were created, he defended the railroads against state regulations but otherwise had few fixed principles and no discernible judicial philosophy. For a short time, he served as McKinley's attorney general. When Stephen Field was finally persuaded to retire, in 1897, McKinley rewarded McKenna's loyalty with nomination to the High Court.

Once there, McKenna proved a little more open to state and federal regulations than might have been expected and supported the rights of unions and laborers who had been injured on the job, and he revealed a social utility view of private property. He joined the majority of the Court at the end of the Fuller era as it began to favor broader federal regulatory powers. At the same time, he was suspicious of regulations that were not well-rooted in the health and police powers of the state, striking down wage and hours legislation when regulators could not prove that the health or welfare of the laborer was at stake. McKenna wrote nearly three hundred opinions for the Court during the Fuller years, but none were landmark cases. He retired in 1925.

Although Court observers have concluded that McKenna was erratic and unpredictable in his judicial views and distant, even formal, in his personality, the grace and clarity of the opinions he wrote suggests otherwise. Good sense and general principles were more important to him than abstract doctrine. A more convincing explanation of his somewhat tangled jurisprudence suggests that his deep Roman Catholic convictions and his youthful intent to join the priesthood left him with a strong commitment to justice. Real harm and practical consequences meant more to him than abstract doctrinal consistency. In this, he was the forerunner of justices like Harry Blackmun and David Souter, men who also did not fulfill the political aims of the presidents who selected them.

Theodore Roosevelt's appointments, drawn from his ideas of robust nationalism and progressive reform, were far more liberal than his predecessors' and filled out the second Fuller Court. The first of these appointments was another of the giants of American jurisprudence, Oliver Wendell Holmes Jr. Raised in the heady cultural atmosphere of upper-middle-class prewar Boston, during the time that it called itself the "Athens of America," he and his entire class at Harvard idealistically volunteered for service in the Union armies. Few returned unscathed. Wounded three times and on one occasion saved by the timely arrival of his physician father, Holmes's idealism withered and his sense of the irony and capriciousness of life grew. He served for a brief time on the Harvard Law School faculty, then accepted appointment to the Massachusetts Supreme Court, becoming chief justice in 1899. Theodore Roosevelt named him to the U.S. Supreme Court in 1902, assuming without thorough investigation that Holmes would support his views on antitrust and labor.

Holmes's brilliance, elegance of phrasing, and deep understanding of the law are unquestionable. His personal views and his personality remain difficult to fathom. He was reserved and bookish and valued intimacy with his friends and feminine companionship despite being a devoted husband. He loved the law as a profession and an intellectual discipline. Whether he was a skeptic who had no fixed ideals, as his critics claimed, or was simply a realist will never be finally settled. Often misperceived as a liberal in sympathy with reform, in fact he believed in deference to legislatures and in a kind of cynical realism. As David Hollinger wrote of the justice, "Holmes was eager to focus on contingent historical forces rather than on timeless, rational structures; he was persistently fatalistic rather than voluntaristic; and he attributed to the objective order of experience supreme authority at the expense of the subjective."

For Holmes, rationality was not based on an abstract reasoning but on real men exercising the rationality that experience taught. As he wrote in *The Common Law* (1881), "The felt necessities of the time, the prevalent moral and political theories, institutions of public policy [and] . . . even the prejudices that judges share with their fellow men" had more to do with the outcome of cases and the path of legal developments than fixed principles or abstract logic. He consistently believed in judicial restraint and deference to the elected branches. He served until 1932 and died in 1934.

William R. Day, the second of Roosevelt's appointments, might easily have fit in Holmes's shadow. Certainly, that is his place in history. A short, slight midwesterner, Day was a cautious progressive who accepted legislative supremacy in all but a few matters. Day allowed Congress and the states to require vaccination, set wages for miners, regulate monopolies, and discipline corrupt officials. In his service during the White Court years, he wrote opinions denying prosecutors the use of illegally gained evidence and voided agreements forcibly segregating residential areas. Day has never gained the attention of historians that he deserves. From the time that he replaced Shiras, in 1903, until 1922, when he retired, he was a hardworking Court centrist.

William H. Moody joined the Court in 1906, three years after the appointment of Day and four after Holmes. He was Theodore Roosevelt's attorney general when the president tapped him for the High Court seat to replace the ailing Justice Brown. Like Holmes, Moody was from Massachusetts. Unlike Holmes, Moody never finished law school. But Roosevelt trusted the stocky outdoorsman, in part because he was personally fearless. At the department of justice, he prosecuted lynch mobs and monopolists. Though a genuine liberal who might have led the Court into a progressive renaissance, Moody was hammered by arthritis and only served for a little over three years. He died in 1917.

Roosevelt's successor in the White House, William Howard Taft, made only one appointment to the Fuller Court. Horace H. Lurton of Tennessee had been a boy when he joined the Confederate army. A Democrat, he gained the attention of Grover Cleveland, who appointed him to sit on the Sixth Circuit Court of Appeals. When Moody resigned, Lurton took his place on the High Court, but, like Moody, Lurton served only a short time. On the Court, Lurton was very much a post–Civil War Democrat: a devotee of limited government, free labor, and states' rights and opposed to bigness. He was also a true son of the Confederate South and closed his eyes to the ill treatment of blacks under Jim Crow. He concurred in 1911 with a Holmes opinion concerning an Alabama law that effectually reenslaved blacks: "Neither public document nor evidence discloses a law which by its administration is made something different from what it appears on its face, and therefore the fact that in Alabama it mainly concerns the blacks does not matter." He died in 1914, leaving little mark on jurisprudence.

THREE LANDMARK CASES AND AN ELECTORAL REFERENDUM

Once Bradley and Miller were gone and the irascible Harlan was isolated, the Fuller-Peckham-White-Brewer core could begin an overhaul of the Waite Court's precedents. Three key cases marked the direction of the new jurisprudence. These touched on labor agitation, antitrust legislation, and the proposed federal income tax—the three legs upon which reform stood. The decisions had the same authors and supporters, cut the same way, and together raised a furor against the Court. The 1896 Democratic Party presidential nominee, William Jennings Bryan, campaigned against the Court and the three decisions. His defeat in the election enabled Fuller and his allies to continue remaking constitutional law.

The first of the three cases arose when the federal government prosecuted the E. C. Knight sugar refining company and other refining operations, all part of the same sugar trust, for violation of the 1890 Sherman Antitrust Act. The act stated that "every contract, combination in the form of trust, or otherwise, or conspiracy in restraint of trade and commerce among the several States is illegal, and that persons who shall monopolize or shall attempt to monopolize, or combine or conspire with other persons to monopolize trade and commerce among the several States, shall be guilty of a misdemeanor." The idea behind the law was that competition was good, and that the market could only govern itself when monopolies were curbed, a throwback to an era of small competing businesses.

But the American Sugar Refining Company was buying up its competitors, including E. C. Knight, in an attempt to control all refining in the country, and following that, all supply and pricing. At least, that is what Richard Olney, attorney general of the United States, alleged. Such activity, whatever its gain in efficiency might be, was a conspiracy to restrain free trade under the act. Olney argued that the stock must be returned to its original owners and the contracts of sale canceled.

The circuit court disagreed in *E. C. Knight. v. U.S.* The sugar trust had not violated the act. Manufacturing did not equate to commerce, and there was no evidence that the combination of companies intended to restrain trade. Control of the market was not in itself a restraint of trade. Fuller wrote the opinion for the High Court at the end of 1894. It seemed as simple as A, B, C. Thus A: "The monopoly and restraint denounced by the act are the monopoly and restraint of interstate and international trade or commerce, while the conclusion to be assumed on this record is that the result of the transaction complained of was the creation of a monopoly in the manufacture [of sugar]." And B: "The fundamental question is, whether conceding that the existence of a monopoly in manufacture is established by the evidence, that monopoly can be directly suppressed under the act of Congress in the mode attempted by this bill." Congress had the power to regulate interstate commerce. But C: "That which belongs to commerce is within the jurisdiction of the United States, but that which does not belong to commerce is within the jurisdiction of the police power of the State." The refineries were manufacturing plants wholly within the states of Delaware, Pennsylvania, and New Jersey.

Fuller understood that a monopoly over manufacturing had as its purpose total control over distribution: "Doubtless the power to control the manufacture of a given thing involves in a certain sense the control of its disposition, but this is a secondary and not the primary sense. . . . Commerce succeeds to manufacture, and is not a part of it." Fuller wrote as though "secondary and primary sense" were well-established legal categories, used to parse the meaning of statutes all the time. But that was not so. Neither did they arise from the language of the statute or from precedent. Fuller invented the distinction and then disguised the novelty. In a final touch, as he stood over the defeated statute, he spoke its eulogy: "Acknowledged evils, however grave and urgent they may appear to be, had better be borne, than the risk be run, in the effort to suppress them, of more serious consequences by resort to expedients of even doubtful constitutionality."

Harlan dissented: "A general restraint of trade has often resulted from combinations formed for the purpose of controlling prices by destroying the opportunity of buyers and sellers to deal with each other upon the basis of fair, open, free competition." He pointed out that precedent ran against Fuller's ingenious argument: "Combinations of this character have frequently been the subject of judicial scrutiny, and have always been condemned as illegal because of their necessary tendency to restrain trade. Such combinations are against common right and are crimes against the public."

The Court, by a vote of 8 to 1, refused to let the government enjoin (legally stop) the combination of the sugar refineries. By the same vote, it upheld a lower court injunction sought by the federal government against the American Railway Union for striking. In the years to come, the "antiunion injunction" would became a standard tactic to break strikes and unions, wielded by federal judges antipathetic to union activities and sanctioned by the High Court. The case involved two of the most remarkable men of the age, George Pullman and Eugene V. Debs. Pullman, who did not have more than a fourth-grade formal education, became one of the richest men in America. Pullman's sleeping cars offered railroad passengers the height of comfort. Debs, who left school at the age of fourteen, became one of the most influential labor leaders in the country. As a leader of the railroad Fireman's Brotherhood, he won concessions from their railroad employers for these highly skilled workers that exceeded even his expectations.

The two would clash when Debs became leader of the industry-wide American Railroad Union, and Pullman, in the midst of the great depression of 1893, cut his workers' pay. Many of these workers lived in the company town of Pullman and had joined the American Railroad Union to gain its aid against their employer. The other members of the union assisted the Pullman workers with a national boycott of the Pullman railcars and refused to attach them to trains. The railroad owners' Managers Association decided that they would not allow the boycott. What should have been a stalemate turned violent when unionized workers tried to prevent replacement workers hired by the railroads from entering the rail yards. The result was the stoppage of much train traffic in the Midwest, South, and Far West.

The railway owners had powerful friends in high places—in particular, in the federal courts and the attorney general of the United States, Richard Olney. Olney arranged for the federal court in Chicago to issue an injunction against the boycott. It was very broad, encompassing any act interfering with the rails, and applied to all persons, unnamed, who might be found in violation. It led to the arrest of the four union leaders, including Debs. In addition, a federal grand jury was called to indict Debs and the union leaders for criminal conspiracy. The whole proceeding was ex parte. Debs found out that his continued leadership of the strike was a contempt of court when he read it in the newspapers.

Debs reached out to a young and upcoming railroad lawyer with pro-labor sympathies, Clarence Darrow, and to a very senior lawyer who had helped to frame the Reconstruction amendments, Lyman Trumbull, to argue his case. They agreed to join Stephen Gregory, counsel for the American Railway Union. In his brief for the Court, Gregory argued the facts, not the law. The labor injunction, unregulated and overbroad, gained ex parte at the behest of any employer, "will turn over the workingmen of this country, bound hand and foot, to the mercy of corporate rapacity and greed in a time when combination rules every market and every great enterprise and dominates all the activities of capital. . . . No more tyrannous and arbitrary government can be devised than the administration of criminal law by a single judge by means of injunction and proceedings in contempt." The injunction was government-by-judiciary, a nonelected judiciary. His brief was powerful as political speech—and would soon resonate for the Democratic Party—but not very persuasive as law.

Olney argued the law. Obedience to lawful commands of the courts was essential to a well-ordered polity. Men could not take the law into their own hands, no matter how oppressed they might feel or be. Olney shared his personal views with the Court, too. Unions, agents, and fomenters of this disorder had upset the natural order of things and violated the laws of the market. Courts had to step in to restore that order.

Darrow argued about justice. "When a body of 100,000 men lay down their implements of labor, not because their own rights have been invaded, but because the bread has been taken from the mouths of their fellows, they are not criminals." They are, instead, the salt of the earth, for whom "this country must so largely depend for its safety, prosperity and progress." He added his own gloss on moral economy by turning the free market ideology upside down— the courts should stay out of the market and let the unions and the owners work out the appropriate solution.

At the Supreme Court, none of Darrow's ingenious inversion of Olney's argument mattered. Justice Brewer wrote: "That the complaint filed in this case clearly showed an existing obstruction of artificial highways for the passage of interstate commerce and the transmission of the mail—an obstruction not only temporarily existing, but threatening to continue; that under such complaint the Circuit Court had power to issue its process of injunction." No one may consciously or inadvertently disobey the legally enunciated order of a federal court. The injunction was such an order. By disobeying it, the strike leadership was in contempt of court.

Brewer, like Fuller in *E. C. Knight*, disposed of *In re Debs* swiftly, then paused to shed a tear over the body of the fallen adversary: "Whatever any single individual may have thought or planned, the great body of those who were engaged in these transactions contemplated neither rebellion nor revolution, and when in the due order of legal proceedings the question of right and wrong was submitted to the courts, and by them decided, they unhesitatingly yielded to their decisions. The outcome, by the very testimony of the defendants, attests the wisdom of the course pursued by the government." Brewer even indulged a wistful sympathy for the workers: "A most earnest and eloquent appeal was made to us in eulogy of the heroic spirit of those who threw up their employment, and gave up their means of earning a livelihood, not in defense of their own rights, but in sympathy for and to assist others whom they believed to be wronged. We yield to none in our admiration of any act of heroism or self-sacrifice."

But Brewer did not sympathize with labor, organized or not. He said as much out of court in lectures and in private correspondence. Organized labor's activity violated the Eighth and Tenth Commandments—taking and coveting the property of others. In short, it was sinful. For this reason, Brewer was willing to concede to the federal government an almost untrammeled discretion to curb unions that ran against all of his previously expressed views on federalism, limitation of government involvement in the economy, and belief in market forces' ability to work without government interference.

The federal labor injunction, which more properly should be termed the antilabor injunction, remained a feature of the federal court's business until the passage of the Norris-LaGuardia Act of 1932. The act specifically protected lawful strikes, including becoming or remaining a member of a labor organization, paying strike or unemployment benefits, assisting a person involved in a labor dispute in a court case, and "giving publicity to the existence of, or the facts involved in, any labor dispute, whether by advertising, speaking, patrolling, or by any other method not involving fraud or violence," including peaceful picketing and assembly.

The third of the controversial cases in which the Fuller Court elucidated its constitutional stance concerned a federal income tax statute. In the 1890s, states and the federal government financed their operations in a variety of fashions. Most of these involved some sort of tax. Democratic voters in rural areas favored the reintroduction of an income tax. The U.S. Congress had passed one during the Civil War. That statute expired in 1872. But in 1894 Congress adopted an income tax that imposed a flat 2 percent on all incomes over $4,000—the equivalent of about $91,000 in 2005 dollars. Under the act, only

2 percent of the country's wage earners would pay. Corporations, regarded as individuals under the law, were to pay 2 percent of their earnings. Mutual savings banks, savings and loans, and mutual insurance companies, all enterprises whose clients were farmers and laborers, were exempt. Bryan, a congressman from Nebraska, strongly supported the measure for reasons similar to Debs's support of the Pullman boycott. He claimed that the rich were parasites while the honest laboring man was enslaved by the corrupt giant corporation.

Defenders of free enterprise, fiscal morality, and the sacredness of private wealth were aghast. The measure brought the nation one step closer to communism, they feared. Arguing against the constitutionality of the act before the High Court in *Pollock v. Farmers Loan and Trust Company* (1895), Rufus Choate Jr., a corporate lawyer, urged the Court to stand fast against "populistic wrath," the very purpose for which the Constitution and the federal courts were created. Moreover, as Choate said in oral argument, "a tax which imposes one rate upon individuals and a higher rate upon corporations, which exempts individuals generally to the extent of $4,000, but practically denies any such exemption to those deriving their income from corporate investments, and which arbitrarily exempts immense accumulations of property in the hands of favored [savings and loan] private corporations and associations" was a class measure.

For Choate, the act privileged one class and imposed upon another, violating both due process in the Constitution's Fifth Amendment and the Tax Clause of Article I that states that all taxes must be uniform. Choate added: " I believe there are private rights of property here to be protected; that we have a right to come to this court and ask for their protection, and that this court has a right, without asking leave of the Attorney General or of any counsel, to hear our plea. . . . if you approve this law . . . this communistic march goes on."

Olney, the government's lawyer, begged the Court to defer to Congress: "I venture to suggest that all this laborious and erudite and formidable demonstration [by Choate] must necessarily be without result on one distinct ground. In its essence and in its last analysis, it is nothing but a call upon the judicial department of the government to supplant the political in the exercise of the taxing power; to substitute its discretion for that of Congress."

James C. Carter, a New York City lawyer reputed to be the most polished courtroom orator of his day, represented the loan company sued. Not given to technical niceties, he confronted the class question directly: "In every community those who feel the burdens of taxation are naturally prone to relieve themselves from them if they can; and the extent of the effort which they make to relieve themselves is, in general, proportionate to the extent of the burden which they suppose has been laid upon them." Carter continued with a lesson on political economy 101: "One class struggles to throw the burden off its own shoulders. If they succeed, of course it must fall upon others. They also, in their turn, labor to get rid of it, and finally the load falls upon those who will not, or cannot, make a successful effort for relief." And this time, Congress stood with the many poor against the few—the rich: "This is, in general, a one-sided struggle, in which the rich only engage, and it is a struggle in which the poor always go to the wall. This struggle on the part of the wealthy and highly organized classes of society constantly, unceasingly exerted, must necessarily succeed, either completely or partially, and it does everywhere succeed. The consequence is that in every country and in every age the principal burdens of taxation have been borne by the poor." Carter reminded the Court that his disquisition was not mere theory: "At the same time another impressive and startling fact . . . has also been receiving more and more of the attention of the people of the country   I mean the growing concentration of large masses of wealth in an ever diminishing number of persons."

A warning, but not one the Fuller Court majority found convincing. Fuller, writing for the Court in *Pollock*, set aside the entire act of Congress, not just the offending corporate provisions. This is a somewhat technical but highly important question that the Court periodically faces. If one portion of an act is unconstitutional, does the entire act fail? The Court's majority found that any tax falling upon the real estate holdings—in this case the bulk of the assets of the loan company—was a "direct tax" and had to be apportioned according to the population of the states. It also declared that the tax upon municipal bonds was unconstitutional because the bonds were creations of the states, and the federal government could not tax the states. The personal income tax provision went down with the rest of the law.

The Court split 4 to 4 the first time the case was argued, with Justice Jackson, ill in Nashville, favoring the act. By the time Jackson returned, in 1895, Fuller had found another vote against the tax, and the Court split 5 to 4 to strike it down. Fuller assigned himself the opinion. It repeated the logic of *E. C. Knight*: There may have been an evil, and Congress may have desired to remedy it, but "if, by calling a tax indirect when it is essentially direct, the rule of protection could be frittered away, one of the great landmarks defining the boundary between the Nation and the States of which it is composed, would have disappeared, and with it one of the bulwarks of private rights and private property."

Field agreed, turning Carter's argument on its head. Congressional efforts to reduce the maldistribution of wealth would only contribute to class war: "If the provisions of the Constitution can be set aside by an act of Congress, where is the course of usurpation to end? The present assault upon capital is but the beginning. It will be but the stepping-stone to others, larger and more sweeping, till our political contests will become a war of the poor against the rich; a war constantly growing in intensity and bitterness."

All three of the High Court's opinions were grist for the Populists' mill. Bryan, who had been their leader, captured the Democratic Party nomination in 1896, winning over a much-divided convention in part with an attack on the Court's dismissive view of the workingman:

The man who is employed for wages is as much a businessman as his employer. The attorney in a country town is as much a businessman as the corporation counsel in a great metropolis. The merchant at the crossroads store is as much a businessman as the merchant of New York. The farmer who goes forth in the morning and toils all day, begins in the spring and toils all summer, and by the application of brain and muscle to the natural resources of this country creates wealth, is as much a businessman as the man who goes upon the Board of Trade and bets upon the price of grain.

Bryan made it crystal clear that he was attacking the Court:

They tell us that the income tax ought not to be brought in here; that is not a new idea. They criticize us for our criticism of the Supreme Court of the United States. My friends, we have made no criticism. We have simply called attention to what you know. If you want criticisms, read the dissenting opinions of the Court. That will give you criticisms. . . . It was not unconstitutional when it went before the Supreme Court for the first time. It did not become unconstitutional until one judge changed his mind; and we cannot be expected to know when a judge will change his mind.

But Bryan sounded like a dangerous radical in a decade filled with radicalism. A widely circulated cartoon depicted him naming to the High Court a band of cutthroats, crooks, and violent men. Better financed and supported by all but the labor and farmer newspapers, and with the depression of 1893 finally on the wane, the Republicans and McKinley won a landslide victory, with 271 electoral votes to Bryan's 176. The popular vote was 7,102,246 to 6,492,559. The Court's course seemed to be validated by the election results.

RACE STILL MATTERS

The retreat from civil rights for minorities begun in the Waite Court accelerated in the Fuller era. It began early, with the *Chinese Exclusion Case* (1889) and

Louisville, New Orleans, and Texas Railway Co. v. Mississippi (1890). The Chinese Exclusion Act of 1882 barred the importation of Chinese laborers, whose contribution to the country had included much of the work of mining and laying railroad track in the Far West. Motivating the act, which had a ten-year renewable clause, was animosity toward the "yellow races." The Chinese already in the country before the act were not required to leave but found it increasingly difficult to prove that their residence antedated 1882. What was more, additional acts of Congress in 1884 and 1888 abrogated the promises made to the Chinese in the 1882 legislation.

Justice Field, whose California experience had put him in touch with the state's anti-Chinese feeling, went far beyond narrow statutory interpretation to uphold the exclusion of a returning laborer in *Chae Chan Ping v. U.S.* (1889). For Field, more important than treaty obligations to the Chinese government or contractual implications of the 1882 act was the very nature of the Chinese laborer: "The competition between them and our people was for this reason altogether in their favor, and the consequent irritation, proportionately deep and bitter, was followed, in many cases, by open conflicts, to the great disturbance of the public peace." It was inevitable, he thought, that

the differences of race added greatly to the difficulties of the situation. . . . [The Chinese] remained strangers in the land, residing apart by themselves, and adhering to the customs and usages of their own country. It seemed impossible for them to assimilate with our people or to make any change in their habits or modes of living. As they grew in numbers each year the people of the coast saw, or believed they saw, in the facility of immigration, and in the crowded millions of China . . . great danger that at no distant day that portion of our country would be overrun by them.

Field was mindful that the exclusion of the Chinese was more than physical. Even when permitted to remain in the United States, they were second-class citizens under the law. Such status was not unique to the Chinese, as Field knew from his participation in civil rights cases. In a sly but telling dictum, he defended the treatment of the newcomers by linking it to the Court's handling of African American suits: "The control of local matters being left to local authorities, and national matters being entrusted to the government of the Union, the problem of free institutions existing over a widely extended country, having different climates and varied interests, has been happily solved." Fuller agreed about "the vital importance of the preservation of local self-government through the states," in a speech he delivered on December 11, in the same year.

The stage was now set for the Court to revisit the question of segregation. In *Louisville*, railroad lines ran over a number of state borders, but the carrier did not want to add or change cars in Mississippi to accommodate the state's law that black passengers could only ride in specially designated cars. The Court, in the voice of Brewer, with Bradley and Harlan in dissent, held that the Mississippi law applied only within the state, so it did not come under the Commerce Clause of the federal Constitution. Nor did the Fourteenth Amendment apply.

Brewer had to explain the difference between this case and the Court striking down state regulation of freight rates for the very same rail lines because the lines crossed state boundaries and interstate commerce belonged exclusively to Congress: "Obviously whether interstate passengers of one race should, in any portion of their journey, be compelled to share their cabin accommodations with passengers of another race, was a question of interstate commerce, and to be determined by Congress alone." But the Mississippi rules only applied within the state, and "if it be a matter respecting wholly commerce within a State, and not interfering with commerce between the States, then, obviously, there is no violation of the commerce clause of the Federal Constitution."

Harlan's dissent espied a different kind of distinction: "It is made an offence against the State of Mississippi if a railroad company engaged in interstate commerce shall presume to send one of its trains into or through that State without such arrangement of its cars as will secure separate accommodations for both races." But in *Hall v. Decuir*, the Court found that the state could not burden interstate travel (by steamboat) with a requirement of equal accommodations. That pro–civil rights state statute overstepped the state's powers and intruded upon Congress's:

In its application to passengers on vessels engaged in interstate commerce, the Louisiana enactment forbade the separation of the white and black races while such vessels were within the limits of that State. The Mississippi statute, in its application to passengers on railroad trains employed in interstate commerce, requires such separation of races, while those trains are within that State. I am unable to perceive how the former is a regulation of interstate commerce, and the other is not.

A state law that required equal treatment of passengers, regardless of color, must fall, and a state law that required discriminatory treatment of passengers, based on color, must prevail, even though both involved transportation that was interstate in nature.

In *Plessy v. Ferguson* (1896), the Court, with Harlan dissenting, went further, explaining why state-mandated segregation was both moral and necessary, as well as legal. White supremacy was assumed in the generation after Reconstruction. Even Harlan conceded this: "The white race deems itself to be the dominant race in this country. And so it is, in prestige, in achievements, in education, in wealth and in power. So, I doubt not, it will continue to be for all time, if it remains true to its great heritage and holds fast to the principles of constitutional liberty." The "ruling race" was Anglo-Saxon or Teutonic or Nordic, and whiteness literally was in the blood. The darker races of Africa and the yellow races of Asia could not rule—a perfect justification for England, France, Germany, and, in 1898, the United States to assert their natural as well as political right to rule over the inferior peoples. The Reconstruction amendments merely confirmed this inferiority in the minds of segregationists like Tennessee senator John Tyler Morgan, writing in 1890. Some legal protection was needed "to save the negroes from the natural decay of their new-born liberties, which would result, necessarily, from their natural inability to preserve their freedom."

The very essence of this decline was race mixing, whether in education, travel, accommodations, business, politics, and, above all, marriage. It was taken as scientific fact, according to the German-born insurance executive Frederick L. Hoffman, that "the children of colored women and white men, of whatever shade of color, are morally and physically the inferiors" of both pure races. Even education did not close the gap in the moral sensibilities of "the inferior race." Hence the races must be strictly segregated. Only segregation would avert the corruption of the blood of the ruling race.

Plaintiff Homer Plessy and counselor Albion Tourgeé tested Louisiana's version of this ideology in 1892. Two years before, the state had passed a railroad car segregation law. Plessy, who could have passed for white, agreed with the conductor and a detective to be detained and then arrested after he bought his first-class ticket and refused to switch to the black car. It was a "test case." Plessy, already a civil rights leader, aided by a citizens committee, a local forerunner of the National Association for the Advancement of Colored People (the NAACP), lost in the Louisiana courts but appealed to the High Court on Thirteenth and Fourteenth Amendment grounds.

Justice Brown wrote for the Court, not only dismissing both of the constitutional grounds for the suit but also continuing on to explain the need for segregation: "The object of the amendment was undoubtedly to enforce the absolute equality of the two races before the law, but in the nature of things it could not have been intended to abolish distinctions based upon color, or to enforce social, as distinguished from political equality, or a commingling of the two races upon terms unsatisfactory to either." A law that limited where a person of one color could sit on a train and did not so restrain a person of another color did not disparage, harm, or make any assertion about the first person:

If this be so, it is not by reason of anything found in the act, but solely because the colored race chooses to put that construction upon it. . . . We think the enforced separation of the races, as applied to the internal commerce of the State, neither abridges the privileges or immunities of the colored man, deprives him of his property without due process of law, nor denies him the equal protection of the laws, within the meaning of the Fourteenth Amendment.

Brown's legal reasoning used one set of contemporary white social values. The "colored man" was not "lawfully entitled to the reputation of being a white man," and the state "is at liberty to act with reference to the established usages, customs and traditions of the people, and with a view to the promotion of their comfort, and the preservation of the public peace and good order."

Some modern commentators have suggested that *Plessy* was a missed opportunity for this Court to limit or roll back Jim Crow, but, according to Brown, the presumption of the naturalness and properness of segregation dictated that it could never have imposed integration of the races on whites: "If the two races are to meet upon terms of social equality, it must be the result of natural affinities, a mutual appreciation of each other's merits and a voluntary consent of individuals." The alternative, that "social prejudices may be overcome by legislation, and that equal rights [be] secured to the negro . . . by an enforced commingling of the two races" was a social impossibility more than a legal one. "Legislation is powerless to eradicate racial instincts or to abolish distinctions based upon physical differences, and the attempt to do so can only result in accentuating the difficulties of the present situation. . . . If one race be inferior to the other socially, the Constitution of the United States cannot put them upon the same plane."

Harlan's dissent in *Plessy* echoed his dissent in the *Civil Rights Cases*:

In respect of civil rights, common to all citizens, the Constitution of the United States does not, I think, permit any public authority to know the race of those entitled to be protected in the enjoyment of such rights. . . . I deny that any legislative body or judicial tribunal may have regard to the race of citizens when the civil rights of those citizens are involved. Indeed, such legislation, as that here in question, is inconsistent not only with that equality of rights which pertains to citizenship, National and State, but with the personal liberty enjoyed by every one within the United States. [The federal laws,] if enforced according to their true intent and meaning, will protect all the civil rights that pertain to freedom and citizenship. . . . These notable additions to the fundamental law were welcomed by the friends of liberty throughout the world. They removed the race line from our governmental systems.

Harlan accepted the dominant social ideas of the time: "Every true man has pride of race, and under appropriate circumstances when the rights of others, his equals before the law, are not to be affected, it is his privilege to express such pride and to take such action based upon it as to him seems proper, but such attitudes should not be embodied in law." Harlan's dissent continued: "In view of the Constitution, in the eye of the law, there is in this country no superior, dominant, ruling class of citizens. There is no caste here. Our Constitution is color-blind, and neither knows nor tolerates classes among citizens. In respect of civil rights, all citizens are equal before the law."

Harlan, as was his custom, considered the intent of the statute in weighing its constitutionality.

It was said in argument that the statute of Louisiana does not discriminate against either race, but prescribes a rule applicable alike to white and colored citizens. But this argument does not meet the difficulty. Every one knows that the statute in question had its origin in the purpose, not so much to exclude white persons from railroad cars occupied by blacks, as to exclude colored people from coaches occupied by or assigned to white persons.

Harlan's willingness to speculate about the motives of the legislators, that is, to try to determine "legislative intent," was not shared by his brethren. Although Harlan had introduced the legislative intent argument in his *Civil Rights Cases* dissent, Brown refused to ask what the legislators had in mind when they wrote laws. He wrote in a later opinion:

It is unnecessary to enter into the details of this debate. The arguments of individual legislators are no proper subject for judicial comment. They are so often influenced by personal or political considerations, or by the assumed necessities of the situation, that they can hardly be considered even as the deliberate views of the persons who make them, much less as dictating the construction to be put upon the Constitution by the courts.

There is a final twist to Harlan's dissent in *Plessy*. It was Harlan who repeated the language of the state statute that the railroads "are required to have separate but equal accommodations for white and colored persons." The term "separate but equal" did not appear in the majority opinion at all. Like "substantive due process," a term that came into fashion over fifty years after the Fuller Court routinely began to adopt the doctrine, "separate but equal" did not come into vogue until nearly twenty years after the High Court decided *Plessy*.

To be fair to Brown, even had Harlan carried the Court to the opposite conclusion, that, as a matter of law, state-mandated segregation of any kind violated the Equal Protection Clause, how would the Court have enforced its order? Seven years after *Plessy*, Holmes, ever the realist, explained the limited reach of the Court's decisions in civil rights cases. In *Giles v. Harris* (1903), a black petitioner sought an order to add his name to the Alabama voting lists. Holmes wrote for the Court denying the request. Even if the petitioner had such a constitutionally protected right, could the Court compel the state to obey? If it issued the injunction, could it oversee every registrar's office?

The [petitioner's] bill imports that the great mass of the white population intends to keep the blacks from voting. To meet such an intent something more than ordering the plaintiff's name to be inscribed upon the lists of 1902 will be needed. If the conspiracy and the intent exist, a name on a piece of paper will not defeat them. Unless we are prepared to supervise the voting in that State by officers of the court, it seems to us that all that the plaintiff could get from [a court order] would be an empty form.

The only prospect of relief depended upon political action: "Relief from a great political wrong, if done, as alleged, by the people of a state and the State itself, must be given by them or by the legislative and political department of the Government of the United States." In short, either the federal government would have to summon up the political will, or the blacks of Alabama, denied the right to vote, would have to find political allies in the state who could participate in its politics, to vindicate what Holmes knew was their legal right. Neither seemed likely in 1903.

But Harlan was not willing to concede that problems with enforcement outweighed the injustice of racial discrimination. His dissent in the *Berea College Case* (1908) was his last. This private college in Kentucky was integrated, but Kentucky state law forbade race mixing in any educational institution chartered by the state: "It shall be unlawful for any white person to attend any school or institution where negroes are received as pupils or receive instruction, and it shall be unlawful for any negro or colored person to attend any school or institution where white persons are received as pupils or receive instruction." Berea was a corporation under state law, and the college was fined $1,000 under the statute for allowing black and white students to sit in the same classrooms.

Justice Brewer found the case to be not one of civil rights but of contracts. Kentucky had not violated the Constitution of the United States by imposing certain restrictions upon all corporations it chartered. Had the school been run by an individual (without tax or other benefits of a state charter), the seg-regation law would not have applied to it.

Harlan's dissent showed his frustration, his deep religious commitment to equality, and one way in which moral and legal concepts could be fused. The Court had made the distinction between the corporate "creatures" of the state and private individuals, but Harlan asked the Court to look behind the neutral language of the state's counsel to the intent of the legislators: "It is absolutely certain that the legislature had in mind to prohibit the teaching of the two races in the same private institution, at the same time by whomsoever that institution was conducted." Indeed, "the state court upheld the authority of the State, under its general police power, to forbid the association of the two races in the same institution of learning." Harlan finished as he had begun in the *Civil Rights Cases*: "In the view which I have as to my duty I feel obliged to express my opinion as to the validity of the act as a whole. I am of opinion that in its essential parts the statute is an arbitrary invasion of the rights of liberty and property guaranteed by the Fourteenth Amendment against hostile state action and is, therefore, void."

The question of the civil rights of persons of color was raised obliquely in *Downes v. Bidwell* (1901). This was the first of the *Insular Cases*, a series of suits that determined whether the full panoply of rights and guarantees under the Constitution extended to the country's territorial and foreign possessions. The majority found that Puerto Rico, captured from the Spanish in the Spanish-American War of 1898, was a territory to which the full rights and privileges of the Constitution did not extend. Behind that was a pervasive vision of civiliza-tion and barbarism that was tied to race.

An importer of Puerto Rican oranges did not want to pay U.S. customs on the fruit, arguing that Puerto Rico was no longer a foreign country and its fruit was no longer a foreign import. An act of Congress passed after the war imposed duties nonetheless. Five of the justices held that the act was constitu-tional and that the duties must be paid, but only three members of the Court agreed on a theory to support the finding. Two other justices subscribed to the result but wrote their own concurring opinions. The four dissenters also each wrote for themselves.

Brown made insidious references to racial inferiority a core part of the majority decision in *Downes*: "We are also of opinion that the description of this power to acquire territory by treaty implies not only the power to govern such territory, but to prescribe upon what terms the United States will receive its inhabitants, and what their status shall be in what Chief Justice Marshall termed the 'American Empire.'" Some people in that empire were not eligible to be full citizens: "There seems to be no middle ground between this position and the doctrine that if their inhabitants do not become, immediately upon annexation, citizens of the United States, their children thereafter born, whether savages or civilized, are such, and entitled to all the rights, privileges and immunities of citizens." The rule for citizenship was birth in the United States. Treat the newly obtained imperial possessions of Puerto Rico and the Philippine Islands as part of the United States and the dark-skinned peoples of the territories would, in a generation, have the same rights and privileges as Brown: "If such be their status, the consequences will be extremely serious. Indeed, it is doubtful if Congress would ever assent to the annexation of territory upon the condition that its inhabitants, however foreign they may be to our habits, traditions and modes of life, shall become at once citizens of the United States."

Opponents of America's imperial experiment raised this issue during and after the Spanish-American War, but Brown did not worry about it: "Grave apprehensions of danger are felt by many eminent men—a fear lest an unrestrained possession of power on the part of Congress may lead to unjust and oppressive legislation, in which the natural rights of territories, or their inhabitants, may be engulfed in a centralized despotism. These fears, however, find no justification in the action of Congress in the past century." (Congress's many compromises with slavery in the first part of that century were not examples of "unjust and oppressive legislation," nor did the masters of slaves, protected and comforted by these laws, enjoy a regime of "centralized despotism.")

MECHANICAL JURISPRUDENCE

In an influential 1908 law review article, Professor Roscoe Pound took Fuller's Court to task for its "mechanical jurisprudence." He insisted that modern, enlightened courts should bow to legislatures when the representative branches were accommodating public needs. Pound had in mind a series of cases in which the majority of the justices had overturned labor legislation. On Pound's side one could find the Progressives, including many social scientists and legal reformers. Their case was rooted in the new politics of the 1900s.

A new group of political leaders had come to prominence at the end of the nineteenth century. These so-called Progressives—professionals, social scientists, efficiency experts, managers, journalists, and reformers—lived in cities, opposed corruption in government, resented monopolies, and demanded a cleaner and healthier world. Some denounced immigration, fearing that the newcomers would be abused by city bosses and unscrupulous employers; others welcomed it and set about raising the educational level of the arrivals. In the main, the Progressives were pro-labor, but they divided over their support for unions. They agreed, however, that state governments should protect both workers and consumers with wage, hours, and inspection regulations and with compensation for injuries on the job. And they believed that law should foster competition and restrain monopoly.

Theodore Roosevelt was the nominal leader of the movement. He favored a rugged individualistic approach to getting things done, a bully determination to impose his will on recalcitrant nature, political foes, and economic problems. But this approach did not bar government activity. Indeed, he wanted government to inject itself into the economy with vigor—regulating food and drug companies, creating a national wilderness, and cutting down the size of monopolistic corporations.

Roosevelt's New York was a leader in progressive reform. Typical of the legislative initiatives was the Bakeshop Act of 1895. It limited the hours a baker could be made to work to ten per day or sixty per week. A coalition of New York City Democrats, upstate Republicans, and health reformers had joined the Bakers Union and other labor advocates to promote the act. More important, unlike some of its predecessors, it had a mechanism for enforcement and imposed criminal penalties for offenders.

Joseph Lochner, whose bakery in Utica did not quite fit the image of the horrible conditions of the tenement bakeries the act's promoters had portrayed, resented the imposition. He refused to obey and refused to pay his fines, arguing that the act violated his and his workers' freedom to enter into contracts, a freedom protected from a state's interference by the Fourteenth Amendment. Although the state legislature twice passed the act unanimously and the state's courts declined to honor his claims, the High Court agreed to hear the case.

At stake was the doctrine of "freedom" or "liberty" of contract, a foundational notion of the pre–Civil War free labor movement, as well as a collection of ideas about the free market and the fear of a paternalistic state. In its brief and in oral argument, New York did not make the best case for its own laws, failing to produce sufficient evidence that working longer hours was detrimental to the bakers' health or to the cleanliness of their product. Such evidence could have been compiled, as it happened, for most small family bakeries were dark, dank, overheated, filled with flour dust, and overrun by insects (the bakers used sugar) and required the bakers to work through the night. Contracting tuberculosis was an occupational hazard. In a wide variety of cases, by far the majority that came to it, the High Court allowed the states and the federal government to regulate hazardous industries, for example, mining.

But another line of cases held that the Court, as the guardian of the Due Process Clause, was required to review state legislation that unduly interfered with private businesses. In *Chicago, Milwaukee, and St. Paul Railway v. Minnesota* (1890) and *Reagan v. Farmer's Loan and Trust* (1894), the Court found that state regulations of railroads were subject to the Court's supervision. Too severe a curtailment of the rails' profits was an unconstitutional taking of private property. But did that reasoning apply to ordinary labor relations?

Peckham wrote for the majority in *Lochner v. New York* (1905), which included Fuller, Brewer, Brown, and McKenna: "The statute necessarily interferes with the right of contract between the employer and employees, concerning the number of hours in which the latter may labor in the bakery of the employer. The general right to make a contract in relation to his business is part of the liberty of the individual protected by the Fourteenth Amendment of the Federal Constitution." State regulation of economic activities or individual rights was not unconstitutional per se, but "there is a limit to the valid exercise of the police power by the State. . . . Otherwise the Fourteenth Amendment would have no efficacy and the legislatures of the States would have unbounded power."

To the objection that the exercise of such minute supervision over state laws made the High Court a super legislature, a concern of the Populists, Progressives, and all advocates of legislative reform measures, Peckham had a ready answer: "This is not a question of substituting the judgment of the Court for that of the legislature. If the act be within the power of the State it is valid, although the judgment of the court might be totally opposed to the enactment of such a law. But the question would still remain: Is it within the police power of the State? and that question must be answered by the court."

Peckham assumed that the New York State law did not have a rational relationship to its stated purpose, although the purpose was a legitimate one. On one level, this was the state's burden—to show that limiting the hours a baker worked protected his health. On another level, this early enunciation of a rational-relation test had no clear boundary, and for Peckham the state police power was very narrow indeed: "It is a question of which of two powers or rights shall prevail—the power of the State to legislate or the right of the individual to liberty of person and freedom of contract." The state's assertion must pass through the eye of the Court's needle "before an act can be held to be valid which interferes with the general right of an individual to be free in his person and in his power to contract in relation to his own labor."

Harlan dissented. Freedom of contract was hedged by legitimate state regulations, and the Court had already found that "the right to contract in relation to persons and property or to do business, within a State, may be 'regulated and sometimes prohibited, when the contracts or business conflict with the policy of the State as contained in its statutes.'" When could and should a Court override the state? Rarely and with great trepidation: "Upon this point there is no room for dispute; for, the rule is universal that a legislative enactment, Federal or state, is never to be disregarded or held invalid unless it be, beyond question, plainly and palpably in excess of legislative power."

Harlan then presented a mini-brief, drawn from a variety of social science and government reports, to show that the bakery industry was indeed dangerous to its employees. However other members of the High Court elected to read these reports, Harlan argued that the Court should defer to the legislature's reading of them: "Let the State alone in the management of its purely domestic affairs, so long as it does not appear beyond all question that it has violated the Federal Constitution." White and Day agreed.

Holmes, who had no love lost for laboring men's rights, joined the dissenters. He did not see why Peckham's economic ideology should be constitutionalized, any more than any judge's personal views of liberty should trump a legislature's. In a way, this reflected Holmes's willingness to let southern legislatures read segregation into the Fourteenth Amendment and the civil rights acts. Here, he wrote:

This case is decided upon an economic theory which a large part of the country does not entertain. If it were a question whether I agreed with that theory I should desire to study it further and long before making up my mind. But I do not conceive that to be my duty, because I strongly believe that my agreement or disagreement has nothing to do with the right of a majority [in a legislature] to embody their opinions in law. . . . The Fourteenth Amendment does not enact Mr. Herbert Spencer's Social Statics.

But it did enact Victorian sensibilities. Every member of the Court agreed, three years later, that an Oregon law forbidding laundry operators from making women work over ten hours a day was constitutional. Women had joined the commercial labor pool in huge numbers at the end of the nineteenth century. Many of these lower-class, often immigrant, women found themselves in especially wearying jobs, at lower pay and with longer hours than their menfolk. Pressed by reform groups, including the National Consumers League that lawyer-activist Florence Kelley had founded in 1898, twenty states had laws limiting daily and weekly work hours for women by 1903. Oregon's was one of these.

On September 4, 1905, Curt Muller, of Portland, Oregon, demanded that one of his laundry workers work overtime, violating the Oregon law. The laundress, Emma Gotcher, was having none of it and reported him for the infraction. He hired William Fenton, a corporate lawyer, to represent him, but lost in the trial courts. Fenton believed that his client's plea was a winner under newly decided *Lochner* and argued to that effect before the Oregon Supreme Court in 1906. But it upheld the conviction.

State supreme courts in Nebraska and Washington had earlier heard claims like Muller's and brushed them aside. But that was before *Lochner*. Representing Oregon as a special counsel was Louis D. Brandeis. Florence Kelley had recommended Brandeis, a well-to-do Boston lawyer with a difference. He was a progressive warrior, believing that the best kind of legal counsel mediated between labor and capital. Against utilities that overcharged and railroads that would not compensate their injured workers, he often represented the underdog without charging a fee.

His brief in *Muller v. Oregon* would become famous—indeed, it would come to be called the "Brandeis Brief." One hundred and thirteen pages long, it devoted but two pages to the legal precedents and the rest to evidence of the harms to women due to excessively long work days. He documented how arduous working in a commercial laundry was and added evidence that long hours at hard labor not only harmed women workers but also resulted in stunted children. He argued that the mothers of the next generation deserved special protection from the state. Kelley and her research aides had done their job well. (A second, conventional brief that Brandeis and the state's attorneys submitted argued that the Oregon law, unlike the New York Bakeshop Act, was a legitimate expression of the state's concern for the health and welfare of a particularly vulnerable group of workers.)

Fenton took the position that the law should treat men and women the same, a curiously modern-sounding argument. Men in the same industries as women were not especially protected by Oregon. Its law thus violated the Fourteenth Amendment in two ways—denying to women employees the freedom of contract that the Constitution gave to all workers, as the Court held in *Lochner*, and denying to women the rights and liberties (to work longer hours) that men had.

Both the factual and the legal claims for the state would prove to be decisive in the Court's view. The justices agreed that womanhood and motherhood deserved special consideration. At the turn of the century, women were regarded as morally purer than men but physically and mentally inferior. Distinctions in law coming out of that viewpoint were allowable, because without the paternal protection of the state, women could not be healthy mothers. Writing for the Court, Brewer, for whom the "paternal state was odious," had no qualms about a paternal state protecting maternity:

The legislation and opinions referred to in the margin may not be, technically speaking, authorities, and in them is little or no discussion of the constitutional question presented to us for determination, yet they are significant of a widespread belief that woman's physical structure, and the functions she performs in consequence thereof, justify special legislation restricting or qualifying the conditions under which she should be permitted to toil.

Brewer acknowledged that liberty of contract was protected by the Fourteenth Amendment but that exceptions must be made:

That woman's physical structure and the performance of maternal functions place her at a disadvantage in the struggle for subsistence is obvious. This is especially true when the burdens of motherhood are upon her. Even when they are not, by abundant testimony of the medical fraternity continuance for a long time on her feet at work, repeating this from day to day, tends to injurious effects upon the body, and as healthy mothers are essential to vigorous offspring, the physical well-being of woman becomes an object of public interest and care in order to preserve the strength and vigor of the race.

The justices concluded that, like Oregon, the Court must protect the woman, who naturally turns to her father or husband or brother. She was not equal, and the law could recognize that inequality: "She will still be where some legislation to protect her seems necessary to secure a real equality of right. Doubtless there are individual exceptions, and there are many respects in which she has an advantage over him; but looking at it from the viewpoint of the effort to maintain an independent position in life, she is not upon an equality."

The Court split over the second of the Progressive economic objectives— antitrust. Roosevelt's presidency featured his "trust-busting," the attempt to break up the most monopolistic of the giant industries. In *Northern Securities* (1904), the Roosevelt administration's attempt to restore competition among midwestern carriers was approved by the High Court. The government had argued that the creators of the Northern Securities railroad holding company had restraint of trade uppermost in their minds when they arranged the deal: "The testimony of defendants shows that the incorporation of the Securities Company, and its acquisition of a large majority of the stock of both railway companies were the designed results of a plan or understanding between the defendants . . . which was carried out to the letter by the parties thereto."

J. P. Morgan, the leading New York City investment banker, had helped to organize the monopoly, and many of the so-called robber barons had a piece of it. But the holding company's claim that busting it interfered with intrastate commerce was not persuasive to Justice Harlan:

Underlying the argument in behalf of the defendants is the idea that, as the Northern Securities Company is a state corporation, and as its acquisition of the stock of the Great Northern and Northern Pacific Railway Companies is not inconsistent with the powers conferred by its charter, the enforcement of the act of Congress, as against those corporations, will be an unauthorized interference by the national government with the internal commerce of the states creating those corporations. This suggestion does not at all impress us. . . . No state can, by merely creating a corporation, or in any other mode, project its authority into other states, and across the continent, so as to prevent Congress from exerting the power it possesses under the Constitution over interstate and international commerce, or so as to exempt its corporation engaged in interstate commerce from obedience to any rule lawfully established by Congress for such commerce.

But how far could the government carry this burden? Could it—should it—dissolve the myriad of interlocking financial and industrial and transportation institutions that by 1910 owned and controlled over 50 percent of the nation's wealth? Would that not go beyond the competitive ideal to one of redistribution of wealth? Would it not be, to the horror of all advocates of corporate interests, "class legislation," a first step toward communism? No one could call Harlan a believer in collectivism, and Harlan dismissed dire predictions of economic collapse following trust-busting: "Many suggestions were made in argument based upon the thought that the anti-trust act would, in the end, prove to be mischievous in its consequences. Disaster to business and wide-spread financial ruin, it has been intimated, will follow the execution of its provisions. Such predictions were made in all the cases heretofore arising under that act. But they have not been verified."

Justice Brewer, concurring, reassured business interests of the Court's continuing goodwill: The Northern Securities trust had gone too far, for "under present conditions a single railroad is, if not a legal, largely a practical, monopoly; and the arrangement by which the control of these two competing roads was merged in a single corporation broadens and extends such monopoly. I cannot look upon it as other than an unreasonable combination in restraint of interstate commerce." But, he "felt constrained to make these observations for fear that the broad and sweeping language of the opinion of the court might tend to unsettle legitimate business enterprises, stifle or retard wholesome business activities, encourage improper disregard of reasonable contracts, and invite unnecessary litigation."

Fuller, Peckham, White, and Holmes dissented. The first two men's thinking needs no explication. For White, the plan was just a stock swap, hardly a matter of interstate commerce: "The very definition of the power to regulate commerce, as announced in *Gibbons v. Ogden*, excludes the conception that it extends to stock ownership."

Holmes, nominated by Roosevelt in part because the president assumed that the new justice would support the trust-busting program, infuriated Roosevelt with his dissent. But Holmes worried that the government had opened a Pandora's box: "Great cases like hard cases make bad law. For great cases are called great, not by reason of their real importance in shaping the law of the future, but because of some accident of immediate overwhelming interest which appeals to the feelings and distorts the judgment." Holmes believed that the Sherman Act was so vague in its language and so broad in its potential application that every business might at one time or another fall afoul of it: "What we have to do in this case is to find the meaning of some not very difficult words." The key to that effort, for Holmes, lay in the recognition that the Sherman Act should be read as criminal law: "The statute of which we have to find the meaning is a criminal statute. The two sections on which the Government relies both make certain acts crimes. That is their immediate purpose and that is what they say." In criminal law, intent was paramount, which shifted the burden on the government to that of proving that a business combination was formed to restrain trade, not just to combine or manage larger units of production or commerce.

The vigor of the Fuller Court core, including the chief justice, Peckham, and Brewer, found its voice in cases like *Lochner*. These justices had staked out their ideological ground ten years before and defended it against all comers with consistent and powerful logic. But by the closing years of the decade, Fuller, Peckham, and Brewer were showing their age. All were ailing. What was more, their worldview, rooted in the free market moralism of the Victorian age, ill fit the new and potent progressive program.

When the majority opinions of the High Court began to lag far behind evolving public opinion and leading politicians like Roosevelt began to openly turn on the Court, it became harder for it to justify its rulings. The Progressives were calling for a "recall" amendment that would have turned life tenure for judges into a popularity contest, and such a contest the Fuller Court majority could not win. But within three years, Fuller, Peckham, and Brewer were gone, and their colleague, Justice White, was occupying the center chair. His Court would make concessions to the administrative and regulatory state that Fuller, Brewer, and Peckham would never have countenanced. Within a few years of their passing, their legacy was under attack from all sides.

CHAPTER 8

The White Court, 1910–1921

With Fuller's passing, newly elected President William H. Taft reached into the Court itself and nominated Justice Edward White for the chief justiceship. Taft, a former federal appeals court judge, liked what he saw in the heavyset, courtly White, but more important, Taft himself wanted the job when he stepped down in 1912, as the 1910 election rout of the Republican Party hinted would happen. Taft and White may even have agreed that the job would be Taft's after he was out of office and a Republican president again sat in the White House.

Taft considered compatibility a key value in the operation of an appellate court. He seemed to enjoy, as well, the entire process of naming justices. Many of his candidates were personal friends or social acquaintances. In these men, Taft looked for "soundness," which to him meant steady and trustworthy character but to critics seemed to mean conservative. And White's nationalism appealed to Taft. Like Taft, White believed that the independence and dignity of the judicial branch must be maintained at all costs. In any case, White's elevation was the first time that an associate justice had assumed the chief justice's job.

WHITE'S COURT

White had already demonstrated his caution with regard to most matters of federalism, government regulation of the economy, and court-legislative relations. He would not innovate, nor would he challenge the settled law. He was, however, a zealous defender of the discretion and authority of courts. When a Toledo newspaper was held in contempt for criticizing a federal court's actions, White voted to uphold the contempt citation. The federal code on courts' contempt powers explicitly stated that "such power shall not be construed to extend to any cases except the behavior of persons in their presence, or so near thereto as to obstruct the administration of justice." White construed this narrow power broadly and "compatibly with the sacred obligation of courts to preserve their right to discharge their duties free from unlawful and unworthy influences . . . [and with] the power to restrain acts tending to obstruct and prevent the untrammeled and unprejudiced exercise of the judicial power given by summarily treating such acts as a contempt and punishing accordingly."

White was comfortable on the Court. He had settled into Washington society, marrying for the first time after joining the Court. White even liked the Court's setting—the old Senate chamber, still close and clubby in its atmosphere, with backlighting of the bench through the windows giving the justices a kind of halo, but too dark for some of the justices to see beyond the first row of counsels' desks beneath the raised platform on which they sat. At least they could hear counsel (a plus, since some of them were nearly deaf). A floor below, their first Capitol chamber, now their library and conference room, was so dank that the justices kept their conferences in it short.

White and the associate justices worked at home because they had no offices in the Capitol to which they could return after their sessions. Congress allowed them a $2,000 home office subsidy to complement their $14,500 salaries (the chief justice made $500 more) and provided another $2,000 for them to hire clerks or secretaries. Some used these funds to pay for stenographers, but others, notably Holmes and later Brandeis, hired Harvard Law School honor graduates and treated the young men as protégés.

White's elevation might be read as an omen that the Fuller Court legacy would march on undisturbed, but national politics and international strife had other plans for the Court. The White Court had to face cases of great popular concern, a people and a Congress that did not trust the High Tribunal, and a president whose agenda did not square with Fuller's. Continued episodes of labor versus capital, coalescing in union strikes and antiunion injunctions, prosecutions of the Standard Oil holding company, the American Tobacco Company's monopoly, and the International Harvester Company and U.S. Steel, all under the Sherman Antitrust Act, and a world war forced White and his Court to move toward the left, though always grudgingly.

Taft's first selection for the White Court was the Republican governor of New York, Charles Evans Hughes, a genuine progressive. In New York, he had begun to engineer the same kind of liberal reform regime as Robert La Follett in Wisconsin and other progressive executive leaders were putting together. Formerly a professor of law at Cornell, an advocate of investigating and uncovering wrongdoing in industries like insurance and utilities, and a believer in the rightful role of government in the economy, Hughes could have been a major player on the bench had he not interrupted his service in 1916 to run for the presidency. He returned to the Court in 1930 as President Herbert Hoover's choice for chief justice.

Taft had political reasons for selecting Hughes. He was a Republican—indeed, he was the leader of the liberal wing of the party, and Taft sought to undercut Roosevelt's appeal to those Republicans. At the same time, Taft saw Hughes as a potential rival, and moving him to the Court removed him from the electoral lists. To sweeten the deal, Taft even hinted that Hughes would be his choice for the center seat, should that become vacant. For his part, Hughes was profoundly tired of campaigning and did not intend to stay on as governor. The appointment suited both men, and Congress approved.

Joseph R. Lamar was the next of Taft's choices, a Georgia Democrat whose practice and legal career had not required him to leave his state. Taft came to know Lamar through personal contact—a chance encounter at a spa followed by socializing and golf. Lamar served from 1910 to 1914, replacing Moody and lasting on the Court about the same amount of time as Moody. His record was not especially noteworthy and was even quixotic. He favored employers, Native Americans, Chinese workers, and other less fortunate Americans—but not his section's own blacks. He became ill in 1915 and died in 1916, a year after resigning his post.

Some saw Lamar's appointment as a last and concluding gesture in restoring the South to the Union. Though still recovering its infrastructure and its fiscal stability, the South was once again a dominant force in Congress and on the Court. Lurton, White, and Lamar were all southerners, though the Deep South had but one of the federal circuits. Indeed, insofar as the rest of the nation had retreated from the goals of Reconstruction, one could say that the white South had won the Civil War. Southerner Woodrow Wilson's victory in the 1912 presidential contest confirmed this triumph.

When Fuller died and White was elevated, Taft tapped Wyoming Republican Willis Van Devanter for the vacant seat. A former senator and power in his state and an able craftsman as both lawyer and federal circuit judge, he lobbied for the seat and then occupied it for twenty-six years. He was no particular friend to railroads, unlike so many of the members of the Fuller Court, and he bowed to Congress when it limited its regulations to interstate commerce, except in Congress's penalization of child labor. He opposed civil rights and First Amendment liberties. Throughout his career, he could be counted on to take the least liberal position possible. He is often ranked as one of the weakest of the justices, in part because he had writer's block, or "pen paralysis" as he called it, and he did not do his share of the Court's opinion writing. He died in Washington, D.C., in 1941, four years after his retirement.

Mahlon Pitney of New Jersey was Taft's final appointment, in 1910. He was not Taft's first choice. But he had been a solid Republican member of Congress in the 1890s, and he had served with distinction on the New Jersey Supreme Court from 1901 to 1908, after which he became the chancellor of the state's equity court. That court, along with Delaware's, handled many of the most complex business matters, for New Jersey's laws, like Delaware's, encouraged corporations to register in the state. Tax benefits and the absence of state antitrust laws were enticements, as was the unsavory and sometimes outwardly corrupt pro-business outlook of the state government. Much of this would end with the election of Woodrow Wilson as a reform governor in 1910. Pitney's appointment had another advantage—Taft needed Pitney's aid in securing the New Jersey delegates' support at the 1912 Republican presidential convention.

To the Court, Pitney brought his consistently pro-employer perspective. He rarely dissented, for he rarely had to dissent; and in his ten years on the bench, he wrote 244 majority opinions. The most famous of these was *Coppage v. Kansas* (1915), which overturned a progressive Kansas statute that barred "yellow dog" (open shop) contracts. For Pitney, the law had to protect "personal liberty" or it could not defend "the right of private property." He also approved injunctions against union organizers and against primary and secondary boycotts by unions.

When he dissented, as he did in opposing the eight-hour-day laws for railroad workers, his dissent again sounded like strict construction of the Commerce Clause, but behind that legal doctrine was the same liberty-of-contract ideology that infused his majority opinions. He joined the majority in upholding convictions of radicals for speech and writings that the federal government found dangerous or critical of government policies. Only on racial justice matters did Pitney side with the liberal bloc. He had a stroke in 1922 and retired, dying two years later.

Woodrow Wilson's first appointment was his attorney general, James McReynolds. By the time of the appointment, there was no love lost between Wilson and this narrow-minded, often blunt, and increasingly eccentric Tennessean. McReynolds had proven to be a dogged antitrust prosecutor under Roosevelt and Taft, a characteristic that hid for a time his bigoted views of minorities. A longtime bachelor, he was rude to other justices and almost obsessive in his personal habits. In later years, one of his clerks described him as "selfish to an extreme, vindictive, almost sadistically inclined at times, inconceivably narrow, temperamental, and heaven knows what." To his credit, he was gallant with women, had many women friends, and was generous to children. In a 1972 survey ranking the justices, eight were rated as "failures," including McReynolds. In a 1993 survey, he ranked dead last. Gossip at the time claimed that Wilson proposed his name to the Senate to rid the cabinet of him.

Wilson's second appointment, Louis Brandeis, was a "fearful shock" (Taft's words) to the advocates of conservative jurisprudence. For Brandeis had emerged as "the people's advocate," a defender of social justice who used the courts for liberal ends. In speaking for consumer groups and labor unions in legislative hearings and court cases, Brandeis made plain his views—for example, on labor unionism: "The disclosures incident to the labor policies of the strong trusts and particularly the hours of labor, wages, and conditions . . . are making many Americans recognize that unions and collective bargaining are essential to industrial liberty and social justice."

Wilson held Brandeis dear and adopted many of Brandeis's ideas. "The new freedom" that carried Wilson to victory in 1912 was largely Brandeis's creation. As Brandeis explained, in 1911, "No economic problem in America is as important today as that presented by the Money Trust—the control which a few financiers exercise over the capital of America. . . . the greatest economic menace of today is . . . these few able financiers who are gradually acquiring control over our quick capital." But so odious did many find Brandeis's relentless advocacy (and his Judaism) that Wilson did not dare bring the Boston lawyer into his cabinet.

Instead, in 1916, he proposed that Brandeis replace the retiring Lamar. The confirmation battle was incredibly bitter, and both Taft and McReynolds lobbied against the appointment. For four months, witnesses for and against Brandeis trooped up to Capitol Hill. In particular, railroad interests stung by Brandeis's testimony in favor of Interstate Commerce Commission rate-setting, corporate leaders furious at Brandeis's role in framing the Clayton Antitrust Act, and banking spokesmen determined to pay Brandeis back for such articles as "Breaking the Money Trust" saw the confirmation as the occasion to vent their spleen.

The argument against him was that he was no lawyer and not fit to be a judge—for, according to one newspaper, "Mr. Brandeis is a radical, a theorist, impractical, with strong socialistic tendencies. That he is given to extravagance in utterance, inspired by prejudice and intolerance. That he is a self-advertiser, reckless in his methods of seeking personal exploitation." A petition of fifty-five Boston lawyers, most of whom had crossed swords with Brandeis and lost, pronounced that Brandeis did not have "their confidence."

But Wilson stood by his man and wrote to the committee: "I perceived from the first that the charges were intrinsically incredible by anyone who had really known Mr. Brandeis. I have known him. . . . He is a friend to all just men and a lover of the right, and he knows more than how to talk about the right—he knows how to set it forward in the face of his enemies." Wilson and his allies in the Senate lined up Democratic and Progressive votes, and the nomination was confirmed on June 5, 1916, by a vote of 47 to 22.

On the Court, Brandeis would prove to be a man of exquisite personal probity, recusing himself whenever a case touched any of his earlier interests or his financial holdings, treating his colleagues with genuine respect and courtesy, and taking great pains with every case that came the Court's way. His opinions were predictably liberal, and often he found himself in dissent, particularly in matters of racial justice, civil liberties, free speech, and labor unions, and he almost always favored deference to legislative acts and judicial restraint. Holmes found in Brandeis a personal friend, and Brandeis was able to persuade Holmes to soften some of his hard-edged realism. Brandeis also cultivated a special relationship with young Harvard Law professor Felix Frankfurter, the latter selecting Brandeis's clerks from among the law school's brightest men, and Brandeis using his own funds to pay Frankfurter for research services. In modern rankings of justices, Brandeis always appears in the "great" or top category.

The last of Wilson's nominees was John H. Clarke, to replace Hughes, who departed in August to run for the presidency on the Republican ticket. Clark was an Ohio Democratic lawyer and newspaperman. He had represented, among other corporate clients, the Pullman Palace Car Company. But by 1900, he had cast his lot with the progressives in his party, and he ran, unsuccessfully, for the Senate on a reform ticket. He supported a woman's right to vote, organized labor, and reforms in tort law to protect workers, children, and consumers. Wilson named him to the federal bench in 1914 and to the High Court in 1916. Taft again opposed the appointment, fearing that Clarke's views were too close to Brandeis's.

Taft was right, for Clarke often agreed with Brandeis, especially in dissent. Clarke and Brandeis dissented in the *U.S. Steel* case and in *Hammer v. Dagenhart*, and the two men joined the majority in upholding the eight-hour workday for railroad workers and workers' compensation laws. Both men opposed the antiunion injunction. The two disagreed about free speech issues, however, with Clarke joining the majority to uphold convictions of anarchists and socialists who opposed U.S. entry into World War I. He left the Court in 1922 to work for greater American participation in international peace efforts. He later supported President Franklin D. Roosevelt's plan to reorganize the Supreme Court (the "packing plan") to protect New Deal legislation. Clarke, a deeply religious man and a philanthrope, never married and left public life in 1927, to live on his earnings in southern California. He died in 1945.

BUSINESS AS USUAL

In two vital areas of law, the White Court's conservative majority struggled to hold its own against the rising tide of progressive reform. The first was in labor law. The second was in antitrust law. The Fuller Court's labor precedents, with *Lochner* and *Muller* facing off, gave no clear signals for the White Court, nor did *Northern Securities* in the antitrust area.

Progressive forces in Congress and in state legislatures had acted to protect workers' health and welfare, through liability (workplace injury) laws, workers' compensation laws, minimum wage laws, and child labor laws. Employers responded by seeking refuge in the same catch-22 that enabled advocates of Jim Crow to maintain segregation in the South. They argued that the federal government could not protect workers if the workers were not directly engaged in interstate commerce or if they worked in the manufacturing economy (*F. C. Knight*, among other precedents). Then they argued against state protection for workers engaged in interstate commerce, on the grounds that only the federal government could provide these protections.

When Congress or the states acted to set a minimum wage or to violate the liberty of contract of workers, even of those who were too young to be able to enter into contracts legally, the Court struck down the legislation. The most fiercely contested of these cases was *Hammer v. Dagenhart* (1918). Despite widespread support in the country for some limitation on child labor, powerful industrial interests, particularly southern textile mills and mines, did not want such limitation. These mills and mines, closed to black workers by the racism of both owners and white employees, needed child labor to operate profitably. Poor southern white families, strapped for cash, reluctantly sent out sons, including preteens, to work in dangerous places with few safety controls. Because these were manufacturing enterprises, rather than commercial ones, *E. C. Knight* prevented Congress from forbidding child labor in them directly. Congress moved instead to criminalize the interstate shipment of products that came from child labor, in the Keating-Owen Child Labor Act of 1916.

The majority of the Court was not fooled by Congress's sleight of hand. Using the Commerce Clause, the Court concluded, was just a screen to intrude into the sole province of state government. If North Carolina did not want to protect its children, then Congress could not—even if those children were also citizens of the United States and had the privileges and immunities of all U.S. citizens. Justice Day wrote:

By means of a prohibition against the movement in interstate commerce of ordinary commercial commodities, [Congress seeks] to regulate the hours of labor of children in factories and mines within the States, a purely state authority. Thus the act in a two-fold sense is repugnant to the Constitution. It not only transcends the authority delegated to Congress over commerce but also exerts a power as to a purely local matter to which the federal authority does not extend.

Holmes, dissenting, urged deference to Congress: "The act does not meddle with anything belonging to the States. They may regulate their internal affairs and their domestic commerce as they like. But when they seek to send their products across the state line they are no longer within their rights." Holmes allowed himself a brief contrary-to-fact analysis of the majority's logic: "If there were no Constitution and no Congress [the products' ability] to cross [another state's] line would depend upon their neighbors. Under the Constitution such commerce belongs not to the States but to Congress to regulate." The Court would strike down child labor laws repeatedly thereafter, and child labor was not prohibited by federal law until 1938, by which time two more generations of young people had lost their childhoods in the mill and the mine, and many had died or been crippled as well.

Ironically, had North Carolina acted to bar child labor, the plaintiff, a father who wanted his two underage sons to work in a North Carolina mill, could have brought suit in federal court against the state. *Lochner* was precedent. His counsel would have argued that the law violated the children's liberty of contract. (Of course, in contract law that argument made no sense, for as minors they lacked the power to enter or enforce contracts.) Could the state have replied that its law protected the morals or the health of minors (as in *Muller*)?

Relying on *Lochner*, the Court gave its assent to "yellow dog contracts." In *Adair v. U.S.* (1908) and again in *Coppage v. Kansas* (1915), the Court found that neither Congress nor the states could pass laws barring employers from insisting that no worker could be a member of a union. To allow governments to do this was to violate the liberty of contract of workers, although the logic of that reading of liberty of contract escaped labor advocates. Did it not deny to workers who wanted to be in a union the right to belong to it? The answer was no—they could belong, they just could not work for employers who would not take them. In effect, these decisions protected the liberty of contract of the employers only.

Antitrust was a second area in which the Fuller Court's precedents failed to settle key issues. What was the reach of the Sherman Antitrust Act? *Northern Securities* did not say. The greatest trust in the land was the monster oil combination fabricated by John D. Rockefeller. In *Standard Oil v. U.S.* (1911), the federal government alleged that Rockefeller "purchased and obtained interests through stock ownership and otherwise . . . entered into agreements with, various persons, firms, corporations, and limited partnerships . . . for the purpose of fixing the price of crude and refined oil and the products thereof, limiting the production thereof, and controlling the transportation therein, and thereby restraining trade and commerce among the several States, and monopolizing the said commerce." White agreed with that assessment. The oil trust was an illegal combination in restraint of trade.

But as in his dissent in *Northern Securities*, White's opinion for the Court defined "restraint" not in absolute but in relative terms. He rendered the purpose of the act as the restraint of "unreasonably restrictive" conduct, "of such a character as to give rise to the inference or presumption that they had been entered into or done with the intent to do wrong to the general public and to limit the right of individuals, thus restraining the free flow of commerce and tending to bring about the evils, such as enhancement of prices, which were considered to be against public policy."

Hidden in this maze of words—White's writing embodied a number of the worst features of nineteenth-century prose style—were three tests that White supplied but the statute did not specify. First, to violate the act, the conduct must be an "undue limitation on competitive conditions." This implied that there were certain "due" limitations on competition. That was not unrealistic—for the government allowed monopoly in certain communications fields already. Bigness itself, as Roosevelt had conceded, was not the enemy—it was evil bigness. There was no doubt in any of the justices' minds that Rockefeller and his cohorts had intentionally tried to get around the Sherman Antitrust Act.

The second test White imposed was that the conduct must be "unreasonably restrictive." This language had appeared in Brewer's concurrence in *Northern Securities*. White's adoption of this test was later called the "rule of reason" and was given pride of place in commentaries on him and the case (although credit should go to Brewer).

Finally, White insisted that the acts of forming and operating the monopoly must have the intent of restraining trade—not just of making a business more efficient or increasing its productivity. The statute nowhere mentioned intent, but Holmes's dissent in *Northern Securities* had firmly placed the idea in White's head that the Sherman Antitrust Act was a criminal law. Here, the intent must be to restrain trade.

White's tests gave room to the Court in which to exercise its reasoning powers: "The merely generic enumeration which the statute makes of the acts to which it refers and the absence of any definition of restraint of trade as used in the statute leaves room for but one conclusion . . . to leave it to be determined by the light of reason." White might have regarded the statute as a strict liability law, like going through a stoplight. If there is restraint of trade, the defendant is liable. Instead, he reached the opposite conclusion, that the Court had to find evil "purpose and intent."

As chief justice voting with the majority, White could assign himself the opinion in the case, and thus he was able to import key elements of his dissenting opinion from *Northern Securities*. Harlan had to concur in the result, but he was furious with White. Instead of inventing tests that were not in the text of the act, Harlan looked at the debates and hearings in Congress on the act to find its legislative intent:

All who recall the condition of the country in 1890 will remember that there was everywhere, among the people generally, a deep feeling of unrest. The Nation had been rid of human slavery—fortunately, as all now feel—but the conviction was universal that the country was in real danger from another kind of slavery sought to be fastened on the American people, namely, the slavery that would result from aggregations of capital in the hands of a few individuals and corporations controlling, for their own profit and advantage exclusively, the entire business of the country.

Congress had expressly forbidden "every" kind of contract or combination in restraint of trade. As Harlan remembered, and White should have known,

Fifteen years ago, when the purpose of Congress in passing the Antitrust Act was fresh in the minds of courts, lawyers, statesmen and the general public, this court expressly declined to indulge in judicial legislation, by inserting in the act the word 'unreasonable' or any other word of like import. It may be stated here that the country at large accepted this view of the act, and the Federal courts throughout the entire country enforced its provisions.

The Court next heard the American Tobacco Company case and found that it too was a combination in restraint of trade. Its practices had been far more predatory than Standard Oil's, including buying up tobacco supplies to deny them to competitors, monopolizing sales and distribution, driving down the prices that tobacco farmers were paid for their crops, and concluding unfair deals with foreign companies. But the American Tobacco Company did not fully comply with the High Court's ruling, and the monopoly was only dissolved after a second round of cases, in 1940.

Antitrust prosecutions of the International Harvester and U.S. Steel cases dragged on through the lower courts and then were delayed at the High Court until the end of the decade. In the end, International Harvester negotiated a settlement with the government that allowed it to divest itself of unprofitable divisions—thus cutting its costs, increasing its profits, and avoiding paying any penalties. U.S. Steel was found to have no evil intent in its business practices, and its share of the market had dropped by the time that the High Court finally decided on the government's appeal. The Court, in 1921, found no violation of the Sherman Act.

After extensive hearings in 1912 and 1913, Congress responded to the Court's opinions on antitrust by passing the Clayton Antitrust Act of 1914. Congress did not accept the Court's narrowing of the Sherman Antitrust Act or the imposition of judicial tests. Instead, the legislators reaffirmed and President Woodrow Wilson signed into law the more precise definitions that Holmes wanted:

It shall be unlawful for any person engaged in commerce, in the course of such commerce, either directly or indirectly . . . to discriminate in price between different purchasers of commodities of like grade and quality, where either or any of the purchases involved in such discrimination are in commerce . . . where the effect of such discrimination may be substantially to lessen competition or tend to create a monopoly in any line of commerce, or to injure, destroy, or prevent competition with any person who either grants or knowingly receives the benefit of such discrimination.

The burden that the Court in *Standard Oil* had shifted to the shoulders of the government prosecutors the Clayton Act laid on the accused: "Upon proof being made, at any hearing on a complaint under this section, that there has been discrimination in price or services or facilities furnished, the burden of rebutting the prima-facie case thus made by showing justification shall be upon the person charged with a violation of this section." The act added, against rate fixing, dumping, special discounts, and kickbacks: "It shall be unlawful for any person engaged in commerce, in the course of such commerce, to be a party to, or assist in, any transaction of sale, or contract to sell, which discriminates to his knowledge against competitors of the purchaser."

In the ongoing back-and-forth of the often-adversarial legislative-judicial relations stretching all the way back to *Marbury*, Congress sought to curb the Court's interference in Congress's prerogatives.

MORE REGULATIONS

Congress was just as unhappy with the Court's reading of the charter for the Interstate Commerce Commission (ICC). Responding to the Court's overturning ICC rate setting, Congress passed the Elkins Act (1903), the Hepburn Act (1906), and the Mann-Elkins Act (1910), which explicitly gave to the ICC the authority to oversee and set railroad haulage rates. With Hughes leading, the Court conceded that these emendations of the Interstate Commerce Act were constitutional, so long as the ICC compiled an adequate record to support its actions. Writing in the *Shreveport Rate Cases* (1914), Hughes opined:

The use of the instrument of interstate commerce in a discriminatory manner so as to inflict injury upon that commerce, or some part thereof, furnishes abundant ground for Federal intervention. . . . Having this power, Congress could provide for its execution through the aid of a subordinate body; and we conclude that the order of the [Interstate Commerce] Commission now in question cannot be held invalid upon the ground that it exceeded the authority which Congress could lawfully confer.

This was a robust reading of Congress's authority, national economic priorities, and administrative delegation.

The Court's broader reading of the ICC's powers came in an era of agency formation, beginning with the creation of the Food and Drug Administration under the Pure Food and Drug Act of 1906. One of the progressives' goals had been to shift oversight of key industries from courts to independent regulatory commissions. Exposés like Upton Sinclair's searing *The Jungle* demonstrated that mass-market food processing concealed unhealthy practices. The Court upheld the provisions of the act and the activities of the agency in a series of cases, although Holmes dissented until Congress modified certain portions of the act.

MORE MESSAGES FROM THE SOUTH

In a private conversation with the producer of D. W. Griffith's openly racist movie, *Birth of a Nation*, White admitted that he had been a member of the Ku Klux Klan and had, in the violent closing days of Reconstruction in New Orleans, "walked my sentinel's beat through the ugliest streets of New Orleans with my rifle on my shoulder." The Klan, despite congressional legislation banning hooded vigilantism, had made a strong comeback in the White Court era. President Wilson believed in segregation and reversed the Roosevelt and Taft policies of desegregation of federal offices. An alliance of white and black reformers created the NAACP in 1909 and the next year began to bring cases to the High Court.

In *Franklin v. State of South Carolina* (1910), the first of the NAACP cases, the White Court followed the precedent of Fuller Court opinions on minority rights, deferring to local juries and state courts. Pink Franklin was a sharecropper who refused to plow a field until later in the day. A constable, acting under a South Carolina law that made such refusals criminal, burst without warning or warrant into Franklin's home, and Franklin killed the constable. The all-white trial jury found Franklin guilty of murder, even though key pieces of evidence were withheld from Franklin's defense counsel. But the High Court, as in *Giles*, was not about to oversee every criminal trial in which a claim of racial discrimination was made. Conduct of trial "rests in the sound discretion of the trial court, and its action in that respect is not ordinarily reviewable. It would take an extreme case to make the action of the trial court in such a case a denial of due process of law." Justice Day concluded,

> Even if one attempted to be arrested under process issued under a void and unconstitutional law has the right to resist arrest, even to the taking of human life, a point we do not find it necessary to decide, the case could not have been taken from the jury upon the testimony disclosed in this record. The right to make such resistance to the officer, under the circumstances here shown, must have been left to the determination of the jury under proper instructions.

Franklin was executed.

But flickers of hope for civil rights reformers came in *Bailey v. Alabama* (1911), *Reynolds v. U.S.* (1914), *Guinn and Beal v. U.S.* (1915) and the other *Grandfather Clause Cases*, and *Buchanan v. Warley* (1917). In all of these cases, the Court refused to openly admit the extent or nature of the oppression of blacks by whites. But, at least, the majority found technical grounds upon which to invalidate discriminatory laws without exploring the racial nature of the discrimination.

At the beginning of the 1900s, to ensure that its white planters had a ready supply of cheap black labor, Alabama had made it a crime to receive an advance for labor under a contract and then either fail to perform the labor or fail to continue to labor for the period of time stated in the contract. Failure to complete the contract subjected the laborer to a term of forced labor. Conviction turned a free labor relationship into peonage—effectually slavery.

The Alabama statute also included an instruction the judges were to make to the jury—that nonperformance of the agreed-upon labor was presumptive evidence of the intention to defraud, in effect making the defendant guilty until proven innocent: "The refusal of any person who enters into such contract to perform such act or service, or refund such money, or pay for such property, without just cause, shall be prima facie evidence of the intent to . . . defraud . . . his employer." This 1907 addition to the 1903 criminal statute closed any avenues the laborer had to escape conviction. Because many of these "contracts" were verbal, and because the only witnesses were the (black) laborer and the (white) boss, the evidentiary burden the new law placed on the laborer was almost insurmountable. Not surprisingly, all-white juries routinely found the accused guilty. Alabama had found its way back to the black codes the state's legislature had passed in 1865.

The state's attorney general explained the judge's instruction to the High Court justices: "The statute was to punish fraudulent practices and not mere failure to pay a debt. . . . if a rule of evidence which excludes the defendant from testifying as to his motives has the effect of making the rule of evidence prescribed by the statute a conclusive rule, it is due to the particular facts and not to the statute itself." He added that Alabama did not violate federal law against peonage, because the Alabama law did not mention peonage.

Hughes's opinion for the majority turned on the Alabama trial court's instructions. There might not be "a particle of evidence of the intent to defraud." Ordinarily, it was the burden of the state to produce such evidence. Here it simply took the word of the employer, the person who would directly benefit from the conviction. Hughes also noted that the penalty for conviction was forced labor for a term far longer than it would take to repay the advance. The labor was due to a private individual—the employer—even though the offense was against the state (as in all criminal cases). So the state, in effect, had reduced a free laborer to a peon working for a private employer.

But the Thirteenth Amendment denied to Alabama and its master class the power to re-enslave, and federal law barred peonage for debt: "What the state may not do directly, it may not do indirectly. It cannot punish the servant as a criminal for the mere failure or refusal to serve without paying his debt. It is not permitted to accomplish the same result" by changing the criminal law to make the defendant in such cases guilty until proven innocent and then exclude all evidence of his innocence.

Hughes declined to attribute the Alabama law to illicit racism or to condemn it as part of a regime of racial discrimination. Thus the Court left open the door for Alabama to adjust its peonage laws, and it did. Instead of the criminal prosecution of the laborer for failing to perform the contract, satisfied by selling him to a private employer, Alabama law gave to the payer of a surety after conviction—a bond for the repayment of a debt—the right to put a person convicted of the very same Alabama law found unconstitutional in *Bailey* into forced labor.

Alabama's attorney general explained that "the offense of peonage does not exist" in the Alabama code, and "the sentence of imprisonment [the alternative to which was forced labor for the surety] for embezzlement in lieu of his restoring to the injured party the amount embezzled is not regarded as imprisonment for the debt." Indeed, "the statute is a humane one. If the convict does his duty according to his contract [serving as forced labor for the surety rather than doing hard time for the state] there is no reminder of his convict state, save at the end of each month when his wage is withheld. He is practically a free man and the law delights in the liberty and the happiness of the citizen." Failure to perform the forced labor, however, would result in another round of trial, automatic conviction, and a longer term of forced labor.

Justice Day, who had declined to reopen Pink Franklin's murder trial, this time tore into Alabama for thumbing its nose at the Court's decision in *Bailey*: "Under this statute, the surety may cause the arrest of the convict for violation of his labor contract. He may be sentenced and punished for this new offense, and undertake to liquidate the penalty by a new contract of a similar nature, and, if again broken, may be again prosecuted, and the convict is thus kept chained to an everturning wheel of servitude. . . . The hirer becomes the transferee of the right of the State to compel the payment of the fine and costs, and by this exaction of involuntary servitude the convict has only changed masters." The Court unanimously reversed the conviction and struck down the statute.

Jim Crow state governments found a variety of subterfuges to deny the most basic right of citizenship to their black citizens—that of voting. The literacy test, the poll tax, the all-white primary, and the grandfather clause were four of these pernicious and ingenious uses of law to violate higher law and undermine the principles of democratic republicanism that were intentionally deployed by white legislators from 1880 to 1910.

In time, all would fall. The literacy test was supposedly neutral and could theoretically disqualify voters of all races, but who passed the test was at the discretion of white voter registrars. It was restricted in the 1965 Voting Rights Act. The poll tax applied to everyone as well, but it affected blacks disproportionately because they represented the poorest of the population. It was outlawed for federal elections by constitutional amendment in 1964 and later for all elections. The all-white party primary, achieved by declaring political parties to be private organizations and thus exempt from Fourteenth Amendment "state action" analysis, fell in 1944.

Oklahoma was new to the Union, but its government assayed the same system of racial injustice as its southwestern neighbors. The process of reenfranchisement of blacks was slow going, but the Oklahoma *Grandfather Clause Cases* were a beginning. In 1910, Oklahoma added a clause to its constitution imposing a literacy test on all new voters, but an exception was made for those whose grandfathers could vote in 1866. Oklahoma was not a state in 1866. Why then the date? It was before the ratification of the Fifteenth Amendment in 1871, and in the Oklahoma Territory in 1866 no person of color could vote. Thus whites, whose grandfathers could vote, did not face the literacy test, but every black citizen of the state did.

John W. Davis, Woodrow Wilson's solicitor general, looked behind the racially neutral language and saw that

the necessary effect and operation of the Grandfather Clause is to exclude practically all illiterate negroes and practically no illiterate white men, and from this its unconstitutional purpose may legitimately be inferred. The census statistics show that the proportion of negroes qualified under the test imposed by the Grandfather Clause is as inconsiderable as the proportion of whites thereby disqualified. In practical operation the amendment inevitably discriminates between the class of illiterate whites and illiterate blacks as a class, to the overwhelming disadvantage of the latter.

Davis was not an enemy of segregation, nor was President Wilson. Davis would run for president in 1924 on a platform that condoned segregation, and he argued for it in *Briggs v. Elliot* (1954), one of the school segregation cases accompanying *Brown v. Board of Education*. But the grandfather clause of the Oklahoma Constitution was an open affront to the Fifteenth Amendment and could not be overlooked.

The High Court unanimously agreed, but White, who assigned himself the opinion (as he had in *Standard Oil*), avoided the larger question of racial discrimination: "We have difficulty in finding words to more clearly demonstrate the conviction we entertain that this standard has the characteristics which the Government attributes to it than does the mere statement of the text." White was not going to go beyond what the government had briefed. Though usually long-winded, he was terse here. White exculpated the state of any racist motive and placed the Court's seal of approval on literacy tests: "No time need be spent on the question of the validity of the literacy test considered alone since as we have seen its establishment was but the exercise by the State of a lawful power vested in it not subject to our supervision, and indeed, its validity is admitted."

White read his states' rights version of the Constitution into the decision: "Whether this test is so connected with the other one relating to the situation on January 1, 1866, that the invalidity of the latter requires the rejection of the former is really a question of state law." White severed the offending portion of the state law—the grandfather exception—from the rest of it (rather than strike down the entire law, as the Court did in *Pollock*), effectively preserving for the state voter registrars the discretion to administer literacy tests unfairly: "We are of opinion that neither forms of classification nor methods of enumeration should be made the basis of striking down a provision which was independently legal and therefore was lawfully enacted because of the removal of an illegal provision with which the legal provision or provisions may have been associated."

The last of the quartet of these *Civil Rights Cases* came from Louisville. A white homeowner had sold his house and lot to a black purchaser, and he sought payment. The black purchaser could not take title because a city ordinance that he had not known about stated that

to prevent conflict and ill-feeling between the white and colored races in the City of Louisville [it shall be] 'unlawful for any colored person to move into and occupy as a residence, place of abode, or to establish and maintain as a place of public assembly any house upon any block upon which a greater number of houses are occupied as residences, places of abode, or places of public assembly by white people than are occupied as residences, places of abode, or places of public assembly by colored people.'

The law exhibited the same kind of upside-down equality as the Alabama adultery statute in 1881. It was just as unlawful for "any white person to move into and occupy as a residence . . . upon any block upon which a greater number of houses are occupied as residences . . . by colored people."

The Court knocked down the ordinance, but not because it legalized Jim Crow housing patterns. Instead, the ordinance violated the right to sell and acquire private property. As Justice Day, again writing for a unanimous Court, put it, "Property is more than the mere thing which a person owns. It is elementary that it includes the right to acquire, use, and dispose of it. The Constitution protects these essential attributes of property." The ordinance violated the Due Process Clause of the Fourteenth Amendment in denying the white owner the right to dispose of his or her property as he or she saw fit.

The city of Louisville "said such legislation tends to promote the public peace by preventing racial conflicts; that it tends to maintain racial purity; that it prevents the deterioration of property owned and occupied by white people, which deterioration, it is contended, is sure to follow the occupancy of adjacent premises by persons of color." Day agreed that public order, racial peace, and property upkeep were positive goods that a city might protect: "There exists a serious and difficult problem arising from a feeling of race hostility which the law is powerless to control, and to which it must give a measure of consideration." But a homeowner's right to sell outweighed these considerations, and the state could not deprive "citizens of their constitutional rights and privileges."

Could the Court have done more to ensure racial equality had it so desired? The Klan had come to Indiana and New Jersey, holding rallies in the open. States passed laws against any mixing of the races at schools, in domestic relationships, and in public places. Residential segregation went on even after *Warley.* White Populist leaders like Tom Watson in Georgia and James K. Vardaman in Mississippi found in racism the ladder to step up to southern governorships and federal elective office. As South Carolina senator Benjamin Tillman told the upper house in 1900:

We did not disfranchise the negroes until 1895. Then we had a constitutional convention convened which took the matter up calmly, deliberately, and avowedly with the purpose of disfranchising as many of them as we could under the fourteenth and fifteenth amendments. We adopted the educational qualification as the only means left to us, and the negro is as contented and as prosperous and as well protected in South Carolina to-day as in any State of the Union south of the Potomac. He is not meddling with politics, for he found that the more he meddled with them the worse off he got.

Roosevelt refused to put a civil rights plank on his Progressive Party platform. Taft thought that the white South could be won over to the Republican Party if the party abandoned its protection of blacks. Wilson segregated the U.S. Postal Service and other federal agencies. Against this tide, what could a willing Court have done to help African Americans?

THE FIRST AMENDMENT IN WAR AND PEACE

The world went to war in 1914. The United States attempted a policy of neutrality, but it clearly favored the Allies—giving nearly $2.3 billion in loans to Britain and France and only $27 million to the Central Powers. So long as Germany refrained from sinking passenger ships with its submarines, Wilson hoped to stay out of the conflict. He won reelection in part with the slogan "he kept us out of war." But when Germany's submarine campaign struck at all vessels heading for Allied ports, including American ships, in early 1917, Wilson finally asked Congress for a declaration of war.

The nation was not prepared to fight. The armed forces numbered under 250,000 men. By the end of the war, nearly five million men would be in uniform, twenty-four million men would be registered for the draft, and the federal budget would approach $25 billion. Wilson, formerly an exponent of small government, exercised presidential powers exceeding those of Lincoln in the Civil War. When the railroads became hopelessly tangled, he took charge of the rails and combined a number of companies into a national transportation system. The prospect of financing the war was equally challenging. Wilson deployed the newly introduced income tax (the Seventeenth Amendment had just been ratified), as well as a package of "liberty bonds" and increased estate taxes.

The mobilization rivaled the Civil War era in legal dilemmas and legal innovations. The draft was not new, but enforcement mechanisms for it were far more comprehensive than in the Civil War. Congress and the president conferred unparalleled discretion on administrative appointees. Wilson asked financial wizard Bernard Baruch to manage a new War Industries Board, and, using the carrot and the stick, this first federal administrative czar convinced manufacturers to dedicate themselves to production of war materials. The newly established National War Labor Board, led by William Howard Taft, had the authority to intervene in labor disputes and did so by recognizing the unions' right to organize. Herbert Hoover, an Iowa Quaker and mining engineer, headed the Food Administration and persuaded Americans to do without so that starving Europeans could share in the bounty of American farms.

Wilson's innovations included a Committee on Public Information, a propaganda organ to drum up support for the war. The result was widespread anti-German feeling. Commissions to hear pleas of conscientious objectors followed the largest draft law in the nation's history. When socialists and anarchists joined peace advocates and German and Irish groups in publicly opposing the war, Wilson used the full extent of new laws to prohibit protests and banish aliens.

Socialist and anarchist criticism of state and federal government was not new, nor were cases in which states and the federal government prosecuted these marginal political players for criticism of public figures and government policies. The High Court heard two of these cases in the years prior to the war. The first arose when John Turner, an English anarchist, challenged his deportation. In 1903, during a speaking tour, he lectured on the essentials of anarchism and criticized the execution of the Haymarket defendants. Under the newly enacted Alien Immigration Act, anyone who entered the country and advocated the overthrow of the government could be summarily deported. The Free Speech League raised money for his defense and hired Clarence Darrow to conduct it.

When the case arrived at the Supreme Court, Darrow argued that the act was unconstitutional because it violated the First Amendment guarantee of free speech. The expression of mere beliefs was always protected. James McReynolds represented the government during oral argument. He called Darrow's First Amendment claims "incomprehensible," sneering that the deportation of anarchists had nothing to do with free speech and that "the right to talk is no more sacred than the right to work."

Darrow's argument that freedom of speech was explicitly guaranteed in the Constitution did not persuade the Court. Fuller, writing for a unanimous Court, professed to be as amazed as McReynolds. Nothing in the act itself or in the deportation of Turner "abridged the freedom of speech or the press." If an alien was ordered out of the country, plainly, he is "in fact cut off from . . . speaking or publishing . . . in the country, but that is merely because of his expulsion therefrom"—another dose of Fuller's wry brand of logic. Congress had the power to deny entry or to expel anyone it chose, and if it chose to expel anarchists because of what they said or published, then their loss of speech or publication was an incidental result of the exercise of a legitimate power. The power to decide to deport him was given by Congress to the immigration board, and that discretion was untouchable. If Congress did the same for the ICC, however, that conferral of discretion was not only reviewable by the Fuller Court, but subject to revision. Fuller's closing words had no bearing on the holding of the case and rang as false as Brewer's crocodile tears for the strikers in *Debs*: "We are not to be understood as depreciating the vital importance of freedom of speech . . . or as suggesting limitation on the spirit of liberty, in itself unconquerable, but this case does not involve those considerations."

Brewer concurred in the result but, consistent with his ICC opinions, added that "I do not believe it within the power of Congress to give to ministerial officers a final adjudication of the right to liberty or to oust the courts from the duty of inquiry respecting both law and facts." To make a plain point plainer, he added: "Congress is not authorized in all things to act for the nation."

The second prewar precedent came from Colorado's prosecution of one of its own U.S. senators, newspaper owner Thomas Patterson. In 1902, he published a series of cartoons attacking the state supreme court for its politics. No case was pending at the time, and the attacks did not discuss any case on the court's docket. Patterson was a Populist and the court was heavily Republican. His expression was political rather than juridical. Nevertheless, the attorney general, acting for the state supreme court, filed proceedings against Patterson for libel, which the court upheld. The state's libel law made truth a positive defense, but the court did not offer Patterson the chance to prove the truth of his words. Nor was it concerned that it was a judge in its own cause.

When the case came to the U.S. Supreme Court, Patterson having claimed that Colorado violated his federal constitutional rights, Holmes wrote for the majority. Although the First Amendment was not a centerpiece of Patterson's defense, Holmes paused to consider the issue himself:

Even if we were to assume that freedom of speech and freedom of the press were protected from abridgement on the part not only of the United States but also of the States (that is, if the Fourteenth Amendment incorporated the First Amendment), still we should be far from the conclusion that the plaintiff . . . would have us reach. . . . The main purpose of such constitutional provisions is to prevent all such previous restraints upon publications as had been practiced by other governments and they do not prevent the subsequent punishment of such as may be deemed contrary to the public welfare.

The source for Holmes's reading of the First Amendment as limited to prior censorship was Blackstone's *Commentaries*, published in 1759 and offering an English view of libel. Holmes imported this doctrine into opinions he wrote as chief judge of the Massachusetts Supreme Judicial Court. The test of impermissible speech was speech that "would tend to obstruct the administration of justice." Thus even the truth would not avert punishment for such speech, because a truthful criticism of the courts would undermine their authority even more profoundly than wildly and unbelievably false attacks.

Harlan and Brewer dissented. Harlan applied the analysis he had used to explain the Fourteenth Amendment in the *Civil Rights Cases*: The First Amendment had a "reflex character" that applied it to all the citizens of the United States, hence to all citizens of the states, hence to the state governments. The Fourteenth Amendment incorporated the First Amendment and imposed it on the states. Nor would he "assent" to the view that the First Amendment only prevented "previous restraints" on publications. They "constituted essential parts of every man's liberty."

As the war approached, Department of Justice lawyers begged Congress to pass an act that would punish "political agitation" that undermined, or might undermine (with discretion left to federal prosecutors to decide what actions fit that category), the "safety of the state." The safety of the state translated into support for the Wilson administration's war policies. The act was to be used against those who spread "disloyal propaganda." Some members of Congress, particularly Progressive senator William Borah, objected that too broad a statute would stifle all political speech. He was reassured that it would not by the author of the act, constitutional scholar and Harvard Law School professor Charles Warren. His draft originally included a censorship provision, but members of Congress rejected this, in part because the president was to be the censor.

The Espionage Act of 1917 and the Sedition Act of 1918 were wartime measures. They could not have been passed by Congress without the war, but they remained on the books after the war. In addition to spelling out the varieties of espionage, the first act had an omnibus section three, part of which read: "Whoever, when the United States is at war, shall wilfully make or convey false reports or false statements with intent to interfere with the operation or success of the military or naval forces of the United States or to promote the success of its enemies and whoever when the United States is at war, shall wilfully cause or attempt to cause insubordination, disloyalty, mutiny, refusal of duty, in the military or naval forces of the United States, or shall wilfully obstruct the recruiting or enlistment service of the United States, to the injury of the service or of the United States" was liable to prosecution, fine, imprisonment, and other penalties.

There was, in addition, a penalty for conspiracy to violate the act that was so broadly defined that it could include anyone who met with or agreed with someone who acted in furtherance of the conspiracy: "If two or more persons conspire to violate the provisions of section two or three of this title, and one or more of such persons does any act to effect the object of the conspiracy, each of the parties to such conspiracy shall be punished." The reach of the statute was longer and more powerful than the antilabor injunction in *Debs* and just as subject to whim, animus, and abuse.

Judge Learned Hand, of the federal district court for the southern district of New York, a brilliant, tough-minded, and realistic judge, heard the first case under this law. The federal government was prosecuting a radical magazine, *The Masses*, that openly opposed the war and accused the giant corporations of fostering it to make a profit out of the carnage. The "merchants of death" theme was hardly un-American, and the writers for the magazine, including leading literary talents like Sherwood Anderson, were not unpatriotic, but the message was all the more threatening to the Wilson administration for its persuasive elegance.

Hand found that the prosecution did not make its case because it misread the statute. Nothing he read in the magazine would "cause" Americans to refuse to fight, unless the statute intended to make all criticism of the government a crime. This surely was not what Congress had in mind, Hand reasoned. Such an interpretation "is so contrary to the use and wont of our people that only the clearest expression of such a power justifies the conclusion that it was intended." Words might be so remote from action, and protest meetings might be so peaceful in their conduct, that no intelligent man could see them as violating the law. Hand did not rely upon the First Amendment, but his reasoning provided a test for what might and might not be seen as "inciting" mischief under the Espionage Act.

The Court did not follow Hand's wise and prudent cue. The full bench of the second circuit reversed him, and the High Court adopted its own standard—then later, according to the author of that standard, misused it. The cases are *Schenk v. U.S.* (1919), *Debs v. U.S.* (1919), *Frohwerk v. U.S.* (1919), and *Abrams v. U.S.* (1919). They were all short decisions, for the applicable law seemed easy. Holmes wrote for a unanimous Court in the first three and then dissented in the fourth. There was no extended First Amendment analysis until Holmes revisited his own views.

Charles Schenk was the secretary general of the Socialist Party and oversaw the printing and mailing of circulars to men eligible for the draft. One circular urged that the men not report for the draft and declared the war illegal. It called for readers to petition the government against the Conscription Act. The First Amendment, read literally, explicitly sanctions petition, free speech, and free press. But the mailing violated the Espionage Act and was sent after the act was passed. Thus the case was a test of the constitutionality of the Espionage Act, not the Conscription Act.

By 1919, when the Court heard the appeal, the war was over and the issue might have been considered moot. Instead, Holmes, in part motivated by the government's rejection of his Blackstonian definition of the First Amendment, used the case to clarify his views. For him, the case was interesting as an intellectual vehicle. He was in no way at this time a civil libertarian: "It may well be that the prohibition of laws abridging the freedom of speech is not confined to previous restraints" (Holmes's position in *Patterson*). And "We admit that in many places and in ordinary times the defendants in saying all that was said in the circular would have been within their constitutional rights . . . [but] the character of every act depends upon the circumstances in which it is done. The most stringent protection of free speech would not protect a man in falsely shouting fire in a theater and causing a panic."

Holmes had replaced one Blackstonian tenet with another. Forced to drop no-prior-restraint, he offered up an "evil tendency" test in its place. The time and place of the speech determined whether it had an evil tendency. Darrow and others believed that it is at just such times, when political opposition to a war expressed in orderly speech may save a nation from its own immorality, that speech needs and deserves constitutional protection. In any case, it was unlikely that Schenk's circular would have had any impact on the draft. Holmes disagreed:

When a nation is at war many things that might be said in time of peace are such a hindrance to its effort that their utterance will not be endured so long as no Court could regard them as protected by any constitutional right. . . . The question in every case is whether the words used are used in such circumstances and are of such a nature as to create a clear and present danger that they will bring about the substantive evils that Congress has a right to prevent.

The Debs case was now easily disposed. Debs, a Socialist by this time, told a Canton, Ohio, audience that the war was illegal. He was indicted, tried, and convicted under the Espionage Act and sentenced to ten years in jail. Represented by Darrow, he appealed, resting his case squarely upon the First Amendment. Speech inciting riot, like libel and slander, Darrow conceded, is not protected by the amendment, but Debs was merely defending socialism and attacking capitalism, a political argument.

No riot followed Debs's talk. There was no "clear and present danger" to the nation or the war effort. But the tenor of the speech triggered Holmes's ire. In it "there followed personal experiences and illustrations of the growth of socialism, a glorification of minorities, and a prophecy of success." Notably in this supposed litany of evils was Holmes's reference to the "glorification of minorities." To be sure, Holmes need not have added any of this, for he opined that the case was wholly within the *Schenk* precedent, and the Court agreed.

Jacob Frohwerk was a copyeditor at a St. Louis, Missouri, German language newspaper, who prepared articles for publication that were critical of the country's entry into the war. What might not be mailed or said in public surely could not be printed in a newspaper, Holmes concluded. Frohwerk might not himself have written or printed the words, but he, and presumably everyone else at the newspaper, was part of a conspiracy, and the Espionage Act defined conspiracy loosely. Holmes relented a little, admitting that "it might be that all this might be said or written even in time of war in circumstances" that would not amount to a crime. "We do not lose our right to condemn either measures or men because the Country is at war." But even if Frohwerk was merely churning out what his publisher wanted, he was guilty under the act and subject to ten years at hard labor in a federal penitentiary.

Nothing in any of this explains Holmes's turnabout in *Abrams*, but turn about he did. Holmes never explained himself, but events and men were working on him. The Court had helped unleash a "Red Scare," an antiradical sweep inaugurated by Wilson's attorney general, A. Mitchell Palmer, after the war ended. Holmes's young protégé, Harvard Law School professor Felix Frankfurter, joined with Harvard Law School dean Roscoe Pound to document the evils of the Red Scare. Holmes himself found Palmer's campaign troubling. Leading intellectuals who were not socialists, men like John Dewey, were making the case for a broad reading of First Amendment liberties, and Holmes respected these men. Learned Hand was corresponding with Holmes, as were Harvard Law School professors like Zechariah Chafee and Ernst Freund. Freund's blast at the *Debs* decision was as powerful as Pound's blast at *Lochner*. Then there was Brandeis, a friend and ally on the Court, whose influence on Holmes was growing. Brandeis would join in the dissent, and the two men would dissent in every prosecution of a political speech case thereafter.

The five defendants in *Abrams v. U.S.*, all young anarchists born in Russia, had dropped leaflets in English and Yiddish in Manhattan from a Lower East Side window that criticized President Wilson's silence about the Allies' opposition to the Bolshevik Revolution. There was no clear and present danger to the country, but the majority, with Justice Clarke citing the three Holmes opinions, found that the leaflets violated the Espionage Act.

Without saying so, Clarke had reached into a far earlier period of English law than had Holmes. The English treason act of Edward III had a provision that any individual who fomented unrest or called the government into disrepute was "constructively" levying war against the crown. Clarke found that "the purpose of this [leaflet] obviously was to persuade the persons to whom it was addressed to turn a deaf ear to patriotic appeals in behalf of the government of the United States" and that was tantamount to a conspiracy to defeat the war effort.

By contrast, Holmes found that these leaflets "in no way attack the form of government of the United States," nor that the authors intended any such act. A strict reading of the Espionage Act must find real intent: "The principle of the right to free speech is always the same. It is only the present danger of immediate evil or an intent to bring it about that warrants Congress setting a limit to the expression of opinion." These were "silly" publications, and, in any case, political speech was privileged. "Congress certainly cannot forbid all effort to change the mind of the country." No act or call to action accompanied the opinions in the leaflets, and the Court was wrong to assume such calls to action.

If the creed of the anarchists was abhorrent to him, a "creed of ignorance and immaturity when honestly held," jail sentences for holding such opinions violated Holmes's faith in democracy. "Persecution for the expression of opinions seems to me perfectly logical." Those with power will want to "sweep away all opposition." But history—the history of a great democracy—offered a different lesson to Holmes:

When men have realized that time has upset many fighting faiths, they may come to believe even more than they believe the very foundations of their own conduct that the ultimate good desired is better reached by free trade in ideas—that the best test of truth is the power of the thought to get itself accepted in the competition of the market, and that truth is the only ground upon which their wishes safely can be carried out. That at any rate is the theory of our Constitution.

Nothing in the Constitution described such free markets of ideas (any more than the Constitution incorporated laissez-faire doctrines), but Holmes added this potent idea to the store of constitutional truths: The Constitution "is an experiment, as all life is an experiment. Every year if not every day we have to wager our salvation upon some prophecy based upon imperfect knowledge." This was a living constitution, one that grew and embraced larger truths and freedoms. It was a tolerant constitution and had room for many contradictory opinions. Brandeis concurred.

By the end of the decade, White's fading powers and refusal to step down irritated the man who had elevated him to the chief justiceship. Taft still hungered for the post himself. White obliged Taft in May 1921, dying from complications of a bladder operation. Taft, with his fellow Ohioan and Republican president Warren Harding's full support, was immediately nominated as chief justice.

It is difficult to assess White's legacy on the Court. Grudgingly, he had moved from a sectional to a national jurist. He had accepted reasonable legislative regulations and rejected the most obvious illegalities of Jim Crow. He was the last of the justices to have welcomed the prospect of a Confederate nation, honored the Klan's operations in Reconstruction, and wished for redemption of the South from meddling outsiders, do-gooders, and race mixers; and his passing was the passing of an age. But under his aegis, if not entirely with his enthusiasm, the Court had taken the first steps since Reconstruction toward one nation under law.

CHAPTER 9

The Taft Court, 1921–1930

President Woodrow Wilson hoped that the Treaty of Versailles ending World War I between the Allies and the Central Powers would bring lasting world peace. The Fourteen Points he had enunciated as the grounds for American entry into the war included the self-determination of peoples, and during his stay at Versailles to write the treaty, he helped turn the ruptured Austro-Hungarian Empire into a congeries of new and independent nations. But his subsequent efforts to get the United States into the League of Nations failed, leaving him broken and ill.

The nation, too, was beset. An influenza epidemic that began in the American heartland spread with the troops to Europe and then throughout the world, killing as many as sixty million people. Returning veterans found that their sacrifice was neither understood nor fully appreciated. They became a "lost generation." Writers and artists in this generation, including e. e. cummings, F. Scott Fitzgerald, Ernest Hemingway, and John Dos Passos, shared the sense that America had lost its way. Some found Europe more congenial, while others burrowed into imagined pasts. Europe was also more welcoming to black artists and musicians, though the notables of the "Harlem Renaissance," like Langston Hughes, Countee Cullen, and Claude McKay, turned the Upper Westside of Manhattan into an oasis of black arts.

African Americans had distinguished themselves in the American Expeditionary Force but found that racism still ruled in the United States. Returning from their stint abroad and seeking employment in northern cities, they were the victims of race riots. The Chicago race riot of 1919 lasted four days and left dozens dead and hundreds wounded. Other riots erupted in southern cities. In East St. Louis, Missouri, and Tulsa, Oklahoma, riots and arson destroyed entire black neighborhoods.

NOT QUITE "NORMALCY"

With Wilson ailing and the Democratic Party in tatters, newly elected Republican president Warren G. Harding and his successors, Calvin Coolidge and

Herbert Hoover, returned the nation to the politics of McKinley—high tariffs, low taxes, an aversion to public services, and windfalls for the business and investor classes. As the new chief justice, William Howard Taft, would write in one of his first opinions, "Business is a property right" entitled to all the protections of the federal Constitution. In the culture of the 1920s, the successful businessman was the epitome of Americanism, an advisor to presidents and judges. One best-selling book, Bruce Barton's *The Man Nobody Knows* (1925), even called Jesus history's foremost businessman. All this the Republicans celebrated as a "return to normalcy."

But nothing was normal. Runaway consumer purchasing, based on giant department stores in the cities and mail-order sales in the country, reached a peak. So did personal debt. The new science of consumer psychology fostered a new kind of advertising, and it turned the pages of glossy national magazines into come-ons. The buy-now, pay-later, credit mentality of these advertisements fit nicely into a stock market boom resting on margin purchases. Often the buyer put up no more than 10 percent of the value of the stock, further inflating an already-inflated market. Brilliant schemers like Carlo Ponzi conceived new kinds of "get rich" scams to con investors, and urban gangs fought turf wars to control illegal liquor and drug distribution.

Harding was a small town man, a former newspaper editor, and he yearned for what he believed were the true values of small town Americana. But the most admired man in the nation was not Harding but Henry Ford. Ford's mass-produced automobiles changed the face of America. Cheap and easy to run, Ford cars and their competitors enabled the rubber, machine tool, and steel industries to take up the slack of lost war contracts and spurred local and state road-paving projects. Detroit became the model of the new industrial city, and by the end of the decade, the number of cars, trucks, buses, and other gasoline vehicles on the roads neared twenty-seven million.

Though some called the 1920s the automobile age, there were other contenders for the title. Although movies were popular entertainment before the war, in the 1920s the industry moved from Long Island, New York, to Hollywood, California, and movie stars like Mary Pickford and Douglas Fairbanks became national icons. It was an age of sports heroes as well, as major sports went professional. New electronic technologies brought the sounds of radio into the home, and the number of stations jumped from thirty to six hundred during the decade. Radio personalities like Will Rogers, the cowboy humorist, became household names. Ten million Americans who had never before heard jazz could now enjoy it.

In the rural areas of the country, often without electrical power, indoor plumbing, or farm machinery, the 1920s wore a different aspect. Overproduction had driven agricultural prices so low that many family farmers and sharecroppers fell deeply into debt. Responding to the urbanization and industrialization of the nation that preceded the war, and the excesses of hedonism that followed it, many of these rural Americans became angry. Religious fundamentalism surged, aiming its guns at science and secularism. Under its influence, some states passed laws against the teaching of evolution. Rural and small town moral reformers reached back into the nineteenth century to demand an end to the sale of alcoholic spirits. Congress and state legislatures agreed—the Eighteenth Amendment banned the manufacture and sale of wine and beer. Prohibitionists convinced Congress to pass the Volstead Act, making violation of the amendment a federal felony, which clogged the federal courts dockets so badly that cases averaged two or three years before coming to trial.

TAFT'S RELIABLE MEN

No lawyer himself, Harding wanted men of experience, conservative tastes, and judicial temperament to fill vacancies on the Court. The one man he knew from their common Ohio roots who fit this bill was Taft. No man was better suited by experience or personal inclination to be chief justice than Taft. With amiability, firmness, and honesty, he had served his country as solicitor general (under Benjamin Harrison), federal appellate court judge, governor general of the Philippines, secretary of war (under Roosevelt), president (1909–1913), and diplomat.

He found time before he went to the Philippines in 1901 to act as dean of the Cincinnati School of Law (from 1897 to 1900). After he left the White House he taught at Yale Law School. Above all, he loved being a judge and yearned to be the chief justice of the Supreme Court. Physically imposing (he could have held his own with Miller, Swayne, or Clifford), an able manager and efficient executive, he demanded and returned loyalty, perhaps even playing favorites.

When Harding fulfilled Taft's often expressed "hope and ambition" by naming him chief justice, Taft inherited a Court that was very different from the one he had envisioned when he was president. Lurton and Lamar were gone. And the Court was still overwhelmed with unfinished business. Taft set about changing both of these situations. He arranged with Harding's attorney general, Ohio politician Harry Daugherty, to have a say in every federal judicial appointment and then lobbied for the men he wanted on the High Court. Most often, he got his way. He urged his colleagues to work as a team, show courtesy to one another, and not dissent. Following his own advice, Taft dissented in only 1.2 percent of the cases his Court heard.

Taft pressed Congress for a more efficient federal courts bureaucracy and got what he wanted. The 1922 Judicial Circuit Conferences Act enabled the High Court justices to work with the judicial circuits in reducing and managing appeals. In 1925, Congress, again at Taft's request, amended the Judiciary Act of 1789 to allow the High Court to select those cases it wanted to hear. Taft wanted the Court to deal with constitutional issues only, and henceforth the bulk of the Court's business would concern the Constitution. Finally, he pleaded with Congress for a Supreme Court building, with offices for each justice, a conference room and separate library, and a courtroom whose dignity would match the Court's own. Congress acceded to his wishes, and he threw himself into planning the new "marble palace."

Taft's impact on the Court's membership was immediately evident. On September 5, 1922, Harding asked Congress to confirm George Sutherland to the High Court, replacing Clarke, and the Senate obliged by a voice vote the next day. Like Taft, Harding chose men for the Court based on personal assessment. The English-born Utah politician had been Harding's close advisor during the campaign, a conservative whose views matched Harding's and Taft's own.

Though he had served in both houses of Congress, Sutherland had no love for legislative solutions to economic or social woes, nor for the supremacy of the federal government over the states. His reading of the Fourteenth Amendment's protection for private enterprise barred federal and state social and labor legislation. He found room in the Constitution to protect the right to fair trial and to oppose prior censorship. To his credit, he was a fine writer and clear thinker, and some of his opinions for the Court remain good law today. He retired in January 1938, as the Court and the country swung away from his economic views, and died in 1942.

Pierce Butler of Minnesota joined the Court in December 1922 when Day retired. Like Sutherland, Butler remained on the Court well into the 1930s—he died in office in 1939—and also like Sutherland, he joined McReynolds, Van Devanter, and the chief justice nearly 90 percent of the time. Thus he rarely found himself in dissent until the last two years of his tenure. Like the other conservatives, he voted to invalidate nearly twenty acts of Congress, a number exceeding all previous years' total.

Butler was a Democratic local politician and lawyer, with railroads as clients—much like Brewer. Taft knew his work and respected it and prodded

Harding to name Butler as Day's replacement. Butler was a Democrat and a Roman Catholic, but his conservative views mollified the conservative Republicans. His nomination did run into some trouble in the Senate from progressives, who knew how conservative he was, and from labor advocates. A capable lawyer, but not especially gifted as a jurist, he left little mark on the law.

Edward Sanford was the last of Harding's nominees, replacing Mahlon Pitney in January 1923. Like Butler, Sanford had a local career rather than a national one and little reputation as a jurist or legal scholar. After graduation from Harvard Law School, he had returned to his native Tennessee to practice. In 1908, he was named to the federal district court, and Taft personally selected him for the High Court. Unlike Butler, Sanford believed that some federal regulation of business was necessary—particularly in antitrust matters. He applied this theory to labor unions, however, narrowing the meaning of the Clayton Antitrust Act of 1914. Sanford was more liberal in protecting the rights of religious and racial minorities, immigrants, and laborers, and he was sensitive to First Amendment claims. He died in 1930, leaving behind indications that he might have joined a new kind of majority, more concerned with individual rights than property rights.

The last of the Taft Court appointees was Harlan Fiske Stone, named in 1925 by Calvin Coolidge to replace McKenna. McKenna, addled and exhausted, left only after Taft pressured him, much as Field had left because of peer pressure. Stone was a New Hampshire man, granitelike in his probity, intellectually inquisitive (he was a professor and then dean of Columbia Law School), and capable of great warmth and friendship (Coolidge had been his classmate at Amherst). On the Court, he demonstrated time and again that he could hold his own with any of his brethren, sometimes driving Taft to distraction. Expected to be as conservative as his predecessor, Stone would instead join with Brandeis, Sanford, and Holmes to form a liberal minority on the Court. His opinions would become the bedrock of a new kind of substantive due process, based not on property but on democratic empowerment.

LOOKING BACKWARD

But Stone, along with Brandeis and Holmes and occasionally Clarke and Sanford, could not prevent the majority from reimposing the rules in *Lochner* and *E. C. Knight*, and even the minority opinion in *Munn*. It began with the Court's majority reading of the fact-finding powers of the Federal Trade Commission. The FTC was created in 1914, in the heyday of progressive agency formation, and its charter included the power to prohibit "unfair or deceptive acts or practices in commerce." Like the language of the antitrust acts, the enabling legislation could be loosely or strictly interpreted by the commission's members. Mindful of the Court's concerns about the reach and reasonableness of the antitrust acts and the rule in *Munn*, Congress limited the FTC to practices affecting interstate commerce having some impact on the public good. The FTC was an information-gathering agency only—it could not punish violators but it could seek civil penalties in federal court. To conform to the High Court's curbs on the Food and Drug Administration (FDA), the commission had to hold full and fair hearings.

In addition to these self-imposed limitations on the FTC's discretion, in *Federal Trade Commission v. Curtis Publishing Company* (1923) the Court announced that every commission finding of fact was subject to court review, and that additional evidence might be produced in court. The practical impact was that a well-financed corporation might entangle the agency in years of back-and-forth hearings and court proceedings, effectively hamstringing any action. Trying to put some of the toothpaste back into the tube, Taft and Brandeis concurred with the holding but agreed that "if it clearly appears that there is no substantial evidence to support additional findings necessary to justify the order of the Commission complained of, the court need not remand the case for further findings."

As Taft hinted in *Curtis*, the majority of the Court had come to accept the legitimate power of the federal government in certain areas of commerce, whether inter- or intrastate. Taft in particular thought that the federal government, through congressional enactments, might regulate commerce as if there were no states. Taft envisioned a national marketplace, tied together by railroads, communications, and grants-in-aid to promote local programs. The idea was as old as Alexander Hamilton's concepts of bounties to industry and Henry Clay's American Plan for internal improvements.

The Court entertained Taft's notion in *Massachusetts v. Mellon* (1923). The state challenged a federal program to aid infant and maternity care under the Sheppard-Townes Act. Justice Sutherland, writing for all the members of the Court, disposed of the challenge by announcing that the Court lacked jurisdiction. Congress could impose on the taxpayers of the United States expenditures for programs that might go only to a few states (not every state had to accept the grants for the program). The precedent would have wide application after the Civil Rights Act of 1964, when states accepted federal grant money for higher education, for example.

The decision reflected a compromise on the Court. Taft's considerable powers of persuasion levied against Butler's and Van Devanter's concern for states' rights. McReynolds, whose personal morality included a tender place for children, may have found the purpose of the act laudable enough to ignore its centralizing tendency. *Mellon* rested on a loose reading of the constitutional powers of Congress, but that reading cut both ways—for it gave to the federal courts the authority to strike down state laws without having to rely on the Fourteenth Amendment.

At the same time, the Taft Court majority adopted a robust reading of the Fourteenth Amendment's protection of private property rights against government intervention. Indeed, the 1920s were the heyday of substantive due process jurisprudence. In case after case, Taft, joined by Van Devanter, McReynolds, Sutherland, and Butler, upheld the rights of employers and businesses to carry on without the burdens of wage, hour, or safety regulations.

The conservatives' suspicions of labor unions and insistence that all employer-employee relations reflect bargaining among equals led to a tortured reading of the Clayton Act to reimpose the antilabor injunction. In *Duplex Printing Press Company v. Deering* (1921), Justice Pitney, a sworn enemy to all unions, explained that a secondary boycott was an illegal action, and even if in support of an otherwise legal strike, the boycott could still be enjoined as a restraint of trade under the Sherman Antitrust Act. Thus the first antitrust act was used to undermine the clear purpose of the second antitrust act.

When coal miners struck southern mines during a union drive, the Court in the *Coronado Coal Company Cases* (1925) announced that, although coal mining might be local, the union had interfered with interstate commerce, and thus the Sherman Act applied to the union. The violent acts of the union organizers meant that the Clayton Act provisions against the injunction did not apply. Here *E. C. Knight* and *Debs* came together to facilitate the injunctive relief to the mine owners. Even in a purely local strike on a company, as in *Bedford Cut Stone Company v. Journeyman Cutters Association* (1927), the cutters union could be brought under the Sherman Act's provisions by calling their actions a restraint of interstate trade. Plainly, the majority of the Court simply refused to accept Congress's power to limit injunctive relief to employers against unions. States could not pass laws limiting antilabor injunctions or legalizing strikes that interfered with businessmen's profits if the business involved interstate commerce.

Brandeis dissented in *Deering* and was joined by Holmes and Clarke. Brandeis opined that the Clayton Act's provision on antilabor injunctions "was the fruit of unceasing agitation, which extended over more than twenty years and was designed to equalize before the law the position of workingmen and employer as industrial combatants." Congress leveled the playing field, letting the market instead of the Courts or the violence of one side or the other decide the issue. But in *Deering*, "due largely to environment, the social and economic ideas of judges, which thus became translated into law, were prejudicial to a position of equality between workingman and employer." Brandeis lectured the majority that "instead of leaving judges to determine according to their own economic and social views whether the damage inflicted on an employer in an industrial struggle" justified the injunction, Congress instructed the courts not to issue injunctions unless the unions violated some other law. Congress said nothing about the illegality of boycotts. The Court should not add that language.

In *Bedford*, Brandeis alone dissented. He marshaled facts, cited empirical studies, repeated learned treatises, and pleaded for the underdog: "If, in the struggle for existence, individual workingmen may, under any circumstances, co-operate in this way for self-protection even though the interstate trade of another is thereby restrained, the lower courts were clearly right in denying the injunction sought by plaintiffs." The other aspect of the *Coronado Coal Company Cases* did not apply, because "the manner in which these individual stonecutters exercised their asserted right to perform their union duty by refusing to finish stone . . . was confessedly legal. They were innocent alike of trespass and of breach of contract. They did not picket. They refrained from violence, intimidation, fraud and threats."

Taft and the majority rolled back the concept of "affected with a public interest," used as a rule of thumb to review state regulations, so that *Munn* might never have existed. In the contest of the rejuvenated economic substantive due process versus the notion of reasonable regulation, the Court split, with the conservatives winning every battle. The first of these cases was *Wolff Packing Company v. Court of Industrial Relations* (1923), a Kansas appeal. In 1920, the state's legislature had passed an act defining for its own courts the term "affected with a public interest": "First, manufacture and preparation of food for human consumption; second, manufacture of clothing for human wear; third, production of any substance in common use for fuel; fourth, transportation of the foregoing; fifth, public utilities and common carriers." Wolff, faced with an order to raise wages at the company under the state law, appealed to the U.S. Supreme Court on Fourteenth Amendment due process grounds.

Taft wrote that the act "curtails the right of the employer on the one hand, and of the employee on the other, to contract about his affairs. This is part of the liberty of the individual protected by the guaranty of the due process clause of the Fourteenth Amendment." For Taft, as for Fuller, the key question was not just what a law did, but how that law was to be interpreted: "The mere declaration by a legislature that a business is affected with a public interest is not conclusive of the question whether its attempted regulation on that ground is justified. The circumstances of its alleged change from the status of a private business and its freedom from regulation into one in which the public have come to have an interest are always a subject of judicial inquiry."

Taft's claiming for the Court finality in matters of constitutional interpretation went back to Marshall's opinions in *Marbury* and *McCulloch*. Taft felt confident of his history on this occasion, having been bombarded with recitations on history by Brandeis in prior cases: "It has never been supposed, since the adoption of the Constitution, that the business of the butcher, or the baker, the tailor, the wood chopper, the mining operator or the miner was clothed with such a public interest that the price of his product or his wages could be fixed by State regulation." The state could regulate the slaughterhouses, inspect the meat, and ensure that the premises were clean, but not set wages. It could regulate common carriers and their appurtenances (rails and inns, for example), public utilities, and monopolies, but nothing else.

But even Taft balked in the most notorious case of substantive due process in his tenure, *Adkins v. Children's Hospital* (1923), though it fit the substantive due process rubric. Felix Frankfurter, counsel for the District of Columbia, explained to the Court how Congress set minimum wages for women working in the District: The "Senate and House Committees held hearings on the needs of this legislation, in view of the conditions prevailing in the District. No one appeared to oppose the bill. An organized body of employers endorsed the bill and urged its passage. The Committees unanimously recommended the legislation." The result, minimum wages for women working in public jobs, "was to provide for the deficit between the cost of women's labor, i.e., the means necessary to keep labor going—and any rate of women's pay below the minimum level for living, and thereby to eliminate all the evils attendant upon such deficit upon a large scale. There is no dispute that Congress was acting in good faith, after mature deliberation." In short, Congress was acting in a reasonable manner in an area in which it was constitutionally empowered.

Counsel for the hospital replied to facts with law, just as Olney had to Darrow in *Debs*: "The Minimum Wage Law of the District of Columbia is unconstitutional because it is a price-fixing law, directly interfering with freedom of contract, which is a part of the liberty of the citizen guaranteed in the Fifth Amendment, and no exercise of the police power justifies the fixing of prices either of property or of services in a private business, not affected with a public interest, and as a permanent measure." Justice Sutherland agreed, as did Justices Butler, Van Devanter, McReynolds, and Day: "There is, of course, no such thing as absolute freedom of contract. It is subject to a great variety of restraints. But freedom of contract is, nevertheless, the general rule and restraint the exception; and the exercise of legislative authority to abridge it can be justified only by the existence of exceptional circumstances."

The *Muller* precedent that women were deserving of special protection fell because "the ancient inequality of the sexes, otherwise than physical, as suggested in the Muller Case has continued 'with diminishing intensity.' In view of the great—not to say revolutionary—changes which have taken place since that utterance, in the contractual, political and civil status of women, culminating in the Nineteenth Amendment, it is not unreasonable to say that these differences have now come almost, if not quite, to the vanishing point." Sutherland was no more advocating the legal equality of women than Brewer was advocating labor unionism in *Debs*. This was faint praise for *Muller*'s logic, and it did not persuade the chief justice.

Taft, writing for himself, Sanford, and Holmes, dissented. Taft's defense of the statute lay in the same Victorian, paternalistic values as the unanimous Court had expressed in *Muller*. Women "are not upon a full level of equality of choice with their employer and in their necessitous circumstances are prone to accept pretty much anything that is offered. They are peculiarly subject to the overreaching of the harsh and greedy employer." Congress had protected women just as had Oregon, and the Court should not interfere. "If it be said that long hours of labor have a more direct effect upon the health of the employee than the low wage, there is very respectable authority from close observers, disclosed in the record and in the literature on the subject quoted at length in the briefs, that they are equally harmful in this regard. Congress took this view and we can not say it was not warranted in so doing."

Holmes wrote his own short dissent. He had dissented in *Lochner* and rightly saw this case as a reprise of that one: "The earlier decisions upon the same words in the Fourteenth Amendment began within our memory and went no farther than an unpretentious assertion of the liberty to follow the ordinary callings. Later that innocuous generality was expanded into the dogma, Liberty of Contract." The Court should defer to the legislative branch and the expertise of the witnesses at the congressional hearings: "When so many intelligent persons, who have studied the matter more than any of us can, have thought that the means are effective and are worth the price, it seems to me impossible to deny that the belief reasonably may be held by reasonable men."

INCORPORATION OF THE BILL OF RIGHTS

The notion that the Fourteenth Amendment might impose certain portions of the Bill of Rights on the states was not new by the time that Taft occupied the center chair. Harlan had wanted it and Holmes had mentioned it in *Patterson*—and now Brandeis's dissent in *Gilbert v. Minnesota* (1920) openly argued for it. The majority opined that a state law criminalizing "teaching or advocating by printed matter, writing or word of mouth, that men should not enlist in the military or naval forces of the United States" was punishable by fines and jail time. Brandeis responded that "the prohibition is made to apply whatever the motive, the intention, or the purpose of him who teaches. It applies alike to the preacher in the pulpit, the professor at the university, the speaker at a political meeting, the lecturer at a society or club gathering." The law was vague and overly broad. "Young men considering whether they should enter these services as a means of earning a livelihood or as a career, may not be told that, in the opinion of the speaker, they can serve their country and themselves better by entering the civil service of State or Nation, or by studying for one of the professions."

In defense of its law, counsel for the state argued that "the guaranty against abridging freedom of speech contained in the First Amendment of the Federal Constitution applies only to federal action." Brandeis answered: "The matter is not one merely of state concern. The state law affects . . . rights, privileges and immunities of one who is a citizen of the United States; and it deprives him of an important part of his liberty." If the Due Process Clause of the Fourteenth Amendment applied to the states' economic regulations, it applied to the states' regulation of free speech: "I cannot believe that the liberty guaranteed by the Fourteenth Amendment includes only liberty to acquire and to enjoy property."

Renewed examination of incorporation doctrine arrived from an unlikely source—Justice McReynolds. McReynolds did not follow Brandeis's lead (McReynolds would not even shake Brandeis's hand, as was customary at the conference), but McReynolds applied the Fourteenth Amendment to what amounted to state suppression of free speech in *Meyer v. Nebraska* (1923) and to freedom of worship in *Society of Sisters v. Pierce* (1925). In *Meyer*, the state forbade the teaching of German in elementary schools. A German language teacher sued. McReynolds saw the right of the teacher to ply his trade as a property right guaranteed by the Due Process Clause, similar in one sense to *Lochner*: "Mere knowledge of the German language cannot reasonably be regarded as harmful. Heretofore it has been commonly looked upon as helpful

and desirable. Plaintiff in error taught this language in school as part of his occupation. His right thus to teach and the right of parents to engage him so to
instruct their children, we think, are within the liberty of the Amendment."

So far, no news. But McReynolds continued that the Due Process Clause "without doubt . . . denotes not merely freedom from bodily restraint but also the right
of the individual to contract, to engage in any of the common occupations of life,
to acquire useful knowledge, to marry, establish a home and bring up children, to
worship God according to the dictates of his own conscience." Among these
rights was speaking one's native language: "The individual has certain fundamental rights which must be respected. The protection of the Constitution
extends to all, to those who speak other languages as well as to those born with
English on the tongue." McReynolds verged on saying that the right to speak a
foreign language was protected by the First Amendment. He did not complete
this chain of reasoning, but it was the foundation of his argument.

It applied in *Pierce* as well. The state's public school law as amended in
1922 required "every parent, guardian or other person having control of a child
between the ages of eight and sixteen years to send him to the public school in
the district where he resides." No child might be sent to a parochial school, in
effect outlawing Catholic schools. Behind the new law was a Klan attack on the
Catholic Church, to which the legislature had capitulated. The Society of Sisters,
a Roman Catholic orphanage and school, sued. The legislature argued that the
new law would lower crime rates and dissipate any religious animosity among
children, but McReynolds judged that "under the doctrine of *Meyer v. Nebraska* . . . we think it entirely plain that the Act of 1922 unreasonably interferes
with the liberty of parents and guardians to direct the upbringing and education of children under their control. As often heretofore pointed out, rights
guaranteed by the Constitution may not be abridged by legislation which has
no reasonable relation to some purpose within the competency of the State."

McReynolds relied upon a version of the rational-relation test developed
in *Lochner* to weigh the Oregon law against the federal Constitution. A state
law had to have a rational relation to a public good to pass muster in a First
Amendment challenge. McReynolds pulled the case into the orbit of *Lochner*:
"Plaintiffs asked protection against arbitrary, unreasonable and unlawful interference with their patrons and the consequent destruction of their business
and property."

But again the hidden issue was whether the Free Exercise Clause of the First
Amendment applied to the states. As counsel for the Society of Sisters argued,
"The statute in suit trespasses, not only upon the liberty of the parents indi-
vidually, but upon their liberty collectively as well. It forbids them, as a body,

to support private and parochial schools and thus give to their children such education and religious training as the parents may see fit." Reynolds's formulation of the rights of the parochial schools did move the Court a step closer to Brandeis's more global and more compelling definition of personal rights. Equally important, the entire Court subscribed to his opinion.

A door was now opened for other claims for incorporation of basic rights. The Taft Court did not allow other plaintiffs to pass through that door, but in subsequent cases, individual justices peered through the opening. The first of these cases was *Gitlow v. New York* (1925), and the issue was squarely free speech. New York State passed a "criminal anarchy" law "punishing those who advocate, advise or teach the duty, necessity or propriety of overthrowing or overturning organized government by force, violence, or any unlawful means, or who print, publish, or knowingly circulate any book, paper, etc., advocating, advising or teaching the doctrine that organized government should be so overthrown." Benjamin Gitlow and others from the "Left Wing Section" of the Socialist Party distributed a pamphlet that the state prosecutors decided violated the law.

Justice Sanford's opinion for the majority quoted large blocks of the manifesto, whose language was inflammatory and, in retrospect, absurd: "'The old order is in decay. Civilization is in collapse. The proletarian revolution and the Communist reconstruction of society—the struggle for these—is now indispensable. This is the message of the Communist International to the workers of the world. The Communist International calls the proletariat of the world to the final struggle!'" But the Bolshevik Revolution in Russia and the beginnings of the Soviet Union were not absurd, and Gitlow's rallying cry hinted that general strikes and other forms of direct action in the United States would bring about a similar upheaval to that in Russia. Gitlow's counsel argued that the statements were meant as factual rather than hortatory, or in the alternative, mere advocacy of one system over another, and that the defendant did not do anything in furtherance of the revolution, other than publish and speak.

Sanford found that the purpose of the manifesto was immediate and violent action, bringing it under the New York statute, and that the statute did not penalize mere speech, but only speech that had the evil tendency of promoting armed insurrection. But Sanford, who sometimes voted with Brandeis and Holmes in dissent, went on to state that "for present purposes we may and do assume that freedom of speech and of the press—which are protected by the First Amendment from abridgment by Congress—are among the fundamental personal rights and 'liberties' protected by the due process clause of the Fourteenth Amendment from impairment by the States."

Gitlow stayed in jail, however, even though there was no evidence that anything had come of his fulminations. Sanford applied the *Meyer* rational-relation test to the New York law and found that "we cannot hold that the present statute is an arbitrary or unreasonable exercise of the police power of the State unwarrantably infringing the freedom of speech or press; and we must and do sustain its constitutionality." Holmes and Brandeis dissented, preferring the clear and present danger test that Holmes had developed and concluding that "it is manifest that there was no present danger of an attempt to overthrow the government by force on the part of the admittedly small minority who shared the defendant's views."

In California, the Criminal Syndicalism Act of 1919, passed at the height of the Red Scare, made the New York law seem tame. California prohibited belonging to an organization that advocated the violent overthrow of the United States government. More than 250 individuals were prosecuted between 1919 and 1924, the first of whom was Anita Whitney. She had attended an organizational meeting of the Communist Labor Party and wrote the platform for the party. Other than that, she had done nothing to further revolution—writing no pamphlets, handing out no manifestos, marching in no parades, and setting fire to nothing. But she had done enough to violate the law, the California courts concluded.

Sanford was convinced that the High Court could hear the case, because the equal protection and due process questions were raised by Whitney's counsel and denied in the California Supreme Court hearing. But in *Whitney v. California* (1927), Sanford found that the matter was simply a police regulation, reasonable on its face to preserve law and order: "It is settled by repeated decisions of this Court that the equal protection clause does not take from a State the power to classify in the adoption of police laws, but admits of the exercise of a wide scope of discretion, and avoids what is done only when it is without any reasonable basis and therefore is purely arbitrary."

The California law did not violate the First Amendment because "freedom of speech which is secured by the Constitution does not confer an absolute right to speak, without responsibility, whatever one may choose, or an unrestricted and unbridled license giving immunity for every possible use of language, . . . and . . . a State in the exercise of its police power may punish those who abuse this freedom by utterances inimical to the public welfare, tending to incite to crime, disturb the public peace, or endanger the foundations of organized government and threaten its overthrow by unlawful means."

But where was the clear and present danger? Brandeis concurred in the result, but did not care for Sanford's reasoning: "The novelty in the prohibition introduced is that the statute aims, not at the practice of criminal syndicalism, nor even directly at the preaching of it, but at association with those who propose to preach it." The First Amendment right to peaceably assemble might well have shielded Whitney and others who attended a conference, so long as what was said or agreed to there did not pose an immediate threat to public safety. "To justify suppression of free speech there must be reasonable ground to fear that serious evil will result if free speech is practiced. There must be reasonable ground to believe that the danger apprehended is imminent"—the clear and present danger test. After all, "the fundamental personal rights of free speech and assembly" were privileged and should not be easily set aside.

Brandeis also returned to Holmes's notion of a free marketplace of ideas in *Abrams* to exculpate Whitney: "Those who won our independence believed that the final end of the State was to make men free to develop their faculties. ... They believed that freedom to think as you will and to speak as you think are means indispensable to the discovery and spread of political truth." Then he went beyond Holmes to argue that "to courageous, self-reliant men, with confidence in the power of free and fearless reasoning applied through the processes of popular government, no danger flowing from speech can be deemed clear and present, unless the incidence of the evil apprehended is so imminent that it may befall before there is opportunity for full discussion." Holmes signed on to Brandeis's concurrence.

Buck v. Bell (1927), a bad decision based on poor and hasty reasoning, showed that incorporation had its limits, even for the dissenters in *Gitlow* and *Whitney*. The most basic of human rights is the right to have a family, decide whether or not to have children, and rear the children in the family. So said McReynolds in *Meyer*. But the popular pseudoscience of "eugenics" posed another theory entirely of who should be allowed to procreate. The English founder of the eugenics movement, Francis Galton, a geologist and statistician of note, called for improvement of the human species by selective breeding but did not argue for forced sterilization of any group. Nevertheless, his somewhat naive and even hopeful faith in voluntary breeding programs among the "ruling races," widely shared by the beginning of the twentieth century among upper-class intellectuals in Europe and the United States, appealed as well to those who feared the spread of supposedly inferior races and the reproduction of "dysgenic" traits among individuals. These advocates of genetic engineering saw birth control methods as a way of ensuring that the Anglo-Saxon "ruling race" and its "good blood" would not be corrupted by African, Asian, or inferior European strains.

In 1907, Indiana introduced the first law for the sterilization of habitual criminals, because criminal conduct was supposedly genetic. By 1917, fourteen more states had passed such laws. Included among the "defectives" scheduled for neutering were epileptics, mentally ill persons, and persons who scored low on the newly introduced IQ tests. The assumption behind the program was that such traits were inheritable. In 1924, Virginia passed a "model" statute in which asylum inmates to be sterilized were entitled to a hearing and an appeal to the state's supreme court.

Albert S. Priddy, the superintendent of the state Colony for the Feeble-minded, was not only an advocate of the new law and of eugenics—he even promoted an aggressive program of institutionalizing the mentally ill and the feebleminded so that they could be sterilized. Young Carrie Buck entered his unkind care when she was committed by her foster father. In fact, she had been raped by a relative of her foster father, and the foster father knew that incarceration would prevent her from making an accusation. Tested for intelligence and found at the same low end of the scale as her natural mother, it was assumed that her newborn was also subpar after a visiting nurse announced that the infant had a peculiar "look" about her. (In fact, none of these tests, and the assumptions that followed from them, were accurate. Carrie and her daughter were of above-average intelligence.) But Priddy sought and gained an order to sterilize Carrie Buck, which the state courts approved. With the connivance of the state authorities and her counsel, the case went to the High Court.

Counsel for Buck laid her case squarely on the Fourteenth Amendment and implied that somewhere in the Bill of Rights the right to start a family and have children must exist. "The salpingectomy, as provided for in the Act of Assembly, is illegal in that it violates her constitutional right of bodily integrity and is therefore repugnant to the due process of law clause of the Fourteenth Amendment." The same invasion of the body was not required for criminals of other kinds, or for people of average intelligence. "The Act denies to the plaintiff and other inmates of the state colony for epileptics and feeble minded the equal protection of the laws guaranteed by the Fourteenth Amendment." The Due Process Clause argument had already won success in *Meyer* and *Pierce*. The Equal Protection Clause argument was one of the first of its kind and would prove even more potent in years to come.

The state's attorney general relied on the rational-relation test: "The State may and does confine the feeble minded, thus depriving them of their liberty. When so confined they are by segregation prohibited from procreation—a further deprivation of liberty that goes unquestioned. The appellant is under the Virginia statutes already by law prohibited from procreation." If Virginia's defense of its sterilization laws bore more than a passing resemblance to Alabama's defense of its peonage laws, that resemblance was not coincidental. Both states had adopted sterilization laws and both states had strict segregation laws.

Holmes wrote for seven of his brethren:

We have seen more than once that the public welfare may call upon the best citizens for their lives. It would be strange if it could not call upon those who already sap the strength of the State for these lesser sacrifices, often not felt to be such by those concerned, in order to prevent our being swamped with incompetence. It is better for all the world, if instead of waiting to execute degenerate offspring for crime, or to let them starve for their imbecility, society can prevent those who are manifestly unfit from continuing their kind.

Race culling was a public good to which the statute had a rational relationship: "Three generations of imbeciles are enough." Virginia responded to the High Court's opinion by sterilizing Carrie Buck and, for good measure, her sister.

Holmes was deferring to the state legislature, as he had in *Giles*. He had dissented in *Meyer*. He brushed aside the constitutional question of equal protection. Butler dissented without an opinion. A devout Roman Catholic, he knew that the church had set its face resolutely against eugenics and sterilization. Holmes privately assumed that that was the reason for Butler's dissent. Brandeis and Stone silently concurred in Holmes's opinion.

The next year Brandeis wrote a ringing defense of a constitutional right of privacy exceeding even Bradley's in *Boyd*. Read closely, it appears to be completely at odds with his willingness to let a surgeon remove Carrie Buck's fallopian tubes. In *Olmstead v. U.S.*, Brandeis waxed eloquent in opposition to a warrantless tapping of telephone conversations. The framers "conferred, as against the Government, the right to be let alone—the most comprehensive of rights and the right most valued by civilized men. To protect that right, every unjustifiable intrusion by the Government upon the privacy of the individual, whatever the means employed, must be deemed a violation of the Fourth Amendment." Stone, Holmes, and Butler agreed.

THE AMERICAN DILEMMA CONTINUES

The Taft Court stance on civil rights was similar to the White Court's; indeed, it continued the slow movement toward protection of black voting rights and the unwillingness to touch segregation. In *Nixon v. Herndon* (1927), the NAACP joined with local counsel to strike down a Texas law providing for an all-white

Democratic Party primary. The state replied in its own defense: "Because the Democratic party holds a nominating primary, can it be contended that outsiders can be forced upon the party over its expressed dissent? If the party should abandon the primary and go back to the convention or the caucus system, could it be consistently maintained that the courts could force upon the convention or upon the caucus, the plaintiff in error?"

Holmes wrote for the majority. Although he had found the Alabama peonage law unexceptionable, he rejected the white primary: "We find it unnecessary to consider the Fifteenth Amendment, because it seems to us hard to imagine a more direct and obvious infringement of the Fourteenth. That Amendment, while it applies to all, was passed, as we know, with a special intent to protect the blacks from discrimination against them." Would not the same reasoning have applied to the peonage laws that Holmes had found unobjectionable? Here was the difference: "The statute of Texas . . . forbid negroes to take part in a primary election the importance of which we have indicated, discriminating against them by the distinction of color alone." Alabama peonage laws said nothing about color or race—though, in fact, they were passed and enforced on the basis of race.

In *Gong Lum v. Rice* (1927), racial discrimination was as obvious as it was in *Nixon*. Mississippi law segregated schools on the basis of white and nonwhite, a policy that a Chinese family challenged. The petitioners slyly explained why segregation was imposed: "The basic assumption is that if the children of two races associate daily in the school room the two races will at last intermix; that the purity of each is jeopardized by the mingling of the children in the school room; that such association among children means social intercourse and social equality." This they found to be unfair to the Chinese, for if exposure to blacks was bad for whites, it was bad for all other races. "The white race creates for itself a privilege that it denies to other races; exposes the children of other races to risks and dangers to which it would not expose its own children. This is discrimination." Apparently, racial prejudice was not a vice confined to any one race.

Although Martha Lum was "pure Chinese," whatever that might mean, and not "colored" in her parents' minds, the state's highest court ruled that "the [state] Constitution divided the educable children into those of the pure white or Caucasian race, on the one hand, and the brown, yellow and black races, on the other, and therefore that Martha Lum of the Mongolian or yellow race could not insist on being classed with the whites under this constitutional division." This finding resembled the Alabama Supreme Court's decision in the *Peonage Cases*—the law mandating segregation in schools did not violate the

Equal Protection Clause of the Fourteenth Amendment because the law was based on the state constitution.

Taft wrote for the majority:

> We must assume then that there are school districts for colored children in Bolivar County, but that no colored school is within the limits of the Rosedale Consolidated High School District. This is not inconsistent with there being, at a place outside of that district and in a different district, a colored school which the plaintiff Martha Lum, may conveniently attend. If so, she is not denied, under the existing school system, the right to attend and enjoy the privileges of a common school education in a colored school.

Brandeis, Stone, and Holmes were silent, though Harlan's dissents in the *Civil Rights Cases* and *Plessy* might have been resuscitated and put to use. Harlan had lived through Reconstruction and saw the failing light of its idealism, but then, so had Holmes, and Holmes had referred to that idealism in *Nixon*. Brandeis privately supported the newly formed NAACP and he was no racist. Perhaps he had concluded that the Court had no way to force Mississippi to obey, the same conclusion Holmes had reached in *Giles*.

THE DISSENTERS

Every Court has had its dissenters and dissents. Many of these dissents have become law in the fullness of time and others remain shining examples of courage. Justices like Harlan became famous as dissenters. In the Taft Court, almost 90 percent of the decisions were unanimous, and Taft worked hard to improve that rate, pleading with potential no-votes to come over and pressing the authors of majority opinions to modify their writing to accommodate the concerns of potential dissenters. But Taft's best efforts could not prevent Brandeis, Holmes, and Stone from becoming a block of dissenters, just as Taft, along with Sanford, Van Devanter, Butler, Sutherland, and McReynolds voted as a block.

The three did not always dissent. They joined or concurred in *Buck, Gong Lum, Whitney,* and other contentious cases. Brandeis dissented, on average, about 6.5 percent of the time, Stone, about 5 percent of the time, and Holmes, about 4.5 percent of the time. By contrast, Butler, Sutherland, Van Devanter, and Taft dissented in less than 2 percent of the cases in which they took part. Compared to the Burger and Rehnquist Courts, in which 5 to-4 and 6-to-3 splits were normal, this cleavage was mild indeed.

When one of the three dissented, the others could usually be found in dissent as well. They gave one another comfort in their astonishment that the majority of the Court could set aside so many state and federal enactments on such shoddy legal grounds. Stone could be persuaded to join with the majority. He was, after all, a conservative at heart, but his head told him that Brandeis and Holmes were right, and more and more he resented the condescension and the insistence of Taft's prodding. By the end of Taft's tenure, Stone was firmly in the camp of the liberals.

Stone had moved toward progressive Republicanism. There he found Herbert Hoover, a longtime friend, waiting with an offer to be acting chief justice in place of the ailing Taft. Taft opposed the nomination. Stone had disappointed him. Taft preferred Van Devanter and told Hoover that Stone would be "a great mistake. . . . he is not a leader." But when Stone's mind was made up, it did not come unmade—something very much like Taft's that Taft never admitted.

Brandeis was a progressive, too, a democrat with both a small and a capital D who favored labor and social justice causes. He believed in civil liberties in a profound way, weighing the rights to speech and worship against the commands of the state and finding the former more important, even in wartime. He opposed bigness, seeing it as a corrupting influence even when the intent was efficiency and productivity. He believed in the power of facts, even though he sat on an appellate court whose formal adherence to old legal doctrines ignored obvious facts. He was an educator on the Court as he was before his elevation—adding footnotes to research studies and scholarship to his opinions. He told his confidant and helpmate Felix Frankfurter, in 1928, that a good Court used oral argument to get at legal issues, used the judicial conference to air views, distributed and discussed draft majority and minority opinions to fully air disagreements, limited the number of cases it heard so that it could give due diligence to those it decided, and took account of public opinion. In all these ways, his jurisprudence, his style of judging, and many of his substantive views would become the standard for justices in the future.

Holmes was not a liberal by inclination but had found a niche as the intellectual voice of realistic jurisprudence, and this included the Harvard Law School's idea of deferring to popularly elected legislatures, listening to expert findings, and weighing the consequences of decisions. Taft, who revered Holmes, blamed Holmes's dissents on Brandeis, in one sense a fair statement, since the two men had become both intellectual and social companions. Frankfurter, too, influenced Holmes, as did other visitors, friends, and correspondents like Harold Laski, an English leftist, and Benjamin Cardozo, chief judge of the New York Court of Appeals. Holmes remained a Republican, but his aloofness from ordinary politics and his adherence to a code of honor by then lost in all but yellowing Civil War letterbooks estranged him from the increasingly fierce partisanship of the conservatives.

THE COURT CONFRONTS THE DEPRESSION

Although the majority of the Court's views on the economy and labor may have seemed reasonable during the boom times of the 1920s, the arrival of the nation's worst depression imposed on all branches of government new levels of demand for relief. The Court proved unwilling and unable to see the reality behind these pleas, and the majority continued to cling to an outmoded view of government's role.

The stock market crash of October 1929 neither caused the Depression nor represented the greatest threat to Americans' well-being. The crash attracted notice, however, because, in the short span of a few days, the 2 percent of the population that actually owned stock lost much of its savings. Attempts by financial moguls like J. P. Morgan to shore up the market did not work because structural weaknesses revealed by the crash were so basic. By 1929, increasing maldistribution of wealth and wild speculation in largely worthless stocks and bonds hid the fact of steeply declining middle- and lower-class buying power. Coal, cotton, and other basic industries had long suffered reverses from competition and high tariffs abroad. More banks failed in the 1920s than in the months after the crash. People simply did not have the money to buy American products. Worse, European customers for American farm products were experiencing a crunch of their own.

The economy was ripe for a contraction. Boom and bust was a constant in the largely unregulated American economy, and significant depressions in 1873 and 1893 had caused wages to drop, unemployment to rise, consumer buying power to flag, and production to fall. But these, like the dips in the economy in the 1903–1904 period and the immediate postwar period, were relatively short-lived. Not so the Great Depression of 1929–1939. Unemployment hit one-quarter of the workforce, median income fell by 50 percent, and shock waves passed through every sector of the economy. On city streets, lines of able-bodied men and women snaked up to soup kitchens. In the countryside, farmers dumped milk on the roads because they could not get a decent return for it, while people in the cities were starving. Banks, driven to the edge of collapse, foreclosed on mortgages. There seemed to be no end to the downward spiral.

President Hoover and Congress, misinformed by the business community, continued to insist that prosperity was "just around the corner," but the market continued its free fall, and stopgap government measures were too little and too late. Hoover was a progressive, and, unlike Taft and his "four horsemen of the apocalypse," as they were called in the press, he had seen the impact in Europe of economic disaster. At first, he called for the voluntarism that had marked America's response to European suffering. Next, he proposed temporary measures to ease credit and shore up wages. Finally, he turned to state and local governments and urged public works and other employment programs. He did not seek direct federal subsidies, work programs, or spending, because, above all, he wished to limit spending, though by the end of his term, in 1932, federal spending on work relief had reached peacetime highs.

The problem for him was legal—he was convinced that direct federal action for local distress was unconstitutional. The federal government could lend but not spend, coordinate but not direct. Federalism, limited government, and his pro-business reading of what government could do for its people, along with his personal aversion to an unbalanced budget, made the federal government an observer rather than a central player. In 1930, thirteen hundred more banks crashed. Without their savings, people could not keep their homes. With demand falling, factory owners shut their doors and unemployed workers could not pay for consumer goods. Beneath their feet, hardworking Americans could see only a bottomless pit.

Before the Taft Court could address these problems, both Taft and Sanford died. The legacy of the Taft Court thus had an unfinished quality. Instead of providing a foundation for lasting national unity, prosperity, and progress, the Court seemed bewildered and out of time and place. When it ventured into relatively uncharted territory, for example, in its incorporation jurisprudence, the novelty came in the form of dicta, protected from criticism because they did not affect the outcome of the case.

Responsibility for some of this disappointing legacy must be laid at Taft's door. For him, and for his majority, the law was not an innovator, not a vision of a new, diverse, and progressive society. Though the immigration of the period 1880–1920, the rise of the cities, the growing power of labor organizations, and the increasing gap between rich and poor should have called for an inclusive and flexible vision of law, the majority believed that law must close the floodgates against change. It must protect the status quo. And that no law can do—not for long.

Chief Justice John Jay (1789–1795), the youngest chief justice, forty-four when named but already much experienced as a diplomat, elected official, and lawyer. He refused to let the Court become a servant of the executive branch. (Reproduction of painting by Joseph Wright, courtesy of Library of Congress)

John Marshall, the great chief justice (1801–1835), who raised the Court to its coequal position with the other branches of the federal government and gave teeth to the Supremacy Clause. (Portrait by Thomas Sully, courtesy of Library of Congress)

Associate Justice Joseph Story (1811–1844), a New Englander and a nationalist and author of many leading opinions and treatises on law. He was a law professor at Harvard Law School as well. (1844 daguerreotype, courtesy of Library of Congress)

Chief Justice Roger B. Taney (1836–1864), long serving and controversial in life and still controversial. Perhaps also underrated. (Portrait courtesy of Library of Congress)

Chief Justice Salmon P. Chase (1864–1873), who had a disappointing end to his career as politician, in a time when strong leadership might have made the Court a leading defender of Reconstruction. A series of strokes had already taken their toll. (Photograph, possibly by Matthew Brady, courtesy of Library of Congress)

The Chase Court's first session, 1864, and the first of the group portraits of the Court. Left to right, the clerk, D. W. Middleton, and Justices Davis, Swayne, Grier, Wayne, the chief justice, Nelson, Clifford, Miller, and Field. The newest justices, as today, occupy the seats farthest from the center chair—a chair that both Miller and Field would covet when Chase died. (Photograph courtesy of Library of Congress)

Chief Justice Morrison R. Waite (1874–1888), a workaholic who died in harness. A good man and a solid lawyer but not quite up to the demanding task of Gilded Age jurisprudence. (Photograph by G. W. Thorne, courtesy of Library of Congress)

Waite's Court in the year of his death, 1888, his labors visible in his posture. Left to right, the justices are Bradley, Blatchford, Miller, Mathews, the chief justice, Gray, Field, Lamar, and Harlan. (Photograph courtesy of Library of Congress)

The Fuller Court at the high tide of its efforts to revolutionize constitutional law, 1894. The justices are, left to right, Gray, Jackson, Field, Brown, the chief justice, Shiras, Harlan, White, and Brewer. In the next year, Peckham would replace the ailing Jackson. (Photograph by C. M. Bell, courtesy of Library of Congress)

The Court that decided *Lochner v. New York* (1906), as they entered the old Senate chamber in 1907. Left to right, justices Moody, Holmes, Day, McKenna, Peckham, White, Brewer, Harlan, with Chief Justice Melville W. Fuller in the van. (Photograph courtesy of Library of Congress)

Louis D. Brandeis, the conscience of the White Court, a brilliant lawyer, progressive advocate for the ordinary citizen, and defender of civil rights and civil liberties. This photograph was taken in the year of his arrival on the Court, 1916, after a bitter confirmation fight. (Photograph by Harris and Ewing, courtesy of Library of Congress)

Chief Justice William Howard Taft (1921–1930), who left his impress on the law, law teaching, the executive branch, and finally the High Court. The photograph was taken in 1912, as Taft was preparing to run for reelection to the presidency. (Photograph by Arnold Genthe, courtesy of Library of Congress)

The Taft Court in midcourse, 1924. Left to right, Van Devanter, Butler, McKenna, Brandeis, the chief justice, Sutherland, Holmes, Sanford, and McReynolds. (Photograph courtesy of Library of Congress)

The "godlike" Chief Justice Charles Evans Hughes (1930–1941), in 1930, about to make a courtesy call on President Herbert Hoover. He served in a time of political and legal change, which legal scholar Bruce Ackerman has called a virtual constitutional convention, and guided the Court through it with gentle but firm leadership. (Photograph courtesy of Library of Congress)

Harlan Fiske Stone, long a justice, but only briefly the chief justice. A man of high personal character, intellectual ability, and increasingly liberal sentiments, in dissent on the Taft Court he shone, but he had trouble as chief justice in reining in his "wild horses." This photograph was taken on the eve of his elevation to the center seat. (Courtesy of Library of Congress)

The Stone Court visits with the new president, Harry S. Truman, in October 1945. Left to right, front row, Chief Justice Stone, Truman, Black, and Frankfurter. Behind Frankfurter is Murphy. Douglas stands at the top step on the left. (Photograph from the Harold Hitz Burton collection, Library of Congress)

The Vinson Court pays a courtesy call on President Dwight D. Eisenhower, in February 1953, the chief justice standing to the president's right. Vinson was not a distinguished jurist or effective manager, but who could keep the feuds that had so long divided the justices from spilling over into their opinions? (New York World Telegram and Sun Photo collection, Library of Congress)

The second great chief justice, Earl Warren, in 1948, as governor of California. Warren replaced Vinson in 1953 and led the Court in a period of great creativity and controversy. His personality and his moral authority kept the Court together even when individual justices disagreed with his views. (Courtesy of Library of Congress)

The Warren Court in 1965. From left to right, Justices Clark, White, Black, Brennan, the Chief, Stewart, Douglas, Fortas, and Harlan. Though potentially as divided as the Vinson Court, Warren led or joined majorities to remake civil rights, civil liberties, voting rights, and criminal procedure. (CORBIS)

The Burger Court in 1981. Left to right, Marshall, Stevens, Brennan, Powell, the chief justice, Rehnquist, White, O'Connor, and Blackmun. No Court was more contentious, and Brennan and Rehnquist came to lead opposing factions. (Courtesy of U.S. Supreme Court)

The Rehnquist Court in 1994. From left to right, Justices Scalia, Ginsburg, Stevens, Souter, the Chief, Thomas, O'Connor, Breyer, and Kennedy. Divided by personality and ideological conflicts but arguably the best educated and most intellectually sophisticated Court. (CORBIS)

The first home of the Court was the Merchant's Exchange building in New York City, but the Court had little business to transact there. Pictured here is the second home of the Court, in Philadelphia's town hall, a courtroom shared with the mayor's court and now part of Independence Hall National Historical Site. The Court sat here from 1791 to 1800, when the national capital moved to the District of Columbia. (Courtesy of Library of Congress)

The basement of the old Senate chamber, where the Court
sat in drafty, mildewed, and cramped quarters until the new
Senate wing of the Capitol was finished, in 1861. In this photograph, the basement has been redesigned as the justices' library,
but it was still damp and drafty, and most of the justices preferred to work at home. (Courtesy of Library of Congress)

In 1861, the justices moved to the old Senate chamber. It featured a robing room and space for visitors. The Court sat here until 1935. (Courtesy of Library of Congress)

Chief Justice Taft's "marble palace." The Supreme Court Building is a neoclassical design by Gilbert Cass and occupies an entire city block in the District of Columbia between Union Station and the Library of Congress. (Courtesy of Library of Congress)

CHAPTER 10

The Hughes Court, 1930–1941

Scholars contest everything about the Hughes Court era of our history. The New Deal, from 1933 to 1941, either saved capitalism and democratic republicanism or it introduced unwelcome state intrusiveness. Either the government's efforts to "prime the pump" failed to alter basic patterns of fiscal and industrial instability or they ushered in a new partnership of planners and regulators that profoundly changed the economy. But no one who studies the period can doubt that at the center of the maelstrom sat the Court.

In reality, there were two New Deals, each quite unlike the other. In the first, from Franklin Delano Roosevelt's election to mid-1935, the president, with the compliance of Congress, experimented with fiscal and relief programs. These lacked a clear ideological and structural base and included cost-cutting measures, devaluation of the currency, direct grants to cities and states, and federal works projects. Larger programs ranged from the Agricultural Adjustment Act, with price setting, production quotas, and payments for reduced planting, to the National Industrial Recovery Act, with its commission that managed the manufacturing side of the economy. Most of these acts the Court struck down.

With the Depression largely unaffected by the first New Deal, in 1935 the Roosevelt administration considered more basic egalitarian reforms. Among these were programs to provide jobs (the Works Progress Administration), the Social Security Act, the Rural Electrification Administration, and the National Labor Relations Act. The last of these finally ended the antilabor injunction, in effect overruling the Fuller, White, and Taft Courts' attempts to protect it. Overseen by a supposedly neutral National Labor Relations Board, collective bargaining was supposed to end the war between capital and labor. The Court upheld most of these acts.

What had happened to change the constitutional landscape? In 1937, after a smashing victory at the polls, Roosevelt announced a plan to revise the membership of the Court. Congress had done this before, adding justices or (at the end of the Civil War) reducing the number of justices. Roosevelt wanted to add justices to the court for every justice over the age of seventy, in effect "packing it" with New Deal supporters. From the vantage point of their new building, dubbed "the marble palace" by journalists, all of the justices viewed the packing plan with skepticism. No one knew what Roosevelt's plan would bring, or if Congress would accede to the president's wishes. In fact, the Senate quashed the initiative, but by that time the High Court had shifted its views enough to let key legislation of the second New Deal stand. And with the retirement of one conservative after another, Roosevelt would be able to pack the Court in a more conventional way with New Deal supporters.

A NEW HOME

The setting for the storm and drama of the Court in the New Deal years changed dramatically on October 7, 1935, with the opening of the new Supreme Court building. Taft did not live to see his dream become reality, though he had taken as painstaking an interest in every detail as Wilson had in the peace treaty framed at Versailles. Taft wanted architect Cass Gilbert to cover an entire block between Union Station and the Library of Congress with a white marble, three-story shrine to justice. Its front boasted an imposing set of steps, huge bronze doors, neoclassical columns, and a frieze on the pediment that included figures from myth and American history. Within, a rotunda surmounted imposing statuary in a reception hall bigger than the entire old Court chamber. Gilbert's masterpiece was a Parthenon within which Americans could worship at the altar of the law.

The focal point of the building was the Courtroom. It was theater-sized, seating three hundred spectators. At the far end was an imposing raised bench with high-backed chairs for the justices. The robing room curtained off at the back opened onto the scene, allowing the justices to enter like priests at a temple ceremony. Behind the bench Gilbert placed a row of marble columns separated by rich red curtains, a temple within a temple. Another frieze ringed the Courtroom.

The justices would no longer have to work at home. The building had three-room suites for each justice, a richly wood-paneled conference room, and, on the third floor, a library. If the justices needed more research facilities, the Library of Congress building (later buildings) was a half-block away. The plan also provided a private dining room, parking in the basement area, and exercise facilities. Storage areas for documents—the Court's circulating system pumped out reams of paper—were abundantly provided. The whole project cost a little over $9.7 million, a bargain even during the Depression.

"NINE OLD MEN"

Although the new Courthouse gave the appearance of the unity and majesty of the law, the Hughes Court was the most sharply divided Supreme Court up to its time—in fact, it divided into warring sides so clearly that observers could predict with great accuracy who would vote how. That division had many causes, but first and foremost was that the membership of the Court did not change much from the Taft Court, while the situation of the nation changed drastically from 1929 to 1931. There was no infusion of new justices responsive to the New Deal agenda until the end of the era. Nevertheless, one justice appointed by Hoover changed his voting pattern in time to ensure that the legislation of the second New Deal was not overruled. That "switch in time" saved the Court and the nation much travail.

As he was dying, Taft tried to persuade Hoover not to name Charles Evans Hughes as the new chief justice. Hoover had his mind made up, however, and Hughes became chief justice after a somewhat acrimonious debate in the Senate, on February 24, 1930. Liberal senators like William Borah, George Norris, Robert La Follette, and Burton Wheeler denounced Hughes's private legal practice for representing oil companies and other major corporations. None of these critics doubted Hughes's integrity or ability, but all worried that another conservative chief justice would only continue on Taft's path. By contrast, conservative southern senators were concerned that Hughes might be too liberal.

Hughes proved all the doubters wrong. Robert Jackson, a future member of the Court, recalled that Hughes looked and spoke like God. Hughes certainly had a sense of his own historical importance and great personal dignity. Brandeis appreciated the new chief justice's evenhandedness, not surprising, given the cold formality with which Taft had treated Brandeis. Hughes moved the conference along expeditiously, cutting off tangential comments, something that Taft, for all his businesslike manner, could not manage. He did not hold private conferences at home with a select few of the members, a practice that Taft had adopted. In oral argument, Hughes was at his best, keeping counsel on their toes and turning the occasion into a genuinely informative event.

His thinking was in accord with progressive currents. Despite the liberal senators' fears, his representation of larger corporations during the hiatus in his public life had not turned his head against organized labor. He was a strong advocate of civil rights for minorities and procedural guarantees for those accused of crime. Though he was mindful that overturning recent precedent might call the reputation of the Court and his own leadership into question and preferred to distinguish his opinions from earlier precedents rather than reverse them, he saw law as a framework rather than a stone wall and believed that the Court must take economic and social conditions into account. He accorded state law the same latitude in this regard as he gave to congressional acts.

Hughes was shortly joined by Philadelphia lawyer Owen Roberts. Hoover would have preferred John J. Parker, a judge on the Fourth Circuit Court of Appeals, but Parker's views on labor and civil rights made him unpalatable to liberals in the Senate. Roberts may not have been the best choice for the post. Unsure of his own abilities, he charted an uncertain course on the Court. The genial and easily persuaded Roberts was highly sensitive to both personal and political pressure. Stung by collegial and public criticism of his opinions, he shifted them. For example, he opposed a New York State minimum wage law for women but upheld a New York State law regulating milk prices, even though the precedents equated state regulation of wages and prices. In 1937, he joined Hughes and the liberal justices to find a Washington State law setting minimum wages for women to be constitutional. Roberts agreed with the four conservatives in overturning key parts of the first New Deal, then voted to sustain the National Labor Relations Act and the Social Security Act two years later.

In 1937, Roberts may have been influenced by the size of Roosevelt's reelection victory or by Roosevelt's plan to enlarge the Court, but his voting in 1937 did not match his voting in 1936. In some areas of the law, however, he was comfortable and consistent, for example, in his support for civil rights and his belief that the Fourteenth Amendment incorporated the Free Exercise Clause of the First Amendment and the right to an attorney. At the end of his career, he finally grew into his position. He retired in 1945, became dean of the University of Pennsylvania Law School, and died in 1955.

The last of the Hoover appointees was Benjamin Cardozo, joining the Court on March 14, 1932, to take the place of Holmes. The Senate hearings were brief and laudatory, and he was confirmed unanimously without debate. Yet Cardozo is perhaps the most enigmatic figure ever to serve on the Court. Cardozo's personal life remains something of a mystery because he destroyed many of the letters sent to him, and others were destroyed or lost after he died. He never married, living much of his life with his sister. Though a Democrat, he was never associated with partisan politics, even in the heady political atmosphere of New York City. A nonobservant Jew, he was nonetheless sponsored for judicial office by the Jewish community.

Cardozo was a brilliant lawyer and jurist and one of the most innovative of all legal thinkers, but he often rowed to his destination with muffled oars. Elected to the New York Supreme Court through reform politics in 1913 at the age of forty-two, he refused to acknowledge any partisan obligations. He served eighteen years on the state court of appeals and can be said to be the father of modern mass tort law and products liability. His Storrs Lectures at Yale University, in 1921, on the nature of the judicial process, were a remarkable contribution to legal thinking. He gave a frank and accurate picture of how contemporary ideas, the pressure of external interest groups, personal inclinations, and the precedents of the law came together in judges' minds.

On the Court, he continued his courteous but uncompromising aloofness. Though he admired Brandeis, he and Brandeis were never close. Cardozo paid regular visits to Holmes, his predecessor, but the bond was more intellectual than emotional. With Stone, whom Cardozo had known in New York City, Cardozo was friendly but not warmly so. His relations with McReynolds were cold. McReynolds would hold a piece of paper in front of his face when Cardozo read an opinion on the bench. Though the new Supreme Court building, with generously apportioned offices for all the justices, opened in 1935, Cardozo continued to work alone, at home. Never an especially healthy man, stress on the Court led to a series of heart attacks and then a stroke. He died in office, in 1938. McReynolds alone among the justices did not attend the memorial service for Cardozo. Vain and sensitive, generous and thoughtful, Cardozo's reputation as a jurist has survived the decline of his reputation as a judge.

Cardozo was assigned few opinions, but when he wrote, he was brilliant. Cardozo had no need of rigid legal categories or distinctions. He rejected the direct-versus-indirect-effects test that Fuller introduced to distinguish between commerce and manufacturing and was willing—sometimes eager—for the Court to dump older precedents based on these suspect distinctions. He believed that administrative agencies should have the discretion to perform their functions but objected when too much discretion was given the executive by the legislative branch.

The next appointment to the Court did not come until 1937. In the meantime, the four conservatives on the Court voted against federal programs, both structural and immediate, associated with the New Deal. The "four horsemen of the apocalypse," Butler, McReynolds, Sutherland, and Van Devanter, never broke ranks, shared the opinion writing among themselves, and articulated a view of law rooted in the ideas of the Fuller, White, and Taft Courts.

Why did these men not concede occasionally, given the dire circumstances? One answer would be that their politics were conservative, and their view of law and economics followed that conservatism. Or that, drawn from the ruling classes, they did not find democratic government or redistribution of wealth attractive. Much of the New Deal legislation was redistributive—it used general taxes to fund specific programs, in effect transferring wealth from the taxpayer to the recipient of the program's benefits. For Sutherland, such transfers were immoral. In addition, the four men saw law as fixed rather than changing and believed that in times of great tribulation, like the Depression, the law must be even more inflexible, or the Constitution itself would become an empty vessel.

The key to this view of law was the boundary between the public sphere, in which some rate fixing, regulation, and even government sponsorship and supervision of programs was permissible, and the private sphere, which under the Constitution was protected from government interference. This strong notion of an absolutely clear line between public and private was itself a doctrine. There was nothing in the Constitution that defined that line or told the justices where it was to be drawn. But precedent—in part the precedent they had crafted under White and Taft—drew the line to expand the area of individual liberty and constrain the area of government intrusion in employment and commercial relations.

JUDGING THE NEW DEAL

The first major cases of the Hughes Court in the Depression era hinted that a majority of the Court might be willing to read the Constitution in a flexible manner. New Jersey law regulated the fees that insurance companies might pay to their agents. The statute seemed to fly in the face of freedom of contract, but Brandeis, writing for Hughes, Stone, Cardozo, and Roberts, upheld it in *O'Gorman and Young v. Hartford Fire Insurance* (1931). He argued that the insurance industry was one charged with a public interest, and the state's police power allowed it to set rates, a finely drawn distinction based on *Munn*. After all, the insurance business in New Jersey was full of "evils" that the statute corrected. Then, in a dictum, Brandeis took the occasion to denounce substantive due process analysis in rate regulation cases. Instead, the Court should defer to the state legislature's fact-based decisions: "As underlying questions of fact may condition the constitutionality of legislation of this character, the presumption of constitutionality must prevail in the absence of some factual foundation of record for overthrowing the statute."

Van Devanter was not buying—*Adkins* had decided the matter otherwise: "This Court has steadfastly upheld the general right to enter into private contract and has definitely disapproved attempts to fix prices by legislative fiat." But only the usual suspects—McReynolds, Butler, and Sutherland—would join Van Devanter.

In 1933, faced with declining prices for their milk, New York State dairy farmers convinced the legislature to set the price of milk for a year. As counsel for the state reported, "Primarily what the Legislature desired to accomplish was to save the dairy industry from destruction, by giving it a price for milk nearer to the cost of production." Leo Nebbia, trying to outfox his retail competition, sold milk below the state's minimum prescribed price and was convicted of violating the statute. Like Lochner, he appealed—the Fourteenth Amendment's Due Process Clause surely applied as much to the milkman as it did to the baker.

Justice Roberts wrote for Hughes, Stone, Brandeis, and Cardozo that the statute fell well within the power of the state to protect the public welfare. Although the dairy industry was not created by the state, nor funded by it, nor directly related to public purposes, "the Constitution does not secure to anyone liberty to conduct his business in such a fashion as to influence injury upon the public at large, or upon any substantial group of people." In addition, Roberts explicitly rejected the substantive due process argument that counsel for the retailer raised, instead deciding that "the guaranty of due process, as has often been held, demands only that the law shall not be unreasonable, arbitrary or capricious, and that the means selected shall have a real and substantial relation to the object sought to be obtained."

McReynolds and the other conservatives dissented in *Nebbia v. People of State of New York* (1934) as they had in *O'Gorman*. Could anything be clearer? "[Nebbia] was convicted of a crime for selling his own property—wholesome milk—in the ordinary course of business at a price satisfactory to himself and the customer." On what basis might the state interfere with this private transaction? "Was the legislation upheld because only temporary and for an emergency; or was it sustained upon the view that the milk business bears a peculiar relation to the public, is affected with a public interest, and, therefore, sales prices may be prescribed?" It did not matter. The law must be fixed, not arbitrary and shifting with every gust of wind. "The Legislature cannot lawfully destroy guaranteed rights of one man with the prime purpose of enriching another, even if for the moment, this may seem advantageous to the public. And the adoption of any 'concept of jurisprudence' which permits facile disregard of the Constitution as long interpreted and respected will inevitably lead to its destruction. Then, all rights will be subject to the caprice of the hour; government by stable laws will pass." Van Devanter, Butler, and Sutherland agreed.

In *Home Building and Loan v. Blaisdell* (1934), Hughes wrote for himself, Roberts, Cardozo, Brandeis, and Stone that the previous year's mortgage moratorium in Minnesota was not a violation of the Contracts Clause of the Constitution. The law helped farm families faced with foreclosure, an emergency the Court allowed the state to consider when the entire economy was faltering. In effect, the opinion created a large exception to *Dartmouth College* and *Charles River Bridge*, but the times were exceptional. Sutherland disagreed. Opening this door to state interference with private contracts might lead to the death of contract itself.

In the first cases of the 1935 term, the narrow majority that had been behind *Blaisdell* and *Nebbia*, both state cases, appeared ready to support Congress's emergency measures. In the *Gold Clause Cases*, the Court's 5-to-4 ruling denied that Congress could simply decide to void payment in gold standard promises in federal bonds, but since the value of the bonds had fallen so far, suits against the United States for failure to pay in gold were moot. In any case, in the national emergency, Congress must have the power to decide how the United States would pay its creditors (as it did in the Emergency Banking Act of 1933) and could delegate this power to the president (later confirming his decisions in the Gold Reserve Act of 1934). Hughes opined: "We are of the opinion that the gold clauses now before us were not contracts for payment in gold coin as a commodity, or in bullion, but were contracts for the payment of money. The bonds were severally for the payment of one thousand dollars." McReynolds's muttering against the majority rose to a crescendo, loud enough for the packed courtroom to hear him say, "This is Nero at his worst."

But McReynolds and his three cohorts found allies in the other camp in *Panama Refining Company v. Ryan* (1935). Federal officials, obeying orders from Hugh Johnson, boss of the National Recovery Administration, to enforce the "hot oil" provisions of the National Industrial Recovery Act, were enjoined by the federal district court, injunctions that the appeals court reversed. The oil companies were distributing oil in excess of the limits the National Recovery Administration had prescribed under an executive order. The oil companies sought relief from the High Court and got it.

The case looked similar to the operation of the New York Milk Act that the Court had approved in *Nebbia*. But Hughes, writing for the majority, found that the provision in the congressional act "does not state whether, or in what circumstances or under what conditions, the President is to prohibit the transportation of the amount of petroleum or petroleum products produced in excess of the State's permission. It establishes no criterion to govern the President's course. It does not require any finding by the President as a condition of his action." In short, it was an open-ended grant of absolute power from Congress to the president.

Whether Congress had such power, or could delegate it to an agency, was a question affecting much of the first New Deal legislation. In White and Taft Court administrative agency cases, clear standards, full hearings, and reports of findings were required. Here, nothing was required. "It gives to the President an unlimited authority to determine the policy and to lay down the prohibition, or not to lay it down, as he may see fit. And disobedience to his order is made a crime punishable by fine and imprisonment." Congress had prefaced the provisions of the National Industrial Recovery Act with a general statement that the national emergency required such open-ended grants. But Hughes wrote: "This general outline of policy contains nothing as to the circumstances or conditions in which transportation of petroleum or petroleum products should be prohibited,—nothing as to the policy of prohibiting, or not prohibiting, the transportation of production exceeding what the States allow." If Congress could not arrogate to itself such untrammeled powers over private property as in the National Industrial Recovery Act, it could not give these to the president and he could not delegate them to the National Recovery Administration.

Cardozo dissented. He found in the record and the briefs of counsel for the government very clear explanations for the policy and limitations upon presidential discretion: "The record is replete with evidence as to the effect of such production and transportation [of oil] upon the economic situation and upon national recovery." Hughes and Cardozo did not get along particularly well, and Cardozo's sharp dissent may have indicated why. Cardozo was lecturing the chief justice, and the chief justice did not appreciate the lesson. Cardozo drove home the point: "Discretion is not unconfined and vagrant. It is canalized within banks that keep it from overflowing." Indeed, it was the president's duty as chief executive to act: "The statute was framed in the shadow of a national disaster. A host of unforeseen contingencies would have to be faced from day to day, and faced with a fulness of understanding unattainable by any one except the man upon the scene. The President was chosen to meet the instant need."

A unanimous Court confirmed *Panama* in *Schechter Poultry v. U.S.* (1935). The Brooklyn, New York, slaughterhouse had violated the live poultry code of the National Recovery Administration. The code was supposed to promote fair practices and competition among firms, protecting them as well as the consumer. The code included minimum wages and maximum hours. Had it been a state code, it would likely have passed muster. But a federal code for intrastate trade was problematic, for under *Adkins* the minimum wage provisions were unconstitutional, and, as in *Panama*, the legislation did not define the standards the National Recovery Administration was to enforce. The National Recovery Administration itself decided what was kosher and what was not, and that made *Schechter* almost a straight replay of *Panama*. Counsel for the company seized on this likeness: "Congress has set up no intelligible policies to govern the President, no standards to guide and restrict his action, and no procedure for making determinations in conformity with due process of law." The lawyers cited *Panama* over and over in their brief, in case the message was lost on the justices.

Hughes wrote for his Court. The code makers had used the Depression crisis as an opportunity to impose administratively what the Fuller, White, and Taft Courts had knocked down: minimum wage, maximum hours, no child labor, no yellow-dog contracts, and the guarantee of collective bargaining. Hughes may have agreed with all of these provisions (he probably did), but the code violated the separation of powers in the Constitution: "We are told that the provision of the statute authorizing the adoption of codes must be viewed in the light of the grave national crisis with which Congress was confronted. . . . But the argument necessarily stops short of an attempt to justify action which lies outside the sphere of constitutional authority. Extraordinary conditions do not create or enlarge constitutional power."

To be precise, Hughes continued, first, "the Congress is not permitted to abdicate or to transfer to others the essential legislative functions with which it is thus vested." The code was created not by Congress or even by the executive office, but by representatives of labor and the industry. Had it been voluntary, it would have satisfied Brandeis's ideal of labor and capital finding common ground. But it rested on federal law, not voluntary compliance. Second, "in determining how far the federal government may go in controlling intrastate transactions upon the ground that they 'affect' interstate commerce, there is a necessary and well-established distinction between direct and indirect effects." Despite Cardozo's admonition, Hughes dragged in Fuller's distinction from *E. C. Knight* and put it to a new use. Finally, Brewer's argument against federal regulation of rates resurfaced in Hughes's opinion: "We are of the opinion that the attempt through the provisions of the Code to fix the hours and wages of employees of defendants in their intrastate business was not a valid exercise of federal power."

Cardozo held his nose and concurred: "I have said that there is no standard, definite or even approximate, to which legislation must conform." But, in this case, what is fair, as thus conceived, is not something to be contrasted with what is unfair or fraudulent or tricky. The extension becomes as wide as the field of industrial regulation. If that conception shall prevail, anything that Congress may do within the limits of the commerce clause for the betterment of business may be done by the President upon the recommendation of a trade association by calling it a code. This is delegation running riot.

Stone joined Cardozo's concurrence.

The National Industrial Recovery Act was hastily drafted and its provisions were unclear, making the power it gave to the president virtually limitless. Moreover, it would expire at the end of the year. But the Court was not done with the legislation of the first New Deal. In *U.S. v. Butler* (1936), the Court struck down the Agricultural Adjustment Act. It violated the Tenth Amendment, Roberts wrote. In *Carter v. Carter Coal Company* (1936), the Court invalidated the Bituminous Coal Conservation Act. Sutherland judged that coal production was not interstate commerce and so could not be regulated by Congress. In *Ashton v. Cameron County Water Improvement District* (1936), the conservative majority struck again, overturning the Municipal Bankruptcy Act. McReynolds wrote for himself, Roberts, Sutherland, Van Devanter, and Butler: "The difficulties arising out of our dual form of government, and the opportunities for differing opinions concerning the relative rights of State and National Governments are many; but for a very long time this court has steadfastly adhered to the doctrine that the taxing power of Congress does not extend to the States or their political subdivisions."

The majority turned next to state emergency measures. In *Morehead, Warden, v. New York ex rel. Tipaldo* (1936), the four conservatives joined Roberts to void a minimum wage law that applied to women and minors. Counsel for Tipaldo's laundry argued: "We have understood, and believe the bench and bar throughout the country have understood, that the Adkins case decided a question much more fundamental than that of the standard involved, namely,— the question of validity of any mere wage-fixing law as applied to adult, legally competent women." New York State's highest court dismissed the indictment against the defendant and found that the law violated the federal Constitution. Exactly right, Butler wrote for himself and the four justices:

It is not an emergency law. It does not regulate hours or any conditions affecting safety or protection of employees. . . . The Adkins case, unless distinguishable, requires affirmance of the judgment below. . . . The right to make contracts about one's affairs is a part of the liberty protected by the due process clause. Within this liberty are provisions of contracts between employer and employee fixing the wages to be paid. In making contracts of employment, generally speaking, the parties have equal right to obtain from each other the best terms they can by private bargaining.

Stone, Cardozo, Brandeis, and Hughes found themselves in the minority over and over again. Cardozo wrote for them in *Ashton*: "To hold that this purpose [of aiding municipalities whose attempts to seek relief were hamstrung by a handful of zealous creditors] must be thwarted by the courts because of a supposed affront to the dignity of a state, though the state disclaims the affront and is doing all it can to keep the law alive, is to make dignity a doubtful blessing."

Hughes's dissent was solemn and admonitory in *Tipaldo*: "We have had frequent occasion to consider the limitations of liberty of contract. While it is highly important to preserve that liberty from arbitrary and capricious interference, it is also necessary to prevent its abuse, as otherwise it could be used to override all public interests and thus in the end destroy the very freedom of opportunity which it is designed to safeguard."

Stone dissented in *Morehead*: "There is grim irony in speaking of the freedom of contract of those who, because of their economic necessities, give their services for less than is needful to keep body and soul together." As Harlan had in *Lochner*, Stone found no equal bargaining power. There was no bargaining at all. The women took whatever scraps the employers left on the table.

THE SWITCH IN TIME

The battle lines on the Court were drawn, and neither side seemed willing to compromise. The nation waited and watched with increasing apprehension to see what would happen to key pieces of legislation coming to the Court in the 1937 session. The legislation the Court had struck down in 1935 and 1936 was of a temporary sort—relief, codes, limitations, rate setting deemed necessary at the time. The next round of cases involved far more profound, permanent, structural reforms. Would the majority nullify them as well?

Indeed, the switch of one vote from the nullifiers could change the entire direction of the Court's reasoning, and that switch came first in *West Coast Hotel Co. v. Parrish* (1937). Washington State had passed a law in 1913 very similar to the New York minimum wage law struck down in *Tipaldo*. The former was not an emergency measure but instead an old Progressive era act, much like the statutory limitation on hours challenged in *Muller*. A commission determined the amount necessary for women to maintain their health and welfare.

Instead of the state indicting a violator of the law, as in *Tipaldo*, Elsie Parrish, a hotel chambermaid, filed suit for back wages, the difference between her pay packet and the commission's set minimum. In *Tipaldo*, the New York State court of appeals had voided the minimum wage law. In Washington, the state supreme court had found for Parrish. Other than that, and Washington State's counsel asking the Court to reverse *Adkins*, there was little difference between *West Coast Hotel* and *Tipaldo*.

If nothing in the two cases seemed to differentiate them, everything in the political arena had changed. Roosevelt had refrained from directly attacking the Court during the 1936 campaign and in the election had won 61 percent of the popular vote and all but two states' electoral votes. With the case up for consideration during the election and decided in conference before Roosevelt announced what he proposed to do with the federal courts, Roberts changed his vote at conference. Was he motivated by the plan to pack the Court? Evidently not—since it came two months after he joined with Hughes, Stone, Cardozo, and Brandeis. Was he motivated in part by the election results? Very probably.

Hughes, writing for the five-justice majority, actually did try to explain his own shift from *Schechter*, but he covered his tracks: "The importance of the question, in which many States having similar laws are concerned, the close division by which the decision in the Adkins case was reached, and the economic conditions which have supervened . . . make it not only appropriate, but we think imperative, that . . . the subject should receive fresh consideration." In so doing, Hughes knocked down the doctrinal pillars that supported *Adkins* and *Tipaldo*: "In each case the violation alleged by those attacking minimum wage regulation for women is deprivation of freedom of contract. What is this freedom? The Constitution does not speak of freedom of contract. It speaks of liberty and prohibits the deprivation of liberty without due process of law."

He then played three-card monte with the dissent in *Adkins*, turning the dissent into the holding in the case: "This array of precedents and the principles they applied were thought by the dissenting Justices in the Adkins case to demand that the minimum wage statute [in *Adkins*] be sustained." Then he argued that, unlike the D.C. wage commission's fixed and arbitrary minimum, "the minimum wage to be paid under the Washington statute is fixed after full consideration by representatives of employers, employees and the public." But that was true of the prices fixed in *Schechter* and the wages set in *Tipaldo*. In the end, the telling argument was one of simple numbers—Hughes had a majority at last. "We think that the views thus expressed are sound and that the decision in the Adkins case was a departure from the true application of the principles governing the regulation by the State of the relation of employer and employed."

By 5-to-4 votes, over and over again, the liberal majority upheld federal and state reform statutes. Even though the Court-packing plan had never really gained momentum and soon failed, the Court did not swerve again. Roberts's switch was permanent. Next up were the National Labor Relations Act and the Social Security Act. In *NLRB v. Jones and Laughlin Steel* (1937), the majority dumped the direct/indirect distinction in interstate commerce and allowed Congress to act on anything "in the stream of commerce." Gone was *E. C. Knight*. *Steward Machine Company v. Davis* (1937) reversed a string of cases holding that Congress's power to levy taxes in the general welfare did not extend beyond the four corners—the enumerated powers—of the Constitution. It extended to the social security tax that employers had to pay, along with employees, to fund social security benefits.

Van Devanter saw that the writing on the wall no longer included his name and decided to retire. Perhaps Congress passing a law giving every federal judge over seventy a pension at full pay had a hand in his decision—and perhaps his age had a hand in Congress passing the law. In any case, Roosevelt now had the chance to choose a new justice, and by the end of Hughes's tenure, Roosevelt appointees had remade the Court. For the rest of the period, the Court did not negate a single act of Congress.

ROOSEVELT'S COURT

None of Roosevelt's first round of appointees would have pleased or impressed Taft. None had judicial experience. None were the kind of solid men of conservative views and good golf games that Taft appreciated. Some lacked judicial temperament, the same fault that Taft had denounced in Brandeis. All saw the Constitution as a creative rather than a conservative instrument.

The first of Roosevelt's nominees and perhaps his most controversial was Hugo Black, an Alabama senator and staunch friend of the New Deal. Indeed, the former rural storekeeper's son sometimes embarrassed the New York plutocrat in the White House with his attacks on privilege, corporate arrogance, and special deals. In this sense, Black was a Populist. He even supported the unions, a dangerous position to take in the Deep South, particularly when his wealthy Birmingham friends were fighting so hard to prevent unionization of the mines and mills.

Although at first there were no objections to the nomination, Hiram Johnson, a liberal Republican senator from California, eventually raised one, and the floodgates opened. Conservatives railed about Black's liberal voting record. The *Washington Post* outdid the senatorial critics: "If Senator Black has given any study or thought to any aspect of constitutional law in a way which would entitle him to this preferment, his labors in that direction have been skillfully concealed." Meanwhile, southern senators criticized Black's pro-union stance and bewailed the appointment.

But the most damaging attack arose from the revelation of Black's former membership in the Klan. Black had been an ambitious young man and had found an ally for his rise to the Senate in the Klan, which he joined in 1923. He officially left three years later but did not renounce his Klan membership until a decade later. After all, at least some part of the Klan's message resembled the anti-privilege, anti-elite message of the Populists. In the end, senatorial courtesy saw him through, 63 to 16, but for the next few years critics continued to demand that he step down. He served from 1937 until his death in 1971.

Though an able trial lawyer, Black had little academic background and no experience in appellate courts (though he was for a time a police court judge) and was not a deep thinker. But to his credit, he had the ability to grow intellectually. He was a voracious reader of history and philosophy, and he had the fine litigator's tenaciousness and the ability to find precedent for positions he adopted. The centerpiece of these positions was his belief in the literal meaning of the Bill of Rights. He was an absolutist, and "Congress shall make no law" meant never, not sometimes. He also believed in incorporation of the Bill of Rights. Thus the former Klansman was one of the first and most reliable defenders of civil rights for blacks in the South, of the right to conscience for religious dissenters, and of procedural rights for those accused of crimes. In old age, he retreated somewhat from these positions, particularly in matters of wartime dissent, privacy, criminal procedure, and pornography, but on the Hughes Court he was a liberal, rejecting root and branch the views of the Fuller, White, Taft, and early Hughes Courts' majorities.

When Sutherland retired at the beginning of 1938, Roosevelt nominated his solicitor general, Kentuckian Stanley Forman Reed. Reed was able, loyal, and intelligent and a small town boy like Black, and he had attended but did not finish law school. He did love reading, again like Black. Reed, like Black, was a man whose experience as a practicing attorney trumped lack of academic pedigree (though Reed did finish his undergraduate studies at Yale). Reed had argued and lost a series of cases before the High Court, and this experience bred in him a strong dislike of judicial activism and claims of substantive due process. He was initially a supporter of civil rights litigation, but again, like Black, his later years on the Court were marked by more conservative views.

Black's longtime foe on the Court, ironically, was another New Dealer close to FDR, Felix Frankfurter. Frankfurter took the seat Cardozo had vacated in January 1939. Like Sutherland, Frankfurter was an immigrant, but unlike Sutherland, Frankfurter's family fled to the Lower East Side of Manhattan in 1891 to escape anti-Semitism in Eastern Europe. Although as an adult he was not a religious Jew, from his father, a rabbi, and from his own reading, he became a friend of Zionism like his patron Brandeis. Frankfurter starred at Harvard, again like Brandeis, but unlike his mentor, Frankfurter chose a career as a law professor rather than as a lawyer. At Harvard Law School, Frankfurter introduced a seminar in administrative law, and from it came a stream of able and eager young men ready to enter and reform government. He was greatly loyal to Roosevelt and patriotic to a fault, perhaps as compensation for his Jewish background or his foreign birth.

In person, Frankfurter was mercurial. He was quick to praise, so much so that his flattery of Holmes and later Roosevelt was legendary—but quick also to find fault with those who disagreed with him. His relations with other members of the Court were marked by this Jekyll and Hyde personality. To Jackson and later to John Marshall Harlan II, Frankfurter was a close and trusted ally; of Black and William O. Douglas, he was a backbiting and supercilious critic. There were no neutrals in Frankfurter's world. But he was also capable of real generosity of spirit. His clerks, some of whom, like Alex Bickel, Andrew Kaufman, and David Currie, went on to stellar careers in law schools, were like his children—beloved and challenged. When Cardozo fell ill, it was Frankfurter who came calling. When Black's wife passed away, Frankfurter reached out to console his former adversary. Frankfurter sat from 1939 to 1962, when a major stroke crippled him and he retired. He died three years later.

In conference and oral argument, Frankfurter reverted to his professorial manner, chiding, lecturing, and posing sharp questions. He loved the give-and-take of oral argument. In conference, however, he could go on far too long, treating the other justices as though they were his students. The lectures, like his opinions and comments on other justices' drafts, were carefully crafted. Frankfurter believed in judicial restraint, husbanding the political capital of the Court, and deference, like his idols Holmes and Brandeis. He looked for ways to avoid deciding questions on constitutional grounds, including denying that a plaintiff had standing to sue or finding that suits were moot or unripe for decision.

The next to last of the Roosevelt appointees to the Hughes Court was another former law professor, William O. Douglas. Douglas had battled his way through family difficulties to a successful legal career. Growing up in Yakima, Washington, after the death of his father, Douglas had been crippled by family poverty and polio. He countered the former by hard work and the latter by a vigorous outdoor life. He went on to a storied career as a law professor at Yale and Columbia and then to head the Securities Exchange Commission. He was elevated to the Court in 1939, replacing Brandeis. At forty-one, Douglas was the next-to-the-youngest man to be appointed (Joseph Story was the youngest), and he would serve until 1975, setting the record for longevity (thirty-six years and seven months).

Douglas had ambitions for elective political office, much like Field and Hughes, and considered running for the presidency from his seat on the Court. He was a brilliant writer, giving speeches and publishing essays, in addition to dashing off stunning opinions. Rough on his clerks and sometimes brusque with his colleagues, he preferred to be backpacking in the West rather than sitting in his office. His three divorces and four marriages and the money he accepted for appearances would make him a target of conservative critics in later years. From the first, his consistent support of the New Deal clearly put him in the liberal camp. More important, perhaps, was his alliance with Black and, later, Frank Murphy and Wiley Rutledge, in the campaign to protect civil liberties and civil rights.

The last addition to the Hughes Court was a Detroit, Michigan, Democratic politician, Frank Murphy, who was named to replace Butler in 1940. Unlike Black, Reed, Frankfurter, and Douglas, Murphy was not a Washington, D.C., insider, even though he briefly served as U.S. attorney general in 1939. Quite the contrary. This reforming Catholic mayor and later governor had an almost saintly disdain for favoritism. In Michigan, he proved that local and state government could be responsive to both unions and great corporations, provide relief to the poor in times of trouble, and promote social justice. As governor general and then high commissioner of the Philippines, he left a record of fair dealing and respect for local traditions. In Michigan, during the automotive workers' strikes and sit-downs in 1936 and 1937, Murphy tried to keep the peace, bring labor and industry to the table to negotiate, and broker settlements between militant labor organizations and militant industrial moguls. It did not always work, and the public outcry against the unions, and against Murphy, sidelined for a time any higher political ambitions he might have had.

Murphy was often a showman and sometimes a show-off. He never shunned publicity and never tired of wearing the robes of righteousness and personal virtue. He emerged unscathed from the Senate hearings on his appointment as attorney general in 1939, after he lost his campaign for reelection in Michigan, by demonstrating how he alone had ended the labor wars in his state. As U.S. attorney general, he fought against corruption in government and for civil rights in a highly visible manner. His targets included federal judges who sold justice, political bosses who sold favors, and city machines that sold jobs. He was a member of the boards of the NAACP and the American Civil Liberties Union, groups that led the fight to end Jim Crow and protect the First Amendment. He changed the Department of Justice from an organization that harassed radicals to one that hounded civil liberties violators. The newspapers loved him or hated him, but the publicity fed his ambition to reach the top office.

Frankly instrumentalist in his view of law, Murphy brought conscience to the Court. As he wrote a year before his nomination, "The old conception of law as a system of purely negative rules designed primarily for the maintenance of order is giving way steadily to the broader view that the law is properly a positive instrument for human betterment." Frankfurter was appalled, wondering whether Murphy belonged on a court of law. What most rankled Frankfurter was not Murphy's consistent defense of the underdog so much as his indifference to legal technicalities, categories, and formal reasoning. Murphy did not hesitate to dissent, even when national security was at stake. Perhaps, as a bachelor, he was used to going his own way. He died in his sleep, in 1949.

INCORPORATION OF THE BILL OF RIGHTS

The Hughes Court revisited incorporation, stepping boldly through the door that the Taft Court had opened. In *Stromberg v. California* (1931), the Court returned to the issues in *Whitney* and found that mere expression of opinion, for example, by showing sympathy to an organization that called for the overthrow of the government, was protected by the First Amendment. A nineteen-year-old camp counselor, a member of the Young Communist League, displayed the Soviet flag and taught her young charges that class solidarity alone could save Americans from unscrupulous and predatory capitalism. But no evidence at trial proved that she had sent—or intended to send—the children out to overthrow the government. Instead, she raised a flag and talked about her political views.

Hughes knew that Stromberg's conviction had come under the same state criminal syndicalism law that had felled Whitney and that a similar law had tripped up Gitlow. "There is no question but that the State may thus provide for the punishment of those who indulge in utterances which incite to violence and crime and threaten the overthrow of organized government by unlawful means." At the same time, "the maintenance of the opportunity for free political discussion to the end that government may be responsive to the will of the people and that changes may be obtained by lawful means, an opportunity essential to the security of the Republic, is a fundamental principle of our constitutional system." The California law that passed muster in *Whitney* now appeared "vague and indefinite [and] . . . repugnant to the guaranty of liberty contained in the Fourteenth Amendment." Butler and McReynolds dissented, but Sutherland and Van Devanter joined the majority.

In *Near v. Minnesota* (1931), the Court voided the state's 1925 law permitting injunctive relief against a publication deemed lewd or malicious. The law violated the First Amendment. The injunction amounted to prior censorship. The newspaper charged "that a Jewish gangster was in control of gambling, bootlegging and racketeering in Minneapolis, and that law enforcing officers and agencies were not energetically performing their duties." But, as Hughes wrote for the majority, the "liberty of the press, historically considered and taken up by the Federal Constitution, has meant, principally although not exclusively, immunity from previous restraints or censorship." The only question left was whether the Fourteenth Amendment Due Process Clause incorporated the First Amendment freedom of the press. Hughes added that assertion almost as an afterthought in the very last paragraph of his opinion: "We hold the statute . . . to be an infringement of the liberty of the press guaranteed by the Fourteenth Amendment." Butler dissented, joined by Van Devanter, McReynolds, and Sutherland. Roberts voted with the majority.

The majority found a place in the Fourteenth Amendment for the Sixth Amendment "right to counsel," applying it to one of the most notoriously biased criminal trials in American history. In 1931, eight young black men were tried and convicted of rape in a Scottsboro, Alabama, courtroom. Their prosecution, based upon the perjured testimony of two vagrant women, exhibited all the malice, haste, indifference, and racial prejudice of trials of blacks in Jim Crow southern courts. They patently did not have access to effective counsel in their capital cases, and counsel that the court ordered to represent them did not consult with them or take the time or make the effort to ascertain the truth. Although all that they, in fact, were guilty of was to engage in a fight with white boys on a train, eight of them were condemned to death.

In *Powell v. Alabama* (1932), the Court heard their appeal. Counsel for the state appeared in Court and made a similar argument to that in *Franklin v.*

South Carolina and the Alabama peonage cases. In criminal trials, "no particular form of procedure is required. The question of due process is determined by the law of the jurisdiction where the offense was committed and the trial was had. . . . Here the trials were in accordance with the constitution and statutes of Alabama, the provisions of which are in no way attacked as being unconstitutional. They were conducted in compliance with the rules, practice, and procedure long prevailing in the State."

Justice Sutherland, who wrote for the majority, found that "there is a . . . recital to the effect that upon the arraignment they were represented by counsel. But no counsel had been employed. . . . When the first case was called, the court inquired whether the parties were ready for trial. The state's attorney replied that he was ready to proceed. No one answered for the defendants or appeared to represent or defend them." Moreover, "each of the three trials was completed within a single day."

A rush to judgment in a capital case involving many witnesses and many defendants—with the trial completed in one day and resulting in every one, including an addled boy, sentenced to death—one would think that able defense counsel, if they were trying, could do a little better, particularly because it soon became evident that one of the alleged rape victims was lying, and the other admitted that she had perjured herself. Sutherland sarcastically continued: "That it would not have been an idle ceremony to have given the defendants reasonable opportunity to communicate with their families and endeavor to obtain counsel is demonstrated by the fact that, very soon after conviction, able counsel appeared in their behalf."

Butler, joined by McReynolds, dissented. He found that the defendants were sufficiently provided with counsel and assumed that counsel consulted with them. In any case, the adequacy of counsel in a state criminal trial was not the business of the federal courts: "This is an extension of federal authority into a field hitherto occupied exclusively by the several States. . . . The Court, without being called upon to consider it, adjudges without a hearing an important constitutional question concerning criminal procedure in state courts." Sutherland differed: "The question, however, which it is our duty, and within our power, to decide, is whether the denial of the assistance of counsel contravenes the due process clause of the Fourteenth Amendment to the federal Constitution." It did.

The travail of the nine "Scottsboro Boys" was not over, however. Retried, they were again convicted. Counsel this time came from the New York City offices of the Labor Defense Fund, but the deck was again stacked. No black person was allowed to sit on the jury. At trial and then on appeal to the Alabama Supreme Court, the absence of black jurors from the panel was raised and overruled, and the conviction was upheld.

Once more the High Court heard the appeal and, in *Norris v. Alabama* (1935), once more found merit in it. Hughes wrote for the majority: "At the outset, a motion was made on [Norris's] behalf to quash the indictment upon the ground of the exclusion of negroes from juries. . . . In relation to each county, the charge was of long continued, systematic and arbitrary exclusion of qualified negro citizens from service on juries, solely because of their race and color, in violation of the Constitution of the United States."

The High Court long before, in *Strauder*, had announced that systematic exclusion of African Americans from jury duty by the action of the legislature or the courts was a violation of the federal Constitution, but the Alabama law on jury eligibility—"all male citizens of the county who are generally reputed to be honest and intelligent men, and are esteemed in the community for their integrity, good character and sound judgment"—left wiggle room for the jury commission to exclude black men. And black men were always, with no exceptions, excluded. "It appeared that no negro had served on any grand or petit jury in that county within the memory of witnesses who had lived there all their lives. Testimony to that effect was given by men whose ages ran from fifty to seventy-six years. Their testimony was uncontradicted. It was supported by the testimony of officials." The Court found that there were qualified black men in "direct testimony that specified [that] negroes, thirty or more in number, were qualified for jury service. Among these were negroes who were members of school boards, or trustees, of colored schools, and property owners and householders. It also appeared that negroes from that county had been called for jury service in the federal court."

The Supreme Court of the United States is an appellate court, and not often does it engage in fact finding of its own. But in this case, with the state of Alabama patently lying about its jury selection policies, the Court asked itself what was going on in Alabama jury selection. Was there bad faith in the production of evidence of the jury rolls when counsel for the defendants objected?

The question arose whether names of negroes were in fact on the jury roll. The books containing the jury roll for Jackson County for the year 1930–31 were produced. They were produced from the custody of a member of the jury commission which, in 1931, had succeeded the commission which had made up the jury roll from which the grand jury in question [in the retrial] had been drawn. On the pages of this roll appeared the names of six negroes. They were entered, respectively, at the end of the precinct lists which were alphabetically arranged.

Apparently, to avoid the charge of excluding blacks without cause, the commissioners had altered the jury roll records to conceal the violation.

This malfeasance had not bothered Alabama's judges. "In denying the motion to quash, the trial judge expressed the view that he would not 'be authorized to presume that somebody had committed a crime' or to presume that the jury board 'had been unfaithful to their duties and allowed the books to be tampered with.'" Alabama judges were elected. The same malicious tampering with the evidence that had displayed itself in the rape trials themselves and in the matter of the jury rolls had kept blacks off the voter rolls. White voters would not reelect a judge who conceded that the jury commissioners tampered with evidence.

Justice Hughes had heard enough. "We think that the evidence that for a generation or longer no negro had been called for service on any jury in Jackson County, that there were negroes qualified for jury service . . . and the testimony with respect to the lack of appropriate consideration of the qualifications of negroes, established the discrimination which the Constitution forbids." The Fifth Amendment guarantee of an impartial jury became part of the Fourteenth Amendment's Due Process Clause. Unable to dissent this time, McReynolds simply absented himself. Sutherland, Van Devanter, and Butler joined in Hughes's opinion.

Next, the Court incorporated the First Amendment right to assembly in the Fourteenth Amendment. *DeJonge v. Oregon* (1937) effectively demolished what survived of *Whitney* after *Stromberg*. Oregon had a criminal syndicalism law similar to California's. Oregon argued that the "statute does not prohibit peaceful and orderly opposition to government, but only such conduct as may tend to incite to crime, disturb the public peace, or endanger the foundation of organized government and threaten its overthrow by unlawful means"—the old evil tendency test established in *Abrams* and the other 1919 cases and reaffirmed in *Gitlow* and *Whitney*.

At a rally, Dirk DeJonge "protested against conditions in the county jail, the action of city police in relation to the maritime strike then in progress in Portland and numerous other matters. . . . he told the workers that these attacks were due to efforts on the part of the steamship companies and stevedoring companies to break the maritime longshoremen's and seamen's strike." For attending the meeting and saying what he did, the state court sent him to prison for seven years.

Hughes once again assigned himself the opinion for the Court: "The defense was that the meeting was public and orderly and was held for a lawful purpose; that while it was held under the auspices of the Communist Party,

neither criminal syndicalism nor any unlawful conduct was taught or advocated at the meeting either by appellant or by others." The evil tendency of the
Communist Party's official doctrine was all that mattered to Oregon, for "however reasonable and timely the discussion, all those assisting in the conduct of
the meeting would be subject to imprisonment as felons if the meeting were
held by the Communist Party."

Hughes did not explicitly overrule the earlier cases like *Gitlow*—just as in
West Coast Hotel he had preferred to find the earlier cases in accord with his
present opinion: "These rights may be abused by using speech or press or assembly in order to incite to violence and crime. The people through their legislatures may protect themselves against that abuse. But . . . the rights themselves
must not be curtailed. The greater the importance of safeguarding the community from incitements to the overthrow of our institutions by force and
violence, the more imperative is the need to preserve inviolate the constitutional rights of free speech, free press and free assembly." This time, no justice
dissented.

Segregation cases were not high on the Court's agenda, but one, *State of
Missouri ex rel. Gaines v. Canada* (1938), did hint that the Court might be ready,
in the near future, to revisit *Plessy*. Missouri's state law school refused to admit Peter Lloyd Gaines, an African American, who was otherwise eligible for
admission. "He was refused admission upon the ground that it was 'contrary
to the constitution, laws and public policy of the State to admit a negro as a
student in the University of Missouri'" and advised to apply to nearby states
that did not bar blacks from their law schools.

Although the Court could have relied upon the separate but equal
standard—there was no black law school in the state—and Missouri argued
that Gaines would get a good legal education elsewhere, Hughes was having
none of it: "We think that these matters are beside the point. The basic consideration is not as to what sort of opportunities, other States provide, or whether
they are as good as those in Missouri, but as to what opportunities Missouri
itself furnishes to white students and denies to negroes solely upon the ground
of color." This violated the Equal Protection Clause of the Fourteenth Amendment. McReynolds dissented: "Considering the disclosures of the record, the
Supreme Court of Missouri arrived at a tenable conclusion and its judgment
should be affirmed. That court well understood the grave difficulties of the
situation and rightly refused to upset the settled legislative policy of the State
by directing a mandamus." Butler joined in the dissent.

In *Cantwell v. Connecticut* (1940), the Free Exercise Clause of the First
Amendment was imposed on the states. A state law prohibited solicitation of

money for religious purposes, except within a church or congregation. The purpose was to prevent scams and fraud. Newton Cantwell and his two sons, Jehovah's Witnesses, were distributing pamphlets door-to-door in New Haven when they were arrested. They were soliciting contributions as part of their presentation, the state supreme court believed, and thus their arrests did not violate their right to free speech. Roberts disagreed. Their conduct was protected under the First Amendment and the Fourteenth Amendment: "The First Amendment declares that Congress shall make no law respecting an establishment of religion or prohibiting the free exercise thereof. The Fourteenth Amendment has rendered the legislatures of the states as incompetent as Congress to enact such laws."

In the course of his opinion, he introduced the doctrine of time, place, and manner regulation, a limitation upon First Amendment rights. "It is equally clear that a State may by general and non-discriminatory legislation regulate the times, the places, and the manner of soliciting upon its streets, and of holding meetings thereon; and may in other respects safeguard the peace, good order and comfort of the community, without unconstitutionally invading the liberties protected by the Fourteenth Amendment." Thus Mormon polygamy was still not protected.

The prosecution had another string in its bow, however—that Cantwell's manner of preaching door-to-door was a breach of the peace. Roberts dealt with that claim as well: "We find in the instant case no assault or threatening of bodily harm, no truculent bearing, no intentional discourtesy, no personal abuse. On the contrary, we find only an effort to persuade a willing listener to buy a book or to contribute money in the interest of what Cantwell, however misguided others may think him, conceived to be true religion." Cantwell was a true believer, and sometimes such men resort to "exaggeration, to vilification of men who have been, or are, prominent in church or state, and even to false statement." But such exhibitions of passion and faith were "essential to enlightened opinion and right conduct on the part of the citizens of a democracy." No one dissented.

There were limits to incorporation, however. In *Palko v. Connecticut* (1937), Cardozo found no reason to incorporate the Fifth Amendment bar on double jeopardy. Connecticut had convicted the defendant on second-degree murder charges, then recharged and convicted him under the charge of first-degree murder, a capital offense. Cardozo explained why the Court would not intervene: "There emerges the perception of a rationalizing principle which gives to discrete instances a proper order and coherence. The right to trial by jury and the immunity from prosecution except as the result of an indictment may have value and importance. Even so, they are not of the very essence of a scheme of ordered liberty."

The doctrine of "ordered liberty" did not explain itself (no more than time, place, or manner restrictions did), which left the justices to draw appropriate lines case-by-case. This very problem was put to the test three years later. The majority of the Court, in the first of the *Flag Salute Cases*, determined that the free exercise of one's religious beliefs did not exempt Jehovah's Witnesses from having to salute the flag at the beginning of the school day or else face disciplinary action. Pennsylvania law required the salute, and when "Lillian Gobitis, aged twelve, and her brother William, aged ten," refused to speak the words, they were expelled from the public schools of Minersville, Pennsylvania.

Justice Frankfurter, in *Gobitis v. Minersville School District* (1940), was torn between his personal and his juridical commitment to freedom of religion and "the felt necessities" of the day, including patriotic exercises when the rest of the world had plunged into war. Around and around Frankfurter went, as though he were thinking out loud. His decision could have come out either way, so well did he argue both sides. "Certainly the affirmative pursuit of one's convictions about the ultimate mystery of the universe and man's relation to it is placed beyond the reach of law. Government may not interfere with organized or individual expression of belief or disbelief." Round one went to the children. "But the manifold character of man's relations may bring his conception of religious duty into conflict with the secular interests of his fellow-men." Round two went to the state. "When does the constitutional guarantee compel exemption from doing what society thinks necessary for the promotion of some great common end, or from a penalty for conduct which appears dangerous to the general good?"

Reading the opinion, one would not be able to guess where Frankfurter would end up. But in the end, he deferred to the state legislature: "The wisdom of training children in patriotic impulses by those compulsions which necessarily pervade so much of the educational process is not for our independent judgment." Is it too much to ask schoolchildren to show solidarity with their community in a ceremony as brief and as secular—not favoring one religion over another—as a flag salute, a ceremony "designed to evoke in them appreciation of the nation's hopes and dreams, its sufferings and sacrifices."

Frankfurter had worked long and hard to convince Black and Douglas to join him. Their inclination was to overturn the state law, but they signed on. But Frankfurter could not persuade Stone, and he movingly objected: "The [state flag salute] law which is thus sustained is unique in the history of Anglo-American legislation. It . . . suppress[es] freedom of speech and . . . prohibit[s] the free exercise of religion." Frankfurter's cobbled-together majority vanished in the next of the *Flag Salute Cases* three years later. Black and Douglas would desert him. That desertion rankled, and Frankfurter never forgave the two apostates.

Hughes, aged seventy-nine, retired on July 1, 1941. He wrote to the president: "I had criticized judges for trying to hang on after they were unable to bring full vigor to their task. As I felt that I could not keep the pace I had set for myself as Chief Justice, I decide that the time has come to take my own advice." Encomia flowed in from all directions, even from those media outlets like *The Nation* that had hotly opposed his nomination. He could now be characterized as a judicial statesman who had steered his Court through rough waters. He died on August 27, 1948, in a cottage on Cape Cod, having served his country well and knowing that it thought well of him.

The Court too wore a new face. McReynolds was the last of the four horsemen to leave the Court, resigning on February 1, 1941. He died five years later, alone and unlamented. Not a single justice attended his funeral, and there was no memorial service. Van Devanter and Butler had already died, and Sutherland would be gone a year later.

The new justices shared to some extent a conception of the Constitution different from that of the men they replaced. The shift lay not in deference to legislatures, for Harlan believed in that, as did Holmes, but in a heightened view of individual civil rights and the understanding that law was a product of social, political, and intellectual currents, rather than of a fixed and unchanging polarity.

The key marker of that altered view was nothing more or less than a footnote—the first (or second) most important footnote in Court history (in competition with note 11 in *Brown v. Board of Education*). In *U.S. v. Carolene Products* (1938), Stone's opinion for the Court validating a federal law on milk shipments included a footnote 4. The decision was typical—deferring to the legislature. But the note spelled out, in broad terms, when the Court might not be willing to defer. Indeed, the note would be later cited as the basis for "strict scrutiny" of a certain class of state acts.

It read:

There may be narrower scope for operation of the presumption of constitutionality when legislation appears on its face to be within a specific prohibition of the Constitution, such as those of the first ten amendments, which are deemed equally specific when held to be embraced within the Fourteenth. . . . It is unnecessary to consider now whether legislation which restricts those political processes which can ordinarily be expected to bring about repeal of undesirable legislation, is to be subjected to more exacting judicial scrutiny under the general prohibitions of the Fourteenth Amendment than are most other types of legislation. . . . Nor need we enquire whether similar considerations enter into the review of statutes directed at particular religious . . . or national . . . or racial minorities . . . whether prejudice against discrete and insular minorities may be a special condition, which tends seriously to curtail the operation of those political processes ordinarily to be relied upon to protect minorities, and which may call for a correspondingly more searching judicial inquiry.

The note laid out the ground for a new kind of substantive due process, not to protect economic or private property interests, but to protect personal rights and privileges. Here the Privileges and Immunities Clause of the Fourteenth Amendment, so long ignored, found a new life, though it was not explicitly resuscitated. Instead, the Court hinted that certain kinds of state activities were suspect. As Justice Black later wrote in *Hines v. Davidowitz* (1941), "The rights, liberties, and freedoms of human beings" were not the same as "state pure food laws regulating the labels on cans." It did not matter, thus, that Stone was not the actual author of the words—Louis Lusky, his clerk at the time, may have written the first draft. Far more important is the way that the note became the anthem of the new jurisprudence—capturing the essence of the incorporation cases and combining them into a constitutional outlook.

Part Three

The Modern Courts

The word and the concept "modern" is slippery, shifting from simple chronology—the here and now—to more complex meanings. For us, the "modern" denotes an emphasis on individual freedom, dignity, and equality. The term fits the larger achievements of the Stone, Vinson, Warren, Burger, and Rehnquist Courts. Though every justice did not sign on to the project, overall these Courts profoundly changed the Constitution. They found a larger space for individual worship, privacy, sexual and procreative preference, and literary expression in the penumbras and emanations of the Constitution. They protected symbolic speech and literary satire.

In the process, the Court itself moved into the very center of American politics. Demanding the end of segregation, and then integration, overturning state laws criminalizing abortion, questioning state courts' handling of search and seizure, confessions, and the death penalty in criminal cases, and even determining the outcome of a presidential election, the Court willingly, some would say willfully, confronted public opinion and the other branches of government.

The course of the Court's intervention in the public sphere was not predictable. But the modern High Courts understood power—and its limitations—as never before. They did not hesitate to tell a president that he could not dictate rules to a major industry, or the legislatures and governors of an entire region that they could not run their schools as they had for a hundred years, or the Congress that it could not pass an act restoring religious worship to a central place in our laws. Indeed, in their jurisprudence, these Courts not only reflected modern ideas of political and human rights, they also helped to frame those ideas.

CHAPTER 11

The Stone Court, 1941–1946

By the time that Charles Evans Hughes submitted his resignation from the Court's center chair in April 1941, Franklin Delano Roosevelt had achieved his objective of packing the Supreme Court. From 1937 to 1942, Roosevelt had nine opportunities to shape the High Tribunal to his liking, including the elevation of Stone to chief justice. But the Court had already approved the domestic New Deal, and the nation now faced an entirely different kind of crisis.

The justices that Roosevelt named confronted a far more implacable and wily enemy than the Depression and had to deal with far more complex and troubling issues than perplexed the Taft Court. For soon after Hughes stepped down, the nation went to war. World War II was not only a monumental event, absorbing ten million Americans into the army, four million into the navy, and six hundred thousand into the marines. The conflict entailed the most extensive conversion ever from peacetime to wartime production and finance in American history (over $304 billion were spent on the war effort itself). The administration and the Congress turned warehouses and factories into an "arsenal of democracy." Rationing of gasoline and other war materials reminded every American that patriotism had its costs.

Turning a small peacetime military establishment into a giant war machine and putting a peacetime nation onto a wartime footing had immediate legal ramifications. The Selective Service Act barred racial discrimination in the draft (though the armed forces were still segregated), and the service of minorities in the war effort led directly to President Harry S. Truman's 1948 order desegregating the armed forces. The Department of Justice faced issues of wartime dissent, sabotage, and disloyalty. What was to be done with German and Japanese nationals—a potential fifth column in the country? Opposition to the war and freedom of speech and press were not curbed as they had been during World War I, but the Smith Act of 1940 reimposed some of the restrictions of the Espionage Act.

Even as the United States went to war, new and powerful currents were stirring on the home front. Minorities and labor groups empowered by wartime employment opportunities were gathering strength for the battle for legal equality. Using wartime needs as leverage, these groups sought their rightful place in the nation's economy, politics, and law. State governments did not always concede these rights, particularly when the NAACP and organized labor pressed for reforms.

STONE'S "WILD HORSES"

Was the Stone Court up to the tasks posed by wartime? It soon became apparent that Stone's "wild horses," as he called them, were not easily corralled. In part, the management style of the chief justice did not promote harmony. An academic by training, he allowed everyone to speak more than once at conference and commented himself on every other justice's opinion, and so prolonged discord. Taft had predicted as much of Stone, but at first Roosevelt's elevation of a nominal Republican with over fifteen years' experience as a member of the Court garnered almost universal acclaim. Frankfurter strongly supported Stone, confident that Stone and he would agree.

But perhaps Stone never had a chance, for one of Stone's new colleagues thought he had the better claim, had been promised the job, and was denied it because of a conspiracy. Attorney General Robert H. Jackson, who advised Roosevelt on several of his other appointees, believed the president had promised him the chief justiceship. He could claim many qualifications for the job. Another of the Court's rags-to-riches stories, Jackson had grown up on a farm in upstate New York. After completing high school, he took classes for a year at Albany Law School and observed New York Court of Appeals arguments. In 1913, at the age of twenty-one, he gained admission to the bar. A voracious reader, he consumed books on history, classical literature, and biographies that would later pepper his opinions and make him one of the great literary craftsmen on the Court. He was immensely successful in private practice but took time to represent the poor and downtrodden as well as the well-to-do.

Jackson's reputation as a lawyer and his steadfast Democratic politics brought him to FDR's attention as a friend and advisor, then in 1938 as solicitor general, and in 1940 as attorney general when Murphy went on the Court. A year later, Jackson followed. Because Stone was sixty-nine and he was only fifty, Jackson assumed that would leave him more than enough time. Jackson was content to fill the associate chair vacated when Stone became chief, but soon became restive. Expected, like Murphy, to follow a liberal activist line, he proved much closer to Frankfurter, reliably deferential to government. Jackson believed that in a world filled with fanatics, liberty must make some concessions to order, and the rights that every citizen had did not include the right to undermine elected officials or the Constitution itself. As he wrote, the Bill of Rights was not "a suicide pact."

Like Frankfurter, Jackson found himself increasingly isolated and came to blame much of this on the real and imagined machinations of Hugo Black. The "feud" was simmering from the moment that Jackson joined the Court, but it exploded in public as a result of the harsh exchange in *Jewel Ridge Coal Corp. v. Local 6167 United Mine Workers* (1945), a case interpreting the Fair Labor Standards Act of 1938. The act completed the long course of minimum wage and working conditions legislation and litigation, providing for a federal minimum wage, pay for overtime, and restrictions on child labor. At stake in the case was whether underground traveling time to work in mines should be considered part of the workday and thus be compensated. The majority of the Court agreed that it should.

Jackson and three of his brethren dissented because the statute "either invalidates collectively bargained agreements which govern the matter in difference between these parties or it ignores their explicit terms"; the language of the statute did not authorize it to supersede bargained-for labor conditions; nothing in the legislative history demonstrated that Congress wanted the Fair Labor Standards Act to supersede contracts; it was the miners who demanded that the Fair Labor Standards Act leave in place their contracts with the mine owners; and "the decision necessarily invalidates the basis on which the Government itself has operated the mines and brings into question the validity of the Government's strike settlement agreements and of all existing miners' agreements."

Jackson's dissent had been, in fact, the majority opinion until Reed's vote shifted, and Jackson suspected that Black, whose law practice had included unions, was behind the shift. Moreover, adding to the dispute, Jackson, with Frankfurter pulling the strings, or at least egging him on, made his objections to Black even more personal when the coal company asked Black to recuse himself, for his former law partner had argued the case before the Court on behalf of the union. Jackson saw Black's refusal to recuse himself as unethical. But Jackson's dissent itself violated one of the unwritten canons of how the justices treat one another. For Jackson quoted Black's words from the time when Black was in the Senate and had testified in favor of the Fair Labor Standards Act. "'[Senator] WALSH: Does the bill affect collective-bargaining agreements already made or hereafter to be made between employers and employees? [Senator] BLACK: It does not.'" Black took exception—the quotation had been taken out of context. Jackson did not hide his glee when Congress not only overrode the Court's decision by amending the act but also revised the judicial code of conduct to forbid participation of a judge when said judge had a "relationship to a party's attorney."

When President Truman prevailed upon Jackson to be the chief prosecutor at the Nuremberg Trials that held members of Hitler's Nazi Germany responsible for their war crimes, Jackson jumped at the chance to leave the marble palace for a year. But his diligent efforts in Europe did not result in the posting he so coveted—the chief justiceship. Among other reasons, Black and Frankfurter had advised Truman that Jackson would not be able to lead the Court. When Stone died suddenly of a cerebral hemorrhage, Truman selected a Senate friend, Frederick M. Vinson, to lead the Court. Jackson died shortly after the Warren Court issued its landmark decision in *Brown*, his most lasting contribution to the Court's history an aphorism: "We are not final because we are infallible, but we are infallible only because we are final."

Joining at the same time as Jackson, though confirmed a month earlier, James F. Byrnes replaced McReynolds, the last of the four horsemen to retire. Byrnes had even less formal education than Jackson but made up for it with the same drive, energy, and support for Roosevelt. He had dropped out of school at fourteen to help his widowed mother by working as a clerk in a local law firm in his birthplace, Charleston, South Carolina. The head of the firm, Benjamin H. Rutledge Jr., encouraged his charge to read widely and take stenographic courses. With Rutledge's considerable help, Byrnes secured a position as the official reporter in South Carolina's second judicial circuit. In 1903, after reading law with the chief judge, he gained admission to the bar and began his practice at the age of twenty-one.

From these humble beginnings, he rose through the legal and political ranks, becoming a prosecutor in 1908 and earning a seat in the U.S. House of Representatives which he occupied from 1911 to 1925, when he lost his first bid for the U.S. Senate in a close election. In the House, he favored the progressive, yet segregationist and antilabor, politics of Woodrow Wilson and other forward-thinking politicians of the New South. When he won a Senate seat, he carried these politics into FDR's New Deal. Along with Black, Byrnes was Roosevelt's key man in the Congress, a position that allowed him to stymie any desegregation initiatives. Largely as a reward for services rendered and to put a southerner on the bench, Roosevelt put his name forward when McReynolds decided he was tired of fighting the losing battle against Roosevelt's men.

Byrnes served only one term on the highest tribunal before accepting the post that the president himself called "assistant president"—helping the administration run the war effort. He managed to write sixteen opinions while on the Court, more than any other justice over that amount of time, deferring to the political branches except on the occasional First Amendment case. He earned high praise from Frankfurter, who liked Byrnes's adherence to the doctrine and approach of judicial restraint. His primary contribution to the Court appears to have been his geniality. He often invited his fellow justices over for dinner, conversation, and song. Byrnes ended his national government service as Truman's first secretary of state. In this position, he helped construct the beginnings of the administration's approach to the Soviet Union. In 1947, he stepped down to practice law in the District of Columbia but returned to politics as South Carolina's governor from 1950 to 1955. As governor, he had a mixed record of funding education and leading the effort against desegregation. He frequently spoke out from retirement against the decisions of the Warren Court until his death in 1972. He is remembered largely for his staunch support of Jim Crow and not for his more liberal opinions toward the power of the government to aid, sponsor, and regulate for the benefit of the disadvantaged.

Roosevelt nominated Wiley B. Rutledge to replace Byrnes, giving Black, Douglas, and Murphy a solid fourth vote. Rutledge was one of the Court's great might-have-beens. Felled in 1949 by a massive stroke, he served only six years on the bench but earned the respect of friend and foe alike for his openness and forthright defense of civil liberties. Rutledge was born in Kentucky in 1894, and his father was a Baptist minister. He attended the University of Wisconsin at Madison and majored in ancient languages. Teaching full time in Bloomington, Indiana, while attending Indiana University Law School, he fell gravely ill with tuberculosis, the same disease that had taken his mother when he was nine.

With his law plans on hold, he sought a better climate for his health in New Mexico and then in Colorado, earning his law degree at the University of Colorado Law School in 1922 and two years later becoming a professor there. He then moved to Washington University Law School in St. Louis, Missouri, becoming dean in 1930. Five years later, he became dean of the University of Iowa College of Law. Like Stone, throughout his academic career, Rutledge had a reputation as a generous and personable teacher with strong liberal commitments. He came to Roosevelt's attention as one of the few law school deans who supported the Court-packing plan. Roosevelt picked him to serve on the D.C. Court of Appeals. Alongside his future chief justice, Vinson, Rutledge grew into his new role as a judge and an outspoken liberal.

In 1942, he joined the High Court, in time to cast a deciding vote in *Murdock v. Pennsylvania* (1943), which explicitly named the exercise of religion as a "preferred freedom." Rutledge's own views were best displayed in *Thomas v. Collins* (1945). Not only was a union official's speech to potential union members protected against Texas's law requiring a permit for such speech, but speech itself was a preferred right: "The case confronts us again with the duty our system places on this Court to say where the individual's freedom ends and the State's power begins. Choice on that border, now as always delicate, is perhaps more so where the usual presumption supporting legislation is balanced by the preferred place given in our scheme to the great, the indispensable democratic freedoms secured by the First Amendment." The state's antiunion laws had to face strict scrutiny, not the far-more-permissive rational-relation test: "That priority gives these liberties a sanctity and a sanction not permitting dubious intrusions. . . . The rational connection between the remedy provided and the evil to be curbed, which in other contexts might support legislation against attack on due process grounds, will not suffice. These rights rest on firmer foundation."

The last man to join the Stone Court, Harold H. Burton, replaced Justice Roberts. A conservative who helped bring stability and lower tensions, Burton's appointment constituted one of Truman's attempts to assuage the feelings of Republicans who chafed at their lack of representation on the Court after nearly thirteen years of Democratic appointments. Burton would not arouse significant opposition because the Senate was unlikely to reject one of its own. For Burton was a moderate Republican from Ohio who favored some social programs and an international role for the United States in a post–World War II world. Like Murphy, Burton prized good government, but without any of Murphy's self-righteous grandstanding. Truman knew and liked Burton from their days in the Senate, and like Taft, Truman valued friendship among the qualifications for a seat on the High Court bench.

In addition to his contribution to Court harmony by favoring orderly and respectful discussions, Burton worked long hours mastering the precedents and legislative record of the cases that came before him. In his early years on the bench, Black and Douglas openly wondered about his competence, in part given Burton's ponderous efforts to reach a decision in cases. Burton's approach was one of studious deference to legislatures except when it came to abhorrent violations of basic civil liberties. He, along with Frankfurter, Reed, and, later, John Marshall Harlan II, found no difficulty overruling Jim Crow but rejected the more aggressive liberal stance of Black and Douglas on other First Amendment and Fourteenth Amendment issues. Ultimately, his declining capacities due to Parkinson's disease forced his retirement from the Court in 1958. He died in 1964.

Had the Jackson-Black feud been the only break in the Court's fellowship, Stone might have been able to maintain a semblance of harmony among the members. But even more disruptive was the deteriorating relationship between

Black and Frankfurter. Black drew Douglas to his side, a natural intellectual ally whose earlier willingness to disregard Frankfurter's patronizing attitude soon eroded. Frankfurter used the art of flattery he had honed on Holmes, Brandeis, and Roosevelt to woo Jackson.

Personal disagreeableness reinforced jurisprudential disagreements. Frankfurter's preference for deference had hardened into a philosophy of judicial restraint. Black's equally inflexible reading of the Bill of Rights required strict scrutiny of the legislatures' actions in a wide variety of cases. Black's absolutism fit Douglas's far more loosely worn willingness to read the Constitution to fit his preferred results. In fact, they were the most liberal on the Court, next to Murphy and later Rutledge. Burton found his way into Frankfurter's camp, if not into his circle of admirers.

WAR POWERS

Just as the White Court had given Wilson's wartime administration considerable latitude in the conduct of the war, so even the most independent-minded of Stone's wild horses hesitated to oppose the president and Congress during World War II. With uneasy minds, they concurred, well aware that officials in the Departments of Justice, War, and State might be swayed by misinformation, indifference to legal niceties, or a disregard for individual rights.

The first case to raise these concerns began in June 1942. German U-boats were sinking U.S. commercial ships on the Atlantic coast within sight of the shore. As in World War I, the U-boat had become the symbol of Germany's indifference to international law and morality. In the middle of the night, two U-boats deposited eight German Americans on the shores of Long Island and Florida with explosives, maps, and the express mission of disrupting U.S. war industries. Thanks to second thoughts of two of the men, FBI agents rounded up the entire nest of saboteurs in New York and Chicago.

Roosevelt ordered that the men be tried not in regular civilian courts but before a specially constituted military tribunal. Perhaps he had in mind the fact that the FBI had not found the saboteurs on its own and that consequently the country's shores and military installations were not safe from the enemy. The fact remained that Roosevelt had ordered the special procedure on his own authority. He assigned the attorney general as a prosecutor, a role that the solicitor general would ordinarily have assumed, a trial on the fifth floor of the Justice Department rather than in a regular court of law, and no review of the proceedings by anybody except himself.

The military commission found the eight men guilty of violating the congressionally enacted Articles of War. The defendants' attorneys filed writs of habeas corpus with the Supreme Court, on the grounds that their clients had been denied due process, the right to a public trial, and counsel of their own choosing. The civilian courts were in session at the time, and the precedent of *Ex parte Milligan* should have sent the Nazi saboteur cases to the civil courts. In a per curiam opinion in which Murphy did not participate, *Ex parte Quirin* (1942), Stone wrote for a unanimous Court denying the defendants' petitions. Although he did find that the Court had the authority to review the cases, he upheld the president's and Congress's authority to dispose of their cases by specially created military tribunal. He reasoned that "the detention and trial of petitioners—ordered by the President in the declared exercise of his powers as Commander in Chief of the Army in time of war and of grave public danger—are not to be set aside by the courts without the clear conviction that they are in conflict with the Constitution or laws of Congress constitutionally enacted." He also distinguished between "lawful combatants," those who wore uniforms and were to be treated as prisoners of war, and "unlawful combatants," those who did not wear uniforms and were subject to military tribunals. This language has reappeared in the 2006 Patriot Act.

Stone noted that "all the petitioners were born in Germany; all have lived in the United States. All returned to Germany between 1933 and 1941." Did this entitle them to the rights that citizens had to due process when civilian courts were in operation? Did they fall under the precedent of *Milligan*? Stone cited *Milligan*, but then ignored it. In fact, he ignored as well the Espionage Act of 1917, which provided for trial for offenses like the defendants' in civil courts:

Congress, in addition to making rules for the government of our Armed Forces, has thus exercised its authority to define and punish offenses against the law of nations by sanctioning, within constitutional limitations, the jurisdiction of military commissions to try persons for offenses which, according to the rules and precepts of the law of nations, and more particularly the law of war, are cognizable by such tribunals. And the President, as Commander in Chief, by his Proclamation in time of war has invoked that law.

But Stone had begged the question of whether in this case the tribunal was "within constitutional limitations." In any case, by the time Stone issued the formal opinion, the army had already executed six of the spies.

Secretary of War Henry Stimson, himself a lawyer, objected to the entire procedure. From the start, he had preferred a civil trial to a military tribunal. When Roosevelt told him, "I won't give them up . . . understand," Stimson backed down. When a second group of Germans came ashore in 1945, he insisted on and prevailed in having regular tribunal proceedings, with the result that the two men received commuted sentences from Truman.

In *Cramer v. U.S.* (1945), perhaps because the United States now had the upper hand in the conflict, Jackson wrote for a 5-to-4 majority that found insufficient grounds to convict Anthony Cramer, accused of treason for assisting one of the saboteurs from the *Quirin* case. His opinion rested on a close reading of the treason clauses of the U.S. Constitution that required giving "aid and comfort" to the enemy but also "adherence to" the enemy and specified the testimony of two witnesses in court. Cramer had provided unknowing assistance to a would-be saboteur, and therefore that assistance was not automatically treasonable.

The legal questions raised in *Quirin* survived the war. In the case *In re Yamashita* (1946), Stone, over the dissents of Murphy and Rutledge, upheld the use of military tribunals on foreign (actually U.S.-occupied Japanese) soil, even though the defendant, General Tomoyuki Yamashita, was to be tried after the war for his troops' war crimes in Japanese-held Manila during the war. If tribunals ended with the end of hostilities, "the practical administration of the system of military justice under the law of war would fail." Nuremberg, with its far-more-visible war crimes trials of leading Nazis, loomed over the Japanese case.

Murphy, in dissent, pointed out that Stone's argument failed to take into account that the close of hostilities ended the basis for prosecution outside the regular procedures in the Fifth Amendment. Murphy turned the Bill of Rights into international law: "The immutable rights of the individual, including those secured by the Due Process Clause of the Fifth Amendment, belong not alone to the members of those nations that excel on the battlefield or that subscribe to the democratic ideology. They belong to every person in the world, victor or vanquished, whatever may be his race, color or beliefs."

Somewhat more practically, Rutledge added that

Japan is a defeated power, having surrendered, if not unconditionally then under the most severe conditions. Her territory is occupied by American military forces. She is scarcely in a position to bargain with us or to assert her rights. Nor can her nationals. She no longer holds American prisoners of war. . . . Had one of our soldiers or officers been tried for alleged war crimes, he would have been entitled to the benefits of the Articles of War. I think that Yamashita was equally entitled to the same protection.

In fact, Yamashita had no hand in the atrocities against American soldiers on the Bataan Death March and in the camps—he had only arrived in the Philippines in late 1944. Nor did he have control of the Japanese marines who sacked Manila at the end of the war.

The problems posed by war crimes, suspected sabotage, and terrorism tested the ingenuity of the Court, and will continue to do so as long as the United States engages in police actions abroad or gains custody of those who commit crimes against Americans overseas. In *Duncan v. Kahanamoku* (1946), the Court reasserted the rule in *Milligan*. Black, for the Court, held the governor of Hawaii's declaration of martial law and the exclusive use of military tribunals to be unconstitutional. Black particularly stressed the importance of civilian courts to the rule of law: "Legislatures and courts are not merely cherished American institutions; they are indispensable to our government." Murphy concurred in the result but wanted the Court to forbid the use of military tribunals altogether. Burton, with Frankfurter, dissented on the grounds that the Court should defer to executive authority in such perilous circumstances. In "the fog of war," officials were "entitled to a wide range of discretion if they were to meet the obligations imposed upon them." If the offense occurred outside the United States and the accused were tried by a military commission abroad, they had no habeas corpus rights, per *Johnson v. Eisentrager* (1950). But this was not the last word. The Rehnquist Court would find some of these same issues coming to it after 9/11.

Divisions on the Court appeared in denaturalization and expulsion cases during the war, when the Roosevelt administration attempted to deport persons it believed to be disloyal. Murphy tried to make the standard one of "evidence of a clear and convincing character" in his majority opinion in *Schneiderman v. U.S.* (1943). Frankfurter preferred "weighty proof" and made this the cornerstone of his opinion in *Baumgartner v. U.S.* (1944). The final word came in *Knauer v. U.S.* (1946). Douglas felt no sympathy for Knauer, who repeatedly advocated and worked on behalf of Nazi Germany. Murphy and Rutledge disagreed with a line of reasoning that treated naturalized citizens as "second-class citizens."

Murphy did get to put his stamp on World War II internal security policy in *Hartzel v. U.S.* (1944), a prosecution under the 1917 Espionage Act. Hartzel had mailed hundreds of flyers with his pro-Nazi, anti-Semitic, anti-Roosevelt views to numerous individuals whose addresses he obtained from such diverse sources as the world almanac and other public listings. Murphy found nothing in the flyers that could lead a reasonable jury to conclude that Hartzel had formed the specific intent "to cause insubordination, disloyalty, mutiny or refusal of duty in the military forces or to obstruct the recruiting and enlistment service." He argued that expression needed protection, especially in wartime, regardless of the vitriol in those expressions. Reed, with Frankfurter, Douglas, and Jackson, disagreed.

The Stone Court split on draft cases. In *Falbo v. U.S.* (1944), Black held that all administrative procedures needed to be exhausted before the Court would review a draft board decision, as Congress did not provide for judicial review in the Selective Service Act of 1940. Murphy dissented. Falbo was an ordained minister. "Individual rights have been recognized by our jurisprudence only after long and costly struggles. They should not be struck down by anything less than the gravest necessity." The justices meted out a harsh refinement of *Falbo* in *Estep v. U.S.* (1946). A Jehovah's Witness, who had claimed a ministerial exemption, was denied the exemption. The person refused to submit to induction and was prosecuted. He then challenged both the classification and the conviction and lost in the federal courts. Douglas's opinion reversed the conviction. Frankfurter, who had already lost to Douglas on Jehovah's Witness free speech cases, took the opportunity to whack at Douglas:

Not only is such a result opposed to the expressed will of Congress. It runs counter to the achievement of the great object avowed by Congress in enacting this legislation; it contradicts the settled practice under the Selective Service Act throughout the war years, recognized as such by authoritative Congressional opinion; it reverses all the circuit courts of appeals before whom the matter has come, constituting an impressive body of decisions and expressing the views of more than forty judges.

Stone and Burton also dissented, arguing that the conviction should stand.

Four related cases came to represent all of the foregoing challenges to wartime policy for civilians. In 1942, according to an act of Congress and a presidential order, over one hundred thousand Japanese American citizens were forcibly removed from their West Coast homes and relocated to detention camps in the deserts and mountains of the West and Southwest. Their sole infraction was their Japanese ancestry. The efficiency and completeness of the War Relocation Authority and the Western Civilian Control Administration in establishing and running the internment camps surpassed that of the English detention of Boers in South Africa during the Boer War.

After the shock, panic, and embarrassment of the Japanese attack on Pearl Harbor and a string of successive defeats in the Pacific and at the urging of several military and civilian officials, on February 19, 1942, Roosevelt issued Executive Order 9066 that allowed the secretary of war and military officials to designate areas of the country from which people could be "excluded, expelled, restricted, or otherwise subjected to regulations the appropriate military authorities might impose at their discretion." Acting under this policy, General John L. DeWitt, commander of the Western Defense Command, dictated curfews for all those of Japanese ancestry residing within forty miles of the West

Coast. On March 18, 1942, Roosevelt issued Executive Order 9102 establishing the War Relocation Authority that gave DeWitt the wherewithal to forcibly remove Japanese Americans to "relocation centers" in Colorado, Arizona, and other western states. On March 21, Congress passed legislation codifying this executive order. Within days, DeWitt's military police began forcibly evacuating 112,000 Japanese Americans to the War Relocation Centers. About 70,000 of these were U.S.-born citizens.

The hardship the curfew and later relocation forced upon these individuals was devastating. Psychological trauma, economic devastation from the sale of all of their businesses and homes, and the separation from their communities took a terrible toll on these people. The first challenge to these policies came from Kiyoshi Hirabayashi and Minoru Yasui. Hirabayashi only reluctantly challenged the curfew after initially obeying. Yasui was an activist for the Japanese American Citizens League and mounted his case with the express intent of overturning the policy. Though considered apart, in opinions that Stone crafted, the unanimous Court rejected the challenges to the curfew, without considering the relocation aspect in *Hirabayashi v. U.S.* (1943) or reversing the summary removal of citizenship in *Yasui v. U.S.* (1943).

Stone considered three issues: whether Congress and the president had the authority to apply such a curfew; whether Congress and the president met the constitutional burden in doing so; and whether Congress could properly delegate such an authority to the War Relocation Authority. His answer to all three questions was in the affirmative. He deferred to the decisions of the military and the executive and the legislative branches in considering the overall context of the imminent and immense danger of wartime. The "war power" in the Constitution meant that the political branches must be given the leeway they needed to meet present emergencies: "Where, as they did here, the conditions call for the exercise of judgment and discretion and for the choice of means by those branches of the Government on which the Constitution has placed the responsibility of warmaking, it is not for any court to sit in review of the wisdom of their action or substitute its judgment for theirs." Based on a "reasonableness" standard of review, in effect the rational-relation test, Stone relinquished the judiciary's supervision of the matter.

Although Douglas concurred, he tried to narrow the precedent. He emphasized the immediacy and the threatened danger as well as the difficulties of attempting to enact a more nuanced approach. Murphy's concurring opinion read more like a dissent. Though he too granted the good faith and intentions of the military authorities, he made it clear he found the blanket classification of a group because of race or nationality as liable to punishment without trial abhorrent: "Distinctions based on color and ancestry are utterly inconsistent with our traditions and ideals. They are at variance with the principles for which we are now waging war."

Black delivered the opinion of the Court in *Korematsu v. U.S.* (1944), which upheld forced relocation. Although he, unlike Stone, weighed the congressional enactment under the strict scrutiny standard he had helped formulate, the result was the same:

Like curfew, exclusion of those of Japanese origin was deemed necessary because of the presence of an unascertained number of disloyal members of the group, most of whom we have no doubt were loyal to this country. It was because we could not reject the finding of the military authorities that it was impossible to bring about an immediate segregation of the disloyal from the loyal that we sustained the validity of the curfew order as applying to the whole group.

Like Stone, Black found that the military acted within the authority Congress and the president had lawfully executed: "But exclusion from a threatened area, no less than curfew, has a definite and close relationship to the prevention of espionage and sabotage. . . . when under conditions of modern warfare our shores are threatened by hostile forces, the power to protect must be commensurate with the threatened danger." He denied any racial aspect in the situation: "Korematsu was not excluded from the Military Area because of hostility to him or his race." Frankfurter agreed that this was the "business of the . . . Congress and the executive . . . not ours."

Roberts no longer concurred with his brethren: "I dissent, because I think the indisputable facts exhibit a clear violation of Constitutional rights." He found that relocation on the basis of ancestry, as opposed to the curfew, was a clear violation of the Constitution: "It is the case of convicting a citizen as a punishment for not submitting to imprisonment in a concentration camp, based on his ancestry, and solely because of his ancestry, without evidence or inquiry concerning his loyalty and good disposition towards the United States." Murphy, now dissenting, added: "Such exclusion goes over 'the very brink of constitutional power' and falls into the ugly abyss of racism." Jackson dissented as well:

Korematsu was born on our soil, of parents born in Japan. The Constitution makes him a citizen of the United States by nativity and a citizen of California by residence. No claim is made that he is not loyal to this country. There is no suggestion that apart from the matter involved here he is not law-abiding and well disposed. Korematsu, however, has been convicted of an act not commonly a crime. It consists merely of being present in the state whereof he is a citizen, near the place where he was born, and where all his life he has lived.

After the 1944 election, in which Roosevelt had stormed back into the White House for a fourth term and the war against Japan now raged over its home islands, the military exigencies claimed for relocation vanished like a mist at morning and the injustice alone of the relocation remained. Douglas, explaining the Court's shifting stances in *Ex parte Mitsuye Endo v. U.S.*, neatly skirted the question of how the Court could uphold the detention of Korematsu while invalidating the detention of Endo by ingeniously distinguishing the two cases. Korematsu had challenged the legitimacy of the initial detention order. Endo was challenging its continuation in her particular circumstances. Douglas concluded that she should have been granted leave from the detention center, whereas Korematsu was legally detained:

It is conceded by the Department of Justice and by the War Relocation Authority that appellant is a loyal and law-abiding citizen. They make no claim that she is detained on any charge or that she is even suspected of disloyalty. Moreover, they do not contend that she may be held any longer in the Relocation Center. They concede that it is beyond the power of the War Relocation Authority to detain citizens against whom no charges of disloyalty or subversiveness have been made for a period longer than that necessary to separate the loyal from the disloyal and to provide the necessary guidance for relocation.

Even when the Court provided relief, it did not do so on well-ordered legal grounds: "We are of the view that Mitsuye Endo should be given her liberty. In reaching that conclusion we do not come to the underlying constitutional issues which have been argued." Why not spell out, as Roberts and his brethren had in dissent, the constitutional grounds for Endo's freedom? Because, as Douglas immediately continued, her case was not the same as *Quirin* or even as the other Japanese relocation cases. Instead, "We must assume that the Chief Executive and members of Congress, as well as the courts, are sensitive to and respectful of the liberties of the citizen. In interpreting a wartime measure we must assume that their purpose was to allow for the greatest possible accommodation between those liberties and the exigencies of war."

The concurring opinions in *Endo* took issue with Douglas's exculpation of the executive and the military. Murphy repeated his objections to the entire relocation program: "For the Government to suggest under these circumstances that the presence of Japanese blood in a loyal American citizen might be enough to warrant her exclusion from a place where she would otherwise have a right to go is a position I cannot sanction." Roberts concurred, but disagreed with Douglas's skirting of the constitutional issues: "An admittedly loyal citizen has been deprived of her liberty for a period of years. Under the Constitution she should be free to come and go as she pleases. Instead, her liberty of motion and other innocent activities have been prohibited and conditioned. She should be discharged."

The shadow of the four cases reached into the 1980s. For his part, Justice Black told an interviewer in 1971 that "I would do precisely the same thing today. . . . people were rightly fearful of the Japanese" because "they all look alike to a person not a Jap." Justice Reed also recalled that "maybe it was hysteria . . . but the record shows there were authenticated cases of such treasonable actions." Justice Douglas confessed, in 1974: "I have always regretted that I bowed to my elders and withdrew my opinion" condemning the camps. In a series of suits in federal court beginning in 1983, Peter Irons and other lawyers gained for Korematsu, Yasui, and Hirabayashi the ruling that their convictions under the relocation laws and orders had been illegal. In 1988, Congress appropriated $20,000 for each survivor of the camps as payment for three years of lost lives and suffering. No assessment was made or repayment offered for lost businesses and careers.

CIVIL LIBERTIES

Deference to the military and its commander in chief regarding the civil rights of Japanese Americans did not blind all members of the Court to the civil liberties of other minorities. Though Frankfurter would dissent, the liberals on the Court found their voice, and eventually a majority, in Jehovah's Witness First Amendment cases. The Witnesses were evangelists who refused to conform in their behavior in various ways because of their religious convictions. They could not take oaths, refused service in the armed forces, and insisted on distributing their literature and proselytizing even in hostile areas. As a result, many communities perceived them as unpatriotic or worse. Assaults on Witnesses were common, and, on various occasions, mobs led by local officials, sometimes including police, attacked them viciously. Beginning in the late 1930s, this persecuted sect initiated a series of constitutional challenges to the official restrictions they faced. In *Gobitis*, Frankfurter dealt them a defeat. But the Witnesses were nothing if not persistent.

In *Jones v. Opelika* and its companion cases, *Bowden v. Fort Smith* and *Jobin v. Arizona* (1942), the Witnesses challenged the licensing laws of cities in Alabama, Arkansas, and Arizona, respectively, on the grounds that the fees restricted their free exercise of religion guaranteed through the Fourteenth Amendment's incorporation of the First Amendment. In a 5-to-4 opinion written by Justice Reed, the Court found that the regulation was content neutral and, thus, permissible. He recognized the necessity of protecting belief and knowledge from censorship, but he argued that the fee was merely a tax on the commercial activity of selling the literature. Stone, joined by Black, Douglas, and Murphy, dissented: "The First Amendment, which the Fourteenth makes applicable to the states, declares: 'Congress shall make no law respecting an establishment of religion, or prohibiting the free exercise thereof; or abridging the freedom of speech, or of the press.' I think that the ordinance in each of these cases is on its face a prohibited invasion of the freedoms thus guaranteed, and that the judgment in each should be reversed."

In 1943, the Court reversed its position. The explanation for the shift in the Court's determination was simple. Rutledge had replaced Byrnes. In *Murdock v. Pennsylvania* and seven other cases, Douglas wrote for a five-justice majority that the free exercise of religion occupied a "preferred position," Rutledge's language. Douglas rejected Reed's reasoning that the sale of the literature made it a commercial activity. Douglas posited: "If it did, then the passing of the collection plate in church would make the church service a commercial project." He placed the highest value on the activity and, in turn, rejected the states' interests in no uncertain terms: "A state may not impose a charge for the enjoyment of a right granted by the federal constitution."

In *West Virginia State Board of Education v. Barnette* (1943), Justice Jackson led the Court in reversing Frankfurter's decision in *Gobitis*. Adding insult to the injury of having Douglas and Black abandon him, Frankfurter had Holmes's imminent danger test thrown in his face. Frankfurter's deference to legislatures fell as Jackson placed the burden on West Virginia to show that Witnesses' refusal to salute the flag somehow jeopardized the well-being of the polity. In another of his eloquent phrasings, he maintained, "If there is any fixed star in our constitutional constellation, it is that no official, high or petty, can prescribe what shall be orthodox in politics, nationalism, religion, or other matters of opinion."

The Court did not always rule in the Witnesses' favor. In *Prince v. Massachusetts* (1944), Rutledge wrote for an 8-to-1 majority that Massachusetts could enforce its child labor law against parents or other relatives who had their children selling their literature on public streets. Despite the fact that it was part of the commandments of their faith that all proselytize, the state could substitute its own judgment as to what was in the best interest of the child. Murphy dissented on the grounds that the state had not met the burden of demonstrating a "serious menace to the public." Ironically, the Court had to balance its relatively newfound concern for children (recall the *Child Labor Law Cases*) with its equally newfound solicitousness for religious exercise.

In another line of cases involving Jehovah's Witnesses, the justices grappled with the blurry line between public and private conduct. In *Martin v. Struthers* (1943), they struck down an ordinance forbidding door-to-door solicitation. Free speech protected those giving out literature as well as the homeowners' right to receive it. The "minor nuisance" of unwanted solicitations could not overcome those rights. In *Marsh v. Alabama* (1946) and *Tucker v. Texas* (1946), majorities decided that even company towns and federal government towns, respectively, could not forbid the handing out of religious literature. Black wrote the majority opinion in both cases and gave the activity "preferred position" status, asserting in *Marsh* that the "right to exercise the liberties safeguarded by the First Amendment lies at the foundation of free government by free men." The Witnesses' litigation was forcing the Court into an endorsement of the First Amendment's privileged position.

But the Witnesses' victories were not laid upon free exercise of religion grounds, with the result that the time, place, and manner limitation on free speech in *Cantwell* applied in *Chaplinsky v. New Hampshire* (1942). A Jehovah's Witness with a pugnacious turn of phrase had taken up a position on a city street in Rochester, New Hampshire. As he passed out literature, his disparaging comments about local officials drew an angry crowd. The members of the crowd threatened him, and he responded that organized religion was a "racket." When police officers moved in to arrest him for disturbing the peace, he called one of them "a damned racketeer," a "damned fascist," and other names. New Hampshire had a statute curbing such public disturbances. Stone wrote: "We are unable to say that the limited scope of the statute as thus construed contravenes the Constitutional right of free expression. It is a statute narrowly drawn and limited to define and punish specific conduct lying within the domain of state power, the use in a public place of words likely to cause a breach of the peace." Murphy argued that "fighting words" were not protected by the First Amendment because they "inflict injury or tend to incite an immediate breach of peace" and do not convey ideas and are of "slight social value." This balancing of the value of the speech against its threat to "the social interest in order and morality" violated Black's absolutist approach, but Black joined the opinion.

But even *Chaplinsky* had limits, as seen immediately in *Bridges v. Wixon* (1945). In this case, Douglas, for a 5-to-3 majority, wrote to reverse the decision of the lower court upholding the deportation of a resident alien. Harry Bridges, an Australian resident alien, had been both a leading communist and a labor union organizer in the 1920s and 1930s. An attempt to deport him in 1938 had failed—the statute requiring that he be currently a member of the party. A second hearing resulted in his deportation. He appealed. He had done no more than associate with communists in the process of organizing longshoremen in San Francisco on behalf of the Congress of Industrial Organizations, the militant union that used sit-down strikes to achieve its goals. Rather than strike down the statute for its clumsy attempt to merge thought and deed, Douglas found problems with the administrative ruling's interpretation of congressional intent and the evidence used to convict Bridges. All of the justices were still a substantial distance away from blanket protection of free speech, but they had moved a few steps closer.

The Court ran into similar problems distinguishing unions' right to picket, a mixture of actual and symbolic speech, from pure speech in *Bakery and Pastry Drivers Local v. Wohl* (1942) and *Carpenters' and Joiners' Union v. Ritter's Café* (1942). Much hinged on the reasonableness of the state laws. In *Thomas v. Collins* (1945), Rutledge wrote for the majority in striking down a Texas law that required the preregistration of any would-be union organizer, in this case the president of the United Auto Workers. Frankfurter, Reed, Roberts, and Stone deferred to the state legislature.

Another case involving Harry Bridges, *Bridges v. California, Times-Mirror Co. v. Superior Court* (1941), stemmed from the trial of two union members for assaulting two nonunion truck drivers. Before the judge issued his sentence, the *Los Angeles Times* wrote an editorial calling for harsh punishment and Bridges wrote to the U.S. secretary of labor threatening a strike if the union members received harsh sentences. Black wrote the opinion for the 5-to-4 majority that overturned the contempt citations on the grounds they violated the free press and free speech clauses of the First Amendment.

First, Black applied the clear and present danger test to the fact pattern and found the state of California's assertions that it was protecting the integrity of the court system unsound:

Free speech and fair trials are two of the most cherished policies of our civilization, and it would be a trying task to choose between them. . . . To be sure, the exercise of power here in question was by a state judge. But in deciding whether or not the sweeping constitutional mandate against any law 'abridging the freedom of speech or of the press' forbids [the contempt order] we are necessarily measuring a power of all American courts, both state and federal, including this one.

Nothing Bridges said or the *Times* wrote posed such a danger to the California trial court or its proceedings.

Next, Black's reading of the framers' words told him that freedom of the press was fundamental. With them at his side, he rode roughshod over *Schenk, Gitlow,* and other annoying precedents. *Patterson v. Colorado* (1902) "cannot be taken as a decision squarely on this point," though surely it was. In practical terms, Black knew that "since [the contempt citations] punish utterances made during the pendency of a case, the judgments below therefore produce their restrictive results at the precise time when public interest in the matters discussed would naturally be at its height. Moreover, the ban is likely to fall not only at a crucial time but upon the most important topics of discussion."

Frankfurter's dissent rehashed his deference to state power. He had been assigned the opinion for the majority by Stone, but his prolonged researches on the history of the First Amendment held up its issuance. The case had to be reargued when Jackson and Byrnes joined the bench. In the meantime, Murphy switched his vote, Jackson joined him, and Frankfurter's 6-to-3 majority became a 4 to 5 minority.

CRIMINAL LAW

The Stone Court divided along the same lines in criminal law cases as it did in other areas. Frankfurter's "shock the conscience" approach yielding most often to the state vied with Black's bright-line prohibitions against infringements of the Bill of Rights. While Frankfurter frequently won over a majority, Black occasionally bested his rival. Even when he lost, he lay the foundation for future victories.

In a series of cases involving interrogation of suspects, the justices asked whether the confessions were voluntary. Voluntary meant that the suspect must have knowingly and freely given those statements. The problem with this test was that it did not evaluate police conduct as such. For example, in *McNabb v. U.S.* (1941), the majority found that federal officials violated a federal statute providing for a speedy arraignment. As a result, the statements given were unreliable and should be excluded from trial. In *Lisenba v. California* (1941), Roberts based his analysis on the old common-law rule that said that coerced confessions were unreliable and therefore produced unfair trials—but sleep deprivation and blows to the head were not sufficient to make the statements that followed inadmissible. Black and Douglas dissented, arguing that the misconduct tainted the confession. In *Ashcraft v. Tennessee* (1944), their dissent became Black's majority opinion, finding that thirty-six hours of interrogation under bright lights was "inherently coercive." Jackson wrote for himself,

Roberts, and Frankfurter in dissent, arguing that individual states must be allowed to determine for themselves the extent to which any given defendant confessed voluntarily.

In trying to decide matters of fact on a case-by-case basis, the justices were dancing around a very difficult technical issue. Should the standard be a bright-line one or one that varied with the defendant's situation?—in Jackson's words, "whether [the defendant] was educated or illiterate, intelligent or moronic, well or ill, Negro or white." In *Malinski v. New York* (1945), a majority found that a confession after the defendant spent several hours in a hotel room stripped naked was coerced. The dissenters believed police officers and a prosecutor, who denied that they had used force or the threat of it.

The Stone Court also struggled to adopt a standard in right-to-counsel cases. As in confessions, the majority moved cautiously toward incorporation. Roberts authored the controlling opinion in *Betts v. Brady* (1942). Counsel for defendants was not necessary unless there were "special circumstances." The Due Process Clause of the Fourteenth Amendment did not demand counsel for indigent defendants: "The phrase formulates a concept less rigid and more fluid than those envisaged in other specific and particular provisions of the Bill of Rights. Its application is less a matter of rule." For him and his six-vote majority, research on the practices of the various states throughout their history demonstrated that right to counsel was not considered fundamental.

Black, with Murphy and Douglas, saw a trial in which "a man of little education" was forced to defend himself. In that light no one could reasonably declare that the trial was fair. Black's dissent may have been his finest moment on the Court:

The petitioner, a farm hand, out of a job and on relief, was indicted in a Maryland state court on a charge of robbery. He was too poor to hire a lawyer. He so informed the court and requested that counsel be appointed to defend him. His request was denied. Put to trial without a lawyer, he conducted his own defense, was found guilty, and was sentenced to eight years' imprisonment.

Would the outcome have been different if Betts had had counsel? Impossible to say. But the constitutional command was clear as day: "If this case had come to us from a federal court, it is clear we should have to reverse it, because the Sixth Amendment makes the right to counsel in criminal cases inviolable by the Federal Government. I believe that the Fourteenth Amendment made the Sixth applicable to the states." Even if the Court did not agree that the Fourteenth Amendment incorporated the Sixth Amendment, "a practice cannot be reconciled with 'common and fundamental ideas of fairness and right,' which subjects innocent men to increased dangers of conviction merely because of their poverty." From his experience defending poor men accused of crime in Birmingham, Black knew the difference between adequate counsel and no counsel.

Ultimately, with Rutledge joining the majority in 1944, the Stone Court lurched toward a more expansive reading of the "special circumstances" exception. Even before Rutledge arrived, in *Glasser v. U.S.* (1942), the Court determined that a judge's order for an attorney to represent two alleged co-conspirators instead of just one was a denial of counsel. In *Rice v. Olson* (1945), a plea of guilty without the benefit of counsel in another federal case did not constitute a waiver of counsel. In *Hawk v. Olson* (1945), on a habeas corpus petition from a convicted murderer in Nebraska state prison, Reed wrote for the eight-person court: "We hold that denial of opportunity to consult with counsel on any material step after indictment or similar charge and arraignment violates the Fourteenth Amendment." On similar facts, the Court found *Powell v. Alabama*'s standard applicable and reversed convictions on lack-of-counsel grounds in *House v. Mayo* (1945) and *Tomkins v. Missouri* (1945).

Search-and-seizure cases under the Fourth Amendment presented similar opportunities to expand incorporation, but the Stone Court upheld the *Olmstead* rule that there must be a physical trespass involved. In *Goldman v. U.S.* (1942), the majority found that the use of an eavesdropping device called a detectaphone did not violate the applicable section of federal law forbidding the interception of information transmitted over air or wire, despite the fact that the detectaphone worked by collecting sound that had traveled (by necessity) through the air. In *Goldstein v. U.S.* (1942), the majority demanded that a party challenging the admissibility of an improperly executed interception had to have been a party to that conversation.

The Stone Court broadened protections for defendants in criminal cases in the selection of juries. In *Thiel v. Southern Pacific Co.* (1946) and *Ballard v. U.S.* (1946), the majorities held that excluding wage earners and women, respectively, from juries denied a fair trial. Unlike in *Betts v. Brady*, they discovered ample evidence of the value and widespread belief in a jury of one's peers. As Murphy reasoned in his opinion for the Court in *Thiel*: "Jury competence is an individual rather than a group or class matter. That fact lies at the very heart of the jury system. To disregard it is to open the door to class distinctions and discriminations which are abhorrent to the democratic ideals of trial by jury."

CIVIL RIGHTS

Jim Crow laws raised the same issues that dominated the justices' disputes in other areas: the deference due to democratically elected bodies versus the duty of judges to uphold the supreme law. Following *Strauder* and *Norris*, the Stone Court held discrimination on the basis of race in jury selection to be a violation of the Equal Protection Clause of the Fourteenth Amendment, in *Hill v. Texas* (1942). But it denied a claim of a defendant indicted by a grand jury that included only one African American, in *Akins v. Texas* (1945). Reed concluded for his six-justice majority that an allegation was not enough: "A purpose to discriminate must be present which may be proven by systematic exclusion of eligible jurymen of the proscribed race or by unequal application of the law to such an extent as to show intentional discrimination." At stake was the vital issue of evidence—would a statistical presentation, showing disproportionate numbers of whites on grand juries, be sufficient for the Court to infer intentional racial discrimination, or did the petitioner have to produce a "smoking gun," testimony that local officials intentionally discriminated? The same question would arise in civil rights suits after the passage of the Civil Rights Act of 1964.

The justices agreed that the all-white primary was impermissibly discriminatory even without evidence of a smoking gun. In *Smith v. Allwright* (1944), Reed delivered the opinion of the Court. In *Grovey v. Townsend* (1935), the Court held that the Texas Democratic Party's resolution denying membership to African Americans was not state action and hence could not be challenged under the Fourteenth Amendment. But in *U.S. v. Classic* (1941), the Court found that Louisiana's primary system was a state activity. Reed overruled *Grovey*, coming to the conclusion that "the [political] party takes its character as a state agency from the duties imposed upon it by state statutes; the duties do not become matters of private law because they are performed by a political party." Roberts dissented from what he regarded as a lack of concern for a "steadiness which would hold the balance even in the face of temporary ebbs and flows of opinion," for he had written *Grovey*.

But other cases led to a different conclusion about the Court's reading of the Fourteenth Amendment. One such controversy stemmed from litigation over the Illinois legislature's refusal to redistrict its congressional districts. Frankfurter wrote for himself, Burton, and Reed in *Colgrove v. Green* (1946) that this was a political question in which judges could not intervene: "It is hostile to a democratic system to involve the judiciary in the politics of the people. And it is not less pernicious if such judicial intervention in an essentially political contest be dressed up in the abstract phrases of the law." In addition, he could find no other remedy than disbanding all the districts and replacing them with a statewide ballot.

Black dissented, with Douglas and Murphy joining him. He saw no difficulty in providing for a statewide ballot nor in dismissing the idea that the issues presented were any more political than any other voting rights case. But, because Rutledge too feared Frankfurter's "political thicket," Jackson was away in Germany, and Stone had recently passed away, judicial restraint carried the day. The Court shied away from a fight with a state government. Frankfurter's restraint and deference had carried the day—but this question would be revisited and reversed by the Warren Court.

A majority of the Stone Court also believed that state and local officials must obey federal law, in *Screws v. U.S.* (1945), but not without complications. Douglas wrote for himself and three other justices in the majority that, when the Georgia sheriff and his deputies, who were white, beat Robert Hall, an African American, to death after arresting him for stealing a tire, the United States could prosecute them under the Civil Rights Act of 1866. At the same time, Douglas demanded that the jury instructions needed to include the statute's "willfully" element. That is, there must be an "evil motive." Rutledge concurred in Douglas's opinion, but Murphy dissented. Willfulness did not matter. Roberts dissented, joined by Frankfurter and Jackson. Rutledge agreed with Murphy, but to dissent would have denied Douglas a majority, with the result that the opinion would not be binding precedent.

In *Morgan v. Virginia* (1946), the Stone Court turned its attention to the issue of segregation on interstate buses. Unlike the steamboats in *Hall v. Decuir* and the rails in *Louisville, New Orleans and Texas Railroad Company,* buses on interstate routes were not to have segregated seating. Reed's majority opinion, however, did not base the ruling on the Equal Protection Clause but instead on the Interstate Commerce Clause, whereby "where uniformity is essential for the functioning of commerce, a state may not interpose its local regulation." He reasoned that the shifting of passengers as the bus crossed state lines in order to comply with differing local rules unduly burdened interstate travel. Burton dissented, and Black and Frankfurter concurred on separate grounds. Rutledge could concur in the result only—he wanted equal protection to ensure the end of segregation. Because of these weaknesses, *Morgan* did not end segregation, even on interstate bus travel, but it could serve as a basis for the Freedom Rides more than fifteen years later.

California's attempt to deny entrance to migrants escaping from the Dust Bowl, men and women commonly known as "Okies" after their primary state of origin, prompted the Stone Court to hold that no state could impede travel of persons for reasons economic or otherwise. In *Edwards v. California* (1941), Byrnes's opinion for the Court based the ruling on the grounds of interference with interstate commerce. Douglas, with Black and Murphy in agreement, concurred in the result but wanted to base the judgment on a right to travel inherent in the Privileges and Immunities Clause of the Fourteenth Amendment. If Douglas's view had carried a majority, it might have resuscitated the status of that clause, moribund since the *Slaughterhouse Cases*.

Douglas did get to write the majority opinion in a case overturning *Buck v. Bell*. In *Skinner v. Oklahoma* (1942), he found that Oklahoma's habitual criminal sterilization law impinged on a basic right: "We are dealing here with legislation which involves one of the basic civil rights of man. Marriage and procreation are fundamental to the very existence and survival of the race." Strict scrutiny of the state law found that it violated the Equal Protection Clause, because the Oklahoma law exempted embezzlement convictions, but not regular larceny, from its three-strikes-and-you-are-out-of-reproductive-rights rule.

A newfound skepticism about the acts of certain state legislatures with regard to fundamental liberties was creeping into the Court's jurisprudence. Racial discrimination lay just below the surface of the state's law, just as it had in the *Grandfather Clause Cases*. As Douglas hinted, he suspected that the statute, which depended upon both prosecutorial discretion and a jury finding, might have the same motive as the state's voting legislation: "In evil or reckless hands it can cause races or types which are inimical to the dominant group to wither and disappear. . . . Oklahoma deprives certain individuals of a right which is basic to the perpetuation of a race—the right to have offspring." *Skinner* would become a precedent in a wide range of cases, from abortion rights to restrictions on capital punishment to striking down state laws against interracial marriage.

The Stone Court's body of work had an unfinished quality. Although Stone had served for many years, most of his colleagues were relatively new to the Court when he became chief justice. His rock-solid self-assurance, an asset in the wars of the 1930s, ill suited him to broker peace between the factions of the Court that emerged in the war years. His own views led him to vote with different sides on different occasions, leaving the impression that he did not have strong opinions of his own.

But the Stone Court had taken the first steps toward the jurisprudence of "insular and isolated minorities," in the language of Stone's *Carolene* footnote. In free speech and civil rights cases, the majority of the wild horses pulled in the same direction—toward a broader conception of individual rights, a more potent role for the federal government in protecting those rights against discriminatory state action, and the imposition of the Bill of Rights on the states. The Taft Court had glanced in this direction and the Hughes Court had taken a tentative step or two, but the Stone Court proved that the Court must strictly scrutinize states and federal officials when preferred freedoms are threatened.

CHAPTER 12

The Vinson Court, 1946–1952

World War II and its aftermath dominated the Stone Court's agenda until the chief justice's untimely death in 1946. President Harry S. Truman then received his chance to shape the Court. In one of his many endearing asides, he admitted that he had tried to pack the Court but was disappointed with the results. It was impossible for the president to impress his will upon the justices, he concluded. His predecessors in the White House, starting with Washington, could have told him as much. Moreover, Truman's own liberal policy initiatives—the "fair deal," full employment, desegregation of the armed forces, the rebuilding of the world's economy, and support for the United Nations—did not particularly resonate with his selections for the Court.

Truman's appointments, starting with Fred Vinson to succeed Stone, could not prevent further disintegration of the Court into bitter division, acrimony, and dysfunction. Nor could or did they offer a distinctive jurisprudential voice. Instead, Frankfurter's war with Black and Douglas, setting New Dealer against New Dealer, continued to dominate the Court. The Court went this way and that way throughout the Vinson years, as jurisprudential disagreements became personal ones and personal quarrels made judicial consensus less and less likely.

The dissension on the Court mirrored the growing disharmony in the postwar nation, as conservatives, fed up with New Deal programs, decried them as "creeping socialism." Making the accusation even more pointed was the rise of the Cold War, a struggle for domination of world politics between free world countries and the Soviet Union. In its atmosphere of heightening suspicion and accusation, former members of the American Communist Party and those who had sympathized with the propaganda of the party became targets of partisanship.

During the second Red Scare, led at first by the members of the House Un-American Activities Committee and then by Wisconsin senator Joseph McCarthy, a broad and mean-spirited brush tarred anyone who would not denounce the communists. McCarthy had little use for due process or even basic fairness in his smear campaign, but local, state, and federal enactments and policies, including the "black list" barring employment for those accused, divided Americans and perplexed the courts. The High Court heard a number of these cases and divided over them as it did over other issues.

When Stone suffered a fatal cerebral hemorrhage while announcing a dissent in a naturalization case on April 22, 1946, he left behind a Court whose jurisprudence was as fractured as the relationships among the justices. This was not a good time for the justices to war among themselves. The United States had emerged from the conflict as the most powerful nation in the world but one not yet accustomed to international leadership. In Joseph Stalin's Soviet Union, the country faced what Winston Churchill described as "a riddle wrapped in a mystery inside an enigma." Was this the benign "Uncle Joe" and ally of World War II or an aggressive, paranoid monster bent on establishing global communism?

One of the first propaganda targets of the Soviets was American racial injustice. American diplomats abroad and policy makers at home found the race question unavoidable. Did equality mean separate but equal or the rollback of Jim Crow? Were communists behind the drive for racial equality, or was it a patriotic goal? What should be the role of the judicial branch in these questions? Or were they the job of the elected branches? Should the federal government take the lead in a reform movement, or should it be left to the states?

TRUMAN'S COURT

To answer these questions, Truman selected a personal friend and advisor, Fred M. Vinson. When word reached Jackson of Vinson's appointment and the possible involvement of Black in the decision, Jackson blew up and secretly issued a fifteen-hundred-word cable to Truman and then to the chairs of the House and Senate judiciary committees, giving his side of the story. Although the fireworks subsided after Jackson's return from Germany, the divisions remained.

Vinson was not the man to heal them. Born in 1890 in the small town of Louisa, Kentucky, Vinson had overcome many obstacles to reach the pinnacle of American judicial office. He demonstrated academic excellence, athletic prowess, and personableness wherever he went, earning scholarships and finding part-time work, some of it as a semiprofessional baseball player, to work his way up. He returned to Louisa to practice law in 1911 with a bachelor's degree in law from Centre College in Kentucky and began a moderately successful practice until U.S. entry into World War I.

Vinson was the quintessential local politician—easy to know and work with—and he earned election as commonwealth attorney in 1921 and then successive terms in Congress from 1924 to 1938, with the exception of the 1928 election, when the national Democratic Party's stand on prohibition briefly cost him his seat. In the Congress, his skills with tax law and his ability to forge coalitions led to service on the Pensions, Flood Control, Public Lands, Military Affairs, and Appropriations committees in support of the New Deal. Roosevelt appointed him to the D.C. Circuit Court of Appeals, like the appointments of Black, Reed, Murphy, and Jackson, based on political compatibility, loyal service, and friendship rather than demonstrable legal expertise. On the circuit court, Vinson sided with the government and deferred to the legislative branch. In May 1943, he became a full-time administrator as head of the Office of Economic Stabilization, fighting mounting inflationary pressures through price controls. After a brief stint in March 1945 as administrator of the Federal Loan Agency, he replaced James F. Byrnes as director of the Office of War Mobilization and Reconversion. In July of 1945, President Truman appointed him secretary of the treasury.

But nothing in this fine career suggested that Vinson should be chief justice or prepared him for that role. Indeed, his skills and outlook betokened some other career cap. On the Court, he saw himself as an administrator, maximizing efficiency by evenhandedly passing out assignments and reducing the caseload. Used to the camaraderie of the Senate and the obedience of administrative leadership, he never understood how to manage personalities on the Court. His relationship with Frankfurter deteriorated rapidly. At the time of Vinson's sudden death, Frankfurter quipped that it was the first time he had evidence that there was a God.

Nor did Vinson's limited education or his brief federal court service prepare him for the complexities of constitutional adjudication. Black became so frustrated with Vinson's inability to lead that he suggested rotating the job among the justices "as some state courts do." Jackson saw Vinson's lack of opinion writing as "just plain lazy." Although almost all of the justices liked the affable, sociable Vinson, they did not see him as one of their own, much less accede to his leadership role.

Vinson's role changed with the sudden deaths of Murphy and Rutledge. Additional Truman appointees gave him, for a short time, a solid five-vote majority (with Burton and Reed) on all issues except segregation. What was more, the new justices shared something of his background and approach to law, drawn as they were from government service. The first of these was Truman's attorney general, Tom C. Clark, to replace Murphy. Truman would later remark that "Tom Clark was my biggest mistake. . . . He was no damn good as Attorney General, and on the Supreme Court . . . he has been even worse. . . . it isn't so much that he's a *bad* man. It's just that he's such a dumb son of a bitch." Truman's disillusionment notwithstanding, Clark possessed a fine legal mind and a distinguished record in the Justice Department and fulfilled Vinson's request for a friend on the Court he could count on. It is entirely possible that Clark's vote against Truman in the *Steel Seizure Case* affected the elderly ex-president's recollection.

Born in Dallas, Texas, in 1899, Clark attended the Virginia Military Institute until financial reasons forced him home. Like Vinson and Burton, he volunteered for service in World War I, but he did not see combat. After a stint in the National Guard, he earned his bachelor's degree and then his law degree from the University of Texas. He joined his father and brother in the family law firm before becoming a successful assistant district attorney.

Local politics led to federal office. In 1937, after another stint in private practice, he went to Washington as special assistant in the War Risk Insurance Office, the first of a series of offices that he held that included civilian coordinator for Japanese internment. Much later in life, he admitted that this was "the biggest mistake of my life." Clark returned to the capitol to work with Truman and his Senate committee on the war frauds unit, next to head the Antitrust Division of the Department of Justice, and then its Criminal Division in 1944. Truman made Clark attorney general. In this capacity, he continued his antitrust work and, unlike Vinson, vigorously aided the civil rights movement, filing amici (friends of the court) briefs in NAACP lawsuits, urging the FBI to investigate racial violence, and supporting an antilynching bill in Congress.

Clark also undertook a thorough campaign against communism through Smith Act prosecutions of American Communist Party leaders. But by 1948, he had soured on red-baiting, now a cause championed by Republican-dominated organs like the House Un-American Activities Committee. From this platform of friendship and service to Truman, Clark ascended to the Court. There he compiled a record nearly identical to Vinson's. Although at first he was an unswerving vote against civil liberties for dissidents, he accompanied this with a strong concern for civil rights for African Americans.

As his career on the Court matured and the Vinson Court turned into the Warren Court, Clark made considerable contributions to incorporation of the Bill of Rights. In *Mapp v. Ohio* (1961), he applied the Fourth Amendment's search-and-seizure requirements and the exclusionary rule to the states. In *School District of Abington v. Schemp* (1963), he wrote for the majority that mandatory Bible reading in public schools violated the First Amendment's separation between church and state. In *Heart of Atlanta Motel v. U.S.* and *Katzenbach v. McClung* (1964), he upheld the provisions of the Civil Rights Act of

1964, which forbade racial discrimination in public accommodations. In 1967, he resigned from the Court to avoid the appearance of impropriety when his son, the new attorney general, argued cases before the Court. He spent the last ten years of his life aiding federal courts, improving judicial training through the establishment of the National Judicial College, working for modernization of the judicial system with the founding of the Federal Judicial Center in 1967, and becoming the first chair of the Board of Trustees for the Supreme Court Historical Society in 1974. Clark died in 1977.

A few months after the Clark nomination, Truman put another friend, Sherman "Shay" Minton, forward to replace Rutledge. Liberal groups favored the former senator from Indiana whose 1934 Senate campaign featured the slogan, "You can't eat the Constitution." Concerns about Minton's health convinced the Judiciary Committee to request his testimony in person. On Frankfurter's advice, Minton declined. The committee and the full Senate approved his appointment anyway, on October 12, 1949.

Opponents and supporters had a shock when Minton did an about-face and joined the judicial restraint bloc, consistently voting to uphold government actions. Minton, like Frankfurter, saw his role in conservative terms. He believed that the political branches were the ones to secure the people's liberty and that his role was to respect precedent and stay out of their way. His gregarious, folksy manner made him many friends on the bench but earned little respect. He voted with Vinson, Reed, Burton, and Clark regularly, but he was one of the four justices who agreed to hear the litigation that became *Brown v. Board of Education* (1954). In 1956, he resigned from the bench due to ill health, leaving behind an undistinguished record. He died in 1965.

NATIONAL SECURITY

The Vinson Court took up national security cases where the Stone Court had left them, in an uncertain and increasingly anxious state. In *Haupt v. U.S.* (1948), the Court modified *Cramer* to uphold a treason conviction for the father of one of the German would-be saboteurs. Although experts disagree as to the exact requirement Jackson's majority opinion applied, it was clear the Court no longer held to the two-witness rule in the Constitution, at least for proving the intent of the defendant. Douglas concurred. Murphy continued to oppose such trials on general principles, and in particular because in this case the father had not in any way forwarded the cause of an enemy power. He had merely provided a bed and board and a job reference for his son: "An act of providing a meal to an enemy agent who is also one's son retains the possibility of having a non-treasonable basis. . . . it cannot qualify as an overt act of treason."

The war crimes trials continued. American occupation of Japan and Germany provided forums for these trials. The Court distinguished between trials of U.S. nationals and those conducted by U.S. personnel, in *Hirota v. McArthur* (1948) and *Johnson v. Eisentrager* (1950), for Japan and Germany, respectively. In 1951, the Vinson Court participated obliquely in the Rosenberg case. Two American communists, Julius and Ethel Rosenberg, were tried and found guilty of violating the Espionage Act for passing atomic bomb secrets to the Soviet Union, ending U.S. monopoly on the super weapon. Despite perjured testimony, some evidence of collusion between the judge and the prosecutor, and questions of FBI falsification of some testimony and documents, Frankfurter and Black could never get the votes they needed for the Court to review the case.

Douglas was willing to order a stay of execution for the married couple, knowing that Ethel was most likely innocent and that her indictment and trial was a ploy to get Julius, who likely was guilty, to admit to the crime. Douglas then left for his annual summer trip to the wilds of the West. A majority, meeting in special session on June 18, 1953, vacated the stay. FBI agents later admitted some improprieties and their plan to get Ethel or Julius to cooperate by pressing for execution of both. When the records of the Soviet spy system were opened after the fall of the Soviet Union, evidence exculpated Ethel and revealed that Julius Rosenberg had had a limited role in the passing of atomic secrets. The betrayal of trust had largely come from Klaus Fuchs, another scientist at Los Alamos, and from a British spy ring run by the KGB.

The Rosenberg trial was only the most deadly aspect of the nation's hysteria during the second Red Scare. But the Court did not interpose itself between the hunters and their prey in the *Loyalty Oath Cases*. The Truman administration had introduced widespread use of loyalty oaths in order to put in place a cheap, public, and efficient way of finding out whether federal employees had connections to communist or communist-affiliated organizations. Certainly, some of these employees had far-left-of-center histories. J. Robert Oppenheimer, who headed the Manhattan Project that developed the atomic bomb during the war, was a leftist, a stance common in some intellectual and reform circles before World War II. In those same years, the Soviet Union carried on a skillful propaganda campaign, portraying itself as the champion of the underdog. Young people flirted with communism before the horrors of Soviet-style collectivism became public knowledge. Now all of these individuals were at risk for their past conduct. Politicians, most notably Senator Joseph McCarthy, a Republican from Wisconsin, made their political reputations through unfounded but highly visible accusations of continuing communist infiltration of government and society.

Taking its cue from the reasoning and precedents of actual times of war, the Vinson Court extended deference to political bodies on national security matters during the early Cold War. At the time, it seemed that the conflict between the United States and the Soviet Union would be conducted not between military personnel, but by spies, in the media, through proxies in other countries, and in the courts. The Korean War, from 1950 through the Armistice in 1953, pitted the U.S.-led United Nations forces against a Soviet proxy, North Korea (although some diplomatic historians regard the North Korean invasion of South Korea as part of a civil war). Ironically, the real war actually cooled the nation's search for internal enemies. But as long as the loyalty oath requirements contained some element of *knowingly* belonging to an organization dedicated to the overthrow of the U.S. government, the justices generally upheld these severe impingements on freedom of thought and association. In such cases as *Gerende v. Board of Supervisors* (1951), the Court upheld Maryland's loyalty oath law for political candidates. *Garner v. Board of Public Works* (1951) upheld a Los Angeles ordinance requiring loyalty oaths for city workers.

Deference reached its apogee in *Adler v. Board of Education* (1952). A majority of the Court upheld New York's Feinberg Act, which stated that belonging to any organization on a previously published list of proscribed organizations constituted a prima facie case for dismissal or disqualification as a public school teacher. The law was comprehensive and unforgiving, a throwback to the language of the World War I Espionage Act. Proscribed conduct included saying or writing anything that "wilfully and deliberately advocates, advises or teaches the doctrine that the government of the United States or of any state or of any political subdivision thereof should be overthrown or overturned by force"; and printing, publishing, editing, or selling any book, newspaper, or other writing "in any form containing or advocating, advising or teaching the doctrine that the government of the United States or of any state or of any political subdivision thereof should be overthrown by force, violence or any unlawful means." Even more broadly and vaguely, whoever "advocates, advises, teaches, or embraces the duty, necessity or propriety of adopting the doctrine contained therein" or joined an organization that so advocated, could not teach in the state. No one could teach Karl Marx. No one could print or sell the Communist Manifesto. No one could join a social group or reading circle that touched on such books and keep a public school teaching job.

The determination as to which organizations and publications violated the law was left to the board of regents of the state, making it the prosecutor, judge, and jury in the case. A last sharp barb in the law regarded those men and women who no longer belonged to such a proscribed organization: "Evidence of membership in such an organization prior to said day [of the passage of the Feinberg Act] shall be presumptive evidence that membership has continued, in the absence of a showing that such membership has been terminated in good faith." In other words, in order to avoid penalties, someone who was no longer a member had to admit, in public, that he or she had been a member and had ended the relationship. Otherwise, simply belonging to an organization, or quoting or saying anything in private conversation fitting, in the opinion of the state, any of these categories, was grounds for dismissal from a public school teaching position, whether or not the opinions were published or spoken in the course of one's employment or in the classroom.

The statute, rooted in the fear that mere words could overturn worlds, could be seen as a violation of the First Amendment. Clearly, it raised the same questions that the Court had supposedly answered during the Taft and Hughes years. But here the state was not demanding criminal penalties, merely denial of a benefit—a job. Of course, there were other penalties for being fired in this way—loss of reputation, loss of the ability to get another job in teaching, and the danger that other agencies of government would begin investigation of the individual's past life. Indeed, the requirement that a suspect prove that he or she was no longer a member recalled the old and much-hated "oath ex officio" by which English courts had prosecuted religious dissenters and Catholics. If one denied that one belonged to the wrong church, one could be prosecuted for lying under oath. If one admitted to such membership, one would be prosecuted for belonging to the wrong church. The law's provisions "blacklisted" the teachers, just as an informal "blacklist" drove former communists, fellow travelers, and those who refused to testify to their former allies' political views from the entertainment industry. Refuse to testify and one is guilty of refusing to testify, even if one had the right to refuse on Fifth Amendment (self-incrimination) grounds. The Inquisition had arrived on American shores.

The majority of the Court found the Feinberg Act acceptable. Although the law did not specify, indeed did not care, whether the suspect brought any of his or her opinions into the classroom, the Court presumed that the dangerous words or ideas were close by. In any case, it was too dangerous to let such a person teach, even if the subject was mathematics or car repair or was in the metal shop. Minton wrote for Vinson, Burton, Jackson, Reed, and Clark: "A teacher works in a sensitive area in a schoolroom. There he shapes the attitude of young minds towards the society in which they live. In this, the state has a vital concern. It must preserve the integrity of the schools. That the school authorities have the right and the duty to screen the officials, teachers, and employees as to their fitness to maintain the integrity of the schools as a part of ordered society, cannot be doubted. One's associates, past and present, as well as one's conduct, may properly be considered in determining fitness and loyalty."

Even if the individual removed from his or her job by the law did not hold to any of the proscribed notions, "From time immemorial, one's reputation has been determined in part by the company he keeps. In the employment of officials and teachers of the school system, the state may very properly inquire into the company they keep, and we know of no rule, constitutional or otherwise, that prevents the state, when determining the fitness and loyalty of such persons, from considering the organizations and persons with whom they associate." Guilt by association was constitutional.

Did the dismissed teacher forfeit his or her First Amendment rights? "His freedom of choice between membership in the organization and employment in the school system might be limited, but not his freedom of speech or assembly, except in the remote sense that limitation is inherent in every choice. Certainly such limitation is not one the state may not make in the exercise of its police power to protect the schools from pollution and thereby to defend its own existence."

The dissenters worried that in the passions of the moment the Court exaggerated the threat to students in metal shop from a teacher who belonged to a radical fringe organization. Black, Frankfurter, and Douglas dissented. Black saw fundamental principles of intellectual inquiry and freedom at stake, much as Holmes and Brandeis did in *Gitlow* and *Whitney*: "This is another of those rapidly multiplying legislative enactments which make it dangerous—this time for school teachers—to think or say anything except what a transient majority happen to approve at the moment. Basically these laws rest on the belief that government should supervise and limit the flow of ideas into the minds of men."

Frankfurter had done some research into the matter and, in a closely reasoned and much longer dissent, struck at the incongruity between the actual danger and the overbreadth of the Feinberg Act:

During the thirty-two years and ten years, respectively, that these laws have stood on the books, no proceedings, so far as appears, have been taken under them. In 1949 the Legislature passed a new act, familiarly known as the Feinberg Law, designed to reinforce the prior legislation. The Law begins with a legislative finding, based on "common report" of widespread infiltration by "members of subversive groups, and particularly of the communist party and certain of its affiliated organizations," into the educational system of the State and the evils attendant upon that infiltration.

But where was the evidence of the spreading, insidious evil? Nowhere.

Douglas's dissent featured his usual dash and style: "I have not been able to accept the recent doctrine that a citizen who enters the public service can be forced to sacrifice his civil rights. I cannot for example find in our constitutional scheme the power of a state to place its employees in the category of second-class citizens by denying them freedom of thought and expression. The Constitution guarantees freedom of thought and expression to everyone in our society. All are entitled to it; and none needs it more than the teacher." The evil the law perpetuated, censorship, was far worse than the potential evil the law sought to prevent: "Indeed the impact of this kind of censorship on the public school system illustrates the high purpose of the First Amendment in freeing speech and thought from censorship." What was worse, the law introduced an obnoxious concept of evidence: "The present law proceeds on a principle repugnant to our society—guilt by association. A teacher is disqualified because of her membership in an organization found to be 'subversive.' The finding as to the 'subversive' character of the organization is made in a proceeding to which the teacher is not a party and in which it is not clear that she may even be heard."

The logic of such powerful dissents, based on such fundamental concepts, did sway enough of the justices so that in *Wieman v. Updegraf* (1951) the Court vacated an Oklahoma statute on the grounds that, per Clark's majority opinion, "indiscriminate classification of innocent with knowing activity must fall as an assertion of arbitrary power." But the six justices in the majority in *Joint Anti-Fascist Refugee Committee v. McGrath* (1951) could not agree on a rationale for why the attorney general's list improperly included this Spanish Civil War group. Like the Court's later inability to define pornography as a legal category, the justices knew that the organization should not be there, but if the attorney general had the legally untrammeled discretion to add or subtract groups, how could the Court object? The attorney general did not have the authority? The list violated the First Amendment? Due process grounds? All of the preceding. Reed, Vinson, and Minton dissented.

When the Congress spoke clearly, so did the Vinson Court—in *American Communications Association v. Douds* (1950) and, more notably, in *Dennis v. U.S.* (1951). The legislation at issue in *Douds* was section 9(h) of the Republican-generated, antiunion Taft-Hartley Act, which required union leaders to file affidavits swearing they were not members of the Communist Party and did not believe in the violent overthrow of the U.S. government, with the penalty being "derecognition" of their unions by the National Labor Relations Board. Vinson wrote for the majority that Congress could restrict political freedom under its authority to regulate interstate commerce. He found the threat of communist-controlled labor unions ordering politically motivated strikes to be of sufficient concern to warrant the measure. Frankfurter and Jackson concurred in part, but both wrote independently that the Court should have found the parts of 9(h) that restricted the right to have a political opinion, or to reject one, to be invalid.

The following year, Vinson directly confronted the free speech issue in *Dennis*. The case arose out of Clark's orders to prosecute the leaders of the Communist Party–USA for violating the 1940 Smith Act, which forbade any advocacy or conspiracy to advocate the violent overthrow of the government. Although this was only one of many cases stemming from the so-called Foley Square Trials in the federal district court in New York City, the Court had yet to rule on the First Amendment issues involved.

Instead of basing his opinion on the decision in *Gitlow*, which allowed Congress to bar certain kinds of speech to protect the nation, Vinson decided to adopt Judge Learned Hand's modification of the "clear and present danger test." Hand's views went all the way back to his 1917 opinion in *The Masses* case, and Hand had repeated his views when the Second Circuit Court of Appeals upheld *Dennis*. In this version of the test, "imminence" dropped out of the formula and became "remoteness," the probability that the danger would come to pass. Thus, in Hand's formula, which Vinson would parrot: "In each case, they must ask whether the gravity of the 'evil,' discounted by its improbability, justifies such invasion of free speech as is necessary to avoid the danger." In effect, Hand had applied a tort (civil harm or wrong) standard that he had pioneered (in *Carroll Towing*, a Hudson River barge collision case) to politically dangerous speech. If the harm was so great (and here it presumably was), even its unlikelihood (for the communists were few and powerless) meant that the danger of communist subversion outweighed the communists' free speech rights. The test did not go to the constitutionality of the statute itself.

Writing for three of his colleagues, Vinson warned that government did not have to wait to act as the Communist Party organized, infiltrated, and gathered strength. The Smith Act was clear and constitutional—and the Communist Party to which Dennis and the others indicted under the act belonged had as its policy the violent overthrow of the government. The communists were known to conspire and subvert in secret. The trial in the lower court had been fair, and the appeals court had rightly turned down the appeal. But, because only Burton, Reed, and Minton joined Vinson's opinion, Vinson's opinion did not create a precedent, and the concurring opinions carried great weight.

Frankfurter's concurrence was tortured, much like his opinion in *Gobitis*. He offered a history of free speech doctrine and its various rationales (he even appended a series of case summaries), but in the end, he deferred to Congress's judgment (in the Smith Act) and the fact that his mentor and friend, Judge Learned Hand, sustained the conviction. One can also find clear evidence of Frankfurter's disdain for the craftsmanship of the chief justice. Frankfurter thought that Vinson did not understand what Holmes and Brandeis meant when they wrote about clear and present danger.

Jackson's concurrence concluded that, although the Court might need to step in at some point to prevent a tyrannous suppression of political speech, now was not that time: "This prosecution is the latest of never-ending, because never successful, quests for some legal formula that will secure an existing order against revolutionary radicalism. . . . The judicial process simply is not adequate to a trial of such far-flung issues. The answers given would reflect our own political predilections and nothing more." Although his opinion sounds as if he was leaning toward dissent, in the end he bowed to the judgment of the government.

Black's dissent was powerful and uncompromising. Congress shall make no law meant "no law." Douglas conceded some power to the government: "If this were a case where those who claimed protection under the First Amendment were teaching the techniques of sabotage, the assassination of the President, the filching of documents from public files, the planting of bombs, the art of street warfare, and the like, I would have no doubts." But that was not what the government proved, for all its thousands of pages of testimony and its truckload of evidence. "So far as the present record is concerned, what petitioners did was to organize people to teach and themselves teach the Marxist-Leninist doctrine contained chiefly in four books." Douglas, who wrote books, would be the first to concede that printed words could lead to action, and he made plain his dislike of the communists' required reading list: "Those books are to Soviet Communism what Mein Kampf was to Nazism," but the books were not outlawed by the law. They remained on library shelves. "If the books themselves are not outlawed, if they can lawfully remain on library shelves, by what reasoning does their use in a classroom become a crime?"

In language far closer to what Holmes and Brandeis had meant in *Abrams* and *Gitlow* than Frankfurter's concurrence, Douglas's dissent explained why the conviction must be overturned:

Free speech has occupied an exalted position because of the high service it has given our society. Its protection is essential to the very existence of a democracy. The airing of ideas releases pressures which otherwise might become destructive. When ideas compete in the market for acceptance, full and free discussion exposes the false and they gain few adherents. Full and free discussion even of ideas we hate encourages the testing of our own prejudices and preconceptions. Full and free discussion keeps a society from becoming stagnant and unprepared for the stresses and strains that work to tear all civilizations apart.

Within a decade, Douglas's views would triumph.

THE LAW IN WARTIME, AGAIN

The communist menace at home was largely spectral, but communists abroad were waging war on American interests. On June 25, 1950, Kim Il Sung's communist North Korea invaded the undemocratic, but capitalist and American-allied, South Korea. Within a few weeks, North Korean forces had taken control over most of the peninsula, including the South Korean capital, Seoul. The shock of the invasion and its early success stunned a Truman administration already reeling from the "loss" of China to the communist forces of Mao Zedong in 1949. Under the newly formulated policy of containment embodied in National Security Council document 68, the situation in this remote and relatively unimportant area was now seen as a significant threat to U.S. security, which was defined as dependent on preventing any communist advances anywhere in the world. Under the auspices of the United Nations (the Soviet Union was absent from the Security Council as a protest against the denial of China's seat to Mao's People's Republic), a mostly American force entered into the conflict on a scope the country had not experienced since World War II.

As the war ground on into a stalemate, with Mao's Chinese and Kim Il Sung's Korean forces on one side and U.S.-led forces on the other, the U.S. economy began to strain under the pressure. At this critical juncture, the independent steel plant owners decided to exert pressure on the unions, relying on the Taft-Hartley Act to prevent the unions from retaliating.

When the steelworkers threatened to strike, Truman decided to not use the Taft-Hartley Act, legislation the Republican Congress had passed over his veto, but instead his executive power as president and commander in chief of the armed forces to seize the steel mills. The actual reasoning was even more complicated. Truman wanted a fair deal for the steelworkers without jeopardizing the U.S. economy in the process. He believed and was advised that precedent supported the move. After all, FDR and Theodore Roosevelt had often used this device in order to bring management and labor to the bargaining table. Why could he not do the same?

In spite of the fact that Truman had appointed four of the justices, the Court demurred to the steel company seizure, in *Youngstown Sheet and Tube Company v. Sawyer* (1952). The first blow to Truman's action came when the Court gave expedited review to take the case, not waiting for the lower courts to hold full hearings on the subject. This gave the management of the steel mills the excuse they wanted to walk away from the tentative agreement Truman had helped them reach with the union. The second and fatal blow came with the Black-led 6-to-3 majority, which declared that Truman's seizure of the steel mills was unconstitutional.

Black reasoned that there were two possible rationales for Truman's action: a statute or the Constitution itself. Because Truman had avoided using Taft-Hartley, in Black's view the controlling statute in the situation, any successful argument must rest with his powers as president during a time of war. Black found this to be unsupportable: "Even though 'theater of war' be an expanding concept, we cannot with faithfulness to our constitutional system hold that the Commander in Chief of the Armed Forces has the ultimate power as such to take possession of private property in order to keep labor disputes from stopping production. This is a job for the Nation's lawmakers, not for its military authorities." In concurring opinions, Frankfurter, Douglas, Jackson, Burton, and Clark emphasized, each in his own way, that Congress's action precluded the president's action.

The chief justice, joined by Reed and Minton, would have deferred to executive authority in the matter. In what could have been a Frankfurter opinion, albeit with fewer didactic excursions, Vinson laid out the reasons why judges should not second-guess the decisions of political branches: "History bears out the genius of the Founding Fathers, who created a Government subject to law but not left subject to inertia when vigor and initiative are required." Vinson also pointed out the context of a global war against aggression, congressional support for this particular war, and presidential actions in the past akin to this one.

Given the Court's restraint during World War I and World War II on such matters, it is legitimate to wonder why the majority found Truman's steel seizure different. More likely than not, the answer lies in Truman's decision to wage a limited war rather than a declared conflict (technically, he classified it as a police action) with full mobilization. This, plus the fact that Congress had not given its assent, led the majority to find against the president. But it should be noted that Black and Douglas might well have dissented even if Congress had declared war.

INDIVIDUAL LIBERTIES

In marked contrast to most of its communism-related cases, the Vinson Court was opposed to prior restraint of public speech by state and local authorities. In *Saia v. New York* (1948), a Douglas-led majority invalidated an ordinance that required a permit from a city official before a speaker could use a loud-speaker in a public place. The Court allowed a Trenton, New Jersey, ban on sound trucks and loudspeakers altogether because it was not a restriction on content, but instead on means, in *Kovacs v. Cooper* (1949). Time, place, and manner still mattered. But in a Vinson opinion, in *Kunz v. New York* (1951), the Court held that a New York City ordinance requiring the police commission-er's approval of any outdoor worship meeting was an unconstitutional prior restraint on speech. As in the Jehovah's Witness cases, the case turned on free-dom of speech, not on free exercise of religion.

The justices did, however, maintain the distinction between regular speech and "fighting words." When Father Arthur Terminiello, a former priest, gave a vituperatively anti-Semitic and anti-Roosevelt speech inside a hall in Chicago in 1946, a crowd rioted outside. The police arrested Terminiello and his follow-ers on disorderly conduct charges. Through a Douglas opinion, the Court re-versed the convictions, in *Terminiello v. Chicago* (1948). Although Terminiello's attorneys did not raise the issue at trial or on appeal, Douglas argued that the Illinois statute defining breach of peace was overly broad: "It permitted convic-tion of petitioner if his speech stirred people to anger, invited public dispute, or brought about a condition of unrest. A conviction resting on any of those grounds may not stand." This struck at the heart of free speech's rationale, the protection of controversial ideas. Vinson, Frankfurter, and Jackson, with Bur-ton joining, wrote dissents. Local authorities' ability to preserve order deserved the Court's deference.

In *Feiner v. New York* (1951), the Court reached the seemingly opposite re-sult. The case involved a pro-communist student convicted of disorderly con-duct after giving an emotional speech before an increasingly irritated crowd on a street corner in Syracuse, New York. Now in the majority, Vinson wrote for the Court that this was a legitimate exercise of the police power. He distinguished this situation from a situation like that in *Terminiello* by applying a form of the imminent danger test: "When as here the speaker passes the bounds of argument or persuasion and undertakes incitement to riot," the government can act.

Black, now in the minority, saw the situation completely differently. In his version of events, "The [police] duty was to protect petitioner's right to talk, even to the extent of arresting the man who threatened to interfere. Instead, they shirked that duty and acted only to suppress the right to speak." The Court had empowered the "heckler's veto"—in this case a man who told the arresting officer that if the officer did not act he would. The two cases could, of course, be distinguished not by time, place, and manner, but by content. Feiner was a communist.

The question of local authority over freedom of expression became even more confusing with Frankfurter's majority opinion in *Beauharnais v. Illinois* (1952), which upheld an Illinois statute forbidding what Frankfurter called "group libel." In this controversy, the object of state concern was a pamphlet from the White Circle League arguing against African Americans moving into white neighborhoods. The prosecution alleged that the defendant "did unlawfully . . . exhibit in public places lithographs, which publications portray depravity, criminality, unchastity or lack of virtue of citizens of Negro race and color and which exposes citizens of Illinois of the Negro race and color to contempt, derision, or obloquy." The accompanying literature was uncompromising on the importance of preventing "the white race from becoming mongrelized by the negro" and described the "rapes, robberies, knives, guns and marijuana of the negro."

Frankfurter, writing for the Court, regarded the pictures and words as libel. But the offender was not an individual (grounds for a civil suit against Beauharnais or his comrades) but a group. One might regard Jim Crow as such a libel. Certainly tobacco companies, sheet music printers, and other purveyors of goods had depicted black people in unflattering and, more important, untrue fashion. Could the state make the distribution of such malign stereotypes into a criminal offense? Frankfurter thought it could:

No one will gainsay that it is libelous falsely to charge another with being a rapist, robber, carrier of knives and guns, and user of marijuana. The precise question before us, then, is whether the protection of "liberty" in the Due Process Clause of the Fourteenth Amendment prevents a State from punishing such libels—as criminal libel has been defined, limited and constitutionally recognized time out of mind directed at designated collectivities and flagrantly disseminated.

History has demonstrated that the diffusion of hurtful stereotypes has corresponded or led to interracial violence. The state could claim an interest in preventing riots and mayhem. Did the state have to wait for someone to punch Beauharnais in the nose before it ordered him to pack up his pictures?

Black, Reed, Jackson, and Douglas dissented, largely on the grounds that this was a content-related restriction and merited a higher level of scrutiny than Frankfurter applied. Beauharnais was trying to petition the state legislature—a basic right safeguarded in the First Amendment, along with free speech and freedom of the press. Frankfurter had not even mentioned the First Amendment in his opinion for the Court, a fact that Black, in his dissent, emphasized. Jackson dissented separately because he opposed using the same standard for both the states and the federal government and because he found, through his reading of the historical record, that the framers of the Fourteenth Amendment did not intend to incorporate the First Amendment. Instead, he would have reversed the conviction based on the denial of a fair trial.

THE COURT AND MATTERS OF FAITH

The unwillingness of the Stone Court to base the Jehovah's Witness holdings on the Free Exercise Clause rather than the Free Speech Clause hinted that the former was a thicket the Court did not wish to enter. The First Amendment not only told Congress not to interfere with the free exercise of religion, it also barred Congress from establishing a religion. The two clauses were perfectly clear in themselves, but did not fit together easily. Would allowing the free exercise of religion, for example, in a school, amount to the establishment of religion? Would preventing prayer in the public schools on establishment grounds be tantamount to denial of free exercise?

The first of these cases, *Everson v. Board of Education of Ewing Township* (1947), concerned a local reimbursement plan to parents for transportation costs, including to parents who elected to send their children to parochial school. Black wrote for the majority that the law did not violate the intended "wall of separation between Church and state" because it was a general measure. The Establishment Clause only required government "to be neutral in its relations with groups of religious believers and nonbelievers; it does not require the state to be their adversary."

Frankfurter saw another opportunity to hound Black, whose position in the Jehovah's Witness cases seemed to conflict with his opinion in *Everson*. Black redrafted his opinion several times in response to Frankfurter's criticisms. Frankfurter had, however, found an ally in Rutledge. Rutledge asserted that the wall of separation meant that the "prohibition is absolute." Sounding more like Black than Black, he criticized the compromise at the core of the majority opinion. Jackson, often Frankfurter's ally, filed a dissent that emphasized similar themes, warning that religious groups should be wary of state involvement: "Many groups have sought aid from tax funds only to find that it carried political controls with it." The separation protected both sides from inappropriate contacts.

The logic of these dissents was the core of the majority opinion in *McCollum v. Board of Education* (1948). The Court found that a school board could not allow religious instruction in the classroom during school hours, even when the classes were voluntary. Black's opinion for the Court refused to disavow his contrary reasoning in *Everson*. Jackson and Frankfurter concurred in the result but insisted that the present case was not consistent with *Everson*—as much to shake a finger at Black as to explain why *Everson* was wrong in the first place. Frankfurter was even more furious with Burton and Rutledge, who decided to join Black's opinion instead of holding out for reversal of *Everson*.

In retrospect, Frankfurter may have had the better claim. The Champaign, Illinois, law at issue in *McCollum* provided for an hour per week when outside clergy would come into the school to conduct Bible study. For Black, the key distinction between this plan and the school buses that Ewing Township hired rested with the fact that Illinois truancy laws required students to be in school during the entire school day. Thus, the state was forcing students to attend Bible classes conducted by clergy.

In *Zorach v. Clausen* (1952), a six-justice majority that Douglas led validated New York's reaction to *McCollum*, moving religious instruction off school grounds in a "release time" program that students did not have to attend. He went further to make it clear the Court did not demand hostility to religion: "We are a religious people whose institutions presuppose a Supreme Being." The Establishment Clause commanded only that government show "no partiality to any one group and that [it] lets each flourish according to the zeal of its adherents and the appeal of its dogma."

This time, Black joined Frankfurter and Jackson in dissent. Jackson dismissed the Douglas opinion as resting on "nonessential details" and as missing the "compulsion which was the underlying reason for invalidity." But when *Zorach* is viewed alongside the Court's decision in *Doremus v. Board of Education* (1952)—issued a month before *Zorach*—in which the majority dismissed a suit against New Jersey's mandated Bible reading in school, one gets the impression the justices wanted to back away from the controversy. Editorial response to the two cases favored a high wall between religion and the state, and the justices were well aware of the potential for furious public outcry. Hence the careful, almost mincing reasoning in these cases, compared to the robust and fulsome language of the Court in free speech cases.

CRIMINAL PROCEDURE

The Vinson Court also took a cautious line on criminal procedure cases, but each case spurred Black and his allies to develop their ideas on the meaning of the Due Process Clause of the Fourteenth Amendment. The first significant case in this area for the Vinson Court, *Adamson v. California* (1947), presented a similar situation to the one that the Hughes Court had considered in *Palko*. A defendant, Admiral Dewey Adamson, declined to take the stand in a murder trial. California state law allowed the state to instruct the jury that it could infer guilt from the defendant's refusal to testify. A hidden subtext of the case did not make it into the opinions, but the defendant was African American and the victim was an elderly white woman. Reed wrote the majority opinion upholding the conviction on the grounds that due process in the Fourteenth Amendment did not incorporate the Fifth Amendment right against self-incrimination.

Reed relied on Cardozo's test in *Palko*, which was whether the trial on the whole was a fair one: "We are of the view, however, that a state may control such a situation in accordance with its own ideas of the most efficient administration of criminal justice. The purpose of due process is not to protect an accused against a proper conviction but against an unfair conviction." The framers' federalism, even as modified by the Fourteenth Amendment, did not require the incorporation of every part of the Bill of Rights.

The noteworthy aspect of *Adamson* was not the outcome but Black's dissent. Read the Fifth Amendment through the eyes of its framers, he insisted. Forget Cardozo's ideas of "natural law," notions of "civilized decency," and "fundamental principles of liberty and justice." The historical record—in reality, his take on the historical records, which differed from Reed's—told him "that history conclusively demonstrates that the language of the first section of the Fourteenth Amendment, taken as a whole, was thought by those responsible for its submission to the people, and by those who opposed its submission, sufficiently explicit to guarantee that thereafter no state could deprive its citizens of the privileges and protections of the Bill of Rights." This so-called total incorporation approach never gained ascendance, but Black's advocacy of it pushed the other justices to reconsider the dictates of due process, specifically why the higher level of constraints on the national government should not apply to the states.

Murphy, with Rutledge concurring, registered a separate dissent in which he rejected the Court's stance as too loose and Black's as too rigid. He wanted the Court to have the ability to raise the floor above the minimum guarantees of the Bill of Rights: "Occasions may arise where a proceeding falls so far short of conforming to fundamental standards of procedure as to warrant constitutional condemnation in terms of a lack of due process despite the absence of a specific provision in the Bill of Rights." This more expansive reading of the Due Process Clause revived, albeit in a different form for different purposes, the substantive due process of the *Lochner* period. The core of their dissent, that somewhere in the Constitution one must and could find fundamental rights not explicitly named, would reappear in the privacy cases of the Warren and Burger Courts.

There were some violations of due process the Court could not ignore. *In re Oliver* (1948) found the justices vacating the sentence of a man whose sentencing judge was also a one-man grand jury and trial jury. In *Haley v. Ohio* (1948), they determined that the "relay interrogation" was coercive, and they set aside a murder conviction of a fifteen-year-old African American. These could be fit under the existing "we know what is fair and what is not" standard, a variant of the "shock to the conscience" test that Frankfurter deployed in criminal procedure cases and the "we know what it is when we see it" test later assayed in pornography suits.

The refusal to incorporate any additional Bill of Rights provisions more often led to judgments as in *Louisiana ex rel. Francis v. Resweber* (1947), in which the Court allowed Louisiana to use the electric chair a second time against Willie Francis after it had failed the first time. In a concurrence, Frankfurter expressed his opposition to the death penalty but could not conclude that the execution would "shock the conscience." The Eighth Amendment's prohibition on "cruel and unusual punishments" was not applicable to a state's proceeding. That Francis was a minor and that the police and prosecution may have acted in a biased fashion did not rise to the level of a constitutional issue.

For federal officers who ran afoul of the Fourth Amendment's search-and-seizure warrant requirements, the Vinson Court set a more lenient standard in *Harris v. U.S.* (1947). The chief justice allowed in evidence the results of a search of a dresser drawer in the apartment of a just-arrested suspect because of the immediacy and because the premises were under the suspect's "control." Then the Court seemingly reversed itself in *U.S. v. Di Re* (1948), *Johnson v. U.S.* (1948), *Trupiano v. U.S.* (1948), and *McDonald v. U.S.* (1948), in which the justices faulted the federal officers for not securing a warrant, despite their opportunity to do so. The thread running through the cases seems to be what Douglas referred to in *McDonald* as the absence of "exceptional circumstances" for not bothering to secure the warrant. But we should note that these mandates were only for federal officers.

State criminal procedure remained a different matter. In *Wolf v. Colorado* (1949), a deputy sheriff entered a doctor's office without a warrant and seized an appointment book. The prosecutor later used this book as evidence in the trial, as well as the testimony of witnesses obtained through the use of the book. Wolf appealed his conviction on the grounds that the seizure violated his due process rights under the Fourteenth Amendment. Frankfurter, applying the *Palko* test, agreed in his majority opinion and, in doing so, incorporated the Fourth Amendment's provisions against the states. However, he refused to impose the exclusionary rule applied in federal cases—instead allowing the states to determine their own remedies. Black concurred, emphasizing that the exclusionary rule was a judge-made, not a constitutional requirement. Douglas, Murphy, and Rutledge each filed separate dissents arguing that the absence of the exclusionary rule vitiated the impact of the decision. In marked contrast, when police had a local hospital pump the stomach of a narcotics suspect they had taken into custody after entering his bedroom and observing him swallowing two pills that were in plain sight, Frankfurter wrote for the Court in *Rochin v. California* (1952) that this conduct "shocked the conscience." But again, he did not require that the state courts exclude such evidence on constitutional grounds.

With the departure of Murphy and Rutledge, the Court's view of warrantless searches by federal officials shifted. Replacing the *Trupiano* practicability standard with the more traditional reasonableness one, Minton wrote for the Court in *U.S. v. Rabinowitz* (1950) that the Fourth Amendment did not impose "any fixed formula" on federal officers or courts. The fact that the search occurred incidental to an arrest in an office that was small, open to the public, and under Rabinowitz's control meant it was a reasonable search under the circumstances.

Black dissented. Why not simply apply *Trupiano*? "The framers of the Fourth Amendment" wanted to protect against "invasion of private premises" without warrants. Frankfurter's dissent was more elegant. He made the distinction between "the arrest," which was "an incident to a warrantless search," and a "warrantless search," which was "an incident to an arrest." In the end, the Vinson Court simply chased its own tail. Frankfurter's deference and soul-searching alternated with Black's desire for bright-line rules. The end result of the struggle advanced the rights of criminal suspects to a degree, but the practical impact was extraordinarily limited.

CIVIL RIGHTS

The Vinson Court's greatest contribution to the development of American law rested with its gradual chipping away at the separate but equal doctrine of *Plessy*. Although most of the justices had already developed an antipathy for racism in the law before World War II, the postwar association of Hitler's purge of the Jews with Jim Crow raised the stakes of complaisance. Jackson, in particular, after his stint at the Nuremberg Trials, could not avoid the fact that Nazi sterilization; segregation of Jews, homosexuals, and the mentally retarded; and, ultimately, their mass murder stemmed from German laws that Hitler had described as being directly copied from those in the South. Mounting evidence from scholars that the pseudoscientific racism of previous generations was flawed, if not fabricated, undermined the basic social notions of separation of the races. Respected and objective studies like Gunnar Myrdal's *An American Dilemma: The Negro Problem and American Democracy* (1944) were widely read and approved of on and off the Court. The Soviet Union's trumpeting of its own supposedly nonracist polity, especially to the non-Caucasians of the Third World, made segregation a diplomatic embarrassment.

Throughout the 1930s, the NAACP's Legal Defense Fund had focused its energies on ensuring that separate but equal was actually equal. Charles Hamilton Houston, from his post as the dean of Howard University Law School, recruited young lawyers for the cause and looked for suitable plaintiffs. It was not easy. A black man or woman who sued Jim Crow was likely to face retaliation from white neighbors. As his health declined, Houston passed on the baton to his able student, Thurgood Marshall. Marshall's legal team, with the financial support of ordinary African Americans and white liberal groups committed to their cause, sought to engineer a legal revolution.

The suits targeted four areas of segregation: transportation, housing, unions, and higher education. The transportation decisions began with the Stone Court's *Morgan* decision. On the same interstate commerce grounds, in a Rutledge opinion, the Vinson Court upheld Michigan's Civil Rights Act when the Bob-Lo ferry company denied an African American girl and classmates transportation from Detroit to Bois Blanc Island, Canada. The segregation of the line had led to riots in Detroit already. In *Bob-Lo Excursion Company v. Michigan* (1948), despite the fact that the ferry was operating in extrastate commerce, Rutledge reasoned that the island was "economically and socially, though not politically, an amusement adjunct of the city of Detroit." Therefore, it fell under the proper ambit of Michigan's authority. Douglas concurred in an opinion that emphasized the race element and the age-old obligations of common carriers—a hint that he was ready to overturn *Plessy.* Jackson, joined by Vinson, dissented. They thought that only Congress should be allowed to regulate commerce with foreign nations.

Justice Burton's opinion for the Court in *Henderson v. U.S.* (1951), reversing a decision of the Interstate Commerce Commission allowing segregated dining cars on the Southern Railway, avoided the constitutional issue and placed the ruling squarely on section 3(1) of the Interstate Commerce Act. In response to a complaint from an African American passenger who could not receive dinner because only whites-only seating was available, the Southern Railway increased the number of seats for African Americans to four. Burton announced that "the denial of dining service to any such passenger by the rules before us subjects him to a prohibited disadvantage." The segregation of dining car passengers was invalid.

Housing was next. In an opinion by Vinson, the Court struck down racially restrictive covenants in *Shelley v. Kraemer* (1948), in effect overruling the Taft Court decision in *Corrigan v. Buckley* (1926): "Among the civil rights intended to be protected from discriminatory state actions by the Fourteenth Amendment are the rights to acquire, enjoy, own, and dispose of property." Shades of *Warley*, this time without the racist asides.

Because covenants are not state laws or state decisions as such, many scholars and courts have shied away from the implications of a ruling that blurred the boundaries between public and private action. If enforcing a private agreement was a public act, then could a property owner exclude anyone from the premises? The justices answered this question in the companion case to *Shelley*, *Hurd v. Hodge*, in which the Court invalidated racially restrictive covenants in Washington, D.C. The property owner's rights included the power to exclude unwanted visitors, but that same right protected the owner's decision to sell the property.

The majority's hostility to these covenants extended to allowing a claim from someone whose rights were not at issue. In *Barrows v. Jackson* (1953), her fellow California homeowners sued Jackson for selling her home to non-Caucasians in violation of a covenant "running with" the property (in other words, imbedded in the terms of her purchase). The state court dismissed the suit, and the High Court affirmed the dismissal. Allowing the suit to go forward would have resulted in a violation of *Shelley*. Minorities would have been denied the chance to buy and Jackson her right to sell, on impermissible racial grounds (a violation of the Equal Protection Clause). Minton, writing for a majority, reasoned: "We are faced with a unique situation in which it is the action of the state court which might result in a denial of constitutional rights and in which it would be difficult if not impossible for the persons whose rights are asserted to present their grievance before any court." That is, the minority buyers would not have standing to bring a suit to vindicate their constitutional right to acquire property. In general, the Court did not allow a party to a suit to claim, in its defense, the rights or privileges of individuals or groups who were not parties to the suit or did not have standing to bring a suit. But in this case, to allow the Court's own rules on standing to effectually bar Jackson from claiming the buyers' rights in her own defense would be to rob *Shelley* of much of its impact. Thus, Burton asserted, "Under the peculiar circumstances of this case, we believe the reasons which underlie our rule denying standing to raise another's rights, which is only a rule of practice, are outweighed by the need to protect the fundamental rights which would be denied by permitting the damages action to be maintained."

Burton's somewhat tangled prose provoked a dissent from Vinson, the author of the *Shelley* opinion. Vinson argued that the rest of the Court had gone too far: "This case, we are told, is 'unique.' I agree with the characterization. The Court, by a unique species of arguments, has developed a unique exception to an otherwise easily understood doctrine." Although he himself did not agree with the social policy at issue, he refused to undo years of precedent on standing.

The Court's willingness to actively rectify racial discrimination, despite earlier precedent, found its way into Black's majority opinion in *Brotherhood of Railroad Trainmen v. Howard* (1952). In it, the Court found that a labor agreement between an all-white union and the railroads to eliminate African American jobs violated the Railway Labor Act. Although both white and black train workers shared a similar history of union busting and scab strikebreakers and had fought similar legal battles against the same opponents, racism was rampant in whites-only conductors', engineers', and other railworkers' unions. Black firemen, brakemen, and switchmen thus faced double prejudice. The black railroad porters' union had a potent leader in A. Philip Randolph, however, and he and other black labor leaders saw that the High Court, along with Congress and the executive, could order fair treatment.

Relying on the Court's prior decision in *Steele v. Louisville & N. R. Co.* (1944), that the law required "fair representation" of all unions, Black argued that these train porters are threatened with loss of their jobs because they are not white and for no other reason. The job they did hold under its old name would be abolished by the agreement; their color alone would disqualify them for the old job under its new name. . . . The Federal Act thus prohibits bargaining agents it authorizes from using their position and power to destroy colored workers' jobs in order to bestow them on white workers. And courts can protect those threatened by such an unlawful use of power granted by a federal act.

Vinson, Reed, and Minton dissented. Minton explained: "I do not understand that private parties such as the carrier and the Brotherhood may not discriminate on the ground of race. Neither a state government nor the Federal Government may do so, but I know of no applicable federal law which says that private parties may not."

The last of the Legal Defense Fund campaign fronts was higher education. The first two cases came from Oklahoma. Basing its decision on the Hughes Court ruling in *Gaines,* the Vinson Court issued a per curiam opinion in *Sipuel v. Board of Regents of the University of Oklahoma* (1948) ordering the state to provide Ada Sipuel with a legal education "in conformity with the equal protection clause of the Fourteenth Amendment and provide it as soon as it does for the applicants of any other group." This decision came down just four days after Thurgood Marshall and the other attorneys involved participated in oral argument.

Oklahoma sought to preserve segregation by hastily opening up a law school for "coloreds" with three attorneys they quickly hired and three rooms in the state capitol with the use of the capitol law library—hardly equal though obviously separate. Marshall did not challenge *Plessy* directly. Only Rutledge filed a dissent that would have gone farther than his brethren, arguing that "the equality required was equality in fact, not in legal fiction." Although Oklahoma successfully evaded integration of its premier law school, the maneuver only lasted one year. In 1949, state authorities conceded, the makeshift law school closed, and Sipuel entered the real one. She graduated in 1951.

In the meantime, the justices faced another case even more egregious than the Sipuel case. George McLaurin gained admission to the doctoral program in education at the University of Oklahoma under *Sipuel,* but the university, per special state law, "required [him] to sit apart at a designated desk in an anteroom adjoining the classroom; to sit at a designated desk on the mezzanine floor of the library, but not to use the desks in the regular reading room; and to sit at a designated table and to eat at a different time from the other students in the school cafeteria." A unanimous Court ruled that these special arrangements failed all constitutional tests. In *McLaurin v. Oklahoma State Board of Regents* (1950), one can hear the same tone of sharp rebuke as in the Court's second Alabama peonage case: "The Fourteenth Amendment precludes differences in treatment by the state based upon race." But again the Court limited its holding to the circumstances of the case.

On the same day, the justices dealt with the University of Texas Law School's whites-only policy, in *Sweatt v. Painter* (1950). In many ways, the facts presented a much more difficult situation than the obvious deficiencies in facilities and treatment of black students in *Sipuel* and *McLaurin*. The state of Texas was not only going to provide an appendage of the University of Texas Law School but also was opening another law school at the university reserved for African Americans, the Texas State University for Negroes, in several months' time. But once more, a unanimous Court, speaking through Vinson, found these accommodations unacceptable. Vinson compared the state's premier school with the other institutions, not only in terms of accreditation, number of faculty, library, and facilities, but also in terms of the job opportunities available from attending each law school. Vinson declared that the "petitioner may claim his full constitutional right: legal education equivalent to that offered by the State to students of other races. Such education is not available to him in a separate law school as offered by the State." No mention was made of *Plessy*.

Divisions among the justices prevented them from considering *Plessy* anew, but plaintiffs in these suits seeking the end of segregation could not be put off indefinitely. Black, Douglas, Burton, and Minton favored destroying *Plessy* outright; Vinson and Reed were reluctant to dismiss such an important precedent. Frankfurter and Jackson pleaded for special arrangements so that the Court could properly address what was a deeply divisive local matter. Waiting for the Court were challenges to state-mandated or state-permitted segregation in elementary school education, a series of cases that local and national civil rights groups had brought to district federal courts. Led by *Brown v. Board of Education* and *Briggs v. Elliott*, from Kansas and South Carolina, respectively, these cases struck directly at segregation in all the schools. Consistent with their concern about the local passions invested in segregation, the justices (led by Frankfurter) consolidated the cases but made the lead case the Kansas suit. Thus they took the southern edge off the question.

After the first oral argument in 1952, the Court heard further oral argument in spring 1953. Again led by Frankfurter, the Court asked for reargument on the questions of what the framers of the Fourteenth Amendment intended for public schools and what remedies were possible considering the numbers of students, jurisdictions, and local conditions involved. Before reargument on these questions took place, Vinson died, on September 9, 1953. Eisenhower's nominee to replace him in the center chair would have the challenge and the opportunity to resolve the matter, and Earl Warren would play a decisive role in that resolution.

The Legal Defense Fund campaign against racial discrimination did not spill over into another category the Court might have regarded as suspect—legal discrimination against women. When it came to discrimination against women, the Vinson Court refused to regard sex as a category that was suspect. Following *Adkins*, the celebration of the equality of women did not lead the Court to suspect laws that discriminated against women solely because they were women. Indeed, by inverting *Muller* to allow state laws that denied to women an occupation that men performed, the Court approved of sex discrimination, in *Goesaert v. Cleary* (1948). Michigan law prohibited women bartenders unless they were the wives or daughters of the male owner. Frankfurter wrote: "The Constitution does not require legislatures to reflect sociological insight, or shifting social standards, any more than it requires them to keep abreast of the latest scientific standards." Rutledge, in dissent, joined by Douglas and Murphy, quoted Frankfurter's coy language back to him: "While the equal protection clause does not require a legislature to achieve 'abstract symmetry' or to classify with 'mathematical nicety,' that clause does require lawmakers to refrain from invidious distinctions of the sort drawn by the statute challenged in this case." Rutledge's views would be vindicated in a series of Burger Court cases.

The Vinson Court left behind a mixed legacy. At the same time as it laid the groundwork for a significant expansion of civil liberties, the Court either reinforced or deferred to some of the worst abuses of individual rights in the nation's history. It was not that the majority of justices was callous or insensitive to the victims of wartime persecutions or Cold War hysteria. Perhaps no Court, however wise or bold, could have found safe passage through the partisans' claims. Doctrines of deference to legislatures, framed in the New Deal era, were inadequate to deal with the postwar due process and equal protection claims of parties. The Vinson Court cautiously inched toward a new kind of substantive due process—unsure of where it would lead and how forcefully to apply it. Along the way, dissents that spared little in courtesy and concurrences that undercut the majority (in all except racial segregation matters) undermined the Court's authority and caused every member of the Court grief.

CHAPTER 13

The Warren Court, 1953–1969

The Supreme Court term that began in October 1953 ushered in the most stunning period in the history of the Court. In more ways than one, its bold and controversial rulings changed not only American law, but also American society, and played a central role in what has been called the civil rights revolution. The irony of this depiction of an activist liberal Court driven by its chief justice's sense of simple justice is that the members of the Court, from Chief Justice Earl Warren to its newest members, did not see themselves as revolutionaries. They saw themselves as judges, not reformers in robes. They simply found in the law its better self.

American constitutionalism has many strands. One of these gives to all federal judges the power to provide equitable remedies when the strictures of law may do injustice. Article III of the Constitution confers this authority explicitly on the High Court with the phrase "in law and equity." When a blue ribbon panel wrote and the Congress approved new rules for civil procedure in the federal courts, in 1938, the role of equity in pretrial process ("discovery" of evidence), pleading a case (for example, class action suits), and providing injunctive relief (commanding a party to do something or to stop doing something) expanded and merged with legal pleading. The two dockets were combined, with every case to begin with equity's simple "complaint" and request for a remedy rather than the law's "writ pleading." Many of the Warren Court's key decisions, in particular those involving civil rights and reapportionment of electoral districts, entailed equitable remedies. What is more, justices like William O. Douglas and William Brennan referred to equity in their opinions. Though they referred to well-established equitable remedies like the injunction, the overall direction of their thinking encompassed the deeper philosophical foundations of equity.

CONFORMITY

The Warren Court years spanned two of the most dissimilar decades in American history—the conformist 1950s and the counterculture 1960s. The first of these began in widespread anxiety that the Cold War abroad and another Red Scare at home spurred. The last days of the Korean War were covered live on television, a technological and consumer marvel whose nightly news broadcasts brought all the world's problems to the American living room. Jim Crow laws still divided the country in two by region and race, a wound that the goodwill of moderates in the South and North seemed unable to heal.

The refuge from the storm was conformity. Television programs like *Father Knows Best*, a celebration of the perfect middle-class white family, reassured viewers. The only black people on television were Amos and Andy, caricatures of urban blacks. Marriage rates increased, as did birthrates. The FBI's long-serving director, J. Edgar Hoover, told mothers that their child rearing contributed to the war on communism. Father, mother, and two perfect children lived in postwar suburban sprawl. Housing developments were connected to the cities (and jobs) by a new network of "superhighways." Car production and car use boomed. By 1952, there were over fifty-two million cars on the road, a number that would double within a generation. But people of color could not get service in restaurants or at motels along the new roads. As taxes went into highway construction and repair instead of mass transit, businesses left city cores and followed the exodus to the suburbs. So did people of color, leading to housing riots in Detroit and other northern cities.

Dwight David Eisenhower, World War II commander of Allied forces in Europe, handily won election over Democratic senator Adlai Stevenson in 1952 on a platform of ending the war in Asia and winning the war against communism. There was nothing in his platform about racial injustice or the problems of the poor. But in fact, he did not roll back the social and economic welfare programs of the New Deal, though many of his supporters, including members of his cabinet, wished him to do so. More so than any president before him, he brought corporate leaders into his government. Secretary of the Treasury George Humphrey and Secretary of Defense Charles Wilson had both been CEOs of major companies. Wilson's famous lines, explaining why he did not see a conflict of interest between his place at the top of General Motors and his new role as cabinet member, captured the close tie between business and the new Republican administration: "I thought what was good for the country was good for General Motors and vice versa."

And maybe it was. The gross national product increased some 37 percent during the decade, with inflation low and unemployment under the 4 percent mark. With the eradication of polio and the widespread introduction of antibiotics and other new medicines, life expectancy rose for most Americans, from sixty-three to seventy. But life expectancy for minorities did not keep pace, nor did educational opportunities. Unions, though curbed by new laws, were able to negotiate "cost of living" provisions in their contracts, and many companies included pension plans in their benefits—but it was not until the 1970s that most unions desegregated. When newsman Edward R. Morrow revealed to the country the plight of migrant workers and civil rights leader Martin Luther King led boycotts and protests, they captured the headlines, but real progress on the ground was slow.

Had the president added his prestige to these efforts, they might have born fruit sooner, but Eisenhower was hobbled by a heart condition and did not see these problems as the most pressing for his administration. In 1956 and 1957, he presented civil rights bills to Congress, but there a bloc of southern Democrats disemboweled the legislation. Instead of funding federal voting registrars, the bills created a civil rights commission with no power. Civil rights proponents did have a friend within Eisenhower's administration, however—Attorney General Herbert W. Brownell, a New York lawyer and Republican Party leader who had been Eisenhower's campaign manager. Brownell would suggest to his boss two appointments to the High Court that would, in time, help change the civil rights landscape.

THE EISENHOWER JUSTICES

Although courts, according to conventional wisdom, are the least able and the least likely to lead the country toward major social and economic change, it would fall to the Warren Court to lead the attack on racism. Though the president was later quoted as saying that the nomination of Earl Warren for the center seat was "the worst mistake I ever made," more than any other chief justice, Earl Warren led the Court toward racial justice. His personality, experiences, philosophy, and political talents gave the Court's output its unique combination of liberalism through compromise. A moderate Republican, Warren's views became a principled activism when translated into a judicial philosophy.

The chief justice, like Taft and Hughes, learned his politics on the executive side of government. He brought to the Court a willingness to experiment, a concern for all the people, and a can-do attitude that marked the best in the American executive tradition. Like Frankfurter, Black, Jackson, and Rutledge, Warren worked his way up to high office. His parents were the children of Norwegian immigrants. His father repaired Southern Pacific Railroad cars. There were no silver spoons on this family's dinner table. Warren distinguished himself at school and went on to the University of California at Berkeley for a bachelor's and a law degree. Volunteering for service in World War I, he spent the duration of the conflict stateside, much like Black. When the war ended, he practiced law for a time. Thanks to his politic manner and work ethic, he gained appointment as an assistant district attorney for Alameda County in California. He began his career in public service in his characteristic way: public-spirited, patriotic, and energetic and with a mind toward bipartisan reform.

In a series of election campaigns, Warren overwhelmed his opponents, winning votes from both Democrats and Republicans, until he eventually became California's first attorney general in 1938, a position his lobbying helped create. The secret to his success lay in a mixture of organizational acumen and clever positioning. During these years, he joined the Native Sons of the Golden West, a nativist organization, much as Black had joined the Klan, and worked with law enforcement officials throughout the state to professionalize law enforcement, never hesitating to involve the media in his efforts.

He could not have been characterized as a liberal. He had little sympathy for the radicalism that lay at the edge of California politics and used his office to fight communist-influenced labor organizations. When World War II began, deeply concerned that the Japanese Americans of the West Coast might form a fifth column ready to aid the Japanese empire, he became California's most prominent civilian official to campaign for relocating Japanese Americans to the interior of the country. Only in his memoirs, published shortly after his death, did he admit to an error in this regard. Though he regretted it after the war, it was not politic to admit to an error so egregious.

Political advancement seemed to be his lodestar. He won the governorship in 1942, an office he would retain with ever-increasing vote margins in 1946 and 1950. As California moved a little to the left, so did he, seeking, for example, to convince the legislature to create a state health insurance plan. By the end of the decade, he was one of the most prominent Republicans in the country, and he was named Thomas E. Dewey's running mate in the 1948 presidential campaign. When it became clear at the Republican National Convention of 1952 that Eisenhower would win the nomination, Warren released the California delegation from its commitment to him to vote for Eisenhower.

Was there a reward for Warren? Though many disagree as to whether the convention politics played a role, what is certain is that candidate Eisenhower, at Brownell's urging, promised Warren an appointment to the Court at some time. When Chief Justice Fred Vinson died suddenly, Warren sought the slot. Eisenhower agreed, somewhat reluctantly. Despite the fact that Warren had never served as a judge in any capacity, he sailed through the Senate confirmation process.

On the Court, Warren found the Black-Frankfurter feud simmering. He asked Black to run the conference until he got his bearings. Black did and wrote to a son that Warren was a "fine attractive man. . . . he is a novice here . . . but a man with his . . . practical hard common sense and integrity . . . should be able to give good service." Warren solicited Frankfurter's advice, and Frankfurter was delighted to supply it. The feud would go on, but Warren had found a way to manage, for a time, both men. Instead of imposing a command style of administration (the mistake that Vinson made), Warren consulted and listened. He made up his own mind and his writing featured little of the technical sophistication of some of his brethren—but his demeanor, his warmth, and his clear convictions gained his colleagues' admiration (except for Frankfurter, who soon grew frustrated that he could not dictate the law to Warren).

The philosophy that governed his views defies traditional categories. Justice Abe Fortas, who served with Warren at the end of his chief justiceship, called it a "basic-value approach." Others regarded it as results oriented. He knew where he wanted to go. The question was how to get there. His pursuit of justice and fairness overrode any particular interpretative strategy. If anything, he adopted an equitable view of the Constitution and the role of judging. Some commentators looked at the process and mistook it as balancing interests. True, sitting in equity, the judge is required to find win-win solutions, balancing the harms and benefits of all parties. Much of Warren's thinking and the jurisprudence of his Court exhibited this quality. Other commentators simply regarded Warren as a liberal activist, indifferent to the proper, restrained role of judging. Some scholars accused him and his majorities of reinventing substantive due process. However he is viewed, the fact is that he dedicated himself to fundamental changes in American law.

Later additions to his Court might buy into this agenda or not, but all grew to respect Warren. Following the sudden death of Robert H. Jackson from heart failure, Eisenhower nominated John Marshall Harlan II, the grandson of the great dissenter, to replace Jackson. Some southern senators used objections to the nomination to express their displeasure with the ruling in *Brown*. Other senators objected on the grounds that Harlan's undergraduate and graduate degrees from Oxford made him a part of the one-world conspiracy of the United Nations and its supporters.

But even the most cursory examination of his life story reveals a lawyer of the highest quality and one with conservative instincts and broad sympathies. Harlan's studies at Princeton in 1920, where he was class president for three years, editor of the *Princetonian*, and chair of the Senior Council, prefigured Samuel Alito's career there. His exemplary performance at Oxford's Balliol

College on a Rhodes Scholarship added luster to his credentials. Harlan attended New York Law School at night while he worked as a paralegal at a firm during the day. One year later he had his law degree. In New York, Harlan compiled a distinguished record as a prosecutor and legal counsel for various city, state, and federal offices—including assistant U.S. attorney for the Southern District of New York, special assistant to the New York attorney general, chief of the Operational Analysis Section of the Eighth Air Force during World War II, and chief counsel to the New York State Crime Commission in 1951. In private practice, he had clients like the DuPont Corporation, for whom he argued before the U.S. Supreme Court. At the same time, he volunteered for the Legal Aid Society.

He was, in short, a lawyer's lawyer with a conscience—a believer in hard and careful work and the value of lawyering. He left private practice for good when Eisenhower appointed him to the Second Circuit Court of Appeals, a position he occupied for only eight months before he rose to the Supreme Court. On it, Harlan gained a reputation as one of the Court's ablest opinion writers. He apparently relished the task, for he penned over 600 opinions, almost half of them in dissent, and 149 concurrences. He was Frankfurter's natural ally. They respected one another, and during the time they sat together on the bench they agreed in 80 percent of the cases. One wag went so far as to declare that Harlan was Frankfurter without the mustard. When Frankfurter retired, Harlan became the standard bearer of judicial restraint, federalism, and deference to legislatures, but he shared with his grandfather a concern for civil rights, especially those of African Americans, and free speech. Much respected by his brethren, he exercised great influence well into the Burger Court. He retired on September 23, 1971, due to the onset of spinal cancer and died later that year.

When Sherman Minton announced his retirement in late 1956, Eisenhower had another chance to shape the supreme tribunal. Largely in order to demonstrate his bipartisanship in an election year, he determined to nominate a Democrat. Brownell had come to like and admire a New Jersey Supreme Court justice, William J. Brennan Jr., and Ike went along with his attorney general's recommendation. Brennan was hesitant, but Brownell told him, "You can't say no to the president of the United States." Brennan would exercise an immense influence over American law for the next thirty-four years, and his cherubic optimism, his immense delight in the politics of coalition building, and his sense of right and wrong came through in every decision in which he took part.

Commitment to liberal reform came naturally to Brennan. Born on April 25, 1906, in Newark, New Jersey, to Irish immigrants, Brennan grew up amid the boom, turbulence, and corruption of the industrial Northeast. His father became a staunch supporter of organized labor, a foe of dirty dealings, and a crusading politician. His family sacrificed so that Bill Jr. could attend Wharton and then his first two years at Harvard Law School. At this point, the sudden death of his father would have ended this shining career but for the intervention of his professors, who arranged for a scholarship so that Brennan could complete his degree. In 1931, he graduated in the top 10 percent of his class. Upon his return to Newark, he joined the firm of Pitney, Hardin, and Skinner. In a move that might have stunned his father, he ably represented the firm's corporate clients in labor negotiations.

He joined the army at the outset of World War II. With the peace, he rejoined his firm as a named partner, but public service beckoned again, and Brennan became the protégé of the prominent jurist and legal reformer Judge Arthur T. Vanderbilt. When Republican governor Alfred Driscoll created the convention to rewrite New Jersey's constitution in 1947, Vanderbilt gave his young charge the responsibility for overhauling the state's antiquated, complex, and malfunctioning judicial system. In recognition of his effort, Driscoll appointed Brennan to the superior court in 1949, the appellate division of the superior court in 1950, and the New Jersey Supreme Court in 1952. Appointment to the High Court followed in 1956.

He did not always impress law professors and other pundits with the elegance of his writing style, but Brennan was greatly admired by most experts for his grasp of the nub of legal issues, for his vision, and for his ability to bring together majorities around the extension and protection of civil liberties and civil rights. As he wrote in 1961, "Judicial self restraint which defers too much to the sovereign powers of the states and reserves judicial intervention for only the most revolting of cases [Frankfurter's 'shock the conscience standard'] will not serve to enhance Madison's priceless gift of 'the great rights of mankind [the Bill of Rights].'" Brennan's judicial philosophy ultimately became known as the "living Constitution school." In the justice's words, the Constitution's "genius . . . rests not in any static meaning it might have had in a world that is dead and gone, but in the adaptability of its great principles to cope with current problems and current needs." He would author over 1,200 opinions, of which over 450 were for the majority. He served until 1990 and died in 1997.

Eisenhower's fourth appointment came when Reed announced his retirement in early 1957. In order to balance the court geographically with a solid Republican, he chose the Court's first native-born Kansan, Charles E. Whittaker. A farm boy who worked his way up from rural poverty to the highest court in the land might well have represented one of the great success stories of all time—except, by his own admission, his years as a justice were some of the worst of his life. All the qualities that enabled him to overcome his hardships—hard work, drive, and concentration—could not help with the intellectually demanding work of the Court. This able trial lawyer and judge had risen above his level of competence. As his term on the Court progressed, he became more and more anxious. Douglas recalled that in the case of *Myers v. U.S.* (1960) Whittaker became so distressed at having to write the majority opinion that he gave the task to his friend, Douglas, a dissenter in the case. For perhaps the first and only time in its history, a justice wrote both a majority and a dissenting opinion. In 1962, the stress reached critical levels, and his doctors at Walter Reed Medical Center advised him to retire in order to recover his health. On March 29, 1962, he did. He died thirteen years later.

Potter Stewart, Eisenhower's fifth and last appointment, replaced Burton, taking his seat on May 15, 1959. Stewart hailed from Cincinnati. His father, a councilman, mayor, and justice of the Ohio Supreme Court, served as a role model. Stewart attended exclusive private schools and Yale. After a year's study in England at Cambridge, he returned to Yale for his law degree, which he received with honors. He practiced corporate law in New York City and saw active service in World War II. After the war, he returned to Cincinnati to practice law, excelling at trial litigation and becoming active in Republican Party politics. On Senator John W. Bricker's recommendation, Eisenhower nominated Stewart to the Sixth Circuit Court of Appeals in 1954. When the Senate confirmed him for the Supreme Court in October of 1958, he gained the distinction of being the youngest to serve as federal judge at the time and the youngest justice since the Civil War.

Perhaps because his jurisprudential philosophy was more traditional and supposedly more value free than the Court in general, his conservative pragmatism defied labels. Like the more erudite Harlan, Stewart believed in a limited role for judges in a democratic society but also sought a color-blind society. He tended to defer to the judgments of legislators and law enforcement officials while maintaining an adaptive stance toward constitutional problems. Unfortunately for his popular reputation, his remark about refusing to define obscenity in *Jacobellis v. Ohio* (1964), "but I know it when I see it," outweighed his more important contributions in cases like *Katz v. U.S.* (1967), in which his majority opinion extended Fourth Amendment search-and-seizure protection to eavesdropping. His over six hundred opinions made a substantial, if unclassifiable, contribution to the development of American law.

"THE TIMES THEY ARE A-CHANGING"

In the 1960s, Stewart and his brethren found their values and experience put to the test. Folk rocker Bob Dylan described the new era: "The times they are a-changing." The election of John F. Kennedy, in 1960, was a celebration of youth and vigor, a "Camelot" that brought a promise of change. Though, in fact, Kennedy was a conservative in many respects, a Cold Warrior who did not press hard for the end of segregation, fearing to split the Democratic Party into antagonistic northern and southern wings, a new generation of young people came to regard his election as a signal to explore personal independence and to protest injustice.

Out from New York City radiated the pulse of the "beat" poets, their howl of protest against convention joining the sounds of rock and roll coming from the heartland and the marching feet of civil rights workers in the South. Movements to save the environment and to preserve older architecture from urban renewal joined the reform agenda. A counterculture featuring beads, free love, and communes overlapped student-led movements for civil rights and peace. The counterculture and the protest movements once again raised questions about the time, place, and manner restrictions on free speech and free press.

After an assassin's bullet killed Kennedy, President Lyndon Johnson pushed through civil rights and equal opportunity programs, envisioning a "Great Society" in which there was no poverty or unemployment. But American involvement in the Vietnam War, a conflict that had raged in one form or another since the end of World War II, drafted millions and sent hundreds of thousands of young men into the deltas, jungles, and mountain plateaus of Indochina. Over fifty thousand never returned.

The antiwar protests grew in numbers, flowing into a more confrontational civil rights movement, as voluntaristic reforms in the antebellum era flowed into uncompromising abolitionism. A new feminism, which coalesced in nationwide organizations like the National Organization for Women, demanded equal pay for equal work and reproductive autonomy—birth control and abortion rights.

Kennedy's first appointment to the Court, a 1962 replacement for Whittaker, had little in common with and no great sympathy for these sea changes in social and cultural values. Instead, Byron R. White more resembled the doomed president. A "New Frontier" justice, White was admirable in person, tough-minded and realistic in his thinking, and pragmatic in his view of the law. He graduated first in his class at Yale Law School after a magna cum laude career at the University of Colorado, where he lettered in three sports and excelled on the gridiron. Postponing his term at Oxford on a Rhodes Scholarship, he signed a professional football contract with the Pittsburgh Pirates of the American Football League. He led the league in rushing for two years and is the only justice to be in a sports Hall of Fame. During the 1940 and 1941 football seasons he attended Yale Law School, until Pearl Harbor and the beginning of World War II curtailed his athletic career. As an intelligence officer in the Pacific theater, he earned commendations and promotions. At the war's close he was a decorated officer who wrote the report on the sinking of Jack Kennedy's PT 109.

He returned to Yale Law School to complete his degree, earning first-in-his-class distinction. In 1946, he clerked for Chief Justice Fred Vinson and then returned to Colorado to practice law. His general practice for mostly corporate and wealthy clients earned him a comfortable living. A man blessed with these athletic and intellectual gifts might have sought a political career, but White chose not to do so, at least in part a reaction to the assault by the press during his college and professional football-playing days. He developed an almost virulent distaste for the press and those seeking to publicize his life, including historians. In 1986, as his twenty-fifth anniversary on the Court approached, he and a clerk spent weekends shredding his papers at the Court.

His judicial philosophy was honed when he served as an assistant to Attorney General Robert Kennedy. He favored vigorous enforcement of the law to counter resistance to civil rights for African Americans but deference to political bodies in other matters. He had little sympathy for the downtrodden accused of crime and those who protested on their behalf. He believed in "neutral principles," a philosophy of judging in which only fair procedures and a commitment to the legal process should govern the outcome of a case. Straightforward to the point of brutal honesty, incisive in his opinions, a realist and an intellectual, he would serve until 1993. He died in 2002.

Kennedy's second and last appointment, Arthur J. Goldberg, rose from humble origins to great political influence and legal office, like the man he replaced, Frankfurter. Goldberg never forgot those humble beginnings or abandoned his advocacy of the rights of organized labor. As a child on Chicago's lower-class West Side, he held several jobs in order to help keep his Russian immigrant family afloat. His intellectual gifts and hard work enabled him to graduate from high school at age fifteen. He attended Crane Junior College during the day and DePaul University at night. At Northwestern University, he graduated first in his class and then earned his law degree in 1930, the next year.

He began his distinguished law career clerking for Pritzker and Pritzker in Chicago and after a time started his own practice, focusing on labor law. He successfully represented the American Newspaper Guild in its strike against the William Randolph Hearst newspaper empire. In World War II, Goldberg became chief of the labor division in the Office of Strategic Services. He used his familiarity with organized labor to arrange for resistance activities in Nazi-occupied Europe. After the war, he became general counsel for the United Steelworkers of America in 1948 and represented the Congress of Industrial Organizations. Goldberg played an integral part in the merger of the CIO with its rival, the American Federation of Labor, in 1955. The joint constitution came largely from his pen. He served as the new organization's special counsel until 1961 when Kennedy tapped him to become the secretary of labor. In this capacity, he displayed the same qualities that characterized him as a lawyer and would later as a justice. He sought fair solutions to disputes that increased opportunities for historically disadvantaged groups.

When Frankfurter announced his intention to retire from the bench after failing to recover fully from a stroke, Kennedy had little difficulty putting Goldberg into the so-called Jewish seat. Although he would only occupy it for three terms, from 1962 to 1965, his vote and opinions constituted the high-water mark of the Warren Court's civil rights revolution. His majority opinion in *Escobedo v. Illinois* (1964), giving those accused of crimes the right to be informed of the right to remain silent, remains a pillar of criminal procedure, and his invocation of the Ninth Amendment as the constitutional source of privacy rights was a brilliant insight. He died of a heart attack in 1990.

President Lyndon Johnson pressed Goldberg to trade his seat on the Court for the ambassadorship to the United Nations, ostensibly to help negotiate an end to the Vietnam War. In fact, Johnson wanted to place his confidant, Abe Fortas, in the Jewish seat. Though he would have a rewarding career as a diplomat and D.C. lawyer, Goldberg always regretted his short stay at the marble palace. Fortas's appointment did not tilt the balance of the bench. He was as liberal and as much an activist as Goldberg.

Like some Shakespearian tragic hero, Fortas possessed the makings of a great justice, perhaps a great chief justice, but circumstance and his own personal failings conspired to bring about his fall. The child of orthodox Jewish immigrants from Russia and from Lithuania, Fortas grew up in Memphis, Tennessee, and attended Yale Law School after graduating first in his class at Southwestern College in Memphis. It was the high tide of legal realism at Yale, led by the energetic dean, Charles Clark. Clark sponsored and participated in a wide variety of legal reform projects, including those leading to no-fault car insurance, the end of prohibition, no-fault divorce, and the merger of law and equity in federal courts. Fortas's mentor at Yale was Professor William O. Douglas. Douglas encouraged Fortas to apply social conscience to public service, even if he elected to remain in private practice. Although he accepted an appointment to his law school's faculty, he soon followed in his mentor's footsteps into Franklin D. Roosevelt's New Deal agencies.

Fortas was a success everywhere he turned in his administrative posts. Recognizing his prodigious talents, Harold Ickes, the secretary of the interior, named Fortas to be director of the Division of Power, then, a year later in 1942, to be undersecretary of the department. There he became known as Ickes's "field marshal." In 1946, Fortas quit government work to form the highly successful D.C. law firm of Arnold, Fortas, and Porter. But he did not abandon public service even though he represented large corporate interests. In 1962, he won his most notable Supreme Court victory on behalf of a Florida indigent, Clarence Earl Gideon, convicted of a felony without representation. In *Gideon v. Wainwright* (1963), the Court overturned *Betts v. Brady* and mandated that the state provide attorneys for destitute defendants in felony cases.

Through his personal connections, in particular, his services to Lyndon Johnson, Fortas became the ultimate inside-the-beltway operator. Without his permission, Johnson submitted his name to be a justice of the Supreme Court in July 1965. Fortas was reluctant to join the Court, for it would mean a huge loss of income, but he agreed. On the bench, he proved to be an able judicial craftsman. He wrote the majority opinion in *In re Gault* (1967), which extended self-incrimination and right-to-counsel rights to juveniles, and in *Tinker v. Des Moines* (1969), which recognized the symbolic speech rights of grade school and high school students.

When Johnson learned, in 1968, of Warren's intention of retiring at the end of the Court's spring term, the president nominated Fortas to be Warren's successor. At his hearing, Fortas failed to anticipate the sharp attacks on his character (for advising Johnson while on the Court), his morality (for extending constitutional free speech protections to lurid films), and, most devastating, his ethical judgment (for accepting money for teaching a law course paid for by the clients at his former law firm). Although none of these activities could have been prosecuted or were, in and of themselves, particularly damaging, a battered, besmirched, and weary Fortas withdrew himself from consideration for the center chair.

This did not end his travails. *Life* magazine broke a story on Fortas's acceptance, later returned, of $20,000 from a charitable foundation established by a shady former client named Louis Wolfson. Assailed for this lapse in judgment, with threats of impeachment emanating from Congress, Fortas resigned from the Court on May 14, 1969. He died on April 5, 1982.

Johnson's second appointee was even more consistently liberal and loyal to the Warren Court's liberal jurisprudence than Goldberg or Fortas. The confirmation of Solicitor General Thurgood Marshall broke the color barrier on the Court. Appropriately, Marshall had been a key player in breaking many of the color barriers in the country. Marshall's appointment made it past the segregationists, who threatened to filibuster in the Senate, on August 30, 1967. Thurgood Marshall replaced Clark and thus gave the Warren Court liberals their solid majority for the two terms they had left.

If Whittaker's rise from poverty to power was inspiring, Marshall's was awesome. This grandson of a former slave grew up in Jim Crow Baltimore, with a father who worked as a dining car waiter and a mother who taught in the segregated elementary school. Marshall worked as a bellhop to put himself through college at Lincoln University in Pennsylvania and then Howard University Law School, both all-black schools, because Maryland denied blacks admission to its premier undergraduate and graduate institutions. At Howard, Marshall found two mentors: Dean Charles Hamilton Houston and William Hastie. Under Houston's direction, Marshall joined the NAACP's litigation team, the Legal Defense Fund.

"Mr. Civil Rights," as he came to be known, knew that the Court's enforcement decision to proceed with school desegregation "with all deliberate speed" in 1955 made the desegregation of schools much harder. At this time he also lost his first wife, Vivian Burey, to cancer. He remarried in December of 1955 and continued with his work. In 1961, Kennedy appointed him to the Second Circuit, a move that doubled his salary but removed him from the cause he valued so highly. Despite an eleven-month confirmation fight and bespattered with the vitriol of southern Democrats, he gained Senate approval. He was the first African American to sit on the federal circuit courts of appeal.

On the circuit court, his 118 opinions made lasting contributions to the law. Finding himself in harmony with the Warren Court, none of his 98 majority opinions were faulted at the highest level. When Johnson made Marshall solicitor general of the United States, he solidified his reputation as one of the nation's ablest advocates, winning 14 of 19 cases. Many of those cases protected the landmark civil and voting rights legislation of the Johnson presidency.

In Marshall's tenure on the Warren Court, he helped advance the causes of the weak, the underprivileged, and the vulnerable. He wrote for the Court in *Stanley v. Georgia* (1969), protecting the privacy rights of individuals with regard to obscene material, and in *Benton v. Maryland* (1969), applying the double-jeopardy protection of the Bill of Rights to the states. From the Fortas debacle to Marshall's retirement in 1991, he increasingly found himself in the minority, but this did not deter him from writing stirring dissents. As the only justice who faced invidious racism every day of his life, including once being mistaken for the elevator operator in the marble palace, Marshall wrote with real authority on injustice. A man of good humor who enjoyed the bully pulpit his seat on the Court provided (once frankly telling a gathering of lawyers and judges that he thought little of the Rehnquist Court's civil rights jurisprudence), he reluctantly left the bench due to growing health problems on June 1, 1991. Marshall died on January 24, 1993.

CIVIL RIGHTS AND THE RULE OF LAW

In many ways, the first decision of note in the Warren Court, *Brown v. Board of Education* (1954), showed both the promise and the limitations of the liberalism of the Court. Warren deserves much of the credit for fashioning the approach to *Brown* and its many progeny, as well as some criticism for how the Court handled one of the most controversial cases in its history.

As Justice Oliver Wendell Holmes noted, hard cases make bad law. No case could have been harder than undoing at a stroke what nearly one hundred years of segregation had done in elementary education. The system of separate schools was rooted in the fiscal, social, and psychological life of much of the South. Frankfurter's argument that courts were inadequate to deal with these kinds of problems had much truth. Courts would play a vital role in the end of segregation, but there were obstacles that the best intentioned of courts could not, by themselves, overcome.

Thurgood Marshall and the NAACP's Legal Defense Fund devised a class-action lawsuit to undo segregation in public schools all at once. Federal courts asked to handle class actions have to certify that the issues in every case under a class action are essentially the same, and the relief sought has to be acceptable to all the winning parties. The class-action lawsuit against segregated schools was not the first class action, but it was the most sweeping by far, an issue lawsuit on a broad spectrum initiated in order to change the law of the land. It was not an assignment any of the justices relished, even though almost all of them knew that segregation had done harm and that the Court had the power to declare state-mandated separate schools unconstitutional. Although a majority of Americans, and hence public opinion, favored such a step, the reception of any sweeping decision in the South, where Jim Crow ruled in education, access to public facilities, local transportation, restaurants, movie theaters, and even ballparks, could not be predicted.

The justices worried about enforcement from the first moment that lawyers argued the five cases under Chief Justice Vinson and again when Warren replaced him. Frankfurter brooded that Minton and Reed might not be enthusiastic about the Court sweeping aside what southern legislatures and local school boards had fashioned over so many years. Warren was in favor of ending segregation and had no hesitation about the Court so ordering but, like Frankfurter and Jackson, understood that enforcement was the real problem for consensus on the Court. Frankfurter was right. Justice Reed required special attention. According to one of his law clerks at the time, Warren persuaded Reed to sign on when he appealed to both his patriotism and his isolation from the rest of the Court. Thus Warren had his unanimous Court, but he had to pay a substantial price for that consensus. The opinion would rule only on segregation in education and did not explicitly overrule *Plessy*, and the implementation decision, *Brown II*, would come in the fall term of the next year. This would give the southern legislatures and school boards time to accommodate themselves to the new order.

The opinion of the Court was unanimous, and Warren wrote it. From its emphasis on the importance of public schooling to American life, to the plain language that took its reasoning from one point to the next, to the forward-thinking rejection of segregation as a moral wrong, the California progressive shone. It was a short opinion—barely ten pages—that Warren read. The cases presented slightly different fact patterns: "In the Kansas case, *Brown v. Board of Education*, the plaintiffs are Negro children of elementary school age residing in Topeka. They brought this action in the United States District Court for the District of Kansas to enjoin enforcement of a Kansas statute which permits, but does not require, cities of more than 15,000 population to maintain separate school facilities for Negro and white students." *Brown* was the lead case, "joined" by the Court with four other cases decided at the same time.

Segregation was not voluntary in South Carolina. "In the South Carolina case, *Briggs v. Elliott*, the plaintiffs are Negro children of both elementary and high school age residing in Clarendon County." The case had cost its original plaintiff in the rural community his farm and livelihood. To save the lawsuit, hundreds of black parents and children signed the petition when the case was refiled. "They brought this action in the United States District Court for the Eastern District of South Carolina to enjoin enforcement of provisions in the state constitution and statutory code which require the segregation of Negroes and whites in public schools." The federal panel that first heard the case ordered equalization of facilities but refused to overturn the state's segregation law. The lower court also accepted the state government's promise to pass legislation providing more funds for the black schools and so delayed any relief to the petitioners.

Prince Edward County in Virginia had some of the same characteristics as Clarendon County. Fifty miles west of Richmond, today the county is still largely rural. Race relations there were not as hostile as in Clarendon County. "In the Virginia case, *Davis v. County School Board*, the plaintiffs are Negro children of high school age residing in Prince Edward County. They brought this action in the United States District Court for the Eastern District of Virginia to enjoin enforcement of provisions in the state constitution and statutory code which require the segregation of Negroes and whites in public schools." Unlike the case in South Carolina, "the court found the Negro school inferior in physical plant, curricula, and transportation, and ordered the defendants forthwith to provide substantially equal curricula and transportation and to 'proceed with all reasonable diligence and dispatch to remove' the inequality in physical plant." But the federal district court, following *Plessy*, would not override the state law and would not order white schools to admit black students.

There was one ray of light. In Delaware, Chancellor Collins Seitz, whose powers included the provision of equitable remedies, took a step that the federal judges in South Carolina and Virginia refused to take (though they too had equitable powers): "In . . . *Gebhart v. Belton*, the plaintiffs are Negro children of both elementary and high school age residing in New Castle County. They brought this action in the Delaware Court of Chancery to enjoin enforcement of provisions in the state constitution and statutory code which require the segregation of Negroes and whites in public schools. . . . The Chancellor gave judgment for the plaintiffs and ordered their immediate admission to schools previously attended only by white children." The Delaware Supreme Court affirmed Seitz's decision. The defendants—the school board—appealed to the High Court to prevent desegregation.

Warren reported that historical investigation of the Reconstruction congressional records could not guide the Court. They were inconclusive. But history did show that "in the first cases in this Court construing the Fourteenth Amendment, decided shortly after its adoption, the Court interpreted it as proscribing all state-imposed discriminations against the Negro race." The notion of "separate but equal" was a later retreat from the goals of Reconstruction in general and the Fourteenth Amendment in particular. John Marshall Harlan's voice in the *Civil Rights Cases* and *Plessy* had not been lost after all, despite the cacophony of racism that had drowned him out at the time.

Warren and his Court read the Fourteenth Amendment simply: "What is this but declaring that the law in the States shall be the same for the black as for the white; that all persons, whether colored or white, shall stand equal before the laws of the States, and, in regard to the colored race, for whose protection the amendment was primarily designed, that no discrimination shall be made against them by law because of their color?" While this reading might be viewed as the continuation of the *Ex rel. Gaines* (1938) line of cases, Warren went far beyond those precedents. He read the Fourteenth Amendment in light of the Thirteenth Amendment, following the steps that the Reconstruction Congress itself had taken, to find "the right to exemption from unfriendly legislation against them distinctively as colored—exemption from legal discriminations, implying inferiority in civil society, lessening the security of their enjoyment of the rights which others enjoy, and discriminations which are steps towards reducing them to the condition of a subject race."

Warren opined that education was the key to success in American society. No one could disagree. "It is doubtful that any child may reasonably be expected to succeed in life if he is denied the opportunity of an education. Such an opportunity, where the state has undertaken to provide it, is a right which must be made available to all on equal terms." Then he asked,

Does segregation of children in public schools solely on the basis of race, even though the physical facilities and other "tangible" factors may be equal, deprive the children of the minority group of equal educational opportunities? We believe that it does. . . . To separate them from others of similar age and qualifications solely because of their race generates a feeling of inferiority as to their status in the community that may affect their hearts and minds in a way unlikely ever to be undone.

Segregated education placed an indelible mark of inferiority on black schoolchildren. In 1954, common sense revealed what in 1896 prejudice had denied: "The policy of separating the races is usually interpreted as denoting the inferiority of the negro group." The impact in education, particularly in the lower grades, could be predicted: "A sense of inferiority affects the motivation of a child to learn. Segregation with the sanction of law, therefore, has a tendency to [retard] the educational and mental development of negro children and to deprive them of some of the benefits they would receive in a racial[ly] integrated school system."

Warren's clerk added a footnote to the written opinion at this point citing social science studies of the psychological impact of segregation on young people. The Legal Defense Fund had either commissioned the studies or introduced them into the arguments, so the note was one sided. The studies cited included "K. B. Clark, Effect of Prejudice and Discrimination on Personality Development (Midcentury White House Conference on Children and Youth, 1950)," the famous white and black dolls study. Later critics of the Court's supposed reliance on "sociological jurisprudence" and later critics of the methodology of the doll study (no controls, no repetition) have misunderstood or exaggerated the importance of the evidence and note 11. The note, and the studies, were not crucial in Warren's thinking. He did not need to know that black children thought that the white dolls were good and the black dolls were not to know that forced separation was a stigma in itself.

Warren and the Court concluded that "in the field of public education the doctrine of 'separate but equal' has no place. Separate educational facilities are inherently unequal. Therefore, we hold that the plaintiffs and others similarly situated for whom the actions have been brought are, by reason of the segregation complained of, deprived of the equal protection of the laws guaranteed by the Fourteenth Amendment." This applied to all four state cases. In *Bolling v. Sharpe*, the Court relied on the Fifth Amendment to knock down segregated schools in the District of Columbia. The Fourteenth Amendment only applied to the states.

But Warren did not explicitly overrule *Plessy*, a fact that had great significance. He said that the rule in *Plessy* did not apply to public education. *Plessy* was not concerned with education, though it would become the precedent on which segregation of schools was based. Instead, it concerned transportation. To overrule *Plessy* would have been tantamount to saying that all state segregation was unconstitutional. The Court would follow this path in the years to come, but for the present, it was more cautious.

Indeed, the caution extended to *Brown* and its sister cases. Because of the "considerable complexity" involved in desegregating tens of thousands of schoolchildren in thousands of school buildings in multiple jurisdictions specifically arranged for segregation, Warren's opinion invited not only the parties to the class action but also the U.S. attorney general and the attorneys general of the states involved to reargue the case on implementation.

From the time Warren read the opinion of the Court on Monday, May 17, 1954, reaction was sharply mixed. Those opposed to Jim Crow hailed the decision as the correction of a wrong long in coming. The *New York Times* linked the decision to the Declaration of Independence, and other papers in the North trumpeted that the decision would "stun" our communist enemies. Black newspapers were even more delighted. The *Chicago Defender* predicted that "this means the beginning of the end of the dual society in American life."

But some die-hard southern segregationists feared a race war. The *Daily News* in Jackson, Mississippi, warned ominously that "human blood may stain Southern soil in many places because of this decision. . . . white and negro children in the same schools will lead to miscegenation . . . and mongrelization of the human race." "Impeach Earl Warren" signs popped up along some rural southern roads. Southern congressmen and politicians joined in a "Declaration of Constitutional Principles" on March 12, 1956, that announced a well-organized, government-sponsored massive resistance to the decision. The Court was guilty of a "clear abuse of judicial power" that would undo the "habits, customs, traditions and way of life" of southerners, that were "founded on elemental humanity and commonsense." It would create chaos and confusion, "destroying the amicable relations between the white and Negro people of both races." Desegregation would plant "hatred and suspicion where there has been heretofore friendship and understanding." In short, almost every southern state's member of Congress (for almost every southern member of Congress signed the manifesto) believed that the heckler's veto—massive resistance—would force the Court to back down or change course.

Eisenhower never came out in favor of *Brown*. In fact, he privately indicated that he was not opposed to segregated schools. Only the fact that his attorney general, Herbert Brownell, favored the end of segregation and sent the solicitor general of the United States to present this position to the Court put the weight of the federal government behind its highest court. Eisenhower's opponent in the 1956 presidential campaign, Adlai E. Stevenson, urged gradualism. He needed and hoped for Democratic votes in the South and could not afford to offend its segregationists. Most northern liberals agreed that southern blacks must exercise patience, a remarkable feat given the violence the white mobs and vigilantes routinely exercised in opposition to the Court's order. Even Warren despaired that desegregation would not come until "we are all long dead."

In the academy, where the Court might have expected support from liberal law professors, criticism took one of two forms: the Herbert Wechsler "neutral principles" school or the John Hart Ely democracy school. Columbia Law School's Wechsler argued that Warren's reasoning elevated just outcomes over the means he used to achieve them—and that Warren had used a form of reasoning more suited to a legislature than a court. Ely's objections stemmed from his concern about the proper role of judges in a constitutional democracy. Although courts must act to protect individual liberties as a last resort, decisions like desegregating should be left to the political branches. Majorities must be left free to determine the course and pace of social change.

Brown II (1955), the implementation decision, with its call for individual suits and "all due deliberate speed," was not what the Legal Defense Fund team wanted. The Court had turned to an equitable remedy to the problem but left the management of the remedy in the hands of federal district court judges. These men were white southerners who had grown up with segregation. Some, like Elbert Tuttle, in the Fifth Circuit, would press hard for the end of segregation. Others dragged their feet. The problem was that all equitable remedies require the good faith of the parties before the court. If they do not carry out the court's orders, the judge can hold them in contempt, but what federal judge was going to send an entire school board to jail? Knowing this, and determined not to follow the High Court's lead, local and state school boards delayed, denied, and disobeyed *Brown II* with ill-concealed dodges like pupil placement plans.

At first the Court did little to force inferior federal tribunals to act with anything like deliberate speed. When a state governor finally openly defied the Court, however, the justices had little choice but to speak. In *Cooper v. Aaron* (1958), Brennan crafted the opinion for the entire Court. He elected to focus on Arkansas governor Orville Faubus rather than the school board and on the federal/state supremacy issues rather than race itself. Faubus refused to obey a court order to desegregate the high school in Little Rock, Arkansas. He interposed himself and the state government, much as John C. Calhoun told South Carolina to do in the Tariff Nullification Controversy of 1828–1833. In the per curiam opinion, the Warren Court reasserted their ultimate authority to interpret the Constitution: "No state legislator or executive or judicial officer can war against the Constitution without violating his undertaking to support it." But Eisenhower's resort to airborne troops to protect the African American students trying to integrate the high school bespoke volumes about the difficulty of the effort and the judicial branch's ineffectiveness when backed up by tepid executive and legislative branches.

It was not until five years later that Warren and his fellow justices began to take the reins from the hands of the district courts. In *Goss v. Board of Education* (1963), they invalidated a plan that would have allowed voluntary one-race-only schools. In *Griffin v. Prince Edward County School Board* (1964), they forced a Virginia county to reopen its schools that the county had closed in order to avoid integration. Justice Black's majority opinion made it plain the tribunal would no longer accept delays. Finally, in *Green v. County School Board* (1968), Brennan wrote a majority opinion that laid out the specifics demanded of all integration plans: they must be results-oriented, not intent-focused, and the particular elements of each plan must meet judicial approval. Federal judges would be required to use the full extent of their equity powers to take over and run the schools if need be.

UNDOING PLESSY

In a series of cases after *Brown*, the Court deployed the Equal Protection Clause to knock down state and local segregation. In *McLaughlin v. Florida* (1964), it struck down a law prohibiting the cohabitation of interracial couples. In *Loving v. Virginia* (1967), Warren's opinion for a unanimous Court eliminated miscegenation laws, the restrictions on interracial marriage. Echoing the language of *Brown*, he stated: "Restricting the freedom to marry solely because of racial classification violates the central meaning of the Equal Protection Clause." The time seemed ripe for such a decision. Led by Frankfurter, the Court had refused to hear a case challenging the very same Virginia law, in *Naim v. Naim* (1955).

What had changed? The rule against mixed marriages was rooted in history. Warren conceded that "Penalties for miscegenation arose as an incident to slavery and have been common in Virginia since the colonial period. The present statutory scheme dates from the adoption of the Racial Integrity Act of 1924, passed during the period of extreme nativism which followed the end of the First World War." After the war, southern states stiffened the rule—changing from one-eighth or one-sixteenth black ancestry to "one-drop" of Negro blood. Well into the civil rights era, the rule was still prevalent. In 1966, Alabama, Arkansas, Delaware, Florida, Georgia, Kentucky, Louisiana, Mississippi, Missouri, North Carolina, Oklahoma, South Carolina, Tennessee, Texas, and West Virginia—in addition to Virginia—all had laws that penalized mixed marriages.

Arguing for its own law, Virginia insisted that "the question of constitutionality would thus become whether there was any rational basis for a State to treat interracial marriages differently from other marriages. On this question, the State argues, the scientific evidence is substantially in doubt and, consequently, this Court should defer to the wisdom of the state legislature in adopting its policy of discouraging interracial marriages." In short, defer to Virginia. But what evidence was there of a legitimate state purpose? Nothing but the old idea that interracial marriage corrupted the blood, or as the law put it, harmed the "racial integrity" of the white race. Warren and the rest of the Court replied that "the clear and central purpose of the Fourteenth Amendment was to eliminate all official state sources of invidious racial discrimination in the States." *Pace v. State* (1881) was finally overruled in 1970.

But the unanimity in the Court over civil rights fractured over increasingly disruptive civil protests. The sit-in cases of the early 1960s put the consensus to the test. The Court spoke with one voice in *Edwards v. South Carolina* (1963), holding that a peaceable march down a city street "reflect[ed] an exercise of these basic constitutional rights in their most pristine and classic form." But in *Bell v. Maryland* (1964), a divided Court dismissed the convictions of sit-ins. Brennan's convoluted reading of Maryland's recently passed public accommodations law was an attempt to find common ground. It failed. Concurrences and dissents ran to 120 pages. Only Brennan's outmaneuvering of Black's opinion that the sit-ins went too far saved the day for the protesters.

But not every protest was acceptable. In *Adderley v. Florida* (1966), Black outmaneuvered Brennan, as well as his former liberal ally Douglas, to uphold the convictions of trespassing against a group of Florida A&M students rallying outside a county jail:

Students of the Florida A. & M. University in Tallahassee, had gone from the school to the jail about a mile away, along with many other students, to "demonstrate" at the jail their protests of arrests of other protesting students the day before, and perhaps to protest more generally against state and local policies and practices of racial segregation, including segregation of the jail. The county sheriff, legal custodian of the jail and jail grounds, tried to persuade the students to leave the jail grounds. When this did not work, he notified them that they must leave, that if they did not leave he would arrest them for trespassing, and that if they resisted he would charge them with that as well.

Common sense dictates that courts should uphold law and order, particularly when legal institutions are threatened. But were the students not assembling on public grounds, under their First Amendment right? Did this right not bear upon the state of Florida under Black's own earlier absolutist reading of the First Amendment and incorporation doctrine? Florida law against such assembly with intent to do mischief was clear—but was it not so broad that it might bar any assembly? So thought Douglas, joined by Warren, Brennan, and Fortas: "The jailhouse, like an executive mansion, a legislative chamber, a courthouse, or the statehouse itself is one of the seats of government, whether it be the Tower of London, the Bastille, or a small county jail. And when it houses political prisoners or those who many think are unjustly held, it is an obvious center for protest." The protestors were young, poor, and black. "Those who do not control television and radio, those who cannot afford to advertise in newspapers or circulate elaborate pamphlets may have only a more limited type of access to public officials. Their methods should not be condemned as tactics of obstruction and harassment as long as the assembly and petition are peaceable, as these were."

By the early 1960s, the Court was no longer alone in promoting the federal government's civil rights program. President Johnson made Kennedy's stalled civil rights bill a tribute to the fallen president and urged it through Congress with the help of liberal Republicans like Everett Dirksen, an old Senate friend. After some acrimonious debate, Congress passed the Civil Rights Act of 1964. In *Heart of Atlanta Motel v. U.S.* (1964) and *Katzenbach v. McClung* (1964), announced on the same day, the Court upheld the public accommodations provisions in a broad reading of the Interstate Commerce Clause.

The Civil Rights Cases (1883) were precedent to strike down the 1964 act, for its provisions were very similar to the 1875 Civil Rights Act. The Court could not uphold the 1964 act on the basis of the Fourteenth Amendment because owners of restaurants, golf courses, movie houses, and motels were no more state agents in 1964 than they were in 1875. Instead, the Court found constitutional grounds for congressional power over public accommodations in the Interstate Commerce Clause. It was fancy footwork, but it has stood the test of time. Of course, before 1954, one might have said the same for *Plessy*.

Congress had also acted to protect the voting rights of minorities with the Voting Rights Act of 1965. In a unanimous opinion by Warren, the justices took the Voting Rights Act of 1965 challenge by South Carolina on its original jurisdiction so that they could quickly dispose of the matter. In *South Carolina v. Katzenbach* (1966), the chief justice employed a form of the rational basis test when he found that Congress chose "appropriate means of combating the evil."

Black dissented when Douglas and the Court struck down state poll taxes, in *Harper v. Virginia Board of Elections* (1966). Under both a "fundamental interests" and a "suspect classification" test of the Equal Protection Clause, Douglas argued that "lines drawn on the basis of wealth or property, like those of race, are traditionally disfavored." Further, he adopted a flexible view of the Equal Protection Clause: "Notions of what constitute equal treatment for purposes of the Equal Protection Clause do change." Douglas was at his best in finding novel and clever ways to expand the meaning of equality.

Black's dissent took particular umbrage at this assertion. His absolutist views did not accommodate the new liberality: "I did not join the opinion of the Court in *Brown* on any theory that segregation . . . denied equal protection in 1954 but did not similarly deny it in 1896." The new liberalism did not appeal to him personally, but his challenge to Douglas's reading of the Equal Protection Clause showed the fissures separating the Warren Court's view of rights and the Stone Court's handling of similar questions. Black was still the great dissenter, but now his dissents looked back instead of ahead.

POLITICAL RIGHTS AND WRONGS

In similar fashion to its enlightened gradualism in civil rights, the Warren Court acted gingerly when it came to what may be loosely referred to as political rights. These are First Amendment rights asserted in public context, for example, political speech and assembly. Other governments, like those of West Germany, France, and Japan, had to confront these issues head-on following World War II and wrote constitutions conferring expansive political rights, but the United States had a Bill of Rights that was largely untouched since the late eighteenth century. The Supreme Court needed to improvise a series of balancing tests, categories, and levels of scrutiny to decide when a government could impair these rights, if at all.

During the Red Scare of the 1950s, the Court, with the exception of the free speech absolutists Black and Douglas, conceded to the authorities the power to curb or silence radical political expression. The adoption of versions of Holmes's clear and present danger did not clarify the boundaries of these concessions, however, particularly when the speech did not fit old categories.

Only haltingly did Warren's increasingly solid liberal majority move to stop the worst of the Red Scare practices. The Court upheld most of the House Un-American Activities Committee's investigatory powers but warned there were limits, including when the committee ventured into "private affairs unrelated to a valid legislative purpose," in *Quinn v. U.S.* (1955), *Emspak v. U.S.* (1955), and *Bart v. U.S.* (1955). The next year the justices struck down a state version of the Smith Act, in *Pennsylvania v. Nelson*, arguing that federal action preempted state action. It was a neat twist in the liberal direction on the way in which the Fuller Court had used Commerce Clause analysis to validate segregation in interstate transportation.

The majority still refused to back entirely away from *Dennis*. In *Yates v. U.S.* (1957), on June 17, 1957, a day some labeled "Red Monday," Harlan's opinion squelched prosecutions under the Smith Act while upholding the law in general. Harlan based the ruling in part on the doctrine that speech rules needed to apply to all, not just to communists, and that the targets must be moving toward action, not just "believ[ing] in something." On the same day, hence the nickname, in *Watkins v. U.S.*, *Sweezy v. New Hampshire*, and *Service v. Dulles*, the Court struck down convictions in three more Red Scare cases. Just as in

Yates, Warren, in *Watkins*, dismissed the charges on more limited grounds than he might have, in particular that Congress did not authorize the House Un-American Activities Committee "to expose for the sake of exposure."

In 1961, the Court announced another set of Janus-faced decisions in Smith Act and Red Scare cases. In *Scales v. U.S.*, the justices upheld the Smith Act's criminalization of membership in any group advocating violent revolution. On the same day, in *Noto v. U.S.*, Harlan's opinion threw out a conviction under the Smith Act for just such a membership because the prosecution did not prove in court that the Communist Party was such a group. In the same year, Frankfurter wrote for a bare majority that the McCarran Act's membership list provisions passed constitutional muster despite the intimidation factor such a move intended. The case, *Communist Party v. Subversive Activities Control Board*, demonstrated that communism could still stir extraordinary emotions. On the other hand, after Frankfurter left the Court, its majority threw out the denial of passports to known communists and the bar on employing them in defense industries, in *Aptheker v. Secretary of State* (1964), and invalidated convictions of communists refusing to register, in *Albertson v. Subversive Activities Control Board* (1965).

When freedom of association and the civil rights movement converged, the Warren Court found it easier to speak with a single voice. In a series of cases beginning with *NAACP v. Alabama* (1958), the justices denied Alabama the authority to command the NAACP to hand over its membership lists. The state had alleged it needed the membership lists to sift through for communists. In *Bates v. City of Little Rock* (1960), Potter Stewart commanded a majority for the proposition that even state tax laws requiring the disclosure of membership lists violated the NAACP's members' freedom of association rights. In *Gibson v. Florida Legislative Investigating Committee* (1963), Justice Goldberg's majority reversed the conviction of the head of the Miami chapter of the NAACP for not handing over his membership list to a state legislative committee, even though the committee was supposedly investigating communists.

The Court's last significant statement on association, expression, and speech came in a ruling that involved a rally of the Ku Klux Klan in Ohio. A per curiam opinion in *Brandenburg v. Ohio* (1969) invalidated Ohio's 1919 syndicalism law's provisions as overly broad and in the process expressly overruled *Whitney*. Though Black's concurring opinion wanted to apply Holmes's imminent danger test and Douglas's concurrence wanted a blanket prohibition, the rest of the justices were content to limit state prohibitions to "such advocacy ... directed to inciting or producing imminent lawless action and ... likely to incite or produce such action." The crafting of a balancing test, necessary for consensus, instead of enunciating a clear rule, meant that later Courts had to weigh the circumstances of individual cases and might balance the weights according to their own preferences.

Indeed, each foray into new political rights territory produced another line of cases to be argued, studied, and modified. This was especially true when Warren and his brethren turned to voting rights and voter district apportionment. From its roots in the "political question doctrine" that Taney had created in *Luther v. Borden* (1849) to its more recent adoption in Frankfurter's plurality opinion in *Colgrove v. Green* (1946), judges had shied away from apportionment as a "political question." By the 1950s, urbanization led to increasingly maldistributed state legislatures. Sparsely populated rural districts sent more representatives to state legislatures than did densely populated urban districts. Legislative majorities perpetuated the maldistribution because the constituents of the two kinds of districts very often had dissimilar aims—rural districts were more socially and politically conservative.

The Court's self-imposed "political question" jurisprudence began to crack with Frankfurter's own majority opinion in *Gomillion v. Lightfoot* (1960). The Court invalidated under the Fifteenth Amendment an Alabama redistricting plan that marginalized African American voters. He distinguished it from *Colgrove*: "When a State exercises power wholly within the domain of state interest, it is insulated from federal judicial review. But such insulation is not carried over when state power is used as an instrument for circumventing a federally protected right." The Court's consensus on race logically included the political right of representation. Did it extend to nonminorities as well?

In *Baker v. Carr* (1962), Brennan wrote for a 6-to-2 majority declaring that the Equal Protection Clause of the Fourteenth Amendment allowed the federal bench to hear cases involving state legislative districting. The Court had now entered the "political thicket." The Court, as in desegregation, was once again ahead of Congress and the federal executive. Over the strenuous objections of Frankfurter and Harlan, who berated the majority for their disregard of their proper—limited—role within a democratic system, Brennan reasoned that the Court was ensuring democracy. What was more, *Baker*, a Tennessee state legislative case, did not involve a new legal principle. It simply extended the logic of *Gomillion*.

Once the door was open to Court scrutiny of apportionment, cases poured in to the Court. Douglas's majority opinion in *Gray v. Sanders* (1963) included a formulation so simple and resonant—"one person, one vote"—that ordinary Americans could understand what the Court was doing. The Georgia "unit" districts at issue in *Gray*, designed to make the black vote for members

of Congress disappear, soon gave way to other challenges, leading to a revolution in reapportionment of both state legislatures and congressional districts
that rivaled the civil rights movement itself in importance. The notion of one
person, one vote, gave to previously isolated and insulated urban populations
their rightful share of political power.

Lawyers brought suits in Alabama and Colorado to see if state legislatures
would act without waiting for the High Court to intervene. Both went to the
Court on appeal, and in *Reynolds v. Sims* (1964) and *Lucas v. Forty-fourth General Assembly of Colorado* (1964), a majority put the Court's seal on the reapportionment drive. Countering two different defenses from state officials, one
a majoritarian argument, the other a regionalist one, Warren declared in *Lucas:*
"The weight of a citizen's vote cannot be made to depend on where he lives,"
and "certain rights exist which a citizen cannot trade, barter, or even give away."
The chief justice's most direct statement came in *Reynolds:* "Citizens, not history or economic interests, cast votes. People, not land or trees or pastures
vote."

Brennan's controversial opinion in *New York Times v. Sullivan* (1964) confronted another aspect of political rights. As with many High Court decisions,
the implications mattered more than the facts. The majority found that the
First Amendment protected the media against libel suits by public figures provided there was no "actual malice," that is, a reckless disregard for the truth
by the media. The Alabama court had upheld a libel suit against a civil rights
advertisement in the *Times* brought by L. B. Sullivan, police commissioner in
Montgomery. He alleged that the advertisement damaged him by containing
falsehoods about his officers' treatment of civil rights marchers.

The Court could have dismissed the suit against the newspaper on the
grounds that it had no responsibility for an advertisement's truth, or that the
claims in the advertisement were true, but Brennan looked to the larger issue involved—the role of the press in a free society—and found the state's
law wanting. With *Sullivan*, the Court protected political speech against "the
chilling effect" of civil liability. Black and Douglas wrote separately in order to
advocate an even broader standard.

Brennan's balancing approach lent itself to further refinements. In *Garrison v. Louisiana* (1964), Brennan clarified the holding in *Sullivan*. *Garrison* involved a district attorney in New Orleans who is best known today for his role
in Oliver Stone's movie on the assassination of President Kennedy. Because no
one had demonstrated actual malice on the part of James Garrison in his accusations against suspected conspirators in the assassination, the conviction
could not stand. In *Curtis Publishing Co. v. Butts* and *Associated Press v. Walker*

(1967), the Court added "hot news" and "public figure" exemptions to the libel law. "Hot news" could be forgiven for inaccuracies because of its immediacy. Even people who were not public officials, but who were "public figures" and had gained a higher level of access to the media, needed to show actual malice, "a reckless disregard" for the truth, to win libel suits against the media.

The end result of the Warren Court's forays into political rights was a stream of cases that substantially expanded the realm of publicly protected speech, in which balancing tests won out over bright-line rules. By 1969, precedents guarded a robust democracy, but the complex and often innovative terminology in which the political rights were elucidated left the edges of those rights vague.

INDIVIDUAL LIBERTIES, PRIVATE RIGHTS

Private rights may be distinguished from public rights by their relationship to the functioning of the society. The Warren Court could take on cases involving segregation, public speech, voting, and the public media precisely because they were public, but topics such as religious belief and expression, the purchase or sale of personal reading material, and private consensual sexual relations were all matters of private behavior that entered into the public realm only when government agencies attempted to censor or impose criminal penalties. Governments, to protect public morals from private misconduct, regulated this behavior on a regular basis. And individuals and groups seeking relief from this regulation occasionally found friends on the High Tribunal.

Religious establishment cases raised such questions. In *Engel v. Vitale* (1962), Black wrote for a six-person majority that a New York State regents prayer for schools at the start of each day was an unconstitutional mixing of church and state. The Warren Court abandoned the Vinson Court precedents to hold that even a nondenominational, voluntary prayer—"Almighty God, we acknowledge our dependence upon Thee, and we beg Thy blessings upon us, our parents, our teachers and our Country"—impermissibly imposed a state religion.

In *Engel*, a small circle of Nassau County parents and students objected to the New York Regents model prayer, and despite peer group and public pressure to conform, they sued the head of the school board. Black's reasoning rested on two larger principles, that of compulsion of religious minorities and the danger to society from official religion: "[A] union of government and religion tends to destroy government and degrade religion." Black returned to his favorite sources, the founding fathers, to ground the need for separation.

Despite the fact that Black's originalist opinion sought to protect religion, many religious leaders denounced the ruling as irreligious, godless, and radical. Billy Graham, the evangelist who advised presidents, and Francis Cardinal Spellman, perhaps the most important leader in the Catholic Church in America at the time, joined forces to lament the Court's attempt to remove God from public life. Politicians who already despised the Court's "social engineering" with regard to integration voted to put godly messages everywhere they could.

Justice Clark responded for the Court in an 8-to-1 decision in *Abington School District v. Schempp* (1963), which struck down a Pennsylvania requirement for the reading of ten Bible verses at the beginning of each school day. Only "a secular legislative purpose and a primary effect that neither advances nor inhibits religion" was acceptable. The decision came from a reading of the Establishment Clause. But the Pennsylvania legislature allowed students to opt out and leave the room, and thus Clark could not argue that the Free Exercise Clause had been violated. Justices wrestled with the competing interests involved in this area as well.

Very few Americans would have taken issue with Stewart's dissent in *Abington* that "religion and government must interact in countless ways." Certain associations, like the recognizing of privileged communications between an individual and his or her religious advisor, were necessary to the functioning of society. Public funding of religiously affiliated activities seemed another obvious good. But what happened when government funding crossed over that invisible line and became state support of religion? Although the Warren Court would leave that messy issue to its successors, Warren's opinion in *Flast v. Cohen* (1968) allowed taxpayers to sue on such matters.

In a similar vein, some forty-five years after the so-called Scopes Monkey Trial resulted in Tennessee's Supreme Court upholding a state law prohibiting the teaching of evolution in its schools, a unanimous High Court overturned a similar Arkansas law. In fact, the law was pretty much a dead letter, but, in *Epperson v. Arkansas* (1968), Fortas's opinion for the Court struck it down for advancing in the classroom "a particular interpretation of the Book of Genesis by a particular religious group." Black's concurrence pointed out the problems with such a test. What if, for example, a state neutrally required that all theories about human origins be taught in biology classes?

In two cases in 1961, the Warren Court proved that neutrality, not secularism, drove its decisions in religious belief cases. In *McGowan v. Maryland* and *Braunfeld v. Brown*, Warren upheld Sunday closing laws as achieving a neutral purpose: granting a day of rest to all. In what Brennan's dissent described as "exalted administrative convenience," the chief justice dismissed the claims of the Jewish Orthodox merchants in *Braunfeld* with the insensitive aside that their beliefs were their problem.

By contrast, Brennan applied a "compelling interest" standard in *Sherbert v. Verner* (1963). South Carolina's unemployment checks made no accommodation for a Seventh Day Adventist dismissed from her job because she refused to work on Saturday—the Seventh Day Adventist's Sabbath. But what seemed to be a simple principle of fairness (the state cannot hold the religious beliefs of its citizens against them) was itself problematic. Did *Sherbert* subsidize Seventh Day Adventism by giving its adherents a special subsidy? Was that a violation of the Establishment Clause?—especially when viewed in conjunction with *McGowan*'s affirmation of Sunday closing laws.

The Warren Court faced a different set of issues in its decisions over government's power to restrict reading material and other media deemed "obscene." An individual's ability to make choices about what books to read and what films to see and other such decisions are as much matters of privacy as they are of consumer choice. Such choices define each person's identity. Can government, by censoring and penalizing such choices, dictate who we are? Historians know that societies often define themselves by what is prohibited. Knowing who the deviant is (by defining deviance) gives comfort and reassurance to people uncertain of who belongs in their community and who does not.

In obscenity cases, the justices felt the need to balance two competing interests. In *Butler v. Michigan* (1956), Frankfurter wrote for a unanimous court that a Michigan law forbidding publication of material "tending to the corruption of the morals of youth" abridged the First Amendment. The ability of adults to make these decisions for themselves constituted one of the "indispensable conditions for the maintenance and progress of a free society." Justice Brennan's majority opinion went further in *Roth v. U.S.* (1957). Brennan personally found pornography abhorrent, defiling women and violating morality. In *Roth* he offered a test for obscenity undeserving of protection as "whether to the average person, applying contemporary community standard, the dominant theme of the material taken as a whole appeals to prurient interest."

Because Brennan's *Roth* test demanded an evaluation of the whole work, it expanded constitutional protection of private decisions over access to reading material while drawing a line (somewhere) beyond which pornography could be censored. The film version of D. H. Lawrence's classic, *Lady Chatterley's Lover,* did not meet the definition of obscene in *Kingsley International Pictures Corp. v. Regents* (1959), but magazines catering to homosexuals possessed "patent offensiveness," in Harlan's words in *Manual Enterprises v. Day* (1962).

Brennan made it clear in *Jacobellis v. Ohio* (1964) that he meant for national community standards to define obscenity, which occasioned Stewart's concurrence that "I know it when I see it and the motion picture involved in this case is not that." Brennan tried again to create a workable test in *Memoirs v. Massachusetts* (1966). This time he added the requirement that "the material [be] utterly without redeeming value" to the *Roth* criteria—but still could not command a majority. The sadomasochistic material at issue in *Mishkin v. New York* (1966) did not merit protection, and neither did the magazine *Eros*, in *Ginzburg v. U.S.* (1966). The Court could not agree on a substance-based test.

In *Redrup v. New York* (1967), a per curiam memorandum dismissing several obscenity convictions offered a different standard. This time the justices would look at the state's purpose and the danger to the First Amendment involved rather than to the inherent value, or lack of value, of the work itself. Brennan's opinion in *Ginsberg v. New York* (1968) pointed the way. Although the private reading of adults might be acceptable, the state had a legitimate interest in protecting minors. If the state could demonstrate a reasonable basis for its action, it would be permitted to close bookstores and penalize booksellers.

But more qualifications followed. In an opinion by Marshall in *Stanley v. Georgia* (1969), the Supreme Court accepted the privacy rights of an individual caught possessing obscene films in his home: "If the First Amendment means anything, it means that a State has no business telling a man, sitting alone in his own home, what books he may read or what films he may watch." In effect, the Fourth Amendment was deployed to explain the First.

In 1873, led by the lobbying of Anthony Comstock, Congress had classed birth control materials and information as obscene and barred its transmission through the mails. Many states passed "little Comstock Acts" that penalized the distribution of such information within the state, even by doctors to their patients. In *Griswold v. Connecticut* (1965), family-planning advocates finally got the High Court to overturn the Connecticut birth-control-ban laws. They had begun their battle against the state's 1879 birth-control-is-obscenity law in the 1930s. But neither the state courts nor the state legislature would budge. A powerful Roman Catholic presence in the state senate ensured that any doctor giving out information or assisting a married couple to practice birth control faced fines.

Planned Parenthood in the state, led by its new head, Estelle Griswold, did not give up. She arranged for a married couple seeking counseling and a doctor providing it at the Planned Parenthood clinic to be prosecuted under the law. Again the state courts gave no relief. She appealed her conviction and that of the couple seeking counseling to the High Court, aided by the American Civil

Liberties Union and Planned Parenthood of America. It was the third time that opponents of the state law had brought the case to the High Court. Twice it had been dismissed for want of a real controversy. This time the Court heard and decided it for the petitioners.

A 7-to-2 majority agreed that the law violated the couple's constitutional rights. Harlan thought that married couples should not be prohibited from planning their families. Brennan agreed. Douglas wrote for the majority. He found a constitutional right of privacy in the "penumbras" of the Bill of Rights, a shadowy place for such a potent source of constitutional light. Goldberg— joining with Douglas but writing a concurrence for himself, Brennan, and Warren—argued that privacy antedated the Constitution and could, therefore, be found in the reserved rights of the Ninth Amendment. White agreed with the result but warned that the Court was tiptoeing back toward a new kind of substantive due process, finding basic rights in the Constitution without any textual basis. Stewart dissented because, although he believed the statute "an uncommonly silly law," judges should defer to legislatures in these matters. Black dissented because his absolutist reading of the Bill of Rights was a strict constructionist one. He could not find privacy in any of the amendments. *Griswold* was not the last word on the subject of birth control. In 1983, a unanimous High Court finally nailed down the lid on that coffin. In *Bolger v. Youngs Drug Products*, Marshall announced that the U.S. Postal Service could not seize unsolicited advertisements for contraceptives.

LAW ENFORCEMENT

The most controversial of the Warren Court precedents concerned criminal procedure. Beginning in 1961 with *Mapp v. Ohio*, majorities on the Court nationalized police and criminal court practices and imposed on every police force basic procedural guarantees. Building on cases such as *Wolf* that had already incorporated portions of the Bill of Rights, *Pointer v. Texas* (1965) incorporated the right to confront witnesses, *Malloy v. Hogan* (1964) incorporated the Fifth Amendment's right against self-incrimination, and *Duncan v. Louisiana* (1968) incorporated the right to a jury trial.

However, it was the *Mapp* Court's initiation of the use of the exclusionary rule against the states that gave these decisions their foundation. The police burst into Dollree Mapp's home in Cleveland, Ohio, to search for "policy slips" (gambling materials). They found pornography. At no time did they produce a warrant for their search or for the seizure of the evidence. But a Cleveland trial court and the Ohio Supreme Court allowed the evidence at trial against Mapp for violating the state's pornography laws and found no harm in the circumstances of the search and seizure. Had this been a federal case, the evidence the police obtained could not have been introduced at trial. It was the fruit of the poisoned tree.

In *Mapp*, writing for a 5-to-4 majority, Clark applied the same principle to the states. Although the incorporation of the Fourth Amendment was a small step in a long process, Clark said explicitly what the Court had not yet admitted. The purpose of keeping out the illegally obtained evidence was to force the police, and the state, to obey the Constitution. In the words of Clark's majority opinion, "To hold otherwise is to grant the right but in reality to withhold its privilege and enjoyment." The overall idea was to deter law enforcement misconduct. From their authority over courts, the justices had taken a giant step, not a small one, toward a more uniform criminal justice system.

The fact that Dollree Mapp was black, and that Ohio local police forces, like many others in the country, seemed to treat minority suspects in discriminatory fashion, was not lost on the Court. For the police and the police courts, blacks and Hispanics were "the usual suspects," and their rights were not so assiduously protected as those of other suspects. Thus what seemed on its face to be a simple extension of the exclusionary rule was in fact part of a much larger political controversy, and the case generated a great deal of criticism of the Court. Local politicians and law enforcement officers claimed that the decision would hamstring their war on crime. Justice Clark had anticipated these criticisms and in his *Mapp* opinion had written: "Nothing can destroy a government more quickly than its failure to observe its own laws, or worse, its disregard of the charter of its own existence." Beginning with *Mapp*, the Warren Court's decisions were not just attempts to redress the imbalance between the largely poor and minority suspects and the state—they represented a deep understanding that law enforcement requires ethical strictures in order to be law.

Not all of the Court's criminal justice decisions met with massive protest. Stewart's position in *Katz v. U.S.* (1967), declaring that warrantless eavesdropping using electronic devices was a violation of the search and seizure provisions of the Fourth Amendment, in the process overturning Taft's opinion for the Court in *Olmstead*, seemed appropriate to the other justices. His insistence that "the Fourth Amendment protects people, not places," also reflected Americans' concerns about "Big Brother" watching everyone and played a role in its acceptability. Similarly, the unanimous Court's overruling of *Betts v. Brady* in *Gideon v. Wainwright*, giving indigent defendants the right to an attorney in criminal trials, struck a chord with a society that liked an underdog. The

Anthony Lewis best seller, *Gideon's Trumpet* (1964), an allusion to the biblical story in the book of Judges, and the subsequent TV movie with Henry Fonda as Clarence Earl Gideon played to the common man element so deeply embedded in American society. Ordinary Americans could sympathize with the innocent man trapped in the impersonal bureaucracy that was the criminal justice system.

Greater difficulty arose when the Court tried to fashion rules for treatment of suspects in police custody. Like the tactics of Cleveland's police in *Mapp*, officers operated with a wide-ranging latitude under the principle of ends justifying the means. Police often have strong feelings about a particular suspect's guilt or innocence. Police suppression of evidence, lying under oath, and planting of evidence happens too often to be regarded as an aberration. Starting with cases like *Spano v. New York* (1959) and *Massiah v. U.S.* (1964), the Court haltingly moved from a deferential "totality of the circumstances" test on confessions to a more stringent one.

They solidified this new line of thought with *Escobedo v. Illinois* (1964). Goldberg wrote the opinion of the Court: When a suspect is brought in for questioning and requests an attorney, the suspect must be granted immediate access to that attorney under the Sixth Amendment's right to counsel and the Fifth Amendment's right against self-incrimination. The very fact that police gained a significant portion of confessions at this stage, rather than later in the suspect's confinement, made the ruling necessary. "The right to counsel would indeed be hollow if it began at a period when few confessions were obtained," reasoned the justice. The justices were trying to prevent coerced confessions as well as evincing their concern with the plight of those "discrete and insular minorities" who were most vulnerable to these law enforcement tactics.

The pinnacle of these Court-imposed protections arrived with Warren's opinion for the majority in *Miranda v. Arizona* (1966). In a decision widely criticized for its lack of coherence and obvious public policy objectives, the chief justice laid out the warnings that became the staple of movies, TV, and literature: "You have the right to remain silent. Anything you say can and will be used against you in a court of law. You have the right to an attorney. If you cannot afford one, one will be appointed for you. Do you understand these rights as they have been explained to you?" Although the exact warnings vary from jurisdiction to jurisdiction, the message remained the same. Police officers and other law enforcement officials must advise suspects of their rights or risk not being able to use in court whatever evidence they obtain from a confession. Warren's objectives were to lay out an easy-to-follow rule for judges and promote an informed citizenry. In effect, the 5-to-4 majority tried to make interrogation rules clearer. "Our decision in no way creates a constitutional straitjacket," he optimistically declared.

Unfortunately, the more the Court applied its prudential strictures to interrogation, search and seizure, and confessions cases, the more complicated the law became. In the field of the Fourth Amendment's warrant requirement, *Aguilar v. Texas*'s (1964) necessity of probable cause to issue a warrant led to *Spinelli v. U.S.* (1969), which demanded that statements on the reliability of any informant be used in a warrant application, leading in turn to *Chimel v. California* (1969), that police needed a warrant to arrest a suspect in his home. Lest the progression seem logical and linear, in *Terry v. Ohio* (1968), the Court upheld a police officer's frisking of two men he suspected of "casing" a store. The so-called *Terry* stops seemed a retreat from the Court's march to greater protections. Were the justices responding to political outrage? Or to the Omnibus Crime Control and Safe Streets Act of 1968, which legislated away many of the decisions they had so carefully crafted? The Warren Court was no more indifferent to the election returns than its predecessors.

Still, taken together, the Warren Court decisions in the field of criminal procedure led to more fair, just, and effective law enforcement—but only if those in charge of directing policing agencies accepted them and acted in good faith. In later years, police departments would find that the various Warren Court rulings could be turned to their advantage. For example, the Miranda warning could be fit into a new style of interrogation: "We cannot help you until you sign the Miranda form." In the final analysis, law enforcement did become more professional, more cognizant of if not compliant with constitutional guarantees, and more circumspect. At the same time, the Warren Court's effort to simplify the law failed. Each new precedent spurred litigation to clarify further, modify, expand, or overturn what had come earlier.

As the 1960s became increasingly, or at least visibly, more violent, with urban riots, gang wars, the conflagration of entire city neighborhoods, and shocking statistics on lawlessness, many otherwise middle-of-the-road voters worried that permissiveness led to perversion. The Great Society political coalition that Johnson had forged for his 1964 reelection campaign was coming apart at the seams. Race had reentered American politics, as Republicans came up with a "southern strategy" to pull white voters away from their traditional Democratic affiliations. For the courts to allow supposedly guilty people to go free on what some labeled "a technicality" aroused fears in some and enabled others to orchestrate campaigns against the Court—and against everyone else who was "soft on crime." It was a tactic that Richard Nixon's handlers would deploy brilliantly in the 1968 elections. Nixon called these middle-of-the-road voters "the silent majority," which he promised to represent if elected president in 1968.

In retrospect, one may discern two substantial threads of legal thinking in the precedents of the Warren Court—a concern with robust democracy and an assertion that the Court could do a great deal to improve the lot of the disadvantaged. These ran all through the three distinct phases of the Court's jurisprudence. The first phase ended with its consensus on matters of race. The second phase ended in the middle of the 1960s when Black became disenchanted with the increasingly turbulent protests. The third phase ended with Johnson's failure to replace Warren and then the subsequent and related loss of Fortas. The line of cases followed a similar path: a precedent breaks open a new field of law, the justices then struggle to define their terms, and, finally, the majority settles the question by leaving subsequent Courts to struggle with the consequences.

Nevertheless, the vast expansion of civil rights and civil liberties under the Warren Court profoundly changed American law. At the same time, the Warren Court's willingness to hand down the decisions it did reflected the changes in America since World War II. The Court's nationalization of American law and the accompanying centering of its own authority within that law would not have been possible without the nationalization of society and economy, the immense increase in the power of the national government, and the liberal optimism that coalesced in Washington, D.C., during the Warren Court era. All of its forays into new constitutional territory were interconnected if not always coherent expressions of wider public opinion on desegregation, privacy, the political processes, and law enforcement.

CHAPTER 14

The Burger Court, 1969–1986

It was perhaps inevitable that the Warren Court's rights revolution would end. All revolutions give way to periods of consolidation and retrenchment. And so it seemed with the election of Republican Richard M. Nixon as president and the replacement of Earl Warren with Warren Burger. Nixon's campaign denounced the Warren Court's criminal justice jurisprudence, and Johnson's botching of Fortas's candidacy gave Nixon the opportunity to fill both the center seat and appoint an associate justice. Warren Burger was far more restrained in his view of the role of courts and far closer to Nixon's law-and-order stance than Warren and his majority.

Nixon, a lawyer himself, recognized the importance of the Supreme Court in achieving his policy objectives. But he did not have the impact on the Court that he wished. His first two nominations to replace Fortas crashed and burned, and his third choice, Harry Blackmun, moved from the right to the left on the Court. William H. Rehnquist would prove to be an able ally, but Warren Burger and Lewis Powell turned out to be conservative centrists. President Gerald Ford's nominee, John Paul Stevens, would join the liberal wing of the Court, and President Ronald Reagan's first appointee to the Burger Court, Sandra Day O'Connor, proved to be a liberal on a number of issues and a moderate on many more.

As a result, the Burger Court defies easy characterization. It did retreat from the high-water mark of activist judging, but it did not abandon all the frontiers that the Warren Court had pioneered, and, in some areas of law, the Burger Court's liberal activism actually exceeded the Warren Court's. The output of the Burger Court in civil rights and civil liberties cases was remarkable, and its fashioning of a middle level of scrutiny between the rational-relation test and strict scrutiny of legislative acts was a signal accomplishment. In the words of one of the Burger Court's foremost observers, Bernard Schwartz, Burger's tenure marked a "counter-revolution that wasn't."

NIXON'S COURT, BURGER'S WAY

At its inception, the Burger Court was the Nixon Court. And the ambiguities of Nixon's presidency would reflect themselves in his Court. Though he had selected Burger because the future chief justice had a strong law-and-order record, and Nixon ran on a law-and-order platform, the new president assented to clean air and water legislation, to the Endangered Species Act of 1973, and to the creation of the Environmental Protection Agency, in which lawyers worked alongside scientists to monitor compliance with congressional acts. Congress created and Nixon acceded to a "Superfund" program to clean up chemical wastelands.

The addition to the administrative state and to the regulatory functions of the federal government by a conservative president would have puzzled older generations of conservatives on the Court like a Peckham or a Brewer, but Taft and Hughes would have understood. Nixon was not an advocate of women's rights, but during his presidency women won key court battles for equal pay, protection against discrimination, and safe abortion. Although he did not support these causes, he did not make his opposition to them a centerpiece of his policies. For example, the equal rights amendment, approved in the House in 1971 and the Senate in 1972, would have ensured that "equality of rights under the law shall not be denied or abridged by the United States or by any state on account of sex." Nixon supported it. Though it failed to gain the necessary three-quarters state ratification, in piecemeal fashion the Burger Court found that the Equal Protection Clause of the Fourteenth Amendment could accomplish much the same goals as an equal rights amendment.

Had Burger been another Warren, his and his Court's reputation for progressive legal innovation might thus have rivaled his predecessor's. Indeed, the opportunities for bold activism presented themselves. With his impressive stature, demeanor, and flowing white mane and his sense of his own dignity and the dignity of the Court, Warren Earl Burger certainly looked and acted the part of chief justice. However, Burger's take-charge management style produced ill will among the justices. His refusal to follow convention in assigning opinions (often hiding his own views or voting against them in order to be in the majority so that he could assign the opinion for the Court), his inability to frame issues clearly when he was writing for the Court, and his pettiness when crossed brought unfavorable comparisons to his predecessor. To be fair, his wry sense of humor, his capacity for friendship, and his genuine commitment to the job should have gained him a higher rating among Court watchers, if not the respect of his colleagues.

Burger's sports ability had earned him a scholarship to Princeton. But he did not feel it was right for him to leave his family without his income. So, instead, he worked as an accountant for an insurance company by day while he took pre-law classes at the University of Minnesota and then law classes at St. Paul College of Law (now William Mitchell) at night. In 1931, the twenty-four-year-old received his law degree magna cum laude and an appointment to teach a contracts course, an appointment he held until 1946. He also joined a law firm, where he specialized in probate, corporate, and real estate law.

Burger helped Republican Harold Stassen run for the Republican presidential nomination in 1948, and when Stassen again came up short in his try for the nomination, in 1952, Burger helped Eisenhower secure Minnesota's crucial delegates. President Eisenhower took notice and appointed him an assistant attorney general in 1953. In this capacity, he made a name for himself toeing the administration's line on loyalty oaths in *Peters v. Hobby* (1955) and fighting corruption in the shipyards. His solid competence led to a place on the D.C. Circuit Court of Appeals. There he displayed progressive views on civil rights and a distaste for the Warren Court's criminal justice decisions.

Burger's dream was an efficient legal system, and his appointment as chief justice in late spring 1969 gave him the platform he needed to call for reform. He aimed at speeding cases through the system and reducing overcrowded dockets. At his urging, the Institute for Court Management trained court officers and state-federal judicial councils consolidated state and federal concurrent cases. From 1971, the National Center for State Courts fostered the sharing of information among the jurisdictions, and expansion of the Federal Judicial Center, an institution founded in 1967, promoted proper legal practice. He oversaw improvements to the Court's grounds, equipment, and procedures, limited oral argument to one hour instead of two, and eliminated the reading of opinions from the bench unless there were exceptional circumstances. He even changed the shape of the bench from straight to the three sides of a hexagon in order to maximize the justices' visibility.

But he never felt truly comfortable in the marble palace or at the head of the Court. Shortly after he was installed, he wrote a memo to himself—"I must pace myself." He never did, and his impatience sometimes led to unexpected flaps. When he took over an unused conference room to provide an adequate reception area for his visitors, his colleagues complained. When he suggested that all the justices' court chairs be uniform, they complained. Sometimes he deserved the criticism. Because he wanted to lead, he hedged his votes at conference to put himself in the majority even when he did not see the case that way. His opinion writing showed him more concerned with the individual facts of a case than with the principles involved—which did not impress his colleagues. In the end, after seventeen years of often frustrating service, Burger resigned to become head of the nation's commission to commemorate the bicentennial of the Constitution. Burger died in 1995.

Nixon's attempts to fill the Fortas seat did not proceed as smoothly as the Burger appointment, at least in part because Nixon's "southern strategy," designed to swing votes from the Democratic Party to the Republican side, included a promise to choose a conservative southern justice. His first try, in 1969, Clement F. Haynsworth Jr. of South Carolina, seemed assured of confirmation until questions arose over his handling of a case in which he had a personal stake. He was denied the seat, in a 55-to-45 vote. Nixon's second choice, G. Harrold Carswell of Georgia, fared even less well. The American Bar Association was concerned about his lack of experience and overall lack of distinction. This prompted Republican senator Roman Hruska of Nebraska to defend the nomination: "Even if he is mediocre, there are a lot of mediocre judges and people and lawyers, and they are entitled to a little representation, aren't they? We can't have all Brandeises and Cardozos and Frankfurters and stuff like that." Carswell's own words came back to haunt him. In a speech he made while on the hustings for a seat in the Georgia legislature before he gained a federal judgeship, he said: "I yield to no man as a fellow candidate or as a fellow citizen in the firm, vigorous belief in the principles of White Supremacy, and I shall always be so governed." The Senate rejected him 51 to 45.

Beaten down by these battles, Nixon and the Senate embraced a relatively uncontroversial conservative from Minnesota, Harry A. Blackmun. He was confirmed by a 94-to-0 vote on May 12, 1970. Modest and genuinely warm and self-effacing, Blackmun represented what Hruska really meant—a people's justice. He did not, at first, seem very impressive on the bench, and the liberals thought him a lightweight. But he knew how to take notes at conference and he was a quick study. He did not simply put his head into the law books and keep it there—he also listened to public opinion, his family, and his friends. When new justices appeared, he was the first to greet them. He never lorded it over anyone else; he did not know how. Slow to write when he was assigned a case and capable of some stubbornness when a case he had written was ignored or narrowed, he would leave the Court as one of its most beloved members, in 1994—"the shy person's justice," as his fellow Minnesotan Garrison Keillor called him. He died five years later, leaving his papers, a treasure trove for scholars and proof of his down-to-earth virtues, to the Library of Congress.

Though he was a boyhood friend and longtime colleague of Burger—both were from the Minneapolis–St. Paul area and both seemed to share philosophies of law—Blackmun's career differed in key ways from Burger's. Blackmun attended Harvard College and Harvard Law School (working tables in order to pay for his education). At both institutions he excelled. He clerked for Judge John B. Sanford of the U.S. Court of Appeals for the Eighth Circuit and then became resident counsel for the famous Mayo Clinic in 1950. He taught courses at St. Paul College of Law and then at the University of Minnesota Law School. In 1959, Eisenhower nominated him for the Eighth Circuit. Blackmun gained a reputation there as a conservative of conscience and as sympathetic to immigrants, the laboring poor, and women.

When Hugo Black's poor health led him to retire, Nixon nominated another southerner, the gentlemanly Richmond attorney Lewis F. Powell Jr. Although Nixon had followed Eisenhower's example (with Brennan) of nominating someone from the opposite party, Powell did not disappoint his president. In civil rights, like Nixon, Powell was a moderate. Though he resisted desegregation while chair of the Richmond School Board from 1952 to 1961, he kept the schools open as they integrated. The NAACP rated him an acceptable candidate, and he was confirmed by the Senate in 1972, with only one dissenting vote.

The popular and soft-spoken Powell had grown up in comfortable circumstances in Richmond, attending private schools and then Washington and Lee University, where he was elected class president and earned his law degree. Powell earned a masters at law from Harvard the next year and returned to Richmond to practice law for the next thirty-seven years, except for a stint during World War II with the Army Air Corps' intelligence unit. As a partner in Richmond's largest law firm, he represented tobacco companies and other large firms headquartered in the city. As his reputation as an upstanding member of the legal community blossomed, so did his public service commitments. As president of the American Bar Association, in 1964–1965, he oversaw the creation of the Legal Services Corporation to help fund impoverished client representation and a commission to set forth uniform standards for criminal law.

On the Supreme Court, Powell advocated judicial restraint and deference. He believed that the Constitution and the Civil Rights Act of 1964 protected minority rights but did not require states or the federal government to fund those rights. Poverty was not a suspect category, requiring strict scrutiny of legislation that appeared to disfavor the poor, whether in education, abortion rights, or other contexts. He became a key swing vote on an often deeply divided Court.

The same could not be said about Nixon's appointee to replace Harlan, William H. Rehnquist. He joined the Court on the same day as Powell in January

1972. Rehnquist was a veteran of the Nixon White House Counsel's Office. He voted with Burger over 80 percent of the time and the rest of the time dissented (because the chief justice had gone with the majority in order to shape the opinion of the Court).

Most grade schoolers in the suburbs of Milwaukee, Wisconsin, lionized, or at least respected, Franklin D. Roosevelt, but this son of a paper salesman preferred Alf Landon and Herbert Hoover. He attended Stanford on the GI bill. With bachelor's and master's degrees in political science in hand, he went on to get another master's, in government, and then a Stanford law degree in 1952. First in his class at Stanford, he made a reputation for himself as a brilliant conservative.

Thanks at least in part to a Stanford connection, he became a clerk for Justice Robert H. Jackson and continued to impress with both his abilities and his opposition to anything resembling civil rights. For Jackson, during the first *Brown* hearings, Rehnquist wrote a memo urging that the Court reaffirm *Plessy*. He later claimed he was merely writing what Jackson wanted, but an earlier Jackson draft on the case shows that the justice never intended to uphold *Plessy*. In 1957, in an opinion piece for *U.S. News and World Report*, Rehnquist berated his fellow clerks' "extreme solicitude for the claims of Communists and other criminal defendants, expansion of federal power at the expense of State power, great sympathy toward any government regulation of business—in short, the political philosophy now espoused by the Court under Chief Justice Warren." While unusual for a former clerk to blast his Court (indeed, Chief Justice Rehnquist would impose a rule of silence on all serving and former clerks), young Rehnquist's broadside was typical of the man—candid, consistent, and conservative.

Rehnquist combined his private practice with activism for political causes in his adopted city of Phoenix, Arizona. These brought him to the attention of another Republican in Arizona, Richard Kleindienst, who recommended Rehnquist to be Nixon's assistant attorney general in charge of the Office of Legal Counsel. In this position, Rehnquist gave his stamp of approval to mass surveillance of the antiwar movement, an expansive view of the strictures of international law that allowed the extension of American military operations to Thailand, Laos, and Cambodia, as well as the executive branch's resistance to all of the Warren Court's criminal justice rulings. Because of his ardent participation in everything the Nixon White House did, he recused himself when the Court considered Nixon's executive privilege claims in cases such as *U.S. v. Nixon* (1974).

Unlike Powell's smooth confirmation process, Rehnquist's stirred a great deal of controversy. Affidavits from Arizona alleged he had interfered with minority voters in the 1950s. Others protested his views on civil rights and executive powers. His memorandum for Justice Jackson advocating the retention of *Plessy* caused several in Congress to demand that the Judiciary Committee reconsider its vote. Despite these protests, the Senate confirmed the extraordinarily able and amiable government lawyer, 68 to 26.

Rehnquist's conservatism made him a target of liberal scholars. Reclusive in his private life, he was not shy about his views and he battled for them. When he refused to recuse himself in *Laird v. Tatum* (1972), a suit against the COINTELPRO domestic surveillance program—as a government lawyer he had played a role and then he cast the deciding vote on the Court to dismiss the suit—critics added a charge of unethical conduct to the indictment. He replied in a memo to the Court and later in a public speech that he had no actual bias in the suit, and, moreover, that the suit was entirely political from its inception.

Rehnquist believed that constitutional law and hence the High Court had no business promoting egalitarian ends but instead should preserve order, secure fundamental liberties, and show a healthy respect for the other branches' decisions. A form of legal positivism, in which law is seen as the command of the state, his jurisprudence was rich in reverence for the Court's history, a reverence he displayed with his extensive writings on that history.

With the demise of Nixon's presidency in the wake of the Watergate scandal, Gerald Ford had the opportunity to fill the seat vacated by the ailing Douglas. Ford, who was not elected to his place in the White House, felt that the choice should be as uncontroversial as possible. He chose John Paul Stevens, a Seventh Circuit judge who earned the American Bar Association's highest rating. Stevens demonstrated a proficiency and moderation that justified Ford's faith. He came from the same school of jurisprudence as Stewart and Blackmun, favoring restraint, judging on the individual case, and seeking a balance among interests, which made predicting his positions difficult. And, like Blackmun, Stevens appeared more and more liberal as the Court became more and more conservative.

He was a Chicagoan through and through—his father had been a successful businessman in Chicago who was brought low by the Great Depression. Still, young Stevens possessed an assurance and a mild manner, extraordinary intelligence, and instinctual sociability. He earned highest honors at the University of Chicago, graduating in 1941. With the onset of war, he volunteered for duty and served out the war in the navy's intelligence unit as a code breaker. After the war, he returned to Chicago and graduated first in his class from Northwestern Law School. He clerked for Justice Rutledge in the 1947–1948 term, which exposed him to one of the foremost liberals in the history of the Court. Stevens then entered private practice in Chicago.

He started his own firm in Chicago with other lawyers in 1951 and gained a national reputation as one of the country's experts on trusts and monopolies, advising a House subcommittee on monopolies and the attorney general's committee on antitrust law. He also taught courses on the topic at the Northwestern and the University of Chicago law schools. When a vacancy opened on the Seventh Circuit Court of Appeals in 1970, Nixon appointed Stevens, a registered Republican, to his hometown court. There, Stevens demonstrated an expertise and prudence that Ford's attorney general, Edward Levi, who knew Stevens from the University of Chicago, brought to Ford's attention. The Senate confirmed the nomination unanimously on December 17, 1975.

Stevens quickly established a reputation as a maverick. His penchant for authoring concurring opinions and dissents suited a Court that rivaled Stone's in its cliques and divisions. The independent-minded Stevens also gained supporters for his balanced approach, even though at times his empathy for those involved in litigation seemed misplaced. Under his process-oriented technique (similar to the one that Edward Levi had championed when he had been Stevens's dean at the University of Chicago), each case's outcome stemmed from its own particular facts. Because the Court received the vast majority of its cases on appeal, the justices were far removed from the fact-finding stage. Therefore, according to Stevens, justices should defer to other branches and to the states unless those parties' actions somehow shocked the conscience. However, Stevens did not always follow his own rule. He preferred instead to weigh the interests involved. In the words of Illinois senator Charles Percy, Stevens's sponsor in the Senate, he was a "lawyer's lawyer" in private practice and a "judge's judge" when on the bench.

The final addition to the Burger Court was Sandra Day O'Connor of Arizona. When California governor Ronald Reagan ran for the presidency in 1980, he promised that his first appointee to the Court would be a woman. It was a calculated move—in a campaign full of calculated moves—to assure female voters in a close election that Reagan's ultraconservative views did not make him a misogynist. When Potter Stewart announced his retirement in 1981, Reagan fulfilled this promise.

O'Connor's views were close to Reagan's on most matters except one. She was a conservative, but not a doctrinaire one, and would become a swing vote on the Court. Indeed, because she was in tune with the politics of the Court and the political mood of the nation, she was almost always in the majority on the Court. As it moved to the right, she was comfortable with much of its jurisprudence, but in questions of discrimination against women, a subject that would come to occupy the Burger Court more than any before—or after—she joined the liberals.

O'Connor had spent her early childhood on her parents' ranch in southeastern Arizona. Struggling through the Depression, young Sandra learned to rope, ride, shoot, and all the other necessary duties of a ranch hand on a sprawling 155,000-acre enterprise. Isolated from other children, she read voraciously and eclectically, including such diverse publications as the *Wall Street Journal* and the *New Yorker*. She spent six years at Stanford, earning her undergraduate degree in economics with honors in 1950 and her law degree two years later, third in her class.

But despite her academic record and service as an editor of the law journal, her only offer of employment was as a legal secretary at a large firm in Los Angeles. She had found that personal achievement did not overcome the prejudice against women in the professions. O'Connor finally became a deputy county attorney in San Mateo, California. When her husband, John O'Connor, graduated from Stanford Law School one year later and began work for the U.S. Army Judge Advocate General Corps in Frankfurt, West Germany, she went with him as a civilian lawyer for the Quartermaster Corps. In 1957, the O'Connor family settled in Maricopa County, Arizona, where she raised three boys and became active in local politics and public service.

By 1965, she had established a reputation as a sharp, able, and conservative Republican and for the next four years served as assistant state attorney general. From 1969 to 1974, when she successfully ran for a state judgeship on the Maricopa County Superior Court, she was appointed to and then gained election to the state senate, where, in 1972, she became the first female majority leader in the country. In 1979, due at least in part to her refusal to run against him for governor, Democrat Bruce Babbitt appointed O'Connor to the Arizona Court of Appeals. Her nomination to the Supreme Court went through smoothly, with the Senate voting to confirm her 99 to 0. The only substantial opposition came from those who favored overturning *Roe* and were worried about the otherwise right-wing Republican's qualified support for abortion rights while in the Arizona legislature.

As it turned out, they had good reason for concern. O'Connor's conservative positions on criminal law, federalism, and legislative authority were offset by her process-oriented stance on affirmative action, free speech, and the right to an abortion. Her swing vote made her one of the more important justices on the Burger Court, and she became even more important on the Rehnquist Court. Her concurring opinions diluted the effect of conservative majorities. Her respect for certain precedents, combined with her naturally ingrained restraint, produced a jurisprudence that disappointed many who wanted a clearer picture from the highest bench. She was a realist with a soft heart, a counterweight to White's hard-headed realism. Although her opinions lacked an overriding passion, the relentlessly upbeat O'Connor made a very strong impression on the law before she retired in 2006.

SUSPECT CATEGORIES

Those conservatives expecting the Burger Court to break with Warren Court school integration jurisprudence regarded *Swann v. Charlotte-Mecklenburg Board of Education* (1971) with dismay. A unanimous Court spoke through the chief justice, admitting what had become obvious: "District courts and courts of appeals have struggled in hundreds of [desegregation] cases with a multitude and variety of problems. . . . courts had to improvise and experiment without detailed or specific guidelines." The school board plan in Charlotte, North Carolina, would have resulted in a central district with 90 percent of its students black, while integrating the other schools with small numbers of black students. An expert the district court named had suggested that a portion of the nearly all-black district's students be bused into the other school zones. In addition, the children from the inner-city black schools would be bused into the nearly all-white suburban schools within the consolidated (countywide) school system.

Burger, impatient to end the implementation impasse, reminded school boards that, "in fashioning and effectuating the decrees, the courts will be guided by equitable principles. Traditionally, equity has been characterized by a practical flexibility in shaping its remedies and by a facility for adjusting and reconciling public and private needs." Such equity required "clean hands" on the part of all concerned—with school boards and parents all acting in good faith. But Burger also conceded what everyone knew. "White flight" had taken white families out of cities with large numbers of black schoolchildren, and whites who stayed but did not want their children to go to school with blacks established private academies that resegregated the classroom, "sometimes neutralizing or negating remedial action before it was fully implemented." His own inclination was to limit the role of the courts in public education, and he voted with the majority in order to assign himself the opinion. He was not arguing for an integrated society but "to eliminate from the public schools all vestiges of state-imposed segregation."

As the firestorm over busing spread to the North, Burger's views led in the opposite direction from *Swann*. Led by Burger, a majority in *Keyes v. School District* (1973) set up a distinction between de jure (by law) segregation and de facto (in fact) segregation. This was in fact a revival of the state action question, and the Court would now require that a wrong be committed before it would apply a remedy. The Court's limit on integration plans to single districts in *Milliken v. Bradley* (1974) signaled the full retreat in judicial attempts at integration. In *Milliken*, the Court refused the city of Detroit's request to extend a busing plan to the nearly all-white suburbs.

In 1974, Detroit was a city in trouble, with its population declining, its employment opportunities and tax base falling, its infrastructure failing, and its white population fleeing beyond the city limits. As historian Thomas Sugrue has written, the city had been residentially segregated since the beginning of the black migration. Residential segregation meant de facto school segregation. The city school board made de facto school segregation worse by continuously redrawing the "catchment" lines of schools so that no whites had to go to schools in black areas and no blacks could attend schools in white areas. Official desegregation in 1970 was met with white boycotts and a campaign to oust school board members who supported the plan. Whites whose opposition was strongest simply left the city. *Milliken* meant that these parents did not have to go far to ensure that their children did not have to sit next to blacks. Sugrue writes: "In the short period between 1967 and 1978, the Detroit public School District lost 74 percent of its white students."

Affirmative action cases raised parallel questions of the role of courts in countering racial and gender discrimination. Litigants could rely on the Civil Rights Act of 1964 and the Educational Amendments Act of 1972—Title IX—as statutory ground for suit, rather than having to tie their claims to the Equal Protection Clause. Burger wrote for a unanimous Court in *Griggs v. Duke Power Company* (1971) that employers violated Title VII of the 1964 Civil Rights Act when they administered tests that were unrelated to the job and that discriminated against minorities, even if inadvertent. In *Griggs*, a statistical or "disparate impact" test sufficed to prove impermissible racial discrimination.

The issue of intent and numerical disproportion came to a head in a case involving the University of California Medical School at Davis. The Nixon Justice Department had settled on quotas for remedying racial disparities in employment because they were easy to use, enforce, and evaluate. Educational institutions, government agencies, and businesses liked them for the same reasons. By the middle 1970s, racial quotas had spread to public and private institutions, but nonminority applicants to schools and for jobs felt they had become victims of improper racial and gender discrimination. Although the nonminority candidates were not responsible for past injustices, and might be highly qualified for the slot or post, minority candidates, aided by the quota system, got the opening. Anti–affirmative action groups looked for a test case, and disappointed nonminority candidates looked for assistance in bringing legal action.

Allan Bakke was turned down by the University of California Medical Center at Davis at the same time that less-qualified African Americans were admitted according to a quota system. Bakke would have been admitted but for the set-aside the regents of the medical school at Davis had provided for minority applicants. The regents believed that this set-aside of places for minorities would provide a pool of minority physicians to work in minority locales, a public interest that would pass the strict scrutiny test. But the Civil Rights Act did not provide for such race-based set-asides. Thus the plan might pass a Fourteenth Amendment equal protection test but fail the statutory requirement. The California Supreme Court found for Bakke, ordered him admitted, and told the regents to end the set-aside. The regents appealed to the High Court. In friends of the court briefs, an array of elite schools, including Harvard and Princeton, pleaded for the affirmative action program. An array of conservative groups decried it as reverse discrimination—as loading the guilt of past generations onto the shoulders of individuals who had taken no part in the injustices.

In *Regents of the University of California v. Bakke* (1978), Justice Powell agreed in part with those who believed that the Davis plan violated Title VI of the Civil Rights Act of 1964 (Burger, Stevens, Stewart, and Rehnquist) and in part with those who thought the plan was acceptable (Brennan, Marshall, White, and Blackmun). The Court ruled that quotas violated Title VI but that schools could take race into account to ensure diversity. The opinions ran to over one hundred pages, involved many amicus applications, and demonstrated that affirmative action questions had profoundly and permanently ended the Warren Era unanimity on civil rights.

For Powell, Burger, Rehnquist, and Stewart, Stevens argued that quotas or affirmative action constituted reverse discrimination. Citing Harlan's dissent in *Plessy*, he pleaded for a color-blind Constitution. Read in this light, the Civil Rights Act barred racial discrimination in admissions. Although Congress might have been concerned with racial discrimination, the plain language of the statute reached far beyond that specific problem: "Just as Congress responded to the problem of employment discrimination by enacting a provision that protects all races . . . so, too, its answer to the problem of federal funding of segregated facilities stands as a broad prohibition against the exclusion of any individual from a federally funded program 'on the ground of race.'" Discrimination was simply that, and whether exclusion because of race carried a stigma or not did not matter.

Brennan, writing for Marshall, Blackmun, and White, recognized the dilemma for those seeking to rectify racial disparities through government action that benefited individuals simply because of their race: "Against this background, claims that law must be 'colorblind' or that the datum of race is no longer relevant to public policy must be seen as aspiration rather than as description of reality . . . for reality rebukes us that race has too often been used by those who would stigmatize and oppress minorities." There could be benign racial classifications creating privileges, so long as those denied or excluded were not stigmatized by it.

Marshall wrote for himself, from the heart of his own experience: "It must be remembered that, during most of the past 200 years, the Constitution as interpreted by this Court did not prohibit the most ingenious and pervasive forms of discrimination against the Negro. Now, when a State acts to remedy the effects of that legacy of discrimination, I cannot believe that this same Constitution stands as a barrier." For Marshall, history as well as the Fourteenth Amendment mandated the set-aside.

Blackmun added his own short dissent in part and concurrence in part. From his experience as counsel for the Mayo Clinic and his lifelong interest in the medical profession in America, he concluded: "At least until the early 1970's, apparently only a very small number, less than 2%, of the physicians, attorneys, and medical and law students in the United States were members of what we now refer to as minority groups." The set-aside would fulfill a compelling state interest in preparing minorities to practice medicine. Like Marshall, Blackmun had no answer to the Civil Rights Act's uncompromising language, but he insisted, "If ways are not found to remedy that situation, the country can never achieve its professed goal of a society that is not race conscious."

Powell agreed that there was a social value in more minority doctors and that programs could take race into account, but strict quotas and admission based wholly or in large measure on race violated the law. Thus he agreed in part with Burger and his side, and in part with Brennan and his side. The result, however, was a flood of cases asking exactly how race might be taken into account. After *Bakke*, affirmative action only accelerated as a public issue—and thus as an issue for the Court.

In *United Steelworkers Union v. Weber* (1979), Brennan's majority found that a private employer's affirmative action plan did not violate Title VII because it did not fire whites, it was temporary, and it rectified obvious disparities. In *Fullilove v. Klutznik* (1980), a majority found congressional set-asides in the minority business enterprise clause of the Public Works Employment Act of 1977 constitutional. Burger's opinion emphasized Congress's broad powers. Brennan's concurrence favored the important-objective rationale. Rehnquist, Stewart, and Stevens in dissent demanded a remedy only in cases of "actual effects of illegal race discrimination." The nation was fiercely divided, and the Court could not give a clear statement of the law.

"REMEMBER THE LADIES"

But in one area of civil rights, the Burger Court came together. By the beginning of the 1970s, a new feminist movement had entered mainstream American political life. Women began to agitate for equal treatment in the workplace, an activity that brought women together outside the home and empowered them to explore the roots of their frustration. Small groups of women met to "raise their consciousness." In the process, they gained an identity other than homemaker and mother, and that in turn changed the structures and expectations of family life. Women who had long before abandoned hopes of a career began to return to college or professional schools. In 1967, as the effects of the Civil Rights Act's Title VII litigation mounted, President Lyndon Johnson finally added the term "sex" to executive orders forbidding discrimination in federal offices. More indirectly, Johnson's Great Society initiative in 1965 also empowered women. Federal commitment to family planning, welfare, jobs, and educational aid reached down to the lower half of society. Whatever the limitations of that initiative, and there were many, it did result in government commitment to reform for women on a scale that dwarfed all previous programs. In 1966, author and activist Betty Friedan called a conference to "take action to bring women into full participation in the mainstream of American society now." The last word in her address to the conferees became the name of the organization: the National Organization for Women (NOW).

According to NOW's program, the "liberation" of women from unfair treatment in private life was tied to the equality of women in the public sphere. NOW lobbied for day care centers for working women and for election of women candidates to Congress. NOW helped form a woman's political caucus and pushed for the equal rights amendment (ERA) to the Constitution.

The amendment, first proposed to Congress in 1923, began: "Equality of rights under the law shall not be denied or abridged by the United States or by any state on account of sex." Congress would pass it in 1972, and at first it looked as though it would get the necessary three-quarters of the states' ratification.

The long shadow of the ERA hung over the Court as, beginning with several cases involving Title VII, the Court struck down gender distinctions in Idaho's estate law and private employment, in *Reed v. Reed* (1971) and *Phillips v. Martin Marietta Corporation* (1971). By an eight-to-one majority, the Court also struck down discriminatory clauses in the Equal Pay Act and Title VII with regard to the military but did not unite around the proposition that gender was a suspect category akin to race, in *Frontiero v. Richardson* (1973).

In *Craig v. Boren* (1976), the Court elevated gender-specific legislation to the intermediate level of scrutiny. The Oklahoma law in question allowed women to purchase low-alcohol beer at age eighteen but restricted male purchasers to age twenty-one and over. Brennan's opinion struck down the statute, but the test he introduced was far more important than the holding simply equalizing the age at which young people could buy near beer. To pass the new test for equal protection under the Fourteenth Amendment (though Brennan, writing for a 7-to-2 majority, insisted that he had not created anything new), a state law that discriminated against women "must serve important government objectives and must be substantially related to those objectives."

Around Brennan's opinion sailed the usual Burger Court flotilla of concurrences. Blackmun did not think that the Brennan test was entirely satisfactory. Powell insisted on slightly different language for the test of impermissible discrimination, and Stevens would have preferred three levels for the test. Stewart concurred in the result, under the old rational-relation test. Burger and Rehnquist did not buy the decision or its rationale at all, insisting that males did not need special solicitude from the Court and the rational-relation test should apply, because sex was not a suspect category.

The decision was a triumph for lawyer Ruth Bader Ginsburg. Filing a friend of the court brief against the Oklahoma statute on behalf of the American Civil Liberties Union, Ginsburg was fast becoming one of the most successful advocates for legal equality for women. In 1972, she became the first director of the ACLU's Women's Rights Project. In 1971, she was cocounsel in *Reed v. Reed* and entered a winning amicus brief in *Frontiero v. Richardson*, which resulted in equal treatment of housing allowances for married women in the armed services. In *Cleveland Board of Education v. LaFleur* (1974), she helped end discriminatory pregnancy leave policies; and in *Corning Glass Works v. Brennan* (1974), she played a key role in ensuring that businesses pay women the same as they pay men for the same work under the Equal Pay Act. Her ACLU team reversed the sex discriminatory policies of the Social Security Administration, in *Weinberger v. Weisenfeld* (1975). A year after *Craig* she would argue *Califano v. Goldfarb*, which ensured that widowers were not denied benefits that widows would have gained under federal law. Blackmun gave her high marks for her skills but confessed that he was getting a little tired of hearing her use cases about men disfavored by the law to promote equal rights for women.

In its last term, the Burger Court expanded the reach of Title VII's prohibitions on discrimination against women into an entirely new field of law—employment. In general, except for union labor and contractual employment, most Americans worked without a safety net. They were hired at will and could be dismissed at will. *Meritor Savings Bank v. Vinson* (1986) was a fairly simple employment case as procedural matters go. A bank teller named Mechelle Vinson sued her employer, the Meritor Savings Bank, for fostering a "hostile work environment." Her supervisor had allegedly threatened to fire her unless she had sex with him. His defense, and that of the bank, was that her participation in the affair was "voluntary" and that moreover this was not a form of discrimination covered under Title VII.

In an opinion by Justice Rehnquist, a unanimous court disagreed. Not only did they find that the law covered the alleged threat, but the intent of the supervisor was not the standard for judgment for determining whether a workplace was a hostile environment. The perception of the recipient, a subjective test favoring would-be plaintiffs, was the relevant standard. This expansive reading of Title VII in effect created a federal common law against "sexual harassment."

The Court recognized that the intermediate level of scrutiny of *Craig* created thorny constitutional questions. In *Rostker v. Goldberg* (1981), Rehnquist authored a majority opinion deferring to Congress's judgment with regard to women in the military. Under it, Congress could legitimately exclude women from the Selective Service Act. O'Connor's majority opinion in *Mississippi University for Women v. Hogan* upheld a man's claim for admission to an all-female nursing school. Reverse discrimination suits had come to gender.

Biological differences raised the question of whether equal protection meant equal treatment. Or did women's particular needs, for example, in childbirth and child rearing, mandate special treatment? One of these unique issues for women was pregnancy. But the Court's landmark decision in this area was not based on equal protection grounds, but rather on a torturous due process rationale.

Burger knew the importance of *Roe v. Wade* and its companion case, *Doe v. Bolton*, from the moment they arrived in 1971 at the High Court as two class action suits challenging Texas and Georgia's abortion laws, respectively. Texas had a very old law that made the performance of an abortion a felony. The woman undergoing the procedure was not a party to the offense. There was no exception for rape, incest, or the health of the mother. Georgia had recently "reformed" its law, following guidelines from the American Bar Association, the American Medical Association, and the Model Penal Code, permitting abortions if a panel of doctors agreed that the health of the patient was at stake in the continued pregnancy. In both cases, federal district court panels of three judges (petitioners had sought injunctive relief against the states, and federal rules provided that such cases be heard before a panel of judges) had struck down the state laws as violating the federal Constitution's protection of a woman's privacy rights under *Griswold*.

At the conference after the case was first argued, Burger agreed that the young woman bringing the suit, called "Jane Roe" in the litigation to protect her reputation, did have a case and should have injunctive relief if the state law was indeed unconstitutional, but he was not convinced that the state law was unconstitutional. For Douglas, the state law was patently unconstitutional, and Roe's pregnancy, whether or not she would be pregnant when the Court announced its opinion, gave her standing to bring the suit. Brennan seconded Douglas. So did Stewart. Justice White thought that the state had a compelling interest in protecting the potential life of the unborn child. For him, the question concerned what form the state's interest might take. Could it regulate the doctors? Could it bar the abortion, except when the mother's health was at stake? On a deeper level, when did life—human life protected by the Fourteenth Amendment—begin? Clearly he was opposed to so-called abortion on demand. Marshall suggested that the state's interest might appear stronger as the pregnancy grew longer. Surely abortion of an infant at the moment of birth would be murder. But abortion at a very early stage of the pregnancy should be permitted. Justice Blackmun also balanced the interests of the mother with those of the fetus, arguing that there is no absolute right to reproductive autonomy. He was, however, concerned that doctors' privileges and practices not be harmed by the laws against abortion.

Burger counted himself in the majority in overturning the Texas and Georgia laws and assigned the cases to Blackmun. Burger also set the cases down for reargument after Powell and Rehnquist had taken their seats. In the meantime, Brennan had some ideas of his own. He told Douglas that the Court should rely upon privacy as a core constitutional right and from it derive three kinds of liberty: the liberty to be free from bodily restraint; the liberty to make basic decisions like marrying and having or not having children; and the liberty to express one's own personality. It was not the doctor's right to speak freely or practice medicine that must be defended but the fundamental freedoms that all people had from interference by the state. The Court should not take a position on when fetal life began and tell states they could not interfere with abortions in early stages of pregnancies, other than to require doctors performing them to be licensed and facilities to be sanitary. "The decision is that of the woman and hers alone."

After reargument in October 1972, with Powell and Rehnquist taking part, Blackmun claimed to be ready to circulate draft opinions in the two cases. He would rest the right to an abortion upon the Due Process Clause of the Fourteenth Amendment but wanted to root the opinion in the doctor-patient relationship. From his research into the latter, he had proposed the division of a pregnancy into trimesters. In the first of these, a woman only needed the consent of her doctor. In the second and third, after the twentieth week, the state's interest in the potential life allowed it to impose increasingly strict regulations on abortions. Blackmun began these drafts with the stark reminder that Texas and Georgia had made abortion into a crime, although the two statutes had "a different cast," with the latter reflecting "advancing medical knowledge, and . . . new thinking about an old issue." In the time between the passage of the former and the adoption of the latter, changing legal and social ideas on population growth, pollution, poverty, and race had intervened. The Court recognized the fundamentally differing views of the parties and wished to avoid all imputation of emotion.

As he revised his drafts, the choice of ending a pregnancy in its early stages became a fundamental right of a woman's privacy protected by the Fourteenth Amendment. But the right to privacy, however derived and however fundamental, did not grant the absolute right to abortion. States also had a right to protect incipient human life that grew as the pregnancy continued, so that "at some point in time [in the pregnancy]" the state could assert a compelling interest in protecting the potential life of the fetus. But neither Blackmun nor the majority of the Court for whom he wrote "was in a position to speculate" on the medical question of when life began, nor did the Court think that the states could turn religious or moral presumptions into medical facts.

Blackmun had a majority with him, but three of these wrote concurrences, and two of his colleagues dissented. Chief Justice Burger's concurrence was barely longer than a page in print and agreed that the Texas and Georgia statutes violated the Fourteenth Amendment. But he reassured the dissenters—White and Rehnquist—that the Court's decision would not open the door to "abortion on demand" or corrupt the medical profession. Douglas joined

Blackmun but wrote a short concurrence of his own to lay the result squarely on the right of privacy that he had elucidated in *Griswold*. The Texas and Georgia statutes were not constitutional. They deprived women of their "preferred life style" and forced them to accept an "undesired future." Justice Stewart entered a third concurrence. He was still troubled, as he had been in his *Griswold* dissent, with the recrudescence of this new version of substantive due process analysis. But now he conceded that it was proper. The meaning that the Court assigned to the word "liberty" in the Fourteenth Amendment had to change with the times. It had to be broader than the rights enumerated by name in the Bill of Rights. Freedom of choice was an idea whose time had come.

Justice White, as he had promised, dissented, and Justice Rehnquist joined in the dissent. White saw the most troubling cases as those in which women simply wanted to end a pregnancy that did not endanger them. They might be motivated by shame, convenience, economics, or "dislike of children." The Court had turned women's "whim or caprice" into a constitutional principle, although there was nothing in the Constitution's language to sustain that judgment. To convenience a mother, and for little more, the Court had "disentitled" the legislatures of all fifty states from weighing the "relative importance of the continued existence and development of the fetus on the one hand against a spectrum of possible impacts on the mother on the other hand."

Rehnquist's opinion was short, and like White's, powerfully phrased: "Roe" was not pregnant at the time of the decision, so the Court overreached itself in providing her with a relief she did not need and could not claim. There was no right of privacy involved, for the abortion was not a private act. If liberty was lost, it was lost through "due process of law." The state's regulation of abortion did not have to rest upon a compelling interest, only a rational one, and the states' statutes surely had a rational relationship to the goal of saving the unborn child.

The 7-to-2 decision invalidated most of the abortion laws in the country and nationalized what had been a very local, very personal issue. *Roe* would become the most controverted and controversial of the Court's opinions since *Dred Scott*, to which some of its critics, including Justice Antonin Scalia, would later compare it. Women's rights advocates got a decision that recognized a right—but only barely, with qualifications, and that was based on a constitutional theory that was ripe for attack. Opponents of abortion ridiculed a decision that recognized a state interest in the fetus but denied that life began at conception. They would mobilize and wage holy war against the desecration of religion, motherhood, and the family that the decision represented to them. The position a nominee took on *Roe* became a litmus test for the choice of judges for the federal bench and for the High Court itself. Congressional and presidential elections turned on the abortion rights question, as new and potent political action groups, in particular religious lobbies, entered the national arena for the first time, to battle over *Roe.*

The Court itself added to this furor with its moderate, procedurally based balancing tests in subsequent abortion cases. Particularly when it came to minors, even Blackmun tolerated parental notification, additional hurdles to determine the girl's maturity, and the state's interest in minors seeking abortions, in *Bellotti v. Baird I* (1976), *Bellotti v. Baird II* (1979), and *H. L. v. Matheson* (1981), respectively. These cases, along with *Planned Parenthood of Missouri v. Danforth* (1976), which struck down a law restricting abortion and requiring the recording in a state archive of the name of the woman, seemed to indicate that there was no end to the battle in sight, at least no end that the Court could provide.

NOT SO SUSPECT CATEGORIES

Although women's rights might rise to the level of those rights that are fundamentally protected because sex itself was a suspect category, poverty and sexual preference were not. When the debate over abortion rights shifted to the funding of abortions, the moderates like Powell and Stevens joined the conservatives to argue that women's reproductive rights did not require state or federal funding of abortions. In *Maher v. Roe* (1977), Powell wrote for a 6-to-3 majority that Connecticut could elect to use Medicaid funds for birth care but not for abortions: "Nothing in the [federal Medicaid] statute suggests that participating states are required to fund every medical procedure that falls within the delineated categories of medical care." States need only have rational standards for including and excluding categories of medical assistance. It was reasonable, Powell continued, for the state to protect fetal life as much as it did, and to prefer live birth to abortion. Marshall wrote a stinging dissent against what he believed to be the Court's callous disregard for the plight of poor women. Not so hidden in it was Marshall's disdain for Powell himself, going back to Powell's views on Richmond school segregation.

While states and localities were seeking ways to deny abortions, Illinois congressional representative Henry Hyde added a rider to a Health, Education, and Welfare funding bill that prohibited the use of federal funds for abortions for any reason, whether medically necessary or not. The Hyde amendment, as it would be called, led to *Harris v. McRae* (1980). Writing for a 5-to-4 majority,

Stewart could find no fundamental right at stake in the denial of funding for abortions. Just as states could use federal matching funds as they wished, so could the federal government use its own funds as it wished. Denial of funding did not deny women the right to an abortion—merely the ability to get one. "Indigency" was not a problem that Congress was constitutionally mandated to remedy.

A second and new claim that petitioners lodged against the Hyde amendment was that it violated separation of church and state. Stewart's opinion for the majority refused to consider the legislative intent behind the Hyde amendment. If an act had some secular purpose, the religious motives of its framers, even when expressed in the floor debates, were irrelevant. The Hyde amendment had a secular purpose—the protection of fetal life.

The Court underlined the point that poverty was not a suspect category nor eligible for equal protection relief in Justice Powell's opinion on the constitutionality of underfunded school districts in Texas. In Texas, school district funding was based on property taxes. In *San Antonio Independent School District v. Rodriguez* (1973), petitioners claimed that the state did nothing to equalize the funding of districts, with the result that majority Mexican American districts often were unequally supported. Powell held that although access to the courts and basic services should be accessible to the poor, education "is not among the rights afforded explicit protection under our Federal Constitution." Marshall dissented against what he categorized as a "rigidified approach to equal protection analysis."

A similar setback in privacy rights arose out of the gay rights movement's attempt to end discrimination against homosexuals. Its test case arose when police in Atlanta, Georgia, were let into Michael Hardwick's apartment and discovered him engaged in fellatio sex. In *Bowers v. Hardwick* (1986), Justice White wrote the majority opinion that held that no privacy right existed regarding this activity. White declared, "No connection between family, marriage, or procreation on the one hand and homosexual activity on the other has been demonstrated, either by the Court of Appeals or by respondent." Sexual preference was not a suspect category.

EXECUTIVE PRIVILEGES

As the Vietnam War entered its final stages, the Nixon administration was engaged in sophisticated foreign policy negotiations with the Soviet Union, the People's Republic of China, and communist North Vietnam. Unfortunately for this plan, a former staffer for the Pentagon, Daniel Ellsberg, leaked a confidential report he had helped write for the Pentagon to the *New York Times* and the *Washington Post*. It contained information embarrassing to the administration. The administration sought a court order to prevent publication of what was soon termed the "Pentagon Papers."

The 6-to-3 per curiam opinion in *New York Times v. U.S.* (1971) simply stated that the government's request did not meet the heavy burden for prior restraint on the press. But the majority divided on several issues, reflecting the divisions on the Court. Douglas and Black argued against any restraint. Brennan would have allowed restriction of publication if and only if the government could show a clear and present danger. Marshall and White wanted an explicit congressional authorization and not the Nixon administration's mere assertion of national security concerns. For them, it was a question of checks and balances.

Burger, Harlan, and Blackmun dissented. Although their dissents differed, they all agreed that the president had the authority to protect the nation from learning such information. As Burger wrote for all three, there was no constitutional "right to know," as the *Times* had asserted in its appeal from an injunction barring publication. Harlan joined Burger, but wrote for himself that he felt rushed—and that the case should go back to the district court from which it had been taken in the middle of the litigation by the High Court. The variety of dissents, added to the variety of concurring opinions, demonstrated, if anyone needed another demonstration, the dissension on the Court. Burger could not even hold the dissenters together.

The not-so-hidden issue, raised by Nixon's lawyers, was "the question of inherent power of the Executive to classify papers, records, and documents as secret, or otherwise unavailable for public exposure." Other events would soon prove that this claim of "executive privilege" could be extended to internal documents and conversations that might constitute evidence of misconduct in the Oval Office.

The Court's second and biggest political test of executive privilege began with the botched break-in at the Watergate Hotel's offices of the Democratic National Committee on June 17, 1972. Congress investigated the matter and forced President Nixon to appoint an independent prosecutor. The nation learned that the Watergate break-in was part of the Nixon White House's campaign of dirty tricks, slush funds, and cover-up.

The most substantial revelation at the congressional hearings came from Alexander Butterfield, a Nixon appointments secretary, who revealed to the congressional committee the existence of a recording system in the Oval Office. The special prosecutor at this time, Leon Jaworski, subpoenaed the tapes, but the president refused, based on the argument, among others, that "executive privilege" protected him from handing over confidential material. In essence, Nixon claimed that the courts did not have the authority to compel the chief executive officer of the country to participate in a legal proceeding involving the activities of his office. The D.C. trial court judge, John Sirica, who was handling the break-in and cover-up cases, ordered the president to produce the tapes.

In *U.S. v. Nixon* (1974), a unanimous Court, in an opinion written by the chief justice, declared that Nixon must hand over the tapes. No one was above the law. Although the Court's decision was almost universally acclaimed, Burger's actual opinion was much more deferential to the president's position than its popular resonance would suggest. In it he asserted *Marbury*'s continued validity, namely that the courts possessed the authority to review the actions of the other branches; but the Court also recognized the need to give "presidential confidentiality" "the greatest protection consistent with the fair administration of justice." Behind the scenes, the justices had argued heatedly over Burger's original draft, which was even more deferential to executive authority.

The concession to the executive in the opinion notwithstanding, the tapes ultimately confirmed Nixon's involvement in the break-in and the subsequent attempt at a cover-up. Before the House of Representatives could vote on the articles of impeachment that included his obstruction of justice, Nixon resigned the presidency on August 9, 1974, the only time this has happened. A full review of the tapes (minus the eighteen minutes that somehow got erased) revealed a great many reasons why Nixon did not want them released, and none of them involved the sanctity of the presidency or national security. Combined with the scars from the repeated lies about the Vietnam War, Watergate shattered many Americans' trust in the national government.

THE FIRST AMENDMENT

Rather than stay with the Warren Court's imminent danger test of *Brandenburg*, the majority of the Burger Court chose to evaluate the nature of the restraint or the penalty imposed on defendants in free speech cases. If it was the least restrictive means to advance a legitimate and compelling government interest, they would uphold the conviction for public disorderliness involving speech. In a courtroom, where a defendant on the witness stand referred to his alleged assailant as "chicken s—," or on a public street, when a protester exclaimed, "We'll take the f—ing street later," as his group was being cleared from the area, speech was protected (*Clark v. Community for Creative Non-Violence* [1984], *Eaton v. City of Tulsa* [1974], and *Hess v. Indiana* [1973]). The Burger Court preferred its decisions to turn on the details of specific cases rather than on the broader principles. As the Court said, per curiam, in *Eaton*: "This single isolated usage of street vernacular, not directed at the judge or any officer of the court, cannot constitutionally support the conviction of criminal contempt."

The Warren Court recognized symbolic acts as protectable speech. Beginning a line of cases that would reach fulfillment in the Rehnquist Court, the Burger Court justices recognized mistreatment of the flag as a form of protected speech. The continuation in the 1970s of the large protests of the 1950s and 1960s sorely tested public authorities' toleration of marches other than patriotic publicly organized parades. One feature of these marches, the burning of flags, was particularly provocative. But the Court found a Massachusetts statute banning "contemptuous treatment" of the flag to be unconstitutional. Powell explained that the law was too vague for a reasonable person to understand what it did and did not cover. Justice Rehnquist, in dissent, reasoned that the state had a substantial interest in preserving "the physical integrity of a unique national symbol."

The Burger Court upended precedent when it extended constitutional protection to commercial speech in *Bigelow v. Virginia* (1975) and *Virginia Bd. of Pharmacy v. Virginia Consumer Council* (1976). Blackmun's opinion in *Virginia Bd. of Pharmacy* explained that states and localities wishing to curtail commercials faced a four-part test: If the commercial speech's activity was lawful and not misleading, it was protected, and the government's regulation was valid only if it sought a substantial government interest and was no more restrictive than necessary to accomplish the objective. Rehnquist's dissent worried how far the new test would go, and he was proven correct when bans on lawyers advertising their services fell in *Bates v. State Bar of Arizona* (1977). The results can be seen in the Yellow Pages—with entire sections devoted to elaborate law firm advertising. But the right to offer services did not meant the right to directly solicit clients (for example, "ambulance chasing"), as the Court found in *Ohralik v. Ohio State Bar Ass'n* (1978) and *Zauderer v. Office of Disciplinary Counsel* (1985).

In the area of pornography, the Burger Court wrestled with the same slipperiness of definitions, varieties of standards, and measures of toleration as the Warren Court. In *Miller v. California* (1973), the chief justice argued that localities might impose their own standard of what defined "serious literary, artistic, political or scientific value." In effect, this left every nationally distributed book, magazine, and film to the not-so-tender mercies of local prosecutors and juries. A community might find nudity in classical art, Victorian photography, and Renaissance love poetry without serious value. Were, for example, the nude cherubs in High Renaissance paintings pornographic? Were the depictions of sexual congress in D. H. Lawrence's novels pornographic? Was the fleeting preadolescent nudity in Francois Truffaut's now-classic French movie, *The Four Hundred Blows*, pornography? The flaws in the standard became plain when the justices held that appellate courts could overturn jury determinations of what is obscene in one case—but in the companion case on the same day ruled that juries could apply local standards. Which was it—the Circuit Court of Appeals standard of *Jenkins v. Georgia* (1974) or the local jury of *Hamling v. U.S.* (1974)?

Though the Court had ruled, in Harlan's eloquent words, that "one man's vulgarity is another man's lyric," regarding a jacket worn in a courthouse with "F— the Draft" on it in *Cohen v. California* (1971), Justice Stevens found that George Carlin's repeated use of the s-word and f-word and five others in his comedy routine "Filthy Words" could be censored by the Federal Communications Commission, in *Federal Communications Commission v. Pacifica Foundation* (1978). Because the listener could not censor the broadcast before he or she heard it, the government had a legitimate interest, which FCC censorship rationally fulfilled. That the broadcast was to be during regular programming and during the afternoon when children might be listening made the government's regulation all the more reasonable to the Court.

Censorship protecting children from adult-oriented materials undergirded *New York v. Ferber* (1982). Justice White wrote for a unanimous Court that child pornography was not a protected form of expression. The two films in question featured children under the age of sixteen masturbating and were sold to an adult undercover officer. White argued that the state's interest in protecting children from the pornography industry was "beyond the need for elaboration."

Freedom of speech played into political campaigns in more complex fashion. *Buckley v. Valeo* (1976) declared several congressional limitations on contributions to candidates' political campaign chests valid but limitations on other forms of political contributions unacceptable. The Federal Election Campaign Act of 1971 had curbed perceived campaign-giving abuses by limiting the amount of giving that certain individuals and groups could make to congressional and presidential campaigns. In 1975, two senators, James Buckley of New York and Eugene McCarthy of Wisconsin, brought suit against the act on First Amendment grounds.

The court of appeals sustained the act, but the High Court went in all directions. A majority of the Court accepted the idea of limits on and the recording of contributions to candidates but not on payments for advertising and promotion of candidates' views on issues: "By contrast with a limitation upon expenditures for political expression, a limitation upon the amount that any one person or group may contribute to a candidate or political committee entails only a marginal restriction upon the contributor's ability to engage in free communication." The $1,000 limit on individual giving to a candidate did not unduly restrict free speech, but an "expenditure ceiling" on what campaigns might spend limited access to information or the ability to share information. These limitations violated "associational freedoms," which might or might not be equated with freedom to petition and assemble.

The opinion was per curiam, but there were concurrences and dissents in part from Burger, White, Marshall, Blackmun, and Rehnquist. The Court conceded that Congress had the power to set the rules for federal elections, but that power was not without constraints, when "the specific legislation that Congress has enacted interferes with First Amendment freedoms or invidiously discriminates against nonincumbent candidates and minor parties in contravention of the Fifth Amendment."

Another First Amendment arena in which the Burger Court subtly but not greatly refined the Warren Court's jurisprudence was the separation of church and state. Once again the cases involved public schools. The Old Order Amish community of New Glarus, Wisconsin, challenged the state's compulsory high school attendance laws. Its attorneys argued that the Amish should be allowed to homeschool their children in accordance with their religious beliefs after the eighth grade. Wisconsin replied that Amish schools and Amish homeschooling of adolescents "would not afford Amish children 'substantially equivalent education' to that offered in the schools of the area." In effect, the state was arguing that it, rather than the students' parents, had the students' best interests at heart.

Chief Justice Burger, writing for the Court in *Wisconsin v. Yoder* (1972), indicated that the Old Order Amish presented a special case: "As a result of their common heritage, Old Order Amish communities today are characterized by a fundamental belief that salvation requires life in a church community separate and apart from the world and worldly influence." Any test for the best interests of the child must rest upon Amish, not state of Wisconsin or national, educational standards: "The Amish succeed in preparing their high school age children to be productive members of the Amish community. . . . The evidence also showed that the Amish have an excellent record as law-abiding and generally self-sufficient members of society."

White and Brennan concurred but did not buy into Burger's reasoning. Instead, White balanced legitimate interests of state and sect and noted that only the final two years of public schooling were affected: "Cases such as this one inevitably call for a delicate balancing of important but conflicting interests." Douglas alone dissented, because, "despite the Court's claim, the parents are seeking to vindicate not only their own free exercise claims, but also those of their high-school-age children." For him, the children should be able to make their own choices.

Chief Justice Burger wrote the majority opinion that established the test for whether or not a religious practice would be exempt from otherwise neutral state laws. Known as the *Lemon* test, after *Lemon v. Kurtzman* (1971), he opined that the laws or regulations must have a secular purpose, a neutral primary effect that neither advanced nor harmed religion, and should not create an excessive entanglement between church and state.

The posting of the Ten Commandments in a classroom was impermissible even though privately funded and not read aloud, per *Stone v. Graham* (1980), but Nebraska's legislature could employ a chaplain, per *Marsh v. Chambers* (1983), because it was a tradition the chief justice and his six-vote majority could trace back to the earliest practices of Congress. Although the justices fairly consistently determined that direct funding arrangements for parochial schools either violated the primary-effect prong or the excessive-entanglement prong of *Lemon*, in *Committee for Public Education and Religious Liberty v. Nyquist* (1973) and *Sloan v. Lemon* (1973), they ruled that taxpayers could deduct the cost of parochial school education for their children for purposes of state income tax, in *Mueller v. Allen* (1983).

In *Lynch v. Donnelly* (1984), Chief Justice Burger applied the *Lemon* test to a Pawtucket, Rhode Island, nativity scene and found it a permissible exercise of civic pride. It was neutral, accompanied by "a Santa Claus house, reindeer pulling Santa's sleigh, candy-striped poles, a Christmas tree, carolers, cutout figures representing such characters as a clown, an elephant, and a teddy bear, hundreds of colored lights, a large banner that reads 'Seasons Greetings' and the creche at issue here." As for the wall of separation, "There is an unbroken history of official acknowledgment by all three branches of government of the role of religion in American life from at least 1789."

On the brink of saying that Christianity was the official religion of the United States (a comment that Justice Brewer had made in an opinion for the Court some one hundred years earlier), Burger drew back: "Rather than mechanically invalidating all governmental conduct or statutes that confer benefits or give special recognition to religion in general or to one faith—as an absolutist approach would dictate—the Court has scrutinized challenged legislation or official conduct to determine whether, in reality, it establishes a religion or religious faith, or tends to do so."

O'Connor concurred on the grounds that the display did not persuade anyone to adopt the Christian faith. She used a subjective test ("what was in the minds of the viewers of the creche") and found that the display did not promote religion. Did the city have a religious intent? "I would find that Pawtucket did not intend to convey any message of endorsement of Christianity or disapproval of non-Christian religions."

The four dissenters took religion more seriously, at least in this case. They wondered how celebrations of Christmas could possibly be construed as nonreligious. As Burger himself admitted, "The creche, which has been included in the display for 40 or more years, consists of the traditional figures, including the Infant Jesus, Mary and Joseph, angels, shepherds, kings, and animals." Even if these were "traditional figures," was not the tradition a religious one, and the holiday the celebration of the birth of Jesus Christ? If Christmas was a national holiday, did Congress have the authority to establish a religion by making one of its most important days into a national holiday? As Brennan wrote for the dissenters, "It is plainly contrary to the purposes and values of the Establishment Clause to pretend, as the Court does, that the otherwise secular setting of Pawtucket's nativity scene dilutes in some fashion the creche's singular religiosity."

Lynch saved a religious display from removal by asserting that it was not religious, but *Goldman v. Weinberger* (1986) ruled that an ordained rabbi serving as a U.S. Air Force officer had to remove a yarmulke (a skullcap) because it was a religious object. This form of dress was forbidden under the military's need to maintain uniformity. As the dissenters in *Goldman* noted, the balancing of the interests lacked "a credible explanation" as to why a skullcap so much interfered with the government interest that it could be forbidden, but a town could put up a crèche.

Free exercise and establishment analyses bounced off one another in the Court's 6-to-3 decision to overturn Alabama's "moment of silence" law for its public schools. In *Wallace v. Jaffree* (1985), Justice Stevens's majority opinion favored the idea of periods of reflection in school but was suspicious that Alabama's silence was meant to be filled with prayer.

THE COURT AND THE OTHER BRANCHES OF GOVERNMENT

The High Court has always been sensitive to its place in the federal government. In general, it leaves foreign policy to the president and domestic policy making to Congress. The Burger Court did not bow to Nixon's claims of executive privilege but was hospitable to a Democratic chief executive in a case stemming from President Jimmy Carter's handling of the Iran hostage crisis.

Carter froze Iranian assets under the International Economic Emergency Powers Act, after Islamic fundamentalists, with the support and direction of the Ayatollah Ruhollah Khomeini's government, held American embassy personnel hostage. As part of the settlement, Iran not only received its $8 billion worth of assets but also immunity from lawsuits stemming from the incident. In an opinion by Justice Rehnquist in *Dames & Moore v. Regan* (1981), the Court upheld the executive orders enforcing these terms against a lawsuit by a claims agency suing on behalf of some of the former hostages.

Rehnquist based his reasoning for the Court on the inherent necessities of the situation, stating, in part: "Where, as here, the settlement of claims has been determined to be a necessary incident to the resolution of a major foreign policy dispute between our country and another, and where, as here, we can conclude that Congress acquiesced in the President's action, we are not prepared to say that the President lacks the power to settle such claims."

The Burger Court did not defer to Congress when it claimed a quasi-judicial role, however, under the authority of a "legislative veto." Congress used this device to give itself the ability to pass judgment on administrative agency actions. In *I.N.S. v. Chadha* (1983), Jaghish Rai Chadha, a Kenyan with a student visa, was to be deported but was reprieved by the attorney general. Using the legislative veto, the House of Representatives reversed the attorney general's recommendation. Chadha asked the federal courts to review Congress's power to intervene. The appeals court agreed—the legislative veto was unconstitutional because it violated basic separation of powers. For the High Court, Blackmun agreed. Marshall, Brennan, and Stevens joined Blackmun. Powell, worried about the impact of the case, asked for a reargument. Burger, pulled in all directions, could not decide where he stood. Late in the next term, the case was reargued, and only White and Rehnquist voted to let the legislative veto stand. Rehnquist believed that it was "too bad" but that Chadha had to bear this "misfortune."

Chief Justice Burger assigned himself the opinion. "With all the obvious flaws of delay, untidiness, and potential for abuse, we have not yet found a better way to preserve freedom than by making the exercise of power subject to the carefully crafted restraints spelled out in the Constitution," he wrote, defending the separate and independent role of the judiciary. Burger also wrote in part: "Convenience and efficiency are not the primary objectives—or the hallmarks—of democratic government." Congress could not give one of its houses administrative authority without the consent of the other house and the president on a particular item.

ADJUDICATING ADMINISTRATION

Post-Watergate disenchantment with the trustworthiness of the Nixon administration also played a significant role in the Burger Court's reading of administrative law. Beginning at the close of World War II and gaining momentum in the late 1960s and early 1970s, the power and reach of the administrative state moved toward its apogee. Congress reacted to the public clamor for safety and succor by creating more agencies producing even more regulations. Despite his conservative Republican stance on most issues, Nixon signed and then gave force to a number of these enactments, including for worker safety, environmental preservation, pollution, and product safety. Administrative courts served as watchdogs for these administrative agencies and their wealth of regulations. On top of this outpouring of administrative statutes was another layer of laws governing the enforcement of the administrative statutes. But under the Federal Administrative Procedure Act of 1946, a disgruntled party could ask for federal court review of the administrative courts. By the late 1970s, the *Code of Federal Regulations* had become several large volumes.

It was inevitable that the High Court would be drawn into this maze. The first case, *Goldberg v. Kelly* (1970), arose out of an administrative denial of welfare benefits. Were government benefits legally enforceable entitlements? Was the right to question denial of such benefits also an entitlement? A culture of entitlements—the welfare state safety net—included Social Security, Medicare, and other basic programs. In an opinion by Justice Brennan that seemed to signal a revolution in entitlements, payments from programs like Social Security could not be terminated without a court hearing. Due process extended deep into the administrative state. Bureaucratic convenience was subject to due process. "Termination of aid pending resolution of a controversy over eligibility may deprive an eligible recipient of the very means by which to live while he waits." Behind Brennan's reasoning lay his understanding that administrative agencies could not content themselves with efficiency for efficiency's sake—the same argument that Burger would make in *Chadha*. Determinations must be accurate and fair and based on procedural rights, just as in criminal prosecutions.

But there was no entitlement rights revolution following *Goldberg*. In a case involving the termination of disability benefits, *Mathews v. Eldridge* (1976), Justice Powell wrote for the Court that due process must be weighed against cost effectiveness: "But the Government's interest, and hence that of the public, in conserving scarce fiscal and administrative resources is a factor that must be weighed. At some point the benefit of an additional safeguard to the individual affected by the administrative action and to society in terms of increased assurance that the action is just, may be outweighed by the cost." Calculation of opportunity costs and marginal returns mattered more than the "dignity and well-being" of a few individuals.

In a high-inflation, high-unemployment, economy known as "stagflation," valuing each individual's rights seemed too expensive. Powell's test laid out the new calculus of due process in entitlement cases: "First, the private interest that will be affected by the official action; second, the risk of an erroneous deprivation of such interest through the procedures used, and the probable value, if any, of additional or substitute procedural safeguards; and finally, the Government's interest, including the function involved and the fiscal and administrative burdens that the additional or substitute procedural requirement would entail." A balancing test replaced Brennan's constitutional principle.

The idea that law should be married to the so-called dismal science of economics, the law-and-economy approach made popular in the same era by economists and jurists, had come of age. Law schools began to hire joint J.D. and Ph.D.s in economics, and those hires taught the Coase Theorem and the Mathews formula as the proper goals of the law to a new generation of law clerks and litigators. Justice was a scarce resource like any other, and it needed to be allocated on the most efficient basis, not as a limitless entitlement from the state.

The cost analysis could come out in favor of suitors. When Secretary of Transportation John A. Volpe approved the construction of an interstate highway through Overton Park outside Memphis, the community sued in federal court on the grounds that the secretary had violated section 4(f) of the 1968 highway act. In *Citizens to Preserve Overton Park, Inc. v. Volpe* (1971), the Court agreed that section 4(f) and the Administrative Procedure Act's provisions required the agencies involved to consider alternatives to the route. Moreover, the Court declared the action of the agency reviewable by the regular courts, based on the full administrative record available to the administrator when he made that decision. The result for Overton Park advocates was a complete victory. Ultimately deciding that construction would be too costly, the Department of Transportation arranged for other connecting routes that did not cross the park. Though hailed by environmentalists, *Overton Park* did not represent a novelty in administrative law. The Court, as far back as the first Federal Drug Administration cases, had required agencies to hold hearings and compile records.

A second agency case was better known. Although *TVA v. Hill* (1978) seemed an open-and-shut reading of the Endangered Species Act of 1973, Chief Justice Burger's majority opinion affirming the enjoining of the Tellico Dam project (80 percent complete at this point at a cost of tens of millions of dollars) in order to save an endangered three-to-five-inch fish called the snail darter, was controversial. For developers, mine owners, timber companies, and opponents of extreme environmentalism, the decision seemed to be a result of an environmental movement run amok—the very antithesis of cost effectiveness. In fact, the litigation was the end of a much longer process in which Indian peoples whose burial grounds and farmers whose homes would be flooded by the dam were losing to developers who wanted to build expensive resorts on lakeside plots aided by the Tennessee Valley Authority.

When the Court proved unreceptive to the developers, they turned to Senator Howard Baker (R-Tenn.), the minority leader, and Congressman John Duncan, also from Tennessee. The congressmen inserted a rider to an appropriations bill changing the Endangered Species Act. The Tennessee Valley Authority completed the Tellico Dam and destroyed the habitat of the snail darter. Fortunately, discovery of additional snail darters and their habitats removed the snail darter from the extinct list and the endangered list to merely "threatened," but the burial grounds were gone forever.

In stark contrast to *Overton Park* and *Hill*, the Court gave a unanimous signal of support for agency discretion in *Chevron U.S.A. Inc. v. Natural Resource Defense Council* (1984). Stevens thought that, absent the clear intent of Congress, courts needed to show deference to the "reasonable" interpretations of administrative agencies. At dispute was the meaning of "stationary sources" of air pollution in the Clean Air Act Amendments of 1977. Reagan-appointed Environmental Protection Agency officials prompted the litigation when they interpreted the legislation in such a way as to soften the requirements for power plants and other producers of noxious emissions.

Stevens, in wording reminiscent of Frankfurter's deference theory, pointed out that "in such a case, federal judges—who have no constituency—have a duty to respect legitimate policy choices made by those who do." Because congressional language and intent are subject to debate on any given point, the Court's decision gave a great deal of power back to the appointive federal bureaucracy, and behind that, to the policy aims of different presidents who appoint the agency members and senatorial majorities who confirm the appointments.

In a collateral line of cases, the Court dealt with the impact of congressional law on states—the perennial issue of federalism revisited in the context of administrative law. From the New Deal onward, under the Commerce Clause, Congress had passed a series of laws requiring businesses of a certain size to pay a minimum wage, time-and-a-half for overtime, and other benefits. Did these apply to the employees of the state and its agencies? In *League of Cities v. Usery*, a coalition of cities and states asked the High Court to protect them from congressional wages and hours legislation passed in 1974.

Rehnquist wrote for the majority. The original act, in 1938, had exempted the states and their agencies. "This Court has never doubted that there are limits upon the power of Congress to override state sovereignty, even when exercising its otherwise plenary powers to tax or to regulate commerce which are conferred by Art. 1 of the Constitution." Did the sovereignty of the states preclude the extension of the Fair Labor Standards Act to them now? Brennan, White, Marshall, and Stevens dissented. They agreed that this was a policy matter in which the Court ought to defer to the legislative branch. Plainly, they also favored the idea that state employers should pay minimum wages and limit hours. *Adkins* was not cited by either side, but its penumbras fell over the dispute.

Instead of a straightforward explanation of constitutional theory, Rehnquist spent most of his time answering the objections of the dissenters to his opinion. This style of contentious writing characterized almost all of Rehnquist's opinions for the Court, even after 1986, when he became chief justice. The style gave his writing a jerky, fussy, unfinished quality, chopping his arguments into pieces as he responded to the dissenters' arguments. But his argument itself was sound. In the dual federalism system that the founders created, both the federal and the state governments were competent to discipline and reward those who served them. Such powers were essential for any sovereign government: "One undoubted attribute of state sovereignty is the States' power to determine the wages which shall be paid to those whom they employ in order to carry out their governmental functions, what hours those persons will work, and what compensation will be provided where these employees may be called upon to work overtime. The question we must resolve here, then, is whether these determinations are 'functions essential to separate and independent existence,'" of the states. If the Congress could tell states what they could and could not pay their employees, did it not deprive the states of one of the most essential elements of sovereignty?

But Rehnquist did not stop there. In another example of his characteristic style of argument, he found occasion to show how the dissenters' views in the present case cut against their previous opinions. Because Marshall, Brennan, and White favored affirmative action, Rehnquist noted that "this type of forced relinquishment of important governmental activities is further reflected in the complaint's allegation that the city of Inglewood, Cal., has been forced to curtail its affirmative action program for providing employment opportunities for men and women interested in a career in law enforcement." There was no need for this aside. It was gratuitous. One can only ascribe the mention of the Inglewood program to Rehnquist's somewhat wry sense of humor.

MORE CRIMINAL PROCEDURE

The Burger Court's many rulings regarding the Fourth, Fifth, Sixth, Seventh, Eighth, and Fourteenth Amendments carved from the body of the Warren Court's criminal procedure jurisprudence a bewildering array of exceptions, limitations, and qualifications. If the spirit of the Warren Court was concern for the integrity of the justice system, then the Burger Court's was concern for public interest in securing convictions.

When the sufficiency of search warrants was at issue, the Burger Court proposed a "totality of the circumstances" test, in *Illinois v. Gates* (1983). Justice Rehnquist wrote for the 6-to-3 majority that gave the prosecution a chance to use evidence from warrants improperly issued: "Probable cause is a fluid concept—turning on the assessment of probabilities in particular factual contexts—not readily, or even usefully, reduced to a neat set of legal rules."

Gates was a drug case, and the Reagan-era "War on Drugs" vastly increased the number of criminal laws, prosecutions, imprisonments, and seizures. Ultimately, this war involved more cases and more expenditure for jails and trials than any conflict in American history, with the exception of the Civil War and World War II. Because there was more to police, police forces were hard-pressed to handle the tide of criminalized activities, and sloppiness with warrants crept in everywhere.

The Burger Court obliged the police with exceptions to the search-and-seizure requirements. Sometimes this involved confuting the "expectation of privacy" rule, as with the banker's files at issue in *Andreson v. Maryland* (1976).

By the Court's decision in *Washington v. Chrisman* (1982), items within "plain view" could also be seized without warrant. Items found when a person who was uninformed about the purpose of a search gave consent for a search, even if the police did not have probable cause, as in *Schneckloth v. Bustamonte* (1973), were admissible in court.

Containers within cars could be searched, according to *U.S. v. Ross* (1982); as well as cars taken into custody after the arrest of the driver, per *Chambers v. Moroney* (1970); likewise cars impounded so the police could take an inventory to protect themselves against lawsuits for missing property, in *South Dakota v. Opperman* (1976). A majority of justices also agreed to allow for full body searches after a *Terry* stop, in *Adams v. Williams* (1972). Furthermore, if the police could demonstrate urgency, as in *Cupp v. Murphy* (1973), in which the suspect voluntarily walked into a police station with possible evidence under his fingernails, a majority agreed that the police could scrape his nails for evidence before he walked away and use it in court.

On a few occasions, when the police conduct violated the conscience of the Court (the old Frankfurter test) the Burger Court interceded for the defendant. In *Gerstein v. Pugh* (1975), a majority held that the police could not detain someone on a warrantless arrest without formally charging them in a reasonable time. Upon the expiration of a reasonable time, they needed to present a probable cause for the arrest. In *Payton v. New York* (1980), the Court struck down the practice of warrantless entry into a home for a warrantless arrest. Additionally, the justices held that police could not go beyond the owner of an establishment, whose person they had a warrant to search, to search the patrons of the establishment, in *Ybarra v. Illinois* (1980). In the words of Justice Stewart's majority opinion, "A person's mere propinquity to others independently suspected of criminal activity does not, without more, give rise to probable cause to search that person."

U.S. v. Leon (1984) summarized the wrinkles in *Mapp*'s fabric. In *Leon*, the officers seized a large cache of drugs, but only after entering the premises based on a warrant that they may have perjured themselves to obtain. Framing the question in such a way as to make his conclusion inescapable, Justice White argued that admissibility "must be resolved by weighing the costs and benefits of preventing the use in the prosecution's case in chief of inherently trustworthy tangible evidence obtained in reliance on a search warrant issued by a detached and neutral magistrate that ultimately is found to be defective." This was Powell's cost efficiency test for due process applied to criminal procedure.

Other dilutions of the exclusionary rule took place in *U.S. v. Calandra* (1974), in which the Court decided that prosecutors might use evidence before grand juries not admissible at trial; in *U.S. v. Janis* (1976), finding that the exclusionary rule did not apply to civil proceedings involving government agencies; and in *Stone v. Powell* (1976), in which a petitioner could not raise an exclusionary rule claim in a habeas corpus writ (to move a case to the federal court of appeals) if he had not raised the same claim at his trial. The Court recognized an "inevitable discovery" exception to the exclusionary rule in *Nix v. Williams* (1984). Prosecutors could introduce otherwise inadmissible material if they could show that the investigation would have found it anyway.

A similar nibbling away at the edges constrained *Miranda*. In *Harris v. New York* (1971), a majority of the Court ruled that statements excluded because of a defective *Miranda* warning could be used at trial for impeaching credibility (showing that a defendant had lied in his testimony). In *Oregon v. Haas* (1975), the Court ruled that statements gained by repeated questioning after a suspect asserted his or her right to remain silent could be used for impeachment purposes. If the police repeated the *Miranda* warnings each time, there was no limit to how many times they could come back to interrogate a suspect under the ruling in *Michigan v. Mosely* (1975).

The Court's direction became abundantly manifest in an intervening case, *Michigan v. Tucker* (1974), in an opinion by Justice Rehnquist. His contribution to the criminal procedural jurisprudence of the Burger Court was decisive and consistent. In this case, the officers gave all but one of the warnings, the right to appointed counsel, to Tucker before he waived those rights and gave the police the name of another man, Henderson, to corroborate his story. Henderson proved to be an excellent witness for the prosecution at trial. In between the police's questioning of Tucker and the testimony of Henderson at trial, the Court gave its ruling in *Miranda*. The trial judge did not apply the full ruling of *Miranda* and allowed Henderson to testify although he excluded Tucker's statements to the police. Rehnquist argued: "We have already concluded that the police conduct at issue here did not abridge respondent's constitutional privilege against compulsory self-incrimination, but departed only from the prophylactic standards later laid down by this Court in *Miranda* to safeguard that privilege." His depiction of the *Miranda* warnings as a "prophylactic" limited their effectiveness at the same time as it denigrated the precedent. "Just as the law does not require that a defendant receive a perfect trial, only a fair one, it cannot realistically require that policemen investigating serious crimes make no errors whatsoever."

But those expecting *Miranda*'s demise were disappointed. In *Brewer v. Williams* (1977), the Burger Court found that a police officer's conversation with a suspect that drew a confession had violated the suspect's *Miranda* rights.

The Des Moines, Iowa, police were transporting Williams from Davenport to Des Moines where his attorney was waiting for interrogation to begin. Knowing Williams to be a religious man, one of the officers lamented the fact that the girl Williams was suspected of raping and killing would never receive a Christian burial. Justice Stewart wrote for the Court that this was an impermissible interrogation of a suspect in custody. Looking closely at the facts, Stewart concluded that "there can be no serious doubt, either, that Detective Leaming deliberately and designedly set out to elicit information from Williams just as surely as—and perhaps more effectively than—if he had formally interrogated him." It was not unintentional or sloppy police procedure—quite the reverse. Leaming decided that he did not have to follow the rules.

Burger dissented, joined by White, Blackmun, and Rehnquist: The majority opinion "mechanically and blindly keeps reliable evidence from juries whether the claimed constitutional violation involves gross police misconduct or honest human error." Williams was guilty of a heinous crime, and confessed to it. Why should he go free? "I categorically reject the remarkable notion that the police in this case were guilty of unconstitutional misconduct, or any conduct justifying the bizarre result reached by the Court." Marshall, who concurred in the judgment, wrote a concurrence to swipe at the dissents: "The dissenters have, I believe, lost sight of the fundamental constitutional backbone of our criminal law. They seem to think that Detective Leaming's actions were perfectly proper, indeed laudable, examples of 'good police work.'"

The Court divided again in *Rhode Island v. Innis* (1980), this time Stewart joining the chief, Rehnquist, White, Powell, and Blackmun. The police officers' conversation with one another in a patrol car conveying a suspect, leading to a confession, did not violate the suspect's right to counsel. Stewart based his distinction on the definition of interrogation. He reasoned that "since the police surely cannot be held accountable for the unforeseeable results of their words or actions, the definition of interrogation can extend only to words or actions on the part of police officers that they should have known were reasonably likely to elicit an incriminating response."

Another blow to the *Miranda* rule was Rehnquist's "emergency exception" in *New York v. Quarles* (1984). After relating the fact pattern (largely from the police perspective), he found that the officer in question acted properly when, after securing a suspect, he asked the location of the weapon before giving the *Miranda* warnings. Refusing to hem in police officers with handbook procedures for such a fluid situation, Rehnquist argued: "Whatever the motivation of individual officers in such a situation, we do not believe that the doctrinal underpinnings of *Miranda* require that it be applied in all its rigor to a situation in which police officers ask questions reasonably prompted by a concern for the public safety."

In one final area of the criminal law and procedure, the death penalty, the Burger Court took on a subject almost as heated as abortion. In June 1972, the Court stunned the nation and its thirty-eight states that had death penalty statutes with a 5-to-4 opinion in *Furman v. Georgia* that declared the death penalty as administered in Georgia and Texas to be a violation of the Eighth Amendment's prohibition of "cruel and unusual" punishment.

All nine justices wrote opinions in the case, including the members of the majority. Marshall and Brennan joined to argue that "the State, even as it punishes, must treat its members with respect for their intrinsic worth as human beings." The other members of the majority were concerned with capriciousness, arbitrariness, and the disturbingly disproportionate use of the death penalty against African American males.

This split decision forced the states to rewrite their death penalty statutes. They could either mandate the use of the death penalty in every appropriate conviction or separate out the penalty phase from the guilt-finding phase with the separate consideration of both mitigating and aggravating circumstances. In 1976, in *Gregg v. Georgia*, the Court ruled that the new Georgia law, with a separate penalty phase, passed constitutional muster. By this time, Stevens had replaced Douglas, and the moderates on the Court were reassured by the new law's automatic Georgia Supreme Court review of all death sentences. What was more unfortunate, as the chief justice lamented in *Lockett v. Ohio* (1978), states could not bar the defense from introducing any evidence of mitigating factors it thought relevant for jurors to consider.

When the Court overturned the mandatory death penalty statutes of Louisiana and North Carolina, in *Roberts v. Louisiana* and *Woodson v. North Carolina* (1976), it left legislators to ponder the effectiveness of death sentences both as deterrent and as retribution. Because the death penalty issue intersected race issues (statistically, black defendants were, by far, more likely to receive death penalties than white defendants for similar crimes), civil rights groups formed organizations dedicated to eradicating capital punishment. Pro–death penalty advocates organized victims' rights associations to bring relatives and loved-ones into courtrooms, as well as grassroots lobbying campaigns. The Court could not resolve a dispute or forge a consensus on this issue, and neither could Americans.

When Warren Earl Burger left the center chair to head the bicentennial celebrations of the U.S. Constitution, he left behind a mixed record. Burger had presided over one of the most divided Courts, a division that reflected the absence of national consensus on these issues. But many of the Burger Court's contributions to American law still stand—in abortion rights, women's equality, sexual harassment, and the death penalty, for example. The justices modified the criminal procedure jurisprudence of the Warren Court to bring it back into line with popular demands for law and order and police discretion. Often the Court struggled with its own logic. The use of balancing tests never seemed to resolve a dispute, instead bringing more cases to the Court for finer distinctions. But, as law professor Barry Friedman has argued in another context, the High Court must stay close to public opinion, and this Burger and his justices did.

CHAPTER 15

The Rehnquist Court, 1986–2005

After a contentious confirmation hearing and Senate debate, William Rehnquist assumed the center chair at the Court. He was the most persuasive voice for law and order, deference to the executive, and judicial restraint on the Burger Court. Rehnquist believed that the Court had become a rare flower—that its justices lacked the everyday experience in government service that the Court members had had when he clerked for Justice Jackson and that he himself had gained in his career. As Attorney General Edwin Meese wrote sometime after the 66-to-33 vote confirmed the new chief justice, he was "dedicated to the rule of law and to the role of judges as prescribed in the Constitution; that is, to apply the law as it is written in the Constitution and statutes, not to make the law according to their own beliefs, their own biases, or their policy preferences."

But Rehnquist's deference had limits and his judicial philosophy was not as consistently restrained as Meese suggested. He could be an activist when judicial activism seemed necessary to him; an authoritarian when government had to impose itself to keep order; a laissez-faire adherent when government should stand back from the private actor; a moralist when he did not like the conduct of a party seeking the aid of the courts; and an originalist when he had to wage war against "the living Constitution." Over all, Rehnquist was a positivist. He did not have a philosophy of law so much as a philosophy of judging based on desirable ends. In this, he did not differ all that much from Earl Warren or William Brennan.

Rehnquist hoped and wanted to lead the Court, but in the end did not. He could not or would not abandon the choppy, disputatious writing style that characterized his opinions on the Burger Court, with much of the text debating with justices who disagreed with him. Like the Burger Court, Rehnquist's was riven with dissent, and it failed to overturn, and even on a few occasions extended, several of the most controversial liberal precedents of the preceding decades. Public opinion and electoral politics had swung the country in a conservative direction, but Rehnquist's Court followed only at a distance.

THE NEW CONSERVATISM

As the 1960s and the 1970s had been times of cultural and political liberalism, punctuated by right-wing spasms, so the Reagan era was one of retrenchment and reaction, against which liberals struggled largely in vain. In politics, the New Deal Democratic alliance of urban Catholics and rural Democrats finally broke apart. Based on their opposition to abortion rights, evangelical ministers in the South urged their congregations to go to the polls and vote Republican. The same issue split the vote among northern Catholics, long a bastion of Democratic support. The "silent majority" of Nixon's administration had become the "moral majority" undergirding the Reagan era. These trends continued into the presidency of George Herbert Walker Bush, Reagan's vice president and successor in 1988.

What was this new conservatism? President Reagan summed it up—small government, government off the backs of the people. A "new federalism" called for greater deference to the states. A new moralism held individuals to high standards of personal conduct. A new political ideology appeared on the horizon, with old liberals donning the garb of "neocons" and favoring an aggressive foreign policy, strong national security initiatives, and government support for corporate business and tax cuts.

THE NEW JUSTICES

From its inception at Rehnquist's confirmation hearings, his Court had drawn a mixed reception. The hearings were not as contentious as those for Hughes, but the memo endorsing *Plessy* reared its ugly head once more, and so did *Laird v. Tatum*. It was plain that some critics in the Senate were determined to oppose Rehnquist not because he was unfit but because they did not agree with his views. Reports that he had actively participated in intimidating minority voters in Arizona in the 1950s and 1960s circulated. But Rehnquist was confirmed in a 65-to-33 vote.

Because Rehnquist vacated a seat when he rose to the center chair, Reagan had another opportunity to affect the composition of the Court. Attorney General Meese suggested Antonin Scalia. On the D.C. Circuit Court of Appeals, Scalia had never disappointed Meese. His reputation for clear writing, cutting argument, and consistently conservative views of the policymaking role for courts and the limitations the Constitution places on judge-made novelties made him a natural choice to replace Rehnquist. Indeed, few justices can point to as consistent a philosophy of judging and reading of the Constitution as Scalia's. He advocated a plain sense, plain meaning rule for interpreting the Constitution. He did not care for surveys of legislative intent. He would ask, sometimes with asperity, "Where is that in the text," when counsel or academics advanced some novel theory of fundamental law.

Born March 11, 1936, in Trenton, New Jersey, Scalia was the only child of a schoolteacher and a professor. He grew up in Queens, New York, went to a Catholic private school, then to Georgetown, a Jesuit university, and then to Harvard Law School. Always a superior student, he found a job immediately at a Cleveland law firm; in 1967, he became a law professor at the University of Virginia. In 1971, he entered the Nixon administration and stayed on in Gerald Ford's Department of Justice. He taught at the Georgetown University Law Center and then at the University of Chicago from 1977 to 1982. In 1982, Reagan appointed Scalia to the U.S. Court of Appeals for the District of Columbia Circuit. Despite his well-demonstrated antipathy toward Warren-era concepts like the constitutional protection of privacy, Scalia's nomination to the High Court proceeded smoothly, at least in part because of the arduousness of the Rehnquist confirmation.

Scalia's abilities and geniality in person should have made him Brennan's equal in building consensus on the Rehnquist Court. But Scalia had little tolerance for what he perceived as weak logic. He quickly discerned the contradictions in the opinions of his colleagues. Some noted that the first law professor appointed since Frankfurter also exhibited Frankfurter's approach to his colleagues. Scalia was relentless and remorseless in criticizing opposing opinions in his own writings. Unfortunately for his cause, these qualities prevented him from aiding his chief justice in forging alliances on the Court. His relationship with Justice O'Connor occasioned the most virulent and intemperate of these outbursts, but all of the justices, including on occasion the chief justice, bore the brunt of his acerbity.

When Lewis Powell resigned in 1987, Reagan's first two nominees for the slot did not fare well. The second of these, Douglas Ginsburg, had to withdraw after allegations of unethical behavior and marijuana use surfaced, while the confirmation hearings of the first, Robert Bork, created a firestorm of controversy that ultimately led to Senate rejection and a new word in the American right's lexicon, "borked." Bork's supporters claimed that the Senate Democratic majority had introduced politics into the confirmation process instead of judging the nominee on his merits and deferring to the president's choice. Given that the president and his attorney general, Edwin Meese III, had made nominees' positions on certain issues the litmus test for all their choices, this criticism had a pot-calling-the-kettle-black quality.

In the end, Bork's own words undid him. In print, Bork had not only questioned the entirety of Warren Court's jurisprudence, but he had even challenged the icon of that jurisprudence—*Brown* and its legacy. For Bork was an originalist, consistently arguing that the justices should read the text of the Constitution under the strict guidance of its framers' ideas: The framers of the Fourteenth Amendment had no intention of striking down segregation, and thus the Court, in 1954, had no legitimate basis to say that the Equal Protection Clause of the Fourteenth Amendment mandated an end to segregation.

The third nominee, Anthony Kennedy, fared far better. He was born on July 23, 1936, in Sacramento, California, and was throughout his education and legal career a Californian, with the exception of study at Harvard Law School. His father was a lawyer and lobbyist for businesses in the Sacramento area, with effective state government connections. When his father died in 1963, Kennedy assumed the family law practice. He also developed strong ties to the state's Republican establishment, particularly to Ed Meese and, through Meese, to Ronald Reagan. The ties were renewed when Meese became President Reagan's attorney general. President Ford nominated Kennedy for the U.S. Court of Appeals in 1975. In 1987, Kennedy's nomination to the High Court was unanimously confirmed.

Kennedy proved to be another moderate conservative, like Powell and O'Connor. He often joined O'Connor as a swing vote, conservative on national security and criminal justice but liberal on minority and women's rights. Like O'Connor, he was stung by Scalia's acerbity, and like O'Connor, Kennedy was sensitive to criticism in the press. He did not favor affirmative action, saw limits to what Congress might enact, and supported the new federalism. He was the foremost advocate of the Court's primacy in determining the meaning of the Constitution, updating in a 1997 free exercise case the announcement of that primacy that the Warren Court had made in *Cooper v. Aaron.*

The second Rehnquist Court shifted further to the right when Clarence Thomas replaced Thurgood Marshall and David Souter replaced William Brennan. But Souter proved to be another maverick, much like Blackmun. President George Herbert Walker Bush did not insist on the ideological and political tests that Reagan and Meese had imposed on their selections. Bush Sr. tried to steer a moderate conservative course in all things, including in his Court nominees.

Clarence Thomas represented the Republican Party's accommodation with the disparate groups that opposed the rights revolution—with a twist. For, more than any other justice on the Court, his career path was paved by the Warren and Burger Courts' decisions on race and affirmative action. Thomas was an African American Catholic raised in the South but educated in the North at elite institutions, including Holy Cross College in Massachusetts and Yale Law School. These institutions' affirmative action recruitment programs had enabled him to overcome race, poverty, and background. Named to run the Reagan administration's Equal Employment Opportunity Commission, he deflected all affirmative action cases he could and, on the federal bench, upheld Reagan administration policies against affirmative action.

Thomas's defenders paint a portrait of a man with strong personal principles whose convictions accompany a joyful, thoughtful, and loyal character, but Thomas and his jurisprudence have never gained the respect of the academic community. There certainly is something of the trickster in him as well. At his confirmation hearings, Thomas weathered several days of questioning from the Democrat-controlled Senate Judiciary Committee. He was unwilling to express opinions about policies or approaches to constitutional interpretation. He maintained that he had never formulated a position on the controversial abortion decision, *Roe*, even though he had written and published an article criticizing the Court's holding. Once on the Court, Thomas proved to be no one's tool. Though he often agreed with Scalia and Rehnquist, Thomas sometimes went beyond them in his aversion to federal interference in criminal justice. As he wrote in *Doggett v. U.S.* (1992), he opposed transforming "the courts of the land into boards of law enforcement supervision."

But a former employee posed the only real obstacle to his confirmation. Law professor Anita Hill, who had worked under Thomas at the Equal Employment Opportunity Commission, alleged that he had sexually harassed her. In hearings already notable for their bitterness, the charge highlighted the deep divisions in American society over gender relations. Thomas managed to extricate himself from the quagmire with his protest against a "high tech lynching" but could not shake the damage to his reputation. In the end, the Senate voted 52 to 48 to confirm Thomas's nomination to the High Court.

In stark contrast, Souter's confirmation in 1991 sailed through the Senate with nary a dissenting word. A bachelor who enjoyed jogging and hiking his native New Hampshire's wilds, he left next to no paper trail in any of his state legal posts. Indeed, no one on the Court knew who he was—but Bush's trusted advisor, John Sununu, did, and that was sufficient. A moderate conservative like his president and a supreme judicial craftsman, Souter contributed a jovial yet always responsible tone to the Court's deliberations. An avid reader of history, he brought to the Court a sense of its history that differed somewhat from

Rehnquist's. Over time, Souter would prove as unpredictable as Blackmun and Stevens—only hinting at his liberal instincts during the confirmation hearings when he told the senators: "Justice Brennan is going to be remembered as one of the most fiercely principled guardians of the American Constitution that it has ever had or ever will have."

MOVING THE COURT TO THE CENTER

The election of Arkansas Democrat William Jefferson Clinton to the presidency in 1992 did not fundamentally shift the nation's politics. Clinton was, compared to many in his party, fiscally conservative. He believed in cooperation and moderation in government. He agreed to welfare reform, cut government spending in a number of areas, and pleaded for medical coverage for all Americans. But in the congressional elections of 1994, Republican forces led by Congressman Newton Gingrich targeted both Bill and Hillary Clinton and won control of both houses.

In the "Class of 1994's" "Contract with America," the Clintons' support of abortion rights became the central issue but not the only one. A special prosecutor, former Bush solicitor general Kenneth Starr, pressed for indictments against both Clintons on a wide variety of issues. None resulted in a trial, but Clinton's lying under oath in one of the prepresidential cases gave the Republican "class of 1994" in the House the opportunity to impeach him. The Senate found no basis for the charges, but Clinton's second administration was hamstrung by the impeachment and trial.

Clinton was a lawyer and former law professor, and his only two appointments to the High Court were well-known judges with impeccable educational and professional backgrounds. Ruth Bader Ginsburg, in 1993, and, in 1994, Stephen Breyer brought to the High Court distinguished records as judges, lawyers, and writers. Although they were widely viewed as liberals, their voting records would demonstrate a much more conservative view of the law than Brennan's, Thurgood Marshall's, Douglas's, or Warren's.

Ginsburg grew up in New York City, in a family of modest means. Both parents sacrificed the comforts of their later years for their only daughter's education, and Ginsburg made the most of the opportunity. She starred at Cornell, and then at Harvard Law School, finishing at Columbia Law. But even the top women graduates of elite schools could not break into the major New York City firms, just as O'Connor had discovered in California, nor gain important judicial clerkships. As Ginsburg later wrote, "A woman, a Jew, and a mother to boot" was a triple handicap. She found a job teaching at Columbia Law School, then at Rutgers–Newark, and then again at Columbia. President Jimmy Carter named her to the U.S. Court of Appeals for the District of Columbia Circuit in 1980; and, in 1993, the U.S. Senate confirmed her nomination to the Supreme Court, 97 to 3.

Though she would have preferred that *Roe* be decided on equal protection grounds rather than on due process, and that the Court withhold its opinion until the state legislatures and courts were better educated on the issues, at her confirmation hearings she made clear that a woman's right to choose an abortion was "something central to a woman's life, to her dignity. . . . And when government controls that decision for her, she's being treated as less than a full adult human being responsible for her own choices."

Breyer, like Ginsburg, was serving as a federal appellate court judge when Clinton tapped him to replace Blackmun. Like Ginsburg, Breyer had been a law professor, at Harvard. Also like Ginsburg, he had a secular Jewish background and liberal sympathies. But here the outward similarities ended. Breyer grew up in San Francisco in an upper-middle-class family. His father was a prominent lawyer. He graduated from Stanford University in the top rank of his class, went to Oxford University for another degree, and then, in 1961, two years after Ginsburg had left Harvard, went to Harvard Law School. Breyer then clerked for Justice Goldberg, held a post in the U.S. Department of Justice, and was appointed to the Harvard Law School faculty.

All the opportunities that her sex and her family commitments had denied to Ginsburg were open to Breyer. As Ginsburg turned her experiences into a concern for women's rights, so Breyer concluded from his that competition in the free market was the ideal. In late 1980, President Carter nominated Breyer to the U.S. Court of Appeals for the First Circuit. Breyer's views were congenial to Republicans, and he was confirmed easily for a seat on the High Court, on May 14, 1994, by a vote of 87 to 9.

INSIDE THE REHNQUIST COURT

Breyer and Ginsburg soon discovered that Rehnquist prized confidentiality. Blackmun's deposit of his Court memos with the Library of Congress caused the chief justice and several other justices concern. Rehnquist promoted a code of conduct for the justices' clerks, forbidding them ever to reveal the internal workings of the Court.

But the Rehnquist Court was intellectually alive. Questioning of counsel at oral argument and the quality of opinions evidenced the skill and learning of a well-educated bench. In particular, more than ever before, academic law teaching was influencing the Court. Along with Scalia, Breyer and Ginsburg brought their law teaching methods to the bench. And Stevens had taught law, as had Blackmun. What may have been just as important, they had taught at top law schools—Harvard, Columbia, Chicago, and Minnesota. The presence of so many Harvard, Columbia, Stanford, and Yale law school graduates on the Court gave it a polish and literacy rarely before seen. It is almost impossible now to conceive of an appointment to the Court of men with legal educational backgrounds like Jackson or Byrnes.

The elite intellectual character of the Court was also signaled by the quality of the justices' clerks. A small herd (four to a justice) was drawn from the best schools, recommended to the justices by famous professors. The clerks reinforced the law school–like atmosphere of the Court. In a practice traditionalists much lamented, some clerks aided their justices in the writing of the opinions. Clerks who completed their term or terms with the Court went on to the best law schools as professors, to the bench, or to advocacy. Clerkship—like the Roman Republican *cursus honorum* by which city officials might move up the ladder to become consuls—could lead, as it did for Rehnquist, Breyer, Stevens, and Chief Justice John G. Roberts, to a place on the Court itself.

Rehnquist may have been testy about leaks (a problem that plagues all of the government), but testimonials from insiders show a chief justice who tolerated his colleagues' foibles and maintained a wry sense of humor and professionalism. Consistent with his stated aims of efficiency and conservatism, he moved quickly to reduce the docket of cases the Court heard each term. At the behest of the justices, Congress passed a law in 1988 limiting the mandatory appellate jurisdiction of the Court. From 161 in 1985 to under 100 by 1994, a marked drop in cases decided resulted. But a marked increase in cases filed also resulted—from 5,158 in 1985 to 8,100 in 1994, making selection harder. The justices in the conference too felt the stern hand of the new regime. No opinions circulated before the initial vote was taken, and back-and-forth discussion disappeared altogether during conferences. All justices who wanted to speak were heard, but the wandering debates of the Burger era ended.

Even oral arguments happened on schedule. Unlike previous regimes' flexible notion of the one-hour time limit, when the advocate's time expired, the microphone now cut out. Only with the special permission of the Court could an advocate complete a sentence, much less a line of reasoning. Considering that the justices took up advocates' time with queries, quips, and potshots at one another (a silent Justice Thomas being the notable exception), these strict time limits altered the tenor, if not the content, of the exchange. Counsel had to have the quickness of top law professors to keep up (and top law professors became much-wanted attorney for parties at oral argument). Rehnquist's management policies were tough but fair.

At the same time that Rehnquist applied a minimalism to internal procedures, he greatly added to the grandeur of his Court's physical resources and managerial capacity. As head of the federal court administration, the chief justice exercised a great deal of influence over appointments, resources, and the clerical rules that governed the lower courts in the federal system. In 1998, at the request of the Court's reporter of decisions, the chief justice provided increased staffing. The reports are now edited for factual accuracy and grammatical consistency.

But Rehnquist could not command when it counted, in the brokering of clear majorities for his opinions. Precedent became unintelligible, due to fractured majorities, pluralities, and "concurrences in part" in opinions. Given this IIB-or-not-IIB confusion, the Court spoke only rarely with one voice, or in harmony, or even consistently. The conservative majority pledged itself to judicial restraint, deference to the other branches, and the new federalism, but then it embarked on a program of invalidating state and federal legislation. In fact, it exceeded every other Court in invalidating legislative acts. During one eight-year span, it outdid the Warren and Burger Courts' individual totals. This was judicial review with a vengeance.

UNCIVIL LIBERTIES WITH CIVIL RIGHTS?

The voting rights cases posed the first set of difficult yet fundamental questions for the Court. The Stone Court, the Vinson Court, and, most powerfully, the Warren Court had recognized voting, particularly for discrete and insular minorities, as one of the key rights in a democratic republic—and the most easily endangered. But these questions were invariably political in the most partisan sense of the word—forcing the Rehnquist Court to deal with its own politics as well as the country's.

In the Rehnquist Court era, new Republican majorities in southern and western states attempted to eliminate electoral districting that formerly Democratic legislatures had fashioned. In the process, African American voters, largely Democratic, were parceled out into Republican majority districts. Under the Voting Rights Act of 1965, redistricting in states that had a history of racial discrimination—the Jim Crow South—required federal court or Department of Justice approval. In *Shaw v. Reno* (1993) and *Miller v. Johnson* (1995), O'Connor's and Kennedy's majority opinions, respectively, tried to enforce a new race-blind standard for districting plans under the Voting Rights Act.

These first cases came not from Republicans trying to gerrymander black voters out of their votes, however, but from Democratic legislators trying to maximize the impact of black voting. In attempting to redistrict congressional seats after the 1990 census, Democrats in the North Carolina state legislature hit upon the majority-minority district idea. Although 43 percent of the black population of the state went into two snakelike districts along I-85 that were more or less guaranteed to elect blacks to Congress, the districting left enough black voters in contiguous districts to give the Democratic candidate a chance to carry them as well.

After a series of Republican challenges to the new districts failed in lower federal courts, in *Shaw v. Reno* O'Connor wrote that "redistricting legislation that is so extremely irregular on its face that it rationally can be viewed only as an effort to segregate races for purposes of voting, without regard for traditional districting principles and without sufficiently compelling justification," was unconstitutional. The majority-minority districts were impermissible because they were drawn according to racial configurations. In the Voting Rights Act, Congress had told the courts to look for a history of discrimination against minorities at the polls and evidence that the minority population had been denied the power of its numbers by dumping minorities into a single or a few unusually large election districts or by diluting minority voting power by distributing minority voters among numerically larger groups of the majority.

The Court could not coalesce around a majority opinion and could not provide answers to the vital questions of the test to be applied, the standard of review, or the reasoning behind redistricting. Rehnquist noted in his opinion for the Court in *Shaw v. Hunt* (1996) that the bizarre shape of the North Carolina districts alone signaled their invalidity: "We do not see how a district so drawn would avoid [Voting Rights Act] §2 liability." But did the majority concede that there be racial categories whose purpose is benign? That districts could be redrawn to increase the majority of minorities in them?

Stevens and Souter dissented, with Ginsburg and Breyer joining their opinion. Stevens thought the Court should not have taken the case: "As I have explained on prior occasions, I am convinced that the Court's aggressive supervision of state action designed to accommodate the political concerns of historically disadvantaged minority groups is seriously misguided." In short,

Stevens favored deference to the state, while Rehnquist would not defer to the state, belying his avowed adherence to "the new federalism." Stevens's argument had another prong whose sharp end was inserted in the chief justice's craw. For Rehnquist, whose demand for more federalism (hence deference to states) and for a more restrained Court should have led him to adopt Stevens's views, had spent a good part of his opinion refuting Stevens. It was a little war of words, carried on in notes, asides, and oblique thrusts, and was typical of the Rehnquist Court. At last, in *Easley v. Cromartie* (2001), the Court decided that North Carolina's districts, still majority-minority, were within the limits the statute provided. O'Connor had switched sides, joining Stevens, Ginsburg, Souter, and Breyer.

A similar cut and thrust on the Court, leading to a similar ironic inversion of the restrained deference that Rehnquist himself preferred but then declined to follow, awaited those who supported affirmative programs. Affirmative action for women and other disadvantaged groups in employment and in admission to undergraduate and graduate programs had succeeded in significantly rectifying the disparities in these areas. Businesses, schools, and governments—federal, state, and local—had acclimated quite well to the quota systems of the Nixon administration and the Burger Court.

The Rehnquist Court allowed the programs to exist so long as they were narrowly tailored, limited in duration, and a response to demonstrable past disparity. The disparate impact standard, based on pure numbers in *Griggs*, was modified in *Johnson v. Santa Clara County Transportation Agency* (1987). The fact that no women worked as dispatchers for the county road crews suggested that its new affirmative action plan might favor a woman applicant for the post over a man. The agency made that choice, and the loser, Paul Johnson, sued. It was a clear case of reverse discrimination, he thought. Though the county could not admit to its own policies of sex discrimination (that would have opened it to a host of suits), it found a winning argument. Brennan wrote for a majority that the plan, like that in *Weber*, made a "minimal intrusion" into hiring policy, was temporary, and had a legitimate purpose in eliminating past discrimination.

But *Johnson* was soon left standing on its own facts. The Court demanded proof of prior discrimination and the intent to continue it before it would allow an affirmative actions program, in *City of Richmond v. J. A. Croson* (1989), *Ward's Cove Packing Co. v. Atonio* (1989), and *Adarand Constructors, Inc. v. Pena* (1995). O'Connor demanded that the entity "identify that discrimination, public or private with some specificity before they may use race-conscious relief," in *Croson*, and then must narrowly tailor the relief. Scalia, in *Croson*, hinted that the language of the city's set-aside for black subcontractors in all public contracts demonstrated that the city could not show a pattern of prior discrimination.

Marshall, dissenting in *Croson*, countered that anyone who knew the history of Richmond knew that no bank would lend a black laborer enough money to set himself up as a contractor. Hence no black contractors could bid for city contracts. The 30 percent set-aside for black subcontractors was simple recompense for discrimination against them as a group in the past, to which Scalia retorted that the city could not show that Croson or any of the other bidders required to subcontract to black businesses had discriminated against blacks in the past.

Aleuts and other nonwhites were the objects of putative discrimination in *Ward's Cove*. The almost complete absence of Filipinos and Aleuts, who worked dirty and dangerous unskilled jobs on the cannery floor, from the skilled jobs at two plants that were filled almost entirely by whites did not constitute impermissible discrimination, according to the majority of the Court, because there was no official practice (or rather evidence of an official practice) to reserve the better-paying and more prestigious skilled jobs for whites. A violation of Title VII of the Civil Rights Act of 1964 required more than pure statistical evidence, more than "disparate impact," according to Justice White: "It is clear to us that the Court of Appeals' acceptance of the comparison between the racial composition of the cannery work force and that of the noncannery work force, as probative of a prima facie case of disparate impact in the selection of the latter group of workers, was flawed," for it did not take into account the percentage of minority workers who were qualified for the skilled positions.

But the Court refused to slam shut the door on affirmative action. Giving minority applicants to the undergraduate program at the University of Michigan special consideration did not pass muster in *Gratz v. Bollinger* (2003), despite pleas from faculty all over the country that diversity was good in itself and thus a compelling reason for a state university's affirmative action plan. In *Grutter v. Bollinger* (2003), however, the Court allowed the University of Michigan's law school to preserve its rough 12 percent minority goal in recruitment. The swing opinion in both cases was O'Connor's, and she may have been persuaded to distinguish between the two cases because of the fairly visible undergraduate presence of blacks on the University of Michigan campus for many years, which did not match the total absence of blacks in the law school classes until its administration imposed its affirmative action program. She added that in twenty-five years, by her estimate, which was nowhere explained or legally based, affirmative action programs might no longer be needed.

WHEN EXPRESSION IS NOT FREE

In the first years of the Rehnquist Court, Brennan managed to cobble together a majority for his opinions recognizing that flag burning constituted constitutionally protected speech—against the assault first by the state and then by a subsequent federal law, in *Johnson v. Texas* (1989) and *U.S. v. Eichman* (1990), respectively. The dissents of the chief justice, Stevens, White, and Scalia emphasized the importance of the flag as a national symbol and, therefore, that the government could protect it as vital to the nation. Stevens called the flag a "national asset." But if it was a national symbol, was that not because of its expressive value? And if the value of the flag was expressive, then surely its display was no more protected than its misuse under the First Amendment.

The resulting activity in Congress for an amendment to the Constitution protecting the flag ran into snags. Emotionally compelling, it raised the same sort of questions in congressional debate that the Court might have encountered. Henry Hyde compared the flag to "the sacrament in the Catholic Church"—but was that, like the burning of the flag, too extreme an expression? On the other hand, would wearing a flag on a motorcycle gang jacket be desecration? Republicans in Congress seemed to favor the amendment and Democrats to oppose it. Was this simply partisan politics wrapped in patriotic bluster? The argument continued throughout the Rehnquist Court era and after.

After the elder Bush had replaced Brennan and Marshall with more conservative justices, Scalia authored his own explanation of freedom of expression, in *R.A.V. v. City of St. Paul* (1992), joined in whole or in part by the rest of the Court. It was a reprise of *Beauharnais*: the city's ordinances expressly forbade Nazi regalia and Klan cross burning. When the Klan burned a cross on an African American family's lawn, the city prosecuted the Klan members. But the act was symbolic speech, and the code and the prosecution were content-based rather than based on the danger to public order. Although the ordinance contained language about fighting words, it did not require that a disturbance follow the act. Scalia, who believed strongly in free speech, may have overstated himself when he wrote, with his usual panache: "St. Paul has no such authority to license one side of the debate to fight freestyle, while requiring the other to follow Marquess of Queensbury Rules." In any case, every member of the Court weighed in with a concurrence in part or a separate opinion concurring only in the result. Scalia's logic was compelling, but he had lost the majority for his opinion because he would not compromise on it.

Did Scalia's standard apply as well to funded exhibitions? In *National Endowment of the Arts v. Finley* (1998), O'Connor's majority opinion allowed Congress to act as "patron" instead of a "sovereign" to restrict funding of art based on decency standards. Rehnquist's majority opinion in *McConnell v. Federal Election Commission* (2003) allowed Congress to regulate campaign advertisements and funding under the Bipartisan Campaign Reform Act. The chief justice deferred to Congress's "particular expertise" in that area.

One class of free speech cases further complicated these already-tangled rulings—abortion speech. In 1970, the federal government had established a program for family planning under Title X of the Public Health Services Act. It was intended as an alternative to abortion counseling, and one of its provisions required that no funds could go to abortion clinics. In 1988, the last year of Reagan's presidency, personnel, including doctors, at clinics receiving federal money were told that they were not to mention abortion. If asked about it by a client, the health care or social work professional had to say that the clinic did not consider abortion an "appropriate method" of birth control.

Dr. Irving Rust, a New York City practitioner and a recipient of Title X funds, sued the secretary of Health and Human Services, Louis Sullivan, alleging that the regulations the secretary promulgated under the authority of the act violated the terms of the act itself, as well as Dr. Rust's and his patients' free speech and due process rights under the Constitution. The Second Circuit Court of Appeals, sitting in New York City, upheld the restrictions on abortion speech (called a "gag rule" by their opponents) after the First and Third Circuit Courts of Appeals had struck down the same regulations for violating the constitutional rights of doctors and their patients.

When the High Court took the case, Harvard Law School professor Lawrence Tribe argued for Rust. Solicitor General Kenneth Starr argued for the federal government. The majority of the Court concluded that the regulation was not a free speech question. Rehnquist wrote for himself, Souter, White, Kennedy, and Scalia. The act itself was ambiguous on the question of abortion counseling. In light of the ambiguity, the Court had to defer to the interpretation of the statute given it by the federal agency (Health and Human Services) charged with administering the act. The secretary's interpretation was in line with the general purposes of the act and did not violate the free speech rights of the doctors but simply required that referral to abortion services be made outside of the confines of the Title X–funded clinic. The restrictions on doctors' speech did not violate the First Amendment. Nor was the patient's right to an abortion constrained, for she could always go to a family planning center that was not given federal funds—the same option she would have had if Title X did not fund any clinics.

O'Connor dissented. In a single-page opinion, she stated that the secretary had wrongly interpreted his duties under the statute. He had no business telling doctors they could not advise women who needed an abortion that they ought not to have one. O'Connor also joined the first part of a Blackmun and Marshall dissent, in insisting that the government could not attach an unconstitutional requirement to a funding bill and then say, in effect, if you don't want to give up your constitutional rights, don't apply for the funding. The two justices continued, with Stevens now signing on, that the government was using funding as a way to promote one viewpoint on abortion. With heavy-handed irony, they quoted Rehnquist and Scalia opinions that had called free speech a fundamental right.

Abortion speech questions had another side—protests outside clinics. Was that speech protected? Pro-choice litigators used state courts to seek injunctions against anti-abortion rights protestors. In Florida, where the protests were vehement and violent, a state court imposed and the state's highest court upheld an order barring protestors from coming within thirty-six feet of the clinic's entrances or within three hundred feet of individuals entering and leaving, unless the latter indicated their willingness to talk with the protestors. The demonstrators filed suit in the federal courts, alleging that the ban was a violation of their free speech rights. In *Madsen v. Women's Health Center* (1994), the Supreme Court (with Rehnquist writing for himself and for Justices Blackmun, O'Connor, Souter, and Ginsburg, as well as Stevens in part) found that the ban was an acceptable restraint of the demonstrators' speech so long as the ban burdened speech no more than was necessary to serve a "significant government interest." Scalia, Thomas, and Kennedy dissented, arguing that the demonstrators were not engaging in criminal activity and were unlawfully deprived of their free speech rights under the first amendment.

In *Schenck v. Pro-Choice Network* (1997), the Court, voting 8 to 1, invalidated a New York court's "floating buffer zone" of fifteen feet between persons seeking to enter or leave a clinic and all demonstrators. That imposition burdened speech too much. But a fifteen-foot fixed space around entrances was acceptable. Colorado's statute, requiring only eight feet of separation, came before the High Court in January 2000 (*Hill v. Colorado*), on an appeal of the Colorado Supreme Court's decision upholding the law. The Court, in a 6-to-3 opinion, upheld the statute. In his dissent, Justice Scalia asked why a statute could single out antiabortion protestors for restrictions that did not apply to other individuals exercising their right to free speech. When the decision was announced, he read his impassioned dissent in Court. Justices Thomas and Kennedy joined him in dissent.

RELIGIOUS EXERCISES

Free exercise and religious establishment cases continued to bedevil the Court. The majority extended protection to religious films and public money spent for religious purposes, so long as the public authority had opened the space to all or allowed all religious groups to use the funding, in *Lamb's Chapel v. Center Moriches Union Free Schools District* (1993), *Capitol Square Review Board v. Pinette* (1995), *Rosenberger v. Tolerable and Visitors* (1995), *Bowens v. Kendrick* (1988), and *Zobrest v. Catalina Foothills School District* (1993). In a contrary line of cases, the moderates switched sides to strike down a law requiring the teaching of creationism alongside evolution, an invocation at a graduation by a member of the clergy, and a student-led invocation at a football game, in *Edwards v. Aguillard* (1987), *Lee v. Weisman* (1992), and *Santa Fe Independent School District v. Doe* (2000).

The Court found that a judge who prominently displayed the Ten Commandments inside his courthouse violated the Establishment Clause; but public displays of the Ten Commandments along with other Judeo-Christian and Western monuments to law, in *McCreary County, Kentucky v. ACLU* and *Van Orden v. Perry* (2005), were permissible. A crèche inside a courthouse was not allowed, but a menorah outside was, in *County of Allegheny v. ACLU* (1989). Finely calibrated distinctions, like Breyer's between "substantially to promote religion" and "mixed but primarily non-religious purpose," in *McCreary* and *Van Orden*, did not resolve the confusion.

The most striking Court pronouncement on free exercise arose out of an Oregon case. In October 1983, Albert Smith, a Native American drug abuse counselor for an Oregon facility, was fired for using peyote. He had ingested it at an American Indian Church ceremony in which it was part of a regular ritual, but the Oregon Employment Division refused to give him unemployment insurance because peyote use was not legal under state law. He sued, claiming that the state law violated his First Amendment freedom of exercise right. The Oregon courts agreed and ordered that he receive his unemployment insurance, but the attorney general of the state appealed the case to the High Court, insisting that the state's criminal laws were neutral on religion, and that they were police and health regulations that trumped Smith's federal constitutional rights. After two hearings separated by a remand to the Oregon

Supreme Court, on April 17, 1990, Scalia wrote for the majority in *Smith v. Oregon* that Smith's denial of benefits for use of the banned drug was a legitimate exercise of the state's police powers. Only those statutes that directly targeted a particular faith were barred by the First Amendment. Smith and Galen Black, who joined him in the suit, contended "that their religious motivation for using peyote places them beyond the reach of a criminal law that is not specifically directed at their religious practice." This would not fly: "We have never held that an individual's religious beliefs excuse him from compliance with an otherwise valid law prohibiting conduct that the State is free to regulate. On the contrary, the record of more than a century of our free exercise jurisprudence contradicts that proposition."

O'Connor, writing for Brennan, Marshall, and Stevens, concurred in the result but objected to Scalia's sweeping generalization: "The Court today gives no convincing reason to depart from settled First Amendment jurisprudence. There is nothing talismanic about neutral laws of general applicability or general criminal prohibitions, for laws neutral toward religion can coerce a person to violate his religious conscience or intrude upon his religious duties just as effectively as laws aimed at religion." Smith had not made his case for an exemption from the drug laws, but a case could be made, under other facts, that a neutral law on its face could have an unconstitutional impact on religious freedom.

As a result of the case, Oregon changed its law to allow peyote at religious services, and, after much debate, Congress responded with the Religious Freedom Restoration Act, which passed unanimously in the House and 97 to 3 in the Senate. President Clinton signed it into law in November 1993. In the meantime, the federal government amended the American Indian Religious Freedom Act to allow peyote use. But the High Court was not done with the subject. In *City of Boerne v. Flores* (1997), the Court struck down the Religious Freedom Restoration Act as a violation of the principle of separation of powers—Congress assuming an authority to interpret the First and the Fourteenth Amendments that exclusively belonged to the High Court.

FAITH, SEX, AND DEATH

As the doctrinal confusion in *Smith* hinted, the Court had no talismanic answer to religious establishment and religious exercise questions. It found that a law requiring the teaching of creationism in schools was a form of religious establishment, and so violated the First Amendment. But the issues of school vouchers, in *Zelman v. Simmons-Harris* (2002), posed the problem in slightly different fashion. Ohio's state school board, dominated by Republican appointees, and the state legislature, similarly inclined, passed an education bill that would use public funds to pay tuition for private schooling. Many of these schools were religious in orientation and sectarian in focus. Parents who saw the measure as the opening wedge of a religious establishment underwritten by their public tax dollars, brought suit.

The majority of the Court, led by Rehnquist, found that the program was neutral as to religious content, that it had a secular as well as a religious purpose (improving the performance of children in low-rated school districts, particularly black children in financially strapped Cleveland), and that it was entirely based on parental choice. Thus it did not violate the Establishment Clause. Rehnquist ignored the religious question: "Parents who choose a program school in fact receive from the State precisely what parents who choose a community or magnet school receive—the opportunity to send their children largely at state expense to schools they prefer to their local public school."

By contrast, Stevens's dissent went directly to the religious question: "Is a law that authorizes the use of public funds to pay for the indoctrination of thousands of grammar school children in particular religious faiths a 'law respecting an establishment of religion' within the meaning of the First Amendment?" Breyer, Souter, and Ginsburg joined Stevens. The fact that many different religious groups and churches might benefit from the public funds did not matter—the use of public funds for religious education should itself be barred.

The issue of legal recognition for gay and lesbian unions entered the public debate in the late 1980s and early 1990s. The emergence of gay, lesbian, and transgendered activism came too late to be included in the iconic Civil Rights Act of 1964 or in the rights revolution case law—at that time it would have seemed beyond the pale. But these cases began to arrive in the Rehnquist era. They reflected the social and cultural coming-out of an entire segment of the population. TV shows like *Will and Grace*, *Queer Eye for the Straight Guy*, *Queer as Folk*, and *The L Word*, the play *Angels in America*, and sympathetic movie portrayals of gays in *Philadelphia* and *Brokeback Mountain* all publicized the world of gay and lesbian activity.

At the same time, private individuals' quests for constitutional protections against discrimination based on their sexual preferences drew the fire of conservative and evangelical groups, which were concerned that modern gay culture corrupted family values. Sometimes this concern, as when children's characters like Teletubby and SpongeBob SquarePants were targeted by media conservatives, seemed trifling, but efforts to revise state constitutions and pass state laws denouncing gay marriage were anything but trivial. Some political writers claimed that the 2004 presidential election in the end was determined by the issue of gay marriage bans in state constitutions.

The Rehnquist majority put aside its deference to state law when it came to antidiscrimination statutes that included sexual orientation. New Jersey forbade discrimination on the basis of sexual orientation, but the Boy Scouts of America wanted a gay scoutmaster named James Dale out. Although the New Jersey Supreme Court upheld the state law against the Scouts challenge, by a 5-to-4 vote the High Court found that the Scouts had a First Amendment right of association to decide who could be a scoutmaster. The state argued that his dismissal was a form of prejudice, and counsel for the Scouts agreed—prejudice against immorality as the Scouts organization defined morality. Thus a public definition of morality, based on nondiscrimination, confronted a private definition of morality, based on discrimination. The Court had already knocked down a Colorado law that would have prevented any municipality from protecting gays from discrimination from job or housing discrimination—but Colorado was a public entity, not a private association. The Court already had forced the Jaycees and the Rotary to admit female members.

In *Boy Scouts of America v. Dale* (2000), Chief Justice Rehnquist, joined by Kennedy, Scalia, Thomas, and O'Connor, explained. Dale was not just gay, he was openly gay, and he advocated that Boy Scouts need gay role models. The Scouts organization had a First Amendment "freedom of association" right to require that scoutmasters and Scouts conform to the teachings of the organization or leave it. This freedom of association incorporated a freedom of expression that was opposite to the intuitive notion of freedom of speech. In order that the organization be free to impress its "mission" and message on the Scouts, it must have the power to expel those whose words or deeds undermined the Scouting mission, as the national organization defined it. The First Amendment thus became grounds to deny free speech to Dale and assure it to the Boy Scouts of America. "Given that the Boy Scouts [organization] engages in expressive activity, we must determine whether the forced inclusion of Dale as an assistant scoutmaster would significantly affect the Boy Scouts' ability to advocate public or private viewpoints. This inquiry necessarily requires us first to explore, to a limited extent, the nature of the Boy Scouts' view of homosexuality." The national organization regarded homosexuality as unclean and immoral. Rehnquist could not restrain himself from a shot across Stevens's bow: "Justice Stevens's dissent makes much of its observation that the public perception of homosexuality in this country has changed. Indeed, it appears that homosexuality has gained greater societal acceptance. But this is scarcely an argument for denying First Amendment protection to those [the Scout organization] who refuse to accept these views." Ginsburg, Breyer, and Souter joined Stevens's dissent.

The Court's decision in *Lawrence v. Texas* (2003), striking down a Texas law making consensual adult homosexual activity a crime, resembled the Colorado case rather than the New Jersey litigation. Justice Kennedy declared that "liberty protects the person from unwarranted government intrusion into a dwelling or other private places. In our tradition the State is not omnipresent in the home." This overruled White's declaration in *Bowers v. Hardwick* (1986) and extended privacy rights beyond *Griswold.* This time, Rehnquist, Thomas, and Scalia were in the minority.

The High Court's refusal, on six separate occasions, to review the lower federal court ruling, in *Schiavo ex rel. Schindler v. Schiavo* (2005), despite pressure from the Republican Congress, the Republican governor of Florida, Jeb Bush, brother of the president, and the religious right's litigation firms, rested on the Court's earlier right-to-die decisions. The husband's decision, based on his semicomatose wife's wishes, to remove a feeding tube, was much like a do-not-resuscitate clause in a living will.

The Court had already ruled on the constitutional right to die. Rehnquist's majority had held, in *Cruzan v. Director, Missouri Department of Health* (1990), that an individual had a right to a do-not-resuscitate order but that the state could require clear and convincing evidence of a person's wish to die rather than be kept alive artificially. Nancy Cruzan needed to have anticipated this situation and provided a signed, preferably notarized, document to this effect. Washington's law forbidding doctors from participating in euthanasia was upheld, in *Washington v. Glucksberg* (1997). The bottom line was that there was no constitutional right to assisted suicide; it was up to the states to decide.

Terri Schiavo's brother and parents objected to the High Court's refusal to hear the case, however, and the case had become a media circus, complete with high-wire legal acts, three rings of religious supporters, and two chambers of congressmen looking for news-bites. When the feeding tube was removed, on March 18, 2005, she had been brain-dead for years. Her death from dehydration came almost two weeks later. In the interim, led by Republican congressman Tom DeLay, members of both houses demanded that Congress have the power to override any court decision. The movement to so amend the federal Constitution never got off the ground, in part because it was such a clear violation of separation of powers.

EMINENT DOMAIN AND THE TAKINGS CLAUSE

One might have expected that private property would trump public use on the Rehnquist Court. But here, too, the justices sent a mixed message. In the cases of *Nollan v. California Coastal Commission* (1987)—in which householders on the beach fought and won against a state law requiring that they permit public access to the water's edge, *Lucas v. South Carolina Coastal Council* (1992)—in which a Carolina landowner wanted relief from a state environmental law forbidding building on the shore and got it, and *Dolan v. City of Tigard, Oregon* (1994)—in which a businesswoman successfully objected to the city's requirements for a renovation permit, including that a portion of her land be used for a bike and hiking trail, the Court showed a concern for private property rights. Rehnquist wrote in *Dolan* that under a rational-relation test, the lowest level of scrutiny, the 15 percent set-aside for public use might be acceptable, but it was not acceptable to Rehnquist, so he imposed a more rigorous test and found the law, and the set-aside of land, an unconstitutional taking.

In these cases, the Scalia- and Rehnquist-led majorities reinvigorated the Takings Clause. Local and state regulatory procedures that required property owners to provide public accommodations, such as a path to the beach, received a higher level of review than the rational-relation test, under Scalia's "substantially advanced a state interest" test (the middle level of scrutiny originated to hear sex discrimination suits).

Souter, Blackmun, Ginsburg, and Stevens dissented, with Stevens writing in *Dolan* that "the mountain of briefs that the case has generated nevertheless makes it obvious that the pecuniary value of her victory is far less important than the rule of law that this case has been used to establish. It is unquestionably an important case." Why? Because the city of Portland is choked by automobile traffic? Because the Carolina and California coastlines are endangered by private land misusers? "The Court's narrow focus on one strand in the property owner's bundle of rights is particularly misguided in a case involving the development of commercial property." Stevens reasoned that commercial property always has one foot in the public interest.

Stevens had one more string to his bow—deference to the states—and he aimed the arrow at the chief justice. In the ongoing sniping at one another's consistency that he and Rehnquist engaged in, Stevens cited the chief justice's views on federalism and restraint: "The Court has made a serious error by abandoning the traditional presumption of constitutionality and imposing a novel burden of proof on a city implementing an admittedly valid comprehensive land use plan. Even more consequential than its incorrect disposition of this case, however, is the Court's resurrection of a species of substantive due process analysis that it firmly rejected decades ago."

But *Susette Kelo v. City of New London* (2005) seemed to dismantle all that Rehnquist's majority had constructed in the earlier takings cases. New London, Connecticut, had a waterfront that was rusting into decay and dotted with old houses. The city's tax base was shrinking and its infrastructure was deteriorating. One way to upgrade this private property (and increase the city's tax base) was to turn the Long Island Sound waterfront into upscale housing and commercial real estate. Under a permissive state law, the city condemned the houses on the waterfront and offered the site for commercial "redevelopment."

Kelo and the other homeowners on the shore might have expected that the Court's Takings and Due Process Clause precedents would stop the city in its tracks. But in *Kelo*, a Stevens-led majority went in the opposite direction. In short, taking private property "to increase tax and other revenues, and to re-vitalize . . . [the] economically distressed city" was a "public use" exception to the Fifth Amendment, even when the city itself was not the redeveloper. Could the city then take anyone's real estate and give it to a wealthier owner, so long as the city got more taxes from the new owner? "A state may transfer property from one private party to another if future 'use by the public' is the purpose of the taking." But should increased tax revenues constitute such a "public use"?

The property condemned was not in total decay. It simply was not bring-ing in enough income. "There is no allegation that any of these properties is blighted or otherwise in poor condition; rather, they were condemned only because they happen to be located in the development area." What could be more ideal, or idyllic, than family-owned homes well maintained? Stevens had an answer: The city's "determination that the area was sufficiently distressed to justify a program of economic rejuvenation is entitled to our deference. The City has carefully formulated an economic development plan that it be-lieves will provide appreciable benefits to the community, including—but by no means limited to—new jobs and increased tax revenue." Progress trumped the American tradition of home ownership.

O'Connor, Rehnquist, Scalia, and Thomas dissented. O'Connor wrote: "Today the Court abandons this long-held, basic limitation on government power. Under the banner of economic development, all private property is now vulnerable to being taken and transferred to another private owner, so long as it might be upgraded—i.e., given to an owner who will use it in a way that the legislature deems more beneficial to the public—in the process."

But Kennedy had deserted his conservative colleagues. And he was again the swing vote in cases involving abortion rights. These cases, more than downtown redevelopment, had become a critical test for every session of the Court.

THE LITMUS TEST OF ABORTION RIGHTS

It was in the area of women's reproductive rights that the Rehnquist Court most severely and bitterly divided. O'Connor led the Court majority in examining whether a state regulation "unduly burdened" women seeking abortions, in *Webster v. Reproductive Services* (1989). This was followed by *Casey v. Planned Parenthood* (1992), a compromise that failed to overturn *Roe* outright but shifted its basis. Blackmun would not concede to this compromise, however, and neither would Rehnquist and Scalia.

In 1986, Missouri passed the third generation of its antiabortion laws. The new statute included twenty provisions, seven of which had already been struck down by the Court in earlier cases. There was a preamble to the act, labeled a "finding" by the legislature, that the "life of each human being begins at conception" and that "unborn children have protectable interests in life, health, and well-being." Additional provisions required that all abortions after the sixteenth week be performed in hospitals, that no public hospital or public hospital worker was to take part in an abortion, nor were public hospitals to expend funds on abortions, nor were doctors at these facilities to advise anyone to have an abortion, to advise that an abortion was available, or to advise that one might be preferable to continuing the pregnancy, even if the pregnancy was in trouble. This was part of the legislatively scripted "informed consent" that the doctor was required to read to the patient and the patient was required to sign, even though such scripts had been rejected by the Court in earlier cases.

A final provision required doctors to ascertain, through a series of tests, whether a fetus was viable. Missouri required its physicians to determine lung size, and the only sure test for lung size, amniocentesis, was both expensive and dangerous to the mother and the fetus. In effect, the state was telling doctors that it was more important to the state to determine the viability of the fetus than to ensure the health of the woman, or rather, that the potentially viable fetus was the doctor's primary patient until proven otherwise.

Lower federal courts temporarily enjoined enforcement of seven provisions of the act, finding that they were unconstitutional. The Eighth Circuit Court of Appeals affirmed the district court's ruling and made the injunction permanent. The state appealed the lower courts' findings on the preamble, the twentieth-week testing, and the use of public personnel, but did not contest the ban on the scripted informed consent or the ban on the use of hospitals after the sixteenth week of pregnancy. The High Court could reinstate all or part of the provisions of the Missouri law or affirm the lower courts. But William Webster, the attorney general of Missouri, wanted more. He asked the Court to overturn *Roe*.

Advocates for both sides took to the streets. Operation Rescue, a pro-life organization, staged demonstrations in the District of Columbia, and the National Right to Life Committee led a publicity campaign. In January 1989, 65,000 pro-life marchers filled the streets of the District of Columbia. Three months later, pro-choice groups staged their own march, attracting half a million supporters to the Capitol steps and the Mall. Seventy-eight "friends of the Court" submitted briefs, twenty more than any previous case. One of the briefs in favor of upholding the circuit court rested heavily on the work of historian James Mohr, and it had gained support from 286 other historians.

During oral arguments, Charles Fried, the departing U.S. solicitor general, joined Webster's demand for reversal of *Roe*. He did not want the Court to roll back all the privacy rights—he did not challenge *Griswold*—but rather he wanted the Court "to pull this one thread." Frank Susman, a veteran pro-choice counsel, represented St. Louis's oldest abortion clinic, Reproductive Health Services. He began by challenging Fried's metaphorical "single thread"—in his experience, he argued, when he pulled a thread, the whole sleeve unraveled. Wouldn't that happen to privacy rights if *Roe* were reversed?

Chief Justice Rehnquist had waited seventeen years for this case, since his dissent in *Roe*. More recently, he had secured majorities to rewrite *Roe*'s trimester formula. But never, not until *Webster*, had a state attorney general and a former U.S. solicitor general stood before the bench and asked that *Roe* be overturned. At the conference on April 28, he spoke first and announced that he "disagreed with *Roe*." The lower courts' rulings should be reversed. White agreed, but O'Connor was hesitant. *Roe* should not be overturned—the Missouri rules, with the exception of the doctors' tests, fit within *Roe*. Scalia joined Rehnquist and White. Kennedy thought that the Missouri rules passed muster, but he had qualms about saying more, for *Roe* was a long-settled precedent and he believed in stare decisis—"let the prior decision stand"—a pillar of American common-law adjudication. Stevens seemed to waver—perhaps Missouri had not gone too far. Only Blackmun, Brennan, and Marshall would have upheld the lower courts' injunctions against all the rules.

Rehnquist assigned himself the opinion but could only muster White and Kennedy to uphold all of the provisions that the state wanted to retain. And he could not get a majority to topple *Roe*. Only Scalia was willing to join White and the chief justice in that position. Rehnquist had to content himself with a dictum—that the "rigid" trimester formula of *Roe* was wrong. The state's interest in fetal life should commence with conception. But he did not carry the logic of the dictum to its natural end. Instead of writing that the Court had to overrule *Roe*, he backpedaled: The "facts of the present case, however, differ from those at issue in *Roe*. Then the state had made all abortions a crime. Here the state had merely regulated abortion."

O'Connor's refusal to join any opinion overturning *Roe* had reduced Rehnquist's core following from five members of the Court to four. Her concurring opinion agreed that the tests on the fetus were permissible, but she did not read them to narrow *Roe* at all. There was no compulsion involved; a doctor could skip one or more of the tests if he or she did not need them. And if done properly, they did not impose an undue burden on a woman's choice. The preamble would have no effect on women's rights. She approvingly noted Rehnquist's reference to the "undue burden" test she had long before proposed—and reiterated that it did not conflict with *Roe*.

Scalia rejected the "judicial statesmanship" of the chief justice, for it "needlessly prolonged" the Court's entrapment in a field "where it has little proper business." The abortion question was to Scalia a political one, not a legal one, and best left to the legislatures. This posture would allow Missouri to pass any law on abortion, including a permanent and total ban. O'Connor's praise of judicial restraint (whether her own or Rehnquist's) in refusing to overrule *Roe*, Scalia believed "cannot be taken seriously."

Pennsylvania offered the next chance for the Court to decide that a woman had no constitutionally protected right to end a pregnancy. Its 1988 law, like Missouri's, included provisions that the Supreme Court had nullified in earlier cases. In effect, the two states' legislatures treated the Court as just another group of politicians and the Court's precedents as though they were entirely political rather than based on fundamental law. As the Court moved to the right, Pennsylvania hoped that the Court would ignore its own precedents and simply vote its new majority's personal views into law.

The Pennsylvania statute included a twenty-four-hour waiting period—and a scripted informed consent in which the doctor was to review all the alternatives to abortion for his patient and remind her that the state could secure child support from the father. The statute also required a minor to notify her parent and her spouse (with a judicial bypass option according to which a judge could allow the procedure without notification), or to sign a written statement that she had notified or tried to notify her spouse. Also required was the gathering of information on patients that could, under certain circumstances, become public.

Casey arrived at the Supreme Court in 1992 and, given the makeup of the High Court, seemed to be the case that Rehnquist and White, joined now by Thomas, Scalia, Kennedy, and Souter (if not O'Connor), needed in order to reverse *Roe*. U.S. Solicitor General Kenneth Starr joined Pennsylvania to present President Bush's support for the regulations. Starr argued that after twenty years of *Roe* the Court still did not have a governing standard for reviewing abortion cases and hoped that the plurality opinion in *Webster* would become that standard. Justice White stepped in to ask Starr: Why let *Roe* stand at all if the state had an interest in the life of the fetus from its inception? If the state's interest was rational, would not a total prohibition on abortion follow?

For in *Casey*, the anti-*Roe* members of the Court believed they had found a vehicle to narrow *Roe* to its own facts (in short, the state cannot criminalize all abortions), but they were to be disappointed. In private meetings in chambers, O'Connor, Kennedy, and Souter joined Blackmun and Stevens in protecting the right to an abortion. The first three issued a "joint opinion" that accepted all but one of Pennsylvania's regulations (the one on spousal approval), but upheld *Roe*.

Kennedy opened the joint opinion: "A jurisprudence of doubt" pervaded the Court's rulings on abortion. He wanted it ended. "The essential holding of *Roe v. Wade* should be retained and once again reaffirmed." Instead of asserting that the state knew what was best for women, or that men knew what was moral for women, he wrote: "Her suffering [in pregnancy] is too intimate and personal for the State to insist . . . upon its own vision of the woman's role." Souter's portion of the joint opinion on stare decisis followed. When confronted with a call to overturn well-settled precedent, the Court must engage in "a series of prudential and pragmatic considerations." Had related principles of law so changed or the world so altered that the old rule no longer had "significant application or justification"? Clearly not. "The inquiry into reliance [on precedent] counts the cost of a rule's repudiation as it would fall on those who have relied reasonably on the rule's continued application. . . . The ability of women to participate equally in the economic and social life of the Nation has been facilitated by their ability to control their reproductive lives." Justice O'Connor concluded the joint opinion with the reasons why the provisions of the Pennsylvania law (less the spousal notification requirement) passed muster under the "undue burden" test.

But the joint opinion did not settle the issues or quiet the controversy. Abortion rights continued to divide the nation. Pro-life groups would not compromise and pro-choice groups would not abandon *Roe*. During the Clinton presidency, pro-life members of Congress joined with pro-life advocates around the country to focus on the "dilation and extraction" abortion procedure in the second trimester. Calling this a "partial birth abortion" and graphically depicting how it dismembered already formed fetuses in the birth canal (a procedure doctors employed to reduce the risk of damage to the patient's uterus), pro-life legislators banned it in Nebraska. In *Stenberg v. Carhart* (2000), a sharply divided Court found that the poorly drafted Nebraska statute barring the procedure placed an "undue burden upon a woman's right to make an abortion decision." The statute did not have an exception for a woman's health. Clinton vetoed a similar bill when Congress passed it, but, in 2003, George W. Bush signed it.

CRIME AND PUNISHMENT

If constitutionally protected human life began with conception, could a state incarcerate women thought likely to injure their prospective newborns by smoking, drinking alcohol, or failing to obtain proper prenatal care? One state—South Carolina—thought so. It was an addition to American criminal law with frightening potential, a kind of gender-based "1984." How might the Court respond to it? Clues lay in the Rehnquist Court's decisions on criminal procedure.

America's "War on Crime" in the Reagan and Bush years eventually rivaled education in terms of dollars spent, and the list of offenses (primarily drug-related) and people involved grew to be huge. Up to his last days, Rehnquist tried to lead the Court to narrow the reach of *Miranda*, *Mapp*, and other procedural guarantee cases. From 2003 to 2005, the chief justice was in the majority in all eleven criminal justice 5-to-4 decisions expanding exceptions to the exclusionary rule and dissented in all nine of the 5-to-4 cases that reversed or remanded cases in which police or prosecutorial misconduct was alleged. As the splits in voting in these cases indicate, however, his Court disappointed the most extreme of the law and order advocates.

In *Whren v. U.S.* (1996), police officers driving unmarked cars received permission to pull over cars for traffic offenses so they could search for drugs. In *Atwater v. Lago Vista* (2001), arresting, handcuffing, booking, and incarcerating suspects for minor offenses, in this case, for no seat belts, was found constitutional. Majorities fashioned more exceptions to the exclusionary rule. The Court, per a Scalia opinion, extended the doctrine of the "independent source"—federal agents entered a warehouse prior to attaining a warrant, in *Murray v. U.S.* (1988). In *California v. Greenwood* (1988), police could search anything shared with others such as someone's garbage that was inside black, closed bags placed on the curb for pick up.

The Miranda warnings had become such a familiar object in the law and order landscape, as the chief wrote in *Dickerson v. U.S.* (2000), that there was no need to revisit the subject. Rehnquist offered two rationales. First, he did not want to produce chaos in the system. Second, he understood that the general public needed to see at least the semblance of a staged process, a cool deliberation, and the occasional check on authority in order to believe in the system. For the public had seen that the rush to judgment, particularly in capital cases, had led to many miscarriages of justice. The "Innocence Project" deployed DNA evidence to demonstrate that many on death row could not have committed the crimes for which they were convicted. Several state governors and even a few state legislatures were aghast at these prosecutorial errors.

But potential miscarriage of justice was no grounds for reversal or remand. In *Herrera v. Collins* (1993), the majority held that a man who produced exculpatory evidence after he received the death sentence could not get relief from the U.S. Supreme Court. Rehnquist's opinion found that the six affidavits attesting that Herrera's older brother had actually committed the two murders of police officers were not sufficient to convince the Court of "actual innocence." Herrera's confession after being hospitalized for the beating he had received upon arrest did not meet the old shock-the-conscience test. Rehnquist explained: "Herrera's showing of innocence falls far short of the threshold showing which would have to be made in order to trigger relief. That threshold would necessarily be extraordinarily high because of the very disruptive effect that entertaining such claims would have on the need for finality in capital cases, and the enormous burden that having to retry cases based on often stale evidence would place on the States." To intervene would have been to undermine confidence in Texas's criminal justice system and to violate federal-state boundaries. If the Court began to remand such cases, surely it would be inundated with thousands more. Texas executed Herrera.

The sternest test of the Rehnquist Court's law and order jurisprudence came after 9/11. In pursuing the "War on Terror," President George W. Bush not only committed the United States to the invasion of Afghanistan and Iraq, but also to a policy of the indefinite detention of all those the president classified as either enemy combatants or would-be terrorists. Congress passed the Patriot Act in 2003, which gave the president plenary judicial power to search, seize, detain, and interrogate suspected terrorists and illegal combatants without trial, counsel, and the other elements of due process. In four cases, Attorney General John Ashcroft and then Attorney General Alberto Gonzales argued that the Executive Power Clause of Article II of the U.S. Constitution allowed the president to indefinitely detain suspects whom only the president need determine as suspects, without access to attorneys or courts, to conduct surveillance on all foreign telephone calls, and, when the president so decided, to prosecute any or all of these individuals without the use of civil procedural safeguards. He was to be the ultimate judge of his own authority to pursue these actions.

Justice Jackson had written that the constitutional guarantee of rights was not "a suicide pact." The nation's government had legitimate cause to worry about future terrorist attacks. But the Rehnquist Court had mixed reactions to detentions and trials ordered by the president. In *Hamdi v. Rumsfeld, Rasul v. Bush,* and *Al Odah v. U.S.* (2004), the majority opinions held that the detainees must be allowed access to courts to challenge their detentions. O'Connor's majority opinion in *Hamdi* affirmed the president's power to protect the nation from immediate threat but also reminded that "history and common sense teach us that an unchecked system of detention carries the potential to become a means for oppression and abuse of others who do not present that sort of threat." In *Padilla v. Rumsfeld* (2004), the majority's insistence on proper identification of defendants in the lawsuits restated the ideal of due process. The Court's majority did not insist on any standard of substantive, that is either criminal or military justice, but did require a modicum of procedural fairness. However, the Court did not act to prevent the removal by stealth of suspected terrorists to foreign countries, where the suspects might be tortured.

CHECKS AND BALANCE (SHEETS)

President Reagan's new federalism, redressing the perceived imbalance between the national and state governments, had always been close to Rehnquist's heart. This redress took a variety of forms: a resuscitation of state-action doctrine in analysis of Fourteenth Amendment claims, strengthening state immunity from lawsuits, and a renewed interest in the limits of the Interstate Commerce Clause.

State-action doctrine arose under the Enforcement Acts cases *Reese* and *Cruikshank.* For a suit against a state to raise a Fourteenth Amendment claim, a state needs to make some affirmative move that violates the rights of the plaintiff. Simply standing by while a private party behaves abhorrently does not constitute a punishable act. Thus when the Warren Court found the Civil Rights Act of 1964 constitutional, it did an end run around state action, laying the legality of Congress's action on the Commerce Clause.

In addition to resurrecting state action to limit federal intervention in a slew of school districting and personal injury cases, the Rehnquist majority opinion applied it to state agencies themselves, in *DeShaney v. Winnebago County Social Services Dept.* (1989). A county social worker did not remove a little boy from his natural father's care despite the obvious signs of physical abuse and previous complaints. When the four-year-old boy turned up beaten so severely by his father that the boy had permanent mental retardation, his mother, divorced from the father and living in a different state, sued the county in federal court.

Following the district and appeals courts' rulings, Rehnquist's majority agreed that the Due Process Clause served as "a limitation on the State's power to act, not as a guarantee of certain minimal levels of safety and security." The case was a "tragic one," Rehnquist wrote, for the county social services knew of the danger and had intervened before the final beating. The father was convicted for the beating and jailed. But the requirement for state action, triggering due process protection, was missing in *DeShaney*. The father, a private actor, not the state, was at fault: "The Due Process Clauses generally confer no affirmative right to governmental aid, even where such aid may be necessary to secure life, liberty, or property interests of which the government itself may not deprive the individual." For if Wisconsin was liable in this case, might not police forces be liable when they failed to stop a crime of which they had prior knowledge, or a public hospital when it failed to provide any care for a sick or injured person?

Brennan, Marshall, and Blackmun dissented: "It may well be, as the Court decides, that the Due Process Clause . . . creates no general right to basic governmental services. That, however, is not the question presented here." Brennan's dissent looked for other grounds for the suit. In an analogy to old English common-law precepts of tort liability—that when someone has begun to act, and then has stopped, the person is liable for not finishing what was begun—Brennan argued: "I would focus first on the action that Wisconsin has taken with respect to Joshua and children like him, rather than on the actions that the State failed to take. . . . Wisconsin has established a child-welfare system specifically designed to help children like Joshua. Wisconsin law places upon the local departments of social services such as respondent a duty to investigate reported instances of child abuse." Under Wisconsin's own law, Brennan found the state liable. One more step, the fact that the federal district court was required by the Judiciary Acts to apply Wisconsin law in this diversity suit, would have led to victory for the petitioners.

Usrey and *DeShaney* were the harbingers of new federalism on the Rehnquist Court. In the 1990s, the Rehnquist majority reminded litigants that state governments that did not consent to be sued were immune from liability. Under the Eleventh Amendment, no state could be sued in a federal court by a citizen of another state. Rehnquist extended this to citizens suing their own state. The federal government had waived its sovereign immunity under the Tucker Act of 1887 (suits for breach of express or implied contracts) and the Federal Tort Claims Act of 1946 (suits against federal officers who are negligent), and many states had passed similar legislation. But parties could not use the federal courts to sue states under federal laws, according to *Seminole Tribe of Florida v. Florida* (1996), even on a federal question. The same Rehnquist-led majority joined in *Alden v. Maine* (1999): "We hold that the powers delegated to Congress under Article I of the United States Constitution do not include the power to subject nonconsenting States to private suits for damages in state courts." The result was that state governments were increasingly insulated from lawsuits.

Justice Kennedy's opinion for the Court in *Alden* made an originalist claim: "[As] the Constitution's structure, and its history, and the authoritative interpretations by this Court make clear, the States' immunity from suit is a fundamental aspect of the sovereignty which the States enjoyed before the ratification of the Constitution, and which they retain today." Kennedy's history was not quite right (the founders did not regard state sovereignty as conferring immunity from suit—see *Chisholm* in chapter 2). In dissent for himself, Breyer, Stevens, and Ginsburg, Justice Souter raised the banner of the living Constitution: "The Court's federalism ignores the accepted authority of Congress to bind States . . . and to provide for enforcement of federal rights in state court. The Court's history simply disparages the capacity of the Constitution to order relationships in a Republic that has changed since the founding."

In cases like *U.S. v. Lopez* (1995) and *New York v. U.S.* (1992), the new federalism limited what Congress could do under the Commerce Clause. Rehnquist conceded that the later New Deal Court had allowed Congress great latitude under the Commerce Clause: "In part, this was a recognition of the great changes that had occurred in the way business was carried on in this country. Enterprises that had once been local or at most regional in nature had become national in scope. . . . But even these modern-era precedents which have expanded congressional power under the Commerce Clause confirm that this power is subject to outer limits."

Rehnquist's opinion devoted much space to refutation of the dissenters' writing and closed with a barely concealed exasperation: "We decline here to proceed any further. To do so would require us to conclude that the Constitution's enumeration of powers does not presuppose something not enumerated, and that there never will be a distinction between what is truly national and what is truly local. This we are unwilling to do."

Justice Kennedy's concurrence was more measured:

The history of the judicial struggle to interpret the Commerce Clause during the transition from the economic system the Founders knew to the single, national market still emergent in our own era counsels great restraint before the Court determines that the Clause is insufficient to support an exercise of the national power. That history gives me some pause about today's decision, but I join the Court's opinion with these observations on what I conceive to be its necessary though limited holding.

How limited? The Civil Rights Act of 1964 was sacrosanct (Rehnquist explicitly said so in *Lopez*), but into the dustbin went the Violence against Women Act, the Gun Free School Zones Act, an environmental protection regulation concerning the disposal of hazardous waste, and the requirement that local sheriffs perform handgun registration searches under the Brady Act. What states would not do, Congress could not impose on them.

POLITICS BY OTHER MEANS?

Though Rehnquist attempted at all times to keep the Court from acting or even looking like a partisan political body, in at least three cases the Court stepped into the political firestorm of the 1990s. The first case, *Clinton v. Jones* (1997), raised the question of whether a sitting president could be sued for an action entirely unrelated to and antedating his presidency. When the unanimous Court per a decision from Stevens found that the Constitution said nothing directly on the topic, the justices held that a president could be so treated.

Consistent with a line of cases limiting presidential immunity, Stevens wrote: "The burden on the President's time and energy that is a mere by-product of such review surely cannot be considered as onerous as the direct burden imposed by judicial review and the occasional invalidation of his official actions." The subsequent legal proceedings' "mere by-product" nearly brought down the Clinton presidency, preoccupied the nation's news media for well over two years, materially damaged the functioning of the White House for a significant part of that period, pushed Bill Clinton and his wife, Hillary

Rodham Clinton, into near-bankruptcy, and severely damaged the chances for Clinton's vice president, Al Gore, to win the presidency in 2000.

Jones opened the door to a constitutional crisis and allowed the politically supercharged "Class of 1994" in the House of Representatives to impeach the president of the United States for lying under oath in a deposition about events that did not even touch the *Jones* suit, much less his conduct as president. Whipping up public outrage at the president's misconduct with a twenty-two-year-old White House intern into a froth of righteous indignation, the congressional Republicans voted as a bloc to prosecute Clinton for "high crimes and misdemeanors." Historians and law professors warned that there were no grounds for conviction, but the lower house named prosecutors and the Senate held a trial. Chief Justice Rehnquist presided at the Senate trial and ruled that the senators were not only jurors, but also judges. They could decide what in law was impeachable. They declined to find Clinton guilty of any impeachable offenses. The Senate majority and minority leaders presented Rehnquist with a plaque and congratulated him for impartially presiding over the proceeding.

The Court's next opportunity to prove its nonpartisanship was controversial from the moment the justices decided they would hear the case. The election of 2000 ended in splendid confusion, as the key Florida electoral votes seemed up for grabs. Claims of voter fraud flew as early closings of polls denied to African Americans their franchise and senior citizens in South Florida discovered that defective ballots left them voting for a third-party candidate rather than the candidate of their choice. Were Democratic voters in the sunshine state's cities denied their franchise by misleading and defective ballots? The nation sat transfixed as a recount of the "hanging chads" on ballots left election officials cross-eyed and lawyers brought suits to end the recount or extend it in Florida courts.

When *Bush v. Gore* arrived at the High Court, all eyes were on the nine justices. In oral argument and behind closed doors they debated the dictates of the Fifteenth Amendment and the respective jurisdictions of the Florida Supreme Court, the Florida legislature, and the U.S. Supreme Court. In the end, the Court decided that the putative winner of the election, George W. Bush, would be irreparably harmed if the Florida Supreme Court's order for a recount was allowed to proceed differently in each county beyond the state's safe harbor deadline of December 12, a deadline set under the auspices of federal law. Then, the per curiam opinion narrowed the case to its facts: "Our consideration is limited to the present circumstances, for the problem of equal protection in election processes generally presents many complexities."

Frankfurter's insistence that the Court deny itself jurisdiction over political questions here had its most striking test. To Democrats, it looked as if the five justices of the majority (all Republican appointees) substituted their own vote for that of the voters of Florida. Though a news organization–sponsored review of the ballots conducted substantially afterward revealed that Gore could only have won using the least restrictive standard, one he had not asked for, the case cast a pall over the Rehnquist Court legacy.

After September 11, 2001, the Court faced a new set of highly politicized cases. As President George W. Bush and the Republicans stressed the wartime status of the nation, the Court rediscovered executive privilege. It overturned an appellate decision denying Vice President Dick Cheney's claim of privilege. A coalition of environmental and public interest groups sought access to the records of Cheney's energy task force meetings with energy producers in *Cheney v. USDC for District of Columbia* (2004). Kennedy's majority opinion cited both *Nixon v. U.S.* and *Jones v. Clinton* in support of this denial, odd bedfellows surely for a decision extending executive privilege rather than limiting it.

From this line of cases, one might conclude that the Republican majority on the Court constituted the most enduring Republican legacy of the Reagan revolution. The Rehnquist Court found no executive privilege for a Democratic president and then cited the same case to find it for a presidential task force headed by the vice president with no decision-making authority. Some critics observed that a partisan majority of the Court bent over backward to let the Bush administration claim a privilege for information that was advisory on the basis that it was so valuable to the functioning of the executive branch no one might see it. As Alice concluded of the laws of Wonderland, "curiouser and curiouser."

When William Hubbs Rehnquist succumbed to thyroid cancer in September 2005, he left behind a mixed and controversial legacy. The stable divisions on the Court, often splitting 5 to 4, made it the most contentious in the history of the Court, exceeding even the Hughes, Stone, and Burger Courts. Moreover, the case law of the chief justice's majority did not exhibit consistent support for the new federalism, judicial restraint, and private property rights. Instead, a slender majority that the chief justice led followed an instrumentalist, results-oriented course. Constitutional law expert Stephen Gottlieb concluded that this majority "returned the law to the way it stood some seventy years ago, in the early years of the Roosevelt administration."

But when Kennedy or O'Connor joined Souter, Stevens, Ginsburg, and Breyer, the Court seemed entirely modern, protecting antidiscrimination statutes, women's and minorities' rights, and other post–New Deal initiatives. Thus it is not the retrogressive nature of the Rehnquist Court, so much as its weaving and tacking on the law, that remains its most obvious contribution. In other words, it did not leave a legacy. As Peter Irons presciently wrote, ten years before Rehnquist died, "There will never be a 'Rehnquist Court'" in the sense that there was a Marshall Court or a Warren Court.

At the same time, insofar as its wayward course through constitutional law can be tied to the political attachments and policy objectives of the justices themselves, the Rehnquist Court does have a precedent—the Chase Court, in which politics divided the Court and dictated the shape of its jurisprudence.

The Court Today and Tomorrow

You have decided that you want to appeal your case to the Supreme Court. What must you do to be heard? The High Court speaks as an oracle of the law, but it also stands atop a bureaucratic pyramid. At the feet of the justices sit their clerks. The four administrative officials who occupy the next layer are the clerk of the Court, the reporter of its decisions, the marshal, and the librarian. The Court has its own legal affairs office. Each of these miniature bureaucracies has a staff and offices. To reach this level, you must run the gamut of rules for appealing to the Court, in part set by Congress, in part by the Court itself. Of the many thousands of appeals that come to the Court each year (currently nearly ten thousand), only a few hundred will gain the attention of Chief Justice John G. Roberts's Court.

THROUGH THE LABYRINTH

The justices' clerk system emerged at the end of the nineteenth century and has evolved greatly over time. The clerks are the justices' personal helpers. In 1882, Justice Horace Gray began hiring Harvard Law School graduates to assist him. In 1922, Congress provided funds for each justice to select one clerk. Today, each justice has three or four clerks coming from a thousand applicants. Some justices have used law professors to select clerks for them. Professor Frankfurter, while at Harvard, selected clerks for Justices Oliver Wendell Holmes Jr. and Louis Brandeis. Justice Frankfurter asked Professor Henry Hart of Harvard Law School to select his clerks. Today, clerks often interview their potential replacements. Earlier in the twentieth century, clerks sometimes served for a number of years. But now most serve for only one or at most two years. Over one-quarter still come from Harvard Law School. Another 17 percent come from Yale Law School.

Some justices, notably William O. Douglas, were very hard on their clerks. Others, like Frankfurter, helped their clerks to begin their careers in law or politics. Some clerks became justices themselves—notably Chief Justices William Rehnquist and John Roberts and Justices John Paul Stevens and Byron R.

White. Some of the clerks played major roles in helping justices to frame issues, to negotiate with other justices (the clerks forming a kind of underground information network), and to help revise opinions. Some justices, like Frank Murphy and Thurgood Marshall, used them to write first drafts of opinions. Some justices, notably Thurgood Marshall and William Brennan, regarded their clerks as part of an extended intellectual family. All clerks are formally sworn to secrecy and discard all notes in "burn bags" for shredding.

The official Office of the Clerk was created by Congress in 1790. Like the clerk of any other American court, the clerk of the Court is actually an administrative office, handling the submission and distribution of appeals and other records and the calendar of the Court and managing the employees of the Court. At its inception, the office was filled by one man. Today, the clerk of the Court runs an office with over two dozen staff members. The clerk of the Court handles the briefs (written arguments of counsel), appeals, and writs (judicial orders to do something) by which cases come to the High Court. He or she sets the calendar and notifies all parties of due dates. The clerk is also responsible for handling admission to the Supreme Court bar—the list of men and women allowed to argue before the Court. The clerk ensures that drafts and final opinions are accurately printed for distribution among the justices.

The reporter was at one time a private individual who simply published the opinions, sometimes with copies of the briefs of counsel. The first of these, and perhaps the most famous, was Philadelphia attorney Alexander James Dallas. He later served in President Madison's cabinet. His volumes of reports of the High Court were unofficially called Dallas's Reports. William Cranch was the second reporter, but the volume of the cases overwhelmed him, and by 1815 his publications were running late, in part because he was the chief judge of the District of Columbia Circuit Court. The official *United States Reports* commenced in 1817, and Congress provided funds for hiring an official reporter in the Judiciary Act of that year. The job was still a patronage plumb, going to Henry Wheaton and then Richard Peters. Wheaton sued Peters for violating Wheaton's copyright on the reports, but in *Wheaton v. Peters* (1834) the Court determined that the reports were in the public domain and no one, including the reporter, could claim copyright in them. To this day the briefs, opinions, and other materials of the Court—and all federal publications—are in the public domain and no permission is needed to repeat them in whole or in part. The reports continued to bear the names of the reporters, Benjamin Chew Howard, Jeremiah Black, and John William Wallace, and the job continued to be a patronage plum until 1874. But the holders—Howard would serve four terms in Congress and Black would become the U.S. attorney general—were still distinguished men. Thereafter the office became more professional and the reports appeared with more precision and regularity. But the reporters continue to have full-time occupations away from the Court.

Notorious bloopers in the official reports abounded when the justices wrote out their opinions by hand. But modern word processing, in which the reporter and his staff of nearly a dozen men and women have access to the drafts and opinions and can query a justice about grammar, factual accuracy, and spelling, has reduced this source of error. The rule is still, however, that once published, there will be no corrections, even of misspellings. In 1941, the Reports ceased to include arguments of counsel, in part because the reporter, Ernest Kraebel, simply left them out.

The first librarian was hired in 1887. A public information officer joined the librarian in 1935, and a curator of manuscripts appeared in 1974. The staff now includes over two dozen trained burrowers. The Office of the Legal Counsel of the Court, created in 1972, supports the Court in cases of original jurisdiction. The staff lawyers may help the chief with administrative questions (though he has an administrative aide for this purpose). Created in 1867, the marshal is part secretary, part enforcement officer. He and his staff keep order in the Court, protect the justices, serve warrants, and enforce Court orders, much as the old English sheriff did. He or she also keeps track of the funds, including the payroll, and ensures that the janitorial and repair staff and Supreme Court Police perform their duties.

The *Federal Rules of Appellate Procedure* spell out what you must do to get your case into the running for a High Court hearing. The rules include forms you must fill out and submit. The rules are not for the faint hearted or the easily discouraged. They are periodically revised by a blue ribbon committee that Congress and the High Court selects, and they constitute a part of Title 28 of the *United States Code*. At one time there were certain mandatory or obligatory grounds for appeal of a case to the High Court, for example, when lower federal courts disagreed about a matter of law or a state court found against a party's alleged federal constitutional rights.

Under the Judicial Improvement and Access to Justice Act of 1988, a curiously mislabeled piece of legislation, the appellate jurisdiction of the High Court was revised, giving to the justices almost total control over their appellate docket. How this increased access to justice was unclear, except if one thought that the High Court was an unlikely fount of justice and thus best avoided. The act did reduce the number of cases the Court had to hear, however, an outcome for which Chief Justice Burger and Chief Justice Rehnquist campaigned. Thus if the Court hears your case, it is because the Court wants to hear your case.

Most likely, if you are appealing, you will file a writ of certiorari with the clerk of the Court. This asks the Court, in old law Latin, to take up the papers from the lower court and to inform itself of your claims. Certiorari, unlike formal appeal, gives to the Court the power to hear or not hear a case. In 1925, at Chief Justice Taft's behest, Congress lightened the load of mandatory (non-discretionary appeals) and allowed the Court to take most of its cases through cert. Unless you are filing in forma pauperis (as a pauper), you pay a fee of $300. You have to file on the right color of paper, and even if you are poor, you have to submit ten copies of the cert.

About two-thirds of appeals come from federal courts. The Rehnquist Court made every effort to reduce the number of appeals from state court decisions, particularly appeals based on the federal writ of habeas corpus. In his opinion, too many convicted criminals were using this writ to get a new hearing to which they were not entitled on the facts. It is now much harder to get the federal courts to listen to you, even if you are on death row.

Of course, your case has to be a real one, the Court has to have jurisdiction over the subject matter, and you have to have standing to bring the suit (that is, it actually affects you or your legally recognized interest). Various High Courts have disagreed about whether private individuals can bring suits about taxation, the environment, and other issues that might more properly belong to government to prosecute or litigate. Whether the Court will hear, as Judge Jerome Frank called them, "private attorneys general" is still a debated matter. Your case cannot be moot, in which the problem is already resolved, nor can you bring a case in which the Court has already rendered a definitive verdict (res judicata) or on an issue already settled (stare decisis), though this has not stopped the Court from revisiting certain kinds of cases.

Once your petition for cert arrives at the Court, the staff of the clerk determines if it is in proper form. Some justices take a day or two each week to examine new certs and decide for themselves if they are worth hearing. Other justices depend on the "cert pool," in which the clerks of some of the justices presort the petitions, particularly the unpaid ones. The clerks write memos for the justices on the petitions with recommendations as to which cases should move to the next stage of scrutiny. Justices may instruct their clerks to be on the lookout for one or another kind of case.

To be added to the docket requires that at least four of the justices agree that a case is worth hearing. The next steps, filing the briefs, including responding to the briefs of your opponent and soliciting the friend of the court (amicus curiae) briefs of supporters (the Court permitting), and preparing for oral argument, are best done with the assistance of experts. Today, these steps are taken collectively, with various legal-interest groups, law professors, and expert witnesses to help. In this sense, your suit has become part of the democratic process, or rather, has made the judicial branch much more democratic. The great cases of our day, for example, those on criminal rights, abortion, the environment, and the right to die, bring together a wide range of special-interest and advocacy groups. Some of these cases have engendered dozens of amicus briefs, many running to over a hundred pages of argument, citation of authorities, and reproduction of exhibits.

You may want to seek the help of the American Civil Liberties Union, the Center for Individual Rights, the Alliance Defense Fund, or one or more of the other legal advocacy groups to help you prepare your briefs and your oral argument. You may even want them to provide counsel to do this for you, if you are not a member of the Supreme Court bar. Whether they do it or you do it, you will hold minicourts or "moots" to practice and hone your arguments. Perhaps your counsel will use note cards, files, or other aids during oral argument. Fortune favors the prepared.

Each side has a half hour to present its case in oral argument in the Supreme Court courtroom. Those who have done this report that it is among the most exhausting and exhilarating moments in their lives. Even veteran counsel who have often stood before the Court find answering the justices' questions daunting and exciting. The solicitor general of the United States argues the federal government's cases in the Court and may ask to join your case on one side or the other if the executive branch has an interest in the outcome of the case.

In the nineteenth century, oral argument before the Court played a major role in the outcome of cases, and sometimes the oratory of counsel stretched on for days. Rarely did justices interrupt counsel, who included members of Congress like Daniel Webster. Today, seldom does counsel go on for more than a few minutes without a question from one of the justices, and sometimes the questions take up all of the allotted time. Justices ask counsel to explain issues raised in their briefs and to explore points made in oral argument, and they often argue among themselves.

Some justices have seemed to love oral argument—Justices Frankfurter and Scalia, both former professors, kept counsel on their toes. Other justices, like Douglas, seemed uninterested. Justice Clarence Thomas rarely takes an active part in the questioning. Often the tenor of the justices' questions indicates their thinking or their concerns, and participants in the oral argument later join with observers to second-guess how the justices are going to vote on a case, based on their questions and comments. If you reach this stage, you will probably have some idea where most of the justices stand on your case.

Once the oral argument is over, the chief will announce that your case has been "submitted." Now it is fodder for the justices at their twice-weekly conferences. The judicial conference is, in a way, at the heart of the Supreme Court's intellectual operation. Like oral argument, it has its own written and unwritten rules. It is a private meeting, but individual justices' notes, some now deposited at the Library of Congress, reveal much about the conference. The chief justice presides. The business of the conference includes discussion of cases already argued orally, new cases, cases that might or might not be added to the docket, and ordinary administrative business.

At conference, the dance of politics and personalities on the Court is in full swing from the moment the judges arrive. The trading of drafts and ideas among the justices and their clerks begins at the conference as the justices move through the list of cases argued before the Court and try to persuade one another to accept or reject cases for argument. This give-and-take then gives way to formal deliberations on cases already heard. The justices speak in turn, in order of descending seniority, on the cases before them. Chief Justice Stone gave to each justice as much time as he wished. His predecessor, Chief Justice Hughes, ran a tighter ship, beginning with short summaries of his own. The speaking order allowed the chief to impose his personality and his personal views on the conference—or try to. Chief Justice Warren was charming; Vinson and Burger were formal. Burger allowed back and forth. Rehnquist discouraged it.

The justices then vote in ascending order of seniority. The chief justice tallies the votes. If he or she is in the majority, he or she assigns the opinion to one of the members of the majority or to himself. If the chief justice is in the minority, the most senior justice in the majority assigns the opinion. Sometimes the conferences are raucous and contentious, but more often they are a rehearsal for the arguments that will appear in opinions for the Court, dissents, and concurrences. The horse trading on your case has already begun.

THE ROBERTS COURT

Who will hear your case? The death of William Rehnquist led to much speculation about his successor. Many sitting judges were touted for the job, and capsule biographies, along with handicappers' odds, appeared in the media and on the web. On July 20, 2005, President George W. Bush nominated John G. Roberts of the D.C. Circuit Court of Appeals to fill the vacant center chair. On September 29, 2005, the Senate confirmed his nomination.

Roberts's nomination came as a surprise, for he was not the best known of the candidates, but his career path, his views of the law, and his approach to judging were compatible with his predecessor's and with the desires of both the president and key members of the Republican Party in Congress. He was young—at fifty, Roberts became the youngest chief justice since John Marshall. That meant that he would likely lead the Court for many years to come.

His background was comfortable and conservative. He grew up in suburban Indiana—his father was an executive for Bethlehem Steel. He was an athlete and a school politician. At Harvard College and at Harvard Law School, he distinguished himself in academics, and after he earned his law degree he clerked for Republican Judge Henry Friendly of the U.S. Court of Appeals for the Second Circuit and then for Justice Rehnquist of the U.S. Supreme Court. Immediately after his Supreme Court clerkship, in 1981, he was hired by the Reagan administration, first as a special assistant to the U.S. attorney general and then as associate counsel to the president. His Republican Party credentials were impeccable, and key members of the Republican leadership were able to assess his views. These conformed to theirs on abortion, federalism, and, most important, the primacy of private property rights over government regulation.

In 1988, he served as deputy solicitor general. In this capacity, he argued dozens of cases before the Supreme Court on behalf of the federal government, winning well over half of them. When Democrat Bill Clinton won the 1992 presidential election, Roberts returned to private practice. He became a partner at Hogan and Hartson, a prestigious Republican Washington, D.C., firm, where he ran the appellate division and continued to argue cases before the Supreme Court.

In 2001, President George W. Bush nominated Roberts to be a judge on the U.S. Court of Appeals for the District of Columbia Circuit, widely considered the most important intermediate appellate court in the country. Roberts's initial nomination was never voted on by the Democrat-controlled Senate Judiciary Committee and was therefore never addressed by the full Senate. In 2003, President Bush renominated Roberts in a Republican-controlled Senate; he was confirmed by a voice vote with little opposition. During his time on the D.C. Circuit Court of Appeals, Roberts wrote forty-nine opinions. Only two of his decisions were not unanimous, and he only dissented from other judges' opinions three times.

His Senate confirmation hearings for the High Court revealed little more of the man, except his considerable charm and composure and his unwillingness to go beyond generalities and commonplaces in discussing his jurisprudence or his views on upcoming issues. His opening statement and his answers to the senators' questions, however, hinted at those views. He found a right to privacy in the Constitution, and he repeated that he respected precedent. He refused to indicate where he stood on *Roe v. Wade* and promised that he had "no agenda" for himself or for the Court. He saw its role as a limited one, and offered his own "humility" as a promise of his view of judging—an affirmation of the concept of judicial restraint.

Perhaps even more important was the way that the political divisions among the senators questioning Roberts fell out on the nominee. Clearly, the senators were using him as a kind of sounding board, in part for their own opinions, in part to send messages to their constituents. Roberts's own unwillingness to say more than he had to, given that his nomination was guaranteed by the Republican majority in the upper house, allowed him to move into the shadows of the hearing room as the senators did battle with one another.

Perhaps, however, he preferred that place, for, unlike some of his showier predecessors, Roberts's earlier career—including his disinclination for elective office, his ability to work well with others in staff positions, and his aversion to staking out new ground as a judge—reveals characteristics he seems to have carried onto the High Court. In the first half term that he led the Court, it did not strike out in new directions. Roberts's votes were predictable from a political point of view—for example, in the Texas redistricting that gave the Republican Party favorable districts and in supporting Bush administration policies. Roberts did recuse himself, however, when he had taken part in the lower court determinations—something that Rehnquist and Scalia had declined to do.

On January 31, 2006, Roberts was joined on the Court by retiring Justice O'Connor's replacement, Samuel Alito Jr. After the fiasco of attempting to appoint his White House counsel, Harriet Miers, to the Court and discovering that her knowledge of constitutional law did not impress leading members of either party, Bush again surprised Court-watchers with his appointment of Judge Alito of the Third Circuit Court of Appeals.

Named to that post by the elder Bush, Alito had already compiled a record of federal service. His preference was the role of prosecutor. A Trenton, New Jersey, native from a close-knit Roman Catholic family, he excelled at Princeton and then at Yale Law School. As long as he could remember, he was interested in politics. He lionized President Reagan and thought that the Warren Court had far exceeded the powers of a Court in a biased liberal direction. In

1972, newly graduated Alito joined a Princeton alumni group that worked to counter the "leftist urges" at the university.

After clerking on the Third Circuit, he served as an assistant U.S. attorney in the appellate division, where he argued cases before the Third Circuit. From 1981 to 1985, he found a job with the man he so admired, becoming assistant to the solicitor general in Reagan's first administration. From 1985 to 1987, he moved up as deputy assistant attorney general in the Office of Legal Counsel, where he provided constitutional advice for the executive branch, a post even closer to Reagan. His reward was appointment as U.S. attorney for the District of New Jersey. There he compiled a record of convictions in white collar and environmental crimes, drug trafficking, organized crime, and violations of civil rights.

On the Third Circuit, Alito's deeply held religious convictions, for example, in abortion rights cases and cases involving religious displays in public places, on First Amendment bars to hate speech codes, and on restrictions on immigration, placed him squarely in the Scalia camp—so much so that during his Senate confirmation hearings wags referred to the two as one man, "Scalito."

The Senate debate was contentious and partisan, largely because of the abortion question. Alito had, it was true, in 1985 boasted that he was proud of his efforts to remove the constitutional protection for abortion. He was certainly a hard-liner on the death penalty and in criminal matters. On the Court of Appeals, Alito had earned the reputation of a judicial craftsman of conservative leanings but a high degree of professionalism. Thus, for example, he voted to uphold a New Jersey Supreme Court ban on the state's partial abortion law, citing the High Court's opinion in *Stenberg*. But Alito's calm, almost folksy, manner, his quiet self-confidence (he refused to look at a briefing book the White House had prepared for his hearings), and his obvious competence impressed even those who voted against him. Alito was confirmed 58 to 42, with one Republican voting nay and four Democrats, all in states that had voted for Bush in 2004, voting yea.

The record of the first Roberts Court is unclear, but some outlines have emerged. Oral argument and conference are more civil than they have been in years. The chief justice has set an example for the other justices. For example, without the old contentiousness, a Kennedy-led majority upheld an Oregon state law allowing physician-assisted suicide in *Gonzales v. Oregon* (2006), though it would take a bit of contortion. Deferring to the state's physician-assisted suicide stance conformed to the majority's desire to defer to the judgments of states.

In displays of unanimity, the Roberts Court agreed that any law restricting a minor's access to abortion must make exceptions for medical emergencies; that a genuine religious sect may legally import a tea with hallucinogenic properties if it is central to observance of the religion; that a college must allow military recruiters the same access to students as it gives to other potential employers; that those who complain about discrimination or harassment at their place of work should be legally protected against retaliation based on those complaints; and that death row prisoners can raise constitutional challenges to the manner of their execution.

But the old divisions reappeared when the Court divided 5 to 4 or 5 to 3, with Roberts and Alito on the same side, in finding that public employees cannot find safety in the Constitution when their employer demotes them for making derogatory public statements; that the redistricting of Texas's congressional seats substantially increasing Republican majority congressional districts was legal; that limits on campaign spending by candidates and contributions to candidates that Vermont imposed were unconstitutional; and that even if the police failed to "knock and announce" their intention to enter a dwelling, the search was legal if they had a warrant. Roberts and Alito joined in dissent when the majority found that Texas could not tear apart a congressional district with a Latino majority and distribute the votes to dilute that majority; that a defendant who was told that he could not have a lawyer of his choice was entitled to a new trial; and, most important (though Roberts did not take part), that military commissions to try the detainees at Guantanamo violated federal law and internal law precepts.

Thus the course of the Court is unclear for the 2006–2007 term. It has agreed to take up the partial birth abortion ban that Congress voted and the president signed; more immigration cases; an ordinance that used racial quotas to ensure integration in local schools; and a major environmental case. But the Court refused to review a conviction under the Texas "sex toy" law that bans the sale of any "obscene device" designed for "the stimulation of human genital organs" and a California woman's plea that required reading from a portion of the Koran in a world history class violated separation of church and state.

It may be that the Court once again looks for consensus within itself, and with American values. Or it may be that Rehnquist's bludgeon is replaced with Roberts's stiletto. In *Gonzalez v. Arizona* (2006), the Court had before it one of many new state laws requiring proof of citizenship from voters seeking to register, designed to "prevent voter fraud." The lower courts had enjoined enforcement of the new law, which gave to voter registrars the authority to turn away registered voters who, in their opinion, did not have or could not present evidence of citizenship. The voter was allowed to cast a "provisional" vote and required to return within five days with proof of citizenship. Every voter did not have to present such proof, however, with the discretion lying with the registrar. Shades of *Reese* perhaps? Or of the Oklahoma grandfather clauses and literacy tests? Was it a law passed by a white, Republican majority to deny voting to a Hispanic Democratic minority, or at least to deter such voters by being embarrassed at the polling places? Georgia Republicans had passed a similar law, requiring photo identification, a law enjoined by a federal court judge on the grounds that it violated federal voting law and the Constitution (for poor black people were less likely to have such photo identification than other voters).

Arizona had a long history of racial discrimination at the polls and so had to clear its new law with the U.S. attorney general under the Voting Rights Act of 1965. Alberto Gonzales, the Republican attorney general, found no problem with the law, but residents of the state, including Indians and Hispanics, brought a suit to enjoin the law, and the federal court of appeals issued the injunction on October 5, 2006. But when the preliminary injunction went back to the district court, it decided that the election should go forward under the new law. The Supreme Court agreed. The harm that the new law might impose by keeping people away from the polls was outweighed by the danger that there might be voter fraud—a stiletto instead of a bludgeon.

The only major cases the Court faces are old business. In *Parents v. Seattle* and *Meredith v. Jefferson,* the Court must determine whether state-imposed remedies for de facto segregated schools in Seattle, Washington, and Louisville, Kentucky, may juggle enrollments based on racial quotas. In a sense, *Bakke* may have more to do with these cases than *Brown*, for under strict scrutiny standards in affirmative action cases, the two plans, which create a marbled pattern of racial mixing at every public school, fail. They impose an impermissible racial quota. What is more, as Justice Scalia noted in oral argument, once a unitary system (a nonsegregated system) is attained, only "race-neutral" means may be employed in pupil placement. But under the more general notion that integration is a national goal, a reading that follows the spirit of *Brown* and its progeny rather than the letter of the law, some form of quota is a necessity to avoid the resegregation of a school system. Justice Breyer opined during the oral argument that *Swann* stated that remedies could take race into consideration. In any case, hundreds of other school districts have plans resembling the Louisville or Seattle choice/quota systems, and all will have to go back to the drawing board if the two plans are struck down, as seems likely.

Yet, even in these highly charged cases, the outcome seems clear. The two integration plans will fall. What is more, affirmative action may simply cease to be a judicial matter. For example, the University of Michigan affirmative action student recruitment policies, the subject of the closely watched *Grutter* and *Gratz* cases, have led to Proposal 2, an amendment to the Michigan constitution to bar all state agencies and institutions from operating affirmative action programs that grant preferences based on race, color, ethnicity, national origin, or gender. The measure, also called the Michigan Civil Rights Initiative, passed easily, with 58 percent of the vote, at the November 2006 polls.

The so-called partial birth abortion medical procedure returned to the Court in *Gonzales v. Carhart*, a test of the federal ban on the dissection and extraction method used to end a later-term pregnancy. The Court had already ruled that a state ban failed because it did not provide exceptions for the health of the pregnant woman. But this time Kennedy, writing for Roberts, Alito, Thomas, and Scalia, found that the act had a rational relation to a legitimate state interest in the life of the unborn—an interest conceded in *Roe*, and "ethical and moral" considerations outweighted any slight medical advantage the procedure might have over other surgical procedures. Scalia and Thomas wrote a concurring opinion calling for the demise of *Roe*, but Roberts and Alito did not join that opinion. Ginsburg, with Stevens, Souter, and Breyer, dissented. In another abortion case, *Ayotte v. Planned Parenthood* (2006), the Court ruled, unanimously, that laws limiting teenagers' access to abortion must have an exception for medical emergencies.

When the Court split, Justice Kennedy held the middle ground. For example, in an Oregon suit involving a jury's $79.5 million award against Philip Morris, a 5-to-4 vote (with Kennedy in the majority) sent the case back to the trial court but did not find the award excessive on its face. The judge had erred by allowing the jurors to consider the dangers of smoking to men and women not involved in the litigation.

Under Roberts, the Court may be moving away from the spotlight that Rehnquist enjoyed. Certainly, the number of cases the Court has agreed to hear in the 2006–2007 session has dropped sharply, as a number of perennial issues may now be off the table. The Court under Chief Justice Roberts may be wary and weary of highly charged political cases, resuscitating the "political question" doctrine. At the same time, interest group litigants that have in the past sought the aid of the Court may now be wary. Civil rights advocates, on the one hand, and religious special interests, on the other, may find legislative remedies more congenial than judicial rulings. The U.S. solicitor general under President Bush has filed fewer cases with the Court than had his predecessors. Or the drop may simply be a continuation of the reduction of the docket that

Chief Justice Rehnquist began, for under him the number of cases the Court decided fell from two hundred to one hundred per year.

This epilogue ends in the middle of the Court's term in the early stages of what will likely be a long Roberts era. This is as it should be, for the Court's history is neither fixed nor finished. Because the politics on the Court and the politics of the nation will continue to change, because the Court has the ability to revisit its own precedents, distinguishing and changing what it no longer believes to be good law, and because the Constitution is a living document whose health the justices superintend, the Court can rewrite history. And, in the coming years, we have no doubt that the Court will rewrite American law.

Conclusion

What can we now say of the Court's past, its present, and its future? Some conclusions are indisputable. Looking back at the long course of the High Court's history, one can see that the Court's physical and institutional presence has changed greatly. From borrowed, cramped, and uncomfortable quarters, the Court has found a home in a marble palace. From meeting in a short session and then spending most of the year in exhausting circuit riding, the Court now meets most of the year in Washington, D.C. From relative obscurity, the Court has become a focus of extensive media coverage, bloggers' comments, and scholarly examination. From the weakest branch by far, the Court has come to rival Congress and the executive in the impact of its decisions.

The number of the justices rose from six to as high as ten and then fell to the familiar nine. Behind the changes were increases in the business of the Court, the number of circuits the justices had to ride, and, inevitably, politics. President Franklin Roosevelt's plan to add more justices thus had ample precedent, though its purpose was plainly partisan, and as such it was rejected by opponents of the New Deal, every member of the sitting court, and most law school deans.

Accompanying the enlargement of the Court was its administrative elaboration. The two key changes in the Court as an institution were the providing of offices for the justices in the Supreme Court building and the rise of the clerk system. The caseload of the Court grew as well, from a handful at the beginning to over a thousand by 1950. After 1950, the cases filed with the Court exploded in number, increasing from three thousand in 1960, to five thousand in 1970, to over ten thousand a year by the end of the century. The Court, according to a 1988 act of Congress, can almost entirely determine its own docket, but within that docket, the number of opinions has grown as well. The total peaked in the late 1980s at over four hundred per term. Though that number has fallen, the length of opinions has not—straining the facilities of the Court's printing office and the attention span of Court-watchers.

As the shifts in caseload demonstrate, these changes were not linear, following a steady upward progress from amateur to professional and partisan to expert. Instead, there were halts, retreats, and leaps forward. Sometimes the Court was behind public opinion, sometimes ahead, sometimes a moral tutor, sometimes a political liability. On occasion, the Court inflicted wounds on itself, losing public confidence, and at other times, it elevated its decisions above the clamor of popular opinion to point the way to a more just and compassionate regime of law. Lately, the Court has found itself a target of organized protest. As retired Justice Sandra Day O'Connor admitted, in an October 28, 2006, CNN interview, "As I went through the last few years of service here at the Court, I saw increasing indications of unhappiness with judges."

The shape of the justices' decisions has changed, too. As one would expect with the growing number of precedents, opinions have grown longer. Somewhat more surprising, the percentage of unanimous opinions has declined, as individual justices devote themselves to concurrences in part and dissents. The opinions have become more learned, incorporating material from treatises, law review articles, and learned treatises. The result is more technical language with fewer concessions to the untrained reader.

As the Court gained more and more control over its docket, the cases the justices elected to hear and the opinions they rendered focused more and more on the Constitution and on interpretation of state and federal legislative enactments. Although the Court had always taken on the supervision of legislation, its willingness to defer to the elected branches varied over time. Indeed, there were periods of deference followed by periods of far stricter scrutiny. In the process, the Court found (or invented) new prudential doctrines to justify its stances. Among these were substantive due process, liberty of contract, and strict scrutiny. The Court became its own source of rules and standards for interpreting the meaning of the Constitution, just as, in its infancy, it had asserted its preeminence in judicial review.

In the process, some of the justices cast themselves as teachers, and others adopted the pose of oracles. Some found the burden of writing opinions so onerous that they "froze." The roles the individual justices took on varied with their personalities and their view of the Court's proper function. Some greatly valued collegiality; some joined cliques on the Court; some, like the first John Marshall Harlan, Oliver Wendell Holmes Jr., James McReynolds, Benjamin Cardozo, Frank Murphy, and William O. Douglas, preferred not to socialize with their brethren. Some justices saw the Court as the grand tribunal, sitting in judgment of all the laws. Others believed in a more restrained role. But the garments of activism and restraint could be exchanged for the other one when an individual justice wanted a particular outcome.

The history of the Court teaches us that the law the justices promulgated was mutable. It could and did shift over time with changing interpretations of the Constitution. Whether that document should or should not be regarded as a living text, the justices breathed new life into it every term.

And nothing is clearer from the Court's history than that the impact of politics—both personal and national—has shaped the output of the Court. Early party struggles found their way onto the Court's docket, and its decisions reflected the partisanship of the individual justices. That partisanship was muted in later years, and transformed in complex ways. By the time of the twentieth-century Courts, one could no longer predict a justice's view of the law from his or her party affiliation with perfect accuracy—although, overall, politics was not a bad predictor of voting on the Court. But the jurisprudence of members like McReynolds, Stone, Frankfurter, Warren, Brennan, Blackmun, and Souter confounded the pundits. For these men, national politics, and perceived national political needs, trumped earlier political attachments.

Some characteristics of the Court have not changed at all. Throughout its and our history, the Court has reflected the values and assumptions of America's best-educated segment. The least democratic of all the branches is also the most sensitive to shifts in legal opinion. In reverse fashion, despite its occasional stumbles, popular support for the Court reflects Americans' belief in the rule of law in a republican system.

As well, the Court has never backed away from its role as final arbiter of the meaning of the Constitution. Justice Stephen Breyer explained why, in that same CNN interview:

Since for 200 years, people have thought in this country that the best guarantee that minorities will not be oppressed, that the Constitution will be lived up to, is to give the very last word to a group of judges who are independent. . . . Not because they are wiser—they make mistakes—but because, by giving them the last word, there is a better guarantee of that neutrality, insulated from politics, that can help those whom the Constitution wanted to help, that minority that might be oppressed.

Where does the Court's reputation stand today? Felix Frankfurter believed, with much truth, that the Court had only a certain store, a kind of bank account, of prestige or reputation on which it could draw. Although some observers thought that after *Bush v. Gore* the Court was bankrupt, that view was hasty. A more serious danger loomed behind the ruling in that case—for the rise of a powerful executive branch with a High Court at its beck and call posed a genuine threat to the basic notions of separation of powers and checks and balances in the Constitution. The Court's reputation is not related to its individual justices, as fan loyalty to a professional team might be. Ordinary Americans cannot identify individual members. A Findlaw.com study of public ability to identify anyone on the Court, repeated in the years 2003, 2004, and

2005, demonstrated this fact. In 2003, 65 percent of Americans could not name any of the justices. The best-known justice, Sandra Day O'Connor, was named in only 25 percent of the responses, followed by Clarence Thomas, in 21 percent of the responses. Two years later, 43 percent of those polled could not name a single justice, and O'Connor still led, appearing on 27 percent of the replies.

It is the Court, as a body, not the individual justices, that Americans know and respect. How many Americans trust the Court's decisions? The Pew Research Center polls for 2005 found that nearly 65 percent of those asked thought that the Court's opinions in abortion and suspected terrorists' rights were very important. Other polls have found that more than half of the respondents believe that the Court is doing a good job—higher than numbers for Congress and the presidency. In October 2006, an Opinion Research Corporation CNN poll reported that two-thirds of Americans do not want the courts to be more controlled by legislatures than they are now.

Can history and current events help us say something of the future of the Court? Certainly leading American politicians and scholars have made such predictions. Richard Henry Lee, of Virginia, an Anti-Federalist, was the first prognosticator. On October 16, 1787, he wrote a long letter to Virginia governor and Federalist Edmund Randolph, criticizing the draft of the Constitution that Virginia was supposed to ratify. Particularly worrisome to Lee was the proposed U.S. Supreme Court, which would "call people from their own country" where they "will be exposed to endless oppression, and the necessity of submitting in multitudes of cases, to pay unjust demands . . . without a jury." Lee was right—the High Court did create a national law, a law that superseded state laws and courts and that rested not on local sentiment but on the will of nine judges. But his prediction was wrong in its most important aspect. The Court does have the trust of Americans.

Almost two hundred years later, constitutional scholar Raoul Berger wrote: "A prime task of scholarship, therefore, is to heighten public awareness that the Court has been overleaping its bounds." Berger's concern was that the majority of the Court was abusing its constitutional authority, in particular through a broad reading of the Fourteenth Amendment, to impose busing and other managerial solutions on segregated school districts. He opined that it was time for a "rollback" from "policy making" and an end to tinkering with reapportionment, local discretion in criminal justice, and antiobscenity ordinances. The striking similarities between Berger's admonitions and Lee's fears cannot be ignored. Indeed, Berger explicitly pointed to the demand for greater local autonomy by the Anti-Federalists at the Virginia ratification convention. But

Berger was mistaken. The Court has not retreated from its Bill of Rights jurisprudence.

Lee and Berger remind us that predictions about the future of the Court will always be rooted in present concerns—and, most often, in the desires and priorities of the self-appointed seer. Thus most media discussions of the future of the Court look at the upcoming session or perhaps the next few years. The discussants ask what the Court will do with a variety of cases likely to be docketed for review. Taking a longer and less-partisan stance, can one project the past and present into the future of the Court?

Some trends will surely continue. First, the examination of nominees in Congress and in the public arena will become even more searching. Does this mean that more nominees will be rejected? No. President John Tyler's record of four nominees rejected or withdrawn will probably stand. It does mean that nominees will have to sacrifice their privacy in ways that will even exceed the embarrassments of past years. The introduction of committee hearings and, somewhat later, testimony by the nominee at the hearing has given senators the opportunity to place their own views on record—an opportunity they are not likely to forgo in future.

Along with increased scrutiny of nominees, one can anticipate increased partisanship in the naming of justices. This again is nothing new. As we have seen, presidents rarely pick candidates from the opposing party, and senators rarely ignore the party affiliation of the nominees. Partisanship led to fierce confirmation hearings in Brandeis's and Hughes's cases and in the rejection of Robert Bork.

The same partisanship will grow on the Court itself, particularly as it takes up political questions. Frankfurter's plea that the Court leave political matters to the popularly elected branches may not have made sense in the reapportionment cases, where a legislature was not truly popularly elected, but Frankfurter's aversion to political cases could save the Court from dissolving into internal factionalism. The question is, which issues are "political" and which are constitutional? Justice Scalia would put abortion rights in the former category, while the majority of his colleagues on the Rehnquist Court saw them as a constitutional matter.

The Court's opinions are likely to grow longer, more complex, and more intrusive into everyday life. This is particularly true in areas like intellectual property, copyright, and technology; voting rights; education; employment; and immigration. The Court in such cases is merely following the way in which our lives have changed. The same can be said for environmental issues, immigration, and real estate use, as our land becomes more crowded and we have to balance ecological and economic concerns.

As the Court's visibility rises and its decisions reach further into our lives, filling vacancies on the Court will become a more important issue in the election of presidents. This continues a trend reaching back into our history. The composition of the Court was featured among the campaign issues in the re-election of Franklin Roosevelt and the reelection of George W. Bush. To some extent, this was also true of the election of Abraham Lincoln and of Theodore Roosevelt. It is hard to imagine a future presidential race in which the Court's membership will not figure in some fashion.

What of the output of the Court—its contribution to our laws and our sense of lawfulness? Taking a longest view of the legal direction of the Court, we see that the history of the Court cannot be separated from the history of the nation. As that history has unfolded, so has the Court's jurisprudence evolved. Looking at the long course of our history, federal and state government has become more and more a part of our everyday lives; and so has the Court. The operations of our governments have become more open to our inspection; and so has the Court. Our laws and our society have become more aware of the plight of minorities and the poor; and so has the Court. We have become a people committed to the ideal of rights; and so has the Court. We have accepted the role of administrative agencies and regulations; and so has the Court. We have become modern in our outlook and more tolerant of sexual and cultural individualism; and so has the Court.

Bibliographic Essay

The following essay contains the primary and secondary sources we consulted for this volume. We have omitted endnotes to make the volume more readable, inexpensive, and appealing to students and general readers. In adopting this format, the authors are following the precedent of the University Press of Kansas Landmark Law Cases and American Society series and a number of other highly regarded and widely consulted series.

The author of the quotation in the introduction threatening the Court is Rep. Tom De-Lay (R-Tex.), from a March 31, 2005, speech. The issue was the Court's refusal to review a lower-court decision in the Terri Schiavo case.

The bibliography for the preceding pages could easily exceed them in length. With some exceptions, we have omitted the extensive theoretical and philosophical litera-ture, the subjects of which may touch on what we have written but are not central to it. This is not a history of constitutional doctrine. At the same time, there are a number of classic essays on the High Court that cross over the boundary between history and jurisprudence and that any student should be familiar with. These include Benjamin Cardozo, *The Nature of the Judicial Process* (New Haven: Yale University Press, 1921); Je-rome Frank, *Law and the Modern Mind* (New York: Brentano, 1930); Robert H. Jackson, *The Supreme Court in the American System of Government* (New York: Harper, 1963); and John T. Noonan, *Persons and Masks of the Law: Cardozo, Holmes, Jefferson, and Wythe as Makers of the Masks* (New York: Farrar, 1976). Cass Sunstein's *One Case at a Time: Judicial Minimalism on the Supreme Court* (Cambridge, Mass.: Harvard Univer-sity Press, 1999) makes a compelling case for the Court limiting its decisions to the cases at hand. Stephen Breyer, *Active Liberty: Interpreting Our Democratic Constitution* (New York: Knopf, 2005), applies a variant of this theory to a series of modern issues. A nice recent summary of interpretative stances is Jeffrey M. Shaman, *Constitutional Interpre-tation: Illusion and Reality* (Westport, Conn.: Greenwood, 2001). John E. Semonche, in *Keeping the Faith: A Cultural History of the U.S. Supreme Court* (Lanham, Md.: Rowman and Littlefield, 1998), argues that the Court may be likened to a religious body, with the justices as priests and their opinions as scripture.

On the images of the Court in the public mind, see Barbara A. Perry, *The Priestly Tribe: The Supreme Court's Image in the American Mind* (Westport, Conn.: Praeger, 1999); and Norman Rosenberg's essay, "The Supreme Court and Popular Culture: Image and Projection," in *The United States Supreme Court: The Pursuit of Justice*, ed. Christopher Tomlins (Boston: Houghton Mifflin, 2005), 398–422. In fact, all of the essays in this collection are worth reading, particularly Stephen Gottlieb's essay on the Rehnquist Court. Many surveys have ranked the justices, based on the opinions of veteran Court observers, clerks, and scholars. Two of them are Albert P. Blaustein and Roy M. Mersky, "Rating Supreme Court Justices," *American Bar Association Journal* 58 (1972): 1183–1187; and Blaustein and Mersky, "Rating Supreme Court Justices," in *Great Justices of the*

Supreme Court, ed. William D. Pederson and Norman W. Prozier (New York: Peter Lang, 1993). William G. Ross, "The Ratings Game: Factors That Influence Judicial Reputation," *Marquette Law Review* 79 (1996): 401–444, assesses the assessors.

The debate over the "internalist" versus the "externalist" view of the Court's history is not new, but recently law professor G. Edward White has made an unequivocal case for internalism:

The issue of causation in constitutional jurisprudence is closely connected to the issue of what constraints exist on Supreme Court justices as they interpret constitutional provisions. ... The process is collegial, deliberative, and focused on the analysis of legal doctrine. ... The collegial deliberations of the Court are conducted in a specialized professional language, the language of doctrinal analysis. Whatever the sources of a justice's attitude toward the disposition of a case, that justice's arguments on behalf of a given disposition will need to emphasize doctrinal reasons, because doctrinal analysis is the technique employed to justify the Court's decisions.

Scholars who prefer an externalist interpretation of the Court's workings import the justices' political, social, economic, and even psychological outlooks and focus on the surrounding political landscape. G. Edward White's manifesto, William Leuchtenberg's case for the politics of lawmaking, and Laura Kalman's superb commentary appear in "AHR Forum: The Debate over the Constitutional Revolution of 1937," *American Historical Review* 110 (October 2005): 1046–1115.

Perhaps the best introduction to the middle road is the writing of the justices themselves on their roles. See, for example, Norman Dorsen, ed., *The Evolving Constitution: Essays on the Bill of Rights and the U.S. Supreme Court* (Middletown, Conn.: Wesleyan University Press, 1989), with essays by Harry A. Blackmun, William J. Brennan Jr., Abe Fortas, Arthur J. Goldberg, Thurgood Marshall, and John Paul Stevens. The same picture emerges from the justices' Court conference notes and other papers at the Library of Congress. The papers of William O. Douglas, William J. Brennan, Lewis Powell, Thurgood Marshall, and Harry Blackmun are the most recent of those deposited and form the basis for many insider accounts of the Court.

The question of how political the Court really is may be the central one in the literature today. The political scientist who did the most to popularize the Court-as-political-institution thesis was Robert Dahl, in a 1957 article, "Decision Making in a Democracy: The Supreme Court as a National Policy Maker," *Journal of Public Law* 6 (1957): 279–295; and later in a series of books. Dahl first proposed this thesis at the height of criticism of the Warren Court for its desegregation decisions—opinions that looked a lot like policy making rather than lawgiving. Dahl defended the Court by implying that it reflected national consensus. A similar view infuses Robert McCloskey, *The American Supreme Court* (Chicago: University of Chicago Press, 1960). The most recent edition, brought up to date by Sanford Levinson, was published in 2004. Jeffrey Rosen, in *The Most Democratic Branch: How the Courts Serve America* (New York: Oxford, 2006), argues that "bipartisan judicial restraint" should be the norm, but he offers plenty of evidence to the contrary in practice. An enjoyable survey of the politics of and on the Court is David M. O'Brien's *Storm Center: The Supreme Court in American Politics*, 7th ed. (New York: W. W. Norton, 2005).

One law professor has gone even farther down this road than the political scientists have. According to Michael Klarman, the justices "rarely hold views that deviate far from dominant public opinion." Even if this dictum were generally true, a "dominant public opinion" in a nation so diverse in its sectionalism, ethnicity, religious adherence, and politics as ours (a proposition itself open to question) requires a kind of originalism that most historians would not adopt. Michael Klarman, *From Jim Crow to Civil Rights: The Supreme Court and the Struggle for Racial Equality* (New York: Oxford, 2004), is nevertheless essential reading on both the politics of the time and the politics on the Court.

Books on politics and the appointment of justices include Henry Abraham, *Justices, President, and Senators*, rev. ed. (Lanham, Md.: Rowman and Littlefield, 1999); and Michael J. Gerhardt, *The Federal Appointments Process: A Constitutional and Historical Analysis* (Durham, N.C.: Duke University Press, 2000). O'Brien has a splendid chapter on the topic in *Storm Center*.

One may also sample from classic essays on politics, judicial review, and the Court's role in government, for example, Alexander Bickel, *The Least Dangerous Branch: The Supreme Court at the Bar of Politics* (Indianapolis, Ind.: Bobbs Merrill, 1962); Archibald Cox, *The Role of the American Supreme Court in American Government* (New York: Oxford, 1976); John Hart Ely, *Democracy and Distrust: A Theory of Judicial Review* (Cambridge, Mass.: Harvard University Press, 1980); and Laurence Tribe, *Constitutional Choices* (Cambridge, Mass.: Harvard University Press, 1985).

The subject of judicial activism has engendered more than enough highly argumentative tracts (often rooted in the controversies of their time). Examples include Raoul Berger, *Government by Judiciary* (Cambridge, Mass.: Harvard University Press, 1977); Robert Bork, *The Tempting of America* (New York: Free Press, 1990); Arthur Selwyn Miller, *Toward Increased Judicial Activism* (Westport, Conn.: Greenwood, 1982); Richard Neely, *How Courts Govern America* (New Haven: Yale University Press, 1981); and Christopher Wolfe, *Judicial Activism: Bulwark of Freedom or Precarious Security?* (Lanham, Md.: Rowman and Littlefield, 1997).

For constitutional scholars, the concept of original intent is both important and slippery. Does it mean what the framers had in their heads? How are we to recover that with any certainty? According to what they said? Records of the earliest debates are fragmentary and unreliable. According to the plain meaning of what they wrote? Given how bitterly the framers themselves contested those words soon after they were written, such a task is only likely to lead to more controversy. Every one of these approaches subordinates constitutional adjudication to the findings of historians, leaving judges at the mercy of academics. The debate over originalism versus a living Constitution is played out in Robert Bork, *The Tempting of America: The Political Seduction of the Law* (New York: Free Press, 1990); Leonard Levy, *Original Intent and the Framers' Constitution* (New York: Macmillan, 1988); and Mark Tushnet, *Taking the Constitution Away from the Courts* (Princeton, N.J.: Princeton University Press, 1999). A history of the idea of originalism is Jonathan O'Neill, *Originalism in American Law and Politics: A Constitutional History* (Baltimore: Johns Hopkins University Press, 2005).

Indeed, how the Court uses history, or is supposed to use history, can be a vexing issue. Sometimes lawyers and judges do history pretty badly. They look through the past for their friends, finding and taking out of context historical facts that support the argument they want to make. On other occasions, the Court has listened to fine historians and incorporated their findings into opinions. Some notable examples of this are the works of Leonard W. Levy on the First and Fifth Amendments: *Legacy of Suppression: Freedom of Press in Early American History* (Cambridge, Mass.: Harvard University Press, 1960), a book that Justice Hugo Black condemned by name because it confuted his own views of the First Amendment's early history; and *Origins of the Fifth Amendment: The Right against Self-Incrimination* (New York: Oxford, 1968).

There are many ways to periodize the history of an institution as important and long-lived as the U.S. Supreme Court. The tripartite division we have chosen loosely corresponds to that in Bruce A. Ackerman, *Foundations*, vol. 1 of *We the People* (Cambridge, Mass.: Harvard University Press, 1991). Ackerman's division has been criticized for historical inaccuracy and theoretical mischief. See, for example, Edmund S. Morgan, "The Fiction of the People" (review of Ackerman, *We the People*), in *New York Review of Books* 39 (April 23, 1992): 46–48; and Michael McConnell, "The Forgotten Constitutional Moment," *Constitutional Commentary* 11 (1994): 115. Keying the chapters to the tenure of chief justices is so conventional it amounts to a cliché, but it is very serviceable and divides the material into even chronological lengths. For other examples of this form of organization, see Charles Warren, *The Supreme Court in United States History*, 3 vols. (Boston: Little, Brown, 1924); the individual volumes of the Oliver Wendell Holmes Jr. Devise, *History of the Supreme Court of the United States*, now superbly, and on time, edited by Stanley N. Katz; the *ABC-CLIO Supreme Court Handbooks*; the Associated Faculty Press series The Supreme Court in American Life; and the Chief Justiceships of the United States Supreme Court series from the University of South Carolina Press under the editorship of Herbert Alan Johnson. Our source for docket loads is Margaret Meriwether Cordray and Richard Cordray, "The Calendar of the Justices: How the Supreme Court's Timing Affects Its Decisionmaking," *Arizona State Law Journal* 36 (Spring 2004): 183–255.

The standard historical reference work on the High Court is Kermit Hall, ed., *The Oxford Companion to the Supreme Court of the United States* (New York: Oxford, 1992, 2005); but one may also consult Clare Cushman, ed., *The Supreme Court Justices: Illustrated Biographies, 1789–1993* (Washington, D.C.: Congressional Quarterly and the Supreme Court Historical Society, 1993); Gary Hartman, Roy M. Mersky, Cindy L. Tate, eds., *Landmark Supreme Court Cases* (New York: Facts on File, 2004); Melvin Urofsky, ed., *The Supreme Court Justices: A Biographical Dictionary* (New York: Garland, 1994); and Leonard Levy and Kenneth L. Karst, eds., *Encyclopedia of the American Constitution*, 2nd ed. (New York: Macmillan, 2000); as well as Christopher Tomlins, ed., *The United States Supreme Court: The Pursuit of Justice* (Boston: Houghton Mifflin, 2005).

In fact, because much of the history of the Court is in reality its opinions on cases, reference works and textbooks on constitutional history are essential collateral reading on the history of the Court. Textbooks include Alfred H. Kelly, Winfred A. Harbison, and Herman Belz, *The American Constitution: Its Origins and Development*, 2 vols., 7th ed. (New York: Norton, 1991); Melvin Urofsky and Paul Finkelman, *A March of Liberty*, 2 vols., 2nd ed. (New York: Oxford, 2002); and Michael Les Benedict, *The Blessings of Liberty: A Concise History of the Constitution of the United States* (Lexington, Mass.:

D. C. Heath, 1996). A more personal and argumentative but highly readable essay on the Constitution is Akhil Reed Amar, *America's Constitution, A Biography* (New York: Random House, 2005). The modern standard, and classic, work on the framers' Constitution is Jack N. Rakove, *Original Meanings: Politics and Ideas in the Making of the Constitution* (New York: Knopf, 1996).

Full versions of every Supreme Court opinion can be found in the U.S. Reports, the official repository of all these opinions, as well as the West and Lawyer's Cooperative editions of the opinions. In addition, online sources like Westlaw and Lexis have fully annotated versions. Most of the major cases can also be found on the Yale Law School Avalon and the Findlaw websites. Squibs (key portions) of the High Court's jurisprudence can be found in any major constitutional law casebook. A larger portion of the opinions on a smaller and more selective basis can be found in three collections by historians: Herbert A. Johnson, ed., *American Legal and Constitutional History: Cases and Materials*, 2nd ed. (Lanham, Md.: University Press of America, 2001); Stanley I. Kutler, ed., *The Supreme Court and the Constitution: Readings in American Constitutional History*, 2nd ed. (New York: Norton, 1977); and Kermit L. Hall, ed., *The Supreme Court in American Society*, a multivolume reprint series (New York: Garland, 2000). Broader collections of readings that touch on the jurisprudence of the Court include Kermit L. Hall, ed., *Major Problems in American Constitutional History*, 2 vols. (Lexington, Mass.: D. C. Heath, 1992); and Melvin Urofsky and Paul Finkelman, eds., *Documents of American Constitutional and Legal History*, 2 vols., 2nd ed. (New York: Norton, 2002).

There are a number of single-volume histories of the Supreme Court. They range from the chatty William Rehnquist, *History of the Supreme Court*, rev. ed. (New York: Vintage, 2003); to the bare bones of Robert Langran, *The Supreme Court: A Concise History* (New York: Lang, 2004); to the breezy and occasionally opinionated Peter Irons, *A People's History of the Supreme Court* (New York: Viking, 1999); to the anecdotal Bernard Schwartz, *A History of the Supreme Court* (New York: Oxford, 1993). The classic three-volume work by Charles Warren, *The Supreme Court in United States History* (Boston: Little, Brown, 1923), is the source for many of the facts about the Court we now take for granted. It is, however, severely dated and its biases may be off-putting to some readers.

Biographies of leading justices and books on individual cases are included in the sections of this bibliographic essay below, organized by chapter.

For the historical details in the chapters, we in American history are blessed with a cornucopia of textbooks. Among those we relied on were Edward L. Ayers et al., *American Passages: A History of the United States*, 2 vols., 3rd ed. (Belmont, Calif.: Wadsworth, 2007); Paul Boyer et al., *The Enduring Vision: A History of the American People*, 2 vols., 6th ed. (Boston: Houghton, 2005); Alan Brinkley, *American History: A Survey*, 2 vols., 11th ed. (New York: McGraw Hill, 2002); Mark C. Carnes and John A. Garraty, *The American Nation*, 2 vols., 11th ed. (New York: Longman, 2003); Robert A. Divine et al., *America Past and Present*, 5th ed. (New York: Longman, 1999); John Mack Faragher et al., *Out of Many: A History of the American People*, 2 vols., 4th ed. (Upper Saddle River, N.J.: Prentice Hall, 2003); Pauline Maier et al., *Inventing America: A History of the United States*, 2 vols. (New York: Norton, 2003); James Kirby Martin et al., *America and Its Peoples*, 4th ed. (New York: Longman, 2001); John M. Murrin et al., *Liberty, Equality,*

Power: A History of the American People, 2 vols., 3rd ed. (Orlando, Fla.: Harcourt, 2003); and James L. Roark et al., *The American Promise: A History of the United States*, 2 vols. (Boston: Bedford, 1998).

Apart from these general sources, each chapter relied on particular works. Especially useful in the first two chapters were Julius W. Goebel Jr., *Antecedents and Beginnings to 1801*, vol. 1 of *History of the Supreme Court of the United States* (New York: Macmillan, 1971); the first of the Holmes Devise, *History of the Supreme Court*; and William R. Casto, *The Supreme Court in the Early Republic: The Chief Justiceships of John Jay and Oliver Ellsworth* (Columbia, S.C.: University of South Carolina Press, 1995). The one absolutely essential primary source collection is Maeva Marcus et al., eds., *The Documentary History of the Supreme Court of the United States, 1789–1800*, 8 vols. (New York: Columbia University Press, 1980–1998). On the Alien and Sedition Acts, see Leonard W. Levy, *Emergence of a Free Press* (New York: Oxford, 1985); and James Morton Smith, *Freedom's Fetters: The Alien and Sedition Laws and American Civil Liberties* (Ithaca, N.Y.: Cornell University Press, 1956).

The notion of a constitutional regime based on widespread popular participation is the centerpiece of Larry D. Kramer, *The People Themselves: Popular Constitutionalism and Judicial Review* (New York: Oxford, 2004); Mark Tushnet, *Taking the Constitution Away from the Courts* (Princeton, N.J.: Princeton University Press, 1999); and Ahkil Reed Amar, *The Bill of Rights: Creation and Reconstruction* (New Haven: Yale University Press, 1998). The problem for this reading of the populist Constitution is judicial review. On the origins of judicial review, we learned much from Daniel J. Hulsebosch, *Constituting Empire: New York and the Transformation of Constitutionalism in the Atlantic World, 1664–1830* (Chapel Hill: University of North Carolina Press, 2005). The importance of the concept of personal property in the Bill of Rights is a key contribution of Jennifer Nedelsky, *Private Property and the Limitations of American Constitutionalism: The Madisonian Framework and Its Legacy* (Chicago: University of Chicago Press, 1990). On the Eleventh Amendment, see John V. Orth's *The Judicial Power of the United States: The Eleventh Amendment in American History* (New York: Oxford, 1987). On *Elkay*, see Stanton D. Krauss, "New Evidence That *Dred Scott* Was Wrong about Whether Free Blacks Could Count for the Purposes of Federal Diversity Jurisdiction," *Connecticut Law Review* 37 (Fall 2004): 25–65.

For chapter 3, the biographies of John Marshall are many, and some are of exceedingly high quality. The classic anecdotal biography is Albert J. Beveridge, *The Life of John Marshall* (Boston: Houghton Mifflin, 1919). In addition, see R. Kent Newmyer, *John Marshall and the Heroic Age of the Supreme Court* (Baton Rouge: Louisiana State University Press, 2001); Jean Edward Smith, *John Marshall: Definer of a Nation* (New York: Holt, 1996); and Charles F. Hobson, *The Great Chief Justice: John Marshall and the Rule of Law* (Lawrence: University Press of Kansas, 1996). Hobson is the editor of the John Marshall papers, taking over that role from Herbert Johnson. On the Court during Marshall's tenure as chief justice, see Herbert Johnson, *The Chief Justiceship of John Marshall, 1801–1835* (Columbia, S.C.: University of South Carolina Press, 1997); George L. Haskins and Herbert Johnson, *The Foundations of Power: John Marshall, 1801–1815* (New York: Macmillan, 1984); and G. Edward White, with the aid of Gerald Gunther, *The Marshall Court and Cultural Change, 1815–1835*, abridged ed. (New York: Oxford, 1991).

The best modern biography of Justice Story is R. Kent Newmyer, *Supreme Court Justice Joseph Story, Statesman of the Old Republic* (Chapel Hill: University of North Carolina Press, 1985); but Gerald T. Dunne's *Justice Joseph Story and the Rise of the Supreme Court* (New York: Simon and Schuster, 1970) is a diverting read. The only full-length biography of William Johnson is Donald G. Morgan, *Justice William Johnson, The First Dissenter: The Career and Constitutional Philosophy of a Jeffersonian Judge* (Columbia, S.C.: University of South Carolina Press, 1954), but Morgan's work is dated and ignores important sectional issues.

Material on *Marbury*'s legacy appeared in John T. Noonan Jr., "Forward—A Silk Purse? Judging Judicial Review: *Marbury* in the Modern Era," *Michigan Law Review* 101 (August 2003): 2557–2564. A very wide-ranging symposium on *Marbury* appears in *Virginia Law Review* 89 (October 2003), in which the G. Edward White article, "The Constitutional Journey of *Marbury v. Madison*," pp. 1463–1573, is most convincing. Robert Lowry Clinton, *Marbury v. Madison and Judicial Review* (Lawrence: University Press of Kansas, 1989), argues that Marshall intended the decision to relate only to the Court's own jurisdiction. William E. Nelson, *Marbury v. Madison: The Origins and Legacy of Judicial Review* (Lawrence: University Press of Kansas, 2000), follows the impact of the decision.

On *Fletcher v. Peck*, see Peter C. McGrath, *Yazoo, Law and Politics in the New Republic: The Case of Fletcher v. Peck* (New York: Norton, 1967). The business side of the corporations' rise in the nineteenth century is explained in Alfred D. Chandler Jr., *The Visible Hand: The Managerial Revolution in American Business* (Cambridge, Mass.: Harvard University Press, 1977).

The slave cases are featured in Thomas D. Morris, *Southern Slavery and the Law, 1619–1860* (Chapel Hill: University of North Carolina Press, 1996); and A. Leon Higginbotham, *Shades of Freedom* (New York: Oxford, 1996). One should also consult the corpus of Paul Finkelman's extensive analysis and collation of slave law cases, including his edited *Slavery and the Law* (Madison, Wis.: Madison House, 1997), his *Free Blacks, Slaves, and Slaveholders in Civil and Criminal Courts* (New York: Garland, 1988), and his *Fugitive Slaves and American Courts* (New York: Garland, 1988). In *An Imperfect Union: Slavery, Federalism, and Comity* (Chapel Hill: University of North Carolina Press, 1981), Finkelman's view is realistic and persuasive.

The *Cherokee Cases* have found a very able biographer in Jill Norgren: *The Cherokee Cases* (New York: McGraw Hill, 1996). On Indian law, see David E. Wilkins and K. Tsianina Lomawaima, *Uneven Ground: American Indian Sovereignty and Federal Law* (Norman: University of Oklahoma Press, 2001).

For chapter 4, Roger Brooke Taney (pronounced Tawney) deserves a new major biography. Carl Brent Swisher's *Roger B. Taney* (New York: Macmillan, 1935) still reads well; but H. H. Walker Lewis, *Without Fear or Favor: A Biography of Chief Justice Roger Brooke Taney* (Boston: Houghton Mifflin, 1965), resembles a nineteenth-century work. Its treatment of slavery is not only antiquated, it is wrong. A useful corrective is Paul Finkelman's entry on Taney in *The Supreme Court Justices: A Biographical Dictionary*, ed. Melvin Urofsky (New York: Garland, 1994), 465–473. Peter Daniel has an able and friendly biographer in John P. Frank, *Justice Daniel Dissenting: A Biography of Peter V. Daniel, 1784–1860* (Cambridge, Mass.: Harvard University Press, 1964).

Surveys of the Taney Court's personnel and jurisprudence include the comprehensive Carl Bent Swisher, *The Taney Period, 1836–1864* (New York: Macmillan, 1974); and the more recent Timothy S. Huebner, *The Taney Court: Justices, Rulings, and Legacy* (Santa Barbara, Calif.: ABC-CLIO, 2003). Stanley Kutler's *Charles River Bridge* (Philadelphia: Lippincott, 1971) and Tony Freyer's *Harmony & Dissonance: The Swift & Erie Cases in American Federalism* (New York: New York University Press, 1981) are still the standard works on those cases. Don E. Fehrenbacher won the Pulitzer Prize for *The Dred Scott Case: Its Significance in American Law and Politics* (New York: Oxford, 1978).

On the troubled jurisprudence of the Civil War era, see Daniel Farber, *Lincoln's Constitution* (Chicago: University of Chicago Press, 2003); Harold P. Hyman, *Toward a More Perfect Union* (New York: Knopf, 1973); and Mark E. Neely Jr., *The Fate of Liberty: Abraham Lincoln and Civil Liberties* (New York: Oxford, 1991). The farewell of Taney is described in David N. Atkinson, *Leaving the Bench: Supreme Court Justices at the End* (Lawrence: University Press of Kansas, 1999). The prize and piracy cases are discussed in Mark A. Weitz, *The Confederacy on Trial: Piracy and Sequestration Cases of 1861* (Lawrence: University Press of Kansas, 2005).

The most recent biographies of Salmon P. Chase include John Niven, *Salmon P. Chase: A Biography* (New York: Oxford, 1995); and Harold P. Hyman, *The Reconstruction Justice of Salmon P. Chase* (Lawrence: University Press of Kansas, 1997). Analysis of the justices and the case law appears in Jonathan Lurie, *The Chase Court: Justices, Rulings, and Legacy* (Santa Barbara, Calif.: ABC-CLIO, 2004), as well as in the voluminously anecdotal Charles M. Fairman, *Reconstruction and Reunion, 1864–1888*, vols. 6 and 7 of *History of the Supreme Court of the United States* (New York: Macmillan, 1971). Fairman also wrote *Mr. Justice Miller and the Supreme Court, 1862–1890* (New York: Russell, 1966). On Stephen Field, see Paul Kens, *Justice Stephen Field: Shaping Liberty from the Gold Rush to the Gilded Age* (Lawrence: University Press of Kansas, 1997); and Carl Brent Swisher, *Stephen J. Field: Craftsman of the Law* (Washington, D.C.: Brookings, 1930).

The Waite Court deserves more study. A good summary is Donald Grier Stephenson Jr., *The Waite Court: Justices, Rulings, and Legacy* (Santa Barbara, Calif.: ABC-CLIO, 2003). C. Peter Magrath, *Morrison R. Waite: A Study in Character* (New York: Macmillan, 1963), is an admiring look at the man that does not add much on the jurisprudence of his Court. Robert M. Goldman takes on the voting rights cases in *Reconstruction and Black Suffrage: Losing the Vote in Reese and Cruikshank* (Lawrence: University Press of Kansas, 2001). Linda Przybyszewski has given us a fine biography of Harlan in *The Republic according to John Marshall Harlan* (Chapel Hill: University of North Carolina Press, 1999); equally valuable is Tinsley E. Yarbrough, *Judicial Enigma: The First Justice Harlan* (New York: Oxford, 1995).

The Fuller Court's output is far more controversial than its predecessor. Even the commentators take issue with one another. See Owen Fiss, *Troubled Beginnings of the Modern States, 1888–1910* (New York: Macmillan, 1993); John E. Semonche, *Charting the Future: The Supreme Court Responds to a Changing Society, 1890–1920* (Westport, Conn.: Greenwood, 1978); James W. Ely Jr., *The Fuller Court: Justices, Rulings, and Legacy* (Santa Barbara, Calif.: ABC-CLIO, 2003); and Herbert Hovenkamp, *Enterprise and American Law, 1836–1937* (Cambridge, Mass.: Harvard University Press, 1991).

Biographical treatments of the justices are a little more revealing of the motives behind the men. See, for example, Michael J. Brodhead, *David J. Brewer: The Life of a Supreme Court Justice, 1837–1910* (Carbondale: Southern Illinois University Press, 1994); Robert B. Highsaw, *Edward Douglass White: Defender of the Conservative Faith* (Baton Rouge: Louisiana State University Press, 1981); and Matthew McDevitt, *Joseph McKenna: Associate Justice of the United States* (New York: Da Capo, 1974).

Albert W. Alschuler, *Law without Values: The Life, Work, and Legacy of Justice Holmes* (Chicago: University of Chicago Press, 2000), condemns Holmes as the ultimate cynic; G. Edward White, *Justice Oliver Wendell Holmes: Law and the Inner Self* (New York: Oxford, 1993), finds contradictions behind the icon; and Sheldon M. Novick, *Honorable Justice: The Life of Oliver Wendell Holmes* (Boston: Little, Brown, 1989), admires the man and the justice. A series of essays on Holmes that captures his intellectual side is Robert W. Gordon, ed., *The Legacy of Oliver Wendell Holmes, Jr.* (Stanford, Calif.: Stanford University Press, 1992). We have quoted David Hollinger's essay from this anthology.

On Hughes, the standard conventional biography is still Merlo J. Pusey's Pulitzer Prize–winning *Charles Evans Hughes*, 2 vols. (New York: Macmillan, 1951). A more specialized treatment is Samuel Hendel, *Charles Evans Hughes and the Supreme Court* (New York: Russell, 1968).

Most treatments of Brandeis are friendly, including Alpheus T. Mason, *Brandeis: A Free Man's Life* (New York: Viking, 1946); Edward Purcell, *Brandeis and the Progressive Constitution* (New Haven: Yale University Press, 2000); Philippa Strum, *Brandeis: Beyond Progressivism* (Lawrence: University Press of Kansas, 1993); Philippa Strum, *Louis D. Brandeis: Justice for the People* (New York: Schocken, 1984); and Melvin I. Urofsky, *Louis D. Brandeis and the Progressive Tradition* (Boston: Little, Brown, 1981). But Bruce Allen Murphy, *The Brandeis/Frankfurter Connection: The Secret Political Activities of Two Supreme Court Justices* (New York: Oxford, 1982), argues that the collaboration of the two men was illicit.

On McReynolds, John Knox, a former clerk, composed a memoir based on a diary, published as David J. Garrow and Dennis J. Hutchinson, eds., *The Forgotten Memoir of John Knox: A Year in the Life of a Supreme Court Clerk in FDR's Washington* (Chicago: University of Chicago Press, 2002).

For the Court's leading cases, see David Ray Papke, *The Pullman Case* (Lawrence: University Press of Kansas, 1999); Paul Kens, *Lochner v. New York* (Lawrence: University Press of Kansas, 1998); Charles F. Lofgren, *The Plessy Case: A Legal-Historical Interpretation* (New York: Oxford, 1987); Brook Thomas, ed., *Plessy v. Ferguson: A Brief History with Documents* (Boston: Bedford, 1997); and Bartholomew H. Sparrow, *The Insular Cases and the Emergence of American Empire* (Lawrence: University Press of Kansas, 2006).

The standard work on the White Court is Alexander Bickel and Benno Schmidt's *The Judiciary and Responsible Government, 1910–1921* (New York: Macmillan, 1984). Bickel passed away before his magisterial volume was complete, and Schmidt finished its pages on race relations cases in fine style. See also Rebecca S. Shoemaker, *The White Court: Justices, Rulings, and Legacy* (Santa Barbara, Calif.: ABC-CLIO, 2004), a concise work; and the evenhanded Walter F. Pratt Jr., *The Supreme Court under Edward Douglass White, 1910–1921* (Columbia: University of South Carolina Press, 1999).

The old standard on free speech cases was Harry Kalven Jr., *A Worthy Tradition: Freedom of Speech in America*, ed. Jamie Kalven (New York: Harper and Row, 1988). The book is somewhat awkward in its topical arrangement but very clear in its arguments (and no one can miss its stance). The modern standard is David Rabban, *Free Speech in Its Forgotten Years* (New York: Cambridge, 1997). A nice short summary by a master is Paul L. Murphy, *The Shaping of the First Amendment, 1791 to the Present* (New York: Oxford, 1992). Holmes is generally credited with the key role in defining the limits of free speech in the White Court. On his role, see H. L. Pohlman, *Justice Oliver Wendell Holmes: Free Speech and the Living Constitution* (New York: New York University Press, 1991). A wonderful book on the Abrams case is Richard Polenberg, *Fighting Faiths: The Abrams Case, the Supreme Court, and Free Speech* (New York: Viking, 1987).

Taft has relatively few major biographies, given the breadth of his experience. It may be that his outlook and his persona are not congenial to modern scholarly tastes. There are Judith Icke Anderson, *William Howard Taft, an Intimate History* (New York: Norton, 1981), on the family; and Paolo E. Coletta, *The Presidency of William Howard Taft* (Lawrence: University Press of Kansas, 1973). But the standard remains Henry F. Pringle, *The Life and Times of William Howard Taft: A Biography*, 2 vols. (New York: Farrar, 1939).

On Taft's Court, see David H. Burton, *Taft, Holmes, and the 1920s Court: An Appraisal* (Madison, N.J.: Fairleigh Dickinson University Press, 1998); Peter G. Renstrom, *The Taft Court: Justices, Rulings, and Legacy* (Santa Barbara, Calif.: ABC-CLIO, 2003); and the now-dated Alpheus T. Mason, *William Howard Taft, Chief Justice* (New York: Simon and Schuster, 1965). Helpful articles include Donald F. Anderson, "Building National Consensus: The Career of William Howard Taft," *University of Cincinnati Law Review* 68 (1999): 323–356; Peter G. Fish, "William Howard Taft and Charles Evans Hughes: Conservative Politicians as Chief Judicial Reformers," *Supreme Court Review* (1975): 123–145; and Robert C. Post, "Chief Justice William Howard Taft and the Concept of Federalism," *Constitutional Comment* 9 (1992): 199–222.

Our account of *Adkins* and the Court comes in part from Barry Cushman, *Rethinking the New Deal Court: The Structure of a Constitutional Revolution* (New York: Oxford, 1998). The account of *Buck v. Bell* follows that in William E. Leuchtenberg, *The Supreme Court Reborn: The Constitutional Revolution in the Age of Roosevelt* (New York: Oxford, 1995). Both of these superb volumes figure in our Hughes Court discussion as well.

Cardozo has found a biographer to match his insight in Andrew L. Kaufman, *Cardozo* (Cambridge, Mass.: Harvard University Press, 1998); but because many of the justice's personal papers were destroyed, a full biography will never be possible. Biographies of William O. Douglas abound, starting with his two-volume autobiography: *Go East, Young Man: The Early Years; The Autobiography of William O. Douglas* (New York: Random House, 1974); and *The Court Years, 1939–1975: The Autobiography of William O. Douglas* (New York: Random House, 1980). Douglas's letters have a fine editor in Melvyn Urofsky, ed., *The Douglas Letters: Selections from the Private Papers of Justice William O. Douglas*, with the assistance of Philip E. Urofsky (Bethesda, Md.: Adler and Adler, 1987). An admiring former student, Vern Countryman, prepared an anthology of Douglas's leading opinions in *The Douglas Opinions* (New York: Random House, 1977). Biographers not so admiring as Urofsky and Countryman include Bruce Allen Murphy, *Wild Bill: The Legend and Life of William O. Douglas* (New York: Random House, 2003); and James F. Simon, *Independent Journey: The Life of William O. Douglas* (New York: Harper and Row, 1980).

Felix Frankfurter tried to shape history's view of him by sharing his reminiscences with Joseph P. Lash, ed., *From the Diaries of Felix Frankfurter* (New York: Norton, 1975); and *Felix Frankfurter Reminisces, Recorded in Talks with Harlan B. Phillips* (New York: Reynal, 1960). Biographers of Frankfurter, like those of Douglas, paint a more complex picture of the man. They include the ongoing project, Michael Parrish, *Felix Frankfurter and His Times* (New York: Free Press, 1982–); James F. Simon, *The Antagonists: Hugo Black, Felix Frankfurter and Civil Liberties in Modern America* (New York: Simon and Schuster, 1989); Melvyn Urofsky, *Felix Frankfurter: Judicial Restraint and Individual Liberties* (Boston: Twayne, 1991); an ethnic study, Robert Burt, *Two Jewish Justices: Outcasts in the Promised Land* (Berkeley: University of California Press, 1988); and even a stab at psychohistory, H. N. Hirsch, *The Enigma of Felix Frankfurter* (New York: Basic Books, 1981).

The third of this trio, Hugo Black, gives away nothing to Douglas and Frankfurter in scholarly attention but, like both of them, ultimately remains enigmatic. Biographies include Gerald T. Dunne, *Hugo Black and the Judicial Revolution* (New York: Simon and Schuster, 1977); Tony Freyer, *Hugo L. Black and the Dilemma of American Liberalism* (Glenview, Ill.: Scott Foresman, 1990); Roger K. Newman, *Hugo Black: A Biography* (New York: Fordham University Press, 1997); and Tinsley E. Yarbrough, *Mr. Justice Black and His Critics* (Durham, N.C.: Duke University Press, 1988).

Frank Murphy has an admiring biographer in Sidney Fine, *Frank Murphy*, 3 vols. (Ann Arbor: University of Michigan Press, 1975–1984); and an understanding one in J. Woodrow Howard Jr., *Mr. Justice Murphy: A Political Biography* (Princeton, N.J.: Princeton University Press, 1968).

There are two superb books on the Scottsboro Boys cases: Dan T. Carter, *Scottsboro: A Tragedy of the American South* (Baton Rouge: Louisiana State University Press, 1969); and James Goodman, *Stories of Scottsboro* (New York: Pantheon, 1994).

We take the account of legal realism from N. E. H. Hull, *Roscoe Pound and Karl Llewellyn: Searching for an American Jurisprudence* (Chicago: University of Chicago Press, 1997). Other accounts of this intellectual movement include Laura Kalman, *Legal Realism at Yale, 1927–1960* (Chapel Hill: University of North Carolina Press, 1986); John Henry Schlegel, *American Legal Realism and Empirical Social Science* (Chapel Hill: University of North Carolina Press, 1995); and William M. Wiecek, *The Lost World of Classical Legal Thought: Law and Ideology in America, 1886–1937* (New York: Oxford, 1998).

Did the New Deal transform American constitutionalism, and did the apparent shift in the Supreme Court's view of judicial review derive from that transformation? Contemporary works by luminaries like Edward Corwin, echoed by later scholars like Carl Swisher, Robert McCloskey, Loren Beth, and William Leuchtenberg, agreed that politics and constitutional law influenced one another in transformative ways during the 1930s. To them, the "switch in time" confirmed and propelled a genuine revolution in constitutional thinking. In their sophisticated doctrinal analyses, Bruce Ackerman, *We The People*, and Cass R. Sunstein, *The Partial Constitution* (Cambridge, Mass.: Harvard University Press, 1993), found much truth in the transformative thesis. In all these accounts, the Court-packing plan plays some role. But G. Edward White, *The Constitution and the New Deal* (Cambridge, Mass.: Harvard University Press, 2000); Barry Cushman, *Rethinking the New Deal Court: The Structure of a Constitutional Revolution* (New York: Oxford, 1998); and, to a lesser extent, Laura Kalman, *The Strange Career of Legal Liberalism* (New Haven: Yale University Press, 1996), question the transformative thesis, finding the seeds of change much earlier and arguing that their growth was more gradual. Nice summaries of the controversy appear in "AHR Forum: The Debate over the Constitutional Revolution of 1937," *American Historical Review* 110 (October 2005): 1046–1115; and James A. Henretta, "Charles Evans Hughes and the Strange Death of Liberal America," part of "Forum: Liberalism and the Liberal State," in *Law and History Review* 24 (Spring 2006): 115–213.

The Stone and Vinson Courts are treated in Peter G. Renstrom, *The Stone Court: Justices, Rulings, and Legacy* (Santa Barbara, Calif.: ABC-CLIO, 2001); Michal R. Belknap, *The Vinson Court: Justices, Rulings, and Legacy* (Santa Barbara, Calif.: ABC-CLIO, 2004); Jan Palmer, *The Vinson Court Era: The Supreme Court's Conference Votes* (New York: AMS Press, 1990); C. Herman Pritchett, *Civil Liberties and the Vinson Court* (Chicago: University of Chicago Press, 1954); Francis Howell Rudko, *Truman's Court: A Study in Judicial Restraint* (Westport, Conn.: Greenwood, 1988); Melvin I. Urofsky, *Division and Discord: The Supreme Court under Stone and Vinson, 1941–1953*, Chief Justiceships of the United States Supreme Court (Columbia: University of South Carolina Press, 1997); and William M. Wiecek, *The Birth of the Modern Constitution: The United States Supreme Court, 1941–1953*, in Oliver Wendell Holmes Jr. Devise, *History of the Supreme Court of the United States* (New York: Cambridge University Press, 2006).

For biographies of the justices appointed to the Stone and Vinson Courts, see David Robertson, *Sly and Able: A Political Biography of James F. Byrnes* (New York: W. W. Norton, 1994); Mary Frances Berry, *Stability, Security, and Continuity: Mr. Justice Burton and Decision-Making in the Supreme Court, 1945–1958* (Westport, Conn.: Greenwood, 1978); Wallace Mendelson, *Justices Black and Frankfurter: Conflict in the Court* (Chicago: University of Chicago Press, 1961); and James F. Simon, *The Antagonists: Hugo Black, Felix Frankfurter and Civil Liberties in Modern America* (New York: Simon and Schuster, 1989).

For the Jehovah's Witness cases, consult Shawn Francis Peters, *Judging Jehovah's Witnesses: Religious Persecution and the Dawn of the Rights Revolution* (Lawrence: University Press of Kansas, 2000). For the German spy cases, read Louis Fisher, *Nazi Saboteurs on Trial: A Military Tribunal and American Law*, 2nd ed. (Lawrence: University Press of Kansas, 2005). Peter Irons, *Justice at War: The Story of the Japanese Internment Cases* (New York: Oxford, 1983), is a remarkable work.

On the loyalty oaths and education, see Ellen Schrecker, *No Ivory Tower: McCarthyism and the Universities* (New York: Oxford, 1986); and Thomas G. Paterson, *Meeting the Communist Threat: Truman to Reagan* (New York: Oxford, 1988). On editorial response to *Everson* and *McCollom*, see Stuart Nagel and Robert Erikson, "Editorial Reaction to Supreme Court Decisions on Church and State," *Public Opinion Quarterly* 30 (1966–1967): 647–655.

The desegregation cases are featured in Mark V. Tushnet, *The NAACP's Legal Strategy against Segregated Education, 1925–1950* (Chapel Hill: University of North Carolina

Press, 1987); Mark V. Tushnet, *Making Civil Rights Law: Thurgood Marshall and the Supreme Court, 1936–1961* (New York: Oxford, 1994); Clement Vose, *Caucasians Only: The Supreme Court, the NAACP, and the Restrictive Covenant Cases* (Berkeley: University of California Press, 1959); Michael Klarman, *From Jim Crow to Civil Rights* (New York: Oxford University Press, 2004). and Charles L. Zelden, *Battle for the Black Ballot: Smith v. Allwright and the Defeat of the All-White Texas Primary* (Lawrence: University Press of Kansas, 2004). For the Cold War cases, there are Michal R. Belknap, *Cold War Political Justice: The Smith Act, the Communist Party, and American Civil Liberties* (Westport, Conn.: Greenwood, 1977). For the steel seizure case, consult Maeva Marcus, *Truman and the Steel Seizure Case: The Limits of Presidential Power* (New York: Columbia University Press, 1977). On the struggle for black union men's rights, see Eric Arnesen, *Brotherhoods of Color: Black Railroad Workers and the Struggle for Equality* (Cambridge, Mass.: Harvard University Press, 2001).

Some of the many overviews on the Warren Court include Morton J. Horwitz, *The Warren Court and the Pursuit of Justice* (New York: Hill and Wang, 1998); Lucas A. Powe, *The Warren Court and American Politics* (Cambridge, Mass.: Belknap Press of Harvard University Press, 2000); Mark Tushnet, ed., *The Warren Court in Historical and Political Perspective* (Charlottesville: University of Virginia Press, 1993); and Melvin I. Urofsky, *The Warren Court: Justices, Rulings, and Legacy* (Santa Barbara, Calif.: ABC-CLIO, 2001).

Biographies of Earl Warren include G. Edward White, *Earl Warren: A Public Life* (New York: Oxford, 1982); and Bernard Schwartz, *Super Chief: Earl Warren and His Supreme Court—A Judicial Biography* (New York: New York University Press, 1983). Biographies of William Brennan include Hunter R. Clark, *Justice Brennan: The Great Conciliator* (New York: Birch Lane Press, 1995); and Kim Isaac Eisler, *A Justice for All: William J. Brennan, Jr., and the Decisions That Transformed America* (New York: Simon and Schuster, 1993). Books on Brennan's approach to the Constitution include Frank I. Michelman, *Brennan and Democracy* (Princeton, N.J.: Princeton University Press, 1999); and E. Joshua Rosenkrans and Bernard Schwartz, eds., *Justice Brennan's Enduring Influence* (New York: Norton, 1997). A book that we relied on for both Brennan and Chief Justice William Rehnquist was the luminous Peter Irons, *Brennan vs. Rehnquist: The Battle for the Constitution* (New York: Knopf, 1994).

One major work on John Marshall Harlan II is Tinsley E. Yarbrough, *John Marshall Harlan: Great Dissenter of the Warren Court* (New York: Oxford, 1992). For another dissenter from the Warren Court who ultimately found comfort with the more conservative Burger and Rehnquist Courts, see Dennis J. Hutchinson, *The Man Who Was Once Whizzer White: A Portrait of Justice Byron R. White* (New York: Free Press, 1998). Laura Kalman's *Abe Fortas: A Biography* (New Haven: Yale University Press, 1990) is an unflinching but ultimately positive look at the Warren Court's tragic justice. On Thurgood Marshall, see the biography of Michael D. Davis and Hunter R. Clark, *Thurgood Marshall: Warrior at the Bar, Rebel on the Bench* (New York: Birch Lane Press, 1992); and the compilation of biographical essays and edited writings by Roger Goldman with David Gallen, *Thurgood Marshall: Justice for All* (New York: Carroll and Graf, 1992).

School desegregation is treated in Richard Kluger, *Simple Justice: The History of Brown v. Board of Education and Black America's Struggle for Equality* (New York:

Vintage Books, 1977); James G. Patterson, *Brown v. Board of Education: A Civil Rights Milestone and Its Troubled Legacy* (New York: Oxford, 2001); and Robert J. Cottrol, Raymond T. Diamond, and Leland B. Ware, *Brown v. Board of Education: Caste, Culture, and the Constitution* (Lawrence: University Press of Kansas, 2003).

Other key cases of the Warren Court are given treatments by Carolyn N. Long, *Mapp v. Ohio: Guarding against Unreasonable Searches and Seizures* (Lawrence: University Press of Kansas, 2006); John W. Johnson, *Griswold v. Connecticut: Birth Control and the Constitutional Right of Privacy* (Lawrence: University Press of Kansas, 2005); and John W. Johnson, *The Struggle for Student Rights: Tinker v. Des Moines and the 1960s* (Lawrence: University Press of Kansas, 1997).

Fans of the Burger Court will enjoy Vincent Blasi, ed., *The Burger Court: The Counter-Revolution That Wasn't* (New Haven: Yale University Press, 1983); Richard Y. Funston, *Constitutional Counterrevolution? The Warren Court and the Burger Court: Judicial Policy Making in Modern America* (New York: John Wiley, 1977); Earl M. Maltz, *The Chief Justiceship of Warren Burger, 1969–1986* (Columbia: University of South Carolina Press, 2000); Bernard Schwartz, ed., *The Burger Court: Counter-Revolution or Confirmation?* (New York: Oxford, 1998); Bernard Schwartz, *The Ascent of Pragmatism: The Burger Court in Action* (Reading, Mass.: Addison-Wesley, 1990); Herman Schwartz, ed., *The Burger Years: Rights and Wrongs in the Supreme Court, 1969–1986* (New York: Viking Penguin, 1987); Tinsley E. Yarbrough, *The Burger Court: Justices, Rulings, and Legacy* (Santa Barbara, Calif.: ABC-CLIO, 2000); and Stephen L. Wasby, *Continuity and Change: From the Warren Court to the Burger Court* (Pacific Palisades, Calif.: Goodyear, 1976). For a controversial inside look at the Burger Court's workings, see Bob Woodward and Scott Armstrong, *The Brethren: Inside the Supreme Court* (New York: Simon and Schuster, 1979).

For the life of Lewis F. Powell Jr., consult John C. Jeffries Jr., *Lewis F. Powell, Jr.* (New York: Charles Scribner's, 1994). Justice Stevens is the subject of R. J. Sickles, *John Paul Stevens and the Constitution* (College Station: Pennsylvania State University Press, 1988). There are several books on William H. Rehnquist, for example, Peter Irons, *Brennan vs. Rehnquist: The Battle for the Constitution* (New York: Knopf, 1994); Donald E. Boles, *Mr. Justice Rehnquist, Judicial Activist; The Early Years* (Ames: Iowa State University Press, 1987), covering his time before appointment to the Court; and Sue Davis, *Justice Rehnquist and the Constitution* (Princeton, N.J.: Princeton University Press, 1989), covering his time on the Court before he became chief justice. Among the books on Justice O'Connor is Robert W. Van Sickel, *Not a Particularly Different Voice: The Jurisprudence of Sandra Day O'Connor* (New York: Peter Lang, 1998). On Justice Blackmun, see Linda Greenhouse, *Becoming Justice Blackmun: Harry Blackmun's Supreme Court Journey* (New York: New York Times Books, 2005).

For individual cases of the Burger Court, see Shawn Francis Peters, *The Yoder Case: Religious Freedom, Education, and Parental Rights* (Lawrence: University Press of Kansas, 2003); N. E. H. Hull and Peter Charles Hoffer, *Roe v. Wade: The Abortion Rights Controversy in American History* (Lawrence: University Press of Kansas, 2001); Howard Ball, *The Bakke Case: Race, Education, and Affirmative Action* (Lawrence: University Press of Kansas, 2000); Kenneth M. Murchison, *The Snail Darter Case: TVA versus the Endangered Species Act* (Lawrence: University Press of Kansas, 2007); Paul A. Sracic, *San*

Antonio v. Rodriguez and the Pursuit of Equal Education: The Debate over Discrimination and School Funding (Lawrence: University Press of Kansas, 2006); and Augustus B. Cochran III, *Sexual Harassment and the Law: The Mechelle Vinson Case* (Lawrence: University Press of Kansas, 2004). Bernard Schwartz has reported the inside story on *Swann*, in *Swann's Way: The School Busing Case and the Supreme Court* (New York: Oxford, 1986). The report on Detroit's white flight is Thomas J. Sugrue, "Expert Report of Thomas J. Sugrue," *Michigan Journal of Race and Law* 5 (1999): 261–309.

Ex–attorney general Edwin Meese's comments on Rehnquist and the appointment process appeared in "Symposium: Rethinking Rights," *Ave Maria Law Review* 3 (Spring 2005): 305. Solid, though contrasting, books on the Rehnquist Court include Craig M. Bradley, ed., *The Rehnquist Legacy* (New York: Cambridge University Press, 2006); Thomas R. Hensley, *The Rehnquist Court: Justices, Rulings, and Legacy* (Santa Barbara, Calif.: ABC-CLIO, 2006); David G. Savage, *Turning Right: The Making of the Rehnquist Supreme Court* (New York: John Wiley, 1992); Mark Tushnet, *A Court Divided: The Rehnquist Court and the Future of Constitutional Law* (New York: W. W. Norton, 2005); and Tinsley E. Yarbrough, *The Rehnquist Court and the Constitution* (New York: Oxford, 2005). To be fair, there is more division among historical scholars, law experts, and political scientists on this Court than any other.

Accounts of justices that arrived on the Court during the Rehnquist chief justiceship include Richard A. Brisbin Jr., *Justice Antonin Scalia and the Conservative Revival* (Baltimore: Johns Hopkins University Press, 1997); Jan Crawford Greenberg, *Supreme Conflict: The Inside Story of the Struggle for Control of the United States Supreme Court* (New York: Penguin, 2000); John Greenya, *Silent Justice: The Clarence Thomas Story* (Fort Lee, N.J.: Barricade, 2001); and Tinsley E. Yarbrough, *David Hackett Souter* (New York: Oxford, 2005).

For individual cases from the Rehnquist era, see Robert Justin Goldstein, *Flag Burning and Free Speech: The Case of Texas v. Johnson* (Lawrence: University Press of Kansas, 2000); Carolyn N. Long, *Religious Freedom and Indian Rights: The Case of Oregon v. Smith* (Lawrence: University Press of Kansas, 2000); Melvin I. Urofsky, *Affirmative Action on Trial: Sex Discrimination in Johnson v. Santa Clara* (Lawrence: University Press of Kansas, 1997); Melvin I. Urofsky, *Lethal Judgments: Assisted Suicide and American Law* (Lawrence: University Press of Kansas, 2000); Tinsley E. Yarbrough, *Race and Redistricting: The Shaw-Cromartie Cases* (Lawrence: University Press of Kansas, 2002); and Mark V. Tushnet, "The Story of *City of Boerne v. Flores*," in *Constitutional Law Stories*, ed. Michael C. Dorf (New York: Foundation Press, 2004), 505–531.

Bush v. Gore has its own bibliography, dominated by critics of the case. See, for example, Alan Dershowitz, *Supreme Injustice: How the High Court Hijacked Election 2000* (New York: Oxford, 2001). Richard Posner, *Breaking the Deadlock: The 2000 Election, the Constitution, and the Courts* (Princeton, N.J.: Princeton University Press, 2001), defends the decision.

On the conferences, see David M. O'Brien, *Storm Center: The Supreme Court in American Politics*, 7th ed. (New York: W. W. Norton, 2005); and Del Dickson, ed., *The Supreme Court in Conference (1940–1985): The Private Discussions behind Nearly 300 Supreme Court Decisions* (New York: Oxford, 2001). On the clerks of the justices, see Artemas Ward and David L. Weiden, *Sorcerers' Apprentices: 100 Years of Law Clerks at the United States Supreme Court* (New York: New York University Press, 2006). On the reporters of cases, see Frank D. Wagner, "The Role of the Supreme Court Reporter in History," *Journal of Supreme Court History* 26 (2001): 9–13.

Readers will find the letter quoted in the conclusion from Richard Henry Lee to Edmund Randolph, October 16, 1787, in John P. Kaminsky and Gaspare J. Saladino, eds., *The Documentary History of the Ratification of the Constitution*, vol. 8 (Madison, Wis.: State Historical Society, 1988), 63. Raoul Berger, *Government by Judiciary: The Transformation of the Fourteenth Amendment* (Cambridge, Mass.: Harvard University Press, 1977), 415, 413, 401, is hardly the last word on the subject.

Index